Liberalism
Volume II

Schools of Thought in Politics

Series Editor: *Brian Barry*
                Professor of Political Science, London
                School of Economics and
                Political Science

Future titles will include:

Liberalism
Volume II

Edited by

Richard J. Arneson

Professor of Philosophy
University of California, San Diego

An Elgar Reference Collection

Published by
Edward Elgar Publishing Limited
Gower House
Croft Road
Aldershot
Hants GU11 3HR
England

Edward Elgar Publishing Limited
Distributed in the United States by
Ashgate Publishing Company
Old Post Road
Brookfield
Vermont 05036
USA

A CIP catalogue record for this book is available from the British Library

Library of Congress Cataloguing in Publication Data
Liberalism/edited by Richard J. Arneson.
    p. cm. – (An Elgar reference collection) (Schools of
thought in politics; 2)
   1. Political science–History. 2. Liberalism–History.
I. Arneson, Richard J. II. Series. III. Series: Schools of thought
in politics; no. 2.
JA83.L53 1992
320.5'1'09–dc20
91–42041
CIP

ISBN 1 85278 348 6 (3 volume set)

Printed in Great Britain at the University Press, Cambridge

Contents

Acknowledgements

The editor and publishers wish to thank the following who have kindly given permission for the use of copyright material.

Basil Blackwell Ltd. for articles: Philip Pettit (1987), 'Towards a Social Democratic Theory of the State', *Political Studies*, **XXXV** (4), 537–51; Jan Narveson (1984), 'Equality vs. Liberty: Advantage, Liberty', *Social Philosophy and Policy*, **2** (1), 33–60.

Cambridge University Press for articles: Desmond S. King and Jeremy Waldron (1988), 'Citizenship, Social Citizenship and the Defence of Welfare Provision', *British Journal of Political Science*, **18** (4), 415–43; John Rawls (1975), 'A Kantian Conception of Equality', *Cambridge Review*, **96**, 94–99; Julia Annas (1977), 'Mill and the Subjection of Women', *Philosophy*, **52** (200), 179–94.

Fabian Society for article: R.H. Tawney (1920), *The Sickness of an Acquisitive Society*, chapters II–VI, 7–48.

H.J. McCloskey for his own article: (1963), 'Mill's Liberalism', *Philosophical Quarterly*, **13** (51), 143–56.

H.L.A. Hart for his own article: (1979), 'Between Utility and Rights', *Columbia Law Review*, **79** (5), 828–46.

Kluwer Academic Publishers B.V. for article: Robert J. van der Veen and Philippe van Parijs (1986), 'A Capitalist Road to Communism', *Theory and Society*, **15** (5), 635–55.

Princeton University Press for article: David Lyons (1977), 'Human Rights and the General Welfare', *Philosophy and Public Affairs*, **6** (2), 113–29.

The Philosophical Review for article: D.G. Brown (1972), 'Mill on Liberty and Morality', *Philosophical Review*, **81** (2), 133–58.

University of Chicago Press for articles: Michael S. McPherson (1982), 'Mill's Moral Theory and the Problem of Preference Change', *Ethics*, **92** (2), 252–73; Russell Hardin (1986), 'The Utilitarian Logic of Liberalism', *Ethics*, **97** (1), 47–74.

Yale Law Journal for article: Thomas Nagel (1975), 'Libertarianism Without Foundations', *Yale Law Journal*, **85** (1), 136–49.

Every effort has been made to trace all the copyright holders but if any have been inadvertently overlooked the publishers will be pleased to make the necessary arrangement at the first opportunity.

In addition the publishers wish to thank the library of the London School of Economics and Political Science and The Alfred Marshall Library, Cambridge University for their assistance in obtaining these articles.

Introduction

Utilitarian Liberalism

Throughout most of human history the accepted standard of justification for social and political arrangements has been the religious ideology of the rulers. The official justification of policy typically has been 'God wills it' and those who wished to oppose official policy have invoked alternate interpretations of God's will. This is as true of John Locke as of Saint Thomas Aquinas or John Calvin.

Whether because of increasing diversity of religious faiths in European society or increasing skepticism and unbelief among European intellectuals, political theorists throughout the eighteenth century often adopted a secular standpoint. For example, although both Rousseau and Kant avow allegiance to Christian faith in their writings, neither thinker appeals to theological premises in constructing his arguments. Here a qualification should be noted. Kantian ethics forbids any action that uses another person as a mere means even if the predictable consequences of refraining from such action would be catastrophic. Kant supposes that the failure of ethical action to produce acceptable outcomes in all circumstances so far as we can see provides us a rational motive for belief in a God who will set matters right in an afterlife. One might also observe that the moralities professed by Locke, Rousseau and Kant are all self-consciously compatible with the Judeo–Christian tradition in ethics and particularly with the set of rules known as the Ten Commandments and supposed to have been delivered on tablets of stone by God to Moses.

Utilitarianism is an avowedly secular, this-worldly doctrine. It is a response to the issue of how we might conceive standards for assessing and justifying government policy and individual action when society is so splintered in the religious commitments of its members that no religious standard of morality could expect to attract the assent of all reasonable people. John Stuart Mill's writings on religion are clear that ethics must stand on its own feet independent of religious claims. The point is not so much anti-religious as against religion-based ethics. Once we give up the idea that a sacred book can authoritatively tell us how to live, we humans are left to figure out the answers to moral issues as best we can. Invoking a divinity is no substitute for practical reasoning. With a certain relish Mill points out that even the assumption that there is an all-powerful being would not relieve us of the obligation of deciding for ourselves how we ought to live: 'I will call no being good who is not what I mean when I apply that epithet to my fellow-creatures; and if such a creature can sentence me to hell for not so calling him, to hell I will go.'[1]

This pronounced secularism is both a strength and a weakness of Utilitarianism. The aspect of weakness comes into view when one notices that Utilitarianism makes no concessions, at least at the level of abstract principle, to the idea of a morality of absolute prohibitions. But the idea that there are absolute prohibitions – that there are some acts one must absolutely never do whatever the consequences – is central to Judeo–Christian ethics and deeply entrenched in the moral intuitions of most of us, raised in that tradition.

The doctrine of Utilitarianism can be factored into two components: (1) an account of what is worthwhile or good in human existence, morality aside, and (2) the idea that the point of morality is to bring about the maximization of the good. In this view 'utility' is a formal notion. It stands for whatever is worthwhile or valuable in human existence. One obtains different varieties of Utilitarianism depending on how (1) and (2) are further specified and interpreted. Utilitarian theorists have contributed to the philosophy of liberalism both in their accounts of the good and in their accounts of morality as directed toward maximization of the good.

During the 1820s and 1830s in England Utilitarianism was the creed of a loosely organized faction of intellectuals and politicians seeking the reform of English institutions, which were undergoing the prolonged stress and strain of large-scale social change in the form of urbanization, rapid population growth, and industrialization. This small group, the self-styled 'Philosophical Radicals', sought the extension of the franchise toward universal manhood suffrage and worked unsuccessfully for a realignment of the major political parties, both of which were dominated by aristocratic landowning interests – to the detriment of the nation, in the judgement of the Radicals. The Philosophical Radicals were inspired by the writings of Jeremy Bentham and included among their number James Mill and his son, John Stuart Mill.

Bentham proposed that the greatest happiness of the greatest number should be the standard of assessment for social policy and individual actions. Stated somewhat more precisely, his proposal was that the sum total of human happiness (and of nonhuman sentient creatures as well, according to Bentham) should be made as large as possible over the long run. By *happiness* Bentham meant pleasure and the avoidance of pain. The good on this view consists of psychological episodes of enjoyment. The more such episodes there are, the greater their intensity, and the longer their duration, the better is the state of the world from the moral standpoint.

Bentham conceived of the utility standard as a rival to individual rights fulfillment as the standard of social justice. Positive rights specified by existing institutional rules were regarded by Bentham as possible helps or hindrances to the maximization of utility, to be assessed on this basis. Bentham professed not to be able to make sense of the idea of *moral rights* as something distinct from the rights actually established by some institutional scheme. According to Bentham the only possible rational standard of normative assessment was utility.

In the works excerpted in this volume Mill refines the notion of utility, clarifies the relation between utility and morality, and develops a comprehensive liberal social philosophy predicated on the goal of utility maximization under the conditions of modern social life.

In Chapter 1 of *On Liberty* Mill stated that utility was 'the ultimate appeal on all ethical quesions, but it must be utility in the largest sense, grounded on the permanent interests of man as a progressive being'. One might wonder what constitutes utility in the largest sense. Chapter 3 'Of Individuality' provides a partial answer. To live a good life it is not sufficient to satisfy one's preferences. In addition one's preferences must be truly one's own, which means they must be intelligently chosen by oneself under reasonably favourable conditions. Or perhaps the point is that one's preferences must be such that they would withstand informed rational deliberation (whether or not one actually engages in such deliberation), and in a diverse modern society the best way to ensure that one's preferences and values would withstand rational scrutiny is actually to subject them to rational scrutiny.

This individuality ideal might be stated differently. Individual human natures differ, according to Mill. What satisfies one person may not satisfy another. Moreover, our natures are not transparent to ourselves. The true nature of our deepest impulses and traits sometimes lies hidden. For this reason careful observation of oneself and others, cultivated education, and self-chosen experimentation in ways of life are needed in order to form in oneself settled preferences that suit one's nature and would be ratified by one's own rational scrutiny. It would not be far wrong to summarize these points by saying that according to Mill the good is rational preference satisfaction.

In Chapter 2 of *Utilitarianism* (not included in this volume) Mill directly addresses the issue, what utility is. There Mill pours new wine in old bottles. On the one hand he asserts the Benthamite claim that utility is pleasure and the absence of pain. On the other hand he develops an informed preference test for the quantity and quality of pleasure. The result is a hybrid position, which may be unstable. Mill does not seem fully to appreciate the fact that when someone is asked to put moral obligations aside and to determine what she would choose for its own sake, in order to make her life go best, the answer need not be identified with that which would yield her most pleasure. The research scientist might say that her true interest lies in doing good science, and scientific achievement is what she most wants for herself, for its own sake, quite apart from the further consequences such achievement might bring. Saying that is fully compatible with adding that attaining scientific achievement is not (for her) attaining maximal pleasure. What the woman we are imagining most wants is achievement of a certain sort, which is not to be identified with experience of any sort, let alone the specific mode of experience that is pleasurable. One's basic preferences, what one wants for its own sake, morality and obligations to others aside, need not take pleasure as their object and need not be such that satisfaction of the preferences brings satisfaction in the sense of an experience of pleasure. Rational preference satisfaction and pleasure are two rival answers to the question, what is utility. (For a somewhat different but complementary view of Mill's conception of utility, see Michael McPherson, 'Mill's Moral Theory and the Problem of Preference Change' (Chapter 16).)

The identification of utility with rational preference satisfaction has liberal implications. This is a broad and sweeping claim that requires some explication. Suppose that one rejects rational preference satisfaction and instead identifies the good with an *objective list* of states of affairs knowable quite independently of consulting the standpoint of the particular individual for whom one is trying to identify the elements of a good life. This objective list theory of human good has also been called *perfectionism*. In fact Bentham's view that pleasure is the good is one possible specification of an objective list theory: Bentham thought the objective list of goods contained one item, namely, pleasure. If the would-be designer of institutions knows that pleasure is the good, presumably she should design a political constitution and a set of laws and institutional structures and policies that taken together would maximize the sum of human pleasure. On the face of it, there is no basis on this view for deferring to individuals' own judgements of what is good for them. We already know what is good for them. Perhaps one could devise a sophisticated argument that would show that the best way to maximize my pleasure is to give me broad freedom to follow my own lights and lead my life as I choose, but any perfectionist social theory starts with a tilt against deference to individual judgement.

Matters are quite otherwise if we begin with the view that the good is rational preference satisfaction and add Mill's observation regarding the significance of individuality. Individual natures are different, and what any one person's rational preferences are cannot be determined except from that very person's standpoint, in the knowledge of that very person's proclivities, dispositions, and considered value judgements. In general, with respect to many matters crucial to each person's welfare, the individual herself will typically be in the best epistemic position to determine what is good for her, where her true interests lie. It does not follow from this that the individual cannot make mistakes about what for her is good for its own sake. Individuals can and do make mistakes not just about how best to achieve their good but about what it is that constitutes their good. Sometimes others can see an individual's good better than she herself can. But knowing a person's good requires us to see into her soul, as it were, and normally each person is in a better position to see for herself than others are to see for her. So there is a close if complex affinity between the idea that the good is rational preference satisfaction, Mill's views on individuality and personal autonomy, and the policy of antipaternalism: one should never restrict a person's liberty against her will for her own good.

Antipaternalism is one component of the liberty principle that Mill defends in *On Liberty*. Many critics have doubted whether Mill's utilitarian argument for strict antipaternalism in Chapter 3 of *On Liberty* is fully successful in its own terms. Critics have also expressed serious doubts as to whether, leaving Utilitarianism aside, we should decide that strict antipaternalism on its own merits is acceptable social policy. But that Mill's arguments create a substantial presumption in favour of allowing wide individual freedom to individuals and of subjecting proposed paternalist restrictions of liberty to strict scrutiny is undeniable, and undeniably a signal contribution to the political philosophy of liberalism.

On the basis of his Utilitarianism Mill develops a thoroughgoing liberalism. In *On Liberty* he argues for the liberty principle, the doctrine that the only good reason to restrict a sane nonfeebleminded adult individual's liberty is that her activity threatens to cause harm to nonconsenting others. (In an alternative but nonequivalent formulation of the liberty principle, Mill asserts that the only good reason to restrict individual liberty is to prevent harm to others.) In his writings on political economy he defends economic competition and free exchange but proposes for the state the role of providing needed public goods and anticipates the day when workers associating in voluntary cooperatives will gradually replace the capitalist firm as the dominant form of economic enterprise.[2] In *Considerations on Representative Government* (Chapter 8) he argues for representative democracy, with universal suffrage, and proportional representation, but qualified by a plural votes scheme that gives extra ballots to the better educated voters. In *The Subjection of Women* (Chapter 9) Mill argues that the then current legal subordination of women to men 'ought to be replaced by a principle of perfect equality, admitting no power or privilege on the one side, nor disability on the other'.

In each of these cases critics have raised questions both about the viability of Mill's proposals taken on their own and about the consistency of Mill's liberalism and his Utilitarianism.

Mill's views on representative democracy have provoked the complaint that the right to vote and to stand for office in free elections is a simple demand of justice, which ought to be fulfilled regardless of whether a contingent and inevitably uncertain calculation of likely consequences supports this right. Justice not utility is claimed to be the true rationale of equal democratic citizenship. Mill's hedged commitment to democracy as evidenced by his support of plural votes is cited as evidence that his Utilitarian arguments fail to capture the strength and quality of most people's allegiance to democratic principles.[3]

Julia Annas (Chapter 10) finds *The Subjection of Women* to be a confused mixture of a reformist approach to the liberation of women founded on a utilitarian concern for satisfying preferences as they are and a radical approach which takes people's present preferences to be part of the problem and envisages circumstances of equality as shaping people's values and wants for the better. (For a quite different view of the moral significance of present preferences, see Chapter 20 by George Sher in Volume III.)

Consider Mill's defence of the liberty principle. For interestingly diverse views of Mill's argument in *On Liberty* and its relationship to his *Utilitarianism*, see D.G. Brown's 'Mill on Liberty and Morality'(Chapter 11), David Lyons's 'Human Rights and the General Welfare' (Chapter 14), H.J. McCloskey's 'Mill's Liberalism' (Chapter 15), and Michael S. McPherson's 'Mill's Moral Theory and the Problem of Preference Change' (Chapter 16). Mill holds that restriction of individual liberty in violation of the liberty principle is always counterproductive in terms of utility. Somewhat more precisely, he holds that more utility will be generated by resolutely adhering to the liberty principle than could be gained by deciding on a case by case basis whether an exception to the liberty principle should be made here or here or here. But why suppose this? It has seemed to many readers that Mill is being dogmatic on a very uncertain question of fact which should be approached tentatively. Others have claimed that Mill cannot prove that utility will be maximized by absolute conformity to the liberty principle, because this in fact is not true: sometimes restricting people's liberty for their own good does more good than harm. The general issue raised here is that the essence of liberalism as a political doctrine is the assertion of firmly guaranteed individual rights to freedom of expression, prerogatives of democratic citizenship, wide liberty of action, and the like. A firm commitment to individual rights is not obviously consistent with the recommendation always to undertake whatever action or policy will maximize the sum of human happiness.

On this point, see especially Lyons (Chapter 14) and the contribution of Russell Hardin, 'The Utilitarian Logic of Liberalism' (Chapter 12). Lyons explores the issue by clarifying Mill's Utilitarian understanding of moral obligation and moral rights in *Utilitarianism* (Chapter 6). One way to construe Utilitarian morality is the Act-Utilitarian doctrine: when choosing among known risks one morally ought to do that act among the available alternatives which maximizes expected utility. According to Lyons, this is not Mill's view. Mill holds that among the inexpedient acts that fail to maximize utility, the acts that are wrong are those that it would be expedient to punish in some way, and among the morally wrong acts, the unjust acts are those that violate an individual right (a claim that society should honour, in order to maximize the general welfare). Lyons concludes that a Utilitarian can endorse the view that one should not infringe individual moral rights even if doing so would maximize utility on the particular occasion. The utilitarian 'can take rights seriously', asserts Lyons (p. 262).

The question remains whether the sort of rights that can be justified by a general welfare standard or utility-maximizing view will dovetail reasonably well with the sorts of individual rights that are characteristic of the liberal tradition and that Mill works to defend.

The problem can perhaps best be introduced by way of a simple and extreme case. Imagine that there are a very large number of bored and unhappy plebians in ancient Rome. Spectacles can increase their happiness. As it happens, bloody spectacles such as forced gladiatorial contests and the tossing of disliked Christians to the lions are the best sorts of spectacles for the purpose of increasing the happiness of the Roman masses. From a utilitarian standpoint these persecution spectacles are morally costly insofar as they impose terrible unhappiness on a few gladiators and Christians and their friends and relatives. Probably the unhappiness caused by these spectacles outweighs the happiness they cause sufficiently to bring it about that Utilitarianism on balance does not recommend the staging of persecution spectacles. One might also mention the bad effects on the characters of the Roman spectators of taking pleasure in these bloody spectacles; and one might speculate that such character deformation is also likely to be productive of future bad consequences. Nonetheless, according to Utilitarian maximizing calculation, if the number of plebian spectators is sufficiently large and the pleasures they gain sufficiently intense, it could be that the Utilitarian right policy in these circumstances is to stage persecution spectacles. The unhappiness of the few persecuted ones is overbalanced by the offsetting gains in happiness to the many. (Note that this problem could arise on Mill's view of utility and rights as interpreted by Lyons as well as on a straight Act-utilitarianism.)

But for many of us the Utilitarian analysis of this scenario constitutes a decisive objection against Utilitarian principle. We think that the coerced gladiators and the tossed Christians have rights to liberty and physical security which in justice must outweigh any amount of pleasure that violating these rights would cause. Utilitarianism does not take rights seriously.

In one way or another Chapters 12 to 14 are concerned with the conflict between utility and individual rights. H.L.A. Hart's 'Between Utility and Rights' (Chapter 13) both agrees with liberal rights-based criticism of Utilitarianism and criticizes two prominent contemporary rights theorists in a way that raises a general question about whether liberal theory as developed so far contains sufficient resources of its own decisively to supplant Utilitarianism.

Libertarian Liberalism

The political philosophy of libertarianism is probably best characterized as the denial that it is morally permissable for the state to assume any function beyond the protection of persons from murder, assault, physical damage to their persons and property, coercion, theft, fraud and breach of contract (this list is substantially drawn from Nagel (Chapter 21)). At the level of moral obligation, individuals are bound according to libertarianism to refrain from injuring persons or threatening to injure persons in any of these ways, with the qualification that someone who does wrong to others may be subjected to coercion and punishment that it would be wrong to impose except for his wrongdoing. In a slogan, each individual is to be left free to live her life as she chooses so long as she does not wrongfully harm nonconsenting others.

The list of what libertarianism counts as ways of wrongful harming is not very precisely specified. It is fair to say that for libertarians that idea of what individuals may permissibly do without wrongfully harming their fellows is tailored to a certain conception of what people are typically permitted to do in an economy organized around free markets. Harming another person by outdoing her in market competition is not wrongful injury. Failing to offer help to a person who needs it is not wrongful injury. Similarly, if I own a resource which you need badly, and I decline to offer you access to the resource, this failure to share is not wrongful injury. *Caveat emptor* is a libertarian moral principle. So if I offer to sell you a car and I make no guarantee that it has an engine in sound condition or working brakes, I do you no wrong if the price you pay me for the car is influenced by your false beliefs about the car's condition – whereas if I had deliberately induced the false belief in you, the deal would be fraudulent. The same assessment holds for nonfraudulent profitmaking manipulation by a buyer of false beliefs entertained by a seller. *Caveat venditor* is then a libertarian principle as well.

The libertarian frowns on coercive impositions on persons in the absence of prior consent, so free-riding behaviour that does not involve violation of property rights is tolerated. If all my neighbours join together to pay for prompt snow removal on our street, I am not obligated to pay what is deemed my fair share, nor am I forbidden to drive on the plowed street if the others band together without my cooperation to provide the good.

The libertarian also insists on unimpeded free contract. Being the sole rightful owner of myself, I am free to sell myself into serfdom or slavery if I choose. Whether or not such contracts would be ill-advised from my point of view does not give others a right to interfere. By the same token I am free to commit suicide or maim myself or sell my body parts or make no provision for my retirement or for medical disability. I am free to enter into any sort of sexual relation I choose with persons who are willing, including momentary liaisons and permanent marriage contracts with no possibility of divorce.

Libertarianism as I am characterizing it is a view about what the state may permissibly do and what individuals may permissibly do to each other. Such a view might be justified by a variety of more foundational ethical positions. The American Ayn Rand believes that libertarianism can be derived from ethical egoism, the doctrine that each person ought always to act so as to do the best she can for her own interests. Jan Narveson in Chapter 20 pursues a closely related contractarian argument for libertarianism. (He believes that actual people with full information about the circumstances of their lives would unanimously agree to libertarian principles and to nothing further.) Under certain improbable factual conditions, utilitarianism would imply libertarianism. Herbert Spencer appeals to a mixture of utilitarian argument, appeal to natural rights, and to the 'science of life' (Chapters 17 and 18). In *Anarchy, State and Utopia*, the most philosophically sophisticated recent defence of libertarianism, Robert Nozick appeals to a Lockean doctrine of natural rights and hints that this doctrine can be grounded in Kantian moral premises. Chapter 21 by Thomas Nagel is a highly critical review essay on Nozick's book. In short, there are several paths of argument leading to libertarianism.

In Eric Mack's formulation (Chapter 9), libertarianism dissolves the tensions of Lockeanism, by cutting away all its attachments except to the core libertarian rights. The intuitive appeal of this manoeuvre can perhaps best be appreciated by considering the implications of libertarianism for self-ownership. According to the libertarian, each person is the rightful full owner of herself. One has full property rights over one's own body, which means that no other person has any property rights over one's body. Libertarianism upholds the freedom of each individual in this sense. Owning my own body (my self), I am morally free to do whatever I want with it so long as I do not wrongfully harm others with it. I am free to perform self-destructive acts (or what others deem to be such) if I wish. No-one has the right to interfere on the ground that the act I would choose would harm me. My liberty here trumps other people's judgements of what would be good for me. Owning myself, I am not under any enforceable obligation to help any other person unless I have promised or contractually agreed to render assistance. It might be morally nice if I choose to help those less fortunate than myself, but according to libertarianism I have the right not to offer help and no-one has the right to force me to help. Moreover, what no individual or group of individuals may force me to do, the state is not empowered to coerce me into doing either. That is, the state has no valid authority to force individuals to help others by such means as redistributive taxation to aid the needy. (Nozick asserts that redistributive taxation is tantamount to forced labour; Spencer asserts that a *slave* is someone who is forced to labour for the benefit of another.) Owning myself, I am free to behave as I wish so long as I do not wrongfully harm others, even if other people regard my behaviour as scandalous or immoral. For example, I might choose to have sex with someone of my own sex, and if that person consents, since nobody else is wrongfully harmed no-one has the right to coerce me to desist.

In short, libertarian self-ownership forbids paternalistic restriction of liberty, enforced charity, and coercive moralism. Within the liberal tradition the former two limits on individual and state action are controversial, but the third is not. Social-democratic liberals, for instance, countenance forcing someone (a) to wear seat belts in cars for his own good and (b) to pay taxes for the good of others but not (c) to refrain from harmless 'immorality'.

A full libertarian doctrine proceeds beyond the assertion of self-ownership to the claim that self-owning persons may justifiably acquire full private ownership rights over land and the other resources of the earth, either by transfer from a legitimate owner or by initial acquisition of unowned resources. The arguments for this further step are tricky. For some relevant discussion, see the discussion of 'Lockean Property Rights' in the section on Locke and Lockean Liberalism in Volume I. Since initial appropriation of an unowned resource augments the liberty of the appropriator and diminishes the liberty of everyone else, contemporaries and members of future generations who thereafter lack the opportunity to appropriate for themselves, the justification of full private ownership in a world of limited resources is bound to be complex.

Herbert Spencer's essays (Chapters 17 to 19) forcibly urge several lines of argument against expansion of the activities of government beyond those of the classic night-watchman state. One argument opposes sentimental humanitarianism which does more harm than good. Spencer poses the question: 'Is it not manifest that there must exist in our midst an immense amount of misery which is a normal result of misconduct and ought not to be dissociated from it?' (p. 411). In Spencer's view much poverty is the result of dissolute living, fecklessness, laziness and shortsighted spending habits. It is folly for the state to attempt to make happiness rather than unhappiness the outcome of bad conduct; the attempt weakens the incentives to good conduct and must be counterproductive. A variant of this argument asserts that much of the current misery of the poor has been caused by misguided attempts by legislators in the past to intervene on behalf of the poor. The intelligent humanitarian who discerns the causal connections will follow the libertarian path and resist the temptation to institute state activity aimed at 'solving' problems that are better left alone. At some points Spencer stresses the utilitarian point that state charity does more harm than good. At some points Spencer suggests that the productive and wealthy citizens are more worthy and more deserving than the unproductive and impoverished citizens. Spencer's essays published in 1884 eerily anticipate contemporary conservative rhetoric.

A second line of thought energetically pursued by Spencer is that piecemeal state activism has the unintended consequence of building up an ever-larger class of public officials with an interest in further expansion of the state sector, increasing their class pride and assertiveness, encouraging the beneficiaries of piecemeal activism to expect more and more from the state rather than to make do for themselves, and discouraging the private enterprise of productive citizens. The result is a drift over time toward state tyranny.

A third line of Spencerian argument combines the idea that societies tend to move toward one of two poles and a kind of Social Darwinism. The first idea is that a society will inevitably tend either to a system of voluntary cooperation or state-coerced cooperation, a system of contract or status. The Social Darwinist premise is that the laws of life dictate that only the systems of voluntary cooperation will survive in long-run equilibrium and that the more worthy will crowd out the less worthy under these voluntary conditions. This argument might seem only an historical curiosity but I think it retains some influence. A recurrent theme in conservative thought down to the present day is speculation about what causes great empires and great nations to rise and decline, these speculations often fueling laissez-faire policy recommendations.

Jan Narveson's 'Equality vs. Liberty: Advantage, Liberty' (Chapter 20) contrasts equality of condition as a social ideal with a libertarian understanding of the ideal of individual liberty. Narveson offers a contractarian argument for liberty, understood in the libertarian way.

'Libertarianism Without Foundations' (Chapter 21) by Thomas Nagel is a review essay discussing Robert Nozick's arguments for libertarianism. The criticisms developed, if valid, do not take Nozick's position uniquely as their target but have a broader reach.

Social-Democratic Liberalism

In the latter half of the nineteenth century, particularly on the European continent, the movement for political democracy and the extension of the suffrage often revealed rifts between 'straight' republicans in conflict with 'social' republicans or social democrats. Karl Marx's journalistic writings on the French revolutionary conflicts between 1848 and 1851 contain a classic account of this tension interpreted as class conflict between working class, peasant, bourgeois and petit-bourgeois elements in the movement for democracy.[4] For purposes of understanding liberal political theory, it is more important to appreciate the overt substance of such disputes than to speculate about the class interests that supposedly underlay them. However, through much of this period the programmatic differences between left-leaning and right-leaning liberals were often vague and murky. The straight republicans advocated a democratic republic with universal manhood suffrage or a light property qualification for the suffrage. The advocates of the social republic favoured a democratic republic plus something extra, but what exactly this something extra was that would render the republic 'social' was not always clear. In general terms, the social-democratic attitude favoured the adoption of interventionist social and economic policies by a democratic state in order to improve the welfare of the worse off section of the population, especially the working class, compared with the welfare levels this section of the population could expect under a laissez-faire free-market regime.

As I am using the terms, social-democratic liberalism is directly opposed to libertarian liberalism. Both views are defined in terms of their beliefs about the proper role of the state particularly in regard to economic policy under modern conditions. The contrast between Utilitarian and Kantian liberalism is different in kind: here the opposition is between rival foundational moral premises invoked in support of whatever sort of liberal political arrangements are preferred – libertarian, social-democratic, or other.

I will briefly sketch several different types of argument that converge on social-democratic policy conclusions.

1. The ideal of a democratic society as an association of equal citizens who participate with equal power in the making of the laws that all must obey is not automatically achieved by extending the vote to all citizens. A democratic political order might be ruled in accordance with the outcomes of elections in which all citizens have an equal vote, yet the society would be only formally a democracy. For although all have equal votes, access to the media of communication may be strictly limited for most citizens, who lack the financial means that open this access. But lacking effective access to major media, these citizens of limited means have limited opportunities to persuade other citizens in democratic deliberation. Also, politicians may be beholden to wealthy citizens, who make large political contributions to their political campaigns or otherwise are in the position to do important favours for politicians. In short, wealth inequality (and perhaps other socially significant inequalities such as educational inequality) can render ineffective the formal equality of democratic citizenship. So in order to achieve true democracy and substantially equal citizenship, it may be necessary to maintain legally enforced rights of popular access to the print and broadcast media, or establish publicly funded political campaigns, or institute limits on campaign spending, or enforce upper bounds on permissible inequalities of wealth, income, or education.

2. Democracy in the political sphere and capitalist hierarchy in the economic sphere are an unstable combination. At least, the experience of hierarchy in the everyday grind of economic life reduces the willingness of those at the bottom of economic hierarchies to participate actively in democratic politics. Capitalist hierarchy at work breeds attitudes of hierarchy in workers, managers and owners, and these attitudes of deference and command do not consort well with the attitudes and character traits one expects in democratic citizens. Capitalist work arrangements breed passivity and other attitudes at odds with the traits and virtues which individuals should develop in order adequately to fulfill the role of democratic citizen. Hence capitalist hierarchy should be done away with and democratic citizenship rights should be extended to economic enterprises, in the interests of promoting the psychological attitudes and behavioural dispositions on which healthy and vigorous democratic politics depends.

3. Grinding poverty and severe uncertainty about one's economic future are incompatible with successful fulfillment of the responsibilities of democratic citizens. Similarly, lack of education and lack of knowledge about the contemporary world and the history of democratic institutions unfit one for the role of democratic citizen. One option here is to let the distribution of goods and services and income and education and wealth be determined by an unregulated free exchange market. But this is a counsel of despair, for we know that the unregulated market will generate a class of unemployed, barely employed and uncertainly employed citizens whose economic woes and cares will effectively sap their personal resources and drain their self-esteem and leave them little of the free time, energy or gumption that are required for active citizenship. Hence the state has a vital role to play in sustaining for each citizen the economic prerequisites of active citizenzhip. For most citizens, the role of the state will be to provide social insurance against uninsurable bad luck and to provide educational opportunities and a framework of laws that enable the individual to provide for herself. For some unfortunate and unlucky citizens, the role of the state must be greater and more continuously guiding. In all cases the state is to be seen as a mechanism used by all of us that helps each of

us to clasp hands with our neighbours, steadying ourselves and helping to keep those who are wobbling from falling to the gutter.

4. If the aim of the liberal state is to promote and protect the freedom of all citizens, we must distinguish merely 'formal' freedom from 'substantive' or 'effective' freedom and understand that the genuinely liberal state is concerned above all with the latter. This distinction between formal and substantive freedom has been variously construed. One important aspect of the distinction is the contrast between what I am legally permitted to do and what I have the resources to do, so that if I chose to I could do it. I may be legally free to attend the opera or travel abroad but lack the resources for doing either. The resources that render freedom effective may be financial or other. Perhaps in order to appreciate the opera I need some musical training, and to be secure in travel abroad I need some education in map-reading. The same contrast between merely formal and substantive arises also in the context of measuring unfreedom. The law in its majesty may forbid rich and poor alike from sleeping under bridges, but the restrictions of this law bear harder on the poor than on the rich.

The social-democrat is suspicious of focusing attention on formal freedom to the exclusion of seeing beyond it to gauge the quality and range of the effective opportunities that are open to individuals. If one adds to a concern for effective opportunity a special concern for those members of society who are below average or far below average in their allotment of these opportunities, one has a rationale for considerable state intervention in economic life in order to ameliorate the lot of the downtrodden.

Origins

Most of the arguments sketched above can be found in Chapters 22 to 25, excerpts from L.T. Hobhouse's book *Liberalism*, first published in 1911. Hobhouse was not a systematic thinker. C. Wright Mills was doubtless paying tribute to its generosity of spirit rather than to its analytic rigour when he called Hobhouse's *Liberalism* 'the best twentieth-century statement of liberal ideals I know'. Several themes run through this book. By listing some of them one can detect a continuity of concern between Hobhouse's thought and the welfare-state programmes of the British Labour Party instituted after World War II. One can also discern some affinity between Hobhouse's thinking and the economic and social reform policies instituted by the US President Franklin Delano Roosevelt during the Great Depression of the 1930s (although FDR's preoccupation is more with fixing a broken economy than with correcting the inequities in a smoothly functioning market economy).

Many arguments in *Liberalism* aim to rebut the presumption that the government ought not to tamper with the outcomes of an unregulated market economy. Hobhouse writes that even if most competing employers wish to institute health and safety benefits for their employees, they may be constrained by one hold-out employer who would undersell the others, so government regulation mandating health and safety would be misdescribed if called a reduction of liberty. Hobhouse ventures the opinion that nothing guarantees that the market economy will secure to each reasonably enterprising worker a wage that suffices for civilized life, so the shortfall should be made good by all of us collectively through the state. The market economy generates periodic large-scale unemployment, for which the unemployed individual is not responsible, but which the state is bound to alleviate. The free market generates large incomes to property owners that really belong to society and may justly be expropriated by the state for this purpose. His example is the rising value of land in the vicinity of great and growing cities.

Another theme developed by Hobhouse is the legitimacy and proper limits of paternalistic state policy. Hobhouse dissents from Mill's strict antipaternalism. Sometimes restricting someone's liberty for his own good will foster his autonomy, get him on his own feet as it were. The problem is to stop short of paternalism that interferes with the individual's right to live her life in her own way. Again, the state envisaged by Hobhouse provides paternalistic aid to unfortunate citizens, but does so in ways calculated to boost individual initiative and a sense of prudent care for self. As Hobhouse puts it, 'the function of the State is to secure conditions upon which its citizens are able to win by their own efforts all that is necessary to a full civic efficiency' (p. 495).

A third theme in Hobhouse's writing is individualism. In this respect he sees himself pursuing the goals advanced by John Stuart Mill by somewhat different means. The aim is to enhance individual self-development and individual liberty by positive state action and state regulation. On this ground Hobhouse opposes what he calls 'mechanical' and 'official' socialism.

In turning from Hobhouse to R.H. Tawney we find a quite different animating spirit. Something of this spirit is discernible in the title of Tawney's pamphlet 'The Sickness of an Acquisitive Society' (Chapter 26). Tawney sees modern capitalist society as individualism run amok. He hears the property owner asking the ugly rhetorical question 'May I not do what I like with my own?' whenever it is proposed to restrict the prerogatives of private ownership for the public good – to enforce a minimum standard of safety and sanitation in privately owned mines and mills, for example. An acquisitive society Tawney takes to be one whose members are dedicated above all to the acquisition of wealth. A capitalist society tends to become an acquisitive society in part owing to its ideological origin in a glorification of property rights considered without regard to economic functions or service to the community. Tawney thinks this sort of society is inimical to human welfare, but he objects most strongly to the greedy motivations it promotes and the absence of communal regard it fosters.

The socialism that Tawney passionately advocates is a form of community in which individuals are motivated to serve the common welfare and to be liberated from the narrow horizons of endless self-seeking. As he puts it, 'A society which aimed at making the acquisition of wealth contingent upon the discharge of social obligations, which sought to proportion remuneration to service and denied it to those by whom no service was performed, which inquired first not what men possess but what they can make or create or achieve, might be called a Functional Society, because in such a society the main subject of social emphasis would be the performance of functions' (p. 530). Social functions on this view are not just objects of institutional design. These functions would shape individual motivation in a decent society. The spirit of Tawney's thought is akin to the romanticism of the 'Estranged Labour' section of the *Economic and Philosophic Manuscripts of 1844* by Karl Marx. In Tawney and in the early Marx the main objection to capitalism is what it does to the human soul. Tawney's argument is liberal but pushes a strand of liberalism to its outer envelope, close to utopian repudiation of human nature. Tawney harnesses sensible plans of social reform to a vision of society in which human nature will have been gradually transformed for the better, shedding the traces of bad capitalist socialization.

Recent Formulations

John Rawls's work, epitomized in 'A Kantian Conception of Equality', can be regarded as a philosophy of the modern welfare state. The hallmark of the welfare state is that society through the agency of the state takes responsibility for sustaining adequate opportunities for a decent life for each of its members regardless of their marketable skills or lack thereof. On this topic the reader may wish to consult the 'Liberalism and Distributive Justice' section of the Introduction to Volume III and Rawls's essay 'The Idea of an Overlapping Consensus' (Chapter 10) reprinted in that same volume.

One can approach Rawls's thought by noting a vague formulation by Hobhouse. Hobhouse writes that the ideal of equality of opportunity, which he endorses, implies that 'whatever inequality of actual treatment, of income, rank, office, consideration, there be in a good social system, it would rest, not on the interest of the favoured individual as such, but on the common good' (p. 482). But what is the common good? Rawls invokes a Kantian ideal of the dignity of the individual and the inviolability of her freedom to interpret the idea of the common good as requiring equal treatment and tolerating departures from equal treatment only to the extent that the inequalities work to maximize the benefit level of the worst off citizens. Since all are of equal worth, none should enjoy special benefits not enjoyed by others except insofar as these favourable inequalities work maximally to the advantage of the least advantaged. Rawls specifies and sharpens the idea of the common good construed as the standard of justified inequality.

Rawls appeals to the Kantian ideal of a society as an association of free and equal moral persons to support a special concern for freedom of expression and other civil liberties and an insistence that these basic liberties be provided equally to all citizens. Hence Rawls asserts two principles of social justice, a principle of equal liberty and a principle regulating the distribution of social and economic benefits, and gives strict priority to the equal liberty principle. The priority of liberty in Rawls's system of justice is justified by characterizing the idea of a free and equal moral person. Persons differ in the kinds of lives they wish to pursue and they know that they have fundamental interests, such as religious interests, that require a framework of guaranteed civil liberty for their successful pursuit. Moreover, individuals also regard themselves as having a capacity to reason about their interests and values and to revise even their most fundamental interests and they wish to give priority to their liberty in this regard over the instrumental goal of satisfying whatever interests they happen to have at the moment. For this reason the idea of a state-established religion or the secular equivalent in the form of a state-established orthodoxy is anathema to free persons. In the Rawlsian conception an egalitarian state is above all egalitarian in its provision of fundamental civil liberties. Social and economic equality is important, but secondary.

Free persons are regarded as capable of assuming responsibility for their life plans and even for the choice of basic goals that shape life plans. The just society in Rawls's view takes responsibility for providing each citizen a fair share of material means and general-purpose resources according to the terms of the principle that regulates the distribution of social and economic benefits. In turn the individual takes responsibility for shaping her own wants and values and fashioning a reasonable plan of life given her expected circumstances. According to Rawls's principles of justice do not look beyond the fair provision of opportunities to assess the final outcomes that people reach – these are matters for which individuals themselves take responsibility given fair background conditions.

At this point Rawls considers a libertarian-inspired objection. Why not let individuals take full responsibility for their lives including responsibility for gaining the resources they need by voluntary exchange with others (or gifts freely bestowed by private citizens)? Why should free persons be hampered in their contractual freedom by the impositions of a redistributive state? Rawls's response is that the 'free and voluntary' contracts that individuals reach are genuinely free and voluntary only if fair background conditions obtain, so that individual choice is not coerced or compelled or unduly constrained. But nothing in the working of an unregulated free market guarantees that these background conditions will continue to be met over time. Accidents of fortune can make some abjectly dependent on reaching a contractual agreement with others. The basic institutions of society must function justly – must continuously generate tolerable conditions – or else pressures of economic compulsion render it inappropriate to ask individuals to take responsibility for their voluntary choices. Rawls's Kantian conception of equality provides one interpretation of the idea of maintaining fair background conditions as the condition for holding individuals responsible for their voluntary choices.

Philip Pettit's essay 'Towards a Social Democratic Theory of the State' (Chapter 28) concisely illustrates how a consequentialist approach to political theory combines with a traditional liberal ideal to generate a programme for state action. Pettit postulates the norm that every citizen enjoys or ought to enjoy equal respect as common ground between the liberal democrat and the social democrat. The liberal democrat according to Pettit interprets the norm as a deontological requirement, so that respect is to be exemplified whatever the consequences. The social democrat according to Pettit interprets the norm as a goal to be maximized. In the actual world, people are not equally respectable, because variations in ignorance, talent, skill, resources and character traits ensure that different individuals conduct themselves in a manner that is worthy of respect to different degrees. The state then, taking people and conditions as they are, should strive to emancipate and empower individuals so that they become more nearly equally worthy of respect. In this formulation the Kantian norm of equal respect becomes a goal to be maximized by any means necessary. Pettit does not spell out the implications of this consequentialist reading of the equal respect norm for state policy, but he evidently believes these implications in broad outline support the interventionist policies of twentieth-century democratic welfare states and perhaps entail further interventions better described as socialist.

In the late 1970s and throughout the 1980s the panoply of social welfare services provided by modern democratic industrial states in England and on the European continent has suffered retrenchment owing to economic downturns and has come under sharp moral attack as well from right-wing politicians and political theorists. In 'Citizenship, Social Citizenship, and the Defence of Welfare Provision' (Chapter 29) Desmond S. King and Jeremy Waldron develop a moral argument supporting social democratic welfare state policies. They consider three broad lines of defence. One line is that in order to be a full citizen and participating member of society, the individual must have access to a high standard of education, health care, job access, involuntary unemployment relief, and the like. A stable democratic order requires citizens sufficiently free of material care to participate intelligently in public life. The stability of a democratic order also depends on solidarity ties uniting all citizens which extreme poverty and extreme inequalities of wealth tend to erode. The second line they consider is that the actual politics of welfare states in the twentieth century generates legitimate expectations in citizens which ought to be respected or at least not suddenly and drastically violated. The third line of argument they pursue is that if individuals were to choose principles to regulate social life under conditions of complete ignorance about their own wealth or poverty or the marketability of their skills, they would choose principles that provide strong social insurance against the worst possible outcomes for individuals, and this social insurance is tantamount to welfare state policy.

It is perhaps worth mentioning that King and Waldron assume that it is important to the idea of a welfare state that the major benefits it provides are available to all citizens as a matter of right and not a special dispensation granted only to those who can prove their special need. The policy of universal provision of benefits to all citizens is thought to remove the stigma from acceptance of government hand-outs and to foster a sense of solidarity among all citizens. I myself do not see any particular moral advantage in universal provision as opposed to targeted benefits for the needy. Should the state supply health care for all citizens or only for the poor who cannot afford adequate care? Unless there are economies of scale that make society-wide provision more efficient, I would favour targeted aid for the needy. The welfare state is not supposed to be a boondoggle of 'free' benefits for everyone. Rather the moral ideal is that more fortunate individuals should acknowledge strong obligations to those who happen to be less fortunate. But there are complexities lurking in this issue, as the reader will note by considering what might be said for public provision of schooling for all children by the democratic state, as opposed to school aid targeted for the poor.

Beyond the Welfare State?

The development of welfare state policies firmly entrenched changes the nature of a capitalist system. If the state guarantees a minimal level of welfare aid, then an individual deciding whether or not to accept an employment offer is not faced with the choice of 'work or starve'. The higher the level of benefits provided to those who do not work, the more free and voluntary, other things equal, is the decision to accept any employment offer. If the level of benefits is sufficiently high, individuals can afford to choose to forego paid employment and take up self-employment options or collective self-help schemes which would be too risky to undertake in the absence of the state-guaranteed minimum.

The above consideration can be interpreted as an argument that the state should provide a guaranteed minimal income to all citizens at as high a level as is feasible in order to increase the freedom of individuals in labour market transactions. The welfare aid should be given in the form of income that can be spent on anything rather than in the form of particular benefits if the aim is to maximize the freedom of individuals receiving the aid. There are other arguments that seem to favour a guaranteed income or basic income paid by the state to all citizens. Welfare policies targeted for the needy are costly and difficult to monitor. Officials must screen the truly needy from the nonneedy, and this screening can be distasteful and costly. Also, there may be an efficiency loss, as individuals adapt their actions so as to be eligible for the welfare aid or to sustain their eligibility. A guaranteed basic income then recommends itself on the ground that since individuals will receive it whatever they do, no incentive is supplied to undertake socially wasteful or costly activity in order to meet eligibility requirements.

Robert van der Veen and Philippe Van Parijs are advocates of a guaranteed basic income.

In 'A Capitalist Road to Communism' (Chapter 30) they speculate about the transformations in a capitalist market economy that might ensue if a basic income policy were pushed to the limit. The reader will wish to ponder whether their arguments favouring basic income guarantees are sufficiently strong to overturn the suspicion that there is something wrong with a system in which ablebodied willfully unemployed citizens are supported by those citizens who do engage in paid labour. One should also note that there might be legitimate paternalist reasons for providing welfare aid in kind rather than in the form of income. Also, in some cases the state gives aid to families in the form of aid in order to reduce the temptation of adult recipients to turn the aid from its intended use. For example, the state that is concerned for the health of poor children might give milk to poor families instead of money, which might be spent by the parents on beer for themselves.

Notes

1. John Stuart Mill, *An Examination of Sir William Hamilton's Philosophy*.
2. See John Stuart Mill, *Principles of Political Economy*, vols. 2 and 3 of *Collected Works*, ed. J.M. Robson (Toronto and Buffalo: University of Toronto Press, 1965).
3. For this criticism of Mill, see Charles Beitz, *Political Equality* (Princeton: Princeton University Press, 1989).
4. Karl Marx, 'The Class Struggles in France 1848–1850', in Karl Marx and Frederick Engels, *Collected Works*, vol. 10 (New York: International Publishers, 1978), pp. 45–145; Karl Marx, 'The Eighteenth Brumaire of Louis Bonaparte', in Karl Marx and Frederick Engels, *Collected Works*, vol. 11 (New York: International Publishers, 1979), pp. 99–197.

Part I
Utilitarian Liberalism

A
Nineteenth-Century Writings

[1]

Excerpt from *The Collected Works of Jeremy Bentham*, 11–16

CHAPTER I

OF THE PRINCIPLE OF UTILITY

1. Nature has placed mankind under the governance of two sovereign masters, *pain* and *pleasure*. It is for them alone to point out what we ought to do, as well as to determine what we shall do. On the one hand the standard of right and wrong, on the other the chain of causes and effects, are fastened to their throne. They govern us in all we do, in all we say, in all we think: every effort we can make to throw off our subjection, will serve but to demonstrate and confirm it. In words a man may pretend to abjure their empire: but in reality he will remain subject to it all the while. The *principle of utility*[a] recognises this subjection, and assumes it for the foundation of that system, the object of which is to rear the fabric of felicity by the hands of reason and of law. Systems which attempt to question it, deal in sounds instead of sense, in caprice instead of reason, in darkness instead of light.

Mankind governed by pain and pleasure

But enough of metaphor and declamation: it is not by such means that moral science is to be improved.

2. The principle of utility is the foundation of the present work: it will be proper therefore at the outset to give an explicit and determinate account of what is meant by it. By the principle[b] of utility

Principle of utility, what

[a] Note by the Author, July 1822.

To this denomination has of late been added, or substituted, the *greatest happiness* or *greatest felicity* principle: this for shortness, instead of saying at length *that principle* which states the greatest happiness of all those whose interest is in question, as being the right and proper, and only right and proper and universally desirable, end of human action: of human action in every situation, and in particular in that of a functionary or set of functionaries exercising the powers of Government. The word *utility* does not so clearly point to the ideas of *pleasure* and *pain* as the words *happiness* and *felicity* do: nor does it lead us to the consideration of the *number*, of the interests affected; to the *number*, as being the circumstance, which contributes, in the largest proportion, to the formation of the standard here in question; the *standard of right and wrong*, by which alone the propriety of human conduct, in every situation, can with propriety be tried. This want of a sufficiently manifest connexion between the ideas of *happiness* and *pleasure* on the one hand, and the idea of *utility* on the other, I have every now and then found operating, and with but too much efficiency, as a bar to the acceptance, that might otherwise have been given, to this principle.

[b](Principle) The word principle is derived from the Latin *principium*: which seems to be compounded of the two words *primus*, first, or chief, and *cipium*, a

A principle, what

11

is meant that principle which approves or disapproves of every action whatsoever, according to the tendency which it appears to have to augment or diminish the happiness of the party whose interest is in question: or, what is the same thing in other words, to promote or to oppose that happiness. I say of every action whatsoever; and therefore not only of every action of a private individual, but of every measure of government.

Utility, what　　**3.** By utility is meant that property in any object, whereby it tends to produce benefit, advantage, pleasure, good, or happiness, (all this in the present case comes to the same thing) or (what comes again to the same thing) to prevent the happening of mischief, pain, evil, or unhappiness to the party whose interest is considered: if that party be the community in general, then the happiness of the community: if a particular individual, then the happiness of that individual.

Interest of the community, what　　**4.** The interest of the community is one of the most general expressions that can occur in the phraseology of morals: no wonder that the meaning of it is often lost. When it has a meaning, it is this. The community is a fictitious *body*, composed of the individual persons who are considered as constituting as it were its *members*. The interest of the community then is, what?—the sum of the interests of the several members who compose it.

5. It is in vain to talk of the interest of the community, without understanding what is the interest of the individual.[c] A thing is said to promote the interest, or to be *for* the interest, of an individual, when it tends to add to the sum total of his pleasures: or, what comes to the same thing, to diminish the sum total of his pains.

An action conformable to the principle of utility, what　　**6.** An action then may be said to be conformable to the principle of utility, or, for shortness sake, to utility, (meaning with respect to the community at large) when the tendency it has to augment

termination which seems to be derived from *capio*, to take, as in *mancipium, municipium*; to which are analogous *auceps, forceps*, and others. It is a term of very vague and very extensive signification: it is applied to any thing which is conceived to serve as a foundation or beginning to any series of operations: in some cases, of physical operations; but of mental operations in the present case.

The principle here in question may be taken for an act of the mind; a sentiment; a sentiment of approbation; a sentiment which, when applied to an action, approves of its utility, as that quality of it by which the measure of approbation or disapprobation bestowed upon it ought to be governed.

[c] (Interest, &c.) Interest is one of those words, which not having any superior *genus*, cannot in the ordinary way be defined.

THE PRINCIPLE OF UTILITY   CHAPTER I

the happiness of the community is greater than any it has to diminish it.

7. A measure of government (which is but a particular kind of *A measure of*
action, performed by a particular person or persons) may be said *government*
conformable
to be conformable to or dictated by the principle of utility, when *to the prin-*
in like manner the tendency which it has to augment the happiness *ciple of*
utility, what
of the community is greater than any which it has to diminish it.

8. When an action, or in particular a measure of government, is *Laws or*
supposed by a man to be conformable to the principle of utility, it *dictates of*
utility, what
may be convenient, for the purposes of discourse, to imagine a kind
of law or dictate, called a law or dictate of utility: and to speak of
the action in question, as being conformable to such law or dictate.

9. A man may be said to be a partisan of the principle of utility, *A partisan of*
when the approbation or disapprobation he annexes to any action, *the principle*
of utility,
or to any measure, is determined by, and proportioned to the ten- *who*
dency which he conceives it to have to augment or to diminish the
happiness of the community: or in other words, to its conformity
or unconformity to the laws or dictates of utility.

10. Of an action that is conformable to the principle of utility, *Ought,*
one may always say either that it is one that ought to be done, *ought not,*
right and
or at least that it is not one that ought not to be done. One may say *wrong, &c.*
also, that it is right it should be done; at least that it is not wrong *how to be*
understood
it should be done: that it is a right action; at least that it is not a
wrong action. When thus interpreted, the words *ought*, and *right*
and *wrong*, and others of that stamp, have a meaning: when otherwise, they have none.

11. Has the rectitude of this principle been ever formally con- *To prove*
tested? It should seem that it had, by those who have not known *the rectitude*
of this prin-
what they have been meaning. Is it susceptible of any direct proof? *ciple is at*
it should seem not: for that which is used to prove every thing else, *once unneces-*
sary and
cannot itself be proved: a chain of proofs must have their com- *impossible*
mencement somewhere. To give such proof is as impossible as it is
needless.

12. Not that there is or ever has been that human creature *It has seldom,*
breathing, however stupid or perverse, who has not on many, *however, as*
yet, been
perhaps on most occasions of his life, deferred to it. By the natural *consistently*
constitution of the human frame, on most occasions of their lives *pursued*
men in general embrace this principle, without thinking of it: if
not for the ordering of their own actions, yet for the trying of their
own actions, as well as of those of other men. There have been,
at the same time, not many, perhaps, even of the most intelligent,
who have been disposed to embrace it purely and without reserve.

CHAPTER I   THE PRINCIPLE OF UTILITY

There are even few who have not taken some occasion or other
to quarrel with it, either on account of their not understanding
always how to apply it, or on account of some prejudice or other
which they were afraid to examine into, or could not bear to part
with. For such is the stuff that man is made of: in principle and in
practice, in a right track and in a wrong one, the rarest of all human
qualities is consistency.

It can never   **13.** When a man attempts to combat the principle of utility,
be consis-   it is with reasons drawn, without his being aware of it, from that
tently com-   very principle itself.[d] His arguments, if they prove any thing,
bated

---

[d] 'The principle of utility, (I have heard it said) is a dangerous principle:
it is dangerous on certain occasions to consult it.' This is as much as to say,
what? that it is not consonant to utility, to consult utility: in short, that it
is *not* consulting it, to consult it.

Addition by the author, July 1822.

Not long after the publication of the Fragment on Government, anno 1776,
in which, in the character of an all-comprehensive and all-commanding principle, the principle of *utility* was brought to view, one person by whom observation to the above effect was made was *Alexander Wedderburn*, at that time
Attorney or Solicitor General, afterwards successively Chief Justice of the
Common Pleas, and Chancellor of England, under the successive titles of
Lord Loughborough and Earl of Rosslyn.[1] It was made—not indeed in my
hearing, but in the hearing of a person by whom it was almost immediately
communicated to me. So far from being self-contradictory, it was a shrewd
and perfectly true one. By that distinguished functionary, the state of the
Government was thoroughly understood: by the obscure individual, at that
time not so much as supposed to be so: his disquisitions had not been as yet
applied, with any thing like a comprehensive view, to the field of Constitutional Law, nor therefore to those features of the English Government, by
which the greatest happiness of the ruling *one* with or without that of a
favoured few, are now so plainly seen to be the only ends to which the course
of it has at any time been directed. The *principle of utility* was an appellative,
at that time employed—employed by me, as it had been by others, to desig-
nate that which, in a more perspicuous and instructive manner, may, as
above, be designated by the name of the *greatest happiness principle*. 'This
principle (said Wedderburn) is a dangerous one.' Saying so, he said that which,
to a certain extent, is strictly true: a principle, which lays down, as the only
right and justifiable end of Government, the greatest happiness of the greatest
number—how can it be denied to be a dangerous one? dangerous it unquestionably is, to every government which has for its *actual* end or object, the

---

[1] Alexander Wedderburn (1733–1805), Baron Loughborough 1780, Earl of Rosslyn
1801; Solicitor-General 1771–78, Attorney-General 1778–80, Lord Chief Justice of
the Common Pleas 1780–93, Lord Chancellor 1793–1801. Bentham met Wedderburn
at the house of his friend John Lind in February 1777 (*Correspondence*, in *CW*, ii, 18)
and it was almost certainly Lind who told Bentham of Wedderburn's remark. See
also Bentham's account of the matter in the 'Historical Preface' (1828) to the
Fragment on Government, para. v (Bowring, i, 245–6).

prove not that the principle is *wrong*, but that, according to the applications he supposes to be made of it, it is *misapplied*. Is it possible for a man to move the earth? Yes; but he must first find out another earth to stand upon.

14. To disprove the propriety of it by arguments is impossible; but, from the causes that have been mentioned, or from some confused or partial view of it, a man may happen to be disposed not to relish it. Where this is the case, if he thinks the settling of his opinions on such a subject worth the trouble, let him take the following steps, and at length, perhaps, he may come to reconcile himself to it.

Course to be taken for surmounting prejudices that may have been entertained against it

(1) Let him settle with himself, whether he would wish to discard this principle altogether; if so, let him consider what it is that all his reasonings (in matters of politics especially) can amount to?

(2) If he would, let him settle with himself, whether he would judge and act without any principle, or whether there is any other he would judge and act by?

(3) If there be, let him examine and satisfy himself whether the principle he thinks he has found is really any separate intelligible principle; or whether it be not a mere principle in words, a kind of phrase, which at bottom expresses neither more nor less than the mere averment of his own unfounded sentiments; that is, what in another person he might be apt to call *caprice*?[1]

(4) If he is inclined to think that his own approbation or disapprobation, annexed to the idea of an act, without any regard to its consequences, is a sufficient foundation for him to judge and act upon, let him ask himself whether his sentiment is to be a standard of right and wrong, with respect to every other man, or

greatest happiness of a certain *one*, with or without the addition of some comparatively small number of others, whom it is matter of pleasure or accommodation to him to admit, each of them, to a share in the concern, on the footing of so many junior partners. *Dangerous* it therefore really was, to the interest—the sinister interest—of all those functionaries, himself included, whose interest it was, to maximize delay, vexation, and expense, in judicial and other modes of procedure, for the sake of the profit, extractable out of the expense. In a Government which had for its end in view the greatest happiness of the greatest number, Alexander Wedderburn might have been Attorney General and then Chancellor: but he would not have been Attorney General with £15,000 a year, nor Chancellor, with a peerage, with a veto upon all justice, with £25,000 a year, and with 500 sinecures at his disposal, under the name of Ecclesiastical Benefices, besides *et ceteras*.

[1] The emphasis on the word *caprice*, was suggested by Bentham in an Ms. entry in his copy of the 1789 edition, now in the British Museum (see above, Introduction, xl). The suggestion was not followed in 1823.

whether every man's sentiment has the same privilege of being a standard to itself?

(5) In the first case, let him ask himself whether his principle is not despotical, and hostile to all the rest of human race?

(6) In the second case, whether it is not anarchical,[1] and whether at this rate there are not as many different standards of right and wrong as there are men? and whether even to the same man, the same thing, which is right today, may not (without the least change in its nature) be wrong to-morrow? and whether the same thing is not right and wrong in the same place at the same time? and in either case, whether all argument is not at an end? and whether, when two men have said, 'I like this', and 'I don't like it', they can (upon such a principle) have any thing more to say?

(7) If he should have said to himself, No: for that the sentiment which he proposes as a standard must be grounded on reflection, let him say on what particulars the reflection is to turn? if on particulars having relation to the utility of the act, then let him say whether this is not deserting his own principle, and borrowing assistance from that very one in opposition to which he sets it up: or if not on those particulars, on what other particulars?

(8) If he should be for compounding the matter, and adopting his own principle in part, and the principle of utility in part, let him say how far he will adopt it?

(9) When he has settled with himself where he will stop, then let him ask himself how he justifies to himself the adopting it so far? and why he will not adopt it any farther?

(10) Admitting any other principle than the principle of utility to be a right principle, a principle that it is right for a man to pursue; admitting (what is not true) that the word *right* can have a meaning without reference to utility, let him say whether there is any such thing as a *motive* that a man can have to pursue the dictates of it: if there is, let him say what that motive is, and how it is to be distinguished from those which enforce the dictates of utility: if not, then lastly let him say what it is this other principle can be good for?

---

[1] Thus 1789 edn.; 1823 edn. has 'anarchial': see above, Introduction, xl n. 2.

[2]

Excerpt from *The Collected Works of Jeremy Bentham*, 158–64

CHAPTER XIII

CASES UNMEET FOR PUNISHMENT

§ i. *General view of cases unmeet for punishment*

The end of law is, to augment happiness

1. The general object which all laws have, or ought to have, in common, is to augment the total happiness of the community; and therefore, in the first place, to exclude, as far as may be, every thing that tends to subtract from that happiness: in other words, to exclude mischief.

But punishment is an evil

2. But all punishment is mischief: all punishment in itself is evil. Upon the principle of utility, if it ought at all to be admitted, it ought only to be admitted in as far as it promises to exclude some greater evil.[a]

What concerns the end, and several other topics relative to punishment, dismissed to another work

[a] What follows, relative to the subject of punishment ought regularly to be preceded by a distinct chapter on the ends of punishment. But having little to say on that particular branch of the subject, which has not been said before, it seemed better, in a work, which will at any rate be but too voluminous, to omit this title, reserving it for another hereafter to be published, intituled *The Theory of Punishment.** To the same work I must refer the analysis of the several possible modes of punishment, a particular and minute examination of the nature of each, and of its advantages and disadvantages, and various other disquisitions, which did not seem absolutely necessary to be inserted here. A very few words, however, concerning the *ends* of punishment, can scarcely be dispensed with.

Concise view of the ends of punishment

The immediate principal end of punishment is to control action. This action is either that of the offender, or of others: that of the offender it controls by its influence, either on his will, in which case it is said to operate in the way of *reformation*; or on his physical power, in which case it is said to operate by *disablement*: that of others it can influence no otherwise than by its influence over their wills; in which case it is said to operate in the way of *example*. A kind of collateral end, which it has a natural tendency to answer, is that of affording a pleasure or satisfaction to the party injured, where there is one, and, in general, to parties whose ill-will, whether on a self-regarding account,

* This is the work which, from the Author's papers, has since been published by Mr Dumont in French, in company with *The Theory of Reward* added to it, for the purpose of mutual illustration. It is in contemplation to publish them both in English, from the Author's manuscripts, with the benefit of any amendments that have been made by Mr Dumont.[1]

[1] Note added to 1823 edition. For Bentham's *Theory of Punishment* and its relationship to the present work see above, Introduction, xxxviii. The projected publication mentioned here took place in the form of Richard Smith's editions of *The Rationale of Reward* (1825) and *The Rationale of Punishment* (1830).

158

CASES UNMEET FOR PUNISHMENT   CHAPTER XIII

3. It is plain, therefore, that in the following cases punishment ought not to be inflicted.

1. Where it is *groundless*; where there is no mischief for it to prevent; the act not being mischievous upon the whole.

2. Where it must be *inefficacious*: where it cannot act so as to prevent the mischief.

3. Where it is *unprofitable*, or too *expensive*; where the mischief it would produce would be greater than what it prevented.

4. Where it is *needless*: where the mischief may be prevented, or cease of itself, without it: that is, at a cheaper rate.

§ ii. *Cases in which punishment is groundless*

These are,

4. (1) Where there has never been any mischief: where no mischief has been produced to any body by the act in question. Of this number are those in which the act was such as might, on some occasions, be mischievous or disagreeable, but the person whose interest it concerns gave his *consent* to the performance of it.[b] This consent, provided it be free, and fairly obtained,[b] is the best proof that can be produced, that, to the person who gives it, no mischief, at least no immediate mischief, upon the whole, is done. For no man can be so good a judge as the man himself, what it is gives him pleasure or displeasure.

5. (2) Where the mischief was *outweighed*: although a mischief was produced by that act, yet the same act was necessary to the production of a benefit which was of greater value[c] than the mischief. This may be the case with any thing that is done in the way of precaution against instant calamity, as also with any thing that is done in the exercise of the several sorts of powers necessary to be

or on the account of sympathy or antipathy, has been excited by the offence. This purpose, as far as it can be answered *gratis*, is a beneficial one. But no punishment ought to be allotted merely to this purpose, because (setting aside its effects in the way of control) no such pleasure is ever produced by punishment as can be equivalent to the pain. The punishment, however, which is allotted to the other purpose, ought, as far as it can be done without expence, to be accommodated to this. Satisfaction thus administered to a party injured, in the shape of a dissocial pleasure,* may be styled a vindictive satisfaction or compensation: as a compensation, administered in the shape of a self-regarding profit, or stock of pleasure, may be styled a lucrative one. See B. I. tit. vi (Compensation). Example is the most important end of all, in proportion as the *number* of the persons under temptation to offend is to *one*.

[b] See B. I. tit. (Justifications).

[c] See supra, Ch. iv (Value).

* See Ch. x (Motives).

Side notes:

Therefore ought not to be admitted;

1. Where groundless

2. Inefficacious

3. Unprofitable

4. Or needless

1. Where there has never been any mischief: as in the case of consent

2. Where the mischief was outweighed: as in precaution against calamity, and the exercise of powers

CHAPTER XIII   CASES UNMEET FOR PUNISHMENT

established in every community, to wit, domestic, judicial, military, and supreme.[d]

3. —or will, for a certainty, be cured by compensation

6. (3) Where there is a certainty of an adequate compensation: and that in all cases where the offence can be committed. This supposes two things: 1. That the offence is such as admits of an adequate compensation: 2. That such a compensation is sure to be forthcoming. Of these suppositions, the latter will be found to be a merely ideal one: a supposition that cannot, in the universality here given to it, be verified by fact. It cannot, therefore, in practice, be numbered amongst the grounds of absolute impunity. It may, however, be admitted as a ground for an abatement of that punishment, which other considerations, standing by themselves, would seem to dictate.[e]

§ iii. *Cases in which punishment must be inefficacious*

These are,

1. Where the penal provision comes too late: as in, 1. An ex-post-facto law. 2. An ultra-legal sentence

7. (1) Where the penal provision is *not established* until after the act is done. Such are the cases, 1. Of an *ex-post-facto* law; where the legislator himself appoints not a punishment till after the act is done. 2. Of a sentence beyond the law; where the judge, of his own authority, appoints a punishment which the legislator had not appointed.

2. Or is not made known: as in a law not sufficiently promulgated

8. (2) Where the penal provision, though established, is *not conveyed* to the notice of the person on whom it seems intended that it should operate. Such is the case where the law has omitted to employ any of the expedients which are necessary, to make sure that every person whatsoever, who is within the reach of the law, be apprized of all the cases whatsoever, in which (being in the station of life he is in) he can be subjected to the penalties of the law.[f]

[d] See Book I. tit. (Justifications).

Hence the favour shewn to the offences of responsible offenders: such as simple mercantile frauds

[e] This, for example, seems to have been one ground, at least, of the favour shewn by perhaps all systems of laws, to such offenders as stand upon a footing of responsibility: shewn, not directly indeed to the persons themselves; but to such offences as none but responsible persons are likely to have the opportunity of engaging in. In particular, this seems to be the reason why embezzlement, in certain cases, has not commonly been punished upon the footing of theft: nor mercantile frauds upon that of common sharping.*

[f] See B. II. Appendix. tit. III (Promulgation).[1]

* See tit. (Simple merc. Defraudment).

[1] It was presumably material originally intended for this part of the Appendix to the *Plan of a Penal Code* that was used by Dumont for that part of the *Traités de Législation* (1802) which was edited in English for the Bowring edition by Richard Smith as *Essay on the Promulgation of Laws and the Reasons Thereof; with Specimen of a Penal Code* (Bowring, i, 155–68).

CASES UNMEET FOR PUNISHMENT   CHAPTER XIII

9. (3) Where the penal provision, though it were conveyed to a man's notice, *could produce no effect* on him, with respect to the preventing him from engaging in any act of the *sort* in question. Such is the case, 1. In extreme *infancy*; where a man has not yet attained that state or disposition of mind in which the prospect of evils so distant as those which are held forth by the law, has the effect of influencing his conduct. 2. In *insanity*; where the person, if he has attained to that disposition, has since been deprived of it through the influence of some permanent though unseen cause. 3. In *intoxication*; where he has been deprived of it by the transient influence of a visible cause: such as the use of wine, or opium, or other drugs, that act in this manner on the nervous system: which condition is indeed neither more nor less than a temporary insanity produced by an assignable cause.[g]

10. (4) Where the penal provision (although, being conveyed to the party's notice, it might very well prevent his engaging in acts of the sort in question, provided he knew that it related to those acts) could not have this effect, with regard to the *individual* act he is about to engage in: to wit, because he knows not that it is of the number of those to which the penal provision relates. This may happen, 1. In the case of *unintentionality*; where he intends not to engage, and thereby knows not that he is about to engage, in the *act* in which eventually he is about to engage.[h] 2. In the case of *unconsciousness*; where, although he may know that he is about to engage in the *act* itself, yet, from not knowing all the material

Margin notes:
3. Where the will cannot be deterred from any act: as in, Infancy
Insanity
Intoxication
4. Or not from the individual act in question, as in,
Unintentionality
Unconsciousness

[g] Notwithstanding what is here said, the cases of infancy and intoxication (as we shall see hereafter) cannot be looked upon in practice as affording sufficient grounds for absolute impunity. But this exception in point of practice is no objection to the propriety of the rule in point of theory. The ground of the exception is neither more nor less than the difficulty there is of ascertaining the matter of fact: viz. whether at the requisite point of time the party was actually in the state in question; that is, whether a given case comes really under the rule. Suppose the matter of fact capable of being perfectly ascertained, without danger or mistake, the impropriety of punishment would be as indubitable in these cases as in any other.[*]

The reason that is commonly assigned for the establishing an exemption from punishment in favour of infants, insane persons, and persons under intoxication, is either false in fact, or confusedly expressed. The phrase is, that the will of these persons concurs not with the act; that they have no vicious will; or, that they have not the free use of their will. But suppose all this to be true? What is it to the purpose? Nothing: except in as far as it implies the reason given in the text.

[h] See Ch. viii (Intentionality).

[*] See B. I. tit. iv (Exemptions) and tit. vii (Extenuations).

Margin notes:
In infancy and intoxication the case can hardly be proved to come under the rule
The reason for not punishing in these three cases is commonly put upon a wrong footing

CHAPTER XIII CASES UNMEET FOR PUNISHMENT

Missupposal *circumstances* attending it, he knows not of the *tendency* it has to produce that mischief, in contemplation of which it has been made penal in most instances. 3. In the case of *mis-supposal*; where, although he may know of the tendency the act has to produce that degree of mischief, he supposes it, though mistakenly, to be attended with some circumstance, or set of circumstances, which, if it had been attended with, it would either not have been productive of that mischief, or have been productive of such a greater degree of good, as has determined the legislator in such a case not to make it penal.[1]

5. Or is acted on by an opposite superior force: as by, **11.** (5) Where, though the penal clause might exercise a full and prevailing influence, were it to act alone, yet by the *predominant* influence of some opposite cause upon the will, it must necessarily be ineffectual; because the evil which he sees[1] himself about to undergo, in the case of his *not* engaging in the act, is so great, that the evil denounced by the penal clause, in case of his engaging in it, cannot appear greater. This may happen, 1. In the case of *physical danger*; where the evil is such as appears likely to be brought about by the unassisted powers of *nature*. 2. In the case of a *threatened mischief*; where it is such as appears likely to be brought about through the intentional and conscious agency of *man*.[1]

Physical danger

Threatened mischief

6. —or the bodily organs cannot follow its determination: as under **12.** (6) Where (though the penal clause may exert a full and prevailing influence over the *will* of the party) yet his *physical faculties* (owing to the predominant influence of some physical cause) are not in a condition to follow the determination of the will insomuch that the act is absolutely *involuntary*. Such is the case of physical *compulsion* or *restraint*, by whatever means brought about: where the man's hand, for instance, is pushed against some object which his will disposes him *not* to touch; or tied down from touching some object which his will disposes him to touch.

Physical compulsion or restraint

[1] See Ch. ix (Consciousness).

Why the influence of the moral and religious sanctions is not mentioned in the same view [1] The influences of the *moral* and *religious* sanctions, or, in other words, of the motives of *love of reputation* and *religion*, are other causes, the force of which may, upon particular occasions, come to be greater than that of any punishment which the legislator is *able*, or at least which he will *think proper*, to apply. These, therefore, it will be proper for him to have his eye upon. But the force of these influences is variable and different in different times and places: the force of the foregoing influences is constant and the same, at all times and every where. These, therefore, it can never be proper to look upon as safe grounds for establishing absolute impunity: owing (as in the above-mentioned cases of infancy and intoxication) to the impracticability of ascertaining the matter of fact.

[1] Thus 1789. The 1823 text, followed by the Bowring and later editions mistakenly reads 'sets'.

§ iv. *Cases where punishment is unprofitable*

These are,

13. (1) Where, on the one hand, the nature of the offence, on the other hand, that of the punishment, are, *in the ordinary state of things*, such, that when compared together, the evil of the latter will turn out to be greater than that of the former.

14. Now the evil of the punishment divides itself into four branches, by which so many different sets of persons are affected. 1. The evil of *coercion* or *restraint*: or the pain which it gives a man not to be able to do the act, whatever it be, which by the apprehension of the punishment he is deterred from doing. This is felt by those by whom the law is *observed*. 2. The evil of *apprehension*: or the pain which a man, who has exposed himself to punishment, feels at the thoughts of undergoing it. This is felt by those by whom the law has been *broken*, and who feel themselves in *danger* of its being executed upon them. 3. The evil of *sufferance*[k]: or the pain which a man feels, in virtue of the punishment itself, from the time when he begins to undergo it. This is felt by those by whom the law is broken, and upon whom it comes actually to be executed. 4. The pain of sympathy, and the other *derivative* evils resulting to the persons who are in *connection* with the several classes of original sufferers just mentioned.[1] Now of these four lots of evil, the first will be greater or less, according to the nature of the act from which the party is restrained: the second and third according to the nature of the punishment which stands annexed to that offence.

15. On the other hand, as to the evil of the offence, this will also, of course, be greater or less, according to the nature of each offence. The proportion between the one evil and the other will therefore be different in the case of each particular offence. The cases, therefore, where punishment is unprofitable on this ground, can by no other means be discovered, than by an examination of each particular offence; which is what will be the business of the body of the work.

16. (2) Where, although in the *ordinary state* of things, the evil resulting from the punishment is not greater than the benefit which is likely to result from the force with which it operates, during the same space of time, towards the excluding the evil of the offence, yet it may have been rendered so by the influence of some *occasional circumstances*. In the number of these circumstances may

Marginalia:

1. Where, in the sort of case in question, the punishment would produce more evil than the offence would

Evil producible by a punishment – its four branches – viz. Restraint Apprehension Sufferance

Derivative evils

(The evil of the offence being different, according to the nature of the offence, cannot be represented here)

2.–Or in the individual case in question: by reason of

---

[k] See Ch. v (Pleasures and Pains).

[1] See Ch. xii (Consequences) 4.

CHAPTER XIII   CASES UNMEET FOR PUNISHMENT

The multi-tude of delinquents

The value of a delin-quent's service

The dis-pleasure of the people

be, 1. The multitude of delinquents at a particular juncture; being such as would increase, beyond the ordinary measure, the *quantum* of the second and third lots, and thereby also of a part of the fourth lot, in the evil of the punishment. 2. The extraordinary value of the services of some one delinquent; in the case where the effect of the punishment would be to deprive the community of the benefit of those services. 3. The displeasure of the *people*; that is, of an inde-finite number of the members of the *same* community, in cases where (owing to the influence of some occasional incident) they happen to conceive, that the offence or the offender ought not to be punished at all, or at least ought not to be punished in the way

The dis-pleasure of foreign powers

in question. 4. The displeasure of *foreign powers*; that is, of the go-verning body, or a considerable number of the members of some *foreign* community or communities, with which the community in question, is connected.

§ v. *Cases where punishment is needless*

These are,[1]

1. Where the mischief is to be prevented at a cheaper rate: as,

By instruc-tion

17. (1) Where the purpose of putting an end to the practice may be attained as effectually at a cheaper rate: by instruction, for in-stance, as well as by terror: by informing the understanding, as well as by exercising an immediate influence on the will. This seems to be the case with respect to all those offences which consist in the disseminating pernicious principles in matters of *duty*; of whatever kind the duty be; whether political, or moral, or religious. And this, whether such principles be disseminated *under*, or even *without*, a sincere persuasion of their being beneficial. I say, even *without*: for though in such a case it is not instruction that can prevent the writer from endeavouring to inculcate his principles, yet it may the readers from adopting them: without which, his endeavouring to inculcate them will do no harm. In such a case, the sovereign will commonly have little need to take an active part: if it be the inter-est of *one* individual to inculcate principles that are pernicious, it will as surely be the interest of *other* individuals to expose them. But if the sovereign must needs take a part in the controversy, the pen is the proper weapon to combat error with, not the sword.

[1] Bentham evidently intended to deal with a number of examples under this head-ing, as in previous sections, but did not in fact proceed beyond the first case.

CHAPTER XVII

OF THE LIMITS OF THE PENAL BRANCH OF JURISPRUDENCE

§ i. *Limits between private ethics and the art of legislation*

1. So much for the division of offences in general. Now an offence *Use of this chapter* is an act prohibited, or (what comes to the same thing) an act of which the contrary is commanded by the law: and what is it that the law can be employed in doing, besides prohibiting and commanding? It should seem then, according to this view of the matter, that were we to have settled what may be proper to be done with relation to offences, we should thereby have settled every thing that may be proper to be done in the way of law. Yet that branch which concerns the method of dealing with offences, and which is termed sometimes the *criminal*, sometimes the *penal*, branch, is universally understood to be but one out of two branches which compose the whole subject of the art of legislation; that which is termed the *civil* being the other.[a] Between these two branches then, it is evident enough, there cannot but be a very intimate connection; so intimate is it indeed, that the limits between them are by no means easy to mark out. The case is the same in some degree between the whole business of legislation (civil and penal branches taken together) and that of private ethics. Of these several limits however it will be in a manner necessary to exhibit some idea: lest, on the one hand, we should seem to leave any part of the subject that *does* belong to us untouched, or, on the other hand, to deviate on any side into a track which does *not* belong to us.

[a] And the *constitutional* branch, what is become of it? Such is the question which many a reader will be apt to put. An answer that might be given is— that the matter of it might without much violence be distributed under the two other heads. But, as far as recollection serves, that branch, notwithstanding its importance, and its capacity of being lodged separately from the other matter, had at that time scarcely presented itself to my view in the character of a distinct one: the thread of my enquiries had not as yet reached it. But in the concluding note of this same chapter, in paragraphs 22 to the end, the omission may be seen in some measure supplied.[1]

[1] Note added by Bentham to the 1823 edition. His attention had been drawn to the apparent omission of constitutional law very soon after the completion of the 1780 text: cf. his letter to Lord Shelburne of 18 July 1781 and several drafts for that letter in the University College collection (to be published in *Correspondence*, iii, in *CW*).

CHAPTER XVII   LIMITS OF PENAL JURISPRUDENCE

In the course of this enquiry, that part of it I mean which concerns the limits between the civil and the penal branch of law, it will be necessary to settle a number of points, of which the connection with the main question might not at first sight be suspected. To ascertain what sort of a thing *a* law is; what the *parts* are that are to be found in it; what it must contain in order to be *complete*; what the connection is between that part of a body of laws which belongs to the subject of *procedure*; and the rest of the law at large: —All these, it will be seen, are so many problems, which must be solved before any satisfactory answer can be given to the main question above mentioned.

Nor is this their only use: for it is evident enough, that the notion of a complete law must first be fixed, before the legislator can in any case know what it is he has to do, or when his work is done.

Ethics in general, what   **2.** Ethics at large may be defined, the art of directing men's actions to the production of the greatest possible quantity of happiness, on the part of those whose interest is in view.

Private ethics   **3.** What then are the actions which it can be in a man's power to direct? They must be either his own actions, or those of other agents. Ethics, in as far as it is the art of directing a man's own actions, may be styled the *art of self-government*, or *private ethics*.

The art of government: that is, of legislation and administration   **4.** What other agents then are there, which, at the same time that they are under the influence of man's direction, are susceptible of happiness? They are of two sorts: 1. Other human beings who are styled persons. 2. Other animals, which on account of their interests having been neglected by the insensibility of the ancient jurists, stand degraded into the class of *things*.[b] As to other human

Interests of the inferior animals improperly neglected in legislation

[b] Under the Gentoo[1] and Mahometan religions, the interests of the rest of the animal creation seem to have met with some attention. Why have they not, universally, with as much as those of human creatures, allowance made for the difference in point of sensibility? Because the laws that are have been the work of mutual fear; a sentiment which the less rational animals have not had the same means as man has of turning to account. Why *ought* they not? No reason can be given. If the being eaten were all, there is very good reason why we should be suffered to eat such of them as we like to eat: we are the better for it, and they are never the worse. They have none of those long-protracted anticipations of future misery which we have. The death they suffer in our hands commonly is, and always may be, a speedier, and by that means a less painful one, than that which would await them in the inevitable course of nature. If the being killed were all, there is very good reason why we should be suffered to kill such as molest us; we should be the worse for their living, and they are never the worse for being dead. But is there any reason

[1] This term for Hindu seems to have become obsolete during the first half of the 19th century.

LIMITS OF PENAL JURISPRUDENCE CHAPTER XVII

beings, the art of directing their actions to the above end is what we mean, or at least the only thing which, upon the principle of utility, we *ought* to mean, by the art of government: which, in as far as the measures it displays itself in are of a permanent nature, is generally distinguished by the name of *legislation*: as it is by that of *administration*, when they are of a temporary nature, determined by the occurrences of the day.

5. Now human creatures, considered with respect to the maturity of their faculties, are either in an *adult*, or in a *non-adult* state. The art of government, in as far as it concerns the direction of the actions of persons in a non-adult state, may be termed the art of *education*. In as far as this business is entrusted with those who, in virtue of some private relationship, are in the main the best disposed to take upon them, and the best able to discharge, this office, it may be termed the art of *private education*: in as far as it is exercised by those whose province it is to superintend the conduct of the whole community, it may be termed the art of *public education*. *Art of education*

6. As to ethics in general, a man's happiness will depend, in the *Ethics exhibits the rules of, 1. Prudence. 2. Probity. 3. Beneficence*

why we should be suffered to torment them? Not any that I can see. Are there any why we should *not* be suffered to torment them? Yes, several. See B. I. tit. (Cruelty to animals.) The day has been, I grieve to say in many places it is not yet past, in which the greater part of the species, under the denomination of slaves, have been treated by the law exactly upon the same footing, as, in England for example, the inferior races of animals are still. The day *may* come, when the rest of the animal creation may acquire those rights which never could have been withholden from them but by the hand of tyranny. The French have already discovered that the blackness of the skin is no reason why a human being should be abandoned without redress to the caprice of a tormentor.* It may come one day to be recognized, that the number of the legs, the villosity of the skin, or the termination of the *os sacrum*, are reasons equally insufficient for abandoning a sensitive being to the same fate? What else is it that should trace the insuperable line? Is it the faculty of reason, or, perhaps, the faculty of discourse? But a full-grown horse or dog, is beyond comparison a more rational, as well as a more conversible animal, than an infant of a day, or a week, or even a month, old. But suppose the case were otherwise, what would it avail? the question is not, Can they *reason*? nor, Can they *talk*? but, Can they *suffer*?

* See Lewis XIVth's Code Noir.[1]

[1] This code, begun under Colbert, completed by Seignelay, and issued in March 1685, regulated the status of slaves in the French West Indies. It forbade the killing of slaves by their masters, and gave the royal authorities the power to protect slaves from maltreatment. It also provided that a slave freed in the West Indies should become a French citizen without formal naturalisation.

CHAPTER XVII   LIMITS OF PENAL JURISPRUDENCE

first place, upon such parts of his behaviour as none but himself are interested in; in the next place, upon such parts of it as may affect the happiness of those about him. In as far as his happiness depends upon the first-mentioned part of his behaviour, it is said to depend upon his *duty to himself*. Ethics then, in as far as it is the art of directing a man's actions in this respect, may be termed the art of discharging one's duty to one's self: and the quality which a man manifests by the discharge of this branch of duty (if duty it is to be called) is that of *prudence*. In as far as his happiness, and that of any other person or persons whose interests are considered, depends upon such parts of his behaviour as may affect the interests of those about him, it may be said to depend upon his *duty to others*; or, to use a phrase now somewhat antiquated, his *duty to his neighbour*. Ethics then, in as far as it is the art of directing a man's actions in this respect, may be termed the art of discharging one's duty to one's neighbour. Now the happiness of one's neighbour may be consulted in two ways: 1. In a negative way, by forbearing to diminish it. 2. In a positive way, by studying to increase it. A man's duty to his neighbour is accordingly partly negative and partly positive: to discharge the negative branch of it, is *probity*: to discharge the positive branch, *beneficence*.

Probity and beneficence how they connect with prudence

7. It may here be asked, How it is that upon the principle of private ethics, legislation and religion out of the question, a man's happiness depends upon such parts of his conduct as affect, immediately at least, the happiness of no one but himself: this is as much as to ask, What motives (independent of such as legislation and religion may chance to furnish) can one man have to consult the happiness of another? by what motives, or, which comes to the same thing, by what obligations, can he be bound to obey the dictates of *probity* and *beneficence*? In answer to this, it cannot but be admitted, that the only interests which a man at all times and upon all occasions is sure to find *adequate* motives for consulting, are his own. Notwithstanding this, there are no occasions in which a man has not some motives for consulting the happiness of other men. In the first place, he has, on all occasions, the purely social motive of sympathy or benevolence: in the next place, he has, on most occasions, the semi-social motives of love of amity and love of reputation. The motive of sympathy will act upon him with more or less effect, according to the *bias* of his sensibility[c]: the two other motives, according to a variety of circumstances, principally according to the strength of his intellectual powers, the firmness and

[c] Ch. VI (Sensibility) 3.

steadiness of his mind, the quantum of his moral sensibility, and the characters of the people he has to deal with.

8. Now private ethics has happiness for its end: and legislation can have no other. Private ethics concerns every member, that is, the happiness and the actions of every member of any community that can be proposed; and legislation can concern no more. Thus far, then, private ethics and the art of legislation go hand in hand. The end they have, or ought to have, in view, is of the same nature. The persons whose happiness they ought to have in view, as also the persons whose conduct they ought to be occupied in directing, are precisely the same. The very acts they ought to be conversant about, are even in a *great measure* the same. Where then lies the difference? In that the acts which they ought to be conversant about, though in a great measure, are not *perfectly and throughout* the same. There is no case in which a private man ought not to direct his own conduct to the production of his own happiness, and of that of his fellow-creatures: but there are cases in which the legislator ought not (in a direct way at least, and by means of punishment applied immediately to particular *individual* acts) to attempt to direct the conduct of the several other members of the community. Every act which promises to be beneficial upon the whole to the community (himself included) each individual ought to perform of himself: but it is not every such act that the legislator ought to compel him to perform. Every act which promises to be pernicious upon the whole to the community (himself included) each individual ought to abstain from of himself: but it is not every such act that the legislator ought to compel him to abstain from.

Every act which is a proper object of ethics is not of legislation

9. Where then is the line to be drawn?—We shall not have far to seek for it. The business is to give an idea of the cases in which ethics ought, and in which legislation ought not (in a direct manner at least) to interfere. If legislation interferes in a direct manner, it must be by punishment.[d] Now the cases in which punishment, meaning the punishment of the political sanction, ought not to be inflicted, have been already stated.[e] If then there be any of these cases in which, although legislation ought not, private ethics does or ought to interfere, these cases will serve to point out the limits between the two arts or branches of science. These cases, it may be

The limits between the provinces of private ethics and legislation, marked out by the cases unmeet for punishment

[d] I say nothing in this place of reward: because it is only in a few extraordinary cases that it can be applied, and because even where it is applied, it may be doubted perhaps whether the application of it can, properly speaking, be termed an act of legislation. See infra, § iii.[1]

[e] Ch. XIII (Cases unmeet).   [1] See above, 207 n. 1.

CHAPTER XVII   LIMITS OF PENAL JURISPRUDENCE

remembered, are of four sorts: 1. Where punishment would be groundless. 2. Where it would be inefficacious. 3. Where it would be unprofitable. 4. Where it would be needless. Let us look over all these cases, and see whether in any of them there is room for the interference of private ethics, at the same time that there is none for the direct interference of legislation.

1. Neither ought to apply where punishment is groundless

10. (1) First then, as to the cases where punishment would be *groundless*. In these cases it is evident, that the restrictive interference of ethics would be groundless too. It is because, upon the whole, there is no evil in the act, that legislation ought not to endeavour to prevent it. No more, for the same reason, ought private ethics.

2. How far private ethics can apply in the cases where punishment would be inefficacious

11. (2) As to the cases in which punishment would be *inefficacious*. These, we may observe, may be divided into two sets or classes. The first do not depend at all upon the nature of the act: they turn only upon a defect in the timing of the punishment. The punishment in question is no more than what, for any thing that appears, ought to have been applied to the act in question. It ought, however, to have been applied at a different time; viz. not till after it had been properly denounced. These are the cases of an *ex-post-facto* law; of a judicial sentence beyond the law; and of a law not sufficiently promulgated. The acts here in question then might, for any thing that appears, come properly under the department even of coercive legislation: of course do they under that of private ethics. As to the other set of cases, in which punishment would be inefficacious; neither do these depend upon the nature of the act, that is, of the *sort* of act: they turn only upon some extraneous *circumstances*, with which an act of *any* sort may chance to be accompanied. These, however, are of such a nature as not only to exclude the application of legal punishment, but in general to leave little room for the influence of private ethics. These are the cases where the will could not be deterred from any act, even by the extraordinary force of artificial punishment: as in the cases of extreme infancy, insanity, and perfect intoxication: of course, therefore, it could not by such slender and precarious force as could be applied by private ethics. The case is in this respect the same, under the circumstances of unintentionality with respect to the event of the action, unconsciousness with regard to the circumstances, and missupposal with regard to the existence of circumstances which have not existed; as also where the force, even of extraordinary punishment, is rendered inoperative by the superior force of a physical danger or threatened mischief. It is evident, that in

LIMITS OF PENAL JURISPRUDENCE   CHAPTER XVII

these cases, if the thunders of the law prove impotent, the whispers of simple morality can have but little influence.

12. (3) As to the cases where punishment would be *unprofitable*. *How far, where it would be unprofitable* These are the cases which constitute the great field for the exclusive interference of private ethics. When a punishment is unprofitable, or in other words too expensive, it is because the evil of the punishment exceeds that of the offence. Now the evil of the punishment, we may remember,[f] is distinguishable into four branches: 1. The evil of coercion, including constraint or restraint, according as the act commanded is of the positive kind or the negative. 2. The evil of apprehension. 3. The evil of sufferance. 4. The derivative evils resulting to persons in *connection* with those by whom the three above-mentioned original evils are sustained. Now with respect to those original evils, the persons who lie exposed to them may be two very different sets of persons. In the first place, persons who may have actually committed, or been prompted to commit, the acts really meant to be prohibited. In the next place, persons who may have performed, or been prompted to perform, such other acts as they fear may be in danger of being involved in the punishment designed only for the former. But of these two sets of acts, it is the former only that are pernicious: it is, therefore, the former only that it can be the business of private ethics to endeavour to prevent. The latter being by the supposition not mischievous, to prevent them is what it can no more be the business of ethics to endeavour at, than of legislation. It remains to shew how it may happen, that there should be acts really pernicious, which, although they may very properly come under the censure of private ethics, may yet be no fit objects for the legislator to control.

13. Punishment then, as applied to delinquency, may be unprofitable in both or either of two ways: 1. By the expense it would *Which it may be, 1. Although confined to the guilty* amount to, even supposing the application of it to be confined altogether to delinquency: 2. By the danger there may be of its involving the innocent in the fate designed only for the guilty. First then, with regard to the cases in which the expense of the punishment, as applied to the guilty, would outweigh the profit to be made by it. These cases, it is evident, depend upon a certain proportion between the evil of the punishment and the evil of the offence. Now were the offence of such a nature, that a punishment which, in point of *magnitude*, should but just exceed the profit of it, would be sufficient to prevent it, it might be rather difficult perhaps to find an instance in which such punishment would clearly appear to be un-

[f] See Ch. XIII (Cases unmeet) § iv.

CHAPTER XVII   LIMITS OF PENAL JURISPRUDENCE

profitable. But the fact is, there are many cases in which a punishment, in order to have any chance of being efficacious, must, in point of magnitude, be raised a great deal above that level. Thus it is, wherever the danger of detection is, or, what comes to the same thing, is likely to appear to be, so small, as to make the punishment appear in a high degree uncertain. In this case it is necessary, as has been shewn,[g] if punishment be at all applied, to raise it in point of magnitude as much as it falls short in point of certainty. It is evident, however, that all this can be but guess-work: and that the effect of such a proportion will be rendered precarious, by a variety of circumstances: by the want of sufficient promulgation on the part of the law[h]: by the particular circumstances of the temptation[i]: and by the circumstances influencing the sensibility of the several individuals who are exposed to it.[j] Let the *seducing* motives be strong, the offence then will at any rate be frequently committed. Now and then indeed, owing to a coincidence of circumstances more or less extraordinary, it will be detected, and by that means punished. But for the purpose of example, which is the principal one, an act of punishment, considered in itself, is of no use: what use it can be of, depends altogether upon the expectation it raises of similar punishment, in future cases of similar delinquency. But this future punishment, it is evident, must always depend upon detection. If then the want of detection is such as must in general (especially to eyes fascinated by the force of the seducing motives) appear too improbable to be reckoned upon, the punishment, though it should be inflicted, may come to be of no use. Here then will be two opposite evils running on at the same time, yet neither of them reducing the quantum of the other: the evil of the disease and the evil of the painful and inefficacious remedy. It seems to be partly owing to some such considerations, that fornication, for example, or the illicit commerce between the sexes, has commonly either gone altogether unpunished, or been punished in a degree inferior to that in which, on other accounts, legislators might have been disposed to punish it.

2. By enveloping the innocent

14. Second, with regard to the cases in which political punishment, as applied to delinquency, may be unprofitable, in virtue of the danger there may be of its involving the innocent in the fate

[g] Ch. xiv (Proportion) 18. Rule 7.
[h] Ch. xiii (Cases unmeet) § iii. Append. tit. (Promulgation).[1]
[i] Ch. xi (Disposition) 35 etc.
[j] Ch. vi (Sensibility).

[1] See above 160 n. 1.

LIMITS OF PENAL JURISPRUDENCE   CHAPTER XVII

designed only for the guilty. Whence should this danger then arise? From the difficulty there may be of fixing the idea of the guilty action: that is, of subjecting it to such a definition as shall be clear and precise enough to guard effectually against misapplication. This difficulty may arise from either of two sources: the one permanent, to wit, the nature of the *actions* themselves: the other occasional, I mean the qualities of the *men* who may have to deal with those actions in the way of government. In as far as it arises from the latter of these sources, it may depend partly upon the use which the *legislator* may be *able* to make of language; partly upon the use which, according to the apprehension of the legislator, the *judge* may be *disposed* to make of it. As far as legislation is concerned, it will depend upon the degree of perfection to which the arts of language may have been carried, in the first place, in the nation in general; in the next place, by the *legislator* in particular. It is to a sense of this difficulty as it should seem, that we may attribute the caution with which most legislators have abstained from subjecting to censure, on the part of the law, such actions as come under the notion of rudeness, for example, or treachery, or ingratitude. The attempt to bring acts of so vague and questionable a nature under the control of law, will argue either a very immature age, in which the difficulties, which give birth to that danger are not descried; or a very enlightened age, in which they are overcome.[k]

15. For the sake of obtaining the clearer idea of the limits between the art of legislation and private ethics, it may now be time to call to mind the distinctions above established with regard to ethics in general. The degree in which private ethics stands in need of the assistance of legislation, is different in the three branches of duty above distinguished. Of the rules of moral duty, those which seem to stand least in need of the assistance of legislation, are the rules of *prudence*. It can only be through some defect on the part of the understanding, if a man be ever deficient in point of duty to himself. If he does wrong, there is nothing else that it can be owing to but either some *inadvertence*[1] or some *missupposal*,[1] with regard

Legislation how far necessary for the enforcement of the dictates of prudence

---

[k] In certain countries, in which the voice of the people has a more especial control over the hand of the legislator, nothing can exceed the dread which they are under of seeing any effectual provision made against the offences which come under the head of *defamation*, particularly that branch of it which may be styled the *political*. This dread seems to depend partly upon the apprehension they may think it prudent to entertain of a defect in point of ability or integrity on the part of the legislator, partly upon a similar apprehension of a defect in point of integrity on the part of the judge.

[1] See Ch. IX (Consciousness).

CHAPTER XVII   LIMITS OF PENAL JURISPRUDENCE

to the circumstances on which his happiness depends. It is a standing topic of complaint, that a man knows too little of himself. Be it so: but is it so certain that the legislator must know more[m][n]? It is plain, that of individuals the legislator can know nothing: concerning those points of conduct which depend upon the particular circumstances of each individual, it is plain, therefore, that he can determine nothing to advantage. It is only with respect to those broad lines of conduct in which all persons, or very large and permanent descriptions of persons, may be in a way to engage, that he can have any pretence for interfering; and even here the propriety of his interference will, in most instances, lie very open to dispute. At any rate, he must never expect to produce a perfect compliance by the mere force of the sanction of which he is himself the author. All he can hope to do, is to increase the efficacy of private ethics, by giving strength and direction to the influence of the moral sanction. With what chance of success, for example, would a legislator go about to extirpate drunkenness and fornication, by dint of legal punishment? Not all the tortures which ingenuity could invent would compass it: and, before he had made any progress worth regarding, such a mass of evil would be produced by the punishment, as would exceed, a thousand-fold, the utmost possible mischief of the offence. The great difficulty would be in the procuring evidence; an object which could not be attempted, with any probability of success, without spreading dismay through every family,[o] tearing the bonds of sympathy asunder,[p] and rooting out the influence of all the social motives. All that he can do then, against offences of this nature, with any prospect of advantage, in the way of direct legislation, is to subject them, in cases of notoriety, to a slight censure, so as thereby to cover them with a slight shade of artificial disrepute.

– Apt to go too far in this respect

16. It may be observed, that with regard to this branch of duty, legislators have, in general, been disposed to carry their inter-

---

[m] On occasions like this, the legislator should never lose sight of the well-known story of the oculist and the sot. A countryman who had hurt his eyes by drinking, went to a celebrated oculist for advice. He found him at table, with a glass of wine before him. 'You must leave off drinking', said the oculist. 'How so', says the countryman? '*You* don't, and yet methinks your own eyes are none of the best'.—'That's very true, friend', replied the oculist: 'but you are to know, I love my bottle better than my eyes.'

[n] Ch. XVI (Division) 52.

[o] Evil of apprehension: third branch of the evil of a punishment. Ch. XIII § iv.

[p] Derivative evils: fourth branch of the evil of a punishment. Ibid.

ference full as far as is expedient. The great difficulty here is, to persuade them to confine themselves within bounds. A thousand little passions and prejudices have led them to narrow the liberty of the subject in this line, in cases in which the punishment is either attended with no profit at all, or with none that will make up for the expense.

17. The mischief of this sort of interference is more particularly conspicuous in the article of religion. The reasoning, in this case, is of the following stamp. There are certain errors, in matters of belief, to which all mankind are prone: and for these errors in judgment, it is the determination of a Being of infinite benevolence, to punish them with an infinity of torments. But from these errors the legislator himself is necessarily free: for the men, who happen to be at hand for him to consult with, being men perfectly enlightened, unfettered, and unbiassed, have such advantages over all the rest of the world, that when they sit down to enquire out the truth relative to points so plain and so familiar as those in question, they cannot fail to find it. This being the case, when the sovereign sees his people ready to plunge headlong into an abyss of fire, shall he not stretch out a hand to save them? Such, for example, seems to have been the train of reasoning, and such the motives, which led Lewis the XIVth into those coercive measures which he took for the conversion of heretics, and the confirmation of true believers.[1] The ground-work, pure sympathy and loving-kindness: the superstructure, all the miseries which the most determined malevolence could have devised.[q] But of this more fully in another place.[r]

– Particularly in matters of religion

[q] I do not mean but that other motives of a less social nature might have introduced themselves, and probably, in point of fact, did introduce themselves, in the progress of the enterprise. But in point of possibility, the motive above mentioned, when accompanied with such a thread of reasoning, is sufficient, without any other, to account for all the effects above alluded to. If any others interfere, their interference, how natural soever, may be looked upon as an accidental and inessential circumstance, not necessary to the production of the effect. Sympathy, a concern for the danger they appear to be exposed to, gives birth to the wish of freeing them from it: that wish shews itself in the shape of a command: this command produces disobedience: disobedience on the one part, produces disappointment on the other: the pain of disappointment produces ill-will towards those who are the authors of it. The affections will often make this progress in less time than it would take to describe it. The sentiment of wounded pride, and other modifications of the love of reputation and the love of power, add fuel to the flame. A kind of revenge exasperates the severities of coercive policy.

[r] See B. I. tit. (Self-regarding offences).

[1] The revocation of the Edict of Nantes in 1685.

CHAPTER XVII   LIMITS OF PENAL JURISPRUDENCE

18. The rules of *probity* are those, which in point of expediency stand most in need of assistance on the part of the legislator, and in which, in point of fact, his interference has been most extensive. There are few cases in which it *would* be expedient to punish a man for hurting *himself*: but there are few cases, if any, in which it would *not* be expedient to punish a man for injuring his neighbour. With regard to that branch of probity which is opposed to offences against property, private ethics depends in a manner for its very existence upon legislation. Legislation must first determine what things are to be regarded as each man's property, before the general rules of ethics, on this head, can have any particular application. The case is the same with regard to offences against the state. Without legislation there would be no such thing as a *state*: no particular persons invested with powers to be exercised for the benefit of the rest. It is plain, therefore, that in this branch the interference of the legislator cannot any where be dispensed with. We must first know what are the dictates of legislation, before we can know what are the dictates of private ethics.[s]

19. As to the rules of beneficence, these, as far as concerns matters of detail, must necessarily be abandoned in great measure to the jurisdiction of private ethics. In many cases the beneficial quality of the act depends essentially upon the disposition of the agent; that is, upon the motives by which he appears to have been prompted to perform it: upon their belonging to the head of sympathy, love of amity, or love of reputation; and not to any head of self-regarding motives, brought into play by the force of political constraint: in a word, upon their being such as denominate his conduct *free* and *voluntary*, according to one of the many senses given to those ambiguous expressions.[t] The limits of the law on

[s] But suppose the dictates of legislation *are* not what they *ought to be*: what are then, or (what in this case comes to the same thing) what ought to be, the dictates of private ethics? Do they coincide with the dictates of legislation, or do they oppose them, or do they remain neuter? a very interesting question this, but one that belongs not to the present subject. It belongs exclusively to that of private ethics. Principles which may lead to the solution of it may be seen in A Fragment on Government, p. 150. Lond. edit. 1776—and p. 114. edit. 1823.[1]

[t] If we may believe M. Voltaire,[*] there was a time when the French ladies

[*] Quest. sur l'Encyclop. tom. 7. art. Impuissance.[2]

[1] Bentham is referring to para. 21 ff. of Ch. IV of the *Fragment* (Bowring, i, 287 ff.).
[2] Bentham refers to the 1770–1 edition of Voltaire's *Questions sur l'Encyclopédie*.

this head seem, however, to be capable of being extended a good deal farther than they seem ever to have been extended hitherto. In particular, in cases where the person is in danger, why should it not be made the duty of every man to save another from mischief, when it can be done without prejudicing himself, as well as to abstain from bringing it on him? This accordingly is the idea pursued in the body of the work.[u]

20. To conclude this section, let us recapitulate and bring to a point the difference between private ethics, considered as an art or science, on the one hand, and that branch of jurisprudence which contains the art or science of legislation, on the other. Private ethics teaches how each man may dispose himself to pursue the course most conducive to his own happiness, by means of such motives as offer of themselves: the art of legislation (which may be considered as one branch of the science of jurisprudence) teaches how a multitude of men, composing a community, may be disposed to pursue that course which upon the whole is the most conducive to the happiness of the whole community, by means of motives to be applied by the legislator.

Difference between private ethics and the art of legislation recapitulated

We come now to exhibit the limits between penal and civil jurisprudence. For this purpose it may be of use to give a distinct though summary view of the principal branches into which jurisprudence, considered in its utmost extent, is wont to be divided.

§ ii. *Jurisprudence, its branches*

21. Jurisprudence is a fictitious entity: nor can any meaning be found for the word, but by placing it in company with some word that shall be significative of a real entity. To know what is meant by jurisprudence, we must know, for example, what is meant by a book of jurisprudence. A book of jurisprudence can have but

Jurisprudence, expository – censorial

who thought themselves neglected by their husbands, used to petition *pour être embesoignées*: the technical word, which, he says, was appropriated to this purpose. These sort of law-proceedings seem not very well calculated to answer the design: accordingly we hear nothing of them now-a-days. The French ladies of the present age seem to be under no such difficulties.

[u] A woman's head-dress catches fire: water is at hand: a man, instead of assisting to quench the fire, looks on, and laughs at it. A drunken man, falling with his face downwards into a puddle, is in danger of suffocation: lifting his head a little on one side would save him: another man sees this and lets him lie. A quantity of gunpowder lies scattered about a room: a man is going into it with a lighted candle: another knowing this, lets him go in without warning. Who is there that in any of these cases would think punishment misapplied?

CHAPTER XVII   LIMITS OF PENAL JURISPRUDENCE

one or the other of two objects: 1. to ascertain what the *law*[v] is: 2. to ascertain what it ought to be. In the former case it may be styled a book of *expository* jurisprudence; in the latter, a book of *censorial* jurisprudence: or, in other words, a book on the *art of legislation.*

Expository jurisprudence, authoritative – unauthoritative

22. A book of expository jurisprudence is either *authoritative* or *unauthoritative.* It is styled authoritative, when it is composed by him who, by representing the state of the law to be so and so, causeth it so to be; that is, of the legislator himself: unauthoritative, when it is the work of any other person at large.

Sources of the distinctions yet remaining

23. Now *law,* or *the law,* taken indefinitely, is an abstract and collective term; which, when it means any thing, can mean neither more nor less than the sum total of a number of individual laws taken together.[w] It follows, that of whatever other modifications the subject of a book of jurisprudence is susceptible, they must all of them be taken from some circumstance or other of which such individual laws, or the assemblages into which they may be sorted, are susceptible. The circumstances that have given rise to the principal branches of jurisprudence we are wont to hear of, seem to be as follow: 1. The *extent* of the laws in question in point of dominion. 2. The *political quality* of the persons whose conduct they undertake to regulate. 3. The *time* of their being in force. 4. The manner in which they are *expressed.* 5. The concern which they have with the article of *punishment.*

Jurisprudence, local – universal

24. In the first place, in point of extent, what is delivered concerning the laws in question, may have reference either to the laws of such or such a nation or nations in particular, or to the laws of all nations whatsoever: in the first case, the book may be said to relate to *local,* in the other, to *universal jurisprudence.*

[v] The word *law* itself which stands so much in need of a definition, must wait for it awhile, (see § iii[1]): for there is no doing every thing at once. In the mean time every reader will understand it according to the notion he has been accustomed to annex to it.

[w] In most of the European languages there are two different words for distinguishing the abstract and the concrete senses of the word *law*: which words are so wide asunder as not even to have any etymological affinity. In Latin, for example, there is *lex* for the concrete sense, *jus* for the abstract: in Italian, *legge* and *diritto*: in French, *loi* and *droit*: in Spanish, *ley* and *derecho*: in German, *gesetz* and *recht*. The English is at present destitute of this advantage.

In the Anglo-Saxon, besides *lage*, and several other words, for the concrete sense, there was the word *right*, answering to the German *recht*, for the abstract; as may be seen in the compound *folc-right*, and in other instances. But the word *right* having long ago lost this sense, the modern English no longer possesses this advantage.

[1] See above, 207 n. 1.

LIMITS OF PENAL JURISPRUDENCE   CHAPTER XVII

Now of the infinite variety of nations there are upon the earth, there are no two which agree exactly in their laws: certainly not in the whole; perhaps not even in any single article; and let them agree to-day, they would disagree to-morrow. This is evident enough with regard to the *substance* of the laws: and it would be still more extraordinary if they agreed in point of *form*; that is, if they were conceived in precisely the same strings of words. What is more, as the languages of nations are commonly different, as well as their laws, it is seldom that, strictly speaking, they have so much as a single *word* in common. However, among the words that are appropriated to the subject of law, there are some that in all languages are pretty exactly correspondent to one another: which comes to the same thing nearly as if they were the same. Of this stamp, for example, are those which correspond to the words *power, right, obligation, liberty,* and many others.

It follows, that if there are any books which can, properly speaking, be styled books of universal jurisprudence, they must be looked for within very narrow limits. Among such as are expository, there can be none that are authoritative: nor even, as far as the *substance* of the laws is concerned, any that are unauthoritative. To be susceptible of an universal application, all that a book of the expository kind can have to treat of, is the import of words: to be, strictly speaking, universal, it must confine itself to terminology. Accordingly the definitions which there has been occasion here and there to intersperse in the course of the present work, and particularly the definition hereafter given of the word *law*, may be considered as matter belonging to the head of universal jurisprudence. Thus far in strictness of speech: though in point of usage, where a man, in laying down what he apprehends to be the law, extends his views to a few of the nations with which his own is most connected, it is common enough to consider what he writes as relating to universal jurisprudence.

It is in the censorial line that there is the greatest room for disquisitions that apply to the circumstances of all nations alike: and in this line what regards the substance of the laws in question is as susceptible of an universal application, as what regards the words. That the laws of all nations, or even of any two nations, should coincide in all points, would be as ineligible as it is impossible: some leading points, however, there seem to be, in respect of which the laws of all civilized nations might, without inconvenience, be the same. To mark out some of these points will, as far as it goes, be the business of the body of this work.

CHAPTER XVII   LIMITS OF PENAL JURISPRUDENCE

*–internal and
international*

25. In the second place, with regard to the *political quality* of the persons whose conduct is the object of the law. These may, on any given occasion, be considered either as members of the same state, or as members of different states: in the first case, the law may be referred to the head of *internal*, in the second case, to that of *international*[x] jurisprudence.

Now as to any transactions which may take place between individuals who are subjects of different states, these are regulated by the internal laws, and decided upon by the internal tribunals, of the one or the other of these states: the case is the same where the sovereign of the one has any immediate transactions with a private member of the other: the sovereign reducing himself, *pro re natâ*, to the condition of a private person, as often as he submits his cause to either tribunal; whether by claiming a benefit, or defending himself against a burthen. There remain then the mutual transactions between sovereigns as such, for the subject of that branch of jurisprudence which may be properly and exclusively termed *international*.[y]

[x] The word *international*, it must be acknowledged, is a new one; though, it is hoped, sufficiently analogous and intelligible. It is calculated to express, in a more significant way, the branch of law which goes commonly under the name of the *law of nations*: an appellation so uncharacteristic, that, were it not for the force of custom, it would seem rather to refer to internal jurisprudence. The chancellor D'Aguesseau[1] has already made, I find, a similar remark: he says, that what is commonly called *droit* des *gens*, ought rather to be termed *droit* entre *les gens*.[*]

[y] In the times of James I of England, and Philip III of Spain, certain merchants at London happened to have a claim upon Philip, which his ambassador Gondemar did not think fit to satisfy. They applied for counsel to Selden, who advised them to sue the Spanish monarch in the court of King's Bench, and prosecute him to an outlawry. They did so: and the sheriffs of London were accordingly commanded in the usual form, to take the body of the defendant Philip, wherever it was to be found within their bailiwick. As to the sheriffs, Philip, we may believe, was in no great fear of them: but, what answered the same purpose, he happened on his part to have demands upon some other merchants, whom, so long as the outlawry remained in force, there was no proceeding against. Gondemar paid the money.[†][2] This was internal juris-

[*] Oeuvres, Tom. ii. p. 337, Edit. 1773, 12mo.
[†] Selden's Table-Talk, tit. Law.[3]

[1] Henri-Francois Daguesseau (1668–1751) was Chancellor of France under Louis XIV.
[2] Diego Sarmiento de Acuna (1567–1626), Conde de Gondomar, came to England as ambassador of Philip III (1598–1621) in 1613 and remained until 1622. John Selden (1584–1654), the jurist, was called to the bar in 1612.
[3] The *Table Talk* of John Selden (see n. 2 above) was posthumously published in 1689.

LIMITS OF PENAL JURISPRUDENCE　　　　　　CHAPTER XVII

With what degree of propriety rules for the conduct of persons of this description can come under the appellation of *laws*, is a question that must rest till the nature of the thing called *a law* shall have been more particularly unfolded.

It is evident enough, that international jurisprudence may, as well as internal, be censorial as well as expository, unauthoritative as well as authoritative.

26. Internal jurisprudence, again, may either concern all the members of a state indiscriminately, or such of them only as are connected in the way of residence, or otherwise, with a particular district. Jurisprudence is accordingly sometimes distinguished into *national* and *provincial*. But as the epithet *provincial* is hardly applicable to districts so small as many of those which have laws of their own are wont to be, such as towns, parishes, and manors; the term *local* (where universal jurisprudence is plainly out of the question) or the term *particular*, though this latter is not very characteristic, might either of them be more commodious.^z *[Internal jurisprudence, national and provincial, local or particular]*

27. Third, with respect to *time*. In a work of the expository kind, the laws that are in question may either be such as are still in force at the time when the book is writing, or such as have ceased to be in force. In the latter case the subject of it might be termed *ancient*; in the former, *present* or *living* jurisprudence: that is, if the substantive *jurisprudence*, and no other, must at any rate be employed, and that with an epithet in both cases. But the truth is, that a book of the former kind is rather a book of history than a book of jurisprudence; and, if the word *jurisprudence* be expressive of the subject, it is only with some such words as *history* or *antiquities* prefixed. And as the laws which are any where in question are supposed, *[Jurisprudence, ancient–living]*

prudence: if the dispute had been betwixt Philip and James himself, it would have been international.

As to the word *international*, from this work, or the first of the works edited in French by Mr Dumont, it has taken root in the language. Witness Reviews and Newspapers.[1]

　　^z The term *municipal* seemed to answer the purpose very well, till it was taken by an English author of the first eminence, to signify internal law in general, in contradistinction to international law, and the imaginary law of nature.[2] It might still be used in this sense, without scruple, in any other language.

　　[1] Paragraph added in 1823. The first of Dumont's works based on Bentham's manuscripts was *Traités de législation civile et pénale* (Paris, 1802).

　　[2] If, as seems likely, Bentham has Blackstone in mind here, his comment is questionable; for the usage he criticises seems to have been established at a much earlier period.

if nothing appears to the contrary, to be those which are in force, no such epithet as that of *present* or *living* commonly appears.

Where a book is so circumstanced, that the laws which form the subject of it, though in force at the time of its being written, are in force no longer, that book is neither a book of living jurisprudence, nor a book on the history of jurisprudence: it is no longer the former, and it never was the latter. It is evident that, owing to the changes which from time to time must take place, in a greater or less degree, in every body of laws, every book of jurisprudence, which is of an expository nature, must, in the course of a few years, come to partake more or less of this condition.

The most common and most useful object of a history of jurisprudence, is to exhibit the circumstances that have attended the establishment of laws actually in force. But the exposition of the dead laws which have been superseded, is inseparably interwoven with that of the living ones which have superseded them. The great use of both these branches of *science,* is to furnish examples for the *art* of legislation.[a2]

Jurisprudence, statutory—customary

28. Fourthly, in point of *expression*, the laws in question may subsist either in the form of *statute* or in that of *customary* law.

As to the difference between these two branches (which respects only the article of form or expression) it cannot properly be made appear till some progress has been made in the definition of *a* law.

Jurisprudence, civil—penal—criminal

29. Last, The most intricate distinction of all, and that which comes most frequently on the carpet, is that which is made between

---

[a2] Of what stamp are the works of Grotius, Puffendorf, and Burlamaqui?[1] Are they political or ethical, historical or juridical, expository or censorial?— Sometimes one thing, sometimes another: they seem hardly to have settled the matter with themselves. A defect this to which all books must almost unavoidably be liable, which take for their subject the pretended *law of nature;* an obscure phantom, which, in the imaginations of those who go in chase of it, points sometimes to *manners,* sometimes to *laws;* sometimes to what law *is,* sometimes to what it *ought* to be.* Montesquieu sets out upon the censorial plan: but long before the conclusion, as if he had forgot his first design, he throws off the censor, and puts on the antiquarian. The Marquis Beccaria's book,[2] the first of any account that is uniformly censorial, concludes as it sets out with penal jurisprudence.

* See Ch. II (Principles adverse) 14.

[1] Hugo Grotius (1583–1645): *De jure belli ac pacis* (1625). Samuel Puffendorf (1632–94): *Elementa jurisprudentiae universalis* (1661); *De jure naturae et gentium* (1672). Jean Jacques Burlamaqui (1694–1748): *Principes du droit naturel* (1747); *Principes du droit politique* (1751).
[2] *Dei delitti e delle pene* (1764). Cf. above, 166 n. 1.

the *civil* branch of jurisprudence and the *penal*, which latter is wont, in certain circumstances, to receive the name of *criminal*.

What is a penal code of laws? What a civil code? Of what nature are their contents? Is it that there are two sorts of laws, the one penal the other civil, so that the laws in a penal code are all penal laws, while the laws in a civil code are all civil laws? Or is it, that in every law there is some matter which is of a penal nature, and which therefore belongs to the penal code and at the same time other matter which is of a civil nature, and which therefore belongs to the civil code? Or is it, that some laws belong to one code or the other exclusively, while others are divided between the two?[b2] To answer these questions in any manner that shall be tolerably satisfactory, it will be necessary to ascertain what *a law* is; meaning one entire but single law: and what are the parts into which a law, as such, is capable of being distinguished: or, in other words, to ascertain what the properties are that are to be found in every object

Question, concerning the distinction between the civil branch and the penal, stated

[b2] To anyone who should come new to the subject the questions mentioned in the text will naturally appear to be the very A B C of Jurisprudence: they must long ago, he would think, have met with a full and satisfactory solution: to say anything at all about them here would therefore appear idle: to say anything new, impossible. So many ages as have been spent in the study of the laws, so many libraries-full as have been written on them, not know yet what a law is? So many laws as have been made, not know the ingredients they are made of? Incredible—and yet nothing is more true. To write to any purpose a man must begin *ab ovo*: I see no fund open that he can draw from: what he makes use of he must make.

The wonder will cease when it comes to be perceived that the idea of a law, meaning one single but entire law, is in a manner inseparably connected with that of a complete body of laws: so that what is a law and what are the contents of a complete body of the laws are questions of which neither can well be answered without the other. A body of laws is a vast and complicated piece of mechanism, of which no part can be fully explained without the rest. To understand the functions of a balance-wheel you must take to pieces the whole watch: to understand the nature of a law you must take to pieces the whole code.

The subject we are now entering upon belongs to a particular branch of logic, untouched by Aristotle. The main and ultimate business of the school-logic of which that philosopher was the father, is to exhibit the several forms of *argumentation*: the business of the branch now before us is to exhibit the several forms of *imperation*: or (to take the subject in its utmost extent) of sentences expressive of volition: a leaf which seems to be yet wanting in the book of science.

All language whatsoever, every sentence whatsoever, inasmuch as it *expresses* something must *assert* something: something expressive of the state and condition, real or pretended, of the mind of him whose language it is: that is either of his understanding or his will: for at bottom, whatever is said even of external events resolves itself into this. In the first case the sentence expressive of

CHAPTER XVII LIMITS OF PENAL JURISPRUDENCE

which can with propriety receive the appellation of *a* law. This then will be the business of the third and fourth sections: what concerns the import of the word *criminal*, as applied to law, will be discussed separately in the fifth.

it has been styled exclusively a *sentence of assertion*: in the other case, a *sentence of volition** of which latter, a *sentence of interrogation* is a particular species.† 'The robber is killed':—'Kill the robber':—'Is the robber killed?'—This is as much as to say, 'I *understand* or I believe that the robber is killed.'—'My *will* is that you kill the robber': 'My *will* is that you tell me whether the robber be killed or no': that is, that if the robber is killed, you tell me he is killed: if not, that he is not killed. Now it is to sentences of the assertive kind that the logic of the schools has confined itself: those which concern volition it has left untouched. The demesnes of the logical branch of science appear then to be more extensive than has commonly been suspected: the language of the will being a new and unexplored province which, neglected as it has been hitherto, might be cultivated, it is probable to at least as good a purpose as the old. It is the branch here in question that is more particularly applicable to the business of government: that subdivision which concerns the forms of imperation at large having a more particular regard to legislation; that which concerns the forms of interrogation, to the less dignified but not less necessary business of collecting verbal information: a process subservient to the business as well of the legislative as of the executive departments.

Had Aristotle happened to turn his view this way, as many pens might perhaps have been employed on this branch of logic as on the other: like that it might have had its algebraical method of notation, its graphical schemes, and its *memoriter* verses: the *Asserit A negat B* . . .': the '*Barbara, celarent, darii, ferioque*' of the schoolmen might have found their parodies: and every piece of intellectual machinery which the ingenuity of those subtle speculatists has ever invented for the accommodation or affrightment of beginners might here have been initiated and improved.

Had this happened to be the case the subject we are entering upon would it is to be presumed by this time have stood in a much clearer light than that in which in the course of a cursory review, I have been able to place it: the business of a great part of the following pages might in that case have been dispatched by a few references. As it is I mean not to descend any deeper into the subject than is absolutely necessary in order to find the requisite materials for the task actually in hand: content with opening the mine, I leave the working of it out to others.[1]

* Harris's Hermes B. 5 Ch. 2 p. 17.[2]
† Ibid.

[1] For the insertion here of this note on the 'logic of the will', see above, Introduction, xlii.
[2] James Harris (1709–80) published in 1751 his *Hermes, or a philosophical enquiry concerning universal grammar*. For some comments on it by Bentham, see his letter to Samuel Bentham of 9 December 1774 (*Correspondence*, in *CW*, i, 221–2).

[4]

Excerpt from *Utilitarianism, On Liberty, Essay on Bentham*, 65–77

CHAPTER I

INTRODUCTORY

THE subject of this Essay is not the so-called Liberty of the Will, so unfortunately opposed to the misnamed doctrine of Philosophical Necessity; but Civil, or Social Liberty: the nature and limits of the power which can be legitimately exercised by society over the individual. A question seldom stated, and hardly ever discussed, in general terms, but which profoundly influences the practical controversies of the age by its latent presence, and is likely soon to make itself recognised as the vital question of the future. It is so far from being new, that, in a certain sense, it has divided mankind, almost from the remotest ages; but in the stage of progress into which the more civilised portions of the species have now entered, it presents itself under new conditions, and requires a different and more fundamental treatment.

The struggle between Liberty and Authority is the most conspicuous feature in the portions of history with which we are earliest familiar, particularly in that of Greece, Rome, and England. But in old times this contest was between subjects, or some classes of subjects, and the Government. By liberty, was meant protection against the tyranny of the political rulers. The rulers were conceived (except in some of the popular governments of Greece) as in a necessarily antagonistic position to the people whom they ruled. They consisted of a governing One, or a governing tribe or caste, who derived their authority from inheritance or conquest, who, at all events, did not hold it at the pleasure of the governed, and whose supremacy men did not venture, perhaps did not desire, to contest, whatever precautions might be taken against its oppressive exercise. Their power was regarded as necessary, but also as highly dangerous; as a weapon which they would attempt to use against their subjects, no less than against external enemies. To prevent the weaker members of the community from being preyed upon

66   On Liberty

by innumerable vultures, it was needful that there should be
an animal of prey stronger than the rest, commissioned to keep
them down.   But as the king of the vultures would be no less
bent upon preying on the flock than any of the minor harpies,
it was indispensable to be in a perpetual attitude of defence
against his beak and claws.   The aim, therefore, of patriots was
to set limits to the power which the ruler should be suffered to
exercise over the community; and this limitation was what they
meant by liberty.   It was attempted in two ways.   First, by
obtaining a recognition of certain immunities, called political
liberties or rights, which it was to be regarded as a breach of duty
in the ruler to infringe, and which if he did infringe, specific
resistance, or general rebellion, was held to be justifiable.   A
second, and generally a later expedient, was the establishment of
constitutional checks, by which the consent of the community,
or of a body of some sort, supposed to represent its interests,
was made a necessary condition to some of the more important
acts of the governing power.   To the first of these modes of
limitation, the ruling power, in most European countries, was
compelled, more or less, to submit.   It was not so with the
second; and, to attain this, or when already in some degree
possessed, to attain it more completely, became everywhere the
principal object of the lovers of liberty.   And so long as mankind
were content to combat one enemy by another, and to be ruled
by a master, on condition of being guaranteed more or less
efficaciously against his tyranny, they did not carry their
aspirations beyond this point.

A time, however, came, in the progress of human affairs, when
men ceased to think it a necessity of nature that their governors
should be an independent power, opposed in interest to themselves.   It appeared to them much better that the various magistrates of the State should be their tenants or delegates, revocable
at their pleasure.   In that way alone, it seemed, could they have
complete security that the powers of government would never
be abused to their disadvantage.   By degrees this new demand
for elective and temporary rulers became the prominent object
of the exertions of the popular party, wherever any such party
existed; and superseded, to a considerable extent, the previous
efforts to limit the power of rulers.   As the struggle proceeded
for making the ruling power emanate from the periodical choice
of the ruled, some persons began to think that too much importance had been attached to the limitation of the power itself.
That (it might seem) was a resource against rulers whose interests

Introductory   67

were habitually opposed to those of the people.   What was now
wanted was, that the rulers should be identified with the people;
that their interest and will should be the interest and will of
the nation.   The nation did not need to be protected against
its own will.   There was no fear of its tyrannising over itself.
Let the rulers be effectually responsible to it, promptly removable by it, and it could afford to trust them with power of which
it could itself dictate the use to be made.   Their power was but
the nation's own power, concentrated, and in a form convenient
for exercise.   This mode of thought, or rather perhaps of feeling,
was common among the last generation of European liberalism,
in the Continental section of which it still apparently predominates.   Those who admit any limit to what a government may
do, except in the case of such governments as they think ought
not to exist, stand out as brilliant exceptions among the political
thinkers of the Continent.   A similar tone of sentiment might
by this time have been prevalent in our own country, if the
circumstances which for a time encouraged it, had continued
unaltered.

   But, in political and philosophical theories, as well as in persons,
success discloses faults and infirmities which failure might have
concealed from observation.   The notion, that the people have
no need to limit their power over themselves, might seem
axiomatic, when popular government was a thing only dreamed
about, or read of as having existed at some distant period of the
past.   Neither was that notion necessarily disturbed by such
temporary aberrations as those of the French Revolution, the
worst of which were the work of a usurping few, and which, in
any case, belonged, not to the permanent working of popular
institutions, but to a sudden and convulsive outbreak against
monarchical and aristocratic despotism.   In time, however, a
democratic republic came to occupy a large portion of the earth's
surface, and made itself felt as one of the most powerful members
of the community of nations;   and elective and responsible
government became subject to the observations and criticisms
which wait upon a great existing fact.   It was now perceived
that such phrases as " self-government," and " the power of the
people over themselves," do not express the true state of the
case.   The " people " who exercise the power are not always the
same people with those over whom it is exercised; and the " self-
government " spoken of is not the government of each by himself, but of each by all the rest.   The will of the people, moreover,
practically means the will of the most numerous or the most

68   On Liberty

active *part* of the people; the majority, or those who succeed in
making themselves accepted as the majority; the people, consequently *may* desire to oppress a part of their number; and precautions are as much needed against this as against any other
abuse of power. The limitation, therefore, of the power of
government over individuals loses none of its importance when
the holders of power are regularly accountable to the community,
that is, to the strongest party therein. This view of things,
recommending itself equally to the intelligence of thinkers and
to the inclination of those important classes in European society
to whose real or supposed interests democracy is adverse, has had
no difficulty in establishing itself; and in political speculations
"the tyranny of the majority"[3] is now generally included among
the evils against which society requires to be on its guard.

Like other tyrannies, the tyranny of the majority was at first,
and is still vulgarly, held in dread, chiefly as operating through
the acts of the public authorities. But reflecting persons perceived that when society is itself the tyrant—society collectively
over the separate individuals who compose it—its means of
tyrannising are not restricted to the acts which it may do by
the hands of its political functionaries. Society can and does
execute its own mandates: and if it issues wrong mandates
instead of right, or any mandates at all in things with which it
ought not to meddle, it practises a social tyranny more formidable than many kinds of political oppression, since, though
not usually upheld by such extreme penalties, it leaves fewer
means of escape, penetrating much more deeply into the details
of life, and enslaving the soul itself.[4] Protection, therefore,
against the tyranny of the magistrate is not enough: there
needs protection also against the tyranny of the prevailing
opinion and feeling; against the tendency of society to impose,
by other means than civil penalties, its own ideas and practices
as rules of conduct on those who dissent from them; to fetter
the development, and, if possible, prevent the formation, of any
individuality not in harmony with its ways, and compel all
characters to fashion themselves upon the model of its own.
There is a limit to the legitimate interference of collective opinion
with individual independence: and to find that limit, and maintain it against encroachment, is as indispensable to a good condition of human affairs, as protection against political despotism.

But though this proposition is not likely to be contested in
general terms, the practical question, where to place the limit—
how to make the fitting adjustment between individual inde-

Introductory

pendence and social control—is a subject on which nearly everything remains to be done. All that makes existence valuable
to any one, depends on the enforcement of restraints upon the
actions of other people. Some rules of conduct, therefore, must
be imposed, by law in the first place, and by opinion on many
things which are not fit subjects for the operation of law. What
these rules should be is the principal question in human affairs;
but if we except a few of the most obvious cases, it is one of those
which least progress has been made in resolving. No two ages,
and scarcely any two countries, have decided it alike; and the
decision of one age or country is a wonder to another. Yet the
people of any given age and country no more suspect any diffi
culty in it, than if it were a subject on which mankind had always
been agreed. The rules which obtain among themselves appear
to them self-evident and self-justifying. This all but universal
illusion is one of the examples of the magical influence of custom,
which is not only, as the proverb says, a second nature, but is
continually mistaken for the first. The effect of custom, in
preventing any misgiving respecting the rules of conduct which
mankind impose on one another, is all the more complete because
the subject is one on which it is not generally considered necessary that reasons should be given, either by one person to others
or by each to himself. People are accustomed to believe, and
have been encouraged in the belief by some who aspire to the
character of philosophers, that their feelings, on subjects of this
nature, are better than reasons, and render reasons unnecessary.
The practical principle which guides them to their opinions on
the regulation of human conduct, is the feeling in each person's
mind that everybody should be required to act as he, and those
with whom he sympathises, would like them to act. No one,
indeed, acknowledges to himself that his standard of judgment
is his own liking; but an opinion on a point of conduct, not
supported by reasons, can only count as one person's preference;
and if the reasons, when given, are a mere appeal to a similar
preference felt by other people, it is still only many people's
liking instead of one. To an ordinary man, however, his own
preference, thus supported, is not only a perfectly satisfactory
reason, but the only one he generally has for any of his notions
of morality, taste, or propriety, which are not expressly written
in his religious creed; and his chief guide in the interpretation
even of that. Men's opinions, accordingly, on what is laudable
or blamable, are affected by all the multifarious causes which
influence their wishes in regard to the conduct of others, and

On Liberty

which are as numerous as those which determine their wishes on any other subject. Sometimes their reason—at other times their prejudices or superstitions: often their social affections, not seldom their antisocial ones, their envy or jealousy, their arrogance or contemptuousness: but most commonly their desires or fears for themselves—their legitimate or illegitimate self-interest. Wherever there is an ascendant class, a large portion of the morality of the country emanates from its class interests, and its feelings of class superiority. The morality between Spartans and Helots, between planters and negroes, between princes and subjects, between nobles and roturiers, between men and women, has been for the most part the creation of these class interests and feelings: and the sentiments thus generated react in turn upon the moral feelings of the members of the ascendant class, in their relations among themselves. Where, on the other hand, a class, formerly ascendant, has lost its ascendancy, or where its ascendancy is unpopular, the prevailing moral sentiments frequently bear the impress of an impatient dislike of superiority.* Another grand determining principle of the rules of conduct, both in act and forbearance, which have been enforced by law or opinion, has been the servility of mankind towards the supposed preferences or aversions of their temporal masters or of their gods. This servility, though essentially selfish, is not hypocrisy; it gives rise to perfectly genuine sentiments of abhorrence; it made men burn magicians and heretics. Among so many baser influences, the general and obvious interests of society have of course had a share, and a large one, in the direction of the moral sentiments: less, however, as a matter of reason, and on their own account, than as a consequence of the sympathies and antipathies which grew out of them: and sympathies and antipathies which had little or nothing to do with the interests of society, have made themselves felt in the establishment of moralities with quite as great force.

The likings and dislikings of society, or of some powerful portion of it, are thus the main thing which has practically determined the rules laid down for general observance, under the penalties of law or opinion. And in general, those who have been in advance of society in thought and feeling, have left this condition of things unassailed in principle, however they may have come into conflict with it in some of its details. They have occupied themselves rather in inquiring what things society ought to like or dislike, than in questioning whether its likings

Introductory 71

or dislikings should be a law to individuals. They preferred endeavouring to alter the feelings of mankind on the particular points on which they were themselves heretical, rather than make common cause in defence of freedom, with heretics generally. The only case in which the higher ground has been taken on principle and maintained with consistency, by any but an individual here and there, is that of religious belief: a case instructive in many ways, and not least so as forming a most striking instance of the fallibility of what is called the moral sense: for the *odium theologicum*, in a sincere bigot, is one of the most unequivocal cases of moral feeling. Those who first broke the yoke of what called itself the Universal Church, were in general as little willing to permit difference of religious opinion as that church itself. But when the heat of the conflict was over, without giving a complete victory to any party, and each church or sect was reduced to limit its hopes to retaining possession of the ground it already occupied; minorities, seeing that they had no chance of becoming majorities, were under the necessity of pleading to those whom they could not convert, for permission to differ. It is accordingly on this battle field, almost solely, that the rights of the individual against society have been asserted on broad grounds of principle, and the claim of society to exercise authority over dissentients openly controverted. The great writers to whom the world owes what religious liberty it possesses, have mostly asserted freedom of conscience as an indefeasible right, and denied absolutely that a human being is accountable to others for his religious belief. Yet so natural to mankind is intolerance in whatever they really care about, that religious freedom has hardly anywhere been practically realised, except where religious indifference, which dislikes to have its peace disturbed by theological quarrels, has added its weight to the scale. In the minds of almost all religious persons, even in the most tolerant countries, the duty of toleration is admitted with tacit reserves. One person will bear with dissent in matters of church government, but not of dogma; another can tolerate everybody, short of a Papist or a Unitarian; another every one who believes in revealed religion; a few extend their charity a little further, but stop at the belief in a God and in a future state. Wherever the sentiment of the majority is still genuine and intense, it is found to have abated little of its claim to be obeyed.

In England, from the peculiar circumstances of our political history, though the yoke of opinion is perhaps heavier, that of law is lighter, than in most other countries of Europe; and there is considerable jealousy of direct interference, by the legislative or the executive power, with private conduct; not so much from any just regard for the independence of the individual, as from the still subsisting habit of looking on the government as representing an opposite interest to the public. The majority have not yet learnt to feel the power of the government their power, or its opinions their opinions. When they do so, individual liberty will probably be as much exposed to invasion from the government, as it already is from public opinion. But, as yet, there is a considerable amount of feeling ready to be called forth against any attempt of the law to control individuals in things in which they have not hitherto been accustomed to be controlled by it; and this with very little discrimination as to whether the matter is, or is not, within the legitimate sphere of legal control; insomuch that the feeling, highly salutary on the whole, is perhaps quite as often misplaced as well grounded in the particular instances of its application. There is, in fact, no recognised principle by which the propriety or impropriety of government interference is customarily tested. People decide according to their personal preferences. Some, whenever they see any good to be done, or evil to be remedied, would willingly instigate the government to undertake the business; while others prefer to bear almost any amount of social evil, rather than add one to the departments of human interests amenable to governmental control. And men range themselves on one or the other side in any particular case, according to this general direction of their sentiments; or according to the degree of interest which they feel in the particular thing which it is proposed that the government should do, or according to the belief they entertain that the government would, or would not, do it in the manner they prefer; but very rarely on account of any opinion to which they consistently adhere, as to what things are fit to be done by a government. And it seems to me that in consequence of this absence of rule or principle, one side is at present as often wrong as the other; the interference of government is, with about equal frequency, improperly invoked and improperly condemned.

The object of this Essay is to assert one very simple principle, as entitled to govern absolutely the dealings of society with the individual in the way of compulsion and control, whether the means used be physical force in the form of legal penalties, or the moral coercion of public opinion. That principle is, that the sole end for which mankind are warranted, individually or col-

Introductory   73

lectively, in interfering with the liberty of action of any of their number, is self-protection. That the only purpose for which power can be rightfully exercised over any member of a civilised community, against his will, is to prevent harm to others. His own good, either physical or moral, is not a sufficient warrant. He cannot rightfully be compelled to do or forbear because it will be better for him to do so, because it will make him happier, because, in the opinions of others, to do so would be wise, or even right. These are good reasons for remonstrating with him, or reasoning with him, or persuading him, or entreating him, but not for compelling him, or visiting him with any evil in case he do otherwise. To justify that, the conduct from which it is desired to deter him must be calculated to produce evil to some one else. The only part of the conduct of any one, for which he is amenable to society, is that which concerns others. In the part which merely concerns himself, his independence is, of right, absolute. Over himself, over his own body and mind, the individual is sovereign.[7]

It is, perhaps, hardly necessary to say that this doctrine is meant to apply only to human beings in the maturity of their faculties. We are not speaking of children, or of young persons below the age which the law may fix as that of manhood or womanhood. Those who are still in a state to require being taken care of by others, must be protected against their own actions as well as against external injury. For the same reason, we may leave out of consideration those backward states of society in which the race itself may be considered as in its nonage. The early difficulties in the way of spontaneous progress are so great, that there is seldom any choice of means for overcoming them; and a ruler full of the spirit of improvement is warranted in the use of any expedients that will attain an end, perhaps otherwise unattainable. Despotism is a legitimate mode of government in dealing with barbarians, provided the end be their improvement, and the means justified by actually effecting that end. Liberty, as a principle, has no application to any state of things anterior to the time when mankind have become capable of being improved by free and equal discussion. Until then, there is nothing for them but implicit obedience to an Akbar or a Charlemagne, if they are so fortunate as to find one. But as soon as mankind have attained the capacity of being guided to their own improvement by conviction or persuasion (a period long since reached in all nations with whom we need here concern ourselves), compulsion, either in the direct form or in that of

74 On Liberty

pains and penalties for non-compliance, is no longer admissible as a means to their own good, and justifiable only for the security of others.

It is proper to state that I forego any advantage which could be derived to my argument from the idea of abstract right, as a thing independent of utility. I regard utility as the ultimate appeal on all ethical questions; but it must be utility in the largest sense, grounded on the permanent interests of man as a progressive being.* Those interests, I contend, authorise the subjection of individual spontaneity to external control, only in respect to those actions of each, which concern the interest of other people. If any one does an act hurtful to others, there is a *prima facie* case for punishing him, by law, or, where legal penalties are not safely applicable, by general disapprobation. There are also many positive acts for the benefit of others, which he may rightfully be compelled to perform; such as to give evidence in a court of justice; to bear his fair share in the common defence, or in any other joint work necessary to the interest of the society of which he enjoys the protection; and to perform certain acts of individual beneficence, such as saving a fellow-creature's life, or interposing to protect the defenceless against ill-usage, things which whenever it is obviously a man's duty to do, he may rightfully be made responsible to society for not doing. A person may cause evil to others not only by his actions but by his inaction, and in either case he is justly accountable to them for the injury. The latter case, it is true, requires a much more cautious exercise of compulsion than the former. To make any one answerable for doing evil to others is the rule; to make him answerable for not preventing evil is, comparatively speaking, the exception. Yet there are many cases clear enough and grave enough to justify that exception. In all things which regard the external relations of the individual, he is *de jure* amenable to those whose interests are concerned, and, if need be, to society as their protector. There are often good reasons for not holding him to the responsibility; but these reasons must arise from the special expediencies of the case: either because it is a kind of case in which he is on the whole likely to act better, when left to his own discretion, than when controlled in any way in which society have it in their power to control him; or because the attempt to exercise control would produce other evils, greater than those which it would prevent. When such reasons as these preclude the enforcement of responsibility, the conscience of the agent himself should step into the vacant judgment seat, and

Introductory   75

protect those interests of others which have no external protection; judging himself all the more rigidly, because the case does
not admit of his being made accountable to the judgment of his
fellow-creatures.

But there is a sphere of action in which society, as distinguished from the individual, has, if any, only an indirect interest;
comprehending all that portion of a person's life and conduct
which affects only himself, or if it also affects others, only with
their free, voluntary, and undeceived consent and participation.*
When I say only himself, I mean directly, and in the first
instance; for whatever affects himself, may affect others through
himself; and the objection which may be grounded on this
contingency, will receive consideration in the sequel. This,
then, is the appropriate region of human liberty. It comprises,
first, the inward domain of consciousness; demanding liberty of
conscience in the most comprehensive sense; liberty of thought
and feeling; absolute freedom of opinion and sentiment on all
subjects, practical or speculative, scientific, moral, or theological.
The liberty of expressing and publishing opinions may seem to
fall under a different principle, since it belongs to that part of the
conduct of an individual which concerns other people; but, being
almost of as much importance as the liberty of thought itself,
and resting in great part on the same reasons, is practically
inseparable from it. Secondly, the principle requires liberty of
tastes and pursuits; of framing the plan of our life to suit our own
character; of doing as we like, subject to such consequences as
may follow: without impediment from our fellow-creatures, so
long as what we do does not harm them, even though they should
think our conduct foolish, perverse, or wrong. Thirdly, from
this liberty of each individual, follows the liberty, within the
same limits, of combination among individuals; freedom to
unite, for any purpose not involving harm to others: the persons
combining being supposed to be of full age, and not forced or
deceived.

No society in which these liberties are not, on the whole,
respected, is free, whatever may be its form of government; and
none is completely free in which they do not exist absolute and
unqualified. The only freedom which deserves the name, is that
of pursuing our own good in our own way, so long as we do not
attempt to deprive others of theirs, or impede their efforts to
obtain it. Each is the proper guardian of his own health,
whether bodily, *or* mental and spiritual. Mankind are greater
gainers by suffering each other to live as seems good to them-

76 On Liberty

selves, than by compelling each to live as seems good to the rest.

Though this doctrine is anything but new, and, to some persons, may have the air of a truism, there is no doctrine which stands more directly opposed to the general tendency of existing opinion and practice. Society has expended fully as much effort in the attempt (according to its lights) to compel people to conform to its notions of personal as of social excellence. The ancient commonwealths thought themselves entitled to practise, and the ancient philosophers countenanced, the regulation of every part of private conduct by public authority, on the ground that the State had a deep interest in the whole bodily and mental discipline of every one of its citizens; a mode of thinking which may have been admissible in small republics surrounded by powerful enemies, in constant peril of being subverted by foreign attack or internal commotion, and to which even a short interval of relaxed energy and self-command might so easily be fatal that they could not afford to wait for the salutary permanent effects of freedom. In the modern world, the greater size of political communities, and, above all, the separation between spiritual and temporal authority (which placed the direction of men's consciences in other hands than those which controlled their worldly affairs), prevented so great an interference by law in the details of private life; but the engines of moral repression have been wielded more strenuously against divergence from the reigning opinion in self-regarding, than even in social matters; religion, the most powerful of the elements which have entered into the formation of moral feeling, having almost always been governed either by the ambition of a hierarchy, seeking control over every department of human conduct, or by the spirit of Puritanism. And some of those modern reformers who have placed themselves in strongest opposition to the religions of the past, have been noway behind either churches or sects in their assertion of the right of spiritual domination: M. Comte, in particular, whose social system, as unfolded in his *Système de Politique Positive*, aims at establishing (though by moral more than by legal appliances) a despotism of society over the individual, surpassing anything contemplated in the political ideal of the most rigid disciplinarian among the ancient philosophers.

Apart from the peculiar tenets of individual thinkers, there is also in the world at large an increasing inclination to stretch unduly the powers of society over the individual, both by the force of opinion and even by that of legislation; and as the

Introductory   77

tendency of all the changes taking place in the world is to strengthen society, and diminish the power of the individual, this encroachment is not one of the evils which tend spontaneously to disappear, but, on the contrary, to grow more and more formidable. The disposition of mankind, whether as rulers or as fellow-citizens, to impose their own opinions and inclinations as a rule of conduct on others, is so energetically supported by some of the best and by some of the worst feelings incident to human nature, that it is hardly ever kept under restraint by anything but want of power; and as the power is not declining, but growing, unless a strong barrier of moral conviction can be raised against the mischief, we must expect, in the present circumstances of the world, to see it increase.

It will be convenient for the argument, if, instead of at once entering upon the general thesis, we confine ourselves in the first instance to a single branch of it, on which the principle here stated is, if not fully, yet to a certain point, recognised by the current opinions. This one branch is the Liberty of Thought: from which it is impossible to separate the cognate liberty of speaking and of writing. Although these liberties, to some considerable amount, form part of the political morality of all countries which profess religious toleration and free institutions, the grounds, both philosophical and practical, on which they rest, are perhaps not so familiar to the general mind, nor so thoroughly appreciated by many even of the leaders of opinion, as might have been expected. Those grounds, when rightly understood, are of much wider application than to only one division of the subject, and a thorough consideration of this part of the question will be found the best introduction to the remainder. Those to whom nothing which I am about to say will be new, may therefore, I hope, excuse me, if on a subject which for now three centuries has been so often discussed, I venture on one discussion more.

[5]

Excerpt from *Utilitarianism, On Liberty, Essay on Bentham*, 184–204

CHAPTER III

OF INDIVIDUALITY, AS ONE OF THE ELEMENTS OF WELL-BEING

Such being the reasons which make it imperative that human beings should be free to form opinions, and to express their opinions without reserve; and such the baneful consequences to the intellectual, and through that to the moral nature of man, unless this liberty is either conceded, or asserted in spite of prohibition; let us next examine whether the same reasons do not require that men should be free to act upon their opinions—to carry these out in their lives, without hindrance, either physical or moral, from their fellow-men, so long as it is at their own risk and peril. This last proviso is of course indispensable. No one pretends that actions should be as free as opinions. On the contrary, even opinions lose their immunity when the circumstances in which they are expressed are such as to constitute their expression a positive instigation to some mischievous act. An opinion that corn-dealers are starvers of the poor, or that private property is robbery, ought to be unmolested when simply circulated through the press, but may justly incur punishment when delivered orally to an excited mob assembled before the house of a corn-dealer, or when handed about among the same mob in the form of a placard. Acts, of whatever kind, which, without justifiable cause, do harm to others, may be, and in the more important cases absolutely require to be, controlled by the unfavourable sentiments, and, when needful, by the active interference of mankind. The liberty of the individual must be thus far limited; he must not make himself a nuisance to other people. But if he refrains from molesting others in what concerns them, and merely acts according to his own inclination and judgment in things which concern himself, the same reasons which show that opinion should be free, prove also that he should be allowed, without molestation, to carry his opinions into practice at

184

Of Individuality   185

his own cost. That mankind are not infallible; that their truths, for the most part, are only half-truths; that unity of opinion, unless resulting from the fullest and freest comparison of opposite opinions, is not desirable, and diversity not an evil, but a good, until mankind are much more capable than at present of recognising all sides of the truth, are principles applicable to men's modes of action, not less than to their opinions. As it is useful that while mankind are imperfect there should be different opinions, so it is that there should be different experiments of living; that free scope should be given to varieties of character, short of injury to others; and that the worth of different modes of life should be proved practically, when any one thinks fit to try them. It is desirable, in short, that in things which do not primarily concern others, individuality should assert itself. Where, not the person's own character, but the traditions or customs of other people are the rule of conduct, there is wanting one of the principal ingredients of human happiness, and quite the chief ingredient of individual and social progress.

In maintaining this principle, the greatest difficulty to be encountered does not lie in the appreciation of means towards an acknowledged end, but in the indifference of persons in general to the end itself. If it were felt that the free development of individuality is one of the leading essentials of well-being; that it is not only a co-ordinate element with all that is designated by the terms civilisation, instruction, education, culture, but is itself a necessary part and condition of all those things; there would be no danger that liberty should be undervalued, and the adjustment of the boundaries between it and social control would present no extraordinary difficulty. But the evil is, that individual spontaneity is hardly recognised by the common modes of thinking as having any intrinsic worth, or deserving any regard on its own account. The majority, being satisfied with the ways of mankind as they now are (for it is they who make them what they are), cannot comprehend why those ways should not be good enough for everybody; and what is more, spontaneity forms no part of the ideal of the majority of moral and social reformers, but is rather looked on with jealousy, as a troublesome and perhaps rebellious obstruction to the general acceptance of what these reformers, in their own judgment, think would be best for mankind. Few persons, out of Germany, even comprehend the meaning of the doctrine which Wilhelm von Humboldt, so eminent both as a *savant* and as a politician, made the text of a treatise—that " the end of man, or that which is prescribed by the eternal or immutable dictates of reason, and not suggested by vague and transient desires, is the highest and most harmonious development of his powers to a complete and consistent whole;" that, therefore, the object " towards which every human being must ceaselessly direct his efforts, and on which especially those who design to influence their fellow-men must ever keep their eyes, is the individuality of power and development;" that for this there are two requisites, " freedom, and variety of situations;" and that from the union of these arise " individual vigour and manifold diversity," which combine themselves in " originality."[1]

Little, however, as people are accustomed to a doctrine like that of von Humboldt, and surprising as it may be to them to find so high a value attached to individuality, the question, one must nevertheless think, can only be one of degree. No one's idea of excellence in conduct is that people should do absolutely nothing but copy one another. No one would assert that people ought not to put into their mode of life, and into the conduct of their concerns, any impress whatever of their own judgment, or of their own individual character. On the other hand, it would be absurd to pretend that people ought to live as if nothing whatever had been known in the world before they came into it; as if experience had as yet done nothing towards showing that one mode of existence, or of conduct, is preferable to another. Nobody denies that people should be so taught and trained in youth as to know and benefit by the ascertained results of human experience. But it is the privilege and proper condition of a human being, arrived at the maturity of his faculties, to use and interpret experience in his own way.

[1] *The Sphere and Duties of Government,* from the German of Baron Wilhelm von Humboldt, pp. 11-13.

Of Individuality   187

It is for him to find out what part of recorded experience
is properly applicable to his own circumstances and character.
The traditions and customs of other people are, to a certain
extent, evidence of what their experience has taught *them*;
presumptive evidence, and as such, have a claim to his deference : but, in the first place, their experience may be too
narrow; or they may not have interpreted it rightly. Secondly,
their interpretation of experience may be correct, but unsuitable to him. Customs are made for customary circumstances
and customary characters; and his circumstances or his character may be uncustomary. Thirdly, though the customs be
both good as customs, and suitable to him, yet to conform
to custom, merely *as* custom, does not educate or develop
in him any of the qualities which are the distinctive endowment of a human being. The human faculties of perception,
judgment, discriminative feeling, mental activity, and even
moral preference, are exercised only in making a choice.
He who does anything because it is the custom makes no
choice. He gains no practice either in discerning or in desiring
what is best. The mental and moral, like the muscular powers,
are improved only by being used. The faculties are called
into no exercise by doing a thing merely because others do
it, no more than by believing a thing only because others believe
it. If the grounds of an opinion are not conclusive to the
person's own reason, his reason cannot be strengthened, but
is likely to be weakened, by his adopting it : and if the
inducements to an act are not such as are consentaneous to
his own feelings and character (where affection, or the rights
of others, are not concerned) it is so much done towards
rendering his feelings and character inert and torpid, instead of
active and energetic.

He who lets the world, or his own portion of it, choose
his plan of life for him, has no need of any other faculty
than the ape-like one of imitation. He who chooses his plan
for himself, employs all his faculties. He must use observation
to see, reasoning and judgment to foresee, activity to gather
materials for decision, discrimination to decide, and when
he has decided, firmness and self-control to hold to his
deliberate decision. And these qualities he requires and exer-

cises exactly in proportion as the part of his conduct which he
determines according to his own judgment and feelings is
a large one. It is possible that he might be guided in
some good path, and kept out of harm's way, without any
of these things. But what will be his comparative worth as
a human being? It really is of importance, not only what
men do, but also what manner of men they are that do
it. Among the works of man, which human life is rightly
employed in perfecting and beautifying, the first in importance
surely is man himself. Supposing it were possible to get houses
built, corn grown, battles fought, causes tried, and even
churches erected and prayers said, by machinery—by automatons in human form—it would be a considerable loss to
exchange for these automatons even the men and women who
at present inhabit the more civilised parts of the world, and
who assuredly are but starved specimens of what nature
can and will produce. Human nature is not a machine to
be built after a model, and set to do exactly the work prescribed for it, but a tree, which requires to grow and develop
itself on all sides, according to the tendency of the inward
forces which make it a living thing.

It will probably be conceded that it is desirable people
should exercise their understandings, and that an intelligent
following of custom, or even occasionally an intelligent devi-
ation from custom, is better than a blind and simply mechanical adhesion to it. To a certain extent it is admitted that
our understanding should be our own : but there is not the
same willingness to admit that our desires and impulses
should be our own likewise; or that to possess impulses of
our own, and of any strength, is anything but a peril and
a snare. Yet desires and impulses are as much a part of
a perfect human being as beliefs and restraints : and strong
impulses are only perilous when not properly balanced; when
one set of aims and inclinations is developed into strength,
while others, which ought to co-exist with them, remain weak
and inactive. It is not because men's desires are strong that
they act ill; it is because their consciences are weak. There
is no natural connection between strong impulses and a weak
conscience. The natural connection is the other way. To

say that one person's desires and feelings are stronger and more various than those of another, is merely to say that he has more of the raw material of human nature, and is therefore capable, perhaps of more evil, but certainly of more good. Strong impulses are but another name for energy. Energy may be turned to bad uses; but more good may always be made of an energetic nature, than of an indolent and impassive one. Those who have most natural feeling are always those whose cultivated feelings may be made the strongest. The same strong susceptibilities which make the personal impulses vivid and powerful, are also the source from whence are generated the most passionate love of virtue, and the sternest self-control. It is through the cultivation of these that society both does its duty and protects its interests : not by rejecting the stuff of which heroes are made, because it knows not how to make them. A person whose desires and impulses are his own—are the expression of his own nature, as it has been developed and modified by his own culture—is said to have a character. One whose desires and impulses are not his own, has no character, no more than a steam-engine has a character. If, in addition to being his own, his impulses are strong, and are under the government of a strong will, he has an energetic character. Whoever thinks that individuality of desires and impulses should not be encouraged to unfold itself, must maintain that society has no need of strong natures—is not the better for containing many persons who have much character—and that a high general average of energy is not desirable.

In some early states of society, these forces might be, and were, too much ahead of the power which society then possessed of disciplining and controlling them. There has been a time when the element of spontaneity and individuality was in excess, and the social principle had a hard struggle with it. The difficulty then was to induce men of strong bodies or minds to pay obedience to any rules which required them to control their impulses. To overcome this difficulty, law and discipline, like the Popes struggling against the Emperors, asserted a power over the whole man, claiming to control all his life in order to control his character—which society

had not found any other sufficient means of binding. But
society has now fairly got the better of individuality; and
the danger which threatens human nature is not the excess,
but the deficiency, of personal impulses and preferences.
Things are vastly changed since the passions of those who
were strong by station or by personal endowment were in a
state of habitual rebellion against laws and ordinances, and
required to be rigorously chained up to enable the persons
within their reach to enjoy any particle of security. In our
times, from the highest class of society down to the lowest,
every one lives as under the eye of a hostile and dreaded
censorship. Not only in what concerns others, but in what
concerns only themselves, the individual or the family do
not ask themselves—what do I prefer? or, what would
suit my character and disposition? or, what would allow the
best and highest in me to have fair play, and enable it to
grow and thrive? They ask themselves, what is suitable to my
position? what is usually done by persons of my station and
pecuniary circumstances? or (worse still) what is usually
done by persons of a station and circumstances superior to
mine? I do not mean that they choose what is customary in
preference to what suits their own inclination. It does not
occur to them to have any inclination, except for what is
customary. Thus the mind itself is bowed to the yoke : even
in what people do for pleasure, conformity is the first thing
thought of; they like in crowds; they exercise choice only
among things commonly done : peculiarity of taste, eccentricity of conduct, are shunned equally with crimes : until by
dint of not following their own nature they have no nature to
follow : their human capacities are withered and starved :
they become incapable of any strong wishes or native pleasures,
and are generally without either opinions or feelings of home
growth, or properly their own. Now is this, or is it not,
the desirable condition of human-nature?

It is so, on the Calvinistic theory. According to that,
the one great offence of man is self-will. All the good of
which humanity is capable is comprised in obedience. You
have no choice; thus you must do, and no otherwise :
" whatever is not a duty, is a sin." Human nature being

radically corrupt, there is no redemption for any one until human nature is killed within him. To one holding this theory of life, crushing out any of the human faculties, capacities, and susceptibilities, is no evil: man needs no capacity, but that of surrendering himself to the will of God: and if he uses any of his faculties for any other purpose but to do that supposed will more effectually, he is better without them. This is the theory of Calvinism; and it is held, in a mitigated form, by many who do not consider themselves Calvinists; the mitigation consisting in giving a less ascetic interpretation to the alleged will of God; asserting it to be his will that mankind should gratify some of their inclinations; of course not in the manner they themselves prefer, but in the way of obedience, that is, in a way prescribed to them by authority; and, therefore, by the necessary condition of the case, the same for all.

In some such insidious form there is at present a strong tendency to this narrow theory of life, and to the pinched and hidebound type of human character which it patronises. Many persons, no doubt, sincerely think that human beings thus cramped and dwarfed are as their Maker designed them to be; just as many have thought that trees are a much finer thing when clipped into pollards, or cut out into figures of animals, than as nature made them. But if it be any part of religion to believe that man was made by a good Being, it is more consistent with that faith to believe that this Being gave all human faculties that they might be cultivated and unfolded, not rooted out and consumed, and that he takes delight in every nearer approach made by his creatures to the ideal conception embodied in them, every increase in any of their capabilities of comprehension, of action, or of enjoyment. There is a different type of human excellence from the Calvinistic: a conception of humanity as having its nature bestowed on it for other purposes than merely to be abnegated. " Pagan self-assertion " is one of the elements of human worth, as well as " Christian self-denial."[2] There is a Greek ideal of self-development, which the Platonic and Christian ideal of self-government blends with, but

[2] Sterling's *Essays.*

does not supersede. It may be better to be a John Knox than an Alcibiades, but it is better to be a Pericles than either; nor would a Pericles, if we had one in these days, be without anything good which belonged to John Knox.

It is not by wearing down into uniformity all that is individual in themselves, but by cultivating it, and calling it forth, within the limits imposed by the rights and interests of others, that human beings become a noble and beautiful object of contemplation; and as the works partake the character of those who do them, by the same process human life also becomes rich, diversified, and animating, furnishing more abundant aliment to high thoughts and elevating feelings, and strengthening the tie which binds every individual to the race, by making the race infinitely better worth belonging to. In proportion to the development of his individuality, each person becomes more valuable to himself, and is therefore capable of being more valuable to others. There is a greater fulness of life about his own existence, and when there is more life in the units there is more in the mass which is composed of them. As much compression as is necessary to prevent the stronger specimens of human nature from encroaching on the rights of others cannot be dispensed with; but for this there is ample compensation even in the point of view of human development. The means of development which the individual loses by being prevented from gratifying his inclinations to the injury of others, are chiefly obtained at the expense of the development of other people. And even to himself there is a full equivalent in the better development of the social part of his nature, rendered possible by the restraint put upon the selfish part. To be held to rigid rules of justice for the sake of others, develops the feelings and capacities which have the good of others for their object. But to be restrained in things not affecting their good, by their mere displeasure, develops nothing valuable, except such force of character as may unfold itself in resisting the restraint. If acquiesced in, it dulls and blunts the whole nature. To give any fair play to the nature of each, it is essential that different persons should be allowed to lead different lives. In proportion as this latitude has

Of Individuality   193

been exercised in any age, has that age been noteworthy to
posterity. Even despotism does not produce its worst effects,
so long as individuality exists under it; and whatever crushes
individuality is despotism, by whatever name it may be
called, and whether it professes to be enforcing the will of
God or the injunctions of men.

Having said that the individuality is the same thing with
development, and that it is only the cultivation of individuality
which produces, or can produce, well-developed human beings,
I might here close the argument: for what more or better
can be said of any condition of human affairs than that it
brings human beings themselves nearer to the best thing they
can be? or what worse can be said of any obstruction to good
than that it prevents this? Doubtless, however, these considerations will not suffice to convince those who most need convincing; and it is necessary further to show, that these developed
human beings are of some use to the undeveloped—to point
out to those who do not desire liberty, and would not avail
themselves of it, that they may be in some intelligible manner
rewarded for allowing other people to make use of it without
hindrance.

In the first place, then, I would suggest that they might
possibly learn something from them. It will not be denied by
anybody, that originality is a valuable element in human
affairs. There is always need of persons not only to discover
new truths, and point out when what were once truths are
true no longer, but also to commence new practices, and set
the example of more enlightened conduct, and better taste
and sense in human life. This cannot well be gainsaid by
anybody who does not believe that the world has already
attained perfection in all its ways and practices. It is true
that this benefit is not capable of being rendered by everybody
alike: there are but few persons, in comparison with the
whole of mankind, whose experiments, if adopted by others,
would be likely to be any improvement on established practice. But these few are the salt of the earth; without them,
human life would become a stagnant pool. Not only is it
they who introduce good things which did not before exist;
it is they who keep the life in those which already exist.

On Liberty

If there were nothing to be done, would human intellect cease to be necessary? Would it be a reason why those who do the old things should forget why they are done, and do them like cattle, not like human beings? There is only too great a tendency in the best beliefs and practices to degenerate into the mechanical; and unless there were a succession of persons whose ever-recurring originality prevents the grounds of those beliefs and practices from becoming merely traditional, such dead matter would not resist the smallest shock from anything really alive, and there would be no reason why civilisation should not die out, as in the Byzantine Empire. Persons of genius, it is true, are, and are always likely to be, a small minority; but in order to have them, it is necessary to preserve the soil in which they grow. Genius can only breathe freely in an *atmosphere* of freedom. Persons of genius are, *ex vi termini,* more individual than any other people—less capable, consequently, of fitting themselves, without hurtful compression, into any of the small number of moulds which society provides in order to save its members the trouble of forming their own character. If from timidity they consent to be forced into one of these moulds, and to let all that part of themselves which cannot expand under the pressure remain unexpanded, society will be little the better for their genius. If they are of a strong character, and break their fetters, they become a mark for the society which has not succeeded in reducing them to commonplace, to point out with solemn warning as " wild," " erratic," and the like; much as if one should complain of the Niagara river for not flowing smoothly between its banks like a Dutch canal.

I insist thus emphatically on the importance of genius, and the necessity of allowing it to unfold itself freely both in thought and in practice, being well aware that no one will deny the position in theory, but knowing also that almost every one, in reality, is totally indifferent to it. People think genius a fine thing if it enables a man to write an exciting poem, or paint a picture. But in its true sense, that of originality in thought and action, though no one says that it is not a thing to be admired, nearly all, at heart, think that they can do very well without it. Unhappily this is too natural

Of Individuality   *195*

to be wondered at. Originality is the one thing which
unoriginal minds cannot feel the use of. They cannot see
what it is to do for them : how should they? If they could
see what it would do for them, it would not be originality.
The first service which originality has to render them, is that
of opening their eyes : which being once fully done, they
would have a chance of being themselves original. Meanwhile, recollecting that nothing was ever yet done which
some one was not the first to do, and that all good things
which exist are the fruits of originality, let them be modest
enough to believe that there is something still left for it
to accomplish, and assure themselves that they are more in
need of originality, the less they are conscious of the want.

In sober truth, whatever homage may be professed, or even
paid, to real or supposed mental superiority, the general
tendency of things throughout the world is to render mediocrity the ascendant power among mankind. In ancient history,
in the Middle Ages, and in a diminishing degree through the
long transition from feudality to the present time, the individual was a power in himself; and if he had either great
talents or a high social position, he was a considerable power.
At present individuals are lost in the crowd. In politics
it is almost a triviality to say that public opinion now rules
the world. The only power deserving the name is that of
masses, and of governments while they make themselves the
organ of the tendencies and instincts of masses. This is as
true in the moral and social relations of private life as in
public transactions. Those whose opinions go by the name
of public opinion are not always the same sort of public :
in America they are the whole white population; in England,
chiefly the middle class. But they are always a mass, that
is to say, collective mediocrity. And what is a still greater
novelty, the mass do not now take their opinions from
dignitaries in Church or State, from ostensible leaders, or
from books. Their thinking is done for them by men much
like themselves, addressing them or speaking in their name,
on the spur of the moment, through the newspapers. I am not
complaining of all this. I do not assert that anything better
is compatible, as a general rule, with the present low state

of the human mind. But that does not hinder the government of mediocrity from being mediocre government. No government by a democracy or a numerous aristocracy, either in its political acts or in the opinions, qualities, and tone of mind which it fosters, ever did or could rise above mediocrity, except in so far as the sovereign many have let themselves be guided (which in their best times they always have done) by the counsels and influence of a more highly gifted and instructed One or Few. The initiation of all wise or noble things comes and must come from the individuals; generally at first from some one individual. The honour and glory of the average man is that he is capable of following that initiative; that he can respond internally to wise and noble things, and be led to them with his eyes open. I am not countenancing the sort of " hero-worship " which applauds the strong man of genius for forcibly seizing on the government of the world and making it do his bidding in spite of itself. All he can claim is, freedom to point out the way. The power of compelling others into it is not only inconsistent with the freedom and development of all the rest, but corrupting to the strong man himself. It does seem, however, that when the opinions of masses of merely average men are everywhere become or becoming the dominant power, the counterpoise and corrective to that tendency would be the more and more pronounced individuality of those who stand on the higher eminences of thought. It is in these circumstances most especially, that exceptional individuals, instead of being deterred, should be encouraged in acting differently from the mass. In other times there was no advantage in their doing so, unless they acted not only differently but better. In this age, the mere example of non-conformity, the mere refusal to bend the knee to custom, is itself a service. Precisely because the tyranny of opinion is such as to make eccentricity a reproach, it is desirable, in order to break through that tyranny, that people should be eccentric. Eccentricity has always abounded when and where strength of character has abounded; and the amount of eccentricity in a society has generally been proportional to the amount of genius, mental

Of Individuality

vigour, and moral courage it contained. That so few now dare to be eccentric marks the chief danger of the time.

I have said that it is important to give the freest scope possible to uncustomary things, in order that it may in time appear which of these are fit to be converted into customs. But independence of action, and disregard of custom, are not solely deserving of encouragement for the chance they afford that better modes of action, and customs more worthy of general adoption, may be struck out; nor is it only persons of decided mental superiority who have a just claim to carry on their lives in their own way. There is no reason that all human existence should be constructed on some one or some small number of patterns. If a person possesses any tolerable amount of common sense and experience, his own mode of laying out his existence is the best, not because it is the best in itself, but because it is his own mode. Human beings are not like sheep; and even sheep are not undistinguishably alike. A man cannot get a coat or a pair of boots to fit him unless they are either made to his measure, or he has a whole warehouseful to choose from: and is it easier to fit him with a life than with a coat, or are human beings more like one another in their whole physical and spiritual conformation than in the shape of their feet? If it were only that people have diversities of taste, that is reason enough for not attempting to shape them all after one model. But different persons also require different conditions for their spiritual development; and can no more exist healthily in the same moral, than all the variety of plants can in the same physical, atmosphere and climate. The same things which are helps to one person towards the cultivation of his higher nature are hindrances to another. The same mode of life is a healthy excitement to one, keeping all his faculties of action and enjoyment in their best order, while to another it is a distracting burthen, which suspends or crushes all internal life. Such are the differences among human beings in their sources of pleasure, their susceptibilities of pain, and the operation on them of different physical and moral agencies, that unless there is a corresponding diversity in their modes of life, they neither obtain their fair share of happiness, nor grow up to the mental, moral, and æsthetic stature of which their nature is capable. Why then should tolerance, as far as the public sentiment is concerned, extend only to tastes and modes of life which extort acquiescence by the multitude of their adherents? Nowhere (except in some monastic institutions) is diversity of taste entirely un- recognised; a person may, without blame, either like or dislike rowing, or smoking, or music, or athletic exercises, or chess, or cards, or study, because both those who like each of these things, and those who dislike them, are too numerous to be put down. But the man, and still more the woman, who can be accused either of doing "what nobody does," or of not doing "what everybody does," is the subject of as much depreciatory remark as if he or she had committed some grave moral delinquency. Persons require to possess a title, or some other badge of rank, or of the consideration of people of rank, to be able to indulge somewhat in the luxury of doing as they like without detriment to their estimation. To indulge somewhat, I repeat : for whoever allow themselves much of that indulgence, incur the risk of something worse than disparaging speeches— they are in peril of a commission *de lunatico,* and of having their property taken from them and given to their relations.[8]

[8] There is something both contemptible and frightful in the sort of evidence on which, of late years, any person can be judicially declared unfit for the management of his affairs; and after his death, his disposal of his property can be set aside, if there is enough of it to pay the expenses of litigation—which are charged on the property itself. All the minute details of his daily life are pried into, and whatever is found which, seen through the medium of the perceiving and describing faculties of the lowest of the low, bears an appearance unlike absolute commonplace, is laid before the jury as evidence of insanity, and often with success; the jurors being little, if at all, less vulgar and ignorant than the wit- nesses; while the judges, with that extraordinary want of know- ledge of human nature and life which continually astonishes us in English lawyers, often help to mislead them. These trials speak volumes as to the state of feeling and opinion among the vulgar with regard to human liberty. So far from setting any value on individuality—so far from respecting the right of each individual to act, in things indifferent, as seems good to his own judgment and

Of Individuality   199

There is one characteristic of the present direction of
public opinion peculiarly calculated to make it intolerant of
any marked demonstration of individuality. The general
average of mankind are not only moderate in intellect, but
also moderate in inclinations : they have no tastes or wishes
strong enough to incline them to do anything unusual, and
they consequently do not understand those who have, and
class all such with the wild and intemperate whom they are
accustomed to look down upon. Now, in addition to this
fact which is general, we have only to suppose that a strong
movement has set in towards the improvement of morals,
and it is evident what we have to expect. In these days
such a movement has set in; much has actually been effected
in the way of increased regularity of conduct and discouragement of excesses; and there is a philanthropic spirit abroad,
for the exercise of which there is no more inviting field
than the moral and prudential improvement of our fellow-
creatures. These tendencies of the times cause the public to
be more disposed than at most former periods to prescribe
general rules of conduct, and endeavour to make every one
conform to the approved standard. And that standard,
express or tacit, is to desire nothing strongly. Its ideal of
character is to be without any marked character; to maim
by compression, like a Chinese lady's foot, every part of
human nature which stands out prominently, and tends to
make the person markedly dissimilar in outline to commonplace humanity.

As is usually the case with ideals which exclude one-half of
what is desirable, the present standard of approbation produces only an inferior imitation of the other half. Instead of

---

inclinations, judges and juries cannot even conceive that a person
in a state of sanity can desire such freedom. In former days, when it
was proposed to burn atheists, charitable people used to suggest
putting them in a madhouse instead : it would be nothing surprising now-a-days were we to see this done, and the doers applauding
themselves, because, instead of persecuting for religion, they had
adopted so humane and Christian a mode of treating these unfor-
tunates, not without a silent satisfaction at their having thereby
obtained their deserts.

great energies guided by vigorous reason, and strong feelings strongly controlled by a conscientious will, its result is weak feelings and weak energies, which therefore can be kept in outward conformity to rule without any strength either of will or of reason. Already energetic characters on any large scale are becoming merely traditional. There is now scarcely any outlet for energy in this country except business. The energy expended in this may still be regarded as considerable. What little is left from that employment is expended on some hobby; which may be a useful, even a philanthropic hobby, but is always some one thing, and generally a thing of small dimensions. The greatness of England is now all collective; individually small, we only appear capable of anything great by our habit of combining; and with this our moral and religious philanthropists are perfectly contented. But it was men of another stamp than this that made England what it has been; and men of another stamp will be needed to prevent its decline.

The despotism of custom is everywhere the standing hindrance to human advancement, being in unceasing antagonism to that disposition to aim at something better than customary, which is called, according to circumstances, the spirit of liberty, or that of progress or improvement. The spirit of improvement is not always a spirit of liberty, for it may aim at forcing improvements on an unwilling people; and the spirit of liberty, in so far as it resists such attempts, may ally itself locally and temporarily with the opponents of improvement; but the only unfailing and permanent source of improvement is liberty, since by it there are as many possible independent centres of improvement as there are individuals. The progressive principle, however, in either shape, whether as the love of liberty or of improvement, is antagonistic to the sway of Custom, involving at least emancipation from that yoke; and the contest between the two constitutes the chief interest of the history of mankind. The greater part of the world has, properly speaking, no history, because the despotism of Custom is complete. This is the case over the whole East. Custom is there, in all things, the final appeal; justice and right mean conformity to

custom; the argument of custom no one, unless some tyrant
intoxicated with power, thinks of resisting. And we see
the result. Those nations must once have had originality;
they did not start out of the ground populous, lettered, and
versed in many of the arts of life; they made themselves all
this, and were then the greatest and most powerful nations
of the world. What are they now? The subjects or dependents of tribes whose forefathers wandered in the forests
when theirs had magnificent palaces and gorgeous temples,
but over whom custom exercised only a divided rule with
liberty and progress. A people, it appears, may be progressive
for a certain length of time, and then stop : when does it
stop? When it ceases to possess individuality. If a similar
change should befall the nations of Europe, it will not
be in exactly the same shape : the despotism of custom
with which these nations are threatened is not precisely
stationariness. It proscribes singularity, but it does not preclude change, provided all change together. We have discarded the fixed costumes of our forefathers; every one
must still dress like other people, but the fashion may
change once or twice a year. We thus take care that when
there is a change, it shall be for change's sake, and not
from any idea of beauty or convenience; for the same idea
of beauty or convenience would not strike all the world
at the same moment, and be simultaneously thrown aside
by all at another moment. But we are progressive as well
as changeable : we continually make new inventions in
mechanical things, and keep them until they are again superseded by better; we are eager for improvement in politics,
in education, even in morals, though in this last our idea
of improvement chiefly consists in persuading or forcing
other people to be as good as ourselves. It is not progress
that we object to; on the contrary, we flatter ourselves that
we are the most progressive people who ever lived. It is
individuality that we war against : we should think we
had done wonders if we had made ourselves all alike; forgetting that the unlikeness of one person to another is
generally the first thing which draws the attention of either to
the imperfection of his own type, and the superiority of

another, or the possibility, by combining the advantages of both, of producing something better than either. We have a warning example in China—a nation of much talent, and, in some respects, even wisdom, owing to the rare good fortune of having been provided at an early period with a particularly good set of customs, the work, in some measure, of men to whom even the most enlightened European must accord, under certain limitations, the title of sages and philosophers. They are remarkable, too, in the excellence of their apparatus for impressing, as far as possible, the best wisdom they possess upon every mind in the community, and securing that those who have appropriated most of it shall occupy the posts of honour and power. Surely the people who did this have discovered the secret of human progressiveness, and must have kept themselves steadily at the head of the movement of the world. On the contrary, they have become stationary—have remained so for thousands of years; and if they are ever to be further improved, it must be by foreigners. They have succeeded beyond all hope in what English philanthropists are so industriously working at—in making a people all alike, all governing their thoughts and conduct by the same maxims and rules; and these are the fruits. The modern *régime* of public opinion is, in an unorganised form, what the Chinese educational and political systems are in an organised; and unless individuality shall be able successfully to assert itself against this yoke, Europe, notwithstanding its noble ante-cedents and its professed Christianity, will tend to become another China.

What is it that has hitherto preserved Europe from this lot? What has made the European family of nations an improving, instead of a stationary portion of mankind? Not any superior excellence in them, which, when it exists, exists as the effect not as the cause; but their remarkable diversity of character and culture. Individuals, classes, nations, have been extremely unlike one another : they have struck out a great variety of paths, each leading to something valuable; and although at every period those who travelled in different paths have been intolerant of one another, and each would have thought it an excellent thing if all the rest could have been compelled to

travel his road, their attempts to thwart each other's development have rarely had any permanent success, and each has
in time endured to receive the good which the others have
offered. Europe is, in my judgment, wholly indebted to
this plurality of paths for its progressive and many-sided development. But it already begins to possess this benefit in
a considerably less degree. It is decidedly advancing towards
the Chinese ideal of making all people alike. M. de
Tocqueville, in his last important work, remarks how much
more the Frenchmen of the present day resemble one another
than did those even of the last generation. The same remark
might be made of Englishmen in a far greater degree.
In a passage already quoted from Wilhelm von Humboldt,
he points out two things as necessary conditions of human
development, because necessary to render people unlike one
another; namely, freedom, and variety of situations. The
second of these two conditions is in this country every day
diminishing. The circumstances which surround different
classes and individuals, and shape their characters, are daily
becoming more assimilated. Formerly, different ranks, different
neighbourhoods, different trades and professions, lived in
what might be called different worlds; at present to a great
degree in the same. Comparatively speaking, they now read
the same things, listen to the same things, see the same
things, go to the same places, have their hopes and fears
directed to the same objects, have the same rights and liberties,
and the same means of asserting them. Great as are the
differences of position which remain, they are nothing to those
which have ceased. And the assimilation is still proceeding.
All the political changes of the age promote it, since they
all tend to raise the low and to lower the high. Every extension of education promotes it, because education brings people
under common influences, and gives them access to the
general stock of facts and sentiments. Improvements in the
means of communication promotes it, by bringing the inhabitants of distant places into personal contact, and keeping
up a rapid flow of changes of residence between one place and
another. The increase of commerce and manufactures promotes it, by diffusing more widely the advantages of easy

circumstances, and opening all objects of ambition, even the highest, to general competition, whereby the desire of rising becomes no longer the character of a particular class, but of all classes. A more powerful agency than all these, in bringing about a general similarity among mankind, is the complete establishment, in this and other free countries, of the ascendancy of public opinion in the State. As the various social eminences which enabled persons entrenched on them to disregard the opinion of the multitude gradually become levelled; as the very idea of resisting the will of the public, when it is positively known that they have a will, disappears more and more from the minds of practical politicians; there ceases to be any social support for non-conformity—any substantive power in society which, itself opposed to the ascendancy of numbers, is interested in taking under its protection opinions and tendencies at variance with those of the public.

The combination of all these causes forms so great a mass of influences hostile to Individuality, that it is not easy to see how it can stand its ground. It will do so with increasing difficulty, unless the intelligent part of the public can be made to feel its value—to see that it is good there should be differences, even though not for the better, even though, as it may appear to them, some should be for the worse. If the claims of Individuality are ever to be asserted, the time is now, while much is still wanting to complete the enforced assimiliation. It is only in the earlier stages that any stand can be successfully made against the encroachment. The demand that all other people shall resemble ourselves grows by what it feeds on. If resistance waits till life is reduced *nearly* to one uniform type, all deviations from that type will come to be considered impious, immoral, even monstrous and con-trary to nature. Mankind speedily become unable to conceive diversity, when they have been for some time unaccustomed to see it.

[6]

Excerpt from *Utilitarianism*, 296–321

CHAPTER V

ON THE CONNECTION BETWEEN JUSTICE AND UTILITY

In all ages of speculation, one of the strongest obstacles to the reception of the doctrine that Utility or Happiness is the criterion of right and wrong, has been drawn from the idea of Justice. The powerful sentiment, and apparently clear perception, which that word recalls with a rapidity and certainty resembling an instinct, have seemed to the majority of thinkers to point to an inherent quality in things; to show that the Just must have an existence in Nature as something absolute, generically distinct from every variety of the Expedient, and, in idea, opposed to it, though (as is commonly acknowledged) never, in the long run, disjoined from it in fact.

In the case of this, as of our other moral sentiments, there is no necessary connection between the question of its origin, and that of its binding force. That a feeling is bestowed on us by Nature, does not necessarily legitimate all its promptings. The feeling of justice might be a peculiar instinct, and might yet require, like our other instincts, to be controlled and enlightened by a higher reason. If we have intellectual instincts, leading us to judge in a particular way, as well as animal instincts that prompt us to act in a particular way, there is no necessity that the former should be more infallible in their sphere than the latter in theirs : it may as well happen that wrong judgments are occasionally suggested by those, as wrong actions by these. But though it is one thing to believe that we have natural feelings of justice, and another to acknowledge them as an ultimate criterion of conduct, these two opinions are very closely connected in point of fact. Mankind are always predisposed to believe that any subjective feeling, not otherwise accounted for, is a revelation of some objective reality. Our present object is to determine whether the reality, to which the feeling of justice corresponds, is one which needs any such special revelation; whether the justice or injustice of an action is a thing intrinsically peculiar, and distinct from all its other qualities, or only a combination of certain of those qualities, presented under a peculiar aspect. For the purpose of this inquiry it is practically important to consider whether the feeling itself, of justice and injustice, is *sui generis* like our sensations of colour and taste, or a derivative feeling, formed by a combination of others. And this it is the more essential to examine, as people are in general willing enough to allow, that objectively the dictates of Justice coincide with a part of the field of General Expediency; but inasmuch as the subjective mental feeling of Justice is different from that which commonly attaches to simple expediency, and, except in the extreme cases of the latter, is far more imperative in its demands, people find it difficult to see, in Justice, only a particular kind or branch of general utility, and think that its superior binding force requires a totally different origin.

To throw light upon this question, it is necessary to attempt to ascertain what is the distinguishing character of justice, or of injustice : what is the quality, or whether there is any quality, attributed in common to all modes of conduct designated as unjust (for justice, like many other moral attributes, is best defined by its opposite), and distinguishing them from such modes of conduct as are disapproved, but without having that particular epithet of disapprobation applied to them. If in everything which men are accustomed to characterise as just or unjust, some one common attribute or collection of attributes is always present, we may judge whether this particular attribute or combination of attributes would be capable of gathering round it a sentiment of that peculiar character and intensity by virtue of the general laws of our emotional constitution, or whether the sentiment is inexplicable, and requires to be regarded as a special provision of Nature. If we find the former to be the case, we shall, in resolving this question, have resolved also the main problem : if the latter, we shall have to seek for some other mode of investigating it.

To find the common attributes of a variety of objects, it is necessary to begin by surveying the objects themselves in the concrete. Let us therefore advert successively to the various modes of action, and arrangements of human affairs, which are classed, by universal or widely spread opinion, as Just or as Unjust. The things well known to excite the sentiments associated with those names are of a very multifarious character. I shall pass them rapidly in review, without studying any particular arrangement.

In the first place, it is mostly considered unjust to deprive any one of his personal liberty, his property, or any other thing which belongs to him by law. Here, therefore, is one instance of the application of the terms just and unjust in a perfectly definite sense, namely, that it is just to respect, unjust to violate, the *legal rights* of any one. But this judgment admits of several exceptions, arising from the other forms in which the notions of justice and injustice present themselves. For example, the person who suffers the deprivation may (as the phrase is) have *forfeited* the rights which he is so deprived of : a case to which we shall return presently. But also,

Secondly; the legal rights of which he is deprived, may be rights which *ought* not to have belonged to him; in other words, the law which confers on him these rights, may be a bad law. When it is so, or when (which is the same thing for our purpose) it is supposed to be so, opinions will differ as to the justice or injustice of infringing it. Some maintain that no law, however bad, ought to be disobeyed by an individual citizen; that his opposition to it, if shown at all, should only be shown in endeavouring to get it altered by competent authority. This opinion (which condemns many of the most illustrious benefactors of mankind, and would often protect pernicious institutions against the only weapons which, in the state of things existing at the time, have any chance of succeeding against them) is defended, by those who hold it, on grounds of expediency; principally on that of the importance, to the common interest of mankind, of maintaining inviolate the sentiment of submission to law. Other persons, again, hold the directly contrary opinion, that any law, judged to be bad, may blamelessly be disobeyed, even though it be not judged to be unjust, but only inexpedient; while others would confine the licence of disobedience to the case of unjust laws : but again, some say, that all laws which are inexpedient are unjust; since every law imposes some restriction on the natural liberty of mankind, which restriction is an injustice, unless legitimated by tending to their good. Among these diversities of opinion, it seems to be universally admitted that there may be unjust laws, and that law, consequently, is not the ultimate criterion of justice, but may give to one person a benefit, or impose on another an evil, which justice condemns. When, however, a law is thought to be unjust, it seems always to be regarded as being so in the same way in which a breach of law is unjust, namely, by infringing somebody's right; which, as it cannot in this case be a legal right, receives a different appellation, and is called a moral right. We may say, therefore, that a second case of injustice consists in taking or withholding from any person that to which he has a *moral right*.

Thirdly, it is universally considered just that each person should obtain that (whether good or evil) which he *deserves*; and unjust that he should obtain a good, or be made to undergo an evil, which he does not deserve. This is, perhaps, the clearest and most emphatic form in which the idea of justice is conceived by the general mind. As it involves the notion of desert, the question arises, what constitutes desert? Speaking in a general way, a person is understood to deserve good if he does right, evil if he does wrong; and in a more particular sense, to deserve good from those to whom he does or has done good, and evil from those to whom he does or has done evil. The precept of returning good for evil has never been regarded as a case of the fulfilment of justice, but as one in which the claims of justice are waived, in obedience to other considerations.

Fourthly, it is confessedly unjust to *break faith* with any one : to violate an engagement, either express or implied, or

disappoint expectations raised by our own conduct, at least
if we have raised those expectations knowingly and voluntarily. Like the other obligations of justice already spoken
of, this one is not regarded as absolute, but as capable of
being overruled by a stronger obligation of justice on
the other side; or by such conduct on the part of the person
concerned as is deemed to absolve us from our obligation to
him, and to constitute a *forfeiture* of the benefit which he
has been led to expect.

Fifthly, it is, by universal admission, inconsistent with
justice to be *partial*; to show favour or preference to one
person over another, in matters to which favour and preference
do not properly apply. Impartiality, however, does not seem
to be regarded as a duty in itself, but rather as instrumental
to some other duty; for it is admitted that favour and preference are not always censurable, and indeed the cases
in which they are condemned are rather the exception than the
rule. A person would be more likely to be blamed than
applauded for giving his family or friends no superiority in
good offices over strangers, when he could do so without
violating any other duty; and no one thinks it unjust to
seek one person in preference to another as a friend, connection, or companion. Impartiality where rights are concerned is of course obligatory, but this is involved in the more
general obligation of giving to every one his right. A
tribunal, for example, must be impartial, because it is bound
to award, without regard to any other consideration, a disputed object to the one of two parties who has the right
to it. There are other cases in which impartiality means,
being solely influenced by desert; as with those who, in
the capacity of judges, preceptors, or parents, administer
reward and punishment as such. There are cases, again, in
which it means, being solely influenced by consideration
for the public interest; as in making a selection among
candidates for a government employment. Impartiality, in
short, as an obligation of justice, may be said to mean, being
exclusively influenced by the considerations which it is supposed ought to influence the particular case in hand; and
resisting the solicitation of any motives which prompt to

conduct different from what those considerations would dictate.

Nearly allied to the idea of impartiality is that of *equality*; which often enters as a component part both into the conception of justice and into the practice of it, and, in the eyes of many persons, constitutes its essence. But in this, still more than in any other case, the notion of justice varies in different persons, and always conforms in its variations to their notion of utility. Each person maintains that equality is the dictate of justice, except where he thinks that expediency requires inequality. The justice of giving equal protection to the rights of all, is maintained by those who support the most outrageous inequality in the rights themselves. Even in slave countries it is theoretically admitted that the rights of the slave, such as they are, ought to be as sacred as those of the master; and that a tribunal which fails to enforce them with equal strictness is wanting in justice; while, at the same time, institutions which leave to the slave scarcely any rights to enforce, are not deemed unjust, because they are not deemed inexpedient. Those who think that utility requires distinctions of rank, do not consider it unjust that riches and social privileges should be unequally dispensed; but those who think this inequality inexpedient, think it unjust also. Whoever thinks that government is necessary, sees no injustice in as much inequality as is constituted by giving to the magistrate powers not granted to other people. Even among those who hold levelling doctrines, there are as many questions of justice as there are differences of opinion about expediency. Some Communists consider it unjust that the produce of the labour of the community should be shared on any other principle than that of exact equality; others think it just that those should receive most whose wants are greatest; while others hold that those who work harder, or who produce more, or whose services are more valuable to the community, may justly claim a larger quota in the division of the produce. And the sense of natural justice may be plausibly appealed to in behalf of every one of these opinions.

Among so many diverse applications of the term Justice,

which yet is not regarded as ambiguous, it is a matter of some difficulty to seize the mental link which holds them together, and on which the moral sentiment adhering to the term essentially depends. Perhaps, in this embarrassment, some help may be derived from the history of the word, as indicated by its etymology.

In most, if not in all, languages, the etymology of the word which corresponds to Just, points distinctly to an origin connected with the ordinances of law. *Justum* is a form of *jussum*, that which has been ordered. Δίκαιον comes directly from δίκη, a suit at law. *Recht*, from which came *right* and *righteous*, is synonymous with law. The courts of justice, the administration of justice, are the courts and the administration of law. *La justice*, in French, is the established term for judicature. I am not committing the fallacy imputed with some show of truth to Horne Tooke, of assuming that a word must still continue to mean what it originally meant. Etymology is slight evidence of what the idea now signified is, but the very best evidence of how it sprang up. There can, I think, be no doubt that the *idée mère*, the primitive element, in the formation of the notion of justice, was conformity to law. It constituted the entire idea among the Hebrews, up to the birth of Christianity; as might be expected in the case of a people whose laws attempted to embrace all subjects on which precepts were required, and who believed those laws to be a direct emanation from the Supreme Being. But other nations, and in particular the Greeks and Romans, who knew that their laws had been made originally, and still continued to be made, by men, were not afraid to admit that those men might make bad laws; might do, by law, the same things, and from the same motives, which if done by individuals without sanction of law, would be called unjust. And hence the sentiment of injustice came to be attached, not to all violations of law, but only to violations of such laws as *ought* to exist, including such as ought to exist, but do not; and to laws themselves, if supposed to be contrary to what ought to be law. In this manner the idea of law and of its injunctions was still predominant in the notion of justice, even when the laws actually in force ceased to be accepted as the standard of it.

It is true that mankind consider the idea of justice and its obligations as applicable to many things which neither are, nor is it desired that they should be, regulated by law. Nobody desires that laws should interfere with the whole detail of private life; yet every one allows that in all daily conduct a person may and does show himself to be either just or unjust. But even here, the idea of the breach of what ought to be law, still lingers in a modified shape. It would always give us pleasure, and chime in with our feelings of fitness, that acts which we deem unjust should be punished, though we do not always think it expedient that this should be done by the tribunals. We forego that gratification on account of incidental inconveniences. We should be glad to see just conduct enforced and injustice repressed, even in the minutest details, if we were not, with reason, afraid of trusting the magistrate with so unlimited an amount of power over individuals. When we think that a person is bound in justice to do a thing, it is an ordinary form of language to say, that he ought to be compelled to do it. We should be gratified to see the obligation enforced by anybody who had the power. If we see that its enforcement by law would be inexpedient, we lament the impossibility, we consider the impunity given to injustice as an evil, and strive to make amends for it by bringing a strong expression of our own and the public disapprobation to bear upon the offender. Thus the idea of legal constraint is still the generating idea of the notion of justice, though undergoing several transformations before that notion, as it exists in an advanced state of society, becomes complete.

The above is, I think, a true account, as far as it goes, of the origin and progressive growth of the idea of injustice. But we must observe, that it contains, as yet, nothing to distinguish that obligation from moral obligation in general. For the truth is, that the idea of penal sanction, which is the essence of law, enters not only into the conception of injustice, but into that of any kind of wrong. We do not call anything wrong, unless we mean to imply that a person ought to be punished in some way or other for doing it; if not by law, by the opinion of his fellow-creatures; if not by opinion, by the reproaches of his own conscience. This seems the real turning point of the distinction between morality and simple expediency. It is a part of the notion of Duty in every one of its forms, that a person may rightfully be compelled to fulfil it. Duty is a thing which may be *exacted* from a person, as one exacts a debt. Unless we think that it may be exacted from him, we do not call it his duty. Reasons of prudence, or the interest of other people, may militate against actually exacting it; but the person himself, it is clearly understood, would not be entitled to complain. There are other things, on the contrary, which we wish that people should do, which we like or admire them for doing, perhaps dislike or despise them for not doing, but yet admit that they are not bound to do; it is not a case of moral obligation; we do not blame them, that is, we do not think that they are proper objects of punishment. How we come by these ideas of deserving and not deserving punishment, will appear, perhaps, in the sequel; but I think there is no doubt that this distinction lies at the bottom of the notions of right and wrong; that we call any conduct wrong, or employ, instead, some other term of dislike or disparagement, according as we think that the person ought, or ought not, to be punished for it; and we say, it would be right to do so and so, or merely that it would be desirable or laudable, according as we would wish to see the person whom it concerns, compelled, or only persuaded and exhorted, to act in that manner.[1]

This, therefore, being the characteristic difference which marks off, not justice, but morality in general, from the remaining provinces of Expediency and Worthiness; the character is still to be sought which distinguishes justice from other branches of morality. Now it is known that ethical

---

[1] See this point enforced and illustrated by Professor Bain, in an admirable chapter (entitled " The Ethical Emotions, or the Moral Sense "), of the second of the two treatises composing his elaborate and profound work on the Mind.

How Connected with Justice

writers divide moral duties into two classes, denoted by
the ill-chosen expressions, duties of perfect and of imperfect
obligation; the latter being those in which, though the
act is obligatory, the particular occasions of performing it
are left to our choice; as in the case of charity or beneficence, which we are indeed bound to practise, but not towards
any definite person, nor at any prescribed time. In the more
precise language of philosophic purists, duties of perfect obligation are those duties in virtue of which a correlative *right*
resides in some person or persons; duties of imperfect
obligation are those moral obligations which do not give
birth to any right. I think it will be found that this distinction exactly coincides with that which exists between
justice and the other obligations of morality. In our survey
of the various popular acceptations of justice, the term
appeared generally to involve the idea of a personal right
—a claim on the part of one or more individuals, like that
which the law gives when it confers a proprietary or other
legal right. Whether the injustice consists in depriving a
person of a possession, or in breaking faith with him, or in
treating him worse than he deserves, or worse than other
people who have no greater claims, in each case the supposition implies two things—a wrong done, and some assignable person who is wronged. Injustice may also be done by
treating a person better than others; but the wrong in
this case is to his competitors, who are also assignable persons.
It seems to me that this feature in the case—a right in some
person, correlative to the moral obligation—constitutes the
specific difference between justice, and generosity or beneficence. Justice implies something which is not only
right to do, and wrong not to do, but which some individual
person can claim from us as his moral right. No one has a
moral right to our generosity or beneficence, because we are
not morally bound to practise those virtues towards any given
individual. And it will be found with respect to this as to
every correct definition, that the instances which seem to
conflict with it are those which most confirm it. For if a
moralist attempts, as some have done, to make out that
mankind generally, though not any given individual, have a

right to all the good we can do them, he at once, by that
thesis, includes generosity and beneficence within the category
of justice. He is obliged to say, that our utmost exertions
are *due* to our fellow-creatures, thus assimilating them to
a debt; or that nothing less can be a sufficient *return* for what
society does for us, thus classing the case as one of gratitude;
both of which are acknowledged cases of justice. Wherever
there is a right, the case is one of justice, and not of the
virtue of beneficence : and whoever does not place the
distinction between justice and morality in general, where we
have now placed it, will be found to make no distinction
between them at all, but to merge all morality in justice.

Having thus endeavoured to determine the distinctive elements
which enter into the composition of the idea of justice, we
are ready to enter on the inquiry, whether the feeling, which
accompanies the idea, is attached to it by a special dispensation of nature, or whether it could have grown up, by any
known laws, out of the idea itself; and in particular, whether
it can have originated in considerations of general expediency.

I conceive that the sentiment itself does not arise from
anything which would commonly, or correctly, be termed an
idea of expediency; but that though the sentiment does not,
whatever is moral in it does.

We have seen that the two essential ingredients in the sentiment of justice are, the desire to punish a person who has
done harm, and the knowledge or belief that there is some
definite individual or individuals to whom harm has been done.

Now it appears to me, that the desire to punish a person
who has done harm to some individual is a spontaneous out-
growth from two sentiments, both in the highest degree
natural, and which either are or resemble instincts; the
impulse of self-defence, and the feeling of sympathy.

It is natural to resent, and to repel or retaliate, any harm
done or attempted against ourselves, or against those with
whom we sympathise. The origin of this sentiment it is not
necessary here to discuss. Whether it be an instinct or a result
of intelligence, it is, we know, common to all animal nature;
for every animal tries to hurt those who have hurt, or who

it thinks are about to hurt, itself or its young. Human beings, on this point, only differ from other animals in two particulars. First, in being capable of sympathising, not solely with their offspring, or, like some of the more noble animals, with some superior animal who is kind to them, but with all human, and even with all sentient, beings. Secondly, in having a more developed intelligence, which gives a wider range to the whole of their sentiments, whether self-regarding or sympathetic. By virtue of his superior intelligence, even apart from his superior range of sympathy, a human being is capable of apprehending a community of interest between himself and the human society of which he forms a part, such that any conduct which threatens the security of the society generally, is threatening to his own, and calls forth his instinct (if instinct it be) of self-defence. The same superiority of intelligence, joined to the power of sympathising with human beings generally, enables him to attach himself to the collective idea of his tribe, his country, or mankind, in such a manner that any act hurtful to them, raises his instinct of sympathy, and urges him to resistance.

The sentiment of justice, in that one of its elements which consists of the desire to punish, is thus, I conceive, the natural feeling of retaliation or vengeance, rendered by intellect and sympathy applicable to those injuries, that is, to those hurts, which wound us through, or in common with, society at large. This sentiment, in itself, has nothing moral in it; what is moral is, the exclusive subordination of it to the social sympathies, so as to wait on and obey their call. For the natural feeling would make us resent indiscriminately whatever any one does that is disagreeable to us; but when moralised by the social feeling, it only acts in the directions conformable to the general good : just persons resenting a hurt to society, though not otherwise a hurt to themselves, and not resenting a hurt to themselves, however painful, unless it be of the kind which society has a common interest with them in the repression of.

It is no objection against this doctrine to say, that when we feel our sentiment of justice outraged, we are not thinking of society at large or of any collective interest, but only of the individual case. It is common enough certainly, though the reverse of commendable, to feel resentment merely because we have suffered pain; but a person whose resentment is really a moral feeling, that is, who considers whether an act is blamable before he allows himself to resent it—such a person, though he may not say expressly to himself that he is standing up for the interest of society, certainly does feel that he is asserting a rule which is for the benefit of others as well as for his own. If he is not feeling this—if he is regarding the act solely as it affects him individually—he is not consciously just; he is not concerning himself about the justice of his actions. This is admitted even by anti-utilitarian moralists. When Kant (as before remarked) propounds as the fundamental principle of morals, " So act, that thy rule of conduct might be adopted as a law by all rational beings," he virtually acknowledges that the interest of mankind collectively, or at least of mankind indiscriminately, must be in the mind of the agent when conscientiously deciding on the morality of the act. Otherwise he uses words without a meaning: for, that a rule even of utter selfishness could not *possibly* be adopted by all rational beings—that there is any insuperable obstacle in the nature of things to its adoption—cannot be even plausibly maintained. To give any meaning to Kant's principle, the sense put upon it must be, that we ought to shape our conduct by a rule which all rational beings might adopt *with benefit to their collective interest.*

To recapitulate : the idea of justice supposes two things; a rule of conduct, and a sentiment which sanctions the rule. The first must be supposed common to all mankind, and intended for their good. The other (the sentiment) is a desire that punishment may be suffered by those who infringe the rule. There is involved, in addition, the conception of some definite person who suffers by the infringement; whose rights (to use the expression appropriated to the case) are violated by it. And the sentiment of justice appears to me to be, the animal desire to repel or retaliate a hurt or damage to oneself, or to those with whom one sympathises, widened so as to include all persons, by the human capacity of enlarged sympathy, and the human conception of intelligent self-interest. From the latter

How Connected with Justice   309

elements, the feeling derives its morality; from the former, its peculiar impressiveness, and energy of self-assertion.

I have, throughout, treated the idea of a *right* residing in the injured person, and violated by the injury, not as a separate element in the composition of the idea and sentiment, but as one of the forms in which the other two elements clothe themselves. These elements are, a hurt to some assignable person or persons on the one hand, and a demand for punishment on the others. An examination of our own minds, I think, will show, that these two things include all that we mean when we speak of violation of a right. When we call anything a person's right, we mean that he has a valid claim on society to protect him in the possession of it, either by the force of law, or by that of education and opinion. If he has what we consider a sufficient claim, on whatever account, to have something guaranteed to him by society, we say that he has a right to it. If we desire to prove that anything does not belong to him by right, we think this done as soon as it is admitted that society ought not to take measures for securing it to him, but should leave him to chance, or to his own exertions. Thus, a person is said to have a right to what he can earn in fair professional competition; because society ought not to allow any other person to hinder him from endeavouring to earn in that manner as much as he can. But he has not a right to three hundred a-year, though he may happen to be earning it; because society is not called on to provide that he shall earn that sum. On the contrary, if he owns ten thousand pounds three per cent. stock, he *has* a right to three hundred a-year; because society has come under an obligation to provide him with an income of that amount.

To have a right, then, is, I conceive, to have something which society ought to defend me in the possession of. If the objector goes on to ask, why it ought? I can give him no other reason than general utility. If that expression does not seem to convey a sufficient feeling of the strength of the obligation, nor to account for the peculiar energy of the feeling, it is because there goes to the composition of the sentiment, not a rational only, but also an animal element, the thirst for retaliation; and this thirst derives its intensity, as well as its moral justification, from the extraordinarily important and impressive kind of utility which is concerned. The interest involved is that of security, to every one's feelings the most vital of all interests. All other earthly benefits are needed by one person, not needed by another; and many of them can, if necessary, be cheerfully foregone, or replaced by something else; but security no human being can possibly do without; on it we depend for all our immunity from evil, and for the whole value of all and every good, beyond the passing moment; since nothing but the gratification of the instant could be of any worth to us, if we could be deprived of anything the next instant by whoever was momentarily stronger than ourselves. Now this most indispensable of all necessaries, after physical nutriment, cannot be had, unless the machinery for providing it is kept unintermittedly in active play. Our notion, therefore, of the claim we have on our fellow-creatures to join in making safe for us the very groundwork of our existence, gathers feelings around it so much more intense than those concerned in any of the more common cases of utility, that the difference in degree (as is often the case in psychology) becomes a real difference in kind. The claim assumes that character of absoluteness, that apparent infinity, and incommensurability with all other considerations, which constitute the distinction between the feeling of right and wrong and that of ordinary expediency and inexpediency. The feelings concerned are so powerful, and we count so positively on finding a responsive feeling in others (all being alike interested), that *ought* and *should* grow into *must*, and recognised indispensability becomes a moral necessity, analogous to physical, and often not inferior to it in binding force.

If the preceding analysis, or something resembling it, be not the correct account of the notion of justice; if justice be totally independent of utility, and be a standard *per se*, which the mind can recognise by simple introspection of itself; it is hard to understand why that internal oracle is so ambiguous, and why so many things appear either just or unjust, according to the light in which they are regarded.

We are continually informed that Utility is an uncertain standard, which every different person interprets differently, and that there is no safety but in the immutable, ineffaceable, and unmistakable dictates of Justice, which carry their evidence in themselves, and are independent of the fluctuations of opinion. One would suppose from this that on questions of justice there could be no controversy; that if we take that for our rule, its application to any given case could leave us in as little doubt as a mathematical demonstration. So far is this from being the fact, that there is as much difference of opinion, and as much discussion, about what is just, as about what is useful to society. Not only have different nations and individuals different notions of justice, but in the mind of one and the same individual, justice is not some one rule, principle, or maxim, but many, which do not always coincide in their dictates, and in choosing between which, he is guided either by some extraneous standard, or by his own personal pre-dilections.

For instance, there are some who say, that it is unjust to punish any one for the sake of example to others; that punishment is just, only when intended for the good of the sufferer himself. Others maintain the extreme reverse, contending that to punish persons who have attained years of discretion, for their own benefit, is despotism and injustice, since if the matter at issue is solely their own good, no one has a right to control their own judgment of it; but that they may justly be punished to prevent evil to others, this being the exercise of the legitimate right of self-defence. Mr. Owen, again, affirms that it is unjust to punish at all; for the criminal did not make his own character; his education, and the circumstances which surrounded him, have made him a criminal, and for these he is not responsible. All these opinions are extremely plausible; and so long as the question is argued as one of justice simply, without going down to the principles which lie under justice and are the source of its authority, I am unable to see how any of these reasoners can be refuted. For in truth every one of the three builds upon rules of justice confessedly true. The first appeals to the acknowledged injustice of singling out an individual, and making him a sacrifice, without his consent, for other people's benefit. The second relies on the acknowledged justice of self-defence, and the admitted injustice of forcing one person to conform to another's notions of what constitutes his good. The Owenite invokes the admitted principle, that it is unjust to punish any one for what he cannot help. Each is triumphant so long as he is not compelled to take into consideration any other maxims of justice than the one he has selected; but as soon as their several maxims are brought face to face, each disputant seems to have exactly as much to say for himself as the others. No one of them can carry out his own notion of justice without trampling upon another equally binding. These are difficulties; they have always been felt to be such; and many devices have been invented to turn rather than to overcome them. As a refuge from the last of the three, men imagined what they called the freedom of the will; fancying that they could not justify punishing a man whose will is in a thoroughly hateful state, unless it be supposed to have come into that state through no influence of anterior circumstances. To escape from the other difficulties, a favourite contrivance has been the fiction of a contract, whereby at some unknown period all the members of society engaged to obey the laws, and consented to be punished for any disobedience to them; thereby giving to their legislators the right, which it is assumed they would not otherwise have had, of punishing them, either for their own good or for that of society. This happy thought was considered to get rid of the whole difficulty, and to legitimate the infliction of punishment, in virtue of another received maxim of justice, *Volenti non fit injuria;* that is not unjust which is done with the consent of the person who is supposed to be hurt by it. I need hardly remark, that even if the consent were not a mere fiction, this maxim is not superior in authority to the others which it is brought in to supersede. It is, on the contrary, an instructive specimen of the loose and irregular manner in which supposed principles of justice grow up.

This particular one evidently came into use as a help to the coarse exigencies of courts of law, which are sometimes obliged to be content with very uncertain presumptions, on account of the greater evils which would often arise from any attempt on their part to cut finer. But even courts of law are not able to adhere consistently to the maxim, for they allow voluntary engagements to be set aside on the ground of fraud, and sometimes on that of mere mistake or misinformation.

Again, when the legitimacy of inflicting punishment is admitted, how many conflicting conceptions of injustice come to light in discussing the proper apportionment of punishments to offences. No rule on the subject recommends itself so strongly to the primitive and spontaneous sentiment of justice, as the *lex talionis,* an eye for an eye and a tooth for a tooth. Though this principle of the Jewish and of the Mahomedan law has been generally abandoned in Europe as a practical maxim, there is, I suspect, in most minds, a secret hankering after it; and when retribution accidentally falls on an offender in that precise shape, the general feeling of satisfaction evinced bears witness how natural is the sentiment to which this repayment in kind is acceptable. With many, the test of justice in penal infliction is that the punishment should be proportioned to the offence; meaning that it should be exactly measured by the moral guilt of the culprit (whatever be their standard for measuring moral guilt): the consideration, what amount of punishment is necessary to deter from the offence, having nothing to do with the question of justice, in their estimation: while there are others to whom that consideration is all in all; who maintain that it is not just, at least for man, to inflict on a fellow-creature, whatever may be his offences, any amount of suffering beyond the least that will suffice to prevent him from repeating, and others from imitating, his misconduct.

To take another example from a subject already once referred to. In a co-operative industrial association, is it just or not that talent or skill should give a title to superior remuneration? On the negative side of the question it is argued, that whoever does the best he can, deserves equally well, and ought not in justice to be put in a position of inferiority for no fault of his own; that superior abilities have already advantages more than enough, in the admiration they excite, the personal influence they command, and the internal sources of satisfaction attending them, without adding to these a superior share of the world's goods; and that society is bound in justice rather to make compensation to the less favoured, for this unmerited inequality of advantages, than to aggravate it. On the contrary side it is contended, that society receives more from the more efficient labourer; that his services being more useful, society owes him a larger return for them; that a greater share of the joint result is actually his work, and not to allow his claim to it is a kind of robbery; that if he is only to receive as much as others, he can only be justly required to produce as much, and to give a smaller amount of time and exertion, proportioned to his superior efficiency. Who shall decide between these appeals to conflicting principles of justice? Justice has in this case two sides to it, which it is impossible to bring into harmony, and the two disputants have chosen opposite sides; the one looks to what it is just that the individual should receive, the other to what it is just that the community should give. Each, from his own point of view, is unanswerable; and any choice between them, on grounds of justice, must be perfectly arbitrary. Social utility alone can decide the preference.

How many, again, and how irreconcilable, are the standards of justice to which reference is made in discussing the repartition of taxation. One opinion is, that payment to the State should be in numerical proportion to pecuniary means. Others think that justice dictates what they term graduated taxation; taking a higher percentage from those who have more to spare. In point of natural justice a strong case might be made for disregarding means altogether, and taking the same absolute sum (whenever it could be got) from every one: as the subscribers to a mess, or to a club, all pay the same sum for the same privileges, whether they can all equally afford it or not. Since the protection (it might be said) of law and government is afforded to, and is equally required by all, there is no injustice in making all buy it at the same price. It is reckoned justice, not injustice, that a dealer should charge to all customers the same price for the same article, not a price varying according to their means of payment. This doctrine, as applied to taxation, finds no advocates, because it conflicts so strongly with man's feelings of humanity and of social expediency; but the principle of justice which it invokes is as true and as binding as those which can be appealed to against it. Accordingly it exerts a tacit influence on the line of defence employed for other modes of assessing taxation. People feel obliged to argue that the State does more for the rich man than for the poor, as a justification for its taking more from them: though this is in reality not true, for the rich would be far better able to protect themselves, in the absence of law and government, than the poor, and indeed would probably be successful in converting the poor into their slaves. Others, again, so far defer to the same conception of justice, as to maintain that all should pay an equal capitation tax for the protection of their persons (these being of equal value to all), and an unequal tax for the protection of their property, which is unequal. To this others reply, that the all of one man is as valuable to him as the all of another. From these confusions there is no other mode of extrication than the utilitarian.

Is, then, the difference between the Just and the Expedient a merely imaginary distinction? Have mankind been under a delusion in thinking that justice is a more sacred thing than policy, and that the latter ought not to be listened to after the former has been satisfied? By no means. The exposition we have given of the nature and origin of the sentiment, recognises a real distinction; and no one of those who profess the most sublime contempt for the consequences of actions as an element in their morality, attaches more importance to the distinction than I do. While I dispute the pretensions of any theory which sets up an imaginary standard of justice not grounded on utility, I account the justice which is grounded on utility to be the chief part, and incomparably the most sacred and binding part, of all morality. Justice is a name

for certain classes of moral rules, which concern the essentials·
of human well-being more nearly, and are therefore of more
absolute obligation, than any other rules for the guidance
of life; and the notion which we have found to be the
essence of the idea of justice, that of a right residing in
an individual, implies and testifies to this more binding obligation.

The moral rules which forbid mankind to hurt one another
(in which we must never forget to include wrongful interference with each other's freedom) are more vital to human
well-being than any maxims, however important, which only
point out the best mode of managing some department of
human affairs. They have also the peculiarity, that they are
the main element in determining the whole of the social
feelings of mankind. It is their observance which alone
preserves peace among human beings : if obedience to them
were not the rule, and disobedience the exception, every one
would see in every one else an enemy, against whom he must
be perpetually guarding himself. What is hardly less important, these are the precepts which mankind have the strongest
and the most direct inducements for impressing upon one
another. By merely giving to each other prudential instruction
or exhortation, they may gain, or think they gain, nothing :
in inculcating on each other the duty of positive beneficence
they have an unmistakable interest, but far less in degree :
a person may possibly not need the benefits of others; but
he always needs that they should not do him hurt. Thus
the moralities which protect every individual from being
harmed by others, either directly or by being hindered in
his freedom of pursuing his own good, are at once those which
he himself has most at heart, and those which he has the
strongest interest in publishing and enforcing by word and
deed. It is by a person's observance of these that his fitness
to exist as one of the fellowship of human beings is tested
and decided; for on that depends his being a nuisance or
not to those with whom he is in contact. Now it is these
moralities primarily which compose the obligation of justice.
The most marked cases of injustice, and those which give the

tone to the feeling of repugnance which characterises the
sentiment, are acts of wrongful aggression, or wrongful
exercise of power over some one; the next are those which
consist in wrongfully withholding from him something which
is his due; in both cases, inflicting on him a positive hurt,
either in the form of direct suffering, or of the privation of
some good which he had reasonable ground, either of a physical
or of a social kind, for counting upon.

The same powerful motives which command the observance
of these primary moralities, enjoin the punishment of those
who violate them; and as the impulses of self-defence, of
defence of others, and of vengeance, are all called forth
against such persons, retribution, or evil for evil, becomes
closely connected with the sentiment of justice, and is universally included in the idea. Good for good is also one of the
dictates of justice; and this, though its social utility is evident,
and though it carries with it a natural human feeling, has
not at first sight that obvious connection with hurt or injury,
which, existing in the most elementary cases of just and
unjust, is the source of the characteristic intensity of the sentiment. But the connection, though less obvious, is not less
real. He who accepts benefits, and denies a return of them
when needed, inflicts a real hurt, by disappointing one of the
most natural and reasonable of expectations, and one which
he must at least tacitly have encouraged, otherwise the benefits
would seldom have been conferred. The important rank,
among human evils and wrongs, of the disappointment of
expectation, is shown in the fact that it constitutes the principal criminality of two such highly immoral acts as a breach
of friendship and a breach of promise. Few hurts which human
beings can sustain are greater, and none wound more, than
when that on which they habitually and with full assurance
relied, fails them in the hour of need; and few wrongs are
greater than this mere withholding of good; none excite
more resentment, either in the person suffering, or in a
sympathising spectator. The principle, therefore, of giving to
each what they deserve, that is, good for good as well as
evil for evil, is not only included within the idea of Justice

as we have defined it, but is a proper object of that intensity of sentiment, which places the Just, in human estimation, above the simply Expedient.

Most of the maxims of justice current in the world, and commonly appealed to in its transactions, are simply instrumental to carrying into effect the principles of justice which we have now spoken of. That a person is only responsible for what he has done voluntarily, or could voluntarily have avoided; that it is unjust to condemn any person unheard; that the punishment ought to be proportioned to the offence, and the like, are maxims intended to prevent the just principle of evil for evil from being perverted to the infliction of evil without justification. The greater part of these common maxims have come into use from the practice of courts of justice, which have been naturally led to a more complete recognition and elaboration than was likely to suggest itself to others, of the rules necessary to enable them to fulfil their double function, of inflicting punishment when due, and of awarding to each person his right.

That first of judicial virtues, impartiality, is an obligation of justice, partly for the reason last mentioned; as being a necessary condition of the fulfilment of the other obligations of justice. But this is not the only source of the exalted rank, among human obligations, of those maxims of equality and impartiality, which, both in popular estimation and in that of the most enlightened, are included among the precepts of justice. In one point of view, they may be considered as corollaries from the principles already laid down. If it is a duty to do to each according to his deserts, returning good for good as well as repressing evil by evil, it necessarily follows that we should treat all equally well (when no higher duty forbids) who have deserved equally well of *us*, and that society should treat all equally well who have deserved equally well of *it*, that is, who have deserved equally well absolutely. This is the highest abstract standard of social and distributive justice; towards which all institutions, and the efforts of all virtuous citizens, should be made in the utmost possible degree to converge. But this great moral duty rests upon a still deeper foundation, being a direct emanation from the

How Connected with Justice

first principle of morals, and not a mere logical corollary from secondary or derivative doctrines. It is involved in the very meaning of Utility, or the Greatest Happiness Principle. That principle is a mere form of words without rational signification, unless one person's happiness, supposed equal in degree (with the proper allowance made for kind), is counted for exactly as much as another's. Those conditions being supplied, Bentham's dictum, "everybody to count for one, nobody for more than one," might be written under the principle of utility as an explanatory commentary.[2] The equal

[2] This implication, in the first principle of the utilitarian scheme, of perfect impartiality between persons, is regarded by Mr. Herbert Spencer (in his *Social Statics*) as a disproof of the pretensions of utility to be a sufficient guide to right; since (he says) the principle of utility presupposes the anterior principle, that everybody has an equal right to happiness. It may be more correctly described as supposing that equal amounts of happiness are equally desirable, whether felt by the same or by different persons. This, however, is not a *pre*-supposition; not a premise needful to support the principle of utility, but the very principle itself; for what is the principle of utility, if it be not that "happiness" and "desirable" are synonymous terms? If there is any anterior principle implied, it can be no other than this, that the truths of arithmetic are applicable to the valuation of happiness, as of all other measurable quantities.

[Mr. Herbert Spencer, in a private communication on the subject of the preceding Note, objects to being considered an opponent of utilitarianism, and states that he regards happiness as the ultimate end of morality; but deems that end only partially attainable by empirical generalisations from the observed results of conduct, and completely attainable only by deducing, from the laws of life and the conditions of existence, what kinds of action necessarily tend to produce happiness, and what kinds to produce unhappiness. With the exception of the word "necessarily," I have no dissent to express from this doctrine; and (omitting that word) I am not aware that any modern advocate of utilitarianism is of a different opinion. Bentham, certainly, to whom in the *Social Statics* Mr. Spencer particularly referred, is, least of all writers, chargeable with unwillingness to deduce the effect of actions on happiness from the laws of human nature and the universal conditions of human life. The common charge against him is of relying too exclusively upon such deductions, and declining altogether to be bound by the generalisations from specific experience which Mr. Spencer thinks that utilitarians generally confine themselves to. My own opinion (and, as I collect, Mr. Spencer's) is, that in ethics, as in all other

claim of everybody to happiness in the estimation of the
moralist and of the legislator, involves an equal claim to all
the means of happiness, except in so far as the inevitable
conditions of human life, and the general interest, in which
that of every individual is included, set limits to the maxim;
and those limits ought to be strictly construed. As every
other maxim of justice, so this is by no means applied or
held applicable universally; on the contrary, as I have
already remarked, it bends to every person's ideas of social
expediency. But in whatever case it is deemed applicable
at all, it is held to be the dictate of justice. All persons
are deemed to have a *right* to equality of treatment, except
when some recognised social expediency requires the reverse.
And hence all social inequalities which have ceased to be
considered expedient, assume the character not of simple
inexpediency, but of injustice, and appear so tyrannical, that
people are apt to wonder how they ever could have been
tolerated; forgetful that they themselves perhaps tolerate
other inequalities under an equally mistaken notion of expediency, the correction of which would make that which
they approve seem quite as monstrous as what they have
at last learnt to condemn. The entire history of social improvement has been a series of transitions, by which one
custom or institution after another, from being a supposed
primary necessity of social existence, has passed into the rank
of a universally stigmatised injustice and tyranny. So it has
been with the distinctions of slaves and freemen, nobles and
serfs, patricians and plebeians; and so it will be, and in part
already is, with the aristocracies of colour, race, and sex.

It appears from what has been said, that justice is a name
for certain moral requirements, which, regarded collectively,
stand higher in the scale of social utility, and are therefore of
more paramount obligation, than any others; though particular cases may occur in which some other social duty is

---

branches of scientific study, the consilience of the results of both
these processes, each corroborating and verifying the other, is requisite to give to any general proposition the kind and degree of
evidence which constitutes scientific proof.]

How Connected with Justice

so important, as to overrule any one of the general maxims of justice. Thus, to save a life, it may not only be allowable, but a duty, to steal, or take by force, the necessary food or medicine, or to kidnap, and compel to officiate, the only qualified medical practitioner. In such cases, as we do not call anything justice which is not a virtue, we usually say, not that justice must give way to some other moral principle, but that what is just in ordinary cases is, by reason of that other principle, not just in the particular case. By this useful accommodation of language, the character of indefeasibility attributed to justice is kept up, and we are saved from the necessity of maintaining that there can be laudable injustice.

The considerations which have now been adduced resolve, I conceive, the only real difficulty in the utilitarian theory of morals. It has always been evident that all cases of justice are also cases of expediency : the difference is in the peculiar sentiment which attaches to the former, as contradistinguished from the latter. If this characteristic sentiment has been sufficiently accounted for; if there is no necessity to assume for it any peculiarity of origin; if it is simply the natural feeling of resentment, moralised by being made coextensive with the demands of social good; and if this feeling not only does but ought to exist in all classes of cases to which the idea of justice corresponds; that idea no longer presents itself as a stumbling-block to the utilitarian ethics. Justice remains the appropriate name for certain social utilities which are vastly more important, and therefore more absolute and imperative, than any others are as a class (though not more so than others . may be in particular cases); and which, therefore, ought to be, as well as naturally are, guarded by a sentiment not only different in degree, but also in kind; distinguished from the milder feeling which attaches to the mere idea of promoting human pleasure or convenience, at once by the more definite nature of its commands, and by the sterner character of its sanctions.

[7]

Excerpt from *Considerations on Representative Government*, 118–35

CHAPTER II

THE CRITERION OF A GOOD FORM OF GOVERNMENT

THE form of government for any given country being (within certain definite conditions) amenable to choice, it is now to be considered by what test the choice should be directed; what are the distinctive characteristics of the form of government best fitted to promote the interests of any given society.

Before entering into this inquiry, it may seem necessary to decide what are the proper functions of government; for, government altogether being only a means, the eligibility of the means must depend on their adaptation to the end. But this mode of stating the problem gives less aid to its investigation than might be supposed, and does not even bring the whole of the question into view. For, in the first place, the proper functions of a government are not a fixed thing, but different in different states of society; much more extensive in a backward than in an advanced state. And, secondly, the character of a government or set of political institutions cannot be sufficiently estimated while we confine our attention to the legitimate sphere of governmental functions. For though the goodness of a government is necessarily circumscribed within that sphere, its badness unhappily is not. Every kind of degree of evil of which mankind are susceptible may be inflicted on them by their government; and none of the good which social existence is capable of can be any further realised than as the constitution of the government is compatible with, and allows scope for, its attainment. Not to speak of indirect effects, the direct meddling of the public authorities has no necessary limits but those of human existence; and the influence of government on the well-being of society can be considered or estimated in reference to nothing less than the whole of the interests of humanity.

Being thus obliged to place before ourselves, as the test of good and bad government, so complex an object as the aggregate interests of society, we would willingly attempt some kind of classification of those interests, which, bringing them before the mind in definite groups, might give indication of the qualities by which a form of government is fitted to promote those various interests respectively. It would be a great facility if we could say the good of society consists of such and such elements; one of these elements requires such conditions, another such others; the government, then, which unites in the greatest degree all these conditions, must be the best. The theory of government would thus be built up from the separate theorems of the elements which compose a good state of society.

Unfortunately, to enumerate and classify the constituents of social well-being, so as to admit of the formation of such theorems, is no easy task. Most of those who, in the last or present generation, have applied themselves to the philosophy of politics in any comprehensive spirit, have felt the importance of such a classification; but the attempts which have been made towards it are as yet limited, so far as I am aware, to a single step. The classification begins and ends with a

120   REPRESENTATIVE GOVERNMENT

partition of the exigencies of society between the two heads of Order
and Progress (in the phraseology of French thinkers); Permanence
and Progression in the words of Coleridge. This division is plausible
and seductive, from the apparently clean-cut opposition between its
two members, and the remarkable difference between the sentiments
to which they appeal. But I apprehend that (however admissible for
purposes of popular discourse) the distinction between Order, or
Permanence, and Progress, employed to define the qualities necessary
in a government, is unscientific and incorrect.

For, first, what are Order and Progress? Concerning Progress
there is no difficulty, or none which is apparent at first sight. When
Progress is spoken of as one of the wants of human society, it may be
supposed to mean Improvement. That is a tolerably distinct idea.
But what is Order? Sometimes it means more, sometimes less, but
hardly ever the whole of what human society needs except improvement.

In its narrowest acceptation Order means Obedience. A government is said to preserve order if it succeeds in getting itself obeyed.
But there are different degrees of obedience, and it is not every degree
that is commendable. Only an unmitigated despotism demands that
the individual citizen shall obey unconditionally every mandate of
persons in authority. We must at least limit the definition to such
mandates as are general and issued in the deliberate form of laws.
Order, thus understood, expresses, doubtless, an indispensable attribute
of government. Those who are unable to make their ordinances
obeyed, cannot be said to govern. But though a necessary condition,
this is not the object of government. That it should make itself obeyed
is requisite, in order that it may accomplish some other purpose.
We are still to seek what is this other purpose, which government
ought to fulfil, abstractedly from the idea of improvement, and
which has to be fulfilled in every society, whether stationary or
progressive.

In a sense somewhat more enlarged, Order means the preservation
of peace by the cessation of private violence. Order is said to exist
where the people of the country have, as a general rule, ceased to
prosecute their quarrels by private force, and acquired the habit of
referring the decision of their disputes and the redress of their injuries
to the public authorities. But in this larger use of the term, as well as
in the former narrow one, Order expresses rather one of the conditions
of government, than either its purpose or the criterion of its excellence.

For the habit may be well established of submitting to the government, and referring all disputed matters to its authority, and yet the manner in which the government deals with those disputed matters, and with the other things about which it concerns itself, may differ by the whole interval which divides the best from the worst possible.

If we intend to compromise in the idea of Order all that society requires from its government which is not included in the idea of Progress, we must define Order as the preservation of all kinds and amounts of good which already exist, and Progress as consisting in the increase of them. This distinction does comprehend in one or the other section everything which a government can be required to promote. But, thus understood, it affords no basis for a philosophy of government. We cannot say that, in constituting a polity, certain provisions ought to be made for Order and certain others for Progress; since the conditions of Order, in the sense now indicated, and those of Progress, are not opposite, but the same. The agencies which tend to preserve the social good which already exists are the very same which promote the increase of it, and *vice versa*: the sole difference being, that a greater degree of those agencies is required for the latter purpose than for the former.

What, for example, are the qualities in the citizens individually which conduce most to keep up the amount of good conduct, of good management, of success and prosperity, which already exist in society? Everybody will agree that those qualities are industry, integrity, justice, and prudence. But are not these, of all qualities, the most conducive to improvement? and is not any growth of these virtues in the community in itself the greatest of improvements? If so, whatever qualities in the government are promotive of industry, integrity, justice, and prudence, conduce alike to permanence and to progression; only there is needed more of those qualities to make the society decidedly progressive than merely to keep it permanent.

What, again, are the particular attributes in human beings which seem to have a more especial reference to Progress, and do not so directly suggest the ideas of Order and Preservation? They are chiefly the qualities of mental activity, enterprise, and courage. But are not all these qualities fully as much required for preserving the good we have, as for adding to it? If there is anything certain in human affairs, it is that valuable acquisitions are only to be retained by the continuation of the same energies which gained them. Things left to take care of themselves inevitably decay. Those whom success induces to relax their habits of care and thoughtfulness, and their willingness to encounter disagreeables, seldom long retain their good fortune at its height. The mental attribute which seems exclusively dedicated to Progress, and is the culmination of the tendencies to it, is Originality, or Invention. Yet this is no less necessary for Permanence; since, in the inevitable changes of human affairs, new inconveniences and dangers continually grow up, which must be encountered by new resources and contrivances, in order to keep things going on even only as well as they did before. Whatever qualities, therefore, in a government, tend to encourage activity, energy, courage, originality, are requisites of Permanence as well as of Progress; only a somewhat less degree of them will, on the average, suffice for the former purpose than for the latter.

To pass now from the mental to the outward and objective requisites of society; it is impossible to point out any contrivance in politics, or arrangement of social affairs, which conduces to Order only, or to Progress only; whatever tends to either promotes both. Take, for instance, the common institution of a police. Order is the object which seems most immediately interested in the efficiency of this part of the social organisation. Yet if it is effectual to promote Order, that is, if it represses crime, and enables every one to feel his person and property secure, can any state of things be more conducive to Progress? The greater security of property is one of the main conditions and causes of greater production, which is Progress in its most familiar and vulgarest aspect. The better repression of crime represses the dispositions which tend to crime, and this is Progress in a somewhat higher sense. The release of the individual from the cares and anxieties of a state of imperfect protection, sets his faculties free to be employed in any new effort for improving his own state and that of others: while the same cause, by attaching him to social existence, and making him no longer see present or prospective enemies in his fellow-creatures, fosters all those feelings of kindness and fellowship towards others, and interest in the general well-being of the community, which are such important parts of social improvement.

Take, again, such a familiar case as that of a good system of taxation and finance. This would generally be classed as belonging to the province of Order. Yet what can be more conducive to Progress? A financial system which promotes the one, conduces, by the very same excellences, to the other. Economy, for example, equally preserves the existing stock of national wealth, and favours the creation of more. A just distribution of burthens, by holding up to every citizen an example of morality and good conscience applied to difficult adjustments, and an evidence of the value which the highest authorities attach to them, tends in an eminent degree to educate the moral sentiments of the community, both in respect of strength and of discrimination. Such a mode of levying the taxes as does not impede the industry, or unnecessarily interfere with the liberty, of the citizen, promotes, not the preservation only, but the increase of the national wealth, and encourages a more active use of the individual faculties. And *vice versa*, all errors in finance and taxation which obstruct the improvement of the people in wealth and morals tend also, if of sufficiently serious amount, positively to impoverish and demoralise them. It holds, in short, universally, that when Order and Permanence are taken in their widest sense, for the stability of existing advantages, the requisites of Progress are but the requisites of Order in a greater degree; those of Permanence merely those of Progress in a somewhat smaller measure.

In support of the position that Order is intrinsically different from Progress, and that preservation of existing and acquisition of additional good are sufficiently distinct to afford the basis of a fundamental classification, we shall perhaps be reminded that Progress may be at the expense of Order; what while we are acquiring, or striving to acquire, good of one kind, we may be losing ground in respect to others: thus there may be progress in wealth, while there is deterioration in virtue. Granting this, what it proves is not that Progress is generically a different thing from Permanence, but that wealth is a different thing from virtue. Progress is permanence and something more; and it is no answer to this to say that Progress in one thing does not imply Permanence in everything. No more does Progress in one thing imply Progress in everything. Progress of any kind includes Permanence in that same kind; whenever Permanence is sacrificed to some particular kind of Progress, other Progress is still more sacrificed to it; and if it be not worth the sacrifice, not the interest of Permanence alone has been disregarded, but the general interest of Progress has been mistaken.

If these improperly contrasted ideas are to be used at all in the attempt to give a first commencement of scientific precision to the notion of good government, it would be more philosophically correct to leave out of the definition the word Order, and to say that the best govern-

ment is that which is most conducive to Progress. For Progress includes
Order, but Order does not include Progress. Progress is a greater
degree of that of which Order is a less. Order, in any other sense,
stands only for a part of the pre-requisites of good government, not
for its idea and essence. Order would find a more suitable place
among the conditions of Progress; since, if we would increase our sum
of good, nothing is more indispensable than to take due care of what
we already have. If we are endeavouring after more riches, our very
first rule should be not to squander uselessly our existing means.
Order, thus considered, is not an additional end to be reconciled
with Progress, but a part and means of Progress itself. If a gain in one
respect is purchased by a more than equivalent loss in the same or in
any other, there is not Progress. Conduciveness to Progress, thus
understood, includes the whole excellence of a government.

But, though metaphysically defensible, this definition of the criterion
of good government is not appropriate, because, though it contains
the whole of the truth, it recalls only a part. What is suggested by the
term Progress is the idea of moving onward, whereas the meaning of
it here is quite as much the prevention of falling back. The very same
social causes—the same beliefs, feelings, institutions, and practices—
are as much required to prevent society from retrograding, as to
produce a further advance. Were there no improvement to be hoped
for, life would not be the less an unceasing struggle against causes of
deterioration; as it even now is. Politics, as conceived by the ancients
consisted wholly in this. The natural tendency of men and their works
was to degenerate, which tendency, however, by good institutions
virtuously administered, it might be possible for an indefinite length
of time to counteract. Though we no longer hold this opinion;
though most men in the present age profess the contrary creed,
believing that the tendency of things, on the whole, is towards improvement; we ought not to forget that there is an incessant and ever-
flowing current of human affairs towards the worse, consisting of all
the follies, all the negligences, indolences, and supinenesses of mankind;
which is only controlled, and kept from sweeping all before it, by the
exertions which some persons constantly, and others by fits, put forth
in the direction of good and worthy objects. It gives a very insufficient
idea of the importance of the strivings which take place to improve
and elevate human nature and life, to suppose that their chief value
consists in the amount of actual improvement realised by their means,
and that the consequence of their cessation would merely be that we

should remain as we are. A very small diminution of those exertions would not only put a stop to improvement, but would turn the general tendency of things towards deterioration; which, once begun, would proceed with increasing rapidity, and become more and more difficult to check, until it reached a state often seen in history, and in which many large portions of mankind even now grovel; when hardly anything short of superhuman power seems sufficient to turn the tide, and give a fresh commencement to the upward movement.

These reasons make the word Progress as unapt as the terms Order and Permanence to become the basis for a classification of the requisites of a form of government. The fundamental antithesis which these words express does not lie in the things themselves, so much as in the types of human character which answer to them. There are, we know, some minds in which caution, and others in which boldness, predominates: in some, the desire to avoid imperilling what is already possessed is a stronger sentiment than that which prompts to improve the old and acquire new advantages; while there are others who lean the contrary way, and are more eager for future than careful of present good. The road to the ends of both is the same; but they are liable to wander from it in opposite directions. This consideration is of importance in composing the *personnel* of any political body: persons of both types ought to be included in it, that the tendencies of each may be tempered, in so far as they are excessive, by a due proportion of the other. There needs no express provision to ensure this object, provided care is taken to admit nothing inconsistent with it. The natural and spontaneous admixture of the old and the young, of those whose position and reputation are made and those who have them still to make, will in general sufficiently answer the purpose, if only this natural balance is not disturbed by artificial regulation.

Since the distinction most commonly adopted for the classification of social exigencies does not possess the properties needful for that use, we have to seek for some other leading distinction better adapted to the purpose. Such a distinction would seem to be indicated by the considerations to which I now proceed.

If we ask ourselves on what causes and conditions good government in all its senses, from the humblest to the most exalted, depends, we find that the principal of them, the one which transcends all others, is the qualities of the human beings composing the society over which the government is exercised.

126   REPRESENTATIVE GOVERNMENT

We may take, as a first intance, the administration of justice; with
the more propriety, since there is no part of public business in which
the mere machinery, the rules and contrivances for conducting the
details of the operation, are of such vital consequence. Yet even these
yield in importance to the qualities of the human agents employed.
Of what efficacy are rules of procedure in securing the ends of justice,
if the moral condition of the people is such that the witnesses generally
lie, and the judges and their subordinates take bribes? Again, how can
institutions provide a good municipal administration if there exists
such indifference to the subject that those who would administer
honestly and capably cannot be induced to serve, and the duties are
left to those who undertake them because they have some private
interest to be promoted? Of what avail is the most broadly popular
representative system if the electors do not care to choose the best
member of parliament, but choose him who will spend most money
to be elected? How can a representative assembly work for good if its
members can be bought, or if their excitability of temperament, un-
corrected by public discipline or private self-control, makes them
incapable of calm deliberation, and they resort to manual violence
on the floor of the House, or shoot at one another with rifles? How,
again, can government, or any joint concern, be carried on in a tolerable
manner by people so envious that, if one among them seems likely to
succeed in anything, those who ought to co-operate with him form a
tacit combination to make him fail? Whenever the general disposition of the people is such that each individual regards those only of his
interests which are selfish, and does not dwell on, or concern himself
for, his share of the general interest, in such a state of things good
government is impossible. The influence of defects of intelligence in
obstructing all the elements of good government requires no illustration. Government consists of acts done by human beings; and if the
agents, or those who choose the agents, or those to whom the agents are
responsible, or the lookers-on whose opinion ought to influence and
check all these, are mere masses of ignorance, stupidity, and baleful
prejudice, every operation of government will go wrong; while, in
proportion as the men rise above this standard, so will the government
improve in quality; up to the point of excellence, attainable but
nowhere attained, where the officers of government, themselves
persons of superior virtue and intellect, are surrounded by the atmosphere of a virtuous and enlightened public opinion.

The first element of good government, therefore, being the virtue and intelligence of the human beings composing the community, the most important point of excellence which any form of government can possess is to promote the virtue and intelligence of the people themselves. The first question in respect to any political institutions is, how far they tend to foster in the members of the community the various desirable qualities, moral and intellectual; or rather (following Bentham's more complete classification) moral, intellectual, and active. The government which does this the best has every likelihood of being the best in all other respects, since it is on these qualities, so far as they exist in the people, that all possibility of goodness in the practical operations of the government depends.

We may consider, then, as one criterion of the goodness of a government, the degree in which it tends to increase the sum of good qualities in the governed, collectively and individually; since, besides that their well-being is the sole object of government, their good qualities supply the moving force which works the machinery. This leaves, as the other constituent element of the merit of a government, the quality of the machinery itself; that is, the degree in which it is adapted to take advantage of the amount of good qualities which may at any time exist, and make them instrumental to the right purposes. Let us again take the subject of judicature as an example and illustration. The judicial system being given, the goodness of the administration of justice is in the compound ratio of the worth of the men composing the tribunals, and the worth of the public opinion which influences or controls them. But all the difference between a good and a bad system of judicature lies in the contrivances adopted for bringing whatever moral and intellectual worth exists in the community to bear upon the administration of justice, and making it duly operative on the result. The arrangements for rendering the choice of the judges such as to obtain the highest average of virtue and intelligence; the salutary forms of procedure; the publicity which allows observation and criticism of whatever is amiss; the liberty of discussion and censure through the press; the mode of taking evidence, according as it is well or ill adapted to elicit truth; the facilities, whatever be their amount, for obtaining access to the tribunals; the arrangements for detecting crimes and apprehending offenders;—all these things are not the power, but the machinery for bringing the power into contact with the obstacle: and the machinery has no action of itself, but without it the power, let it be ever so ample, would be wasted and of no effect. A similar distinction exists in regard to the constitution of the executive departments of administration. Their machinery is good, when the proper tests are prescribed for the qualifications of officers, the proper rules for their promotion; when the business is conveniently distributed among those who are to transact it, a convenient and methodical order established for its transaction, a correct and intelligible record kept of it after being transacted; when each individual knows for what he is responsible, and is known to others as responsible for it; when the best-contrived checks are provided against negligence, favouritism, or jobbery, in any of the acts of the department. But political checks will no more act of themselves than a bridle will direct a horse without a rider. If the checking functionaries are as corrupt or as negligent as those whom they ought to check, and if the public, the mainspring of the whole checking machinery, are too ignorant, too passive, or too careless and inattentive, to do their part, little benefit will be derived from the best administrative apparatus. Yet a good apparatus is always preferable to a bad. It enables such insufficient moving or checking power as exists to act at the greatest advantage; and without it, no amount of moving or checking power would be sufficient. Publicity, for instance, is no impediment to evil nor stimulus to good if the public will not look at what is done; but without publicity, how could they either check or encourage what they were not permitted to see? The ideally perfect constitution of a public office is that in which the interest of the functionary is entirely coincident with his duty. No mere system will make it so, but still less can it be made so without a system, aptly devised for the purpose.

What we have said of the arrangements for the detailed administration of the government is still more evidently true of its general constitution. All government which aims at being good is an organisation of some part of the good qualities existing in the individual members of the community for the conduct of its collective affairs. A representative constitution is a means of bringing the general standard of intelligence and honesty existing in the community, and the individual intellect and virtue of its wisest members, more directly to bear upon the government, and investing them with greater influence in it, than they would in general have under any other mode of organisation; though, under any, such influence as they do have is the source of all good that there is in the government, and the hindrance of every evil that there is not. The greater the amount of these good qualities which the institutions of a country succeed in organising, and the better the mode of organisation, the better will be the government.

We have now, therefore, obtained a foundation for a twofold division of the merit which any set of political institutions can possess. It consists partly of the degree in which they promote the general mental advancement of the community, including under that phrase advancement in intellect, in virtue, and in practical activity and efficiency; and partly of the degree of perfection with which they organise the moral, intellectual, and active worth already existing, so as to operate with the greatest effect on public affairs. A government is to be judged by its action upon men, and by its action upon things; by what it makes of the citizens, and what it does with them; its tendency to improve or deteriorate the people themselves, and the goodness or badness of the work it performs for them, and by means of them. Government is at once a great influence acting on the human mind, and a set of organised arrangements for public business: in the first capacity its beneficial action is chiefly indirect, but not therefore less vital, while its mischievous action may be direct.

The difference between these two functions of a government is not, like that between Order and Progress, a difference merely in degree, but in kind. We must not, however, suppose that they have no intimate connection with one another. The institutions which ensure the best management of public affairs practicable in the existing state of cultivation tend by this alone to the further improvement of that state. A people which had the most just laws, the purest and most efficient judicature, the most enlightened administration, the most equitable and least onerous system of finance, compatible with the stage it had attained in moral and intellectual advancement, would be in a fair way to pass rapidly into a higher stage. Nor is there any mode in which political institutions can contribute more effectually to the improvement of the people than by doing their more direct work well. And, reversely, if their machinery is so badly constructed that they do their own particular business ill, the effect is felt in a thousand ways in lowering the morality and deadening the intelligence and activity of the people. But the distinction is nevertheless real, because this is only one of the means by which political institutions improve or deteriorate the human mind, and the causes and modes of that beneficial or injurious influence remain a distinct and much wider subject of study.

Of the two modes of operation by which a form of government or

I

130 REPRESENTATIVE GOVERNMENT

set of political institutions affects the welfare of the community—
its operation as an agency of national education, and its arrangements
for conducting the collective affairs of the community in the state of
education in which they already are; the last evidently varies much
less, from difference of country and state of civilisation, than the first.
It has also much less to do with the fundamental constitution of the
government. The mode of conducting the practical business of government, which is best under a free constitution, would generally be best
also in an absolute monarchy: only an absolute monarchy is not so
likely to practise it. The laws of property, for example; the principles
of evidence and judicial procedure; the system of taxation and of
financial administration, need not necessarily be different in different
forms of government. Each of these matters has principles and rules
of its own, which are a subject of separate study. General jurisprudence,
civil and penal legislation, financial and commercial policy, are
sciences in themselves, or rather, separate members of the comprehensive science or art of government: and the most enlightened doctrines
on all these subjects, though not equally likely to be understood,
or acted on under all forms of government, yet, if understood and
acted on, would in general be equally beneficial under them all.
It is true that these doctrines could not be applied without some
modifications to all states of society and of the human mind: nevertheless, by far the greater number of them would require modifications
solely of details, to adapt them to any state of society sufficiently
advanced to possess rulers capable of understanding them. A government to which they would be wholly unsuitable must be one so bad
in itself, or so opposed to public feeling, as to be unable to maintain
itself in existence by honest means.

It is otherwise with that portion of the interests of the community
which relate to the better or worse training of the people themselves.
Considered as instrumental to this, institutions need to be radically
different, according to the stage of advancement already reached.
The recognition of this truth, though for the most part empirically
rather than philosophically, may be regarded as the main point of
superiority in the political theories of the present above those of the
last age; in which it was customary to claim representative democracy
for England or France by arguments which would equally have proved
it the only fit form of government for Bedouins or Malays. The state
of different communities, in point of culture and development, ranges
downwards to a condition very little above the highest of the beasts.

The upward range, too, is considerable, and the future possible extension vastly greater. A community can only be developed out of one
of these states into a higher by a concourse of influences, among the
principal of which is the government to which they are subject.
In all states of human improvement ever yet attained, the nature
and degree of authority exercised over individuals, the distribution of
power, and the conditions of command and obedience, are the most
powerful of the influences, except their religious belief, which make
them what they are, and enable them to become what they can be.
They may be stopped short at any point in their progress by defective
adaptation of their government to that particular stage of advancement. And the one indispensable merit of a government, in favour
of which it may be forgiven almost any amount of other demerit
compatible with progress, is that its operation on the people is favourable, or not unfavourable, to the next step which it is necessary for
them to take, in order to raise themselves to a higher level.

Thus (to repeat a former example), a people in a state of savage
independence, in which every one lives for himself, exempt, unless by
fits, from any external control, is practically incapable of making any
progress in civilisation until it has learnt to obey. The indispensable
virtue, therefore, in a government which establishes itself over a people
of this sort is, that it makes itself obeyed. To enable it to do this, the
constitution of the government must be nearly, or quite, despotic.
A constitution in any degree popular, dependent on the voluntary
surrender by the different members of the community of their individual freedom of action, would fail to enforce the first lesson which
the pupils, in this stage of their progress, require. Accordingly, the
civilisation of such tribes, when not the result of juxtaposition with
others already civilised, is almost always the work of an absolute ruler,
deriving his power either from religion or military prowess; very
often from foreign arms.

Again, uncivilised races, and the bravest and most energetic still
more than the rest, are averse to continuous labour of an unexciting
kind. Yet all real civilisation is at this price; without such labour,
neither can the mind be disciplined into the habits required by civilised
society, nor the material world prepared to receive it. There needs a
rare concurrence of circumstances, and for that reason often a vast
length of time, to reconcile such a people to industry, unless they are
for a while compelled to it. Hence even personal slavery, by giving
a commencement to industrial life, and enforcing it as the exclusive

occupation of the most numerous portion of the community, may accelerate the transition to a better freedom than that of fighting and rapine. It is almost needless to say that this excuse for slavery is only available in a very early state of society. A civilised people have far other means of imparting civilisation to those under their influence; and slavery is, in all its details, so repugnant to that government of law which is the foundation of all modern life, and so corrupting to the master-class when they have once come under civilised influences, that its adoption under any circumstances whatever in modern society is a relapse into worse than barbarism.

At some period, however, of their history, almost every people, now civilised, have consisted, in majority, of slaves. A people in that condition require to raise them out of it a very different polity from a nation of savages. If they are energetic by nature, and especially if there be associated with them in the same community an industrious class who are neither slaves nor slave-owners (as was the case in Greece), they need, probably, no more to ensure their improvement than to make them free: when freed, they may often be fit, like Roman freedmen, to be admitted at once to the full rights of citizenship. This, however, is not the normal condition of slavery, and is generally a sign that it is becoming obsolete. A slave, properly so called, is a being who has not learnt to help himself. He is, no doubt, one step in advance of a savage. He has not the first lesson of political society still to acquire. He has learnt to obey. But what he obeys is only a direct command. It is the characteristic of *born* slaves to be incapable of conforming their conduct to a rule, or law. They can only do what they are ordered, and only when they are ordered to do it. If a man whom they fear is standing over them and threatening them with punishment, they obey; but when his back is turned, the work remains undone. The motive determining them must appeal not to their interests, but to their instincts; immediate hope or immediate terror. A despotism, which may tame the savage, will, in so far as it is a despotism, only confirm the slaves in their incapacities. Yet a government under their own control would be entirely unmanageable by them. Their improvement cannot come from themselves, but must be superinduced from without. The step which they have to take, and their only path to improvement, is to be raised from a government of will to one of law. They have to be taught self-government, and this, in its initial stage, means the capacity to act on general instructions. What they require is not a government of force, but one of guidance. Being, however, in too low a state to yield to the guidance of any but those to whom they look up as the possessors of force, the sort of government fittest for them is one which possesses force, but seldom uses it: a parental despotism or aristocracy, resembling the St. Simonian form of Socialism; maintaining a general superintendence over all the operations of society, so as to keep before each the sense of a present force sufficient to compel his obedience to the rule laid down, but which, owing to the impossibility of descending to regulate all the minutiæ of industry and life, necessarily leaves and induces individuals to do much of themselves. This, which may be termed the government of leading-strings, seems to be the one required to carry such a people the most rapidly through the next necessary step in social progress. Such appears to have been the idea of the government of the Incas of Peru; and such was that of the Jesuits of Paraguay. I need scarcely remark that leading-strings are only admissible as a means of gradually training the people to walk alone.

It would be out of place to carry the illustration further. To attempt to investigate what kind of government is suited to every known state of society would be to compose a treatise, not on representative government, but on political science at large. For our more limited purpose we borrow from political philosophy only its general principles. To determine the form of government most suited to any particular people, we must be able, among the defects and shortcomings which belong to that people, to distinguish those that are the immediate impediment to progress; to discover what it is which (as it were) stops the way. The best government for them is the one which tends most to give them that for want of which they cannot advance, or advance only in a lame and lopsided manner. We must not, however, forget the reservation necessary in all things which have for their object improvement, or Progress; namely, that in seeking the good which is needed, no damage, or as little as possible, be done to that already possessed. A people of savages should be taught obedience, but not in such a manner as to convert them into a people of slaves. And (to give the observation a higher generality) the form of government which is most effectual for carrying a people through the next stage of progress will still be very improper for them if it does this in such a manner as to obstruct, or positively unfit them for, the step next beyond. Such cases are frequent, and are among the most melancholy facts in history. The Egyptian hierarchy, the paternal despotism of China, were very fit instruments for carrying those nations

up to the point of civilisation which they attained. But having
reached that point, they were brought to a permanent halt for want of
mental liberty and individuality; requisites of improvement which
the institutions that had carried them thus far entirely incapacitated
them from acquiring; and as the institutions did not break down and
give place to others, further improvement stopped. In contrast with
these nations, let us consider the example of an opposite character
afforded by another and a comparatively insignificant Oriental people
—the Jews. They, too, had an absolute monarchy and a hierarchy,
and their organised institutions were as obviously of sacerdotal origin
as those of the Hindoos. These did for them what was done for other
Oriental races by their institutions—subdued them to industry and
order, and gave them a national life. But neither their kings nor their
priests ever obtained, as in those other countries, the exclusive moulding of their character. Their religion, which enabled persons of genius
and a high religious tone to be regarded and to regard themselves as
inspired from heaven, gave existence to an inestimably precious
unorganised institution—the Order (if it may be so termed) of Prophets.
Under the protection, generally, though not always, effectual, of their
sacred character, the Prophets were a power in the nation, often more
than a match for kings and priests, and kept up, in that little corner of
the earth, the antagonism of influences which is the only real security
for continued progress. Religion consequently was not there what it
has been in so many other places—a consecration of all that was once
established, and a barrier against further improvement. The remark
of a distinguished Hebrew, M. Salvador, that the Prophets were, in
Church and State, the equivalent of the modern liberty of the press,
gives a just but not an adequate conception of the part fulfilled in
national and universal history by this great element of Jewish life;
by means of which, the canon of inspiration never being complete, the
persons most eminent in genius and moral feeling could not only
denounce and reprobate, with the direct authority of the Almighty,
whatever appeared to them deserving of such treatment, but could
give forth better and higher interpretations of the national religion,
which thenceforth became part of the religion. Accordingly, whoever
can divest himself of the habit of reading the Bible as if it was one book,
which until lately was equally inveterate in Christians and in un-
believers, sees with admiration the vast interval between the morality
and religion of the Pentateuch, or even of the historical books (the
unmistakable work of Hebrew Conservatives of the sacerdotal order),

and the morality and religion of the Prophecies: a distance as wide as between these last and the Gospels. Conditions more favourable to Progress could not easily exist: accordingly, the Jews, instead of being stationary like other Asiatics, were, next to the Greeks, the most progressive people of antiquity, and, jointly with them, have been the starting-point and main propelling agency of modern cultivation.

It is, then, impossible to understand the question of the adaptation of forms of government to states of society without taking into account not only the next step, but all the steps which society has yet to make; both those which can be foreseen, and the far wider indefinite range which is at present out of sight. It follows, that to judge of the merits of forms of government, an ideal must be constructed of the form of government most eligible in itself, that is, which, if the necessary conditions existed for giving effect to its beneficial tendencies, would, more than all others, favour and promote not some one improvement, but all forms and degrees of it. This having been done, we must consider what are the mental conditions of all sorts, necessary to enable this government to realise its tendencies, and what, therefore, are the various defects by which a people is made incapable of reaping its benefits. It would then be possible to construct a theorem of the circumstances in which that form of government may wisely be introduced; and also to judge, in cases in which it had better not be introduced, what inferior forms of polity will best carry those communities through the intermediate stages which they must traverse before they can become fit for the best form of government.

Of these inquiries, the last does not concern us here; but the first is an essential part of our subject: for we may, without rashness, at once enunciate a proposition, the proofs and illustrations of which will present themselves in the ensuing pages; that this ideally best form of government will be found in some one or other variety of the Representative System.

CHAPTER III

THAT THE IDEALLY BEST FORM OF GOVERNMENT IS REPRESENTATIVE GOVERNMENT

IT has long (perhaps throughout the entire duration of British freedom) been a common saying, that if a good despot could be ensured, despotic monarchy would be the best form of government. I look upon this as a radical and most pernicious misconception of what good government is; which, until it can be got rid of, will fatally vitiate all our speculations on government.

The supposition is, that absolute power, in the hands of an eminent individual, would ensure a virtuous and intelligent performance of all the duties of government. Good laws would be established and enforced, bad laws would be reformed; the best men would be placed in all situations of trust; justice would be as well administered, the public burthens would be as light and as judiciously imposed, every branch of administration would be as purely and as intelligently conducted, as the circumstances of the country and its degree of intellectual and moral cultivation would admit. I am willing, for the sake of the argument, to concede all this; but I must point out how great the concession is; how much more is needed to produce even an approximation to these results than is conveyed in the simple expression, a good despot. Their realisation would in fact imply, not merely a good monarch, but an all-seeing one. He must be at all times informed correctly, in considerable detail, of the conduct and working of every branch of administration, in every district of the country, and must be able, in the twenty-four hours per day which are all that is granted to a king as to the humblest labourer, to give an effective share of attention and superintendence to all parts of this vast field; or he must at least be capable of discerning and choosing out, from among the mass of his subjects, not only a large abundance of honest and able men, fit to conduct every branch of public administration under supervision and control, but also the small number of men of eminent virtues and talents who can be trusted not only to do without that supervision, but to exercise it themselves over others. So extraordinary are the faculties and energies required for performing this task in any supportable manner, that the good despot whom we are supposing can hardly be imagined as consenting to undertake it, unless as a refuge from intolerable evils, and a transitional preparation for something beyond. But the argument can do without even this immense item in the account. Suppose the difficulty vanquished. What should we then have? One man of superhuman mental activity managing the entire affairs of a mentally passive people. Their passivity is implied in the very idea of absolute power. The nation as a whole, and every individual composing it, are without any potential voice in their own destiny. They exercise no will in respect to their collective interests. All is decided for them by a will not their own, which it is legally a crime for them to disobey. What sort of human beings can be formed under such a regimen? What development can either their thinking or their active faculties attain under it? On matters of pure theory they might perhaps be allowed to speculate, so long as their speculations either did not approach politics, or had not the remotest connection with its practice. On practical affairs they could at most be only suffered to suggest; and even under the most moderate of despots, none but persons of already admitted or reputed superiority could hope that their suggestions would be known to, much less regarded by, those who had the management of affairs. A person must have a very unusual taste for intellectual exercise in and for itself, who will put himself to the trouble of thought when it is to have no outward effect, or qualify himself for functions which he has no chance of being allowed to exercise. The only sufficient incitement to mental exertion, in any but a few minds in a generation, is the prospect of some practical use to be made of its results. It does not follow that the nation will be wholly destitute of intellectual power. The common business of life, which must necessarily be performed by each individual or family for themselves, will call forth some amount of intelligence and practical ability, within a certain narrow range of ideas. There may be a select class of *savants*, who cultivate science with a view to its physical uses, or for the pleasure of the pursuit. There will be a bureaucracy, and persons in training for the bureaucracy, who will be taught at least some empirical maxims of government and public administration. There may be, and often has been, a systematic organisation of the best mental power in the country in some special direction (commonly military) to promote the grandeur of the despot. But the public at large remain without information and without interest on all the greater matters of practice; or, if they have any knowledge of them, it is but a *dilettante* knowledge, like that which people have of the mechanical arts who have never handled a tool. Nor is it only in their intelligence that they suffer. Their moral capacities are equally stunted. Wherever the sphere of action of human beings is artificially circumscribed, their sentiments are narrowed and dwarfed in the same proportion. The food of feeling is action: even domestic affection lives upon voluntary good offices. Let a person have nothing to do for his country, and he will not care for it. It has been said of old, that in a despotism there is at most but one patriot, the despot himself; and the saying rests on a just appreciation of the effects of absolute subjection, even to a good and wise master. Religion remains: and here at least, it may be thought, is an agency that may be relied on for lifting men's eyes and minds above the dust at their feet. But religion, even supposing it to escape perversion for the purposes of despotism, ceases in these circumstances to be a social concern, and narrows into a personal affair between an individual and his Maker, in which the issue at stake is but his private salvation. Religion in this shape is quite consistent with the most selfish and contracted egoism, and identifies the votary as little in feeling with the rest of his kind as sensuality itself.

A good despotism means a government in which, so far as depends on the despot, there is no positive oppression by officers of state, but in which all the collective interests of the people are managed for them, all the thinking that has relation to collective interests done for them, and in which their minds are formed by, and consenting to, this abdication of their own energies. Leaving things to the Government, like leaving them to Providence, is synonymous with caring nothing about them, and accepting their results, when disagreeable, as visitations of Nature. With the exception, therefore, of a few studious men who take an intellectual interest in speculation for its own sake, the intelligence and sentiments of the whole people are given up to the material interests, and, when these are provided for, to the amusement and ornamentation, of private life. But to say this is to say, if the whole testimony of history is worth anything, that the era of national decline has arrived: that is, if the nation had ever attained anything to decline from. If it has never risen above the condition of an Oriental people, in that condition it continues to stagnate. But if, like Greece or Rome, it had realised anything higher, through the energy, patriotism, and enlargement of mind, which as national qualities are the fruits solely of freedom, it relapses in a few generations into the Oriental state. And that state does not mean stupid tranquillity, with security against change for the worse; it often means being overrun, conquered, and reduced to domestic slavery, either by a stronger despot, or by the nearest barbarous people who retain along with their savage rudeness the energies of freedom.

Such are not merely the natural tendencies, but the inherent necessities of despotic government; from which there is no outlet, unless in so far as the despotism consents not to be despotism; in so far as the supposed good despot abstains from exercising his power, and, though holding it in reserve, allows the general business of government to go on as if the people really governed themselves. However little probable it may be, we may imagine a despot observing many of the rules and restraints of constitutional government. He might allow such freedom of the press and of discussion as would enable a public opinion to form and express itself on national affairs. He might suffer local interests to be managed, without the interference of authority, by the people themselves. He might even surround himself with a council or councils of government, freely chosen by the whole or some portion of the nation; retaining in his own hands the power of taxation, and the supreme legislative as well as executive authority. Were he to act thus, and so far abdicate as a despot, he would do away with a considerable part of the evils characteristic of despotism. Political activity and capacity for public affairs would no longer be prevented from growing up in the body of the nation; and a public opinion would form itself not the mere echo of the government. But such improvement would be the beginning of new difficulties. This public opinion, independent of the monarch's dictation, must be either with him or against him; if not the one, it will be the other. All governments must displease many persons, and these having now regular organs, and being able to express their sentiments, opinions adverse to the measures of government would often be expressed. What is the monarch to do when these unfavourable opinions happen to be in the majority? Is he to alter his course? Is he to defer to the nation? If so, he is no longer a despot, but a constitutional king; an organ or first minister of the people, distinguished only by being irremovable. If not, he must either put down opposition by his despotic power, or there will arise a permanent antagonism between the people and one man, which can have but one possible ending. Not even a religious principle of passive obedience and 'right divine' would long ward off the natural consequences of such a position. The monarch would have to succumb, and conform to the conditions of constitutional

140 REPRESENTATIVE GOVERNMENT

royalty, or give place to some one who would. The despotism, being thus chiefly nominal, would possess few of the advantages supposed to belong to absolute monarchy; while it would realise in a very imperfect degree those of a free government; since however great an amount of liberty the citizens might practically enjoy, they could never forget that they held it on sufferance, and by a concession which under the existing constitution of the State might at any moment be resumed; that they were legally slaves, though of a prudent, or indulgent, master.

It is not much to be wondered at if impatient or disappointed reformers, groaning under the impediments opposed to the most salutary public improvements by the ignorance, the indifference, the intractableness, the perverse obstinacy of a people, and the corrupt combinations of selfish private interests armed with the powerful weapons afforded by free institutions, should at times sigh for a strong hand to bear down all these obstacles, and compel a recalcitrant people to be better governed. But (setting aside the fact, that for one despot who now and then reforms an abuse, there are ninety-nine who do nothing but create them) those who look in any such direction for the realisation of their hopes leave out of the idea of good government its principal element, the improvement of the people themselves. One of the benefits of freedom is that under it the ruler cannot pass by the people's minds, and amend their affairs for them without amending them. If it were possible for the people to be well governed in spite of themselves, their good government would last no longer than the freedom of a people usually lasts who have been liberated by foreign arms without their own co-operation. It is true, a despot may educate the people; and to do so really, would be the best apology for his despotism. But any education which aims at making human beings other than machines, in the long run makes them claim to have the control of their own actions. The leaders of French philosophy in the eighteenth century had been educated by the Jesuits. Even Jesuit education, it seems, was sufficiently real to call forth the appetite for freedom. Whatever invigorates the faculties, in however small a measure, creates an increased desire for their more unimpeded exercise; and a popular education is a failure, if it educates the people for any state but that which it will certainly induce them to desire, and most probably to demand.

I am far from condemning, in cases of extreme exigency, the assumption of absolute power in the form of a temporary dictatorship.

Free nations have, in times of old, conferred such power by their own choice, as a necessary medicine for diseases of the body politic which could not be got rid of by less violent means. But its acceptance, even for a time strictly limited, can only be excused, if, like Solon or Pittacus, the dictator employs the whole power he assumes in removing the obstacles which debar the nation from the enjoyment of freedom. A good despotism is an altogether false ideal, which practically (except as a means to some temporary purpose) becomes the most senseless and dangerous of chimeras. Evil for evil, a good despotism, in a country at all advanced in civilisation, is more noxious than a bad one; for it is far more relaxing and enervating to the thoughts, feelings, and energies of the people. The despotism of Augustus prepared the Romans for Tiberius. If the whole tone of their character had not first been prostrated by nearly two generations of that mild slavery, they would probably have had spirit enough left to rebel against the more odious one.

There is no difficulty in showing that the ideally best form of government is that in which the sovereignty, or supreme controlling power in the last resort, is vested in the entire aggregate of the community; every citizen not only having a voice in the exercise of that ultimate sovereignty, but being, at least occasionally, called on to take an actual part in the government, by the personal discharge of some public function, local or general.

To test this proposition, it has to be examined in reference to the two branches into which, as pointed out in the last chapter, the inquiry into the goodness of a government conveniently divides itself, namely, how far it promotes the good management of the affairs of society by means of the existing faculties, moral, intellectual, and active, of its various members, and what is its effect in improving or deteriorating those faculties.

The ideally best form of government, it is scarcely necessary to say, does not mean one which is practicable or eligible in all states of civilisation, but the one which, in the circumstances in which it is practicable and eligible, is attended with the greatest amount of beneficial consequences, immediate and prospective. A completely popular government is the only polity which can make out any claim to this character. It is pre-eminent in both the departments between which the excellence of a political constitution is divided. It is both more favourable to present good government, and promotes a better and higher form of national character, than any other polity whatsoever.

Its superiority in reference to present well-being rests upon two principles, of as universal truth and applicability as any general propositions which can be laid down respecting human affairs. The first is, that the rights and interests of every or any person are only secure from being disregarded when the person interested is himself able, and habitually disposed, to stand up for them. The second is, that the general prosperity attains a greater height, and is more widely diffused, in proportion to the amount and variety of the personal energies enlisted in promoting it.

Putting these two propositions into a shape more special to their present application; human beings are only secure from evil at the hands of others in proportion as they have the power of being, and are, self-*protecting*; and they only achieve a high degree of success in their struggle with Nature in proportion as they are self-*dependent*, relying on what they themselves can do, either separately or in concert, rather than on what others do for them.

The former proposition—that each is the only safe guardian of his own rights and interests—is one of those elementary maxims of prudence, which every person, capable of conducting his own affairs, implicitly acts upon, wherever he himself is interested. Many, indeed, have a great dislike to it as a political doctrine, and are fond of holding it up to obloquy, as a doctrine of universal selfishness. To which we may answer, that whenever it ceases to be true that mankind, as a rule, prefer themselves to others, and those nearest to them to those more remote, from that moment Communism is not only practicable, but the only defensible form of society; and will, when that time arrives, be assuredly carried into effect. For my own part, not believing in universal selfishness, I have no difficulty in admitting that Communism would even now be practicable among the *élite* of mankind, and may become so among the rest. But as this opinion is anything but popular with those defenders of existing institutions who find fault with the doctrine of the general predominance of self-interest, I am inclined to think they do in reality believe that most men consider themselves before other people. It is not, however, necessary to affirm even this much in order to support the claim of all to participate in the sovereign power. We need not suppose that when power resides in an exclusive class, that class will knowingly and deliberately sacrifice the other classes to themselves: it suffices that, in the absence of its natural defenders, the interest of the excluded is always in danger of being overlooked; and, when looked at, is seen with very different eyes from those of the persons whom it directly concerns. In this country, for example, what are called the working classes may be considered as excluded from all direct participation in the government. I do not believe that the classes who do participate in it have in general any intention of sacrificing the working classes to themselves. They once had that intention; witness the persevering attempts so long made to keep down wages by law. But in the present day their ordinary disposition is the very opposite: they willingly make considerable sacrifices, especially of their pecuniary interest, for the benefit of the working classes, and err rather by too lavish and indiscriminating beneficence; nor do I believe that any rulers in history have been actuated by a more sincere desire to do their duty towards the poorer portion of their countrymen. Yet does Parliament, or almost any of the members composing it, ever for an instant look at any question with the eyes of a working man? When a subject arises in which the labourers as such have an interest, is it regarded from any point of view but that of the employers of labour? I do not say that the working men's view of these questions is in general nearer to the truth than the other: but it is sometimes quite as near; and in any case it ought to be respectfully listened to, instead of being, as it is, not merely turned away from, but ignored. On the question of strikes, for instance, it is doubtful if there is so much as one among the leading members of either House who is not firmly convinced that the reason of the matter in unqualifiedly on the side of the masters, and that the men's view of it is simply absurd. Those who have studied the question know well how far this is from being the case; and in how different, and how infinitely less superficial a manner the point would have to be argued, if the classes who strike were able to make themselves heard in Parliament.

It is an adherent condition of human affairs that no intention, however sincere, of protecting the interests of others can make it safe or salutary to tie up their own hands. Still more obviously true is it, that by their own hands only can any positive and durable improvement of their circumstances in life be worked out. Through the joint influence of these two principles, all free communities have both been more exempt from social injustice and crime, and have attained more brilliant prosperity, than any others, or than they themselves after they lost their freedom. Contrast the free states of the world, while their freedom lasted, with the contemporary subjects of monarchical or

144   REPRESENTATIVE GOVERNMENT

oligarchical despotism: the Greek cities with the Persian satrapies; the Italian republics and the free towns of Flanders and Germany, with the feudal monarchies of Europe; Switzerland, Holland, and England, with Austria or ante-revolutionary France. Their superior prosperity was too obvious ever to have been gainsaid: while their superiority in good government and social relations is proved by the prosperity, and is manifest besides in every page of history. If we compare, not one age with another, but the different governments which co-existed in the same age, no amount of disorder which exaggeration itself can pretend to have existed amidst the publicity of the free states can be compared for a moment with the contemptuous trampling upon the mass of the people which pervaded the whole life of the monarchical countries, or the disgusting individual tyranny which was of more than daily occurrence under the systems of plunder which they called fiscal arrangements, and in the secrecy of their frightful courts of justice.

It must be acknowledged that the benefits of freedom, so far as they have hitherto been enjoyed, were obtained by the extension of its privileges to a part only of the community; and that a government in which they are extended impartially to all is a desideratum still un-realised. But though every approach to this has an independent value, and in many cases more than an approach could not, in the existing state of general improvement, be made, the participation of all in these benefits is the ideally perfect conception of free government. In proportion as any, no matter who, are excluded from it, the interests of the excluded are left without the guarantee accorded to the rest, and they themselves have less scope and encouragement than they might otherwise have to that exertion of their energies for the good of themselves and of the community, to which the general prosperity is always proportioned.

Thus stands the case as regards present well-being; the good management of the affairs of the existing generation. If we now pass to the influence of the form of government upon character, we shall find the superiority of popular government over every other to be, if possible, still more decided and indisputable.

This question really depends upon a still more fundamental one, viz., which of two common types of character, for the general good of humanity, it is most desirable should predominate—the active, or the passive type; that which struggles against evils, or that which endures them; that which bends to circumstances, or that which endeavours to make circumstances bend to itself.

THE IDEALLY BEST POLITY 145

The commonplaces of moralists, and the general sympathies of mankind, are in favour of the passive type. Energetic characters may be admired, but the acquiescent and submissive are those which most men personally prefer. The passiveness of our neighbours increases our sense of security, and plays into the hands of our wilfulness. Passive characters, if we do not happen to need their activity, seem an obstruction the less in our own path. A contented character is not a dangerous rival. Yet nothing is more certain than that improvement in human affairs is wholly the work of the uncontented characters; and, moreover, that it is much easier for an active mind to acquire the virtues of patience than for a passive one to assume those of energy.

Of the three varieties of mental excellence, intellectual, practical, and moral, there never could be any doubt in regard to the first two which side had the advantage. All intellectual superiority is the fruit of active effort. Enterprise, the desire to keep moving, to be trying and accomplishing new things for our own benefit or that of others, is the parent even of speculative, and much more of practical, talent. The intellectual culture compatible with the other type is of that feeble and vague description which belongs to a mind that stops at amusement, or at simple contemplation. The test of real and vigorous thinking, the thinking which ascertains truths instead of dreaming dreams, is successful application to practice. Where that purpose does not exist, to give definiteness, precision, and an intelligible meaning to thought, it generates nothing better than the mystical metaphysics of the Pythagoreans or the Vedas. With respect to practical improvement, the case is still more evident. The character which improves human life is that which struggles with natural powers and tendencies, not that which gives way to them. The self-benefiting qualities are all on the side of the active and energetic character: and the habits and conduct which promote the advantage of each individual member of the community must be at least a part of those which conduce most in the end to the advancement of the community as a whole.

But on the point of moral preferability, there seems at first sight to be room for doubt. I am not referring to the religious feeling which has so generally existed in favour of the inactive character, as being more in harmony with the submission due to the divine will. Christianity as well as other religions has fostered this sentiment; but it is the prerogative of Christianity, as regards this and many other perversions, that it is able to throw them off. Abstractedly from religious considerations, a passive character, which yields to obstacles

K

instead of striving to overcome them, may not indeed be very useful to others, no more than to itself, but it might be expected to be at least inoffensive. Contentment is always counted among the moral virtues. But it is a complete error to suppose that contentment is necessarily or naturally attendant on passivity of character; and useless it is, the moral consequences are mischievous. Where there exists a desire for advantages not possessed, the mind which does not poten- tially possess them by means of its own energies is apt to look with hatred and malice on those who do. The person bestirring himself with hopeful prospects to improve his circumstances is the one who feels good-will towards others engaged in, or who have succeeded in, the same pursuit. And where the majority are so engaged, those who do not attain the object have had the tone given to their feelings by the general habit of the country, and ascribe their failure to want of effort or opportunity, or to their personal ill luck. But those who, while desiring what others possess, put no energy into striving for it, are either incessantly grumbling that fortune does not do for them what they do not attempt to do for themselves, or overflowing with envy and ill-will towards those who possess what they would like to have.

In proportion as success in life is seen or believed to be the fruit of fatality or accident, and not of exertion, in that same ratio does envy develop itself as a point of national character. The most envious of all mankind are the Orientals. In Oriental moralists, in Oriental tales, the envious man is remarkably prominent. In real life, he is the terror of all who possess anything desirable, be it a palace, a handsome child, or even good health and spirits: the supposed effect of his mere look constitutes the all-pervading superstition of the evil eye. Next to Orientals in envy, as in activity, are some of the Southern Europeans. The Spaniards pursued all their great men with it, embittered their lives, and generally succeeded in putting an early stop to their successes.[1] With the French, who are essentially a southern people, the double education of despotism and Catholicism has, in spite of their impulsive temperament, made submission and endurance the common character of the people, and their most received notion of wisdom and excellence: and if envy of one another, and of all superiority, is not more rife among them than it is, the circumstance must be

---

[1] I limit the expression to past time, because I would say nothing derogatory of a great, and now at last a free, people, who are entering into the general movement of European progress with a vigour which bids fair to make up rapidly the ground they have lost. No one can doubt what Spanish intellect and energy are capable of; and their faults as a people are chiefly those for which freedom and industrial ardour are a real specific.

THE IDEALLY BEST POLITY 147

ascribed to the many valuable counteracting elements in the French character, and most of all to the great individual energy which, though less persistent and more intermittent than in the self-helping and struggling Anglo-Saxons, has nevertheless manifested itself among the French in nearly every direction in which the operation of their institutions has been favourable to it.

There are, no doubt, in all countries, really contented characters, who not merely do not seek, but do not desire, what they do not already possess, and these naturally bear no ill-will towards such as have apparently a more favoured lot. But the great mass of seeming contentment is real discontent, combined with indolence or self-indulgence, which, while taking no legitimate means of raising itself, delights in bringing others down to its own level. And if we look narrowly even at the cases of innocent contentment, we perceive that they only win our admiration when the indifference is solely to improvement in outward circumstances, and there is a striving for perpetual advancement in spiritual worth, or at least a disinterested zeal to benefit others. The contented man, or the contented family, who have no ambition to make any one else happier, to promote the good of their country or their neighbourhood, or to improve themselves in moral excellence, excite in us neither admiration nor approval. We rightly ascribe this sort of contentment to mere unmanliness and want of spirit. The content which we approve is an ability to do cheerfully without what cannot be had, a just appreciation of the comparative value of different objects of desire, and a willing renunciation of the less when incompatible with the greater. These, however, are excellences more natural to the character, in proportion as it is actively engaged in the attempt to improve its own or some other lot. He who is continually measuring his energy against difficulties learns what are the difficulties insuperable to him, and what are those which, though he might overcome, the success is not worth the cost. He whose thoughts and activities are all needed for, and habitually employed in, practicable and useful enterprises, is the person of all others least likely to let his mind dwell with brooding discontent upon things either not worth attaining, or which are not so to him. Thus the active, self-helping character is not only intrinsically the best, but is the likeliest to acquire all that is really excellent or desirable in the opposite type.

The striving, go-ahead character of England and the United States is only a fit subject of disapproving criticism on account of the very secondary objects on which it commonly expends its strength. In itself it is the foundation of the best hopes for the general improvement of mankind. It has been acutely remarked that whenever anything goes amiss the habitual impulse of French people is to say, 'Il faut de la patience'; and of English people, 'What a shame.' The people who think it a shame when anything goes wrong—who rush to the conclusion that the evil could and ought to have been prevented, are those who, in the long run, do most to make the world better. If the desires are low placed, if they extend to little beyond physical comfort, and the show of riches, the immediate results of the energy will not be much more than the continual extension of man's power over material objects; but even this makes room, and prepares the mechanical appliances, for the greatest intellectual and social achievements; and while the energy is there, some persons will apply it, and it will be applied more and more, to the perfecting not of outward circumstances alone, but of man's inward nature. Inactivity, unaspiringness, absence of desire, are a more fatal hindrance to improvement than any misdirection of energy; and are that through which alone, when existing in the mass, any very formidable misdirection by an energetic few becomes possible. It is this, mainly, which retains in a savage or semi-savage state the great majority of the human race.

Now there can be no kind of doubt that the passive type of character is favoured by the government of one or a few, and the active self-helping type by that of the Many. Irresponsible rulers need the quiescence of the ruled more than they need any activity but that which they can compel. Submissiveness to the prescriptions of men as necessities of nature is the lesson inculcated by all governments upon those who are wholly without participation in them. The will of superiors, and the law as the will of superiors, must be passively yielded to. But no men are mere instruments or materials in the hands of their rulers who have will or spirit or a spring of internal activity in the rest of their proceedings: and any manifestation of these qualities, instead of receiving encouragement from despots, has to get itself forgiven by them. Even when irresponsible rulers are not sufficiently conscious of danger from the mental activity of their subjects to be desirous of repressing it, the position itself is a repression. Endeavour is even more effectually restrained by the certainty of its impotence than by any positive discouragement. Between subjection to the will of others, and the virtues of self-help and self-government, there is a natural incompatibility. This is more or less complete, according as the bondage is strained or relaxed. Rulers differ very much in the length to which they carry the control of the free agency of their subjects, or the suppression of it by managing their business for them. But the difference is in degree, not in principle; and the best despots often go the greatest lengths in chaining up the free agency of their subjects. A bad despot, when his own personal indulgences have been provided for, may sometimes be willing to let the people alone; but a good despot insists on doing them good, by making them do their own business in a better way than they themselves know of. The regulations which restricted to fixed processes all the leading branches of French manufactures were the work of the great Colbert.

Very different is the state of the human faculties where a human being feels himself under no other external restraint than the necessities of nature, or mandates of society which he has his share in imposing, and which it is open to him, if he thinks them wrong, publicly to dissent from, and exert himself actively to get altered. No doubt, under a government partially popular, this freedom may be exercised even by those who are not partakers in the full privileges of citizenship. But it is a great additional stimulus to any one's self-help and self-reliance when he starts from even ground, and has not to feel that his success depends on the impression he can make upon the sentiments and dispositions of a body of whom he is not one. It is a great discouragement to an individual, and a still greater one to a class, to be left out of the constitution; to be reduced to plead from outside the door to the arbiters of their destiny, not taken into consultation within. The maximum of the invigorating effect of freedom upon the character is only obtained when the person acted on either is, or is looking forward to becoming, a citizen as fully privileged as any other. What is still more important than even this matter of feeling is the practical discipline which the character obtains from the occasional demand made upon the citizens to exercise, for a time and in their turn, some social function. It is not sufficiently considered how little there is in most men's ordinary life to give any largeness either to their conceptions or to their sentiments. Their work is a routine; not a labour of love, but of self-interest in the most elementary form, the satisfaction of daily wants; neither the thing done, nor the process of doing it, introduces the mind to thoughts or feelings extending beyond individuals; if instructive books are within their reach, there is no stimulus to read them; and in most cases the individual has no access to any person of cultivation much superior to his own. Giving him something to do for the public, supplies, in a measure, all these deficiencies. If circumstances allow the amount of public duty assigned him to be considerable, it makes him an educated man. Notwithstanding the defects of the social system and moral ideas of antiquity, the practice of the dicastery and the ecclesia raised the intellectual standard of an average Athenian citizen far beyond anything of which there is yet an example in any other mass of men, ancient or modern. The proofs of this are apparent in every page of our great historian of Greece; but we need scarcely look further than to the high quality of the addresses which their great orators deemed best calculated to act with effect on their understanding and will. A benefit of the same kind, though far less in degree, is produced on Englishmen of the lower middle class by their liability to be placed on juries and to serve parish offices; which, though it does not occur to so many, nor is so continuous, nor introduces them to so great a variety of elevated considerations, as to admit of comparison with the public education which every citizen of Athens obtained from her democratic institutions, must make them nevertheless very different beings, in range of ideas and development of faculties, from those who have done nothing in their lives but drive a quill, or sell goods over a counter. Still more salutary is the moral part of the instruction afforded by the participation of the private citizen, if even rarely, in public functions. He is called upon, while so engaged, to weigh interests not his own; to be guided, in case of conflicting claims, by another rule than his private partialities; to apply, at every turn, principles and maxims which have for their reason of existence the common good: and he usually finds associated with him in the same work minds more familiarised than his own with these ideas and operations, whose study it will be to supply reasons to his understanding, and stimulation to his feeling for the general interest. He is made to feel himself one of the public, and whatever is for their benefit to be for his benefit. Where this school of public spirit does not exist, scarcely any sense is entertained that private persons, in no eminent social situation, owe any duties to society, except to obey the laws and submit to the government. There is no unselfish sentiment of identification with the public. Every thought or feeling, either of interest or of duty, is absorbed in the individual and in the family. The man never thinks of any collective interest, of any objects to be pursued jointly with others, but only in competition with them, and in some measure at their expense. A neighbour, not being an ally or an associate, since he is never engaged in any common undertaking for joint benefit, is therefore only a rival. Thus even private morality suffers, while public is actually extinct. Were this the universal and only possible state of things, the utmost aspirations of the lawgiver or the moralist could only stretch to make the bulk of the community a flock of sheep innocently nibbling the grass side by side.

From these accumulated considerations it is evident that the only government which can fully satisfy all the exigencies of the social state is one in which the whole people participate; that any participation, even in the smallest public function, is useful; that the participation should everywhere be as great as the general degree of improvement of the community will allow; and that nothing less can be ultimately desirable than the admission of all to a share in the sovereign power of the State. But since all cannot, in a community exceeding a single small town, participate personally in any but some very minor portions of the public business, it follows that the ideal type of a perfect government must be representative.

[9]

Excerpt from *The Subjection of Women*, 3–29

CHAPTER I

THE object of this Essay is to explain as clearly as I am able, the grounds of an opinion which I have held from the very earliest period when I had formed any opinions at all on social or political matters, and which, instead of being weakened or modified, has been constantly growing stronger by the progress of reflection and the experience of life. That the principle which regulates the existing social relations between the two sexes—the legal subordination of one sex to the other—is wrong in itself, and now one of the chief hindrances to human improvement; and that it ought to be replaced by a principle of perfect equality, admitting no power or privilege on the one side, nor disability on the other.

The very words necessary to express the task I have undertaken, show how arduous it is. But it would be a mistake to suppose that the difficulty of the case must lie in the insufficiency or obscurity of the grounds of reason on which my conviction rests. The difficulty is that which exists in all cases in which there is a mass of feeling to be contended against. So long as an opinion is strongly rooted in the feelings, it gains rather than loses in stability by having a preponderating weight of argument against it. For if it were accepted as a result of argument, the refutation of the argument might shake the solidity of the conviction; but when it rests solely on feeling, the worse it fares in argumentative contest, the more persuaded its adherents are that their feeling must have some deeper ground, which the arguments do not reach; and while the feeling remains, it is always throwing up fresh intrenchments of argument to repair any breach made in the old. And there are so many causes tending to make the feelings connected with this subject the most intense and most deeply-rooted of all those which gather round and protect old institutions and customs, that we need not wonder to find them as yet less undermined and loosened than any of the rest by the progress of the great modern spiritual and social transition; nor suppose that the barbarisms to which men cling longest must be less barbarisms than those which they earlier shake off.

3

4   THE SUBJECTION OF WOMEN

In every respect the burthen is hard on those who attack an almost universal opinion. They must be very fortunate as well as unusually capable if they obtain a hearing at all. They have more difficulty in obtaining a trial, than any other litigants have in getting a verdict. If they do extort a hearing, they are subjected to a set of logical requirements totally different from those exacted from other people. In all other cases, the burthen of proof is supposed to lie with the affirmative. If a person is charged with a murder, it rests with those who accuse him to give proof of his guilt, not with himself to prove his innocence. If there is a difference of opinion about the reality of an alleged historical event, in which the feelings of men in general are not much interested, as the Siege of Troy for example, those who maintain that the event took place are expected to produce their proofs, before those who take the other side can be required to say anything; and at no time are these required to do more than show that the evidence produced by the others is of no value. Again, in practical matters, the burthen of proof is supposed to be with those who are against liberty; who contend for any restriction or prohibition; either any limitation of the general freedom of human action, or any disqualification or disparity of privilege affecting one person or kind of persons, as compared with others. The *à priori* presumption is in favour of freedom and impartiality. It is held that there should be no restraint not required by the general good, and that the law should be no respecter of persons, but should treat all alike, save where dissimilarity of treatment is required by positive reasons, either of justice or of policy. But of none of these rules of evidence will the benefit be allowed to those who maintain the opinion I profess. It is useless for me to say that those who maintain the doctrine that men have a right to command and women are under an obligation to obey, or that men are fit for government and women unfit, are on the affirmative side of the question, and that they are bound to show positive evidence for the assertions, or submit to their rejection. It is equally unavailing for me to say that those who deny to women any freedom or privilege rightly allowed to men, having the double presumption against them that they are opposing freedom and recommending partiality, must be held to the strictest proof of their case, and unless their success be such as to exclude all doubt, the judgment ought to go against them. These would be thought good pleas in any common case; but they will not be thought so in this instance.

JOHN STUART MILL   5

Before I could hope to make any impression, I should be expected not only to answer all that has ever been said by those who take the other side of the question, but to imagine all that could be said by them—to find them in reasons, as well as answer all I find: and besides refuting all arguments for the affirmative, I shall be called upon for invincible positive arguments to prove a negative. And even if I could do all this, and leave the opposite party with a host of unanswered arguments against them, and not a single unrefuted one on their side, I should be thought to have done little; for a cause supported on the one hand by universal usage, and on the other by so great a preponderance of popular sentiment, is supposed to have a presumption in its favour, superior to any conviction which an appeal to reason has power to produce in any intellects but those of a high class.

I do not mention these difficulties to complain of them; first, because it would be useless; they are inseparable from having to contend through people's understandings against the hostility of their feelings and practical tendencies: and truly the understandings of the majority of mankind would need to be much better cultivated than has ever yet been the case, before they can be asked to place such reliance in their own power of estimating arguments, as to give up practical principles in which they have been born and bred and which are the basis of much of the existing order of the world, at the first argumentative attack which they are not capable of logically resisting. I do not therefore quarrel with them for having too little faith in argument, but for having too much faith in custom and the general feeling. It is one of the characteristic prejudices of the reaction of the nineteenth century against the eighteenth, to accord to the unreasoning elements in human nature the infallibility which the eighteenth century is supposed to have ascribed to the reasoning elements. For the apotheosis of Reason we have substituted that of Instinct; and we call everything instinct which we find in ourselves and for which we cannot trace any rational foundation. This idolatry, infinitely more degrading than the other, and the most pernicious of the false worships of the present day, of all of which it is now the main support, will probably hold its ground until it gives way before a sound psychology laying bare the real root of much that is bowed down to as the intention of Nature and the ordinance of God. As regards the present question, I am willing to accept the unfavourable conditions which the prejudice

*H 825

6   THE SUBJECTION OF WOMEN

assigns to me. I consent that established custom, and the general feeling, should be deemed conclusive against me, unless that custom and feeling from age to age can be shown to have owed their existence to other causes than their soundness, and to have derived their power from the worse rather than the better parts of human nature. I am willing that judgment should go against me, unless I can show that my judge has been tampered with. The concession is not so great as it might appear; for to prove this, is by far the easiest portion of my task.

The generality of a practice is in some cases a strong presumption that it is, or at all events once was, conducive to laudable ends. This is the case, when the practice was first adopted, or afterwards kept up, as a means to such ends, and was grounded on experience of the mode in which they could be most effectually attained. If the authority of men over women, when first established, had been the result of a conscientious comparison between different modes of constituting the government of society; if, after trying various other modes of social organisation—the government of women over men, equality between the two, and such mixed and divided modes of government as might be invented—it had been decided, on the testimony of experience, that the mode in which women are wholly under the rule of men, having no share at all in public concerns, and each in private being under the legal obligation of obedience to the man with whom she has associated her destiny, was the arrangement most conducive to the happiness and well-being of both; its general adoption might then be fairly thought to be some evidence that, at the time when it was adopted, it was the best: though even then the considerations which recommended it may, like so many other primeval social facts of the greatest importance, have subsequently, in the course of ages, ceased to exist. But the state of the case is in every respect the reverse of this. In the first place, the opinion in favour of the present system, which entirely subordinates the weaker sex to the stronger, rests upon theory only; for there never has been trial made of any other: so that experience, in the sense in which it is vulgarly opposed to theory, cannot be pretended to have pronounced any verdict. And in the second place, the adoption of this system of inequality never was the result of deliberation, or forethought, or any social ideas, or any notion whatever of what conduced to the benefit of humanity or the good order of society. It arose simply from the fact that from the very earliest twilight of

JOHN STUART MILL   7

human society, every woman (owing to the value attached to her by men, combined with her inferiority in muscular strength) was found in a state of bondage to some man. Laws and systems of polity always begin by recognising the relations they find already existing between individuals. They convert what was a mere physical fact into a legal right, give it the sanction of society, and principally aim at the substitution of public and organised means of asserting and protecting these rights, instead of the irregular and lawless conflict of physical strength. Those who had already been compelled to obedience became in this manner legally bound to it. Slavery, from being a mere affair of force between the master and the slave, became regularised and a matter of compact among the masters, who, binding themselves to one another for common protection, guaranteed by their collective strength the private possessions of each, including his slaves. In early times, the great majority of the male sex were slaves, as well as the whole of the female. And many ages elapsed, some of them ages of high cultivation, before any thinker was bold enough to question the rightfulness, and the absolute social necessity, either of the one slavery or of the other. By degrees such thinkers did arise; and (the general progress of society assisting) the slavery of the male sex has, in all the countries of Christian Europe at least (though, in one of them, only within the last few years) been at length abolished, and that of the female sex has been gradually changed into a milder form of dependence. But this dependence, as it exists at present, is not an original institution, taking a fresh start from considerations of justice and social expediency—it is the primitive state of slavery lasting on, through successive mitigations and modifications occasioned by the same causes which have softened the general manners, and brought all human relations more under the control of justice and the influence of humanity. It has not lost the taint of its brutal origin. No presumption in its favour, therefore, can be drawn from the fact of its existence. The only such presumption which it could be supposed to have, must be grounded on its having lasted till now, when so many other things which came down from the same odious source have been done away with. And this, indeed, is what makes it strange to ordinary ears, to hear it asserted that the inequality of rights between men and women has no other source than the law of the strongest.

 That this statement should have the effect of a paradox, is in some respects creditable to the progress of civilisation, and

8   THE SUBJECTION OF WOMEN

the improvement of the moral sentiments of mankind.   We now live—that is to say, one or two of the most advanced nations of the world now live—in a state in which the law of the strongest seems to be entirely abandoned as the regulating principle of the world's affairs: nobody professes it, and, as regards most of the relations between human beings, nobody is permitted to practise it.   When anyone succeeds in doing so, it is under cover of some pretext which gives him the semblance of having some general social interest on his side.   This being the ostensible state of things, people flatter themselves that the rule of mere force is ended; that the law of the strongest cannot be the reason of existence of anything which has remained in full operation down to the present time.   However any of our present institutions may have begun, it can only, they think, have been preserved to this period of advanced civilisation by a well-grounded feeling of its adaptation to human nature, and conduciveness to the general good.   They do not understand the great vitality and durability of institutions which place right on the side of might; how intensely they are clung to; how the good as well as the bad propensities and sentiments of those who have power in their hands, become identified with retaining it; how slowly these bad institutions give way, one at a time, the weakest first, beginning with those which are least interwoven with the daily habits of life; and how very rarely those who have obtained legal power because they first had physical, have ever lost their hold of it until the physical power had passed over to the other side.   Such shifting of the physical force not having taken place in the case of women; this fact, combined with all the peculiar and characteristic features of the particular case, made it certain from the first that this branch of the system of right founded on might, though softened in its most atrocious features at an earlier period than several of the others, would be the very last to disappear.   It was inevitable that this one case of a social relation grounded on force, would survive through generations of institutions grounded on equal justice, an almost solitary exception to the general character of their laws and customs; but which, so long as it does not proclaim its own origin, and as discussion has not brought out its true character, is not felt to jar with modern civilisation, any more than domestic slavery among the Greeks jarred with their notion of themselves as a free people.

The truth is, that people of the present and the last two or three generations have lost all practical sense of the primitive

JOHN STUART MILL   9

condition of humanity; and only the few who have studied
history accurately, or have much frequented the parts of the
world occupied by the living representatives of ages long past,
are able to form any mental picture of what society then was.
People are not aware how entirely, in former ages, the law of
superior strength was the rule of life; how publicly and openly
it was avowed, I do not say cynically or shamelessly—for these
words imply a feeling that there was something in it to be
ashamed of, and no such notion could find a place in the faculties
of any person in those ages, except a philosopher or a saint.
History gives a cruel experience of human nature, in showing
how exactly the regard due to the life, possessions, and entire
earthly happiness of any class of persons, was measured by
what they had the power of enforcing; how all who made any
resistance to authorities that had arms in their hands, however
dreadful might be the provocation, had not only the law of
force but all other laws, and all the notions of social obligation
against them; and in the eyes of those whom they resisted,
were not only guilty of crime, but of the worst of all crimes,
deserving the most cruel chastisement which human beings
could inflict.   The first small vestige of a feeling of obligation
in a superior to acknowledge any right in inferiors, began when
he had been induced, for convenience, to make some promise
to them.   Though these promises, even when sanctioned by
the most solemn oaths, were for many ages revoked or violated
on the most trifling provocation or temptation, it is probable
that this, except by persons of still worse than the average
morality, was seldom done without some twinges of conscience.
The ancient republics, being mostly grounded from the first
upon some kind of mutual compact, or at any rate formed by
an union of persons not very unequal in strength, afforded, in
consequence, the first instance of a portion of human relations
fenced round, and placed under the dominion of another law
than that of force.   And though the original law of force
remained in full operation between them and their slaves, and
also (except so far as limited by express compact) between a
commonwealth and its subjects, or other independent commonwealths; the banishment of that primitive law even from so
narrow a field, commenced the regeneration of human nature,
by giving birth to sentiments of which experience soon demonstrated the immense value even for material interests, and
which thenceforward only required to be enlarged, not created.
Though **slaves** were no part of the commonwealth, it was in

10   THE SUBJECTION OF WOMEN

the free states that slaves were first felt to have rights as human beings. The Stoics were, I believe, the first (except so far as the Jewish law constitutes an exception) who taught as a part of morality that men were bound by moral obligations to their slaves. No one, after Christianity became ascendant, could ever again have been a stranger to this belief, in theory; nor, after the rise of the Catholic Church, was it ever without persons to stand up for it. Yet to enforce it was the most arduous task which Christianity ever had to perform. For more than a thousand years the Church kept up the contest, with hardly any perceptible success. It was not for want of power over men's minds. Its power was prodigious. It could make kings and nobles resign their most valued possessions to enrich the Church. It could make thousands in the prime of life and the height of worldly advantages, shut themselves up in convents to work out their salvation by poverty, fasting, and prayer. It could send hundreds of thousands across land and sea, Europe and Asia, to give their lives for the deliverance of the Holy Sepulchre. It could make kings relinquish wives who were the object of their passionate attachment, because the Church declared that they were within the seventh (by our calculation the fourteenth) degree of relationship. All this it did; but it could not make men fight less with one another, nor tyrannise less cruelly over the serfs, and when they were able, over burgesses. It could not make them renounce either of the applications of force; force militant, or force triumphant. This they could never be induced to do until they were themselves in their turn compelled by superior force. Only by the growing power of kings was an end put to fighting except between kings, or competitors for kingship; only by the growth of a wealthy and warlike bourgeoisie in the fortified towns, and of a plebeian infantry which proved more powerful in the field than the undisciplined chivalry, was the insolent tyranny of the nobles over the bourgeoisie and peasantry brought within some bounds. It was persisted in not only until, but long after, the oppressed had obtained a power enabling them often to take conspicuous vengeance; and on the Continent much of it continued to the time of the French Revolution, though in England the earlier and better organisation of the democratic classes put an end to it sooner, by establishing equal laws and free national institutions.

If people are mostly so little aware how completely, during the greater part of the duration of our species, the law of force

was the avowed rule of general conduct, any other being only
a special and exceptional consequence of peculiar ties—and
from how very recent a date it is that the affairs of society in
general have been even pretended to be regulated according to
any moral law; as little do people remember or consider, how
institutions and customs which never had any ground but the
law of force, last on into ages and states of general opinion
which never would have permitted their first establishment.
Less than forty years ago, Englishmen might still by law hold
human beings in bondage as saleable property: within the present
century they might kidnap them and carry them off, and work
them literally to death. This absolutely extreme case of the
law of force, condemned by those who can tolerate almost every
other form of arbitrary power, and which, of all others presents
features the most revolting to the feelings of all who look at it
from an impartial position, was the law of civilised and Christian
England within the memory of persons now living: and in one
half of Anglo-Saxon America three or four years ago, not only
did slavery exist, but the slave-trade, and the breeding of
slaves expressly for it, was a general practice between slave-
states. Yet not only was there a greater strength of sentiment against it, but, in England at least, a less amount either
of feeling or of interest in favour of it, than of any other of the
customary abuses of force: for its motive was the love of gain,
unmixed and undisguised; and those who profited by it were
a very small numerical fraction of the country, while the natural
feeling of all who were not personally interested in it, was unmitigated abhorrence. So extreme an instance makes it almost
superfluous to refer to any other: but consider the long duration
of absolute monarchy. In England at present it is the almost
universal conviction that military despotism is a case of the
law of force, having no other origin or justification. Yet in
all the great nations of Europe except England it either still
exists, or has only just ceased to exist, and has even now a
strong party favourable to it in all ranks of the people, especially
among persons of station and consequence. Such is the power
of an established system, even when far from universal; when
not only in almost every period of history there have been
great and well-known examples of the contrary system, but
these have almost invariably been afforded by the most illustrious
and most prosperous communities. In this case, too, the possessor of the undue power, the person directly interested in it,
is only one person, while those who are subject to it and suffer

12   THE SUBJECTION OF WOMEN

from it are literally all the rest. The yoke is naturally and necessarily humiliating to all persons, except the one who is on the throne, together with, at most, the one who expects to succeed to it. How different are these cases from that of the power of men over women! I am not now prejudging the question of its justifiableness. I am showing how vastly more permanent it could not but be, even if not justifiable, than these other dominations which have nevertheless lasted down to our own time. Whatever gratification of pride there is in the possession of power, and whatever personal interest in its exercise, is in this case not confined to a limited class, but common to the whole male sex. Instead of being, to most of its supporters, a thing desirable chiefly in the abstract, or, like the political ends usually contended for by factions, of little private importance to any but the leaders; it comes home to the person and hearth of every male head of a family, and of everyone who looks forward to being so. The clodhopper exercises, or is to exercise, his share of the power equally with the highest nobleman. And the case is that in which the desire of power is the strongest: for everyone who desires power, desires it most over those who are nearest to him, with whom his life is passed, with whom he has most concerns in common, and in whom any independence of his authority is oftenest likely to interfere with his individual preferences. If, in the other cases specified, powers manifestly grounded only on force, and having so much less to support them, are so slowly and with so much difficulty got rid of, much more must it be so with this, even if it rests on no better foundation than those. We must consider, too, that the possessors of the power have facilities in this case, greater than in any other, to prevent any uprising against it. Every one of the subjects lives under the very eye, and almost, it may be said, in the hands, of one of the masters— in closer intimacy with him than with any of her fellow-subjects; with no means of combining against him, no power of even locally overmastering him, and, on the other hand, with the strongest motives for seeking his favour and avoiding to give him offence. In struggles for political emancipation, everybody knows how often its champions are bought off by bribes, or daunted by terrors. In the case of women, each individual of the subject-class is in a chronic state of bribery and intimidation combined. In setting up the standard of resistance, a large number of the leaders, and still more of the followers, must make an almost complete sacrifice of the pleasures or the alleviations of their

JOHN STUART MILL   13

own individual lot. If ever any system of privilege and enforced subjection had its yoke tightly riveted on the necks of
those who are kept down by it, this has. I have not yet shown
that it is a wrong system: but everyone who is capable of
thinking on the subject must see that even if it is, it was certain
to outlast all other forms of unjust authority. And when some
of the grossest of the other forms still exist in many civilised
countries, and have only recently been got rid of in others, it
would be strange if that which is so much the deepest rooted
had yet been perceptibly shaken anywhere. There is more
reason to wonder that the protests and testimonies against it
should have been so numerous and so weighty as they are.

Some will object, that a comparison cannot fairly be made
between the government of the male sex and the forms of
unjust power which I have adduced in illustration of it, since
these are arbitrary, and the effect of mere usurpation, while it
on the contrary is natural. But was there ever any domination
which did not appear natural to those who possessed it? There
was a time when the division of mankind into two classes, a
small one of masters and a numerous one of slaves, appeared,
even to the most cultivated minds, to be natural, and the only
natural, condition of the human race. No less an intellect,
and one which contributed no less to the progress of human
thought, than Aristotle, held this opinion without doubt or
misgiving; and rested it on the same premises on which the
same assertion in regard to the dominion of men over women is
usually based, namely that there are different natures among
mankind, free natures, and slave natures; that the Greeks were
of a free nature, the barbarian races of Thracians and Asiatics
of a slave nature. But why need I go back to Aristotle? Did
not the slave-owners of the Southern United States maintain
the same doctrine, with all the fanaticism with which men
cling to the theories that justify their passions and legitimate
their personal interests? Did they not call heaven and earth
to witness that the dominion of the white man over the black is
natural, that the black race is by nature incapable of freedom,
and marked out for slavery? some even going so far as to say
that the freedom of manual labourers is an unnatural order of
things anywhere. Again, the theorists of absolute monarchy
have always affirmed it to be the only natural form of government; issuing from the patriarchal, which was the primitive
and spontaneous form of society, framed on the model of the
paternal, which is anterior to society itself, and, as they contend,

14   THE SUBJECTION OF WOMEN

the most natural authority of all. Nay, for that matter, the
law of force itself, to those who could not plead any other
has always seemed the most natural of all grounds for the
exercise of authority. Conquering races hold it to be Nature's
own dictate that the conquered should obey the conquerors, or
as they euphoniously paraphrase it, that the feebler and more
unwarlike races should submit to the braver and manlier. The
smallest acquaintance with human life in the middle ages, shows
how supremely natural the dominion of the feudal nobility over
men of low condition appeared to the nobility themselves, and
how unnatural the conception seemed, of a person of the
interior class claiming equality with them, or exercising authority
over them. It hardly seemed less so to the class held in subjection. The emancipated serfs and burgesses, even in their
most vigorous struggles, never made any pretension to a share
of authority; they only demanded more or less of limitation to
the power of tyrannising over them. So true is it that unnatural generally means only uncustomary, and that everything
which is usual appears natural. The subjection of women to
men being a universal custom, any departure from it quite
naturally appears unnatural. But how entirely, even in this
case, the feeling is dependent on custom, appears by ample
experience. Nothing so much astonishes the people of distant
parts of the world, when they first learn anything about England,
as to be told that it is under a queen; the thing seems to them
so unnatural as to be almost incredible. To Englishmen this
does not seem in the least degree unnatural, because they are
used to it; but they do feel it unnatural that women should
be soldiers or Members of Parliament. In the feudal ages, on
the contrary, war and politics were not thought unnatural to
women, because not unusual; it seemed natural that women
of the privileged classes should be of manly character, inferior
in nothing but bodily strength to their husbands and fathers.
The independence of women seemed rather less unnatural to
the Greeks than to other ancients, on account of the fabulous
Amazons (whom they believed to be historical), and the partial
example afforded by the Spartan women; who, though no less
subordinate by law than in other Greek states, were more free
in fact, and being trained to bodily exercises in the same manner
with men, gave ample proof that they were not naturally disqualified for them. There can be little doubt that Spartan
experience suggested to Plato, among many other of his doctrines,
that of the social and political equality of the two sexes.

But, it will be said, the rule of men over women differs from all these others in not being a rule of force: it is accepted voluntarily; women make no complaint, and are consenting parties to it. In the first place, a great number of women do not accept it. Ever since there have been women able to make their sentiments known by their writings (the only mode of publicity which society permits to them), an increasing number of them have recorded protests against their present social condition: and recently many thousands of them, headed by the most eminent women known to the public, have petitioned Parliament for their admission to the Parliamentary Suffrage. The claim of women to be educated as solidly, and in the same branches of knowledge, as men, is urged with growing intensity, and with a great prospect of success; while the demand for their admission into professions and occupations hitherto closed against them, becomes every year more urgent. Though there are not in this country, as there are in the United States, periodical conventions and an organised party to agitate for the Rights of Women, there is a numerous and active society organised and managed by women, for the more limited object of obtaining the political franchise. Nor is it only in our own country and in America that women are beginning to protest, more or less collectively, against the disabilities under which they labour. France, and Italy, and Switzerland, and Russia now afford examples of the same thing. How many more women there are who silently cherish similar aspirations, no one can possibly know; but there are abundant tokens how many *would* cherish them, were they not so strenuously taught to repress them as contrary to the proprieties of their sex. It must be remembered, also, that no enslaved class ever asked for complete liberty at once. When Simon de Montfort called the deputies of the commons to sit for the first time in Parliament, did any of them dream of demanding that an assembly, elected by their constituents, should make and destroy ministries, and dictate to the king in affairs of State? No such thought entered into the imagination of the most ambitious of them. The nobility had already these pretensions; the commons pretended to nothing but to be exempt from arbitrary taxation, and from the gross individual oppression of the king's officers. It is a political law of nature that those who are under any power of ancient origin, never begin by complaining of the power itself, but only of its oppressive exercise. There is never any want of women who complain of ill-usage by their husbands. There

16   THE SUBJECTION OF WOMEN

would be infinitely more, if complaint were not the greatest of all provocatives to a repetition and increase of the ill-usage. It is this which frustrates all attempts to maintain the power but protect the woman against its abuses. In no other case (except that of a child) is the person who has been proved judicially to have suffered an injury, replaced under the physical power of the culprit who inflicted it. Accordingly wives, even in the most extreme and protracted cases of bodily ill-usage, hardly ever dare avail themselves of the laws made for their protection: and if, in a moment of irrepressible indignation, or by the interference of neighbours, they are induced to do so, their whole effort afterwards is to disclose as little as they can, and to beg off their tyrant from his merited chastisement.

All causes, social and natural, combine to make it unlikely that women should be collectively rebellious to the power of men. They are so far in a position different from all other subject classes, that their masters require something more from them than actual service. Men do not want solely the obedience of women, they want their sentiments. All men, except the most brutish, desire to have, in the woman most nearly connected with them, not a forced slave but a willing one, not a slave merely, but a favourite. They have therefore put everything in practice to enslave their minds. The masters of all other slaves rely, for maintaining obedience, on fear; either fear of themselves, or religious fears. The masters of women wanted more than simple obedience, and they turned the whole force of education to effect their purpose. All women are brought up from the very earliest years in the belief that their ideal of character is the very opposite to that of men; not self-will, and government by self-control, but submission, and yielding to the control of others. All the moralities tell them that it is the duty of women, and all the current sentimentalities that it is their nature, to live for others; to make complete abnegation of themselves, and to have no life but in their affections. And by their affections are meant the only ones they are allowed to have—those to the men with whom they are connected, or to the children who constitute an additional and indefeasible tie between them and a man. When we put together three things--first, the natural attraction between opposite sexes; secondly, the wife's entire dependence on the husband, every privilege or pleasure she has being either his gift, or depending entirely on his will; and lastly, that the principal object of human pursuit, consideration, and all objects

JOHN STUART MILL   17

of social ambition, can in general be sought or obtained by her
only through him, it would be a miracle if the object of being
attractive to men had not become the polar star of feminine
education and formation of character.   And, this great means
of influence over the minds of women having been acquired, an
instinct of selfishness made men avail themselves of it to the
utmost as a means of holding women in subjection, by representing to them meekness, submissiveness, and resignation of
all individual will into the hands of a man, as an essential part
of sexual attractiveness.   Can it be doubted that any of the
other yokes which mankind have succeeded in breaking, would
have subsisted till now if the same means had existed, and
had been so sedulously used, to bow down their minds to it?
If it had been made the object of the life of every young plebeian
to find personal favour in the eyes of some patrician, of every
young serf with some seigneur; if domestication with him, and
a share of his personal affections, had been held out as the prize
which they all should look out for, the most gifted and aspiring
being able to reckon on the most desirable prizes; and if, when
this prize had been obtained, they had been shut out by a wall
of brass from all interests not centring in him, all feelings and
desires but those which he shared or inculcated; would not serfs
and seigneurs, plebeians and patricians, have been as broadly
distinguished at this day as men and women are? and would
not all but a thinker here and there, have believed the distinction
to be a fundamental and unalterable fact in human nature?

The preceding considerations are amply sufficient to show
that custom, however universal it may be, affords in this case
no presumption, and ought not to create any prejudice, in
favour of the arrangements which place women in social and
political subjection to men.   But I may go farther, and maintain that the course of history, and the tendencies of progressive
human society, afford not only no presumption in favour of
this system of inequality of rights, but a strong one against
it; and that, so far as the whole course of human improvement
up to the time, the whole stream of modern tendencies, warrants
any inference on the subject, it is, that this relic of the past is
discordant with the future, and must necessarily disappear.

For, what is the peculiar character of the modern world—
the difference which chiefly distinguishes modern institutions,
modern social ideas, modern life itself, from those of times long
past?   It is, that human beings are no longer born to their
place in life, and chained down by an inexorable bond to the

18   THE SUBJECTION OF WOMEN

place they are born to, but are free to employ their faculties, and such favourable chances as offer, to achieve the lot which may appear to them most desirable. Human society of old was constituted on a very different principle. All were born to a fixed social position, and were mostly kept in it by law, or interdicted from any means by which they could emerge from it. As some men are born white and others black, so some were born slaves and others freemen and citizens; some were born patricians, others plebeians; some were born feudal nobles, others commoners and *roturiers*. A slave or serf could never make himself free, nor, except by the will of his master, become so. In most European countries it was not till towards the close of the middle ages, and as a consequence of the growth of regal power, that commoners could be ennobled. Even among nobles, the eldest son was born the exclusive heir to the paternal possessions, and a long time elapsed before it was fully established that the father could disinherit him. Among the industrious classes, only those who were born members of a guild, or were admitted into it by its members, could lawfully practise their calling within its local limits; and nobody could practise any calling deemed important, in any but the legal manner—by processes authoritatively prescribed. Manufacturers have stood in the pillory for presuming to carry on their business by new and improved methods. In modern Europe, and most in those parts of it which have participated most largely in all other modern improvements, diametrically opposite doctrines now prevail. Law and government do not undertake to prescribe by whom any social or industrial operation shall or shall not be conducted, or what modes of conducting them shall be lawful. These things are left to the unfettered choice of individuals. Even the laws which required that workmen should serve an apprenticeship, have in this country been repealed: there being ample assurance that in all cases in which an apprenticeship is necessary, its necessity will suffice to enforce it. The old theory was, that the least possible should be left to the choice of the individual agent; that all he had to do should, as far as practicable, be laid down for him by superior wisdom. Left to himself he was sure to go wrong. The modern conviction, the fruit of a thousand years of experience, is, that things in which the individual is the person directly interested, never go right but as they are left to his own discretion; and that any regulation of them by authority, except to protect the rights of others, is sure to be mischievous. This conclusion,

JOHN STUART MILL   19

slowly arrived at, and not adopted until almost every possible
application of the contrary theory had been made with disastrous
result, now (in the industrial department) prevails universally
in the most advanced countries, almost universally in all that
have pretensions to any sort of advancement. It is not that
all processes are supposed to be equally good, or all persons to
be equally qualified for everything; but that freedom of individual choice is now known to be the only thing which procures
the adoption of the best processes, and throws each operation
into the hands of those who are best qualified for it. Nobody
thinks it necessary to make a law that only a strong-armed
man shall be a blacksmith. Freedom and competition suffice
to make blacksmiths strong-armed men, because the weak-
armed can earn more by engaging in occupations for which
they are more fit. In consonance with this doctrine, it is felt
to be an overstepping of the proper bounds of authority to
fix beforehand, on some general presumption, that certain
persons are not fit to do certain things. It is now thoroughly
known and admitted that if some such presumptions exist, no
such presumption is infallible. Even if it be well grounded in
a majority of cases, which it is very likely not to be, there will
be a minority of exceptional cases in which it does not hold:
and in those it is both an injustice to the individuals, and a
detriment to society, to place barriers in the way of their using
their faculties for their own benefit and for that of others. In
the cases, on the other hand, in which the unfitness is real,
the ordinary motives of human conduct will on the whole
suffice to prevent the incompetent person from making, or
from persisting in, the attempt.

If this general principle of social and economical science is
not true; if individuals, with such help as they can derive from
the opinion of those who know them, are not better judges
than the law and the government, of their own capacities and
vocation; the world cannot too soon abandon this principle,
and return to the old system of regulations and disabilities.
But if the principle is true, we ought to act as if we believed it,
and not to ordain that to be born a girl instead of a boy, any
more than to be born black instead of white, or a commoner
instead of a nobleman, shall decide the person's position through
all life—shall interdict people from all the more elevated social
positions, and from all, except a few, respectable occupations.
Even were we to admit the utmost that is ever pretended as
to the superior fitness of men for all the functions now reserved

20   THE SUBJECTION OF WOMEN

to them, the same argument applies which forbids a legal qualification for Members of Parliament. If only once in a dozen years the conditions of eligibility exclude a fit person, there is a real loss, while the exclusion of thousands of unfit persons is no gain; for if the constitution of the electoral body disposes them to choose unfit persons, there are always plenty of such persons to choose from. In all things of any difficulty and importance, those who can do them well are fewer than the need, even with the most unrestricted latitude of choice: and any limitation of the field of selection deprives society of some chances of being served by the competent, without ever saving it from the incompetent.

At present, in the more improved countries, the disabilities of women are the only case, save one, in which laws and institutions take persons at their birth, and ordain that they shall never in all their lives be allowed to compete for certain things. The one exception is that of royalty. Persons still are born to the throne; no one, not of the reigning family, can ever occupy it, and no one even of that family can, by any means but the course of hereditary succession, attain it. All other dignities and social advantages are open to the whole male sex: many indeed are only attainable by wealth, but wealth may be striven for by anyone, and is actually obtained by many men of the very humblest origin. The difficulties, to the majority, are indeed insuperable without the aid of fortunate accidents; but no male human being is under any legal ban: neither law nor opinion superadd artificial obstacles to the natural ones. Royalty, as I have said, is excepted: but in this case everyone feels it to be an exception—an anomaly in the modern world, in marked opposition to its customs and principles, and to be justified only by extraordinary special expediences, which, though individuals and nations differ in estimating their weight, unquestionably do in fact exist. But in this exceptional case, in which a high social function is, for important reasons, bestowed on birth instead of being put up to competition, all free nations contrive to adhere in substance to the principle from which they nominally derogate; for they circumscribe this high function by conditions avowedly intended to prevent the person to whom it ostensibly belongs from really performing it; while the person by whom it is performed, the responsible minister, does obtain the post by a competition from which no full-grown citizen of the male sex is legally excluded. The disabilities, therefore, to which women are subject from the

JOHN STUART MILL   21

mere fact of their birth, are the solitary examples of the kind
in modern legislation.   In no instance except this, which compre-
hends half the human race, are the higher social functions closed
against anyone by a fatality of birth which no exertions, and
no change of circumstances, can overcome; for even religious
disabilities (besides that in England and in Europe they have
practically almost ceased to exist) do not close any career to
the disqualified person in case of conversion.

The social subordination of women thus stands out an
isolated fact in modern social institutions; a solitary breach
of what has become their fundamental law; a single relic of an
old world of thought and practice exploded in everything else,
but retained in the one thing of most universal interest; as if
a gigantic dolmen, or a vast temple of Jupiter Olympius, occupied the site of St. Paul's and received daily worship, while the
surrounding Christian churches were only resorted to on fasts
and festivals.   This entire discrepancy between one social fact
and all those which accompany it, and the radical opposition
between its nature and the progressive movement which is the
boast of the modern world, and which has successively swept
away everything else of an analogous character, surely affords,
to a conscientious observer of human tendencies, serious matter
for reflection.   It raises a prima facie presumption on the unfavourable side, far outweighing any which custom and usage
could in such circumstances create on the favourable; and
should at least suffice to make this, like the choice between
republicanism and royalty, a balanced question.

The least that can be demanded is, that the question should
not be considered as prejudged by existing fact and existing
opinion, but open to discussion on its merits, as a question of
justice and expediency: the decision on this, as on any of the
other social arrangements of mankind, depending on what an
enlightened estimate of tendencies and consequences may show
to be most advantageous to humanity in general, without
distinction of sex.   And the discussion must be a real discussion, descending to foundations, and not resting satisfied
with vague and general assertions.   It will not do, for instance,
to assert in general terms, that the experience of mankind has
pronounced in favour of the existing system.   Experience cannot possibly have decided between two courses, so long as there
has only been experience of one.   If it be said that the doctrine
of the equality of the sexes rests only on theory, it must be
remembered that the contrary doctrine also has only theory to

rest upon. All that is proved in its favour by direct experience, is that mankind have been able to exist under it, and to attain the degree of improvement and prosperity which we now see; but whether that prosperity has been attained sooner, or is now greater, than it would have been under the other system, experience does not say. On the other hand, experience does say, that every step in improvement has been so invariably accompanied by a step made in raising the social position of women, that historians and philosophers have been led to adopt their elevation or debasement as on the whole the surest test and most correct measure of the civilisation of a people or an age. Through all the progressive period of human history, the condition of women has been approaching nearer to equality with men. This does not of itself prove that the assimilation must go on to complete equality; but it assuredly affords some presumption that such is the case.

Neither does it avail anything to say that the *nature* of the two sexes adapts them to their present functions and position, and renders these appropriate to them. Standing on the ground of common sense and the constitution of the human mind, I deny that anyone knows, or can know, the nature of the two sexes, as long as they have only been seen in their present relation to one another. If men had ever been found in society without women, or women without men, or if there had been a society of men and women in which the women were not under the control of the men, something might have been positively known about the mental and moral differences which may be inherent in the nature of each. What is now called the nature of women is an eminently artificial thing—the result of forced repression in some directions, unnatural stimulation in others. It may be asserted without scruple, that no other class of dependents have had their character so entirely distorted from its natural proportions by their relation with their masters; for, if conquered and slave races have been, in some respects, more forcibly repressed, whatever in them has not been crushed down by an iron heel has generally been let alone, and if left with any liberty of development, it has developed itself according to its own laws; but in the case of women, a hot-house and stove cultivation has always been carried on of some of the capabilities of their nature, for the benefit and pleasure of their masters. Then, because certain products of the general vital force sprout luxuriantly and reach a great development in this heated atmosphere and under this active nurture and watering, while other shoots from the same root, which are left outside in the wintry air, with ice purposely heaped all round them, have a stunted growth, and some are burnt off with fire and disappear; men, with that inability to recognise their own work which distinguishes the unanalytic mind, indolently believe that the tree grows of itself in the way they have made it grow, and that it would die if one half of it were not kept in a vapour bath and the other half in the snow.

Of all difficulties which impede the progress of thought, and the formation of well-grounded opinions on life and social arrangements, the greatest is now the unspeakable ignorance and inattention of mankind in respect to the influences which form human character. Whatever any portion of the human species now are, or seem to be, such, it is supposed, they have a natural tendency to be: even when the most elementary knowledge of the circumstances in which they have been placed, clearly points out the causes that made them what they are. Because a cottier deeply in arrears to his landlord is not industrious, there are people who think that the Irish are naturally idle. Because constitutions can be overthrown when the authorities appointed to execute them turn their arms against them, there are people who think the French incapable of free government. Because the Greeks cheated the Turks, and the Turks only plundered the Greeks, there are persons who think that the Turks are naturally more sincere: and because women, as is often said, care nothing about politics except their personalities, it is supposed that the general good is naturally less interesting to women than to men. History, which is now so much better understood than formerly, teaches another lesson: if only by showing the extraordinary susceptibility of human nature to external influences, and the extreme variableness of those of its manifestations which are supposed to be most universal and uniform. But in history, as in travelling, men usually see only what they already had in their own minds; and few learn much from history, who do not bring much with them to its study.

Hence, in regard to that most difficult question, what are the natural differences between the two sexes—a subject on which it is impossible in the present state of society to obtain complete and correct knowledge—while almost everybody dogmatises upon it, almost all neglect and make light of the only means by which any partial insight can be obtained into it. This is, an analytic study of the most important department of psychology, the laws of the influence of circumstances on character. For, however great and apparently ineradicable the moral and intellectual differences between men and women might be, the evidence of there being natural differences could only be negative. Those only could be inferred to be natural which could not possibly be artificial—the residuum, after deducting every characteristic of either sex which can admit of being explained from education or external circumstances. The profoundest knowledge of the laws of the formation of character is indispensable to entitle anyone to affirm even that there is any difference, much more what the difference is, between the two sexes considered as moral and rational beings; and since no one, as yet, has that knowledge (for there is hardly any subject which, in proportion to its importance, has been so little studied), no one is thus far entitled to any positive opinion on the subject. Conjectures are all that can at present be made; conjectures more or less probable, according as more or less authorised by such knowledge as we yet have of the laws of psychology, as applied to the formation of character.

Even the preliminary knowledge, what the differences between the sexes now are, apart from all question as to how they are made what they are, is still in the crudest and most incomplete state. Medical practitioners and physiologists have ascertained, to some extent, the differences in bodily constitution; and this is an important element to the psychologist: but hardly any medical practitioner is a psychologist. Respecting the mental characteristics of women; their observations are of no more worth than those of common men. It is a subject on which nothing final can be known, so long as those who alone can really know it, women themselves, have given but little testimony, and that little, mostly suborned. It is easy to know stupid women. Stupidity is much the same all the world over. A stupid person's notions and feelings may confidently be inferred from those which prevail in the circle by which the person is surrounded. Not so with those whose opinions and feelings are an emanation from their own nature and faculties. It is only a man here and there who has any tolerable knowledge of the character even of the women of his own family. I do not mean, of their capabilities; these nobody knows, not even themselves, because most of them have never been called out. I mean their actually existing thoughts and feelings. Many a man thinks he perfectly understands women, because he has had amatory relations with several, perhaps with many of them.

JOHN STUART MILL   25

If he is a good observer, and his experience extends to quality
as well as quantity, he may have learnt something of one
narrow department of their nature --an important department,
no doubt. But of all the rest of it, few persons are generally
more ignorant, because there are few from whom it is so carefully hidden. The most favourable case which a man can
generally have for studying the character of a woman, is that
of his own wife: for the opportunities are greater, and the
cases of complete sympathy not so unspeakably rare. And in
fact, this is the source from which any knowledge worth having
on the subject has, I believe, generally come. But most men
have not had the opportunity of studying in this way more
than a single case: accordingly one can, to an almost laughable
degree, infer what a man's wife is like, from his opinions about
women in general. To make even this one case yield any
result, the woman must be worth knowing, and the man not
only a competent judge, but of a character so sympathetic in
itself, and so well adapted to hers, that he can either read her
mind by sympathetic intuition, or has nothing in himself which
makes her shy of disclosing it. Hardly anything, I believe,
can be more rare than this conjunction. It often happens that
there is the most complete unity of feeling and community of
interests as to all external things, yet the one has as little
admission into the internal life of the other as if they were
common acquaintance. Even with true affection, authority on
the one side and subordination on the other prevent perfect
confidence. Though nothing may be intentionally withheld,
much is not shown. In the analogous relation of parent and
child, the corresponding phenomenon must have been in the
observation of everyone. As between father and son, how
many are the cases in which the father, in spite of real affection
on both sides, obviously to all the world does not know, nor
suspect, parts of the son's character familiar to his companions
and equals. The truth is, that the position of looking up to
another is extremely unpropitious to complete sincerity and
openness with him. The fear of losing ground in his opinion
or in his feelings is so strong, that even in an upright character,
there is an unconscious tendency to show only the best side, or
the side which, though not the best, is that which he most likes
to see: and it may be confidently said that thorough knowledge
of one another hardly ever exists, but between persons who,
besides being intimates, are equals. How much more true,
then, must all this be, when the one is not only under the

authority of the other, but has it inculcated on her as a duty
to reckon everything else subordinate to his comfort and pleasure,
and to let him neither see nor feel anything coming from her,
except what is agreeable to him. All these difficulties stand in
the way of a man's obtaining any thorough knowledge even of
the one woman whom alone, in general, he has sufficient opportunity of studying. When we further consider that to understand one woman is not necessarily to understand any other
woman; that even if he could study many women of one rank,
or of one country, he would not thereby understand women
of other ranks or countries; and even if he did, they are still
only the women of a single period of history; we may safely
assert that the knowledge which men can acquire of women,
even as they have been and are, without reference to what
they might be, is wretchedly imperfect and superficial, and
always will be so, until women themselves have told all that
they have to tell.

And this time has not come; nor will it come otherwise than
gradually. It is but of yesterday that women have either been
qualified by literary accomplishments, or permitted by society,
to tell anything to the general public. As yet very few of
them dare tell anything, which men, on whom their literary
success depends, are unwilling to hear. Let us remember in
what manner, up to a very recent time, the expression, even
by a male author, of uncustomary opinions, or what are deemed
eccentric feelings, usually was, and in some degree still is,
received; and we may form some faint conception under what
impediments a woman, who is brought up to think custom and
opinion her sovereign rule, attempts to express in books anything drawn from the depths of her own nature. The greatest
woman who has left writings behind her sufficient to give her
an eminent rank in the literature of her country, thought it
necessary to prefix as a motto to her boldest work, "Un homme
peut braver l'opinion; une femme doit s'y soumettre." [1] The
greater part of what women write about women is mere sycophancy to men. In the case of unmarried women, much of it
seems only intended to increase their chance of a husband.
Many, both married and unmarried, overstep the mark, and
inculcate a servility beyond what is desired or relished by any
man, except the very vulgarest. But this is not so often the
case as, even at a quite late period, it still was. Literary women
are becoming more free-spoken, and more willing to express their

[1] Title-page of Mme de Staël's *Delphine*.

JOHN STUART MILL

real sentiments. Unfortunately, in this country especially, they are themselves such artificial products, that their sentiments are compounded of a small element of individual observation and consciousness, and a very large one of acquired associations. This will be less and less the case, but it will remain true to a great extent, as long as social institutions do not admit the same free development of originality in women which is possible to men. When that time comes, and not before, we shall see, and not merely hear, as much as it is necessary to know of the nature of women, and the adaptation of other things to it.

I have dwelt so much on the difficulties which at present obstruct any real knowledge by men of the true nature of women, because in this as in so many other things "opinio copiæ inter maximas causas inopiæ est"; and there is little chance of reasonable thinking on the matter, while people flatter themselves that they perfectly understand a subject of which most men know absolutely nothing, and of which it is at present impossible that any man, or all men taken together, should have knowledge which can qualify them to lay down the law to women as to what is, or is not, their vocation. Happily, no such knowledge is necessary for any practical purpose connected with the position of women in relation to society and life. For, according to all the principles involved in modern society, the question rests with women themselves—to be decided by their own experience, and by the use of their own faculties. There are no means of finding what either one person or many can do, but by trying—and no means by which anyone else can discover for them what it is for their happiness to do or leave undone.

One thing we may be certain of—that what is contrary to women's nature to do, they never will be made to do by simply giving their nature free play. The anxiety of mankind to interfere in behalf of nature, for fear lest nature should not succeed in effecting its purpose, is an altogether unnecessary solicitude. What women by nature cannot do, it is quite superfluous to forbid them from doing. What they can do, but not so well as the men who are their competitors, competition suffices to exclude them from; since nobody asks for protective duties and bounties in favour of women; it is only asked that the present bounties and protective duties in favour of men should be recalled. If women have a greater natural inclination for some things than for others, there is no need of laws or social

28

THE SUBJECTION OF WOMEN

inculcation to make the majority of them do the former in preference to the latter. Whatever women's services are most wanted for, the free play of competition will hold out the strongest inducements to them to undertake. And, as the words imply, they are most wanted for the things for which they are most fit; by the apportionment of which to them, the collective faculties of the two sexes can be applied on the whole with the greatest sum of valuable result.

The general opinion of men is supposed to be, that the natural vocation of a woman is that of a wife and mother. I say, is supposed to be, because, judging from acts—from the whole of the present constitution of society—one might infer that their opinion was the direct contrary. They might be supposed to think that the alleged natural vocation of women was of all things the most repugnant to their nature; insomuch that if they are free to do anything else—if any other means of living or occupation of their time and faculties, is open, which has any chance of appearing desirable to them—there will not be enough of them who will be willing to accept the condition said to be natural to them. If this is the real opinion of men in general, it would be well that it should be spoken out. I should like to hear somebody openly enunciating the doctrine (it is already implied in much that is written on the subject)—"It is necessary to society that women should marry and produce children. They will not do so unless they are compelled. Therefore it is necessary to compel them." The merits of the case would then be clearly defined. It would be exactly that of the slave-holders of South Carolina and Louisiana. "It is necessary that cotton and sugar should be grown. White men cannot produce them. Negroes will not, for any wages which we choose to give. *Ergo* they must be compelled." An illustration still closer to the point is that of impressment. Sailors must absolutely be had to defend the country. It often happens that they will not voluntarily enlist. Therefore there must be the power of forcing them. How often has this logic been used! and, but for one flaw in it, without doubt it would have been successful up to this day. But it is open to the retort— First pay the sailors the honest value of their labour. When you have made it as well worth their while to serve you, as to work for other employers, you will have no more difficulty than others have in obtaining their services. To this there is no logical answer except "I will not": and as people are now not only ashamed, but are not desirous, to rob the labourer of his

JOHN STUART MILL 29

hire, impressment is no longer advocated. Those who attempt to force women into marriage by closing all other doors against them, lay themselves open to a similar retort. If they mean what they say, their opinion must evidently be, that men do not render the married condition so desirable to women, as to induce them to accept it for its own recommendations. It is not a sign of one's thinking the boon one offers very attractive, when one allows only Hobson's choice, "that or none." And here, I believe, is the clue to the feelings of those men, who have a real antipathy to the equal freedom of women. I believe they are afraid, not lest women should be unwilling to marry, for I do not think that anyone in reality has that apprehension; but lest they should insist that marriage should be on equal conditions; lest all women of spirit and capacity should prefer doing almost anything else, not in their own eyes degrading, rather than marry, when marrying is giving themselves a master, and a master too of all their earthly possessions. And truly, if this consequence were necessarily incident to marriage, I think that the apprehension would be very well founded. I agree in thinking it probable that few women, capable of anything else, would, unless under an irresistible *entraînement*, rendering them for the time insensible to anything but itself, choose such a lot, when any other means were open to them of filling a conventionally honourable place in life: and if men are determined that the law of marriage shall be a law of despotism, they are quite right, in point of mere policy, in leaving to women only Hobson's choice. But, in that case, all that has been done in the modern world to relax the chain on the minds of women, has been a mistake. They never should have been allowed to receive a literary education. Women who read, much more women who write, are, in the existing constitution of things, a contradiction and a disturbing element: and it was wrong to bring women up with any acquirements but those of an odalisque, or of a domestic servant.

B
Twentieth-Century Commentary

[10]

Mill and the Subjection of Women

JULIA ANNAS

When Mill's *The Subjection of Women* was published in 1869 it was ahead of its time in boldly championing feminism.[1] It failed to inaugurate a respectable intellectual debate. Feminist writers have tended to refer to it with respect but without any serious attempt to come to grips with Mill's actual arguments. Kate Millett's chapter in *Sexual Politics* is the only sustained discussion of Mill in the feminist literature that I am aware of, but it is not from a philosophical viewpoint, and deals with Mill only in the service of an extended comparison with Ruskin. Philosophical books on Mill give the essay short measure. Alan Ryan in *J. S. Mill* heads one chapter '*Liberty* and *The Subjection of Women*', but the former work gets twenty-six pages and the latter only four. Ryan says that 'it is almost entirely concerned with the legal disabilities of women in Victorian England'. H. J. McCloskey, in *John Stuart Mill: A Critical Study*, gives the essay one and a half pages, commenting that it reads 'like a series of truisms' and seems so unimportant today because equality of the sexes has been achieved!

It is, however, simply false to say that Mill's essay is mostly concerned with legal technicalities which have since been changed, and so of no great interest today. *The Subjection of Women* is concerned with women's legal disabilities only in so far as they reflect profound social and economic inequalities between the sexes. While today there are few ways in which women are under legal disabilities compared with men (though it would be a mistake to think there are none) women are still subject to economic and social discrimination in a variety of ways, and it is extraordinary to think that Mill's essay no longer contains anything interesting or controversial just because there have been a few changes in the law. To take only one example: today a battered wife is no longer under legal compulsion to return to her husband, as she was in Mill's day, but until very recently the pressure for her to do so was overwhelming; the informal ways in which society enforces conformity to the institution of the family have never been stronger. Although we are more receptive to the ideal, we are nowhere near achieving in practice the kind of equality between the sexes that Mill looks forward to. It will be a good day when *The Subjection of Women* is outdated, but it is not yet.

[1] It became at once unpopular and neglected; it was the only book of Mill's ever to lose his publisher money (A. Ryan, *J. S. Mill*, p. 125). In 1867, when he was an MP, Mill tried to amend the Reform Bill in such a way as to secure the franchise for women, but only 73 MPs voted with him.

Julia Annas

Ryan has another objection: 'Mill's coolness towards sexual issues makes *The Subjection of Women* an awkward work to place in twentieth-century arguments about sexual equality'. It is true that Mill's actual references to sex are all very Victorian in the worst sense, but it does not follow that this undermines his argument, unless it can be shown that his main contentions are based on his false view of women's sexuality. Since Mill does not put forward purported facts about female sexuality as the main support for any of his conclusions, argument is needed, which Ryan does not provide, to show that what Mill says about women should be revised substantially in the light of our greatly altered beliefs about women's sexuality. Mill has often been dismissed on the ground that, being pre-Freudian, he failed to understand the basic importance of sex in determining personality.[2] However, Mill's non-Freudian approach may nowadays be thought a positive advantage, given the extremely contentious character of Freud's views on women and the history of dispute in the psychoanalytic movement on this topic.

The predominant view seems to be that *The Subjection of Women* is obviously right but of little importance. I believe, on the contrary, that it is of great importance, but, far from being obviously truistic, contains very deep confusions; this paper is an attempt to disentangle some of them. I should say at the outset, however, that the reason why I think this is worthwhile is that Mill's confusions are not shallow ones; they come rather from a desire to have things too many ways at once, to do justice to all the complexities of a topic which even now is far from being adequately clarified. If this were not so, it would indeed be perverse to search for faults in what Millett justly calls his 'splendidly controlled humanist outrage'.

I shall begin by distinguishing two ways in which one might protest at existing sexual inequalities.

1. The reformist approach. One can claim that it is unfair for women to be excluded from opportunities that are open to men, because women are in fact capable of doing what men do, and do in fact resent being excluded. This is a straightforwardly factual claim; the available openings are not in fact commensurate with women's desires and needs, and what is therefore required is reform of the existing social system. The most obvious justification for this is utilitarian: if desires are no longer frustrated, this will lead to greater happiness for women, and if unused abilities are put to work, everyone will benefit; in both cases the benefits are such as to be so regarded already by both men and women. This argument is quite compatible with there being many important empirically established differences of nature

---

[2] Freud translated Mill's essay, and discussed his dislike of it in the famous letter to his fiancée in which he says, 'If . . . I imagined my gentle sweet girl as a competitor it would only end by my telling her . . . that I am fond of her and that I implore her to withdraw from the struggle into the calm uncompetitive activity of my home'.

Mill and the Subjection of Women

between the sexes; all that it excludes is that these differences should justify inferior opportunities for women in the respects in which their contribution can be recognized.

2. *The radical approach.* One can also claim that the subjection of women is unfair, but not from observation of actual frustrated desires and unfulfilled capacities. Rather it may be admitted, and even stressed, that most women lack ambition and serious concentration, but argued that this very fact shows that their natural impulses have been suppressed by a system that brings them up to think submissiveness and dependence virtues, and that what is required is that they (and men) be liberated from this system. This is not a straightforwardly factual claim, for the appeal is to women's nature, but this nature is not something that can be ascertained from women's present behaviour and achievements. This approach is not exactly *a priori*, for it may well appeal to known facts about human nature; but these will be extremely general and theory-laden, as opposed to the sort of facts that can be read off from people's observed behaviour. The radical approach will have little use for reform of the existing system; to a radical, this would be merely futile, enabling a few women to get ahead by adopting male values, but doing nothing for the mass of women whose natures have been systematically thwarted. What is required is a radical change in the whole framework of society's attitudes to the relations between the sexes; and the justification of this radical change will be one of justice and of women's rights, not a utilitarian one. As I am using 'utilitarian' in this connection, a utilitarian justification is one that appeals to the satisfaction of desires that people actually have, not those they would have in some ideal condition.[3] Changes that merely produce the maximum satisfaction of desires in the system as it is will be rejected by the radical, because integral to the system are the institutions and attitudes that according to the radical systematically deform women's natures. In contrast to the reformist, the radical does seem committed to holding that there are no large and interesting differences of nature between men and women, none, at any rate, that could justify any institutionalization of sexual differences.

Mill's argument throughout *The Subjection of Women* is a confused mixture of these two approaches. He lurches from a less to a more radical position and back again, and this creates strain at several points. In what follows I shall try to show that although Mill is clear about what he is

[3] Of course I am not claiming that Mill clearly or consistently thinks of 'utilitarian' arguments as those that confine themselves to desires and needs that people actually have, without reference to any idealizing of the situation. (If he did, there could hardly be room for controversy as to whether he espoused 'act-' or 'rule-' utilitarianism.) My distinction is intended to hold apart two lines of thought which Mill seems to employ in the essay, and they would remain distinct even if both of them were brought under the heading of some very broad conception of utilitarianism.

Julia Annas

opposing he fails to consider that there are different possibilities on the positive side, and that different arguments carry different commitments and can be incompatible.

In the argument of Chapter 1 of the essay, Mill seems to presuppose the radical approach. He objects, for example, that the existence of patriarchy is not something that can count in its favour, because it has no theoretical basis. It is not the case that patriarchy is the result of fair experiment, trials and refutations. Experience shows us only that we *can* survive under patriarchy, not that we could not do a good deal better otherwise. So (p. 129)[4] 'experience, in the sense in which it is vulgarly opposed to theory, cannot be pretended to have pronounced any verdict'. Further, 'the adoption of this system of inequality never was the result of deliberation, or forethought, or any social ideas, or any notion whatever of what conduced to the benefit of humanity or the good order of society'. It arose simply because women have always been weaker, being at a biological disadvantage. It is just 'the primitive state of slavery lasting on'. The opponent presumably wants to argue that biology is destiny; Mill's counter to this is to deny that our present experience of relations between the sexes is morally relevant at all. What matter more are considerations of what is just and right, and these cannot be read off from ordinary experience.

Mill also overrides the objection that women do not object to the present system. While insisting that some do, as is shown by franchise agitation, etc., he admits that most do not; yet insists that 'there are abundant tokens how many *would* cherish [similar aspirations] were they not so strenuously taught to repress them as contrary to the proprieties of their sex' (p. 140). He adds that the fact that each woman complains individually about her husband shows that women would collectively complain about the position of men if their education were not aimed at getting them to think of themselves as dependants with subservience to men as their natural goal. This may well be true, but it is not a datum of experience, and Mill does not think that it is; he is getting us to discount the views of most women as presently expressed. He even gets us to disallow most of what women have written as inauthentic. The desires and interests which women now have are thus not given utilitarian weighting; they are explained away, as not reflecting women's real nature.

That this is the radical and not the reformist approach is made even clearer by Mill's eloquent rejection of the opponent's claim that men and women are naturally fitted for their present functions and positions: 'What is now called the nature of women is an eminently artificial thing—the result of forced repression in some directions, unnatural stimulation in

---

[4] All references to *The Subjection of Women* and *The Enfranchisement of Women* come from the useful collection *Essays on Sex Equality* by John Stuart Mill and Harriet Taylor Mill, edited by A. Rossi (University of Chicago Press, 1970).

Mill and the Subjection of Women

others. It may be asserted without scruple, that no other class of dependants have had their character so entirely distorted from its natural proportions by their relation with their masters . . .' (p. 148). Mill insists that nobody is in a position to know anything about women's nature, because so far we have not seen anything that we could call natural; all we have seen is manifestations of the altogether understandable desire to conform to stereotype. He uses the occasion to criticize men who think, from a negligible basis, that they completely understand women. Consistently with this, Mill, in Chapter 1, uses no argument directly from what women want or can do. His main argument works by analogy: the dissatisfaction that most women feel with marriage shows that they would object to the position of men in general if it were not for the submissiveness inculcated by their education, just as complaints about misuse of tyrannical power by one class against another in the past have always led in the end to demands that the power itself should be abolished. Given Mill's strong assertions about the impossibility of demarcating female nature, this kind of argument from analogy is the most he can consistently offer.[5]

After all this, it comes as a surprise to find that in Chapter 3 Mill defends the suitability of women for public office and private employment from a position that makes quite large concessions to the opponent of Chapter 1.

Mill argues (p. 185) that if even a few women are fit to hold office then legally excluding women 'cannot be justified by any opinion which can be held respecting the capacities of women in general'. He adds, with a connection of thought which is for him uncharacteristically loose and vague, 'But, though this last consideration is not essential, it is far from being irrelevant. An unprejudiced view of it gives additional strength to the argument against the disabilities of women, and reinforces them by high considerations of practical utility.' The progress of Mill's thought here seems to be: to exclude women from jobs, etc., on the ground that they are unfit for them is irrational, because we cannot know whether they are unfit or not (never having tried). But it is *also* actually rebutted by the existence of some women who *are* fit—and if some women are fit, it must surely increase utility to include them among the employables. Mill obviously thinks that he has merely brought in a supplementary argument which will strengthen the first, and so he would have if he had stuck to the above formulation of his point; but Mill in the course of making his appeal to utility makes exactly his opponents' dubious move of arguing from a few examples to the capacity of women in general in a specific respect—e.g.

[5] We should note in passing that this argument depends heavily on our being able to predict a very large-scale change in society from the occurrence of similar changes in the past, and also on the assumption that progress in the required direction will not be blocked by large-scale movements in society based entirely on irrational or destructive forces. Mill could not foresee the inroads made on women's rights by fascism, for example.

Julia Annas

from a few women rulers to women's bent for the practical. Yet he had himself earlier (p. 149) pointed out the fallacy of arguing from the behaviour of a few to the behaviour of all members of a class like women or members of other nations. Worse: if, as Mill has argued at length in Chapter 1, we have no real knowledge of women's natures, then we cannot argue from some cases that women are fit to hold jobs, etc., any more than we can argue from some other cases that women are *not* fit. Indeed, this is dangerous ground for a feminist; as Mill seemed aware earlier on, there have always been many more women who have failed to rise above their education than have succeeded—that was why he was so anxious to argue that in this matter we cannot argue from experience. Yet here he seems not to see that the argument cuts both ways, and cuts more sharply against him than for him.

It seems, then, that in his anxiety to add a utilitarian argument to the argument from rights, Mill is trying to occupy ground already undercut by his own earlier arguments. This emerges strongly in the rest of the arguments of Chapter 3. Throughout them we find Mill in untypically embarrassed and tortuous positions. He demands that we 'make entire abstraction of' all considerations suggesting that differences between the sexes are the product of the suppression by education of women's natures, admitting uncomfortably that this leaves only 'a very humble ground' for women, and apparently unaware that earlier he had argued that such abstraction, far from leading to an unprejudiced view, is illegitimate.

Mill makes much of the fact that women have been excellent rulers when they have had a chance to rule. His case perhaps depends on his selection of examples (the Empresses of Russia and China have been worse, if anything, than their male counterparts); but more disturbing is the fact that he concludes that this fits what we do know of 'the peculiar tendencies and aptitudes characteristic of women' (p. 189). Women in general have a bent towards the practical. They are capable of intuitive perception of situations, 'rapid and correct insight into present fact' (p. 190). This is a talent which, while it does not fit one for scientific thought or abstract reasoning on general principles, is of great use in practical matters, where what is required is sensitivity to the realities of the present situation. Women's intuition is thus a valuable corrective to man's tendency to abstract reasoning. It prevents the latter becoming uselessly over-speculative, and it ensures that sound reasoning is put into practice in a competent way.

Here is the oldest cliché in the book: women are intuitive while men reason. If any cliché has done the most harm to the acceptance by men of women as intellectual equals, it is this, and it is distressing to see Mill come out with it. It is even more distressing to find him patronizingly recommending to any man working in a speculative subject the great value of an intuitive woman to keep him down to earth (p. 102). It is true that Mill

Mill and the Subjection of Women

prefaces these remarks with an awkward and apologetic passage (pp. 189–190) in which he says that they apply only to women in their actual state, not as they could be. None the less, it is his own choice to defend women's supposed intuition on utilitarian grounds; and a very back-handed defence it is. If it were sound, it would actually undermine many radical proposals. There would be no good ground, for example, for giving the sexes the same type of education; it would be appropriate to train boys to go in, at least predominantly, for subjects requiring analytical reasoning and development of theory, and to train women rather for subjects requiring no sustained reasoning but rather 'human contact' and easily appreciable practical applications. We do not need to be reminded that our educational system is still run largely on these assumptions, and that girls are still notoriously inhibited from going in for subjects on the science and mathematics side, particularly in mixed schools, for fear of being thought too 'masculine'.[6] As for the utility of women's famous intuition, Mill unwittingly exposes the catch when he points out its utility for a *man* engaged in speculative thought. Why should a woman be pleased by the fact that she is a usefully earthy check on some man's theories? Instead of claiming the usefulness of this function (which is surely very limited anyway) would it not be more rational for her to claim the right to produce theories too, if she can, just as speculative as a man's, and to have them taken seriously? As long as one admits that women are intuitive and men suited to reasoning, one's best efforts at valuing women's contribution will be patronizing and damaging, encouraging women to think that the most highly regarded intellectual achievements are not for them.

No less unhappy is Mill's treatment of the objection that women have greater 'nervous susceptibility' than men and so are unfit for proper employment (p. 194). Firstly he tries to explain this supposed fact away: much of it is the result of having excess energy unused or wasted on trivia, and much is artificially cultivated as the result of an unhealthy upbringing. But he then adds that some women *do* have nervous temperaments, and tries to present this in as favourable a light as possible. He points out that it is not confined to women, that it often accompanies genius, that if allied to self-control it produces a very strong character. In short, what is wrong with being nervous and excitable? But Mill, in spite of the changed direction of his defence, is too honest to claim that excitability is really a virtue. He admits that women would do as well as men 'if their education and cultivation were adapted to correcting instead of aggravating the infirmities incidental to their temperament'. So it seems that nervous susceptibility, in spite of Mill's awkward praise of it, is a defect after all. As if realizing

---

[6] In 1972, for example, the percentage of girls studying mathematics and science subjects at A-level was higher in single-sex schools than in mixed schools, tiny in both (18·7 per cent as against 13·4 per cent).

Julia Annas

how damaging this admission is, Mill launches on to another type of defence: even if women's minds are more 'mobile' than those of men, and thus less capable of sustained intellectual effort, this does not mean that they are any the less to be valued: 'This difference is one which can only affect the kind of excellence, not the excellence itself.' Mill's confused and tangled attempts to show the useful qualities of women's special way of thinking thus ends up with the dangerous cliché so beloved of inegalitarians: women are not *inferior* to men, just *different*.

It is no accident that efforts to get the position of women improved by praising their special, womanly qualities usually end up in a position very similar to that of the opposition, with merely a difference of emphasis. This is because, as Mill so clearly saw in Chapter 1, the special qualities that are ascribed to women, and for which they are praised, are created within a male-dominated society, and it is very unlikely that the roles that give them content can within that society achieve a genuinely high value. Their qualities are the qualities of the inferior, and praising them will not make their owners equal—indeed, it may well have the opposite effect by encouraging women to fall back lazily on their 'female intuitions' rather than learn to argue on equal terms with men. Mill sees very clearly what is wrong and harmful with the Victorian praise of women for having more moral virtue than men. It is surprising that he does not see what is wrong with his own very similar attempts to praise women as less abstractly rational than men and more sensitive to the human dimension.

Mill's discomforts increase when he comes to deal with the alleged fact that men have bigger brains than women. Firstly he dismisses it quite decisively: the alleged fact is dubious; anyway the principle appealed to is ridiculous, for according to it whales would be much more intelligent than men; further, the relationship between size of brain and quality of mind is, to say the least, not the subject of general agreement. But then, amazingly, he backtracks and admits that probably men do have bigger brains than women, but slower cerebral circulation; this would explain why men's thoughts are slower and steadier, while women's are more rapid and ephemeral! This is the only place in *The Subjection of Women* where the argument is quite pathetic, and one is mainly surprised that Mill feels that he needs to argue at all on this level. That he does can only be put down to his anxiety to add as many arguments as possible based upon women's actual (and supposedly actual) qualities, in spite of having pointed out clearly all the pitfalls of this approach in Chapter 1.

As if unhappy about this argument, Mill repeats his sound earlier point that we can know practically nothing about natural differences, because of the meagreness of the research done so far and the inevitability of cultural prejudices. At once he disregards his own good advice and starts speculating on the possible causes of what is represented as the greatest difference between the sexes, namely that there have been no great women philoso-

Mill and the Subjection of Women

phers, artists, etc. He defends this uneasily: 'I am not about to attempt what I have pronounced impossible; but doubt does not forbid conjecture'. But Mill's tone is not subsequently very tentative; and in any case he has already shown amply the futility of all such conjectures, if women's natures have been systematically deformed by their upbringing in male-dominated society. He now, however, takes seriously the question, 'Why have there been no great women artists, etc.?' as a question to be answered by appealing to actually existing features of women's character.

He begins by saying that it is not surprising that there have been no women geniuses, since it has not been very long since women could even enter the stakes for intellectual excellence. This looks at first like a good argument, but if one looks at the facts more closely a good deal of its force seems to evaporate. It cannot explain why women have been so much more prominent in fields like literature than in fields like the visual arts, when they have been open to them for roughly the same length of time.[7] Mill speaks as though women have made slow but increasing progress on all fronts, uniformly achieving competence so far but nothing great. One begins to suspect that he is dominated by a linear picture of Progress.

Even without any belief in Progress, however, one can agree that women have not so far (even now, to any extent) 'produced any of those great and luminous new ideas which form an era in thought, nor those fundamentally new conceptions in art, which open a vista of possible effects not before thought of, and found a new school' (p. 204). Mill's explanation is strange and forced. He argues that in the past, when 'great and fruitful new truths could be arrived at by mere force of genius' women were socially prevented from artistic expression, and nowadays, when the latter is no longer the case, few women have the erudition required to say something new. In other words, women were not allowed to join in when originality was easy to come by, and now when it is hard to come by they start with an educational handicap. Mill seems to be thinking of culture as cumulative, each generation having more homework to get through before they can add anything new. What is puzzling is why he thinks he needs this bizarre and implausible picture. For he has already made clear at some length why it is unlikely that a woman could come out with a profoundly original idea; women are not brought up to be self-reliant and are much more likely (like Harriet Taylor) to express their best insights through the work of some man.

Equally bizarre is Mill's explanation of why women's literature has been so derivative from that of men. He compares it with that of the Romans,

[7] For some preliminary clarifications on this, see the excellent article by L. Nochlin, 'Why are there no great women artists?' in *Women in Sexist Society*, Gornick and Moran (eds.), also (abbreviated) in *Art and Sexual Politics*, Hess and Baker (eds.).

Julia Annas

who found a whole literature, the Greek, already in existence when they began to write. But surely *all* writers, men and women, stand to earlier literary achievements as the Romans stood to the Greeks. The comparison also renders wholly inappropriate Mill's claim that in time women will come to write their own original literature. But in any case he has already provided us with the real answer, or at least part of it, back in Chapter 1: 'The greater part of what women write about women is mere sycophancy to men' (p. 153). The dependence displayed by women who falsify their own experience to fulfil male expectations is quite unlike the literary dependence of the Romans on the Greeks.

Mill's awkwardness in arguing on his chosen humble ground shows up most clearly when he points out that women fail to achieve works of genius partly because they lack ambition to immortalize their names—'whether the cause be natural or artificial'—this in spite of the fact that he has already shown at length that it is unreasonable to think that women are naturally passive and spiritless, just as it is in the case of serfs or black slaves; the limitations and narrow focus of their standard ambitions are quite adequately explained by their upbringing and the expectations of the roles they fill.

Mill's attempts in Chapter 3 to argue for reform on utilitarian grounds, basing himself on women's natures as they are, amount to total failure. I have dwelt on these arguments at length because they are so unexpectedly bizarre and weak; Mill's awkwardness betrays his confusion as again and again he puts forward grounds which are undermined by his own earlier arguments.

Mill seems unaware of this, as he seems likewise to be unaware that Chapter 3 is not co-tenable with some of the arguments of Chapter 4 either.

In Chapter 4 he argues that great benefits will accrue from the liberation of women, including among these the vast improvement of women's influence over men. He describes how as things are a woman is nearly always a moral drag on her husband; her narrow conception of their interests often forces him to sacrifice principle to money and status. 'Whoever has a wife and children has given hostages to Mrs Grundy' (p. 229). Mill's eulogy of marriage as between equals gives great emphasis to the unsatisfactory nature of marriage as it is, largely on the ground that artificially fostered differences of tastes and inclinations make the marriage something that lowers the husband intellectually and morally. We are told similarly that liberated women will help others in a useful and rational way, rather than putting their energy into harmful and patronizing charity, as at present; again there is much stress on the improvements from others' points of view if women are liberated from their present rigid and thwarted characters. Now even if this long catalogue of women's shortcomings is true, it should make one wonder afresh what the status of the arguments in

Mill and the Subjection of Women

Chapter 3 can possibly be. If women's influence as it stands is baneful, why should we hasten to employ women in public and private jobs? What can be the utility of pressing into service all these narrow and repressed natures? And can women's vaunted intuition and nervous susceptibility be worth very much after all, if their effects are those described in Chapter 4? Mill cannot have it both ways. If women even as they are deserve employment in the same way as men, then there is no reason to think that a fundamental change of the relations between the sexes will bring great benefits. On the other hand, if a great change here *will* bring vast benefits, is it not suspicious to try to increase utility by making use of women in their present corrupted state?

Apart from the conflicts I have tried to draw out between Chapter 3 and Chapters 1 and 4, there are less localized signs throughout the essay that Mill is having trouble in combining his different arguments. One is his struggle with 'nature'. We are told over and over again that we cannot read off women's nature from their present state. On the other hand, we are assured that women are schooled into suppressing their desires for freedom and self-expression 'in their natural and most healthy direction' (p. 238).[8] So we are to be stopped from arguing that it is natural for women to be passive, but we must argue that it is natural for them to want to be free and self-determining in the way that men are. It is not clear, in fact, that there is a real incoherence here. What is needed is a distinction between facts about human nature that can be supported by some very general theory, and supposed facts that are merely superficial inferences from what happens to be observed. But none of this is made clear in *The Subjection of Women* itself; the reader is left with the impression that nature has been expelled from the argument as an enemy only to be brought in again by the back door.

A more troubling problem is that it is constantly unclear, throughout the essay, just what changes Mill thinks *are* appropriate. Since he is so insistent that women are not constrained by natural inferiority, and repeats several times that what is desirable is that the sexes compete on an equal basis, one would assume that he thinks that women and men will tend to fill the same roles; his remarks at the theoretical level would all tend to imply the radical approach. Yet what he actually says on the subject is timid and reformist at best. He assumes that most women will in fact want only to be wives and mothers, 'the one vocation in which there is nobody to compete with them' (p. 183)—which is not even true, if we mean child-rearing and not just the physical process of birth. He thinks it undesirable for the wife to earn as well as the husband, for having a job will make a woman neglect

---

[8] Cf. the quotation on p. 182; and what is said about equality on p. 173: 'society in equality is its normal state'. This is hardly something we can learn from experience, when history presents us with nothing but hierarchies.

Julia Annas

the home and family. He argues that to have self-respect a woman must be *able* to earn her own living, but that in fact few women will, and he seems to envisage jobs being held only by the unmarried, or by middle-aged women whose children have grown up. This is clearly most unsatisfactory. How can women's education be a serious affair if it is known that most will not use it? In any case, how can it be argued that women really do want to be free and equal with men, and have political and educational parity, if it is taken to be a fact that the reformed state of affairs will make no difference to the majority of women? Mill's position here seems to be simply confused, because he is trying to argue both from the way women actually are, and from their right to become entirely different.

So far I have pointed to some confusions that arise from the fact that Mill attempts to combine the radical approach with the reformist approach. I shall finally try to show that the radical argument as it appears in Chapter 4 creates a further problem for Mill if he wants to apply utilitarian considerations.

In Chapter 4 Mill sets himself to answer the question 'which will be asked the most importunately by those opponents whose conviction is somewhat shaken on the main point. What good are we to expect from the changes proposed in our customs and institutions? Would mankind be at all better off if women were free?' (p. 216). This looks like a utilitarian argument, and Mill in fact goes on to list advantages to be gained from the liberation of women. However, though it is clearly an appeal to consequences, the argument cannot be utilitarian in the present restricted sense of taking into account only people's actual desires and needs; for what Mill cites as benefits would often only satisfy people *already* liberated from former attitudes. He first, for example, mentions the benefit of having the most basic human relationship run justly instead of unjustly; but if most people in a society are not liberated, they will presumably not see the present system of relations between the sexes as unjust, nor see anything wrong with the attitudes engendered by it. This comes out clearly from Mill's eloquent passage on the selfish and self-worshipping attitudes encouraged in men under patriarchy (pp. 218–220). The obvious retort to this is that, if it is true, then most men would not think of change as a *benefit*. Why should men want to change a system so favourable to themselves? Mill assumes that they will do so when they see the injustice of it; but that is the whole problem, for he has emphasized the way they are brought up to accept it as perfectly natural and just.

Similar remarks apply to what Mill says about the increase in happiness in marriage when it becomes a union of equals. Mill assumes that men will appreciate the greater preferability of a rational union between equals rather than a marriage where the husband has all the authority and all the wife does is obey. 'What . . . does the man obtain by it, except an upper servant, a nurse or a mistress?' (p. 233). But what if men have been so

Mill and the Subjection of Women

brought up that that is precisely what they do want out of a marriage? Should these desires not count? As we are aware from Rawls,[9] Mill will have trouble finding a utilitarian ground for discounting desires that can only be satisfied in an unjust system because they are engendered within it. Mill clearly thinks that these desires should *not* count, any more than women's expressed desires to remain happily dominated by men should count; they show nothing except how warped the nature of both men and women can get. But his justification for doing this cannot be a utilitarian one.

This means that Mill faces more of a problem than he is aware of when he represents the effects of liberation as uncontroversially benefits. In any society hitherto, Mill's or ours, the number of people, men and women, who are dissatisfied with the present state of relations between the sexes is very small. Not only do most men derive satisfaction from their dominant position, and would resent its removal; most women accept their position and do not see it as unjust.[10] So for the effects of liberation such as Mill details to be generally agreed to be benefits, there would have to be large-scale changes in people's desires, and for this to come about there would have to be fundamental changes in the way both sexes think about sex differences and sex roles. Nowadays we know that this entails changes right from the beginning of education; if girls and boys learn from books where sexual stereotypes are presented, they will naturally tend to perpetuate those stereotypes. Our whole approach to education has to be changed if people are not to continue to learn the attitudes which lead to discrimination even where legal disabilities disappear.

In this respect there is some truth in the accusation that Mill's thinking about sexual differences is shallow. He is not aware of the massive changes required in people's desires and outlooks before sexual equality becomes a reality and its effects something that people see as beneficial. Consequently, he does not pay enough attention to the extensive interference in people's lives necessary to ensure that the liberation of women becomes a real change and not just the same attitudes under another name. He rejects reverse discrimination, and says nothing about re-educating people's desires by reforming school-books, etc. If he had been aware of this, he might, as an individualist, have been disturbed. We know from *On Liberty* how he rejects, as unjustified, state interference in people's lives even

---

[9] Mostly in part 1 of *A Theory of Justice*.

[10] One small but striking example (quoted from the *Daily Telegraph* of 16 December 1963 by J. Mitchell, *Women's Estate* p. 126): 'All four hundred employees at the Typhoo Tea Works, Birmingham, went on unofficial strike yesterday because a forewoman reprimanded a workman. A shop-steward said, "The forewoman should have referred any question of discipline to the man's foreman . . ." '. 470 people, in fact, struck over this issue; 300 of them were women.

Julia Annas

where this would be agreed to lead to moral improvement. He regards Prohibition as completely unjustifiable, though all would agree that it is better and morally preferable to be without drunkenness and its results. Presumably he would feel quite unhappy about state-aided programmes to help women, quotas for employing women, revision of books, etc. There is a real problem here, since the only effective means of removing injustice appears to involve injustice itself. Mill never faces this problem because he does not see the extent to which people have to be forcibly led to make sexual equality work. In this sense Mill *is* too much of a rationalist about sex and sexual roles; what is wrong is not that he lacked Freud's supposed truths but that he assumes that when people clearly perceive the injustice of sexual inequality they will come to desire its removal, and find greater satisfaction in liberation from it. But unfortunately this is not true.

In *The Subjection of Women*, then, Mill is sure what he is against, but he is not sure whether he is committed to a radical or a reformist approach, and in trying to have it both ways blurs what he is saying.[11] He has seen neither the problems inherent in pressing the argument from the benefits of liberation, given his individualistic beliefs, nor the difficulties lurking in his attempt to combine both his main lines of thought.

It is intriguing here to notice the way in which *The Subjection of Women* contrasts with an earlier essay on the same theme, *The Enfranchisement of Women*. There are three points at which, by adopting a more radical position than *The Subjection of Women*, and ignoring or rejecting the reformist approach, it achieves a more consistent and stronger argument.

Firstly, *The Enfranchisement of Women* argues firmly that 'The proper sphere for all human beings is the largest and highest which they are able to attain to. What this is, cannot be ascertained, without complete liberty of choice' (p. 100). It is therefore a complete waste of time to argue about women's peculiar aptitudes or capacities. What women are like, and are able to do, will be decided by what they actually do when they are free to have a choice, and in no other way. Thus we find avoided, and on clear grounds, Mill's various disastrous attempts to argue, in Chapter 3 of *The Subjection of Women*, the usefulness of women's 'special gifts', intuitions, etc. Like Mill, the author of the earlier essay says that it cannot be true that women are incapable of political life on the basis of there having been capable women rulers, but because no attempt is made to argue from a few

---

[11] Commentators generally see one or the other strand, but not the fact that Mill combines both. McCloskey curtly sums up the essay by saying (op. cit., p. 136), 'Obviously the utilitarian arguments [from the abuses of power, etc.] have greater force and relevance here than elsewhere'. Ryan, on the other hand, sums up just as curtly (op. cit., pp. 157–158), 'the argument is essentially the argument from individuality', and notes that arguing 'for the higher and better happiness which stems from self-respect and personal autonomy' is 'not a very obviously utilitarian appeal'.

Mill and the Subjection of Women

examples to a supposed fitness for practical matters on the part of all women, there is no incompatibility with the main line of argument.

Secondly, *The Enfranchisement of Women* argues that women should earn a living (p. 105). Where Mill was confused and cool towards this, the earlier essay argues that it would be a good thing even if the effect on wages were all that the most alarmist suggest. Even if man and wife together earned only what he earns now, 'how infinitely preferable is it that part of the income should be of the woman's earning, . . . rather than that she should be compelled to stand aside in order that men may be the sole earners, and the sole dispensers of what is earned'. Women discover self-respect if they earn, and equality of standing with the man; and this is much more important, from the viewpoint of sound relationships between the sexes, than mere economic improvement in the family position. How much more realistic this is than Mill's timid declaration that a woman should draw self-respect from an ability to earn which she in fact makes no use of when married. His position here is sentimental; the earlier essay is more aware of the realities of power.

It is also clear that if women are really to have equality, their education must be seriously intended to fit them for serious jobs. Here the author foresees conflict with what are called 'the moderate reformers of the education of women', which would appear to include the author of *The Subjection of Women*. Women should be taught 'solid instruction', not 'superficial instruction on solid subjects'. They must be educated in a way that makes them independent beings; it is merely fudging the issue to bring them up to be fit companions for men who will none the less do all the earning and thus retain all the economic power. Mill's confused and senti-mental position is here demolished with a few effective words: 'they do not say that men should be educated to be the companions of women'.

Lastly, *The Enfranchisement of Women* is both frank and clear about the claim that liberation will lead to greater happiness for women (pp. 117 ff.). Women are not in general aware of frustration, and tend not to feel their position intolerable, but this does not matter: Asian women do not mind being in purdah, and find the thought of going about freely shocking, but this does not mean that they should not be liberated from seclusion, or that they would not appreciate freedom once they had it; and the same holds for European women who cannot appreciate why it is important for them to be financially independent. 'The vast population of Asia do not desire or value, probably would not accept, political liberty, nor the savages of the forest, civilization; which does not prove that either of those things is undesirable for them, or that they will not, at some future time, enjoy it' (p. 117). This is a bold but consistent position: people's present desires are discounted in favour of the desires that would be had if their natural selves were not repressed. Here we find the radical approach put forward boldly, with no attempt at compromise with the reformist approach; and the application to

Julia Annas

women is made straightforwardly. 'How does the objector know that women do not desire equality and freedom? He never knew a woman who did not, or would not, desire it for herself individually. It would be very simple to suppose, that if they do desire it they will say so. Their position is like that of the tenants or labourers who vote against their own political interests to please their landlords or employers; with the unique addition, that submission is inculcated on them from childhood, as the peculiar grace and attraction of their character' (p. 118).

The earlier essay is thus more coherent as argument than the later; it quite avoids the struggles that occupy Mill over natural differences, and it avoids his tendency to lapse back into a more timid position than his radical premises would suggest.

I have so far spoken non-committally about 'the author of *The Enfranchisement of Women*' because there is some uncertainty about whom to call the author. It was published under Mill's name, but in an introduction to it Mill says that it is Harriet's work, in a stronger and more definite way than in his customary avowals of general intellectual indebtedness.[12] Taking it to be Harriet's work would certainly offer a neat solution to the problem of the discrepancies I have noted. However, I do not wish here to make a contribution to the debate about the extent of Harriet's contributions to Mill's work, which is too complicated a topic to raise here. What is important is simply that *The Subjection of Women* puts forward a position more complicated (as well as more lengthily expressed) than that of *The Enfranchisement of Women*, and in the process, I maintain, introduces deep confusions. It is certainly true that the position put forward in the earlier essay needs much more argument to back up its basic premises before it can be regarded as defensible; but at least it is clear and provides a basis for a coherent practical programme. In *The Subjection of Women*, I believe, we can see Mill doing something strikingly similar to what he does in *Utilitarianism*. Anxious to do justice to all sides of a question he sees to be complex and important, and unwilling to commit himself definitively to one simple line of thought, he qualifies an originally bold and straightforward theory to the point of inconsistency.[13]

St Hugh's College, Oxford

[12] ' . . . the following Essay is hers in a peculiar sense, my share in it being little more than that of an editor and amanuensis. Its authorship having been known at the time and publicly attributed to her' (p. 91). Rossi (pp. 41–43) discusses other evidence for Harriet's authorship, which she accepts.

[13] I am grateful for helpful comments and discussion to A. O. J. Cockshut, J. Dybikowski and G. Segal.

[11]

MILL ON LIBERTY AND MORALITY

PARTS I and II of this paper set out Mill's theory of liberty in three main principles. Part I tries to establish the content of the leading principle of the theory, the Principle of Liberty, and to show from its form that it requires further principles to go with it. Part II supplies two further principles and comments on the application of the theory.

Parts III and IV argue that there is a tension in Mill's theory of liberty as to what counts as conduct harmful to others, and that this tension is traceable to his conception of morality. In particular Mill needs to reconcile the Principle of Liberty with his belief in the enforceability of morality. The reconciliation he attempts imposes severe constraints on the content of morality and commits him to a more negative conception of morality than is commonly attributed to him. The relevant aspects of his view are embodied in two further principles.

Parts V and VI consider the implications of Mill's conception of morality for the kind of utilitarianism which he could consistently hold, and argue that his ability to reconcile his secondary principles with the Principle of Utility reflects the fact that the Principle of Utility is not itself a moral principle.

A short epilogue suggests that in arriving at a synthesis which embodies all five of the secondary principles referred to, together with some version of the Principle of Utility, Mill has achieved consistency at the cost of truth.

I. The Form of the Principle of Liberty

An account of Mill's theory of liberty must of course begin with the leading principle of the essay *On Liberty*. I first consider just what content the principle has, and show from its very form that it needs to be supplemented by further principles.

The object of this Essay is to assert one very simple principle . . . that the sole end for which mankind are warranted, individually or collectively, in interfering with the liberty of action of any of their number,

D. G. BROWN

is self-protection. That the only purpose for which power can be rightfully exercised over any member of a civilized community, against his will, is to prevent harm to others.[1]

In this official announcement of his principle, in two versions, Mill specifies an end or purpose and a kind of action, and says that the former is the only purpose for which the latter is warranted, or can be rightfully done. The purpose is the self-protection of mankind or the prevention of harm to others. The kind of action is interfering with the liberty of action of the individual, or exercising power over a member of a civilized community against his will. Selecting among the variant readings he offers, we can say: the only purpose for which it is warranted to interfere with the liberty of action of the individual is to prevent harm to others.

The formulation in terms of a purpose which warrants (that is, justifies) action is elegant for this occasion and characteristic of Mill's conception of practical reasoning (compare end of Section VI below). But it is unexplicit about the possibility of overriding considerations. Suppose that the specified purpose can be fulfilled by a particular restriction on the individual; is that a sufficient condition for the restriction to be justified? Clearly Mill thinks not, since the disadvantage to the individual or to society of the loss of freedom may outweigh the prevention of the harm.

It must by no means be supposed, because damage, or probability of damage, to the interests of others, can alone justify the interference of society, that therefore it always does justify such interference [p. 150].

So Mill says that here is a purpose which *can* justify the action, and in conditions yet to be given *will* justify it; and no other purpose *can* justify it.

---

[1] J. S. Mill, *Utilitarianism, Liberty and Representative Government* (London, 1910), pp. 72-73. All page references to *On Liberty* are to this Everyman edition. Those to *Utilitarianism* are double. Pages in this edition, marked "Ev. ed.," are preceded by the page reference to John Stuart Mill, *Essays on Ethics, Religion, and Society* (Toronto, 1969), which is Vol. X of the *Collected Works of John Stuart Mill*.

MILL ON LIBERTY AND MORALITY

A nearly equivalent principle could be simply phrased in terms of reasons. That a restriction on liberty will prevent harm to others is always a good reason for it, and nothing else is ever a good reason.[2] Or again: there is a good reason for a restriction if and only if it will prevent harm to others.

A third type of formulation seems to me to be nearly equivalent and to have a useful familiarity, and I will adopt it for working purposes. I will speak not of the purposes which can justify restriction, or of the considerations which are good reasons for restriction, but rather of the circumstances in which there ought prima facie to be a restriction. Formulated in this way, the principle says that the liberty of action of the individual ought prima facie to be interfered with if and only if the interference will prevent harm to others.

But this formulation, reasonably faithful as it is to the words of this passage, does not quite reflect the interpretation which Mill himself seems to place on them. Mill consistently writes and argues as if he had specified, not that interference with the conduct should prevent harm to others, but rather that the conduct itself should be harmful to others.[3] Accordingly I formulate the leading principle of Mill's theory of liberty as follows:

I. *The Principle of Liberty:* The liberty of action of the individual ought prima facie to be interfered with if and only if his conduct is harmful to others.

Cast in such a form, the principle shows a positive and a negative side. It lays down a sufficient condition, and it lays down a necessary condition, for its being so that the liberty of the

---

[2] Here, and throughout the paper, I ignore needed qualifications dealing with probable rather than actual harm and probable rather than actual effects of restrictions. The principles stated apply only under unrealistic assumptions about certainty. They must be regarded as first approximations, worth dwelling on because of the elegance with which they can sketch the structure of actual practical reasoning.

[3] Thus, in the same paragraph, "the conduct ... must be calculated to produce evil to some one else" (p. 73); on p. 75, "so long as what we do does not harm them"; on p. 150, "damage, or probability of damage, to the interests of others"; and so on. As to the evidence from his way of arguing, see Sec. III below.

D. G. BROWN

individual ought prima facie to be interfered with. I have claimed that this is nearly equivalent to laying down a sufficient condition, and a necessary condition, for there being a good reason to interfere.

What we have just seen about the sufficient condition is that the principle, on its positive side, tell us less than it appears to at first about exactly when restriction of liberty is justified. That which it gives a sufficient (and necessary) condition *for* is not the legitimacy of interference. It is only the existence of a prima-facie case for the legitimacy of interference—or of a good reason for interfering, or of a good reason for saying that others ought to interfere. The principle needs to be supplemented by an account of the possible reasons against restriction and of the principles, if any, on which we are to weigh the reasons for and the reasons against.

On the negative side, however, the principle says all that we could ask of it. By giving this necessary condition for the existence of a reason for restriction, it rules out as irrelevant absolutely everything but the prevention of harm to others. This sharp and unequivocal denial is the cutting edge of Mill's essay. For now, I call attention merely to the generality of the negation. It allows for an indefinitely large number of applications, yielding the exclusion of indefinitely many classes of considerations. The one to which Mill understandably gives prominence is the exclusion of the individual's own good, physical or moral, as a justification for interfering with his liberty of action. He states this corollary immediately after the double statement of the principle (p. 73). Strictly speaking, it is no more a part of the principle itself than those corollaries which exclude the enforcement of aesthetic standards and the enforcement of religious requirements. One enemy, paternalism, so dominates the field of debate on which Mill is fighting that it becomes easy to think of the corollary as actually being the negative half of his principle. This identification, however, Mill always avoids.[4]

---

[4] He does so, e.g., even in his final chapter, when he comes to refer (p. 149) to "the two maxims which together form the entire doctrine of this Essay," and says the first is "that the individual is not accountable to society for his actions, in so far as these concern the interests of no person but himself." This maxim

MILL ON LIBERTY AND MORALITY

II. THE REST OF MILL'S THEORY OF LIBERTY

The question now arises of what, in Mill's view, could provide reasons against interfering with the liberty of the individual. This is the question of what considerations will have to be weighed against the reasons for interference which are provided for by Mill's main principle.

I find two further principles in Mill's theory of liberty. Both yield such contrary reasons, and the second of them also says how we are to weigh conflicting considerations. The three principles together, the Principle of Liberty and these two, constitute Mill's theory of liberty. In this section I complete a brief exposition of the theory and notice some points about the application of the theory.

It would appear, in any case, to be a presupposition of Mill's main principle that some reason against interference is not merely available, but always available. The assertion that only a certain kind of thing can justify interference presupposes that justification is called for; it implies that there is a prima-facie case against interference.

The simplest class of such considerations, and one which obviously answers to the universality of this implication, is provided by Mill's assertion that "all restraint, *qua* restraint, is an evil" (p. 150). From this we can derive, with the help of any reasonable version of the Principle of Utility, that all restraint is prima facie wrong. Taking a formulation in terms similar to those of Principle I, we have as the second main principle of Mill's theory of liberty:

II. All interference with the liberty of action of the individual is prima facie wrong.

We can see that this is Mill's principle, and that he gives it the role which I have assigned to it in his theory, by looking at

I take to be equivalent to the negative half of the principle, except for the vagueness of "concern the interests" and except for a kind of suggestion that only considerations of the interest of persons could ever be pleaded on behalf of restriction. The generality of the exclusion, though obscured by this allusion to the interests of the person himself, is still present.

D. G. BROWN

the passage where the quoted remark occurs. He speaks there
of questions which "involve considerations of liberty, only in so
far as leaving people to themselves is always better, *caeteris
paribus*, than controlling them" (p. 151). The context is relevant
for the present purpose, for Mill is saying about questions of
trade that they do affect the interests of others and that, accordingly, the view that people "may be legitimately controlled for
these ends is in principle undeniable" (p. 151). The Principle
of Liberty being in this sense not involved—that is, its applicability not being in dispute—what remains to provide "considerations of liberty" is this category of reasons on the other
side, namely those which invoke the evil of restraint as such.
In fact, Mill thinks the doctrine of free trade turns on factual
grounds, which show that the legitimate aims of interference
cannot be effectively pursued in that way. This I take to be the
force of his claim that the doctrine "rests on grounds different
from, though equally solid with, the principle of individual
liberty asserted in this Essay" (p. 150). It is consistent with this
interpretation to say that, as far as individual liberty to trade is
concerned, Mill is prepared to weigh the harm to others caused
in the course of trade against the standing evil of restraint as
such. But in practice he thinks the former consideration derived
from the principle of individual liberty breaks down on grounds
of the ineffectiveness of restraint as a means, and leaves the
standing evil of restraint in possession of the field. That the
former consideration breaks down in this way is the doctrine of
free trade.

There is nothing mysterious about the status which Mill
assigns to the assertion that all restraint, qua restraint, is an
evil.[5] There is no doubt that he took it for granted as an obvious

---

[5] Benn and Peters say that Mill offers no justification of it, and treats it as
self-evident (S. I. Benn and R. S. Peters, *Social Principles and the Democratic
State* [London, 1959], p. 220). Surely he merely treats it as evident, which it
is. He is clearly making a judgment of utility, and it is fanciful on their part to
construct an account of this doctrine as "a purely formal, or procedural maxim"
(p. 222), somehow implied in the definition of a moral justification. Mill does
defend the claim that "the onus of making out a case always lies on the
defenders of legal prohibitions," and defends it by an analysis of utilities
(*Principles of Political Economy*, ed. by J. M. Robson, in *Collected Works of*

MILL ON LIBERTY AND MORALITY

and substantial judgment on utilities which, in accordance with the Principle of Utility, provided a permanent prima-facie case against restraint, and made it necessary to define the grounds on which liberty could justifiably be abridged.

To find Mill's general view on the further reasons there can be against restricting liberty, we need to consult a number of passages. Let us begin with the two places in the essay *On Liberty* where Mill explicitly deals with the category of considerations which may counterbalance harm to others.

In the first of these, which occurs in the commentary on the enunciation of his principle, Mill refers to the matters in which the individual "is *de jure* amenable to those whose interests are concerned, and, if need be, to society as their protector" and goes on to say:

There are often good reasons for not holding him to the responsibility; but these reasons must arise from the special expediencies of the case; either because it is a kind of case in which he is on the whole likely to act better, when left to his own discretion, than when controlled in any way in which society have it in their power to control him; or because the attempt to exercise control would produce other evils, greater than those which it would prevent [p. 74].

The second passage, similarly, follows the recapitulation of the doctrine of the essay in two maxims. Mill is offering observations relevant to the application of his principles in detail. In two paragraphs he discusses, respectively, competition and free trade, in illustration of the remark (already quoted) that

it must by no means be supposed, because damage, or probability of damage, to the interests of others, can alone justify the interference of society, that therefore it always does justify such interference [p. 150].

John Stuart Mill [Toronto, 1965], Bk. V, ch. xi, sec. 2, p. 938). The same passage makes clear that there lies behind the assertion that restraint qua restraint is an evil the whole Aristotelian and Humboldtian account of happiness in the first half of the chapter in *On Liberty* "Of individuality, as one of the elements of well-being."

D. G. BROWN

With respect to competition, Mill applies a general statement
that in many cases

an individual, in pursuing a legitimate object, necessarily and
therefore legitimately causes pain or loss to others, or intercepts a
good which they had a reasonable hope of obtaining [p. 150].

With respect to free trade, Mill says that trade is a social act,
affecting the interests of others, and so in principle comes within
the jurisdiction of society (p. 150).

The grounds on which Mill argues nevertheless against interferences with competition or with trade are not obviously the
same in the two cases. In competition, the losers lose.

But it is, by common admission, better for the general interest of
mankind, that persons should pursue their objects undeterred by this
sort of consequences. In other words, society admits no right, either
legal or moral, in the disappointed competitors; and feels called on
to interfere, only when means of success have been employed which
it is contrary to the general interest to permit—namely, fraud or
treachery, and force [p. 150].

In the case of trade, as we have seen, the argument is simply
that the restraints do not really produce the results that it is
desired to obtain by them.

In interpreting these two official discussions, we can also draw
upon two comments made in the central chapter (IV), which
is devoted to exposition and defense of his thesis in its general
form. In the initial exposition he says:

As soon as any part of a person's conduct affects prejudicially the
interests of others, society has jurisdiction over it, and the question
whether the general welfare will or will not be promoted by interfering with it, becomes open to discussion [p. 132].

Later, in defending the distinction between conduct which does
and does not concern others, he introduces finer distinctions
among the ways and degrees in which it may concern others.
But his main distinction is between harm which violates a distinct
and assignable obligation, and harm which does not (p. 137).

MILL ON LIBERTY AND MORALITY

For if harmful conduct does violate a distinct and assignable obligation, then some kind of sanction will be appropriate, either moral sanctions or "punishment by opinion" or, in a restricted range of cases, legal sanctions; whereas if it does not violate such an obligation, it is to be left free. Mill speaks as follows of this residue of harmful conduct:

But with regard to the merely contingent, or, as it may be called, constructive injury which a person causes to society, by conduct which neither violates any specific duty to the public, nor occasions perceptible hurt to any assignable individual except himself; the inconvenience is one which society can afford to bear, for the sake of the greater good of human freedom [p. 138].

Surveying this textual evidence, I think we can discern one main doctrine, together with a variety of points about the application of it. The main doctrine does little more than direct us to utilitarian considerations bearing on the question in hand, with the reference to utilities put in terms of interests (or welfare), thereby reminding us that we must consider all the effects of a proposed restraint. The question in hand, at this stage, is whether conduct ought to be interfered with when we know both that interference is prima facie wrong and that the conduct, being harmful, ought prima facie to be interfered with. The answer Mill gives, however abstract, he seems to regard as the best that can be given, and I formulate it as follows, to provide the third main principle of his theory of liberty:

III. Conduct which is harmful to others ought actually to be interfered with if and only if it is better for the general interest to do so.

By Mill's own conception of his moral theory (compare p. 74), I take it we have arrived at this point by successive applications of the Principle of Utility. The evil of restraint as such, which gives rise to the prima-facie wrongness of restraint (Principle II) and to the demand that restraint be justified, is made relevant by the Principle of Utility. The Principle of Liberty (I) then defines the class of possible justifications, the prevention of harm, but

D. G. BROWN

not of harm to the agent, being again applications of the Principle of Utility. When the Principle of Liberty presents us once again with the question of countervailing considerations, we return to the source, and Principle III reminds us that we are again to invoke the first principle of all.

We can exhibit the rest of Mill's points as concerned with the application in practice of this extremely general and abstract third principle. His problem is to find relevant features of particular cases, or relevant classifications of utilities and disutilities, which will enable him to make useful general statements about when the general interest will or will not be served by restraint. Two examples will be enough. On one occasion, Mill divides the field of application into two parts, according to whether or not there is any available method of control likely to have the desired effect of reducing the harm done by the individual; where there is, the question becomes whether "the attempt to exercise control would produce other evils, greater than those it would prevent" (p. 74). On another occasion, Mill proceeds not by the merits of the methods of control, but by the type and gravity of the harm done. Leaving aside for now the question of whether control should be exercised by law or by less formal pressures, Mill locates the watershed between some control and no control by reference to whether the harm does or does not involve the violation of a distinct and assignable obligation (p. 137; compare p. 138). Without going into further detail, I think we can claim that these two distinctions belong to the application of the theory in practice, and that the theory itself is fairly represented by the three principles stated.

III. Preventing Harm

We have seen that the Principle of Liberty, by its very form, requires for its application to particular cases to be taken in conjunction with other principles, which Mill also supplies. These are Principle II, that all restraint is prima facie wrong, and Principle III, to the effect that conduct which the Principle of Liberty does provide a case for interfering with ought actually

MILL ON LIBERTY AND MORALITY

to be interfered with if and only if it is in the general interest to do so. Let us now return to the Principle of Liberty itself and examine it more closely. In this section I exhibit a difficulty in the interpretation of the principle. In the following section, I offer a resolution which looks to the relation between Mill's theory of liberty and his theory of morality, and invokes in particular his view on the enforceability of moral requirements.

I began from Mill's crisp formulation of the only purpose for which it is warranted to interfere with the liberty of action of the individual: to prevent harm to others. In addition, he uses a variety of expressions that can be taken to be or imply a formulation of his principle. His phrases include: "calculated to produce evil to someone else" (p. 73), "affects prejudicially the interests of others" (p. 132), and "damage, or the probability of damage, to the interests of others" (p. 150). It is evident, as Professor J. C. Rees instructively showed,[6] that Mill is specifying an effect on the interests of other people. It is equally evident that in these phrases he is specifying a negative effect. But the force of his principle becomes problematic when we observe how wide is the full variation among the phrases he does use, when we attend to the main dimension along which variation occurs, and when we inspect the examples which Mill in fact brings within the reach of his principle. At one extreme we find the definiteness of "an act hurtful to others" (p. 74). At the other extreme we find the vagueness of "conduct ... which concerns others" (p. 73); nor can we regard this as a mere lapse, when we encounter the positive statement that a man may be compelled "to bear his fair share ... in any ... joint work necessary to the interest of the society of which he enjoys the protection" (p. 74).

This range of variation is due to a tension between two opposing tendencies. One tendency is to keep strictly to action as distinguished from inaction, and harm as distinguished from failure to help. The other is to include any aspect of conduct which is

---

[6] J. C. Rees, "A Re-reading of Mill on Liberty," *Political Studies*, VIII (1960), 113-129 (reprinted in P. Radcliff [ed.], *Limits of Liberty* [Belmont, 1966], pp. 87-107). But Rees's account of interests needs correction, a process begun but not finished by Ted Honderich, "Mill on Liberty," *Inquiry*, 10 (1967), 292-297.

D. G. BROWN

susceptible of control and in which the public interest is somehow importantly at stake. The range over which Mill appears to hesitate can perhaps be better appreciated by locating a position in each direction which lies beyond the range. One radical form of liberalism would set as the only limit to individual liberty that one's action should not restrict the liberty of anyone else. Mill is far too utilitarian to accept such a view or to ignore the further ways in which it is possible to harm others. One radical kind of utilitarianism would subject the individual to coercion for any purpose the fulfillment of which would contribute substantially to an increase in utility. Mill is far too liberal to think it plausible that widespread positive uses of coercion could really maximize utility. His problem (see p. 74) is to determine what principle governing external control really is authorized by considerations of utility.

On the face of it, his explicit discussion of this problem takes him at once beyond his official formulations (pp. 72-73) to the phrase "those actions of each, which concern the interest of other people" (p. 74), and to the recognition under this heading, along with "acts hurtful to others," of "many positive acts for the benefit of others, which he may rightfully be compelled to perform," apparently including even anything "which . . . it is obviously a man's duty to do" (p. 74). But he immediately tries to reassimilate this account to his original version by saying:

A person may cause evil to others not only by his actions but by his inaction, and in either case he is justly accountable to them for the injury. The latter case, it is true, requires a much more cautious exercise of compulsion than the former. To make anyone answerable for doing evil to others is the rule; to make him answerable for not preventing evil is, comparatively speaking, the exception. Yet there are many cases clear enough and grave enough to justify that exception [p. 74].

I take it Mill implies here a rough identification of harming, injury, and causing evil, and uses the notion of causing evil by inaction to argue that these terms have a wider extension than one might think. He seems to imply both that not preventing evil can in some circumstances be causing evil by inaction

MILL ON LIBERTY AND MORALITY

(certainly it is not always so), and that it is the only way of causing evil by inaction. The general question which confronts Mill's analysis at this point, and which we must now consider, is whether such arguments, or any arguments at all, could stretch the category of "causing evil to others" to cover the whole range of conduct that Mill actually includes.

Mill would be on relatively strong ground with those personal obligations breach of which can be brought under the classification of "disappointment of expectation." In the chapter on justice in *Utilitarianism* he argues that such things as breach of promise and breach of friendship come under justice, even strictly interpreted, on the grounds that there is a violation of right consisting in hurt to an assignable individual (p. 256; Ev. ed. pp. 56-57). But the very examples which Mill gives of rightly exacted acts of individual beneficence resist such treatment. If I do not save a fellow creature's life, or do not protect the defenseless against a third party, even in circumstances in which I could be required to do so, it does not follow that in every such case I cause harm to the neglected person or to anyone at all. It is sufficient to preclude such an inference, and in general to preclude any inference from not preventing evil to causing evil, to consider the agency of other people. A drowning man may have jumped or may have been pushed, and quite ordinary circumstances may require us to assign the agency of some other person than myself as the cause of the evil.

What is still more doubtful is whether Mill can include under causing harm to others the breach of one's responsibilities to society at large. In his two official expositions, Mill presents this latter area of legitimate coercion in similar yet discrepant terms. In the first, a man may be compelled "to bear his fair share in ... any ... joint work necessary to the interest of the society of which he enjoys the protection" (p. 74); in the second, to the "bearing his share (to be fixed on some equitable principle) of the labours and sacrifices incurred for defending the society or its members from injury and molestation" (p. 132), where this is again conceived as a return for the benefit of protection by society. The very discrepancy between Mill's two formulations is evidence of serious hesitation in his doctrine. And it seems clear

D. G. BROWN

to me that Mill fails to show that "causing harm" will stretch as far as he needs it to. That the individual is necessarily injuring others by not bearing his share of protecting them from injury is a relatively arguable if dubious claim. But that he is necessarily injuring them by not bearing his share of any joint work necessary to the interest of the society seems to be a much stronger claim and an indefensible one. There can be no guarantee that joint works necessary to the interest of society will not include institutional care for the mentally defective, urban redevelopment, or foreign aid to countries whose economic condition might otherwise lead to war. I cannot see how refusal to co-operate in such efforts toward alleviation of existing problems could be shown to constitute causing harm to others.

Mill's problem would not be solved even if he were to revert to the original formulation of the Principle of Liberty, in place of the principle he seeks to defend. That formulation allowed interference to prevent harm to others, whether or not the harm was attributable to the individual whose liberty was interfered with. Such a principle would grant him without a struggle certain cases which he feels the need to contest, including compulsion to save a life and compulsion to intervene in an attack on the defenseless. But even the general prevention of harm would not stretch to cover a fair share of every joint work necessary to the interest of society.

IV. ENFORCING MORALITY

There is a doctrine of Mill's which suggests a surprisingly obvious explanation of his tendency to stretch the application of the Principle of Liberty. Even if it did not fill this explanatory role, it would remain a striking doctrine whose relation to the Principle of Liberty would have to be considered. So far as I know, neither critics nor supporters of his principle have taken it seriously, with the exception of Mr. Alan Ryan (see Section VI below).

Mill believes in the enforcement of morality. I mean of course in principle, and subject in practice to countervailing reasons of the kind reviewed above for the Principle of Liberty. Since Mill's

MILL ON LIBERTY AND MORALITY

principle has actually been invoked against the enforcement of morality,[7] it may be a needed corrective to accepted images of Mill to quote in full this passage from *Utilitarianism:*

the idea of penal sanction, which is the essence of law, enters not only into the conception of injustice, but into that of any kind of wrong. We do not call anything wrong, unless we mean to imply that a person ought to be punished in some way or other for doing it; if not by law, by the opinion of his fellow creatures; if not by opinion, by the reproaches of his own conscience. This seems the real turning point of the distinction between morality and simple expediency. It is a part of the notion of Duty in every one of its forms, that a person may rightfully be compelled to fulfil it. Duty is a thing which may be exacted from a person, as one exacts a debt. Unless we think that it may be exacted from him, we do not call it his duty. Reasons of prudence, or the interest of other people, may militate against actually exacting it; but the person himself, it is clearly understood, would not be entitled to complain. There are other things, on the contrary, which we wish that people should do, which we like or admire them for doing, perhaps dislike or despise them for not doing, but yet admit that they are not bound to do; it is not a case of moral obligation; we do not blame them, that is, we do not think that they are proper objects of punishment [p. 246; Ev. ed. p. 45].

---

[7] Professor H. L. A. Hart, in *Law, Liberty and Morality* (New York, 1966), writes:

The fourth question is the subject of these lectures. It concerns the legal enforcement of morality and has been formulated in many different ways: Is the fact that certain conduct is by common standards immoral sufficient to justify making that conduct punishable by law? Is it morally permissible to enforce morality as such? Ought immorality as such to be a crime?
To this question John Stuart Mill gave an emphatic negative answer in his essay *On liberty* one hundred years ago . . . . He said, "The only purpose for which power can rightfully be exercised over any member of a civilised community against his will is to prevent harm to others" [p. 4].

Hart allows exceptions to Mill's principle, and then says: "But on the narrower issue relevant to the enforcement of morality Mill seems to me to be right" (p. 5).

Of course, Hart sees clearly the distinction between "positive" and "critical" morality (pp. 17 ff., 82), and his argument is directed against the enforcement of positive (accepted) morality. But it seems not to occur to him that the distinction is critical for the interpretation of Mill. Not only is it odd for him to invoke as his ally, without comment, a writer who advocates enforcement of morality; it will also be necessary in the long run to disarm the Devlin advocacy of enforcing accepted morality by explicitly dissociating it from Mill's thesis, which sounds so much like it. As it is, one cannot even tell whether Hart would agree with Mill's thesis or not.

147

D. G. BROWN

In this passage Mill moves indiscriminately among duty, obligation, and wrongness, and relies on the reader to select appropriate legal and moral uses of these three terms. But he is clearly insistent (compare pp. 246-247; Ev. ed. p. 46) that he is setting out a characteristic feature of the province of morality in general. It also seems to me clearly the implication of what he is saying, although he is not perfectly explicit, that as long as we take legitimacy of compulsion in a moral sense of "legitimacy" this feature is not only characteristic of morality but also peculiar to it. Accepting this interpretation, and noticing that in fact duties and obligations are things which it is wrong not to do, I think we can state the doctrine of this passage in the following principle:

> IV. *The Principle of Enforcing Morality:* The liberty of action of the individual ought prima facie to be interfered with if and only if his conduct is prima facie morally wrong.

We need the second "prima facie" so that prima-facie wrongness (even when overridden by contrary considerations), and not only actual wrongness, will generate a prima-facie case for interference. The principle relates prima-facie judgments, and says in effect that the moral grounds for interfering with the liberty of action of the individual are precisely the same sorts of thing as tend to make his conduct wrong.

There is evidence that the Principle of Enforcing Morality, stated in *Utilitarianism*, is at least at the back of Mill's mind in the essay *On Liberty*. This evidence consists mainly of places at which Mill identifies the sphere of morality with that of legitimate public control, or contrasts it with that of individual liberty. For example, he says:

Acts injurious to others require a totally different treatment. Encroachment on their rights; infliction on them of any loss or damage not justified by his own rights; falsehood or duplicity in dealing with them; unfair or ungenerous use of advantages over them; even selfish abstinence from defending them against injury—these are fit objects of moral reprobation, and in grave cases, of moral retribution and punishment. And not only these acts, but the dispositions which lead

MILL ON LIBERTY AND MORALITY

to them, are properly immoral. . . . These are moral vices, and constitute a bad and odious moral character: unlike the self-regarding faults previously mentioned, which are not properly immoralities [p. 135].

Again more briefly, the contrast appears in these two sentences:

When, by conduct of this sort, a person is led to violate a distinct and assignable obligation to any other person or persons, *the case is taken out of the self-regarding class and becomes amenable to moral disapprobation in the proper sense of the term.* . . . Whenever, in short, there is a definite damage, or a definite risk of damage, either to an individual or to the public, *the case is taken out of the province of liberty and placed in that of morality or law* [pp. 137-138, my italics].

Both IV and the Principle of Liberty (I) deal with the conditions that are necessary and sufficient for there to be a good moral reason to restrict the liberty of the individual. In I the condition is that he be harming others; in IV the condition is that he be doing something to which there is some kind of moral objection. My suggestion is that Mill is found stretching the application of I, and that he seems to be stretching it toward the full range of IV. Since he holds both, he is committed to the claim that their predicates are extensionally equivalent. Since in fact they are not, and there is morally wrong conduct which does not harm others, his actual drawing of the line of legitimacy cannot satisfy both principles. What I find interesting is that his final partition of kinds of conduct seems to conform more closely to the enforcement of morality and only morality, as he conceives it, than to the prevention of harm, and only harm, as he conceives that.

I remarked that since Mill holds both Principles I and IV, he is committed to holding that their predicates are extensionally equivalent. Let us notice more generally the relations among the principles Mill is committed to. Since harmfulness and prima-facie wrongness are each said to be necessary and sufficient for the same thing—namely, for its being the case that conduct ought prima facie to be interfered with—it will follow that harmfulness and prima-facie wrongness coincide. In other words, Mill is committed to a further principle:

V. Conduct is prima facie morally wrong if and only if it is harmful to others.

The truth of V is a necessary and sufficient condition for I and IV to be extensionally equivalent as principles. As long as V is true, I and IV stand or fall together. But further, the three principles are symmetrically related, in that each of I, IV, and V states a necessary and sufficient condition for the extensional equivalence of the other two. We have three classes of conduct: (*a*) that which ought prima facie to be interfered with, (*b*) that which is harmful to others, and (*c*) that which is prima facie morally wrong; and the three principles assert the coincidence of the pairs of these. It is clear that if any two assertions are true, all three classes coincide, and the third assertion is true. If any one assertion is true, the other two assertions say the same thing of coincident classes, and must stand or fall together. If any one assertion is false, then at least one of the others must also be false. Since any moral theory might fairly be asked for its implications on these central topics, it may be of interest to consider, when dealing with other theories besides Mill's, in which particular way they satisfy these constraints.

V. MILL'S UTILITARIANISM

Granting that Mill accepts the Principle of Enforcing Morality, we find, I think, that the original problem of interpretation is not so much solved as deepened. Mill's arguments and examples raised the question of why, in his application of the Principle of Liberty, he appeared to be stretching the category of conduct which harms others, and the question of what independent standard for legitimacy of interference might be influencing him to do so. Evidently, if he believes that it is legitimate to interfere with any wrongdoing, coherence will require him to exhibit every kind of wrongdoing as the doing of harm. This would help to explain such things as his claim that, where there is a duty to save a life, the neglect of that duty would amount to causing harm by inaction. Even supposing that Mill is right and I am wrong about the inclusiveness of causing harm, Mill's arguments

MILL ON LIBERTY AND MORALITY

would still be explained by his acceptance of the three principles, together with the need to answer predictable skepticism about the coincidence of the three classes of conduct. To this extent, the Principle of Enforcing Morality helps to clarify the text. But it does so at the cost of presenting us with V, which says that only the causing of harm is prima facie wrong. The problem of reconciling this doctrine with the Principle of Utility is as difficult a problem as the one we began with.

Is it conceivable that the principle Mill speaks of as the Principle of Utility is consistent with Principle V? If it is of this kind, it can hardly be a principle which demands the maximization of utility, in the sense of making any action wrong if there is an alternative action the over-all consequences of which include the realization of a higher total utility. It must be a principle with much less exacting moral consequences, and must allow Mill a more restrictive view of morality than has commonly been attributed to him.

That this is at least conceivable is shown by a chapter in Bain,[8] which Mill refers to in that passage in *Utilitarianism* (p. 246; Ev. ed. p. 45) where he is most explicit about enforcing morality. In a footnote Mill calls it "an admirable chapter," in which his point is "enforced and illustrated." There we find clear denials of a more positive form of utilitarianism (phrased, it is true, as criticisms of the principle of utility). For example, Bain says of utility:

Some limit must be assigned to the principle, for it is obvious that we do not make everything a moral rule that we consider useful. . . . A distinction must . . . be drawn between utility made compulsory, and what is left free [p. 276].

In criticism of Bentham's phrase "the greatest happiness of the greatest number" Bain says:

A wrong bias is given from the very outset, in assuming it as Right to take away the happiness of a few to give the greater happiness to

---

[8] Alexander Bain, *The Emotions and the Will,* 3rd ed. (London, 1875). I have not been able to consult the 1859 edition.

D. G. BROWN

the many. Morality ought surely to treat all men alike. In its real
province, which is, not the total Happiness as a whole, but Security
or Protection, it actually does so [p. 275].

Again he says:

Positive beneficence is a merit. So with good offices, and with every
kind of gratuitous labour for beneficial purposes. These are the objects
of esteem, honour, reward, but not of moral approbation. Positive
good deeds and self-sacrifice are the preserving salt of human life; but
they transcend the region of morality proper, and occupy a sphere
of their own [p. 292].

Still more pointedly he remarks:

It will be seen at a glance that one great objection to the enforcement
of utility without exception, or qualification, is the consideration of
individual liberty [p. 277].

All this of course is only a chapter by Bain, which Mill knew
and praised as a chapter without dissociating himself from it.
But it happens that Mill himself, in a remarkable paragraph of
a later essay, suddenly sketches such a limited account of the
demands of morality, the details of which I believe are reconcilable with Principle V:

There is a standard of altruism to which all should be required to come
up, and a degree beyond it which is not obligatory, but meritorious.
It is incumbent on every one to restrain the pursuit of his personal
objects within the limits consistent with the essential interests of
others. What those limits are, it is the province of ethical science to
determine; and to keep all individuals and aggregations of individuals
within them, is the proper office of punishment and of moral blame. . . .
The proper office of those sanctions is to enforce upon every one, the
conduct necessary to give all other persons their fair chance: conduct
which chiefly consists in not doing them harm, and not impeding
them in anything which without harming others does good to themselves. To this of course must be added, that when we either expressly
or tacitly undertake to do more, we are bound to keep our promise.
And inasmuch as every one, who avails himself of the advantages of
society, leads others to expect from him all such positive good offices

MILL ON LIBERTY AND MORALITY

and disinterested services as the moral improvement attained by mankind has rendered customary, he deserves moral blame if, without just cause, he disappoints that expectation. Through this principle the domain of moral duty, in an improving society, is always widening.[9]

Writers in ethics have become accustomed to defining utilitarianism in such a way that it is a moral theory cast in the form of a supreme principle for morality. In one of the most systematic attempts to exhibit possible utilitarianisms, David Lyons has used "wrong" as the normative term in the statement of his principles.[10] Proceeding on these lines, it would be natural to look for a formulation of utilitarianism which might answer to Principle V in such principles as Lyons's negative utilitarianism (p. 211). This may well be the route forward, if we are to consider the question of moral theory on its merits. But if we try to construe Mill's theory in such terms, we encounter obstacles. One is the extreme elusiveness of Mill's text at each point where one hopes to find a precise statement of the Principle of Utility. The other is that, as two recent writers have noticed, Mill apparently holds that the Principle of Utility is not in itself a moral principle at all.

VI. THE TEST OF ALL HUMAN CONDUCT

Alan Ryan has suggested that Mill's account of the Art of Life, given in the concluding section of the *System of Logic*, is presupposed in *Utilitarianism*.[11] In that account, the Principle of

---

[9] *Auguste Comte and Positivism*, in John Stuart Mill, *Essays on Ethics, Religion and Society* (Toronto, 1969 [*Collected Works*, Vol. X]), pp. 337-338. I take this to be a further, ingenious attempt (still unsuccessful) to extend the category of harmful conduct, in this case by a theory of participation in conventions which brings breach of social obligations under breach of promise. On the extent of the obligations compare *Utilitarianism* (pp. 247-248; Ev. ed. pp. 46-47) and a letter to George Grote of 10th January 1862: *The Letters of John Stuart Mill*, ed. by H. S. R. Elliot, I, 249-251.

[10] David Lyons, *Forms and Limits of Utilitarianism* (Oxford, 1965).

[11] Alan Ryan, *John Stuart Mill* (New York, 1970), e.g., p. 192. Ryan sketched his view in "Mr. McCloskey on Mill's Liberalism," *Philosophical Quarterly*, 14 (1964), 253-260, and in "John Stuart Mill's Art of Living," *The Listener*, LXXIV (21 October 1965). The *Listener* talk, whose implications seem to have got lost in the book, is the clearest and most forceful statement of an interpretation similar to mine.

D. G. BROWN

Utility is the supreme principle of all appraisal of human conduct, whether that appraisal belongs to the departments of morality, prudence, or aesthetics. Since the promotion of happiness is the test of all conduct, it is indeed the criterion of morality and yields judgments of right and wrong. But it is equally the test of the expedient and of the beautiful or noble, and we therefore cannot identify the Principle of Utility with any moral principle. This explains the otherwise enigmatic statement of the main conclusion of Chapter IV of *Utilitarianism:*

If so, happiness is the sole end of human action, and the promotion of it the test by which to judge of all human conduct; from whence it necessarily follows that it must be the criterion of morality, since a part is included in the whole [p. 237; Ev. ed. p. 36].

According to Ryan, the differentiae of prudence and morality are that they concern the happiness of the agent and of others, respectively (pp. 215-216).

Ryan's sketch evidently needs development. It will hardly do to assign prudence and morality to the happiness of self and others respectively, since on Mill's view, and in fact, morality requires impartiality between self and others (p. 218; Ev. ed. p. 16). Nor does this principle of division allow a place for the third department of the Art of Life. This third department, indeed, seems unstable in Mill's account as well as obscure in Ryan's.[12] But the most pressing question for this interpretation is one to which Ryan does not address himself: in what terms can the Principle of Utility possibly be stated, if it is to have this inclusiveness and versatility of role?

To this question Professor D. P. Dryer offers an ingenious and textually plausible answer:

Mill also makes it clear that when he speaks of the promotion of happiness as "the test by which to judge of all human conduct," the

---

[12] Ryan points out (*John Stuart Mill*, p. 215) that in the essay on Bentham, Mill gives "moral," "aesthetic," and "sympathetic" rather than "morality," "prudence," and "aesthetics," and he prefers the *Logic* version. He omits to mention that in *Utilitarianism* itself we find a third version (pp. 246-247; Ev. ed. p. 46), where morality is marked off "from the remaining provinces of Expediency and Worthiness."

MILL ON LIBERTY AND MORALITY

aspect of conduct of which he means that it is a test is whether it should be done. . . . Accordingly, the main principle which Mill maintains is that something should be done if and only if it would cause more happiness than would any alternative, and that something should not be done if and only if it would fail to cause as much happiness as would some alternative.[18]

Dryer argues that Mill supports his main principle with the contention that happiness is the only thing desirable for its own sake, relying on the suppressed premise that something should be done if and only if it would have more desirable consequences than any alternative. As to the status of the suppressed premise, he suggests that it is far from implausible to urge that by analysis it amounts to the same thing to say that an action would have more desirable consequences than any alternative and to say that it should be done (p. lxx).

Dryer makes clear that he regards "should be done" as interchangeable with "ought to be done" (p. civ), and shifts to "ought" for his discussion of the relation between utility and morality (pp. xcv ff.). His theory is that according to Mill moral assertions about right and wrong, obligation, rights, and justice are equivalent to sets of ought-statements of various degrees of complexity, but that "ought" is neither ambiguous nor itself a distinctively moral term. Thus the Principle of Utility, on this view, will not itself contain a moral term. At the same time, to take "wrong" as an example, an action will be wrong if and only if it is an action which (i) ought not to be done, (ii) is of a kind which ought in general to be condemned, and (iii) would be contrary to a rule which ought in general to be observed (p. xcviii). Thus, I take it, the moral judgment of wrongness can be arrived at by successive applications of the Principle of Utility, even though that principle is not itself a moral one, but rather a principle of general application in any kind of appraisal of conduct (pp. civ, cxii).

This interpretation has the merit of offering a solution to the problem I have raised, as well as the merit of emphasizing ne-

---

[18] Introductory essay, "Mill's Utilitarianism," in Vol. X of the *Collected Works*, pp. lxiii-lxiv. His one footnote in support of the first assertion is to the *System of Logic*, VI, xii, 6.

D. G. BROWN

glected features of Mill's theory of morality. But the evidence is not kind to it. In a letter of 1859 Mill says:

> Now, as to the still more important subject of the meaning of *ought.* I will endeavour to explain the sense I attach to it. . . . I will . . . pass to the case of those who have a true moral feeling, that is, a feeling of pain in the fact of violating a certain rule, quite independently of any expected consequences to themselves. It appears to me that to them the word *ought* means that if they act otherwise they shall be punished by this internal and perfectly disinterested feeling.[14]

There follows an account of moral feelings, including the remark that their main constituent is the idea of punishment. There might be reasonable doubt whether this theory of "ought," which assimilates it so closely to Mill's official accounts of "wrong not to," should be used in the interpretation of *Utilitarianism,* were it not for an unmistakable reference to the recently finished draft of *Utilitarianism* at the end of the letter:

> This is the nearest approach I am able to make to a theory of the moral feelings. I have written it out, much more fully, in a little manuscript treatise which I propose to publish when I have kept it by me for the length of time I think desirable and given it such further improvement as I am capable of. Perhaps the short statement I have now made will convey some notion of what my opinion is, though a very imperfect one of the manner in which I should support it [p. 231].

On the other hand, the only direct evidence Dryer quotes in support of his reading the Principle of Utility with a non-moral "should" is Section VI, xii, 6 of *A System of Logic.* In fact, Mill there contrasts propositions about what *is* with propositions about what *should be* or *ought to be.* It seems a tenuous inference that the

---

[14] Letter of 28th November 1859 to Dr. W. G. Ward, *The Letters of John Stuart Mill,* I, 229. Dryer himself refers to this letter with respect to Mill's view on the use of "ought" (p. xcix). I cannot see how he reconciles it with his interpretation. Dryer also announces (p. c) that Mill does not acknowledge that the assertion that a man *has a right* to do something ever bears the sense that it would be right—i.e., *not wrong*—for the man to do it. But Mill quotes himself as acknowledging just this, in the *System of Logic,* 8th ed. (London, 1872), II, 398-399.

MILL ON LIBERTY AND MORALITY

main principle of *Utilitarianism* lays down the class of actions that should be or ought to be done.

I am not sure how the Principle of Utility should be formulated, and I think the complex evidence provided by the text of *Utilitarianism* itself is inconclusive. My own positive suggestion, toward an enquiry that this paper has no room for, is that Mill constantly thought of his ultimate principle, and of many very general principles of conduct, as statements about ends. On this view the most likely candidates for literal formulations of the Principle of Utility would be such things as the conclusion quoted above, that "happiness is the sole end of human action" (p. 237; Ev. ed. p. 36) or the passage:

According to the Greatest Happiness Principle, as above explained, the ultimate end, with reference to and for the sake of which all other things are desirable (whether we are considering our own good or that of other people), is an existence exempt as far as possible from pain, and as rich as possible in enjoyments, both in point of quantity and quality [p. 214; Ev. ed. p. 11].

From a principle cast in this form, it remains to be seen how we can derive principles about what ought to be done, or what it would be wrong to do. An intermediate form is exemplified by the Principle of Liberty itself, which specifies the sole end that can justify a particular kind of action, and from which I have ventured to derive a principle about when that kind of action ought prima facie to be done.

Interim Judgment

The upshot of Dryer's interpretation, even after this criticism of it, is that we can see very well how Principle V, that conduct is prima facie wrong if and only if it harms other people, might on Mill's view be derivable from the Principle of Utility. We can at least agree that the Principle of Utility is not a principle about what actions are wrong. Whether or not Dryer has given a completely accurate account of the specific moral concepts in Mill, we can agree that the enforceability of morality is on Mill's view essential to the concept of morality, and that Mill can quite consistently combine his utilitarianism with Principle V.

D. G. BROWN

It seems to me that we now have good grounds for attributing to Mill all the five principles I have listed. They form a consistent theory of liberty and morality. In particular they allow Mill to reconcile the Principle of Liberty with his conception of the enforceability of morality through a substantial moral view, which seems independently acceptable to him, about the limited stringency of the demands which morality makes on us.

As I have remarked, however, it does not seem to me to be true that conduct is prima facie wrong only if it harms other people. I think Mill thought it was true, not so much because he regarded as all right a great many instances of actually wrong conduct, but rather because he regarded as conduct harming others a great many instances of conduct which cannot properly be classed as harming others, but only as failing to help them and the like. In either case, Mill's theory is so structured that if Principle V is let go, it starts a drastic unraveling of the whole fabric.

At once we must give up at least one of the two: the Principle of Liberty (I) or the Principle of Enforcing Morality (IV). Mill seems to imply that Principle IV is a merely verbal, and so analytic, proposition. I think it is not; but I also think it is a very plausible substantial moral principle, and one of Mill's most valuable and neglected insights. I am not myself inclined to give it up, even at the cost of the Principle of Liberty. It seems to me that we have duties to help other people which go beyond the avoidance of harming them; that the performance of such duties can legitimately be exacted from us, very commonly in our roles as citizens and taxpayers; and that such exactions are not permitted by Mill's main principle. I conclude that the general ruin of Mill's impressive synthesis carries with it the Principle of Liberty itself.[15]

D. G. BROWN

The University of British Columbia

---

[15] I am grateful for useful criticisms of earlier drafts of this paper to Jonathan Bennett, J. Dybikowski, Roy Edgley, and Peter Remnant. John Clark and Bonnie Moro pointed out substantial errors which I was grateful to be able to correct.

[12]

The Utilitarian Logic of Liberalism*

Russell Hardin

The chief reason society cannot simply judge the rightness of particular outcomes by their utilities is that, even at egregious costs, institutions for doing so would be unreliable. For example, in the Matthew and Luke problem of Braithwaite and Barry, the utility of Matthew's action of playing his jazz trumpet depends on whether there is a Luke who lives beyond a thin wall from him.[1] Playing a trumpet is not simply an action *tout court*, it is an action with contingent consequences. As a result, the rightness of Matthew's action depends on its effects on Luke. To judge directly from utility in practice in general would require an account in each case of all such effects. A far less expensive set of institutions gets us closer to the "ideally best" outcome: that set which simply establishes rules for conduct in typical cases and which leaves some freedom to the relevant parties to work out their own better solutions or to recur to political institutions to prevent others from violating the rules. We need an institutional structure of rights or protections because not everyone is utilitarian or otherwise moral and because there are severe limits to our knowledge of others, whose interests are therefore likely to be best fulfilled if they have substantial control over the fulfillment.

This is how rights should be understood. They are institutional devices for achieving good outcomes despite the egregious burden of gathering information and calculating consequences. They differ from rules in the lexicon of twentieth-century rule utilitarians in their institutional force, but they are similar to the rules of thumb of some rule utilitarians in their actual function. Unlike rules of thumb that an individual would follow to reduce information and calculation costs, however, such institutional rules as legally defined rights cannot easily be overridden when calculation shows that in a particular case a better outcome would follow

* This paper has benefited from comments by the participants, especially Allan Gibbard and Arthur Kuflik, in the Weingart conference for which it was originally written and by participants in colloquia in the departments of philosophy and political science at the University of Wisconsin—Madison and the Murphy Institute at Tulane University. It has also benefited from extensive written commentaries by Joe Carens, Andrew Levine, Charles Silver, and Duncan Snidal, and an energetic discussion with Richard Epstein.

1. R. B. Braithwaite, *Theory of Games as a Tool for the Moral Philosopher* (Cambridge: Cambridge University Press, 1955); Brian Barry, "Don't Shoot the Trumpeter—He's Doing His Best," *Theory and Decision* 11 (1979): 153–80.

Ethics 97 (October 1986): 47–74

48   *Ethics   October 1986*

from violating the rules. This follows for relatively complex reasons of the strategic structure for the establishment and enforcement of the rules. Again, the reason for not violating relevant institutional rules in practice in particular cases is related to the reasons for having them in the first place: the costs of setting up the devices for deciding on when to violate the rules are too great to be justified by the gains from violation. When this conclusion seems not to follow in a particular case, then we may institutionally, as we do individually, resolve that case against the rules.

Conceiving of rules for individual behavior as rules of thumb to be violated when calculation recommends it gives rule utilitarianism very little force. It is nothing more than simple decision theory applied to moral choosing. Hence, it can be judged to be fully consistent with straightforward act utilitarianism. Much of twentieth-century ethical debate has clearly been motivated by a sense that there is more to rule following than this. In part, one might suppose that the reason for seeing more to rule following is that the individualist focus of deontological ethics, the focus on the rightness of individual actions, has pervaded even the ethical thinking of utilitarians.

If there is any force to the kinds of insights that many have had about rule utilitarianism, however, it cannot be that deontological concerns should pervade utilitarian thinking. Rather, it is that many of the rules that we would commonly accede to in our daily lives are conspicuously utilitarian in their consequences and that we cannot imagine living without such rules. This class of rules is generally the class of institutionally determined and—generally but not always—institutionally enforced rules. Much of the twentieth-century effort to read earlier utilitarians, such as Mill, as really rule utilitarians largely misses the point of the earlier concern, which was with institutional arrangements that would help to secure good consequences and not with individual rule following.[2] To avoid such confusion we should speak not of rule utilitarianism but of institutional utilitarianism. Perhaps the largest concern of institutional utilitarianism in a modern society is with rights legally defined.

Even if one granted all of the above, one might still be bothered by a nagging suspicion that, somehow, concern with rights and concern with outcomes or utility are quite different concerns. Part of the reason for this suspicion is perhaps that rights are generally related to the strategic structure of various interactions and not directly to outcomes in the following sense. Rights are not generally about particular outcomes but about particular classes of action. Hence, they might seem to be preeminently deontological in character. The difference between typical rights theories and utilitarianism on this point is, however, less significant than

2. J. O. Urmson, "The Interpretation of the Moral Philosophy of J. S. Mill," *Philosophical Quarterly* 3 (1953): 33–39. Many discussions of this issue in the interpretation of Mill can be found in *Canadian Journal of Philosophy*, suppl. vol. 5: *New Essays on John Stuart Mill and Utilitarianism*, ed. Wesley E. Cooper, Kai Nielsen, and Steven C. Patten (Guelph, Ontario: Canadian Association for Publishing in Philosophy, 1979).

it might seem. The utilitarian judgment of an action is in fact a judgment of the outcome which the action helps to bring about. But few actions that interest moral theorists bring about outcomes on their own. Generally, outcomes of moral concern result from the interactive effects of the actions of more than one person. But we cannot generally legislate that certain kinds of outcomes should result and not others and also make clear who is responsible for what results. Instead of decreeing that outcomes of type *x* are to happen, we legislate that actions of type *a* are legal, or required, or illegal insofar as they would not hinder, would bring about, or would prevent outcomes of type *x*. In many cases, however, it would be prima facie ludicrous to suppose that we actually care about whether actions of type *a* are undertaken *tout court*. For a trivial but important example, we do not a priori care whether people drive on the right or the left. Rather, we only care whether they drive in such a way as to cause harm. Requiring everyone to drive on the right or, alternatively, requiring everyone to drive on the left is justified merely because it brings about a good outcome in general. We constrain individuals' choices of strategy in order to produce a better outcome than would have resulted from unconstrained choices.

In what follows, I wish to argue that morally defensible rights are sensibly grounded in a concern for consequences and that the character of particular rights therefore depends on more general strategic considerations of the nature of the society and of incentives for action within it. Although some rights might seem to be valuable in almost any society we may know, few if any rights can be given an a priori grounding independently of a fairly articulate account of the society or societies in which they are to be defended. If we have established a system of rights we must, of course, have a set of institutions to guarantee and implement them. The institutions will have roles and norms of their own that are institutionally determined. Hence, there are two general issues of concern in what follows: the grounding of rights and the defense or implementation of them. After considering these, I will take up the problem of conflicts that can arise from one or more persons' exercise of their rights, as in the problem of Matthew's trumpet playing. Finally, I will briefly discuss the apparent implication of Sen's "liberal paradox" that a utilitarian theory of rights is inherently contradictory.

STRATEGIC CLASSES OF RIGHTS

In general, the point of traditional legal rights is to secure the aggregation of individual benefits. We may, however, distinguish three ways in which this is accomplished: we may secure benefits to individuals that are independent of other individuals' benefits, we may secure benefits that are mutual but that are generally available only to dyads or very small numbers independently of benefits to the larger society, and we may secure benefits to larger groups or even the whole society. As will become clearer below, the first of these cases involves protection of some

50   *Ethics*   *October 1986*

against intrusions by others and the latter two involve protection of some against their own strategic incapacities to benefit themselves. To some extent, all can involve the problem of paternalism, which, however, I will not discuss at length here.

All rights protect people against other people. There are no rights against impositions of the laws of physics. Hence, they are all directed at interactions between people. Again, these protections are strategic: they do not directly secure outcomes; rather, they protect individuals by securing them or denying them certain choices or actions. A signal value of the game-theoretic representation of moral (and other) choice problems is to clarify the relationship between actions and outcomes. Hence, it helps us to grasp better the sometimes contrary claims of action-based and consequentialist theories, although this is not a central concern here because I am not here concerned with action-based theories in general. What is of concern is to understand why a fundamentally consequentialist moral theory may, when limits to information, theory, and cognitive capacity are severe, address outcomes indirectly through actions even though classes of actions are not inherently either right or wrong on that theory.

Many of the protections that interest us may plausibly be seen as falling into more than one of the classes above. For example, the freedom of contract is dyadic at base but may have large implications for the whole society, even large enough to justify enforcing it independently of our concern with pairwise exchanges. Similarly, the right of ownership of property may have far more important implications for the larger society than for individual property owners considered separately. Both these rights, as do many others, may have external effects that go far beyond particular relationships. Hence, we may wish to secure them for their particular effects, their more general collective effects, or both.

There is a sense in which one could say that securing any of these benefits is a benefit to the larger society, especially if the way in which the benefits are secured in particular cases is through the workings of an ongoing institution. To secure a right that benefits me is, in this sense, to secure it for everyone or nearly everyone. However, for the present discussion, I wish to speak of securing benefits in particular cases in order to show that the way in which this is done may depend on the strategic structures of the cases. That the same strategic structure recurs commonly is good reason for creating an institutional protection and, one may say, widespread recurrence makes the protection a collective benefit. But the protection may explicitly apply individual by individual, dyad by dyad, or only collectively, and it is useful to keep clear which kind of case is at issue.

Exemplars of the three classes of rights are rights of privacy, rights of voluntary exchange or contract, and rights of freedom of speech or freedom from servitude.[3] At first blush it may not be obvious why these

---

3. There may also be grounds for collective or welfare rights, but I will not discuss this issue here. See further, Russell Hardin, "Collective Rights," in *The Restraint of Liberty,*

should be put in their respective categories, but I hope to make clear that their strategic structures justify the categorizations. In the following three sections I will discuss these three categories by focusing on central examples of each. From the general grounding of liberalism in individual protections I will go on to discuss what is perhaps the best understood of the more complex cases, the protection of the dyadic right of voluntary exchange. This right, like certain of the individual protections, is generally considered to be fundamental to liberalism by utilitarian as well as by deontological rights theorists. Of course, utilitarians typically consider the right to be derivative from concern with consequences, whereas many deontological and natural rights theorists derive it from a consideration of a priori reason, from direct apprehension, or perhaps from a relevant metaphysical cloud of the sort that hangs more commonly over some schools of thought than over others. Finally I will discuss what is strategically the most complex of all the classes of rights, the collective rights, some of which are positively directed at creating a beneficial form of government and some of which, the so-called inalienable rights, are negatively directed at preventing certain failures of collective action.

INDIVIDUAL PROTECTIONS

One ground on which virtually all individual protections can be based is the supposition that individuals are generally the best judges of their own interests. Hence guaranteeing them the control over their lives to determine their own consumptions will generally make them better off. The same grounding can be given for dyadic rights as well. The principle is essentially Paretian and utilitarian: protecting an action that makes someone better off while making no one worse off produces a better state of affairs on the whole. Moreover, protecting certain classes of action can make virtually everyone better off. Ensuring certain rights supposedly has just this effect. For example, as all the great English political philosophers assert, ensuring the right to ownership of property guarantees that actions I take to better my condition will indeed better it. Without the security of expectations inherent in such a right, I would be far less likely to exert myself to create the property and to make myself better off.

Although the protection of property is the central concern of early liberal theory, one can defend virtually any individual protection on the same argument. From the freedom of religious practice that exercised Locke to the right of privacy that has exercised jurists and legal theorists in our century, these protections generally have in their favor that they let people make the best of things for themselves without capricious and destructive intervention by others, particularly by others who have the power of the state with them. These protections represent the simplest of the utilitarian logics of liberalism. Indeed, their violation for the purpose

---

ed. Thomas Attig, Donald Callen, and John Gray, vol. 7 of *Bowling Green Studies in Applied Philosophy* (Bowling Green, Ohio: Bowling Green State University, 1985), pp. 88–101.

Column's Choices

	Yield Car	Keep Car
Yield $1,000	2,2	4,1
Keep $1,000	1,4	3,3

Row's Choices

FIG. 1.—Game 1: exchange (Prisoner's Dilemma with ordinal payoffs)

of imposing values that others hold is the defining instance of paternalism and of the odious implications that that term has. Too easy generalization from the logic of this class of protections produces claims for rights that are inherently contradictory and criticisms of state policy as paternalistic when it is in fact far more complex and difficult to evaluate than that label suggests.

DYADIC PROTECTIONS

The class of dyadic protections is fundamentally concerned with exchange and agreement to exchange. Its chief exemplar is the freedom of contract, which largely grows out of the concern to have fuller control over property.[4] Hence, it is an extension of the private aspect of certain individual protections. The larger role of contract has probably become, rather, the enabling of greater control over future plans of diverse kinds with control over property per se as a relatively small part of the whole body of contract. Let us briefly consider the strategic structure of exchange and then turn to the regulation of future fulfillments of exchanges by contract.

Simple dyadic exchange has the strategic structure of the Prisoner's Dilemma, as represented in game 1 (fig. 1). In this game, you as the column player own a car and I as the row player have $1,000. I would rather have your car than my money, and you would rather have my money than your car. Hence, we can move from the status quo, in which you have the car and I have the money, to the unanimously preferred state of affairs, in which I have the car and you have the money. In the game matrix, the payoffs are ordinal with my most preferred outcome ranked first, or 1, and my least preferred ranked fourth, or 4, and similarly for your preferences over the outcomes. Obviously, either of us would most like to have both the money and the car. But an exchange is better for both of us than the status quo.

The payoffs in game 1 can be used to illustrate two different classes of rights. In securing the right of exchange we must also secure one's

4. P. S. Atiyah, *The Rise and Fall of Freedom of Contract* (Oxford: Clarendon Press, Oxford University Press, 1979), pp. 85–90.

right to keep what one "owns." I can meaningfully have the right to exchange my money for your car only if you have no right to take my money for nothing in return. Hence, we first protect my right of ownership and then we further protect my right to exchange what I own with someone who wants to make a presumptively beneficial exchange with me. If we assume that players in such a game as game 1 will not voluntarily move from an outcome to another that is inferior to it in their preference schedule, then the protection of the right of ownership is guaranteed by blocking the 1,4 and 4,1 outcomes from happening as the result of a move from one of the other outcomes. (One of these, say the 4,1 outcome, might occur as the status quo. But then it would be wrong to represent our "interaction" as including the possibility of my choosing my lower strategy. The protection of your right to own both the money and the car implies that I cannot unilaterally act to put you in the less advantageous position of any of the other payoffs.) Further protection of the right of voluntary exchange then requires that we be permitted to move from the 3,3 outcome to the 2,2 outcome that we both prefer to it.

There are basically three ways such exchanges are regulated. One is for us to face each other in a given moment and make an instantaneous exchange under the threat of violence if either should try to take from the other and run; the second is to have a rich ongoing relationship that guarantees that we will each want to treat the other fairly in order not to jeopardize the future of our relationship; and the third is to have an external power enforce our voluntary agreement on whether to exchange. Macneil calls exchanges regulated in the latter two ways relational exchanges because they involve ongoing relationships, in the first case between the parties themselves, and in the third case between each of the parties and the state.[5] In a complex society, the state typically enforces voluntary agreements through the law of contracts. Indeed, for a very large number of exchanges, it also enforces the reliability of each of us in discrete exchanges of the second type by outlawing and punishing theft so that, as Macneil argues, virtually all exchange is relational and the economists' favored category of discrete exchange is virtually empty.

We want the state to intervene to protect our voluntary exchanges when we exchange with people who are strangers to us, when our exchanges involve unusually large values so that even close associates might not be trustworthy, and especially when either or both of these conditions are coupled with the need to consummate our exchange over time with one of us fulfilling now and the other later. Because all are arguably made better off and no one is harmed by such exchanges, it is a Pareto improvement to have an efficient regulator of exchange, as the state can be (this view can be overstated—see further the discussion below under

---

5. Ian Macneil, *The New Social Contract* (New Haven, Conn.: Yale University Press, 1980); see also Russell Hardin, "Exchange Theory on Strategic Bases," *Social Science Information* 21 (1982): 251–72.

54 *Ethics October 1986*

"Conflicts between Rights"). Indeed, if we are restricted to considering only utilities to individuals without comparisons across individuals, this Paretian concern is virtually all that remains of utilitarianism. We can say that an institutional protection of exchange and of contract is utilitarian if everyone seems likely to be better off with it than without it. In contemporary economics, the grandchild of utilitarianism, one speaks of Pareto-efficient changes in the state of affairs rather than of the maximization of social utility. In its weakest version—unanimity—the Pareto principle is perhaps the most generally accepted principle of social choice. But for Amartya Sen's well-known views, one might suppose it was unanimously accepted.[6]

Since the possible range of states of affairs without state protection of exchange and contract may be quite large, it may not easily be shown that such protection is utilitarian, but this is an issue that goes beyond the present concern, and I will skip over it here. If we were concerned only with a particular exchange of the moment, we might easily conclude that it would be utilitarian as compared with not making the exchange. Surprisingly, much of social and political theory has been argued as though this were the only concern: justifying piecemeal actions against the background of everything else held constant. That this is a fundamentally flawed way to frame political theory is suggested below (under "Institutionalization of Rights").

Suppose now that we have a relatively efficient state empowered to intervene to prevent theft, so that virtually discrete exchange is possible, and to enforce contracts, so that fairly complex exchanges, such as those that must take place over time, are possible. Our original insight and model concerned dyadic exchanges. But there are at least three classes of contracts that the state might enforce. First, there are ordinary contracts for mutual benefit through exchange between two or more parties in cases in which all of the benefits of the contracted action derive from "internal" sources, that is, from and to the contracting parties. Second, there are contracts for mutual benefit between two or more parties when one of the parties is a member of a larger class of people who share a common interest in not being able to enter such contracts. Third, there are contracts such as those among members of a group to enable them to support their interest in a conflict with another party, in which case the benefits of contracting derive from "external" sources, that is, from the conflicting party. The second of these classes is the subject of the following section on "Collective Protections." It is enforcement of only the first of these which seems Pareto efficient in plausible cases. Enforcement of the second and third classes of contract will make some people better off at the expense of other people.

---

6. Sen supposes that the weak Pareto principle violates liberalism, which he thinks counts against it as a general principle of social choice. See further below, under the section "Rights versus Unanimity."

Perhaps, one might suppose, the way to keep to Paretian results is to restrict contracts to dyads and to leave others to their own spontaneous devices by not enforcing group contracts. Alas, to do so is automatically to give advantage to certain interests over others, in particular, to give advantage to the interests of small numbers against those of large numbers. For example, for a large group case, recall the early history of labor unions in the United States. The Supreme Court held that collective efforts by workers to negotiate for higher wages were illegal, that workers must individually enter dyadic contracts with their employers. In principle, of course, workers could all have coordinated on negotiating individually for the same wage level they might have got collectively. But, for reasons of the logic of collective action, one would not expect them to have great success in doing so in factories with large numbers of employees or even more generally in any factory which could draw its workers from a relatively large pool. Restriction of contracts to dyads only therefore virtually guaranteed greater bargaining power to employers over potential employees than they would have had against employees legally capable of bargaining collectively.

For a small group case, consider the Chicago–East Coast railway cartel in the latter half of the nineteenth century. Overlapping dyadic contracts between the very small number of railway companies could easily have been arranged to accomplish anything a group contract could have accomplished. If the state had enforced the dyadic contracts, the result would have been monopolistic pricing in an effectively stable cartel. That the state chose to try to block the cartel did not turn on the fact that its organization was of more than two parties. The frequency of failures of the cartel, given that the state would not enforce its agreements, may well be explained by the fact that there were several parties to it with strong incentives to take advantage of those cooperating. But basing the cartel on dyadic as opposed to group agreements would not have made it a more liberal achievement. One might suppose therefore that the rulings against workers trying to bargain collectively likewise did not turn on the stated concern with the protection of freedom of—implicitly dyadic—contract.

Interestingly, the two kinds of cases, involving small and large number collectives, differ enough strategically that they may finally differ legally. To stop cartelization of some small number industries might require positively outlawing agreements and informal coordination since the relevant firms might each be able to reckon that its gains from cheating on an agreement would be outweighed by its probable losses from the failure of the agreement caused by its own cheating. To stop unionization, however, may require little more than refusing to enforce contractual agreements among workers. The general sense very early on that workers needed the union shop to protect their interests was probably well grounded. As Gompers argued in 1905, "Persons who are desirous of becoming beneficiaries of an agreement should become parties to that

56   *Ethics   October 1986*

agreement, and . . . they should bear the equal responsibility which such an agreement involves."[7]

Is it liberal for the state to intervene as a partisan in a conflict of interests? Since partisanship one way or the other either by enforcing or refusing to enforce contracts is unavoidable, a liberal must either answer this hard question or define it away. One might answer that no one loses from the enforcement of certain classes of contracts and that therefore they should be enforced; but for classes of contracts that bring benefits to some parties at the cost of others, the state should not act as enforcer. Where, then, should it stand with respect to contracts that benefit some at the cost of others but that do not require state enforcement? Should the state intervene to block these? Answers to these questions do not follow straightforwardly from considerations of rights sensibly defined. In the case of the railway cartel one can sensibly argue that much of the monopolisitic pricing of rail transport—for example, to small towns served by only one line—did not directly harm anyone in a way that simply not offering the rail transport would not have harmed them. Hence, running lines into small towns and charging monopolistic prices was clearly a benefit to the small towns. But it would be hard to argue on grounds of liberal rights that the railways were required to serve anyone, so that it is hard to see how any rights were violated by the monopolistic pricing of a railway that chose to serve an isolated community. There may have been violations of justice and utility, but not of rights.

If the state has the power to enforce or not to enforce contracts, it therefore unavoidably has the power to decide for one party against the other in certain conflicts of interest. The liberal's disinterested state cannot be disinterested. More generally, liberal support for the freedom of contract cannot be unlimited. It is not easy to present arguments that are exclusively rights based for why contracts to monopolize prices would be wrong so long as the state does not intervene to prevent competitive entry into the market. A utilitarian account that turned on ordinal comparisons between the benefits to the contractors and the costs to the parties against whom they have contracted could, however, yield relevant qualifications on the freedom of contract. Hence, a derivative theory of utilitarian rights stands up better to the problems we face than does a theory that is nonderivatively, fundamentally rights based. In large part, this is because strategic considerations are of overwhelming importance not merely between any two parties to a transaction that is protected by right but also between them and many others who may be unable to influence the transaction.

COLLECTIVE PROTECTIONS

In traditional views there are at least two basic classes of collective protections, as indicated by the locutions "freedom of " or "right to," and

7. Samuel Gompers, "Discussion at Rochester, N.Y., on the Open Shop—'The Union Shop Is Right'—It Naturally Follows Organization," *American Federationist* 4 (April 1905): 221–23, p. 221.

"freedom from": (1) those that help to bring about particular collective benefits more or less to the whole society, as in the right to vote, freedom of assembly, freedom of speech, freedom of the press, and other such guarantees in the Bill of Rights of the American Constitution; and (2) those that protect particular classes against themselves and against adversary classes, as in various so-called inalienable rights, such as the freedom from servitude. These two classes of protections address somewhat different strategic problems and should generally be kept separate in discussion. Rights or freedoms of the first class are generally permissive for the individual: they simply guarantee that the individual may do certain things if the individual wishes to. Those of the second class are generally binding on the individual: they require that the individual not do certain things. In this sense, rights of the second class are sometimes considered duties.[8] But the label "duty" fits them no more perspicuously than the label "rights" since these protections are not so clearly directed at particular individuals as at classes or groups.

Let us consider these two classes of protections in turn. Those of the first class typically function to establish the form of governance of the society. In typical liberal societies, they tend to make politics and collective decision making more open, less fettered by particular powerful interests. In the vocabulary that many liberals like to use, they help to guarantee that politics takes place in a marketplace of ideas with open debate, careful scrutiny of government action, and strong protection of individual rights of participation. Although formulated as individual protections, they secure the genuinely collective benefits of democratic government. They do so not because they mandate that people act in certain ways but because they give people the freedom to act from their own incentives and on their own initiative.

These protections can be successful in their intendment only if people take advantage of the freedoms they provide to control and direct their government. Moderately egoistic people and reasonably utilitarian people can both be expected, from our experience, to take such advantage of these freedoms. For this contingent reason, the rights can be strongly defended by utilitarians—and perhaps also by most egoists, as libertarians assert (although an egoist with great resources might be expected to want to subvert them rather than to defend them). They can also be strongly defended by contractarians of both actual-consent and rationalist varieties, although one might suppose that such contractarians are very nearly utilitarian.

One can make a sophisticated claim that the protection of private-property falls in this class of collective protections rather than in the class of individual protections discussed above. The overwhelming value of the right of ownership of property is not in the enjoyment of what one has without fear of its being taken away but in the strategic or structural impact of such a right. The protection of private property gives extraor-

8. Peter Gardenfors, "Rights, Games and Social Choice," *Nous* 15 (1981): 341–56.

58   *Ethics   October 1986*

dinary incentive to anyone capable of doing so to enhance the well-being of all or many of us by creating new wealth. This is, of course, the eighteenth-century Whig view of Smith and Hayek. Much of the early concern with freedom of contract is similarly, in fact, a concern with allowing anyone who can satisfy demands of others by producing and selling particular goods to do so without restriction.[9] One might, as libertarians such as Nozick commonly do, simply assert such rights out of direct intuition as strictly justified at the level of the individual independently of their effects on the larger society. But if the economic and social theories of Hume, Smith, Mill, and other political economists are sufficiently correct, they can be solidly grounded in their general utility.[10] On this point, contrary to his own apparent belief, Hayek is utilitarian.[11]

Turn now to the second class of collective protections. A typical view of so-called inalienable rights is that they are, and even must be, grounded in concern for individual autonomy. To quote an unlikely source, Knight says that freedom "is a 'value,' a thing the individual ought to want, even ought to have if he may not choose it, a part of the modern ideal of the dignity of the person. Thus the laws of liberal states do not allow men to sell themselves (or their children) into 'involuntary servitude,' even if they so choose."[12] In fact, however, the strategic case for the inalienability of certain rights is compelling and has long been recognized. These rights protect the interests of relevant *classes* of individuals by changing, in their favor, the terms on which they face other classes.

Consider Mill's example of the problem of reducing the workday from ten to nine hours: "Assuming then that it really would be the interest of each to work only nine hours if he could be assured that all others would do the same, there might be no means of their attaining this object but by converting their supposed mutual agreement into an engagement

---

9. However, "to a considerable degree, freedom of contract began by being freedom to deal with property by contract" (Atiyah, p. 85).

10. Even Blackstone sees this: "Had not therefore a separate property in lands, as well as moveables, been vested in some individuals, the world must have continued a forest, and men have been mere animals of prey" (William Blackstone, *Commentaries on the Laws of England* [Chicago: University of Chicago Press, 1979, facsimile of first edition of 1766], vol. 2, p. 7).

11. Hayek supposes that the utilitarian program necessarily falters on the problem of limits to our knowledge to predict outcomes well enough for us to be act-utilitarians or to construct the rules to be rule-utilitarians. His complaint against utilitarians is not that the moral content of their theory is wrong but that the way they speak of applying it is wrong because they do not take account of human ignorance and social complexity, constraints that a rational chooser must recognize. Hence, his criticism of utilitarians is just his criticism of social theorists more generally (F. A. Hayek, *The Mirage of Social Justice*, vol. 2 of *Law, Legislation and Liberty* [Chicago: University of Chicago Press, 1976], pp. 17–23). Norman Barry accepts Hayek's view of himself as not utilitarian (Norman P. Barry, *Hayek's Social and Economic Philosophy* [Atlantic Highlands, N.J.: Humanities Press, 1979], pp. 129–31).

12. Frank Knight, "The Role of Principles in Economics and Politics," in *On the History and Method of Economics* (Chicago: University of Chicago Press, 1956), pp. 251–81, p. 259.

under penalty, by consenting to have it enforced by law."[13] Because factory workers as a class face a difficult collective action problem, in which the logic is for all to favor the nine-hour day as a general rule but to work ten hours in their particular cases, they will wind up working ten hours for a day's pay if they are not prevented from doing so. Hence, what they need is not the simple right to a nine-hour day but the inalienable right to a nine-hour day. Indeed, the force of the logic of collective action may make the simple right of little value. We might simply extend the freedom of contract to allow the members of such a class to contract among themselves to hold together in seeking their interest against another party. But that freedom would not help a very large group. Hence, Mill's workers would require that their right be effectively inalienable.[14] The problem of involuntary servitude is analogous, as may be the problem of marriage in perpetuity.

In all of these cases, the members of a relevant class are potentially pitted against each other to their collective harm, and the only way to secure them against that collective harm is to deny them singly the right to free ride on the abstinence of other members of the class. If one holds, as many, including Mill,[15] do, that a right is for the benefit of the right holder, one might find it odd that, when it is ever invoked, it is actually invoked to stop the right holder from acting in a particular way. Therefore, libertarians can argue with some force that so-called inalienable rights are not rights but the denial of rights because they impose a duty— such as the duty not to sell oneself into servitude—on the supposed right holder. The notion of an inalienable right is somehow contradictory if it is seen as an individual right. It makes sense only at the group level because whatever benefit comes to an individual under the right comes indirectly through its effects on the relevant larger class. It is unfortunate that it has been given the name "right"—again, protection would be a better term.

Many of the first class of collective protections can be strengthened if they are made in some sense inalienable. For example, one can choose not to exercise the right to vote, but there are good reasons to block one from alienating it in the stronger sense of selling it. Making alienation in this sense virtually impossible secures the right in two ways. On the one hand, it makes the right to vote meaningful by preventing the destruction of the voting process through the buying of votes. On the other,

---

13. John Stuart Mill, *Principles of Political Economy*, ed. J. M. Robson (Toronto: University of Toronto Press, 1965), bk. 5, chap. 11, sec. 12, p. 958. Also see Mill, *On Liberty*, in Mill, *Essays on Politics and Society*, ed. J. M. Robson (Toronto: University of Toronto Press, 1977), pp. 209–13; quote is in vol. 18 of *Collected Works of John Stuart Mill*, ed. J. M. Robson (Toronto: University of Toronto Press, 1963–), chap. 4, par. 20, p. 289.

14. Mill does not recommend doing so (*Principles of Political Economy*, p. 958).

15. John Stuart Mill, "Austin on Jurisprudence," pp. 165–205 in Mill, *Essays on Equality, Law, and Education*, ed. John M. Robson (Toronto: University of Toronto Press, 1984), pp. 162–205; vol. 21 of *Collected Works of John Stuart Mill*, p. 179.

60   *Ethics   October 1986*

it is a strategic device to protect holders of the right against coercions to which those rights would otherwise make them subject. In the case of voting, the requisite inalienability can be secured relatively easily by arranging the actual process of voting so that it is strategically almost impossible for one to prove that one has kept any bargain to sell one's vote. But we may go further and make it a crime to sell one's vote.

While the strategic justification for making such protections as freedom from involuntary servitude inalienable has not forced itself upon the understanding of many critics and defenders of the protection, one suspects that the parallel justification for outlawing the selling of votes would easily be accepted. Presumably no one would think it paternalistic to block the selling of votes—perhaps because this would clearly be a case of protecting a good that is conceived to be important generally to anyone and not only to members of a particular class. But one could imagine in most societies a large block of people who would willingly sell their votes. Hence, protecting the right to vote by making it inalienable is not qualitatively different from protecting the freedom from involuntary servitude by making it inalienable.

It is often claimed or apparently presupposed that people can never be made worse off by being given more possibilities from which to choose. That this claim is specious should be clear in such collective action contexts as those above. Requiring that people *not* take the individual choice that, if taken by all or even many, destroys the possibility of mutually beneficial collective gains helps to secure those gains collectively and hence individually. If I am not required to contribute to a collective benefit, I may prefer along with everyone else not to contribute. But against the outcome of such individualistic actions by all, I might prefer that all, including myself, be required to contribute to the provision of our mutual benefit. The examples I have given are powerful because each involves genuine and important interests of the class that faces a collective action problem. For example, suppose, as Mill assumes, that one of Mill's workers who simply chose to work nine hours while all others worked ten would get nine-tenths the daily wage of all workers if none could work more than nine hours. It follows that all would be significantly better off if they could not work more than nine hours.

One can cite other examples of cases in which more choice—hence more liberty—is worse than less, as Dworkin does when he canvasses such problems as the duel and coed dorms.[16] Alexander Hamilton may have had little choice but to duel Aaron Burr if he wished to keep a political career. Hence, a scoundrel could impose horrendous burdens on someone who would not choose to bear such burdens. Hamilton had worked to block Burr's accidental election to the presidency over Thomas

16. Gerald Dworkin, "Is More Choice Better than Less?" in *Social and Political Philosophy*, ed. Peter A. French, Theodore E. Uehling, Jr., and Howard K. Wettstein, vol. 7 of *Midwest Studies in Philosophy* (Minneapolis: University of Minnesota Press, 1982), pp. 47–62.

Jefferson when the electoral college failed to decide between them in 1800.[17] Had dueling been illegal and socially scorned, Hamilton would likely have been safe against Burr's efforts to revenge him for his action, and Hamilton might have lived much longer. The strategically similar complications of life under the social pressures of coed dorms may be left to the reader's imagination. In these, as in the other cases above, the only way to secure an individual benefit without undue cost may be to secure the collective benefit by denying certain courses of action.

In a minor aside, Rawls says that a person does not "suffer from a greater liberty." But Hart rightly counters that "it does not follow that a liberty which can only be obtained by an individual at the price of its general distribution through society is one that a rational person would still want."[18] For example, I might want to have available to me the recourse to perpetual servitude in the event of severe economic duress. But if the only way to have it available to me is to have it available to everyone, the result might soon be a relatively widespread instance of slavery with substantially poorer prospects overall for hired employment. Hence, Rawls's Difference Principle might require that there be no slavery, as suggested by the following argument.

Suppose there are crudely three conditions into which the worst-off members of our society might fall: destitution without opportunity to work for support but with general freedom otherwise, slavery, and wage labor with general freedom. One can imagine that virtually everyone might prefer these in reverse order. Hence, without an inalienable right to freedom, the destitute might readily consent to slavery. If they were barred from consenting to slavery, however, you who need their labor would choose to hire them while leaving them generally in freedom. We could now apply the Difference Principle to two ways of organizing our society: one that imposes an inalienable right to freedom and one that does not. In both societies, the worst-off class would be destitute. But in the society with the inalienable right to freedom the next worst-off class would be wage laborers while in the society with the right even to alienate one's freedom the next worst-off class would be slaves. By Rawls's

---

17. Under the original constitutional provisions, members of the electoral college cast two votes for president. If the person who received the most votes got votes from more than half the electors, he was elected president. The person who received the second highest vote count, if it represented a majority of the electors, was elected vice president. Jefferson's cleverly organized party did not fit the original provisions because its representatives on the electoral college voted for the ticket of Jefferson and Burr, giving each the same number of votes, so that the election had to be decided in the House of Representatives where the opposition party, led by Alexander Hamilton, was in the majority. Against more destructive sentiments in his party, Hamilton preferred his enemy Jefferson to the scoundrel Burr. It was a fatal preference.

18. John Rawls, *A Theory of Justice* (Cambridge, Mass.: Harvard University Press, 1971), p. 143; H. L. A. Hart, "Rawls on Liberty and Its Priority," *University of Chicago Law Review* 40 (1973): 551.

62   *Ethics*   October 1986

criterion, the first organization of our society, with the inalienable right, is more just.

Many examples of the creation of de facto inalienable rights in the actual laws of the nineteenth century of the United States and England involved breaking the supposed sanctity of the freedom of contract since they involved laws that protected classes against actions by their own individual members in contracting, for example, for longer days. Much of the legislation that protected specific classes of people by giving them legally inalienable rights is generally called paternalistic. That may often have been its stated motivation, but it can easily be understood as, in fact, an effort to redress strategic imbalances. The political rhetoric of the time had liberals such as T. H. Green defending the defenseless in order that they might eventually become autonomous, developed persons and conservatives defending the inviolable freedom of contract.[19] But note what a restrictive quality contract had, perhaps especially in late nineteenth- and early twentieth-century American law. Contracts were dyadic, between individuals, not between a large class and an individual or another large class. To outlaw collective negotiations was inherently to disadvantage that class whose collective action problem was the more severe.

We may not be able to know what were the views of the workers, women, tenant farmers, and children protected by various pieces of supposedly paternalistic legislation over the decades, but it is plausible that, had they been able to express a collective will by voting rather than by individually entering their separate contracts, many of the groups would overwhelmingly have chosen to restrict themselves as the legislation eventually did. If so, then governments eventually took the side of one party against the other after long having defended the other. In these cases government action did not better the lot of the members of the relevant class against the members' own judgment, as paternalistic actions generally are supposed to do but, rather, in support of their judgment of their interests. How one should morally judge such a government change of heart turns on how one would evaluate the distributive justice of the two arrangements. To judge it as a violation of rights would be uninformative because either way, before and after the change of heart, a presumptive right was violated.

INSTITUTIONALIZATION OF RIGHTS

Once we have justified the creation of institutional safeguards for individuals rights we face the problem of individuals who have institutional and not merely act-utilitarian norms to follow. In "The Adventure of the Abbey Grange," Sherlock Holmes explains this problem to Watson when he speaks of why he does not share his clues with Inspector Stanley

---

19. See T. H. Green, "Liberal Legislation and Freedom of Contract," in Green, *Political Theory*, ed. John R. Rodman (New York: Appleton-Century-Crofts, 1964), pp. 43–74.

Hopkins: "You must look at it this way: what I know is unofficial, what he knows is official. I have the right to private judgment, but he has none. He must disclose all, or he is a traitor to his service. In a doubtful case I would not put him in so painful a position, and so I reserve my information until my own mind is clear upon the matter."[20] Those who know Holmes may be wont to ask why then he withholds from Watson and from us, who do not share Hopkins's disability. But we can nevertheless grant that there is a valid moral point in his withholding from Hopkins (as there is a literary point in his withholding from us and, hence, from Watson). Hopkins is rightly not free to act simply on his own momentary judgment of what is best on the whole; rather, he must act according to the norms or rules of his role as a police official. We would not trust a police force whose officers chose to act for justice on their own interpretations. Indeed, in the United States, perhaps justifiably more than in many nations, we want stringent controls on police practice.

There are several utilitarian reasons for wanting such controls, which give officials incentives to act in relevant ways (the incentives are therefore strategic—they focus on actions and not on kinds of outcomes). For one, we may not trust many police officers and others in the criminal and civil justice system. For another, we may suppose from our own behavior that people in such roles are apt to suffer from a professional deformation that might incline them to overzealousness. More generally, we simply want the officers of that system to carry out their charge as we have defined it and not some other way. In a meaningful sense we do not want such role holders to act in their roles as though they were fully autonomous. We create a system to make judgments of guilt or innocence and it cannot sensibly be left up to the individuals within the system to make those judgments on their own.

A commonplace criticism of utilitarianism has been that it cannot in fact justify merely the punishment of the proven guilty but must go further and demand the fraudulent punishment of anyone when the action produces better results on the whole. For instance, Carritt argues, it might be supposed that hanging an innocent after a well-publicized trial would deter actual murderers from killing many other innocents. Surely, then, as utilitarians we would want the one innocent hanged.[21] This argument has been given perhaps its most cogent rebuttal by Rawls in "Two Concepts of Rules."[22] Rawls writes that

> the failure of Carritt's argument lies in the fact that he makes no distinction between the justification of the general system of rules

20. Arthur Conan Doyle, "The Adventure of the Abbey Grange," in *The Annotated Sherlock Holmes*, ed. William S. Baring-Gould (New York: Clarkson N. Potter, 1967), pp. 491–507, quoted in vol. 2, p. 504.

21. E. F. Carritt, *Ethical and Political Thinking* (Oxford: Clarendon Press, Oxford University Press, 1947), p. 65.

22. John Rawls, "Two Concepts of Rules," *Philosophical Review* 64 (1955): 3–32.

64   *Ethics*   October 1986

which constitutes penal institutions and the justification of particular
applications of these rules to particular cases by the various officials
whose job it is to administer them. This becomes perfectly clear
when one asks who the "we" are of whom Carritt speaks. Who is
this who has a sort of absolute authority on particular occasions to
decide that an innocent man shall be "punished" if everyone can
be convinced that he is guilty? Is this person the legislator, or the
judge, or the body of private citizens, or what? It is utterly crucial
to know who is to decide such matters, and by what authority, for
all of this must be written into the rules of the institution. Until
one knows these things one doesn't know what the institution is
whose justification is being challenged; and as the utilitarian principle
applies to the institution one doesn't know whether it is justifiable
on utilitarian grounds or not.[23]

Rawls goes on to underscore his argument by supposing that we had an
institution for fraudulently punishing innocents—an institution of "telishment"—when such actions would produce better outcomes on the
whole. The complaint that utilitarians must want such actions withers in
the face of such apt ridicule.

It was prescient of Rawls to present an argument defending the
creation of institutions on a particular moral ground and defending
practices within the institutions on the ground of their coherence with
the structure of the institutions. His theory of justice requires a similar
move: it is not about particular actions but about the structure of society.
To criticize his principles as inapplicable to particular actions in practice
would be to miss the point of the principles.

If utilitarianism recommends an institution for punishment of properly convicted persons, then that is the kind of institution a utilitarian
would want. We must create institutions to achieve utilitarian ends because
individual actions unconstrained and unguided by institutional structures
will not achieve them as well. There is perhaps no more grievous limit
to individual human reason than this. It is precisely the point of such
an institution as that for criminal justice to override individual reason
for the social good.

Suppose more generally that one believes, as liberals generally do,
that the way to secure the best results for individuals in their own lives
is to protect them in their freedom of action from infringements by others
and by the state. It follows that the relevant freedoms should probably
be protected by law. But this means that, if a certain right may in a
particular application override the general utility, the utilitarian who
defends the institutionalization of the relevant right must also defend its
apparently perverse applications. If enforcing the right of private ownership
of property is generally better than not doing so, then it should be
enforced. If there are specifiable classes of infringement of property that

23. Ibid., pp. 10–11.

would be utilitarian, however, these may also be institutionalized and enforced. But it is implausible that we can design institutions, comparable to Rawls's institution of telishment, that could be used to make exceptions from our generally institutionalized rules. There is likely to be no one or no institution we would be willing to empower to decide to take A's property to benefit B simply because that would make the world better. We can, however, easily imagine laws and institutions to tax all property to benefit all those in B's class. The capricious sorts of individual interventions that many moral theorists pose as counterexamples to institutional utilitarianism can have no institutional home.

But note that Rawls's argument is almost exclusively at the institutional level (although he goes on to apply it to "practices"). One might still ask, what of individuals? Suppose Holmes were Inspector Sherlock Holmes. Should he, acting as a utilitarian in an official role, ever violate the rules of his office? It is at least conceivable that he should. For instance, he might come upon a case in which his private knowledge and judgment of some aspects of an apparently criminal action recommended against punishment. Yet he might well know that his knowledge would have little weight in a trial court and that his reporting the case would likely result in severe punishment. There might be no reason to expect any external bad effects of his failing to report the case other than the slight risk that he himself would be caught derelict in his duty and would be punished with, perhaps, some exceedingly slight effect on the general institution of criminal justice. As a utilitarian, Holmes might conclude both that he should be derelict and that if he be caught he should be punished as a "traitor to his service." His view, as Hume, Bentham, Austin, and presumably Rawls would hold, would not be incoherent.

Incidentally, one suspects that Carritt and other critics of institutional utilitarianism would agree with Holmes's judgment here. To that extent, it seems likely that they have no real objection to individual action on utilitarian grounds contrary to one's official role. Rather, their objection is probably to the kinds of actions they portray, which are actions harming one innocent in order to prevent harm to others. Their real complaint, that is to say, is the usual complaint that utilitarianism violates our concern for fairness. This is generally an issue in distributive justice and as such it goes beyond the present concern. These are not easy issues, but I think any utilitarian would think it right to override fairness in sufficiently gruesome circumstances. One suspects that Carritt would have to agree, as Williams finally does after first implying that utilitarianism is particularly grim on this score.[24]

Another complaint against the unjust action in such cases is more pertinent here: that it violates the rights of someone. But this complaint

24. Bernard Williams, "A Critique of Utilitarianism," in *Utilitarianism: For and Against*, ed. J. J. C. Smart and Bernard Williams (London: Cambridge University Press, 1973), pp. 75–150, pp. 98–99, 117.

must assume some grounding for the affected rights. If rights are derivative from general utility, there can be no objection to overriding them in favor of general utility if there is no institutional complication such as that discussed above. That is to say, there may be no institutional way to override institutionalized rights, but an individual actor may act for the better outcome by violating someone's rights. She may then justifiably suffer institutional sanction, with Inspector Holmes, but she may nevertheless think it morally justifiable to violate the right. Hume, who recognizes that the institutions of justice are artificial, which is to say, in large part contingent and conventional, says that those who use the word *right* "before they have explain'd the origin of justice, or even make use of it in that explication, are guilty of a very gross fallacy, and can never reason upon any solid foundation."[25] An individual may support the creation of institutions for the protection of rights, be unable to imagine an associated institution for overriding rights to produce outcomes better on the whole, think it right to act individually to override them for that reason, and also think it right that those who do violate rights even to produce outcomes better on the whole should still be punished for the violation just because there can be no sensibly designed institutional way to exempt them. This account is familiar from a standard view of civil disobedience, according to which one should disobey a law one thinks bad only if one were then prepared to suffer legal punishment for the disobedience.

The point of the institutionalization of various protections is not to spare us as individuals of the need to make judgments of right and wrong but to secure certain outcomes that would otherwise not be secured. Institutional arrangements must inherently have a certain uniformity. That is a characteristic of their great value, but it can also be the source of their rigidity in cases in which particular knowledge available to some individuals and not to others recommends against rigid adherence to their norms. Sometimes relevant knowledge is not usably available to an institution because the institutional safeguards on collecting knowledge prevent its using the knowledge. Typically this is a problem in American criminal law for the prosecution, which is strategically prevented from collecting information in certain ways by being prevented from using any collected in those ways. As a result, there must be many police officers and prosecutors who are morally certain of the guilt of many legally unconvictable miscreants. In such a case of regularly recurring failure of the system to bring people to justice, it would be wrong to commend to individual police officers that they should see that "justice" is done. In such a case, we design the institution to build in a greater likelihood

25. David Hume, *A Treatise of Human Nature*, ed. L. A. Selby-Bigge and P. H. Nidditch, 2d ed. (Oxford: Clarendon Press, Oxford University Press, 1978), bk. 3, pt. 2, sec. 2, p. 491.

of one kind of failure in order to prevent too great a likelihood of another kind of failure.

If it is supposed that it is utilitarian to fail, specifically for reasons of blocked information, to convict some suspects, then it would be wrong for individuals in the criminal justice system to act against that norm—in large part because such action in standard, recurrent cases would destroy the system. The system that would easily survive the occasional dereliction by an Inspector Holmes on behalf of an accused would soon succumb to the recurrent excess of duty by its several officials against unconvictable miscreants. In some abstract sense one might wish to say that the latter actions would be just, but the sense is one that cannot be brought down to ground in a plausible institutional structure. In a meaningful sense, then, the actions would not be just.

CONFLICTS BETWEEN RIGHTS

Obviously, if there are several rights to be protected, their exercise may come into conflict. There are two general classes of conflicts of rights that are sufficiently common as to cause serious problems for a theory of rights. The first, and more widely understood, is the class in which the protected actions of one party coincidentally bring harm to another party, typically because of external effects of the actions. The second is that in which the protected dyadic right of contract conflicts with collective rights that would deny members of relevant collectivities the right to enter certain dyadic contracts. The first of these problems has historically been the focus of much of Anglo-Saxon common law. The second has more generally been handled by legislation or by default of either legislative or judicial intervention.

Both these classes of conflicts between rights are fundamentally problematic for a rights theory that begins with rights and that therefore has no prior principle from which to resolve the conflict. A utilitarian theory of rights would resolve either kind of conflict in principle by settling on that distribution of rights that produced better results overall. However, in practice, it might be nearly impossible to decide how best to allocate rights in particular classes of conflict. Some rights theorists might resolve conflicts that result from harmful externalities in favor of the harmed party on the presumption that harms and benefits are not morally symmetric. Coase, who counts them as strictly symmetric in his general concern with efficiency of production, argues that overall efficiency is not affected by the allocation of rights.[26] His argument is remarkably simple. He supposes that, if on the one hand, I have a right to prevent you from undertaking a certain activity, you will bargain with me to allow you to undertake it nevertheless—*if* it is worth more to you to do it than

26. R. H. Coase, "The Problem of Social Cost," *Journal of Law and Economics* **3** (1960): 1–44.

68   *Ethics*   October 1986

to me to prevent you from doing it. On the other hand, if you have the right to do it, I will bargain with you to get you to refrain—if preventing you from doing it is worth more to me than doing it is to you. Hence, irrespective of where the right lies, the activity will either be undertaken or not according as it is more valuable to undertake it or to prevent it.

The only effect choosing the one or the other allocation of rights will have is to determine which of the parties in the conflict has the initial advantage in bargaining for the gains from undertaking or not undertaking the relevant activity. Hence, the rights assignment is exclusively a matter of distributive, not productive, concern. Insofar as Coase's argument is correct, a utilitarian who thinks that money per se is an adequate measure of utility has no ground on which to allocate simple rights in conflict. Of course, a utilitarian who thinks money isn't everything faces a tough analytical problem of deciding which allocation of rights produces the better outcome.

Coase's analysis, which has considerable force for the allocation between two individuals, typically fails for the allocation of a right between an individual and a collective. His conditions of perfect information and no bargaining costs are far more unrealistic for a group than for an individual and his analysis fails to consider problems of collective action that undercut the hope that the parties in a collective can simply bargain their way to an efficient outcome.

The more interesting of the two classes of problems in the conflict between rights is conflicts between dyadic and collective rights. Such conflicts can arise either as simple problems of external effects of dyadic exercises of rights or as inherent conflicts between certain collective protections and the exercise of dyadic rights. Since little additional complexity follows from the consideration of the conflicts that arise from simple externalities and since these have been discussed at great length by many moral, political, and legal philosophers while the conflicts between dyadic and collective rights have been less well discussed, I will only briefly consider the former before turning more extensively to the latter.

The general problem of external effects of the exercise of rights may be exemplified by the following. A pattern of exchanges may produce incentives to coercion apart from that inherent in the relative power of the parties to the exchanges. For example, one might argue that free traffic in, say, drugs or prostitution will spawn violence and that, since the state cannot protect innocents against the consequent harms in any other way, it must do so by prohibiting or controlling the relevant exchanges. Such an argument turns, of course, on complex facts and causal relations and often cannot *easily* be supported. Many of the apparently paternalistic regulations of modern states may be motivated at least in part by such concerns and they are therefore not in principle illiberal—although they may be in fact. To decide whether to regulate, one would need an ordering principle to say which right takes precedence or a value judgment about which rights violation produces the greater harm.

Turn now to conflicts between dyadic rights, especially of contract, and collective rights when the latter are secured by directly infringing the former. Much of the politics of the nineteenth century in England and the United States over regulation of contract arose from such conflicts. Ironically, when Maine put the case for the shift from status to contract, it was already being succeeded by a contrary development. As Toynbee put the corrective argument, "The real course of development has been first from status to contract, then from contract to a new kind of status determined by the law,—or, in other words, from unregulated to regulated contract."[27] The latter shift is the result of interventions by the state, partly to protect certain parties to contractual relations against others and partly to protect some of us from contractual (and noncontractual) actions by others. If we protect the rights of renters against landlords or of workers against employers, we generally do so by restricting what can be dyadically contracted. For example, workers may be secured the right collectively to negotiate a wage level with a given employer by blocking the "right" of others to contract with that employer to work for a lower wage. Rental and other contracts have implied clauses that cannot be signed away by mutual agreement, and many clauses in actual contracts are unenforceable.

Because the interests protected by collective rights are inherently subject to problems of the logic of collective action, we cannot generally expect to have relevant classes express their own interests with the force and clarity with which an abused individual or corporation might be expected to express its interests. Hence, if the rights of collectives are to be secured, they will commonly have to be secured by state action on behalf of the affected classes without the kind of general, in-principle agreement that we might expect to support the simpler dyadic rights of freedom of contract. We might suppose that establishing the right of dyadic contract is a very nearly Pareto-superior move from a crude status quo, in which restrictions on contract substantially suppress free exchange and even economic development. But then to establish certain collective rights that infringe the right to dyadic contracts is likely not to be even a nearly Pareto-superior move because it will enhance the power of one group at the expense of another without an offsetting substantial impact on general economic productivity. While libertarians and utilitarians may agree on the establishment of the freedom of contract, they are likely to part company over the establishment of collective rights.

RIGHTS VERSUS UNANIMITY

Rights theorists should perhaps be seen as the original strategic or game theorists. To have a right is to be free to take some particular kind of action in the context of actions by others. Rights are therefore ideally

27. Arnold Toynbee, *Lectures on the Industrial Revolution* (London: Longmans, Green & Co., 1884), p. 31.

suited to game theoretic representation. To say that I have the right to a certain kind of action is to say that my set of available strategies must include that of taking the action. To say that I have an inalienable right such as the right to freedom from slavery is to say that I cannot have available any strategy that includes the possibility of my entering into slavery. When we set up an institution to support particular rights, we basically arrange for outlawing any effort to change the relevant characterization of individual strategy sets. Conflicts of rights occur when the constraints on my strategies constrain your strategies against your rights. For example, your freedom of contract is restricted not to include freedom to contract with me for my perpetual servitude to you.

Sen has argued that liberalism is logically even more muddled than our discussion of conflicts between rights suggests. According to his theorem of the "liberal paradox," or the "impossibility of a paretian liberal," the existence of even one right each for two persons is potentially in conflict with the simple principle of unanimity, or the so-called weak Pareto principle, according to which, if everyone prefers x to y, then x should be preferred by society to y.[28] Assuming an adequate understanding of what x and y imply for everyone, any utilitarian seemingly must accept the weak Pareto principle. Hence, if Sen's theorem is correct, any theory of rights must potentially conflict with utilitarianism. As he says, "The fact that unqualified use of the Pareto principle potentially threatens all rights gives the conflict an extraordinarily wide scope."[29]

It happens that Sen's motivating example for his theorem is, in game theoretic representation, a Prisoner's Dilemma because it is a simple problem of exchange. A slightly mean, lewd fancier of such (somewhat old-fashionedly) pornographic literature as *Lady Chatterley's Lover* would sooner have her prudish neighbor read the novel than read it herself. Prude, the self-appointed protector of society's morals, would sooner read it than have Lewd read it. Lewd has the right to read it and Prude has the right not to read it. But, by unanimous preference they choose to have Prude read it in return for Lewd's not reading it. Hence, Sen concludes, both rights are violated.

Sen's conclusion is transparently wrong for this example. Sen seems to have confused rights with obligatory actions. Liberals do not insist that one must exercise one's rights except in cases of inalienable rights. Indeed, it is obvious that among the most important of all rights in the liberal canon are the right of exchange and its correlative right of contract, rights whose exercise is required for the result of Lewd's and Prude's bargain to work. When I exchange something I own for something you own, I do what I have a right not to do. It is not sensibly said that I

---

28. Amartya Sen, "The Impossibility of a Paretian Liberal," *Journal of Political Economy* 78 (1970): 152–57.

29. Amartya Sen, "Liberty, Unanimity and Rights," *Economica* 43 (1976): 217–45, p. 238.

therefore violate my right of ownership. As Lindsay says, the exchange "relation *is* a peculiar one. In it, A gives B what B wants, in return for B giving A what A wants. . . . A is not responsible for B's wants, nor B for A's; and therefore—in this curious relation not A but B decides what A should do: and not B but A decides what B should do."[30] Sen would have it be not only peculiar but wrong.

For a relevantly chosen example, however, there might be some force to Sen's theorem. Suppose Lewd and Prude struck a bargain to exchange their *inalienable* rights or even merely to override Lewd's inalienable right. This would be a unanimous choice (at least of the two parties most immediately concerned) and yet it would violate a right. On the account of inalienable rights given above, it should be clear why such a violation is blocked even though it might be preferred by the most immediately affected parties. Indeed, on that analysis it is clear that the strategic structure of a utilitarian inalienable right cannot be represented with only two people: it requires consideration of the stake of the larger class of which at least one of the two is a member. If the right is inalienable on other grounds, there is no paradox in a conflict between *that* right and the Pareto principle. Of course, liberalism is fundamentally a rejection of such notions of right, as is its close relative, utilitarianism. Therefore, we should not jump to conclusions so quickly merely from a consideration of unanimous preferences in the matter of Lewd and Prude to say that liberalism is in logical difficulty. Again, we should realize, with Rawls, that there are two kinds of justification at issue here and that the kind on which Sen is relying is ruled out in advance. Having a right at all is like an institution in that it is justified in general. Actions under the right are then judged not simply by preferences but also by conformity with the right.

In the inalienable rights instance of Sen's liberal paradox, it is easily seen that the relevant right is in conflict with the preferences of the two actors. But the point of such rights in a contingent theory, as in the utilitarian theory of rights, is to afford us protections against certain kinds of actions that we could not individually guarantee for ourselves. This is necessary in many cases precisely because relevant preferences in particular moments will lead to a result that, on the whole, we consider worse than if the actions of all parties were restricted in such a way as partly to violate their momentary preferences. It is therefore no surprise that Sen finds his supposedly paradoxical conflict between preferences and—inalienable—rights. Indeed, his paradox boils down to a special case of the more general logic of collective action. All prefer cooperation (the maintenance of a certain right, for example) by all to noncooperation, but each prefers not to cooperate because there are benefits to be had from going against the general agreement. That is why we choose to

30. A. D. Lindsay, *The Modern Democratic State* (New York and London: Oxford University Press, 1947), pp. 103–4.

72   *Ethics*   *October 1986*

enforce the general agreement against our own momentary preferences in specific cases. There is surely no paradox in the action of strategically constraining our own actions in advance in order to make ours a better world, considered from our own interests, in which to live.

Perhaps part of the reason for the confusions of Sen's liberal paradox is that it is expressed in the formulations of Arrowian social choice theory. Hence, it is not about strategy choices but only about actual outcomes.[31] In the Arrowian literature, one simply ranks states of affairs and concludes from rankings of all parties what should be the social or collective ranking of the states of affairs. If this were our business in actual life, we would have no need of rights since we would simply produce a social choice and that would be the end of it (or, in light of all the impossibility results, we might reach impasse and that, alas, would be the end of it). But in actual life we do have need of institutions for getting things done and for ensuring certain rights because we bumble along from day to day and generation to generation trying to make the best of things for ourselves. Since your efforts to make things best for you may tend to make them worse for me, and vice versa, when a little coordination or cooperation might have been better for both, we may both agree to establish certain protections in advance that, in particular moments later on, we might one or the other or both prefer to violate. That is part of the logic of the rights of liberalism.

Consider for a moment the form of Sen's example and ignore the content of it. He shows that unanimity conflicts with two rights in a society of two people. Now put questions like those Rawls put to Carritt to Sen. Who is concerned with the supposed rights violations in Sen's two-person society? Why would anyone in that society have conceived of a need for inalienable rights? And if they ever did establish rights for their society, why would they then object to having an override clause in any case in which they both wanted it? Against whom are they protecting themselves with inalienable rights that block them from acting when they unanimously agree on some action?

If theirs were not a two-person society, we could give sensible answers to these questions. If Lewd's and Prude's rights in a larger society are and ought to be inalienable, that is because of the effects of their violation on others. In our larger society, with our need for protections against certain individually rational but often collectively destructive actions, we need such rights. Once we have them, we may be no more able to design the institution for making specific exceptions for ourselves than we can design a sensible institution for telishment. That present agreements may not seem attractive in the future is so far from being a paradox that it is among the most important of all reasons for law and by far the

31. Russell Hardin, "Rational Choice Theories," in *Idioms of Inquiry: Critique and Renewal in Political Science*, ed. Terence Ball (Albany: State University of New York Press, in press).

most important reason for the law of contracts. When the constraints of our general agreement are further exacerbated by the logic of collective action, we get Sen's odd paradox, so called. It seems paradoxical only because he imposes rights to deal with the kinds of constraints that real societies face—strategic interactions and severe limits to reason and information that require that we create institutional devices to handle them—on a peculiar society or partial society of two people in which such constraints cannot meaningfully be resolved by institutional arrangements, in which rights have no reasonable basis.

CONCLUSION

Rather than summarize the foregoing arguments, I wish briefly to do two things: first, to suggest how this account of rights may clarify confusing aspects of rights theories that often have a claim on our understanding because they seem generally right in certain circumstances; and second, to state one caveat on the apparent claims here.

Against much of this argument, one may still wish to assert that rights are fundamental, that they are not derivative from other considerations, such as consequences. I do not wish to take on such a view here other than to note some advantages of a derivative account of rights. If rights are viewed as metaphysical or abstract rather than contingent, they must be defined very simply without many subclasses, distinctions, or exceptions. Legal rights, as opposed to moral or human rights, do not suffer from this disability. They can be modified to meet new situations or conditions and they can be highly articulated with manifold subclasses, distinctions, and exceptions. If a situation occurs in which the application of a particular right leads to undesirable outcomes, perhaps because suboptimal, then the right can be redefined or slightly altered to fit the relevant situation. Hence, in an institutional system of rights, the persistent occurrence of bad outcomes should be rare, or at least only short-lived until the relevant modifications can be made.

Similarly, on the derivative, utilitarian account of rights presented here, rights may change through time as the conditions of social interaction change, and they may differ across societies in understandable ways to adapt to strategic considerations. What set of rights should be defended will depend on what set will produce desirable results under the circumstances. For example, the right of contract should change as economic conditions change. Perhaps at one time the right of contract should have been nearly untrammeled in order to encourage productive activities under the conditions of the nascent industrial economy and early market of, say, eighteenth-century England. Today, perhaps, the right of contract should be restricted in certain systematic ways to prevent imbalances of economic power from grievously affecting certain kinds of transactions and to prevent certain kinds of external effects, such as air and water pollution and neighborhood destruction. Anyone who tries to defend an

74   *Ethics   October 1986*

unvarnished right of contract for any two parties to do whatever they want to do under any circumstances will be met with vacant stares from most moral and political theorists today.

The derivative, utilitarian view of rights is largely an account of what institutional protections we should have. Hence, it is a normative account of what legal rights we should have. To some extent it may also seem to give an explanation of the system of legal rights and institutional protections we have—*if* we further assume that desirability somehow produces relevant causal forces. To some extent such an assumption may be compelling. If we have constructed institutions that work against individuals' interests, we may expect them under certain circumstances to try to change those institutions. Hence, if some of our legal rights are not utilitarian, we may expect some pressure to change them toward more utilitarian rights. No one could sensibly suppose that such pressure would be overwhelming or that there might not be powerful countervailing pressures toward less utilitarian rights. Therefore we cannot sensibly suppose that a normative and largely conceptual account, such as that presented here, yields easy explanations of actual rights.

[13]

Between Utility and Rights *

H.L.A. Hart**

I.

I do not think than anyone familiar with what has been published in the last ten years, in England and the United States, on the philosophy of government can doubt that this subject, which is the meeting point of moral, political and legal philosophy, is undergoing a major change. We are currently witnessing, I think, the progress of a transition from a once widely accepted old faith that some form of utilitarianism, if only we could discover the right form, *must* capture the essence of political morality. The new faith is that the truth must lie not with a doctrine that takes the maximisation of aggregate or average general welfare for its goal, but with a doctrine of basic human rights, protecting specific basic liberties and interests of individuals, if only we could find some sufficiently firm foundation for such rights to meet some long familiar objections. Whereas not so long ago great energy and much ingenuity of many philosophers were devoted to making some form of utilitarianism work, latterly such energies and ingenuity have been devoted to the articulation of theories of basic rights.

As often with such changes of faith or redirection of philosophical energies and attention, the new insights which are currently offered us seem to dazzle at least as much as they illuminate. Certainly, as I shall try to show by reference to the work of two now influential contemporary writers, the new faith has been presented in forms which are, in spite of much brillance, in the end unconvincing. My two examples, both American, are taken respectively from the Conservative Right and the Liberal Left of the political spectrum; and while the former, the Conservative, builds a theory of rights on the moral importance of the *separateness* or *distinctness* of human persons which utilitarianism is said to ignore, the latter, the Liberal Left, seeks to erect such a theory on their moral title to equal concern and respect which, it is said, unreconstructed utilitarianism implicitly denies. So while the first theory is dominated by the duty of governments to respect the separateness of persons, the second is dominated by the duty of governments to treat their subjects as equals, with equal concern and respect.

---

* A shorter version of this essay was delivered as the John Dewey Memorial Lecture at the Law School of Columbia University on November 14, 1978. I am indebted to Derek Parfit for many helpful suggestions and criticisms of both the style and substance of the present version.

** University College, Oxford.

UTILITY AND RIGHTS   829

II.

For a just appraisal of the first of these two theories it is necessary to gain a clear conception of what precisely is meant by the criticism, found in different forms in very many different modern writers, that unqualified utilitarianism fails to recognize or abstracts from the separateness of persons when, as a political philosophy, it calls on governments to maximise the total or the average net happiness or welfare of their subjects. Though this accusation of ignoring the separateness of persons can be seen as a version of the Kantian principle that human beings are ends in themselves it is nonetheless the distinctively modern criticism of utilitarianism. In England Bernard Williams [1] and in America John Rawls [2] have been the most eloquent expositors of this form of criticism; and John Rawls's claim that "Utilitarianism does not take seriously the distinction between persons" [3] plays a very important role in his *A Theory of Justice*. Only faint hints of this particular criticism flickered through the many different attacks made in the past on utilitarian doctrine, ever since Jeremy Bentham in 1776 announced to the world that both government and the limits of government were to be justified by reference to the greatest happiness of the greatest number, and not by reference to any doctrine of natural rights: such doctrines he thought so much "bawling upon paper," [4] and he first announced them in 1776 in a brief rude reply [5] to the American Declaration of Independence.

What then does this distinctively modern criticism of utilitarianism, that it ignores the moral importance of the separateness of individuals, mean? I think its meaning is to be summed up in four main points, though not all the writers who make this criticism would endorse all of them.

The first point is this: In the perspective of classical maximising utilitarianism separate individuals are of no intrinsic importance but only important as the points at which fragments of what *is* important, *i.e.* the total aggregate of pleasure or happiness, are located. Individual persons for it are therefore merely the channels or locations where what is of value is to be found. It is for this reason that as long as the totals are thereby increased there is nothing, if no independent principles of distribution are introduced, to limit permissible trade-offs between the satisfactions of different persons. Hence one individual's happiness or pleasure, however

---

1. *A Critique of Utilitarianism*, in J. SMART & B. WILLIAMS, UTILITARIANISM, FOR AND AGAINST 108-18 (1973); and *Persons, Character and Morality* in THE IDENTITY OF PERSONS (Rorty ed. 1977).
2. *See* J. RAWLS, A THEORY OF JUSTICE 22-24, 27, 181, 183, 187 (1971).
3. *Id.* at 187.
4. J. BENTHAM, *Anarchical Fallacies*, in 2 WORKS OF JEREMY BENTHAM 494 (Bowring ed. 1843).
5. For an acount of this reply included in *An Answer to the Declaration of the American Congress* (1776) by Bentham's friend John Lind, see my *Bentham and the United States of America*, 19 J.L. & ECON. 547, 555-56 (1976).

innocent he may be, may be sacrificed to procure a greater happiness or pleasure located in other persons, and such replacements of one person by another are not only allowed but required by unqualified utilitarianism when unrestrained by distinct distributive principles.

Secondly, utilitarianism is not, as sometimes it is said to be, an individualistic and egalitarian doctrine, although in a sense it treats persons as equals, or of equal worth. For it does this only by in effect treating individual persons as of *no* worth; since not persons for the utilitarian but the experiences of pleasure or satisfaction or happiness which persons have are the sole items of worth or elements of value. It is of course true and very important that, according to the utilitarian maxim, "everybody [is] to count for one, nobody for more than one"[6] in the sense that in any application of the greatest happiness calculus the equal pains or pleasures, satisfactions or dissatisfactions or preferences of different persons are given the same weight whether they be Brahmins or Untouchables, Jews or Christians, black or white. But since utilitarianism has no direct or intrinsic concern but only an instrumental concern with the relative *levels* of total well-being enjoyed by different persons, its form of equal concern and respect for persons embodied in the maxim "everybody to count for one, nobody for more than one" may license the grossest form of inequality in the actual treatment of individuals, if that is required in order to maximise aggregate or average welfare. So long as that condition is satisfied, the situation in which a few enjoy great happiness while many suffer is as good as one in which happiness is more equally distributed.

Of course in comparing the aggregate economic welfare produced by equal and unequal distribution of resources account must be taken of factors such as diminishing marginal utility and also envy. These factors favour an equal distribution of resources but by no means always favour it conclusively. For there are also factors pointing the other way, such as administrative and transaction costs, loss of incentives and failure of the standard assumption that all individuals are equally good pleasure or satisfaction machines, and derive the same utility from the same amount of wealth.

Thirdly, the modern critique of utilitarianism asserts that there is nothing self-evidently valuable or authoritative as a moral goal in the mere increase in totals of pleasure or happiness abstracted from all questions of distribution. The collective sum of different persons' pleasures, or the net balance of total happiness of different persons (supposing it makes sense to talk of adding them), is not in itself a pleasure or happiness which anybody experiences. Society is not an individual experiencing the aggre-

---

6. *See* J.S. MILL, *Utilitarianism* (ch. 5), in 10 COLLECTED WORKS OF JOHN STUART MILL 157 (1969); J. BENTHAM, *Plan of Parliamentary Reform,* in 3 WORKS OF JEREMY BENTHAM 459 (Bowring ed. 1843).

gate collected pleasures or pains of its members; no person experiences such an aggregate.

Fourthly, according to this critique, maximising utilitarianism, if it is not restrained by distinct distributive principles, proceeds on a false analogy between the way in which it is rational for a single prudent individual to order his life and the way in which it is rational for a whole community to order its life through government. The analogy is this: it is rational for one man as a single individual to sacrifice a present satisfaction or pleasure for a greater satisfaction later, even if we discount somewhat the value of the later satisfaction because of its uncertainty. Such sacrifices are amongst the most elementary requirements of prudence and are commonly accepted as a virtue, and indeed a paradigm of practical rationality, and, of course, any form of saving is an example of this form of rationality. In its misleading analogy with an individual's prudence, maximising utilitarianism not merely treats one person's pleasure as replaceable by some greater pleasure of that same person, as prudence requires, but it also treats the pleasure or happiness of one individual as similarly replaceable without limit by the greater pleasure of other individuals. So in these ways it treats the division between persons as of no more moral significance than the division between times which separates one individual's earlier pleasure from his later pleasure, as if individuals were mere parts of a single persisting entity.

III.

The modern insight that it is the arch-sin of unqualified utilitarianism to ignore in the ways I have mentioned the moral importance of the separateness of persons is, I think, in the main, a profound and penetrating criticism. It holds good when utilitarianism is restated in terms of maximum want or preference satisfaction and minimum want or preference frustration rather than in the Benthamite form of the balances of pleasure and pain as psychological states, and it holds good when the maximand is taken to be average rather than total general welfare. But it is capable of being abused to discredit all attempts to diminish inequalities and all arguments that one man's loss may be compensated by another's gain such as have inspired policies of social welfare; all these are discredited as if all necessarily committed the cardinal sin committed by maximising utilitarianism of ignoring the separateness of individuals. This is I think the basis of the libertarian strongly anti-utilitarian political theory developed by Robert Nozick in his influential book, *Anarchy, State and Utopia.*[7] For Nozick a strictly limited set of near absolute individual rights constitute the foundations of morality. Such rights for him "express the

---

7. R. NOZICK, ANARCHY, STATE, AND UTOPIA (1974).

inviolability of persons" [8] and "reflect the fact of our separate existences." [9] The rights are these: each individual, so long as he does not violate the same rights of others, has the right not to be killed or assaulted, to be free from all forms of coercion or limitation of freedom and the right not to have property legitimately acquired, taken, or the use of it limited. He has also the secondary right to punish and exact compensation for violation of his rights, to defend himself and others against such violation. He has the positive right to acquire property by making or finding things and by transfer or inheritance from others and he has the right to make such transfers and binding contracts. The moral landscape which Nozick explicitly presents contains only rights and is empty of everything else except possibly the moral permissibility of avoiding what he terms catastrophe. Hence moral wrongdoing has only one form: the violation of rights, perpetrating a wrong to the holder of a right. So long as rights are not violated it matters not for morality, short of catastrophe, how a social system actually works, how individuals fare under it, what needs it fails to meet or what misery or inequalities it produces. In this scheme of things the basic rights which fill the moral landscape and express the inviolability of persons are few in number but are all equally stringent. The only legitimate State on this view is one to which individuals have transferred their right to punish or exact compensation from others, and the State may not go beyond the night-watchman functions of using the transferred rights to protect persons against force, fraud, and theft or breaches of contract. In particular the State may not impose burdens on the wealth or income or restraints on the liberty of some citizens to relieve the needs or suffering, however great, of others. So a State may only tax its citizens to provide the police, the law courts and the armed forces necessary for defence and the performance of the night-watchman functions. Taxing earnings or profits for the relief of poverty or destitution, however dire the need, or for the general welfare such as public education is on this view morally indefensible; it is said to be "on a par with" forced labour[10] or making the government imposing such taxes into a "part owner" of the persons taxed.[11]

Nozick's development of this extreme libertarian position is wide-ranging. It is full of original and ingenious argument splendidly designed to shake up any complacent interventionist into painful self-scrutiny. But it rests on the slenderest foundation. Indeed many critics have complained of the lack of any argument to show that human beings have the few and only the few but very stringent rights which Nozick assigns to them to support his conclusion that a morally legitimate government cannot have any more extensive functions than the night-watchman's. But the critics

8. *Id.* at 32.
9. *Id.* at 33.
10. *Id.* at 169.
11. *Id.* at 172.

are wrong: there is argument of a sort, though it is woefully deficient. Careful scrutiny of his book shows that the argument consists of the assertion that if the functions of government are not limited to the protection of the basic stringent rights, then that arch-sin of ignoring the separateness of persons which modern critics impute to utilitarianism will have been committed.   To sustain this argument Nozick at the start of his book envelops in metaphors all policies imposing burdens or restraints going beyond the functions of the night-watchman State, and the metaphors are in fact all drawn from a description of the arch-sin imputed to utilitarianism.   Thus, not only is taxation said to be the equivalent of forced labour but every limitation of property rights, every restriction of liberty for the benefit of others going beyond the constraints imposed by the basic rights, are described as *violating* a person,[12] as a *sacrifice* of that person,[13] or as an outweighing of *one life* by others,[14] or a treatment of a distinct individual as *a resource*[15] for others. So conceptions of justice permitting a graduated income tax to provide for basic needs or to diminish social or economic inequalities are all said to neglect the basic truth "that each individual is a separate person, that his is the only life he has." [16]   To hold that a person should bear costs that benefit others more is represented as a *"sacrifice"* of that person and as implying what is false: namely that there is a single social entity with a life of which individual lives are merely part just as one individual's desires sacrificed for the sake of his other desires are only part of his life.[17] This imputation of the arch-sin committed by utilitarianism to any political philosophy which assigns functions to the state more extensive than the night-watchman's constitutes I think the foundation which Nozick offers for his system.

It is a paradoxical feature of Nozick's argument, hostile though it is to any form of utilitarianism, that it yields a result identical with one of the least acceptable conclusions of an unqualified maximising utilitarianism, namely that given certain conditions there is nothing to choose between a society where few enjoy great happiness and very many very little, and a society where happiness is more equally spread.   For the utilitarian the condition is that in both societies either aggregate or average welfare is the same.   For Nozick the condition is a historical one: that the patterns of distribution of wealth which exist at any time in a society should have come about through exercise of the rights and power of acquisition and voluntary transfer included in ownership and without any violation of the few basic rights. Given the satisfaction of this historical condition, how people fare under the resulting patterns of distribution, whether grossly

---

12. *Id.* at 32.
13. *Id.* at 33.
14. *Id.*
15. *Id.*
16. *Id.*
17. *Id.* at 32-33.

inegalitarian or egalitarian, is of no moral significance. The only virtue of social institutions on this view is that they protect the few basic rights, and their only vice is failure to do this. Any consequence of the exercise of such rights is unobjectionable. It is as if the model for Nozick's basic moral rights were a legal one. Just as there can be no legal objection to the exercise of a legal right, so in a morality as empty as Nozick's is of everything except rights, there can be no moral objection to the exercise of a moral right.

Why should a critic of society thus assume that there is only one form of moral wrong, namely, violation of individual rights? Why should he turn his gaze away from the consequences in terms of human happiness or misery produced by the working of a system of such rights? The only answer apparent in Nozick's work is that to treat this misery as a matter of moral concern and to require some persons to contribute to the assistance of others only makes sense if one is prepared like the maximising utilitarian to disregard the separateness of individuals and share the superstition that those required to make such contributions are merely part of the life of a single persisting social entity which both makes the contributions and experiences the balance of good that comes from such contributions. This of course simply assumes that utilitarianism is only intelligible if the satisfactions it seeks to maximise are regarded as those of a single social entity. It also assumes that the only alternative to the Nozickian philosophy of right is an unrestricted maximising utilitarianism which respects not persons but only experiences of pleasure or satisfaction; and this is of course a false dilemma. The impression that we are faced with these two unpalatable alternatives dissolves if we undertake the no doubt unexciting but indispensable chore of confronting Nozick's misleading descriptive terms such as "sacrifice of one individual for others," "treating one individual as a resource for others," "making others a part owner of a man," "forced labour" with the realities which these expressions are misused to describe. We must also substitute for the blindingly general use of concepts like "interference with liberty" a discriminating catalogue which will enable us to distinguish those restrictions on liberty which can be imposed only at that intolerable cost of sacrificing an individual's life or depriving it of meaning which according to Nozick is the cost of any restriction of liberty except the restriction on the violation of basic rights. How can it be right to lump together, and ban as equally illegitimate, things so different in their impact on individual life as taking some of a man's income to save others from some great suffering and killing him or taking one of his vital organs for the same purpose? If we are to construct a tenable theory of rights for use in the criticism of law and society we must, I fear, ask such boring questions as: Is taxing a man's earnings or income which leaves him free to choose whether to work and to choose what work to do not altogether different in terms of the burden it imposes from forcing him to labour? Does it really sacrifice him or make him or his body just a resource for others? Does the admitted moral impermissibility of wounding or maiming others or the existence of an absolute moral right not to have one's vital organs taken for the benefit of others in any way support a conclusion that there exists an absolute moral right to retain untaxed all one's earnings or all the income accrued from inherited property except for taxes to support the army and the police? Can one man's great gain or relief from great suffering not outweigh a small loss of income imposed on another to provide it? Do such outweighings only make sense if the gain and the loss are of the same person or a single "social entity"? Once we shake off that assumption and once we distinguish between the gravity of the different restrictions on different specific liberties and their importance for the conduct of a meaningful life or the development of the personality, the idea that they all, like unqualified maximising utilitarianism, ignore the moral importance of the division of humanity into separate individuals and threaten the proper inviolability of persons disappears into the mist.

There is of course much of value to be learned from Nozick's ingenious and diverting pages, but there are also many quite different criticisms to be made of its foundations apart from the one which I have urged. But since other critics have been busy with many such criticisms I will here mention only one. Even if a social philosophy can draw its morality as Nozick assumes only from a single source; even if that source is individual rights, so that the only moral wrongdoing consists in wrongs done to individuals that violate their rights, and even if the foundation for such rights is respect for the separateness of persons, why should rights be limited as they are by Nozick to what Bentham called the negative services of others, that is to abstention from such things as murder, assault, theft and breach of contract? Why should there not be included a basic right to the positive service of the relief of great needs or suffering or the provision of basic education and skills when the cost of these is small compared with both the need to be met and with the financial resources of those taxed to provide them? Why should property rights, to be morally legitimate, have an absolute, permanent, exclusive, inheritable and unmodifiable character which leaves no room for this? Nozick is I think in particular called upon to answer this question because he is clear that though rights for him constitute the only source of constraint on action, they are not ends to be maximised;[18] the obligations they impose are, as Nozick insists, "side constraints," so the rights form a protective bastion enabling an individual to achieve his own ends in a life he shapes himself; and *that*, Nozick thinks, is the individual's way of giving meaning to life.[19]

But it is of course an ancient insight that for a meaningful life not only the protection of freedom from deliberate restriction but opportunities

---

18. *Id.* at 28-29.
19. *Id.* at 48-50.

and resources for its exercise are needed. Except for a few privileged and lucky persons, the ability to shape life for oneself and lead a meaningful life is something to be constructed by positive marshalling of social and economic resources. It is not something automatically guaranteed by a structure of negative rights. Nothing is more likely to bring freedom into contempt and so endanger it than failure to support those who lack, through no fault of their own, the material and social conditions and opportunities which are needed if a man's freedom is to contribute to his welfare.

IV.

My second example of contemporary right-based social philosophy is that put forward with very different political implications as one ground for rights in the original, fascinating, but very complex web of theory spun by Professor Ronald Dworkin in his book *Taking Rights Seriously*.[20] Dworkin's theory at first sight seems to be, like Nozick's, implacably opposed to any form of utilitarianism; so much so that the concept of a right which he is concerned to vindicate is expressly described by him as "an anti-Utilitarian Concept." It is so described because for Dworkin "if someone has a right to something then it is wrong for the government to deny it to him even though it would be in the general interest to do so." [21]

In fact the two writers, in spite of this surface similarity, differ on almost every important issue except over the conviction that it is a morality of individual rights which both imposes moral limits on the coercive powers of governments, and in the last resort justifies the use of that power.

Before I turn to examine in detail Dworkin's main thesis I shall summarise the major differences between these two modern philosophers of Right. For Nozick the supreme value is freedom—the unimpeded individual will; for Dworkin it is equality of concern and respect, which as he warns us does not always entail equality of treatment. That governments must treat all their citizens with equal concern and respect is for Dworkin "a postulate of political morality",[22] and, he presumes, everyone accepts it. Consequently these two thinkers' lists of basic rights are very different, the chief difference being that for Dworkin there is no general or residual right to liberty as there is for Nozick. Indeed though he recognizes that many, if not most, liberal thinkers have believed in such a right as Jefferson did, Dworkin calls the idea "absurd." [23] There are only rights to specific liberties such as freedom of speech, worship, association, and personal and sexual

---

20. R. DWORKIN, TAKING RIGHTS SERIOUSLY (1977).
21. *Id.* at 269.
22. *Id.* at 272.
23. *Id.* at 267. Yet "Hercules" (Dworkin's model of a Judge) is said not only to believe that the Constitution guarantees an abstract right to liberty but to hold that a right to privacy is a consequence of it. *Id.* at 117.

relationships. Since there is no general right to liberty there is no general conflict between liberty and equality, though the reconciliation of these two values is generally regarded as the main problem of liberalism; nor, since there is no general right to liberty, is there any inconsistency, as conservatives often claim, in the liberal's willingness to accept restriction on economic but not on personal freedom. This is why the political thrust of these two right-based theories is in opposite directions. So far from thinking that the State must be confined to the night-watchman's functions of protecting a few basic negative rights but not otherwise restricting freedom, Dworkin is clear that the State may exercise wide interventionist functions; so if overall social welfare fairly assessed would be thereby advanced, the State may restrict the use of property or freedom of contract; it may enforce desegregation, provide through taxation for public education and culture; it may both prohibit discrimination on grounds of sex or colour where these are taken to be badges of inferiority, and allow schemes of reverse racial discrimination, if required in the general interest, even in the form which the Supreme Court has recently refused to uphold in *Bakke*'s case.[24] But there is no general right to liberty: so the freedom from legal restriction to drive both ways on Lexington Avenue and the freedom, later regretted but upheld in *Lochner*'s case [25] against State legislation, to enter into labour contracts requiring more than ten hours work a day were, as long as they were left unrestricted, legal rights of a sort; but they were not and cannot constitute moral or political rights in Dworkin's strong "anti-Utilitarian" sense, just because restriction or abolition of these liberties might properly be imposed if it advanced general welfare. Finally, notwithstanding the general impression of hostility to utilitarianism suggested by his stress on the "anti-Utilitarian" character of the concept of a right, Dworkin does not reject it wholly as Nozick does, but, as in the Lexington Avenue and labour contract examples, actually endorses a form of utilitarianism. Indeed he says "the vast bulk of the laws which diminish my liberty are justified on Utilitarian grounds." [26] But the utilitarianism which Dworkin endorses is a purified or refined form of it in which a "corrupting" [27] element which he finds in vulgar Benthamite utilitarianism is not allowed to weigh in determining decisions. Where the corrupting element does weigh it destroys, according to Dworkin, the fair egalitarian character, "everybody to count for one, nobody for more than one," which utilitarian arguments otherwise have. This corrupting element causes their use or the use of a majority democratic vote (which he regards as the nearest practical political representation of

---

24. Regents of the Univ. of Cal. v. Bakke, 438 U.S. 265 (1978); and *see* R. DWORKIN, *supra* note 20, at 223-39, and N.Y. Rev. Books, Nov. 10, 1977, at 11-15.
25. *See* Lochner v. New York, 198 U.S. 45 (1905), and R. DWORKIN, *supra* note 20, at 191, 269-278.
26. *Id.* at 269. It is clear that this means "adequately justified," not merely "said to be justified."
27. *Id.* at 235.

utilitarianism) to violate, in the case of certain issues, the fundamental right of all to equal concern and respect.

Before we consider what this "corrupting" element is and how it corrupts I wish to stress the following major point. Dworkin interestingly differs from most philosophers of the liberal tradition. He not merely seeks to draw a vital distinction between mere liberties which may be restricted in the general interest like freedom of contract to work more than ten hours a day, and those preferred liberties which are rights which may not be restricted, but he attempts to do this without entering into some familiar controversial matters. He does not make any appeal to the important role played in the conduct of individual life by such things as freedom of speech or of worship or of personal relations, to show that they are too precious to be allowed to be subordinated to general welfare. So he does not appeal to any theory of human nature designed to show that these liberties are, as John Stuart Mill claimed, among "the essentials of human well-being," [28] "the very ground work of our existence" [29] or to any substantive ideal of the good life or individual welfare. Instead Dworkin temptingly offers something which he believes to be uncontroversial by which to distinguish liberties which are to rank as moral rights like freedom of speech or worship from other freedoms, like freedom of contract or in the use of property, which are not moral rights and may be overridden if they conflict with general welfare. What distinguishes these former liberties is not their greater substantive value but rather a relational or comparative matter, in a sense a procedural matter: the mere consideration that there is an "antecedent likelihood" [30] that if it were left to an unrestricted utilitarian calculation of the general interest or a majority vote to determine whether or not these should be restricted, the balance would be tipped in favour of restriction by that element which, as Dworkin believes, corrupts utilitarian arguments or a majority vote as decision procedures and causes them to fail to treat all as equals with equal concern and respect. So anti-utilitarian rights essentially are a response to a defect—a species of unfairness—likely to corrupt some utilitarian arguments or a majority vote as decision procedures. Hence the preferred liberties are those such as freedom of speech or sexual relations, which are to rank as rights when we know "from our general knowledge of society" [31] that they are in danger of being overridden by the corrupting element in such decision procedures.

What then is this element which may corrupt utilitarian argument or a democratic vote? Dworkin identifies it by a distinction between the personal and external preferences [32] or satisfactions of individuals, both of which vulgar utilitarianism counts in assessments of general welfare and both of

---

28. J.S. MILL, *supra* note 6, at 255.
29. *Id.*
30. R. DWORKIN, *supra* note 20, at 278.
31. *Id.* at 277.
32. *Id.* at 234-38, 275-78.

which may be represented in a majority vote. An individual's personal preferences (or satisfactions) are for (or arise from) the assignment of goods or advantages, including liberties, to himself; his external preferences are for such assignments to others. A utilitarianism refined or purified in the sense that it counted only personal preferences in assessing the balance of social welfare would for Dworkin be "the only defensible form of Utilitarianism" [33] and indeed it is that which justifies the "vast bulk of our laws diminishing liberty." [34] It would, he thinks, genuinely treat persons as equals, even if the upshot was not their equal treatment. So where the balance of personal self-interested preferences supported some restriction on freedom (as it did according to Dworkin in the labour contract cases) or reverse discrimination (as in *Bakke*'s case), the restriction or discrimination may be justified, and the freedom restricted or the claim not to be discriminated against is not a moral or political right. But the vulgar corrupt form of utilitarianism counts both external and personal preferences and is not an acceptable decision procedure since (so Dworkin argues) by counting in external preferences it fails to treat individuals with equal concern and respect or as equals. [85]

Dworkin's ambitious strategy in this argument is to derive rights to specific liberties from nothing more controversial than the duty of governments to treat their subjects with equal concern and respect. His argument here has a certain Byzantine complexity and it is important in assessing it not to be misled by an ambiguity in the way in which a right may be an "anti-Utilitarian right." There is a natural interpretation of this expression which is not Dworkin's sense; it may naturally be taken merely to mean that there are some liberties so precious for individual human life that they must not be overridden even in order to secure an advance in general welfare, because they are of greater value than any such increase of general welfare to be got by their denial, however fair the *procedure* for assessing the general welfare is and however genuinely as a procedure it treats persons as equals. Dworkin's sense is *not* that; his argument is not that these liberties must be safeguarded as rights because their value has been compared with that of the increase in general welfare and found to be greater than it, but because such liberties are likely to be defeated by an unfair form of utilitarian argument which by counting in external preferences fails to treat men as equals. So on this view the very identification of the liberties which are to rank as rights is dependent on the anticipated result of a majority vote or a utilitarian argument; whereas on the natural interpretation of an "anti-Utilitarian right" the liberties which are to rank as rights and prevail over general welfare are quite independently identified.

Dworkin's actual argument is more complicated [36] than this already

---

33. *Id.* at 276.
34. *Id.* at 269.
35. *Id.* at 237, 275.
36. The main complications are: (1) Personal and external preferences may be intertwined in two different ways. A personal preference, *e.g.*, for the segregated company of white men, may be parasitic on an external preference or prejudice against black men, and

complex story, but I do not think what is omitted is needed for its just assessment. I think both the general form of the argument and its detail are vulnerable to many different objections. The most general objection is the following. What moral rights we have will, on this view, depend on what external preferences or prejudices are current and likely at any given time in any given society to dominate in a utilitarian decision procedure or majority vote. So as far as this argument for rights is concerned, with the progressive liberalisation of a society from which prejudices against, say, homosexual behaviour or the expression of heterodox opinions have faded away, rights to these liberties will (like the State in Karl Marx) wither away. So the more tolerant a society is, the fewer rights there will be; there will not merely be fewer occasions for asserting rights. This is surely paradoxical even if we take Dworkin only to be concerned with rights against the State. But this paradox is compounded by another. Since Dworkin's theory is a response specifically to an alleged defect of utilitarian argument it only establishes rights against the outcome of utilitarian arguments concerning general welfare or a majority democratic vote in which external preferences are likely to tip the balance. This theory as it stands cannot provide support for rights against a tyranny or authoritative government which does not base its coercive legislation on considerations of general welfare or a majority vote. So this particular argument for rights helps to establish individual rights at neither extreme: neither in an extremely tolerant democracy nor in an extremely repressive tyranny. This of course narrows the scope of Dworkin's argument in ways which may surprise readers of his essay "What Rights Do We Have?" [37] But of course he is entitled to reply that, narrow though it is, the reach of this particular argument extends to contemporary Western democracies in which the allegedly corrupting "external preferences" hostile to certain liberties are rife as prejudices. He may say that *that* is good enough—for the time being.[38]

---

such "parasitic" preferences are to rank as external preferences not to be counted. (*Id.* at 236). They are however to be distinguished from certain personal preferences when, although they too involve a reference to others, do so only in an instrumental way, regarding others as a means to their personal ends. So a white man's preference that black men be excluded from law school because that will increase his own chances of getting in (*id* at 234-35) or a black man's preference for reverse discrimination against whites because that will increase the number of black lawyers, is to rank as a personal preference and is to be counted. (2) Though personal and external preferences are in principle distinguishable, in practical politics it will often be impossible to discriminate them and to know how many of each lie behind majority votes. Hence whenever external preferences are likely to influence a vote against some specific liberty, the liberty will need to be protected as an "anti-Utilitarian right." So the "anti-Utilitarian" concept of a right is "a response to the philosophical defects of a utilitarianism that counts external preferences and the practical impossibility of a utilitarianism that does not." (*Id.* at 277). Notwithstanding this "practical impossibility," there are cases where according to Dworkin valid arguments may be made to show that external preferences are not likely to have tipped the balance. See his comments on *Lochner*'s case (*id.* at 278) and *Bakke*'s case (*see* note 23 and accompanying text *supra*) and his view that most of the laws limiting liberties are justified on utilitarian grounds (R. DWORKIN, *supra* note 20, at 269).

37. R. DWORKIN, *supra* note 20, at 266-78.

38. This argument from the defect of unreconstructed utilitarianism in counting external preferences is said to be "only one possible ground of rights" (*id.* at 272 and R. DWORKIN, *supra* note 20, at 356 (2d printing 1977)), and is stated to be applicable only in communities

However, even if we accept this reply, a close examination of the detail of the argument shows it to be defective even within its limited scope; and the ways in which it is defective show an important general failing. In constructing his anti-utilitarian right-based theory Dworkin has sought to derive too much from the idea of equal concern and respect for persons, just as Nozick in constructing his theory sought to derive too much from the idea of the separateness of persons. Both of course appear to offer something comfortably firm and uncontroversial as a foundation for a theory of basic rights. But this appearance is deceptive: that it is so becomes clear if we press the question why, as Dworkin argues, does a utilitarian decision procedure or democratic vote which counts both personal and external preferences, *for that reason,* fail to treat persons as equals, so that when as he says it is "antecedently likely" that external preferences may tip the balance against some individual's specific liberty, that liberty becomes clothed with the status of a moral right not to be overridden by such procedures. Dworkin's argument is that counting external preferences corrupts the utilitarian argument or a majority vote as a decision procedure, and this of course must be distinguished from any further independent moral objection there may be to the actual decision resulting from the procedure. An obvious example of such a vice in utilitarian argument or in a majority vote procedure would of course be double counting, *e.g.,* counting one individual's (a Brahmin's or a white man's) vote or preference twice while counting another's (an Untouchable's or a black man's) only once. This is, of course, the very vice excluded by the maxim "everybody [is] to count for one, nobody for more than one" which Mill thought made utilitarianism so splendid. Of course an Untouchable denied some liberty, say liberty to worship, or a black student denied access to higher education as a result of such double counting would not have been treated as an equal, but the right needed to protect him against this is not a right to any specific liberty but simply a right to have his vote or preference count equally with the Brahmin's or the white man's. And of course the decision to deprive him of the liberty in question might also be morally objectionable for reasons quite independent of the unfairness in the procedure by which it was reached: if freedom of religion or access to education is something of which no one should be deprived whatever decision procedure, fair or unfair, is used, then a right to that freedom would be necessary for its protection. But it is vital to distinguish the specific alleged vice of unrefined utilitarianism or a democratic vote in failing, *e.g.,* through double counting, to treat persons as equals, from any independent objection to a particular decision reached through that procedure. It is necesary to bear this in mind in considering Dworkin's argument.

So, finally, why is counting external preferences thought to be, like the

where the general collective justifications of political decisions is the general welfare. Though Dworkin indicates that a different argument would be needed where collective justification is not Utilitarian (R. DWORKIN, *supra* note 20, at 365 (2d printing 1977)), he does not indicate how in such a case the liberties to be preferred as rights are to be identified.

double counting of the Brahmin's or white man's preference, a vice of utilitarian argument or a majority vote? Dworkin actually says that the inclusion of external preference *is* a "form of double counting." [39] To understand this we must distinguish cases where the external preference is *favourable* to, and so supports, some personal preference or want for some good or advantage or liberty from cases where the external preference is hostile. Dworkin's simple example of the former is where one person wants the construction of a swimming-pool [40] for his use and others, non-swimmers, support this. But why is this a "form of double counting"? No one's preference is counted twice as the Brahmin's is; it is only the case that the proposal for the allocation of some good to the swimmers is supported by the preferences both of the swimmer and (say) his disinterested non-swimmer neighbour. Each of the two preferences is counted only as one; and surely *not* to count the neighbour's disinterested preference on this issue would be to fail to treat the two as equals. It would be "undercounting" and presumably as bad as double counting. Suppose—to widen the illustration— the issue is freedom for homosexual relationships, and suppose that (as may well have been the case at least in England when the old law was reformed in 1967 [41]) it was the disinterested external preferences of liberal heterosexuals that homosexuals should have this freedom that tipped the balance against the external preferences of other heterosexuals who would deny this freedom. How in this situation could the defeated opponents of freedom or any one else complain that the procedure, through counting external preferences (both those supporting the freedom for others and those denying it) as well as the personal preferences of homosexuals wanting it for themselves, had failed to treat persons as equals?

It is clear that where the external preferences are hostile to the assignment of some liberty wanted by others, the phenomenon of one person's preferences being supported by those of another, which, as I think, Dworkin misdescribes as a "form of double counting," is altogether absent. Why then, since the charge of double counting is irrelevant, does counting such hostile external preferences mean that the procedure does not treat persons as equals? Dworkin's answer seems to be that if, as a result of such preferences tipping the balance, persons are denied some liberty, say to form certain sexual relations, those so deprived suffer because by this result their concept of a proper or desirable form of life is despised by others, and this is tantamount to treating them as inferior to or of less worth than others, or not deserving equal concern and respect. So every denial of freedom on the basis of external preferences implies that those denied are not entitled to equal concern and respect, are not to be considered as equals. But even if we allow this most questionable interpretation of denials of freedom, still for Dworkin

---

39. R. DWORKIN, *supra* note 20, at 235.
40. *Id.*
41. Sexual Offences Act, 1967, c. 60.

to argue in this way is altogether to change the argument. The objection is no longer that the utilitarian argument or a majority vote is, like double counting, unfair as a procedure because it counts in "external preference," but that a particular *upshot* of the procedure where the balance is tipped by *a particular kind* of external preference, one which denies liberty and is assumed to express contempt, fails to treat persons as equals. But this is a vice not of the mere externality of the preferences that have tipped the balance but of their content: that is, their liberty-denying and respect-denying content. But this is no longer to assign certain liberties the status of ("anti-Utilitarian") rights simply as a response to the specific defects of utilitarianism as Dworkin claims to do. Yet that is not the main weakness in his ingenious argument. What is fundamentally wrong is the suggested interpretation of denials of freedom as denials of equal concern or respect. This surely is mistaken. It is indeed least credible where the denial of a liberty is the upshot of a utilitarian decision procedure or majority vote in which the defeated minority's preferences or votes for the liberty were weighed equally with others and outweighed by numbers. Then the message need not be, as Dworkin interprets it, "You and your views are inferior, not entitled to equal consideration concern or respect," but "You and your supporters are too few. You, like everyone else, are counted as one but no more than one. Increase your numbers and then your views may win out." Where those who are denied by a majority vote the liberty they seek are able, as they are in a fairly working democracy, to continue to press their views in public argument and to attempt to change their opponents' minds, as they in fact with success did after several defeats when the law relating to homosexuality was changed in England, it seems quite impossible to construe every denial of liberty by a majority vote based on external preferences as a judgment that the minority whom it defeats are of inferior worth, not entitled to be treated as equals or with equal concern and respect. What is true is something different and quite familiar but no support for Dworkin's argument: namely that the procedural fairness of a voting system or utilitarian argument which weighs votes and preferences equally is no guarantee that all the requirements of fairness will be met in the actual working of the system in given social conditions. This is so because majority views may be, though they are not always, ill-informed and impervious to argument: a majority of theoretically independent voters may be consolidated by prejudice into a self-deafened or self-perpetuating bloc which affords no fair opportunities to a despised minority to publicise and argue its case. All that is possible and has sometimes been actual. But the moral unacceptability of the results in such cases is not traceable to the inherent vice of the decision procedure in counting external preferences, as if this was analogous to double counting. That, of course, would mean that every denial of liberty secured by the doubly counted votes or preferences would necessarily not only be a denial of liberty but also an instance of failing to treat those denied as equals.

I do not expect, however, that Professor Dworkin would concede the point that the triumph of the external preference of a majority over a minority is not as such a denial of equal concern and respect for the defeated minority, even if in the face of my criticism he were to abandon the analogy which he uses to support the argument between such a triumph and the procedural vice of double counting, which vice in the plainest and most literal sense of these not very clear phrases certainly does fail to treat all "as equals" or with "equal concern and respect." He would, I think, simply fall back on the idea than any imposition of external preferences is tantamount to a judgment that those on whom they are imposed are of inferior worth, not to be treated as equals or with equal concern and respect. But is this true? Of course that governments should as far as possible be neutral between all schemes of values and impose no external preferences may be an admirable ideal, and it may be the true centre of liberalism, as Dworkin argues, but I cannot see that this ideal is explained or justified or strengthened by its description as a form of, or a derivative from, the duty of governments to show equal concern and respect for their citizens. It is not clear why the rejection of his ideal and allowing a majority's external preferences denying a liberty to prevail is tantamount to an affirmation of the inferior worth of the minority. The majority imposing such external preferences may regard the minority's views as mistaken or sinful; but overriding them, for those reasons (however objectionable on other grounds), seems quite compatible with recognising the equal worth of the holders of such views and may even be inspired by concern for them. In any event both the liberal prescription for governments, "impose no scheme of values on any one," and its opposite, "impose this particular conception of the good life on all," though they are universal prescriptions, seem to have nothing specifically to do with equality or the value of equal concern and respect any more than have the prescriptions "kill no one" and "kill everyone," though of course conformity with such universal prescriptions will involve treating all alike in the relevant respect.[42]

---

42. My suspicions that the ideas of "equal concern and respect" and treatment "as equals" are either too indeterminate to play the fundamental role which they do in Dworkin's theory or that a vacuous use is being made of the notion of equality are heightened by his latest observations on this subject. (*See Liberalism*, in PUBLIC AND PRIVATE MORALITY 127-28, 136-40 (Hampshire ed. 1978)). Here he argues that in addition to the liberal conception of equal concern and respect there is another, conservative, conception which, far from requiring governments to be as neutral as possible between values or theories of the good life, requires them to treat all men as a "good man would wish to be treated," according to some particular preferred theory of the good life. On this view, denials of certain forms of sexual liberty as well as the maintenance of social and economic inequalities, if required by the preferred moral theory, would be the conservative form of treating all as equals and with equal concern and respect. But a notion of equal concern and respect, hospitable to such violently opposed interpretations (or "conceptions of the concept") does not seem to me to be a single concept at all, and it is far from clear why either of these two conceptions should be thought of as forms of equal concern and respect to all. Though the claim that liberal rights are derived from the duty of governments to treat all their citizens with equal concern and respect has the comforting appearance of resting them on something uncontroversial ("a postulate of political morality" which all are "presumed to accept," R. DWORKIN, *supra* note 20, at 272), this appearance dissolves when it is revealed that there is an alternative interpretation of this fundamental duty from which most liberal rights could not be derived but negations of many liberal rights could.

Though the points urged in the last paragraphs destroy the argument that denial of liberty on the basis of external preferences is a denial of equal concern and respect and the attempted derivation of rights from equality, this does not mean that such denials of freedom are unobjectionable or that there is no right to it: it means rather that the freedom must be defended on other grounds than equality. Utilitarian arguments, even purified by the exclusion of external preferences, can produce illiberal and grossly inegalitarian results. Some liberties, because of the role they play in human life, are too precious to be put at the mercy of numbers even if in favourable circumstances they may win out. So to protect such precious liberties we need rights which are indeed "anti-Utilitarian rights" and "anti-" much else, but so far as they are "anti-Utilitarian" they are so in the common and not the Dworkinian sense of that expression, and they are needed as a shield not only against a preponderance of external preferences but against personal preferences also. Freedom of speech, for example, may need to be defended against those who would abridge and suppress it as dangerous to their prosperity, security, or other personal interests.[43] We cannot escape, as Dworkin's purported derivation of such rights from equality seeks to do, the assertion of the value of such liberties as compared with advances in general welfare, however fairly assessed.

It is in any case surely fantastic to suppose that what, for example, those denied freedom of worship, or homosexuals denied freedom to form sexual relations, have chiefly to complain about is not the restriction of their liberty with all its grave impact on personal life or development and happiness, but that they are not accorded *equal* concern and respect: that others are accorded a concern and respect denied to them. When it is argued that the denial to some of a certain freedom, say to some form of religious worship or to some form of sexual relations, is essentially a denial of equal concern and respect, the word "equal" is playing an empty but misleading role. The vice of the denial of such freedom is not its inequality or unequal impact: if that *were* the vice the prohibition by a tyrant of all forms of religious worship or sexual activity would not increase the scale of the evil as in fact it surely would, and the evil would vanish if all were converted to the banned faith or to the prohibited form of sexual relationship. The evil is the denial of liberty or respect; not *equal* liberty or *equal* respect: and what is deplorable is the ill-treatment of the victims and not the relational matter of the unfairness of their treatment compared with others. This becomes clear if we

---

43. Dworkin certainly seems to endorse utilitarian arguments purified of external preferences, yet he states that his arguments against an unrestricted utilitarianism are not in favor of a restricted one. (R. Dworkin, *supra* note 20, at 357 (2d printing 1977)). The contrary impression is given by earlier statements such as that the vast bulk of laws which diminish our liberty are justified on utilitarian grounds, R. Dworkin, *supra* note 20, at 269, and the following comment on the right of liberty of contract claimed in *Lochner*'s case: "I cannot think of any argument that a political decision to limit such a right . . . is antecedently likely to give effect to external preferences and *in that way* offend the right of those whose liberty is curtailed to equal concern and respect. If as I think no such argument can be made out then the alleged right does not exist." *Id.* at 278 (emphasis added).

contrast with this spurious invocation of equality a genuine case of a failure to treat men as equals in the literal sense of these words: namely literal double counting, giving the Brahmin or the white man two votes to the Untouchable's or black man's single vote. Here the single vote given to the latter is indeed bad just because the others are given two: it is, unlike the denial of a religious or sexual freedom, a genuine denial of *equality* of concern and respect, and this evil *would* vanish and *not* increase if the restriction to a single vote were made universal.

V.

I conclude that neither Nozick's nor Dworkin's attempt to derive rights from the seemingly uncontroversial ideas of the separateness of persons or from their title to equal concern and respect succeeds. So in the rough seas which the philosophy of political morality is presently crossing between the old faith in utilitarianism and the new faith in rights, perhaps these writers' chief and very considerable service is to have shown, by running up against them, some of the rocks and shoals to be avoided, but not where the safe channels lie for a prosperous voyage. That still awaits discovery. Much valuable work has been done, especially by these and other American philosophers, but there is much still to be done to identify the peculiar features of the dimension of morality constituted by the conception of basic moral rights and the way in which that dimension of morality relates to other values pursued through government; but I do not think a satisfactory foundation for a theory of rights will be found as long as the search is conducted in the shadow of utilitarianism, as both Nozick's and Dworkin's in their different ways are. For it is unlikely that the truth will be in a doctrine mainly defined by its freedom from utilitarianism's chief defect—neglecting the separateness of persons—or in a doctrine resting, like Dworkin's, everything on "equal concern and respect" as a barrier against an allegedly corrupt form of utilitarianism.

[14]

DAVID LYONS

Human Rights
and the General Welfare

Our Constitution tells us that it aims "to form a more perfect union, establish justice, insure domestic tranquility, provide for the common defense, promote the general welfare, and secure the blessings of liberty to ourselves and our posterity." But these grand words must to some extent be discounted. Because of the "three-fifths rule,"[1] which tacitly condoned human slavery, for example, the original Constitution fell short of promising liberty and justice for *all*. At best, the document seems to represent a compromise. But with what? Consider the other aims mentioned: a more perfect union, domestic tranquility, the common defense—these might easily be viewed as either means to, or else included under an enlarged conception of, the general welfare, and it might be thought that this last-mentioned standard is what the Constitution was truly designed to serve—the general welfare, at the expense, if necessary, of those "inalienable rights" and that universal equality which the Declaration of Independence had earlier maintained governments are supposed to serve. At least in that early, critical period of the republic, it might have been argued that the interests of the nation as a whole could be served only through sacrificing the interests of some, even if those interests—in life, liberty, and the pursuit of happiness—amount to basic rights. The Bill of Rights, after all, had to be added to the original document to secure some of

This essay was originally presented as the Special Bicentennial Invited Address to the Pacific Division A.P.A. Meetings in Berkeley, 25 March 1976. I am grateful to Sharon Hill for her comments on that occasion.
1. In Article 1, section 2—just after the Preamble.

the rights of concern to the drafters of the Declaration of Independence. The general idea behind this interpretation cannot lightly be dismissed; at any rate, critics of utilitarianism have often objected that the general welfare standard condones immoral inequalities, injustice, and exploitation, because the interests of a community as a whole might sometimes most efficiently be served by benefiting some individuals at the expense of others. One might be tempted, therefore, to identify the Declaration of Independence with the doctrine of human rights and the Constitution with a commitment to the general welfare, and then conceive of the differences between these documents as transcending their distinct functions and representing a fundamental conflict between commitment to the general welfare and the principles of rights and justice.

These issues need examination now, not just because this nation's Bicentennial obliges us to acknowledge its original ideologies. Thanks to a convergence of political and philosophical developments—including movements to secure equal rights at home and a less barbaric policy abroad, and the somewhat connected resuscitation of political and legal theory—substantive questions of public policy are being discussed more fully today than they have been for many years. Nevertheless, the philosophical attitudes expressed sometimes threaten to become, in their way, just as trite and unreflective as the average politician's Bicentennial claptrap. It is very widely assumed that the general welfare standard, or more specifically utilitarianism, is essentially defective; but the grounds on which this conclusion is reached are often so slender as to make it seem like dogma, not a proper philosophic judgment. Our professional obligations make it incumbent on us, I believe, to challenge such dogmas.

I wish to explore the connections between human rights and the general welfare (where I assume that commitment to the general welfare standard does not entail commitment to full-blown utilitarianism, which regards all other standards as either derivative or else invalid). These matters were not pursued very deeply in the eighteenth century, so my historical references, indeed the basis for my suggestions on behalf of the general welfare, go back only half way, to John Stuart Mill (who was, fittingly, a champion of rights and liberty as well as of the general welfare). Mill's contributions to this area have been neglected and so, I believe, somewhat misunderstood. I hope to throw some light on Mill while seeking a better grasp upon the principles that our republic in its infancy endorsed.

Rights as well as justice have been problems for utilitarians. Aside from Mill, only Bentham gave much thought to rights, and Bentham thought enforcement was essential. He could conceive of rights within an institution but not of rights one might invoke when designing or criticizing institutions. He thus rejected what we call "moral" rights. Recent views of utilitarianism seem to imply that this neglect of rights is theoretically unavoidable. Critics and partisans alike generally suppose that a commitment to the general welfare means that rights are not to count in our deliberations except as conduct affecting them also affects the general welfare, and critics contend that this fails to take rights seriously.[2] Rights are supposed to make a difference to our calculations, which they fail to do if we hold—as utilitarians are supposed to maintain—that rights may be infringed if that is necessary to bring about the smallest increase in the general welfare. Perhaps there are no rights that may absolutely never be overridden; some rights, at least, may be infringed in order to prevent calamities, for example; but infringement of a right should always count against a policy, a law, or a course of action, even when considerations of the general welfare argue for infringement. And it is not necessarily the case that infringement of a right always detracts significantly from the general welfare. For such reasons, commitment to the general welfare standard seems to conflict with genuine acknowledgment of rights; utilitarianism seems positively to abhor them. In this paper I shall sketch how Mill challenges such a conclusion.

One strategy of response could be built upon the idea of "rule-utilitarianism." In this century, utilitarianism was initially understood, by Moore and others, as requiring one always to promote the general welfare in the most efficient and productive manner possible, any failure to do so being judged as wrong, the breach of one's sole "moral obligation." Faced with objections that this "act-utilitarianism" neglects ordinary moral obligations, which do not require one to "maxi-

2. See, for example, Ronald Dworkin, "Taking Rights Seriously," *New York Review of Books*, 18 December 1970; reprinted in A.W.B. Simpson, ed., *Oxford Essays in Jurisprudence, Second Series* (Oxford: Clarendon Press, 1973).

mize utility" but indeed require contrary conduct, revisionists constructed new kinds of "utilitarian" principles. They required adherence to useful rules and excluded case-by-case appeal to the general welfare, hoping that these requirements would match the assumed obligations while still being based upon the general welfare. In the present context, one might extend this rebuttal by supposing that some useful rules would also confer rights, infringement of which would generally be prohibited, and infringement of which would never be warranted by direct appeal to the general welfare. Something like this is in fact suggested by Mill.

Mill's system does, in part, resemble a kind of rule utilitarianism, with the distinct advantage over recent theories that it explicitly acknowledges rights as well as obligations. It has a further, more general advantage. Recent rule-utilitarian theories seem either to have been concocted to avoid objections to act utilitarianism or else to offer an alternative but equally narrow interpretation of the general welfare standard. Both "act" and "rule" versions of utilitarianism seem arbitrarily to restrict the application of the general welfare standard to just one category of things—acts, say, or rules—among the many to which it might reasonably be applied. In contrast, Mill's endorsement of the general welfare standard leaves him free to judge all things by that measure. But he supplements it with analyses of moral judgments which commit him to acknowledging both moral rights and obligations.

For simplicity's sake, let us postpone examination of Mill's theory of rights and consider first his more famous (and initially simpler) principle of personal liberty.[3] Mill says that the only reasons we should entertain in support of coercive social interference is the prevention of harm to people other than the agent whose freedom may be limited. For example, we should not try to force a person to serve his own happiness or prevent a person from harming himself. In effect, Mill

3. Mill's essay *On Liberty* appears consistent with his essay on *Utilitarianism* (written soon after) on all points relevant to the interpretation I am offering here. My interpretation of *On Liberty* does not so much ignore as render it unnecessary to hypothesize nonutilitarian tendencies in Mill's argument; for an alternative account, see Gerald Dworkin, "Paternalism," in Richard A. Wasserstrom, ed., *Morality and the Law* (Belmont, Calif.: Wadsworth, 1971), section V.

says that we should *not* apply the general welfare standard directly
to such intervention. But how could Mill say this—without forsaking
his commitment to the general welfare standard? Mill recognizes that
his principle of liberty is not entailed by his "general happiness principle" taken by itself. The latter commits him in principle to approv-
ing paternalistic intervention that would serve the general welfare.
And so Mill *argues* for his principle of liberty. But wouldn't such a
principle be emptied of all practical significance by the tacit qualifications that are inevitably imposed by Mill's commitment to the general
welfare?

These questions arise when we assume that Mill's commitment to
the general welfare standard amounts to the idea that one is always
morally bound to serve the general welfare in the most efficient and
productive manner possible. His principle of liberty is then conceived
of as a "summary rule," a rough guide to action that is meant to insure
the closest approximation to the requirements laid down by his principle of utility. This is, I think, mistaken on several counts.

Let me suggest, first, that Mill be understood as reasoning along the
following lines. The general welfare will best be served in the long run
if we restrict social interference, by both legal and informal means, to
the prevention of social harm. Experience shows that less limited
intervention is very largely, and unavoidably, counterproductive. Even
when we try our best to prevent people from harming themselves, for
example, we are in all probability bound to fail. Before embarking
on such intervention we are unable to distinguish the productive from
the counterproductive efforts. We are able to do that later; but later
is always too late. Since the stakes are high for those we coerce, and
nonexistent for us, we *ought to make it a matter of principle* never to
entertain reasons for interfering save the prevention of harm to others.
The general welfare would best be served in the long run by our following such an inflexible rule.

Now this seems to me a perfectly intelligible position, and one
even an act-utilitarian might consistently adopt. One need not reject
the general welfare standard—as a basis, or even the sole basis, for
evaluating things—in order to accept such a principle of liberty. Some
possible objections ought however to be noted, though they cannot
adequately be considered here. First, it may be said that this could

not be a complete account of our objections to paternalism and other forms of social interference (so far as we object to them) because our convictions about the sanctity of liberty are much stronger than our warranted confidence in the factual assumptions required by Mill's argument. This seems to me, however, to prove nothing without independent validations of those judgments. Our moral convictions need justification; they are not self-certifying. If we are uncertain about the relevant facts, then we should retain at least an open mind about the relations between liberty and the general welfare.

Second, the argument attributed to Mill suggests that the general welfare will best be served only if we are something other than utilitarians, for it tells us *not* to apply the general welfare standard. The argument thus seems self-defeating for a utilitarian. But, while this problem might arise for utilitarianism in some other contexts, I do not think it need worry Mill right here. I might make it a matter of principle to avoid certain situations that I know will lead to choices that are self-destructive, though they will not seem such to me at the time. This is compatible with my continuing to appreciate my reasons for that policy. Mill's argument is similar. Indeed, one would expect the Mill of *On Liberty* to insist that we remind ourselves of the rationales for our rules and principles if we do not wish them to become ineffective dogmas. This presumably advises us to keep in mind the utilitarian foundation for the principle of liberty.

Third, it may be said that Mill's principle is too rigid and inflexible, that the general welfare would in fact be served better by a more complex principle, which incorporates some exceptions. It may be argued, for example, that paternalistic legislation within certain clearly defined limits should be tolerated.[4] But this is a point that Mill might easily accept—provided that any proposed qualifications on the principle of liberty would not lead to such abuse as to be counterproductive.

It should be clear, now, that the principle of liberty is no "summary rule," of the sort associated with act-utilitarianism; nor is it one of

4. For some suggestions along these lines, see Gerald Dworkin, "Paternalism," section VI; and, on speech, see Joel Feinberg, "Limits to the Free Expression of Opinion," in Joel Feinberg and Hyman Gross, eds., *Philosophy of Law* (Encino, Calif.: Dickenson, 1975).

119　　*Human Rights and the*
　　　　General Welfare

those ideal rules of obligation obtained by applying some modern rule-utilitarian formula. It results from a direct application of the general welfare standard to the question, What sorts of reasons would it serve the general welfare for us to entertain when framing social rules?

Mill is not obliged to be either a rule utilitarian or an act-utilitarian because he does not conceive of the general welfare standard in so limited a way. His principle concerns ends, specifically happiness, and provides the basis for evaluating other things in relation to that end. It does not concern acts or rules as such. It says nothing about right or wrong, duty or obligation. And it does not require one, in moral terms, to maximize the general welfare.

These points are indicated in Mill's "proof" of the principle of utility (where one would expect him to be careful at least in his formulation of his principle, even if his argument fails). In a typical passage Mill says: "The utilitarian doctrine is that happiness is desirable, and the only thing desirable, as an end; all other things being only desirable as means to that end" (chap. IV, par. 2).[5] At the end of the main part of his "proof" Mill says: "If so, happiness is the sole end of human action, and the promotion of it the test by which to judge of all human conduct; from whence it necessarily follows that it must be the criterion of morality, since a part is included in the whole" (chap. IV, par. 8). The relationship between moral judgments and the general welfare standard is then explained more fully by Mill in the next and longest chapter of *Utilitarianism*, which is devoted to the topic of rights and justice.[6]

Mill maintains that judgments about the justice of acts are a specific form of moral appraisal: acts can be wrong without being unjust. To call an act unjust is to imply that it violates another's right, which is not true of all wrong acts. In a perfectly parallel manner, Mill maintains that moral judgments (about right and wrong, duty and obligation) are a proper subclass of act appraisals in general: acts can be negatively appraised—as inexpedient, undesirable, or regrettable, for example—without being regarded as immoral or wrong. To call an

---

5. All references in the text hereafter will cite chapters and paragraphs of *Utilitarianism*.

6. I discuss this matter more fully in, "Mill's Theory of Morality," *Nous* 10 (1976): 101–120.

act wrong is to imply that "punishment" for it (loosely speaking) would be justified (chap. V, paras. 13–15).

Mill's distinction between immorality and mere "inexpediency" indicates that he is no act-utilitarian and also that his general welfare standard does not lay down moral requirements. There must be some basis within Mill's system for appraising acts negatively even when they are not to be counted as wrong. This is either the general welfare standard or some other. But the general welfare standard is quite clearly Mill's basic, most comprehensive criterion. It therefore seems reasonable to infer that Mill would wish to rank acts according to their instrumental value (their promotion of the general welfare), *preferring* those that rank highest in a set of alternatives, without implying that a merely "inexpedient" act is wrong because it falls below the top of such a ranking and thus fails to serve the general welfare in the most productive and efficient manner possible.

According to Mill, to show that an act is wrong, and not merely inexpedient, one must go further and show that sanctions against it would be justified. For Mill says that to judge an act wrong is to judge that "punishment" of it would be fitting or justified.[7] The "punishment" or sanctions Mill has in mind include not just legal penalties but also public condemnation (both can be classified as "external sanctions") as well as guilt feelings or pangs of conscience (the "internal sanction").[8]

Now, Mill presents this as a conceptual point, independent of his commitment to the general welfare; but it has a bearing on our understanding of that standard. Mill distinguishes between general negative appraisals of the "inexpediency" of acts and moral judgments specifically condemning them as wrong. I have suggested that the criterion of "inexpediency" for Mill is an act's failure to promote the general welfare to the maximum degree possible. If so, this cannot be Mill's criterion of wrongness, for from the fact that an act is inexpedient in this sense it does not follow that sanctions against it could be justified. For sanctions have costs of the sort that a utilitarian always counts, and these costs attach to the distinct acts connected with sanctions.

7. For simplicity's sake, I shall understand Mill to mean "justified" or "warranted."

8. Mill uses the terminology of "sanctions" in chapter III of *Utilitarianism*.

121   *Human Rights and the*
                                            General Welfare

The justification of such acts presumably turns somehow upon *their*
relation to the general welfare, not upon (or not alone upon) the
relation of the act that is to be sanctioned to the general welfare. On
Mill's view, therefore, the general welfare standard *can* be applied
directly to acts, but then it simply determines their expediency (and
enables one to rank them accordingly). However, this is not, according
to Mill, a moral judgment, and it has no direct moral implications.[9]

Mill also seems to hold that a wrong act is the breach of a moral
obligation, at least in the absence of some overriding obligation.[10]
But what differentiates morality from mere expediency, as we have
seen, is the justification of sanctions. Mill appears to regard the internal sanction as basic. His formulations imply that public disapproval may be justified even when legal sanctions are not, and that
pangs of conscience may be warranted when no external sanctions
can be justified. Mill suggests that greater costs and risks attach to
social sanctions (which is plausible so long as conscience is not excessively demanding). It may also be observed that the justification
of external sanctions involves an extra step, since they require distinct acts by other persons, while guilt feelings are triggered more or
less automatically. Errors of judgment aside, to justify the operation
of self-reproach in particular cases one must justify no more than the
internalization of certain values. But to justify external sanctions one
must also justify distinct acts by other persons, based on their corresponding values—acts ranging from expressions of disapproval to legal
punishment. In Mill's view, then, to argue that an act is wrong is
basically to argue that guilt feelings for it would be warranted. Other

9. The act-utilitarian reading of Mill is most strongly suggested in *Utilitarianism*, chapter II, paragraph 2. But, as D.G. Brown has noted, the passage
is ambiguous; see his paper, "What is Mill's Principle of Utility?" *Canadian
Journal of Philosophy* 3 (1973): 1–12.

10. This paragraph has been revised in response to a very helpful comment by
a reader for *Philosophy & Public Affairs*, for which I am grateful. Note, now,
that Mill does not differentiate in *Utilitarianism* between duties and obligations.
He may link both too closely with wrong actions, but he does not hold that an
act is wrong if it simply breaches a moral obligation. This is because he recognizes that obligations can conflict. And when they do, rules or obligations are
ranked by reference to the general welfare standard. Mill does not indicate that
acts are so evaluated directly, even when obligations conflict; see the last
paragraph of chapter II, as well as chapter V.

sanctions may be justified as well, depending on the stakes involved
and on the circumstances.

Following Bentham, Mill clearly thinks of sanctions operating not
just after an act, as responses to a wrong already done, but also beforehand, in order to discourage such conduct.[11] This conception presupposes that sanctions are attached to general rules, which serve as
guides to conduct, and has its more natural application to rules of the
social variety, to which external sanctions are also attached. We can
combine this with the previous point as follows. Internal sanctions
require that the corresponding values be "internalized," thoroughly
accepted by the individual. For external sanctions to be justified they
must work efficiently, and this requires that the corresponding values
be shared widely, within, say, a given community; which amounts to
the existence of a common moral code. A reconstruction of Mill's
account of moral judgments, then, would go something like this. To
argue for a moral obligation is to argue for the widespread internalization (within a community) of a value relevant to conduct; to show
that an act is wrong is to show that it breaches such a rule, in the
absence of an overriding obligation.

Mill thus suggests a fairly sophisticated version of what would now
be called "rule-utilitarianism"—except, of course, that he does not limit
the general welfare standard to rules of conduct, any more than he
limits it to acts. Following Bentham's conception of social rules and
his theory of their justification, Mill also takes into account the costs
of sanctions—the social price of regulating conduct—which most recent
rule utilitarians have ignored.[12] Mill departs from Bentham on two
important and related points. First, Mill acknowledges the internal
sanction, conscience and guilt feelings, which Bentham had neglected,
but which Mill thinks is fundamental to the idea of morality. Second,
while Bentham analyzed the idea of obligation in terms of actual
coercion or institutionally authorized coercion—which might not be
justified—Mill analyzes obligation in terms of sanctions that could

11. Since Mill criticized Bentham's views extensively, but had only praise
for Bentham's theory of punishment, I assume that Mill follows Bentham on
all relevant points except where the evidence and the requirements of a coherent
theory indicate the contrary.

12. An exception is Richard Brandt; see especially his "A Utilitarian Theory
of Excuses," *Philosophical Review* 68 (1969): 337–361.

be justified. That is a much more plausible and promising conception than Bentham's.

I do not mean that Mill's account of moral judgments is adequate as it stands. For example, while Mill seems right in emphasizing the connections between judgments of one's own immoral conduct and guilt feelings, he seems to put the cart before the horse. For we usually think of determining whether guilt feelings would be justified by asking, first, whether one has acted immorally, while Mill finds out whether a given act is wrong by first calculating whether internal sanctions for such an act are justified. Perhaps Mill's analysis of moral judgments is misguided. But his general approach to these matters is instructive.

Since Mill's theory of obligation does not seem inconsistent with his general welfare standard, it seems to show that an advocate of the general welfare standard can take moral obligations seriously. For, on Mill's view, obligations alone determine whether an act is wrong; they alone lay down moral requirements. Even if the general welfare would be served by breaching an obligation, it does not follow, on Mill's account, that one would be morally justified in breaching it.

We are now in a position to consider Mill's account of rights. In distinguishing justice from morality in general, Mill says that obligations of justice in particular, but not all moral obligations, correspond with moral rights. An unjust act is the violation of another's right; but an act can be wrong without being unjust—without violating any person's right. Mill believes that we can act wrongly by failing to be generous or charitable or beneficent, and he treats the corresponding "virtues" as imposing "obligations"; but these do not correspond with anyone's rights. "No one has a moral right to our generosity or beneficence because we are not morally bound to practice those virtues towards any given individual" (chap. V, par. 15).

Though not all obligations involve corresponding rights, Mill seems to hold that rights entail corresponding obligations. Consequently, it seems reasonable to interpret his explicit analysis of moral rights in terms of moral obligations. This analysis is presented as follows:

When we call anything a person's right, we mean that he has a valid claim upon society to protect him in the possession of it, either by the force of law or by that of education and opinion. If he has what we consider a sufficient claim, on whatever account, to have something guaranteed him by society, we say he has a right to it [chap. V, par. 24].

After some elaboration Mill restates the point, and then goes one step further:

To have a right, then, is, I conceive, to have something that society ought to defend me in the possession of. If the objector goes on to ask why it ought, I can give him no other reason than general utility [chap. V, par. 25].

Mill first analyzes ascriptions of rights; his analysis refers to arguments with conclusions of a certain type. After completing this account, Mill resumes his advocacy of utilitarianism; he indicates that, on his view, such arguments are sound if, and only if, they turn entirely upon the general welfare.

Mill holds that someone has a right when he ought to be treated in a certain way, which serves (or refrains from undermining) some interest of his. Combining this with Mill's theory of obligation, we get the view that someone has a moral right when another person or persons are under a beneficial moral obligation towards him;[13] or, in other words, when there are sufficient grounds for the widespread internalization of a value that requires corresponding ways of acting towards him.

Mill's approach seems to me significant. Someone who rejected the general welfare standard could consistently accept Mill's analysis of rights (or something like it) and use a different basis for validating the relevant claims. This is because his analysis of rights, like his analysis of moral obligations, is independent of the general welfare standard.

Now, if something like Mill's approach is correct, then we can say the following. If one's principles actually support the relevant sort of claim, then one is committed to the corresponding rights. Mill believes that some such claims are validated by the general welfare standard—

13. For a fuller discussion of this sort of theory, see my "Rights, Claimants, and Beneficiaries," *American Philosophical Quarterly* 6 (1969): 173–185.

Human Rights and the
                                    General Welfare

that is, that it would serve the general welfare to protect individuals in certain ways—so he believes himself committed to moral rights. Mill's principle of liberty can be construed as a defense of some such rights, and its defense as an argument for—among other things—constitutional protections for them. Since Mill's belief is plausible, it is plausible to suppose that a utilitarian such as Mill—indeed, anyone who accepts the general welfare as a standard for evaluation—is committed to certain categories of rights. And it is vital to observe that this conclusion flows, not from a concocted version of "utilitarianism" designed to yield conclusions that external critics demanded, but from a reasonable interpretation of the general welfare standard coupled with a plausible analysis of rights.

Moreover, since Mill is not committed morally to maximizing welfare—to regarding the failure to so act as wrong—he is not committed to infringing rights whenever it would serve the general welfare in the smallest way to do so. Quite the contrary, since such an act would breach a moral obligation that Mill recognizes, and obligations may be breached only when other obligations override them. In this sense, Mill shows that a proponent of the general welfare standard—even a utilitarian—can take rights seriously.

Mill's account of rights is superior to Bentham's in ways that follow from the differences in their conceptions of obligation. Bentham also held that to have a right is to be someone who is supposed to benefit from another's obligation. But, as I have noted, Bentham analyzed obligation in terms of actual or authorized coercion, which might not be justified. This led to his notorious rejection of unenforced rights, including the rights that we invoke to argue for changes in the social order (as was done most famously in our Declaration of Independence and the French Declaration of the Rights of Man, both of which Bentham consequently criticized). Mill, however, is free to recognize such rights, which would be clearly in the spirit of his discussion.

It may also be noted that defects in Mill's account of obligation do not necessarily transfer to his account of rights. It is possible to understand both Bentham and Mill as embracing the idea that rights are to be understood in terms of beneficial obligations, and to interpret this in terms of an *adequate* account of obligation (whatever that may be). One could, of course, go further and say that the implications of the general welfare standard concerning moral rights cannot be fully understood without applying it to an adequate account of rights. Failing that, Mill has at least given us some reason to believe that utilitarians need not ignore or reject rights.

Let us now look at the specific commitments that Mill thinks utilitarians have towards moral rights. He holds that rules conferring rights take precedence over those that merely impose useful obligations, because they "concern the essentials of human well-being more nearly, and are therefore of more absolute obligation, than any other rules for the guidance of life" (chap. V, par. 32). In particular:

> The moral rules which forbid mankind to hurt one another (in which we must never forget to include wrongful interference with each other's freedom) are more vital to human well-being than any maxims, however important, which only point out the best mode of managing some department of human affairs [chap. V, par. 33].

According to Mill, our most important rights are to freedom of action and security of person; these concern our most vital interests, which must be respected or served if a minimally acceptable condition of life, in any setting, is to be possible. That position, I have tried to show, is not inconsistent with utilitarianism, and may in fact be part of a reasonably developed utilitarian theory. (Other rights concern, for example, specific debts or obligations that are due one and matters of desert.)

Mill's underlying reasoning may be understood as follows. An act is not wrong just because it fails to serve the general welfare to the maximum degree possible. This is because an act's being wrong involves the justification of sanctions, and sanctions (including internal sanctions) have unavoidable costs. The stakes must therefore be high enough so that the benefits to be derived from the redirection of behavior resulting from the existence of the sanctions (including the internalization of the corresponding values) exceed the costs entailed. But this applies to all moral obligations, including those "imperfect" obligations of benevolence which merely require generally helpful, charitable, or compassionate patterns of behavior. The obligations of justice are more demanding, and have greater costs attached, because they are "perfect." In the first place this means that they require one to behave towards certain other individuals in more or less determinate ways—that is, to serve or respect certain interests of theirs—on each and every occasion for so acting. In the second place this means that people are entitled to act in ways connected with their having rights: to demand respect for them, to challenge those who threaten to infringe them, to be indignant and perhaps noisy or uncooperative when their rights are violated or threatened, and so on. The obligations of justice are more demanding on the agent, since they do not leave one nearly as much choice as other moral obligations; they also involve greater liability to internal and external sanctions, as well as to demands by other persons upon one's conduct. This means that on a utilitarian reckoning they have special costs, which must be outweighed by the benefits they bring. The stakes must therefore be higher than for other moral obligations. Thus the interests that they are designed to serve must be more important. Rules concerning them will therefore generally take precedence over other moral rules. Such rights are not "inviolable," but their infringement will not easily be justified.

We can now make some further observations about the general nature of the rights that may be endorsed by the general welfare standard. In the first place, they may be characterized as morally fundamental, since they are grounded on a *non*moral standard and are not derived from some more fundamental moral principle.[11] In the second place, if Mill is correct about the importance to anyone of certain interests (such as personal liberty and security), regardless of particular social settings,[15] some of the rights endorsed by the general welfare standard could reasonably be characterized as "universal human" rights. Mill therefore gives us reason to believe, not only that the general welfare standard would not be hostile to such rights, but that it is positively committed to them—that is, to the sorts of rights associated with the Declaration of Independence. If so, the

14. In this respect they are just like the basic rights endorsed by John Rawls in *A Theory of Justice* (Cambridge, Mass.: Harvard University Press, 1971). Rawls' argument invokes self-interest, not the general interest, but on the view we have been considering the latter is no more a "moral" standard than the former.

15. It is interesting to note that Rawls endorses such a notion with his use of "primary goods."

general welfare standard cannot be blamed for any corresponding injustices that are condoned by arguments invoking the general welfare; for such arguments would simply be mistaken.

I do not wish to imply, however, that Mill's suggestions should be accepted without much more severe scrutiny. I merely wish to emphasize that the matter seems far from settled against the general welfare standard.

One final comment in defense of arguments for rights from the general welfare standard. These rights are grounded upon nonmoral values. This will seem unsatisfactory to someone who thinks that some basic rights, or the principles that proclaim them, are "self-evident," as the Declaration of Independence declares. Now, I am not sure what "self-evidence" amounts to, but I know of no account that makes it plausible to suppose that moral principles can somehow stand on their own feet, without any need for, or even possibility of, supporting argument. So I cannot see this as a serious objection to Mill.

A somewhat related and more familiar objection to Mill's manner of defending rights is to note that it relies upon the facts—not just too heavily, but at all. It is sometimes suggested, for example, that the general welfare standard must be rejected or severely limited because it is *logically* compatible with unjust arrangements. From any reasonable definition of human slavery, for example, it would not follow that such an institution could never satisfy the general welfare standard. It is therefore *logically possible* that enslaving some would sometimes serve the general welfare better than would any of the available alternatives. This objection does not rest on factual assumptions, and a utilitarian who tried to answer it by citing the *actual* disutility of human slavery would be accused of missing its point. Facts are simply irrelevant, for "basic" moral principles are involved.

A utilitarian might answer as follows. If moral principles independent of utilitarianism are assumed, the idea that the general welfare standard is valid is tacitly rejected at the outset; but that simply begs the question. At this point, any friend of the general welfare standard (even one who accepts other basic principles as well) might join in the rebuttal: Why should we assume that the principles of rights and justice are independent of the general welfare standard? Let us see the arguments for them, so that we can determine whether they are not actually grounded on and limited by considerations of utility.

Moreover, if facts cannot be called upon to help us interpret the general welfare standard, they must not be assumed by any objections to it. But it is difficult to see how facts can be excluded both from arguments for moral principles and from their applications. If moral principles are not regarded as self-evident, then they must be defended in some manner. The only plausible arguments that I know of in defense of moral principles—such as Rawls'—make extensive use of facts.[16] Moreover, most general principles require considerable information for their application to the varied circumstances of human life.[17] Someone who believes that facts are thus relevant to morality cannot reasonably object to the general welfare standard on the grounds of its unavoidable consideration of the facts. Until we have established principles of rights and justice on nonutilitarian grounds and also have shown that utilitarian arguments for them are ineffective, we must consider what proponents of the general welfare standard might have to say about such matters.

16. A good example is Rawls' argument for his principles, which makes much more extravagant use of facts than Mill's.

17. This is true, not just of Rawls' principles, but, I think, of all principles of similar scope.

[15]

MILL'S LIBERALISM

In his reply to Devlin's *The Enforcement of Morals*[1] H. L. A. Hart explains " the liberal point of view " as follows :—

> " One of the Committee's (the Wolfenden Committee on Homosexual Offences and Prostitution) principal grounds for this recommendation was expressed in its report in this way : ' There must remain a realm of private morality and immorality which in brief and crude terms *is* not the law's business '. I shall call this the liberal point of view : for it is a special application of those wider principles of liberal thought which John Stuart Mill formulated in his essay on *Liberty*. Mill's most famous words, less cautious perhaps than the Wolfenden Committee's, were :
> ' The only purpose for which power can be rightfully exercised over any member of a civilized community against his will is to prevent harm to others '. . . .".[2]

Because he is aware that if this is really the liberal view, it too is exposed to difficulties, Hart qualifies it thus :—

> " Mill's formulation of the liberal point of view may well be too simple. The grounds for interfering with human liberty are more various than the single criterion of ' harm to others ' suggests : cruelty to animals or organized prostitution for gain do not, as Mill himself saw, fall easily under the description of harm to others. Conversely even where there is harm to others in the most literal sense ; there may well be other principles limiting the extent to which harmful activities should be repressed by the law. So there are multiple criteria, not a single criterion, determining when human liberty may be restricted ".

In so alluding to Mill's writings as landmarks in the development of liberalism and even as reasonably adequate expressions of liberal thought, Hart is typical of contemporary British liberal thinkers. It is important, therefore, to examine Mill's writings to determine what precisely is the nature of Mill's liberal political philosophy and, in particular, his answer to the question, What is the function of the state ? I shall argue that even a superficial reading of Mill's writings reveals that it is a myth that Mill has stated a coherent, defensible, liberal view of the state. It is true, as Hart suggests, that Mill stressed the importance of liberty, and that he gave intelligent, thoughtful answers to specific problems such as the rights to freedom from interference of pimps, brothel keepers, gaming-house owners, and those cruel to animals. But we cannot uncritically accept Mill's high praise of liberty without examining its grounds, as they may qualify the praise, both in general and in particular contexts. Again, because Mill made intelligent comments on awkward social issues it cannot be assumed that he has shown that liberalism can deal with such issues—for Mill's thoughtful answers may involve a departure from the liberal view. A consistent co-

---

[1]Maccabaean Lecture in Jurisprudence of the British Academy, 1959, Oxford University Press, London.

[2]*Immorality and Treason : Listener :* Vol. 62, No. 1583, pp. 162-3. See also, R. Wollheim : *Crime, Sin and Mr. Justice Devlin : Encounter :* Vol. XIII, No. 5, pp. 34ff. Also relevant : *Times Literary Supplement* (Feb. 20, 1959), review of Berlin's *Two Concepts of Liberty.*

herent liberal political philosophy must be set out in terms of general principles about liberty and the rôle of the state ; and not simply as a collection
of conclusions of limited generality and scope, accepted on all sorts of grounds
and subject to various conditions and qualifications which spring from an
unclear acceptance of other basic principles which may collide head-on
with the principle they are said to qualify.

Some liberals have suggested that the question, What is the function
of the state ? misses the point of liberalism, liberalism being concerned with
the different problem, of liberty in the state ; i.e., the liberal is one who is
concerned to insist on the maximum liberty possible and who enquires how
it may best and most fully be realized. But unless the demand for liberty is
qualified by reference to the proper function of government, it would imply
anarchism ; or it would become the view that it is the function of government to maximise liberty. Liberals often suggest the latter to be the true
liberal view, but once it is explicitly stated and developed it would be seen
to involve disregard of considerations of justice, happiness, well-being,
except where concern for liberty coincided with them. Further, no notable
liberal has explained liberalism in this way. All have noted the relevance
of demands of justice, even where they conflict with consideration of liberty ;
and they have admitted some coercion to reduce suffering or to promote
happiness even when such interferences are not with harmful, other-regarding
actions. Liberalism, therefore, can be neither a simple view about the place
of liberty in the state, nor the view that the function of the state consists
solely in the promoting of liberty ; instead, it must be a view which explains
the place of liberty in the context of a general view of the proper function
or functions of the state. Mill's writings have the merit those of so many
liberals lack, of showing some awareness of this.

In his most celebrated and most quoted contribution to political philosophy, the essay *Liberty* (1859), Mill is concerned primarily to argue that
liberty is essential if a state composed of civilized people is to be legitimate.
He explains :—

> " The object of this Essay is to assert one very simple principle as entitled
> to govern absolutely the dealings of society with the individual in the way of
> compulsion and control, whether the means used be physical force in the form
> of legal penalties, or the moral coercion of public opinion. That principle is, that
> the sole end for which mankind are warranted, individually or collectively, in
> interfering with the liberty of action of any of their number, is self-protection.
> That the only purpose for which power can be rightfully exercised over any member
> of a civilized community, against his will, is to prevent harm to others. His
> own good, either physical or moral, is not a sufficient warrant. . . . The only
> part of the conduct of any one, for which he is amenable to society, is that which
> concerns others ".[2]

In defending and circumscribing the right to liberty, Mill implicitly
develops a view of the function of the state ; in brief, that the end of the
state is to maximise the goods of true knowledge, rational belief, self-
direction, self-perfection, moral character and responsibility, happiness and
progress. Mill develops this theory further in his discussion of its applica-

[2] *Liberty* (Everyman, J. M. Dent & Sons, London, 1910), pp. 72-73. All subsequent
references to *Liberty* are to this edition.

tions, suggesting that it is part of the function of the well-run state to restrain people from thoughtless errors in the major decisions of their lives, and, more important, to make moral judgments and to aid morality and to impede immorality, indirectly by non-coercive methods such as education, and directly, by using force to ensure the fulfilling of " assignable duties " and to prevent people profiting from the immorality of others, although on this latter point Mill expresses some uncertainty. Thus, whilst the precise view of the function of the state that Mill assumes or develops in *Liberty* is not always clear, it is obvious that he does not regard liberty as the sole or main end of the state, nor even as always a necessary condition of its legitimacy. The same general view is expressed in *Representative Government* (1861) and *Principles of Political Economy* (1848, People's Edition, 1866), it being most clearly, fully and explicitly developed in the latter work.

In *Liberty* Mill claims that he will justify liberty in terms of its utility (74) ; but the term ' utility ' is misleading and obscures from Mill the character of his own arguments. He does try to defend liberty in terms of its utility, but not in the sense suggested by his utilitarianism, for most of his arguments are directed at showing the utility of liberty as a means to knowledge, truth, rationality, rational belief, progress, moral responsibility, and self-perfection. He also notes some considerations which relate to liberty as an aid to happiness, but more usually the arguments linking liberty and happiness relate to happiness expanded to include liberty as part of rather than as a means to the end.

Mill's best known arguments about liberty relate to freedom of speech ; but he nowhere explains exactly what he is defending, as all his definitions relate to freedom of action. He seems to hold that there should be complete freedom of speech provided that its exercise does not incite others to immediate harmful riotous behaviour, this qualification being added almost as an after-thought (114). Mill's four arguments are : (i) The view being suppressed may be true. A claim to infallibility which cannot be sustained is involved in intolerance. (ii) The view being suppressed may be false, but suppressing it will cause the true view to be held in the manner of a prejudice, with little understanding and appreciation of its grounds. (iii) The view being suppressed may be false, but suppressing it will cause the prevailing favoured view to become enfeebled, lost and deprived of its vital effect on character and conduct. (iv) The view being suppressed may be only partly false, and the prevailing view only partly true, hence complete knowledge of the truth will entail tolerance of both. This is a special application of the first argument and need not concern us further.

(i) The first argument supports liberty (and the state's safeguarding it) on the basis of an evaluation of truth and knowledge—an evaluation which, if Mill's argument is sound, rests on an illegitimate claim by the state to infallible knowledge. As Joad observed, this evaluation of true (and of rational) belief of the masses has been disputed, e.g., by Nazis, Marxists, and others.[4] Besides being self-refuting, this argument implies that all

[4] C. E. M. Joad : *Liberty Today* (Watts & Co., London, 1934), ch. 4.

restrictions on freedom of speech, including censorship in war, are illegitimate, as they presuppose indefensible claims to infallible knowledge. But we shall not be concerned here with the soundness or otherwise of Mill's arguments but solely with the view of the state and of liberty that follow from them. This argument suggests the view of the state as a ' good-producer ' which produces the good of true knowledge by promoting liberty of speech as the means to this good ; and it implies that if true knowledge were better promoted by intolerance, intolerance would be as desirable as Mill thought tolerance to be.

(ii) The second argument also defends liberty as a means of promoting some other good, rational, understanding belief ; and it presupposes the view that it is the function of the state so to act as to ensure maximum rational belief ; and it implies that if it were discovered that freedom of speech impedes the realization of this good, the state should then suppress freedom of speech.

(iii) The third argument entails that the state should interfere to ensure that falsehood have a voice if it has no actual exponents. And it, too, is an argument about the value of knowledge and rational belief, with the further good mentioned, the good of moral improvement, liberty of speech being defended as a means of promoting these goods. And it presupposes the view that the state should concern itself not simply with promoting the goods of knowledge and rational belief, but with right behaviour as well. Hence, if intolerance were shown to produce lively, vital beliefs, which effectively influenced our moral conduct, the argument would imply that the state should suppress freedom of speech. Behind these arguments is the suggestion that the enjoyment of these goods is part of happiness and a means to happiness and that the state's business consists in promoting goods.

Slight and inadequate though it is, the qualification that freedom of speech is permissible only if its exercise does not incite others to riotous behaviour, is nonetheless significant. The arguments about freedom of speech justify it as a means to other goods which the state should promote or safeguard. By contrast, this qualification invokes a principle over-riding liberty and involves an admission that the state cannot always treat adult civilized people as responsible, rational beings, as some forms of public speech will cause them to act irrationally, irresponsibly, violently. It is difficult to determine what the additional principle is that this qualification involves. It is not that of limiting liberty for the sake of liberty, as it is directed at protecting the property or person of another ; nor is it that of limiting freedom of speech whenever such freedom results in harm to an-other's person or property ; for Mill wishes to allow freedom of speech which results in harm to people's persons and property, e.g., by a persuasive communist, provided the harm is not due to immediate violence directly consequent on the speaker's oratory. To become a defensible qualification, it must be enlarged and restated in terms of " speech which causes determinate harm " ; and it then becomes a substantial qualification of freedom of speech.

The qualification in terms of harm to others is made explicit in Mill's account of freedom of action as follows :—

> " The only freedom which deserves the name, is that of pursuing our own good in our own way, so long as we do not attempt to deprive others of theirs, or impede their efforts to obtain it " (75).
> " Acts, of whatever kind, which, without justifiable cause, do harm to others, may be, and in the more important cases absolutely require to be, controlled by the unfavourable sentiments, and, when needful, by the active interference of mankind. The liberty of the individual must be thus far limited ; he must not make himself a nuisance to other people " (114).
> " Each will receive its proper share, if each has that which more particularly concerns it. To individuality should belong the part of life in which it is chiefly the individual that is interested ; to society, the part which chiefly interests society " (132).

Mill urges the limiting of liberty of action for the sake of preventing harm or injury, these being construed very narrowly to mean physical harm or harm in respect to one's property or happiness, not harm in respect to knowledge, moral integrity or virtue. Mill thereby implicitly admits that liberty is a lesser good, and a lesser good than a good commonly regarded as itself a lesser good than other goods. Mill sometimes writes as if he is suggesting that the limitations to freedom of action should be confined to actions which interfere with other people's freedom ; but he does not consistently hold such a view as he contends that causing harm constitutes a ground for restricting liberty, even when the harm is not itself a restriction on liberty. (Not all harm is an impediment to another's freedom.) This suggests that the formula ' coercion to prevent coercion ' used by some liberals is distinct from Mill's ' coercion to prevent harm '. And both are distinct from Mill's other formula in terms of self and other-regarding actions. An action may be other-regarding, not productive of harm, and yet be a proper object of state interference, as Mill acknowledges in his discussion of applications of his theory ; and, as Mill also notes, our actions may harm others, but be such that the state should not interfere with them—e.g., in competitive situations (150). Yet Mill's definition of freedom is intended to indicate at least when the state is not entitled to act, i.e., necessary but not sufficient conditions for state interference.

The qualification of freedom of action in terms of harm to others is substantial, for it may exclude many of the more interesting experiments of living, since most of them often involve harm to others—e.g., asceticism, devotion to art, science or learning to the exclusion of other obligations ; life in accord with most moral theories, e.g., Kantianism, pacificism, or even vegetarianism ; social experiments such as prohibition and legalized betting shops ; *laissez-faire* capitalism, socialism, Nazism, etc.

Mill suggests that the arguments for freedom of speech also hold for freedom of action. Thus, here too, he uses arguments which imply that it is the business of the state to promote goods, in particular, the goods of true belief, self-improvement, rationality and rational belief. Mill argues :—

" That mankind are not infallible ; that their truths, for the most part, are only half-truths ; that unity of opinion, unless resulting from the fullest and freest comparison of opposite opinions, is not desirable, and diversity not an evil, but a good, until mankind are much more capable than at present of recognizing all sides of the truth, are principles applicable to men's modes of action, not less than to their opinions. As it is useful that while mankind are imperfect there should be different opinions, so it is that there should be different experiments of living ; that free scope should be given to varieties of character, short of injury to others ; and that the worth of different modes of life should be proved practically, when any one thinks fit to try them " (114-5).

Thus the arguments imply, as when stated for freedom of speech, that if truth, rational belief and self-perfection can be achieved with greater success through intolerance and coercion, then freedom of action will lose its justification. To show further that freedom of action does achieve these goods, in particular the good of self-perfection, Mill invokes other considerations, including the argument " each is the best judge and guardian of his own interests ". But in *Liberty* it is simply one of a number of supporting considerations. Mill argues that our personal peculiarities constitute a ground for freedom of action, in that individual perfection entails the development of these personal traits, and we should have a better knowledge and a keener interest in our self-perfection, and that, in seeking it freely we should develop and improve further our mental and moral powers :

" It is not by wearing down into uniformity all that is individual in themselves, but by cultivating it, and calling it forth, within the limits imposed by the rights and interests of others, that human beings become a noble and beautiful object of contemplation " (120).

" The interference of society to overrule his judgment and purposes in what only regards himself must be grounded on general presumptions ; which may be altogether wrong, and even if right, are as likely as not to be misapplied to individual cases, by persons no better acquainted with the circumstances of such cases than those are who look at them merely from without. In this department, therefore, of human affairs, Individuality has its proper field of action " (133).

Although it is used as a subsidiary argument in *Liberty*, the argument " each is the best judge " is one of which Mill, in company with other liberals, makes extensive use elsewhere. It receives its clearest statement in *Representative Government*.[5] Interpreted literally, it is an argument for anarchism. It implies even a condemnation of legislation preventing " force and fraud " as Mill noted in *Principles of Political Economy*. It must, therefore, as Mill notes in the latter work, be qualified in various ways, e.g. to allow interference to prevent harm, to promote goods. Again, whether interpreted as claiming that we may secure most effectively our happiness, self-perfection, or simply our selfish interests, the argument defends liberty as a means to other goods, and, in some versions of the argument, also as part of the end. Thus if it could be shown that each was not the best judge, or though the best judge each was not the best guardian of his own interests, the principle of the argument would suggest that liberty be restricted and reliance placed on those who were the best judges or guardians of our interests. Mill himself accepts this implication within a limited area in *Principles of Political Economy*. But before these qualifications be considered, I wish to complete our examination of the view of the function of the state suggested or stated in *Liberty*.

[5] *Representative Government* (Everyman), pp. 208-210.

What new principle, if any, is introduced by the qualification that the state may never interfere with self-regarding, and only sometimes with other-regarding actions ? Mill's critics have suggested that this formula virtually destroys his theory, since few if any actions are self-regarding. Mill noted this objection :—

> "The distinction here pointed out between the part of a person's life which concerns only himself, and that which concerns others, many persons will refuse to admit. How (it may be asked) can any part of the conduct of a member of society be a matter of indifference to the other members ? No person is an entirely isolated being ; it is impossible for a person to do anything seriously or permanently hurtful to himself, without mischief reaching at least to his near connections, and often far beyond them " (136).

Every act has social repercussions which may be beneficial or harmful to others. Does Mill's qualification then allow liberty to be restricted *whenever* the general good requires it ? Mill's reply is unconvincing but important :—

> " I fully admit that the mischief which a person does to himself may seriously affect, both through their sympathies and their interests, those nearly connected with him, and in a minor degree, society at large. When, by conduct of this sort, a person is led to violate a distinct and assignable obligation to any other person or persons, the case is taken out of the self-regarding class, and becomes amenable to moral disapprobation in the proper sense of the term. . . . But with regard to the merely contingent, or, as it may be called, constructive injury which a person causes to society, by conduct which neither violates any specific duty to the public nor occasions perceptible hurt to any assignable individual except himself ; the inconvenience is one which society can afford to bear, for the sake of the greater good of human freedom " (137-8).

Mill then suggests that society can help the individual by non-coercive means, e.g., by education, implying thereby the right of the state to promote these goods provided it does not use direct coercion. Thus Mill meets the difficulty that few if any acts are purely self-regarding by conceding the state's right to make moral judgments, and to enforce " assignable duties " (which his discussion there, and of the application of his theory, suggests to be anything the state regards as a fairly determinate inter-personal duty), and to promote self-regarding moral behaviour (presumably also judged to be so by the state) by non-coercive means. And his ground here for limiting coercion in respect of private morality is the one rarely invoked by him, namely that he sees freedom as a distinct good, which outweighs the good of that private morality which is to be achieved only through state coercion.

Mill's discussion of the *applications* of his theory introduces new qualifications and reaffirms those already noted. The discussion of marriage and the family brings out the importance of the qualification that the state may enforce morality where it takes the form of " assignable duties ". Mill argues that the state may properly enforce the duties of parents in respect to their children. Since adultery and neglect of needy, invalid parents or spouses are as much " assignable duties " as those of parents to young children, the state may on Mill's qualified self-regarding, other-regarding principle interfere with a large area of conduct on moral grounds and repress much immorality. After all, are not lies, cheatings, promise-breakings, etc., breaches of assignable duties ? Thus Mill's liberal theory allows the enforcement of a very considerable amount of morality, when it is expedient so to enforce it ; and equally important, his admission of the right of the state to enforce, and hence to judge our assignable duties, involves a very substantial qualification of his infallibility argument.

In his discussion of gambling and prostitution for gain, Mill virtually qualifies his infallibility argument out of existence, for he suggests that it *may* be right to restrict the liberty of those who make a livelihood out of the immorality of others. He observes :—

> " If people must be allowed, in whatever concerns only themselves, to act as seems best to themselves, at their own peril, they must equally be free to consult with one another about what is fit to be so done ; to exchange opinions, and give and receive suggestions. Whatever it is permitted to do, it must be permitted to advise to do. The question is doubtful only when the instigator derives a personal benefit from his advice ; when he makes it his occupation, for subsistence or pecuniary gain, to promote *what society and the State consider to be an evil* " (154 ; my italics).

The fornicator and gambler must be tolerated, but Mill has grave doubts about the pimp, the prostitute and the gaming-house keeper. He notes the arguments for interference, but states :—

> " There is considerable force in these arguments. I will not venture to decide whether they are sufficient to justify the moral anomaly of punishing the accessary, when the principal is (and must be) allowed to go free " (155).

The fact that Mill so sympathetically considers the possibility of such laws suggests that he was vaguely aware that such state interference may be essential in a well-ordered state. If Mill decides in favour of intolerance here, much possibly harmless immorality would be legally banned. Mill suggests that the gambler could still gamble privately, and presumably that the fornicator could fornicate with amateurs. But obviously, such restrictive legislation would make many immoral activities impossible or less accessible. Artificial methods of birth-control were, until this century, almost universally judged to be immoral ; and they are still widely judged to be so. On Mill's principle, the state might be justified in preventing the manufacture and sale of instruments of birth-control ; and this would be to prevent a very important form of private " immorality ". Thus this suggested solution to the problem of prostitution for gain, etc., would drastically qualify Mill's liberal theory. It confers on the state the right to make moral judgments—and to enforce them up to a point—on every important moral issue. Thus if any religious or moral view—atheism, pacifism, euthanasia, family planning, etc., is judged evil, the state can make illegal the having of paid advocates of the view—e.g., clergy ; and it can ban all gainful manufacture upon which the practice of these immoral views is dependent. That this is not a stupid lapse on Mill's part, but a qualification suggested by the needs of his theory is evident from the fact that much the same principle underlies his discussion of the state's right to tax " stimulants " heavily to gain necessary revenue.

Mill's discussion of the state's right to take steps to prevent crimes and accidents—e.g., by insisting on the signing of a poison register and on warning labels on poisons—is significant only as showing an awareness that the individual may not always be the best judge or guardian of his own interests.

The suggested means test for marriage and Mill's discussion of offences against decency throw light on his qualification of liberty in terms of harm to others. The former brings out the extensive restrictions of liberty " harm to others " might justify, whilst the latter extends the concept of harm, from injury to person, happiness or property, to offences against manners. They are included in the class of acts "—which, if done publicly, are a violation of good manners, and coming thus within the category of offences against others, may rightly be prohibited " (153). Such an extension is needed if Mill is to justify restrictive laws about clothing, from " the liberal point of view ".

Even with all these qualifications, explanations and additions, Mill nowhere in *Liberty* indicates the justification of intolerance of those cruel to animals. However, even without any further additional qualifications to explain this very proper restriction on liberty, it is clear that the liberal point of view expressed in *Liberty* is a very complicated one, and one which allows a great deal of activity by the state towards promoting goods, and in restricting and preventing immoralities.

The essay *Representative Government* touches more directly on the problem of the function of the state. Mill rejects the two prevailing views, in terms of Order and Progress, as inadequate, and suggests that the end of the state is the promotion of the well-being of its members :—

> " We have now, therefore, obtained a foundation for a twofold division of the merit which any set of political institutions can possess. It consists partly of the degree in which they promote the general mental advancement of the community, including under that phrase advancement in intellect, in virtue, and in practical activity and efficiency ; and partly of the degree of perfection with which they organise the moral, intellectual, and active worth already existing, so as to operate with the greatest effect on public affairs ".[6]

That Mill regards the state as very properly concerned with the moral and intellectual well-being of its citizens is further apparent from the many references he makes in *Representative Government* to the danger from bad government to these goods, and from the fact that he so often argues that certain kinds of measures are good or bad by reference to well-being so conceived.

In spite of the celebrity of *Liberty* and *Representative Government*, it is *Principles of Political Economy* that contains Mill's most thoughtful treatment of the problem. In Bk. V, ch. 1, Mill explicitly considers the problem of the proper sphere of activity of the state and of state interference, and rejects many formulae relating to it, including various of those used by himself in his later writings. He drastically qualifies the formula ' each is the best judge and guardian of his own interests ', and rejects the " force and fraud " formula popular with earlier liberals, and he seriously qualifies the self-regarding, other-regarding formula he himself so often uses. His discussion of " the province of government " throws light on the movement of his thought, and his lack of clarity and certainty in his other writings. Mill observes :—

[6] *Representative Government*, p. 195.

> " But enough has been said to show that the admitted functions of govern-
> ment embrace a much wider field than can easily be included within the ring-
> fence of any restrictive definition, and that it is hardly possible to find any
> ground of justification common to them all, except the comprehensive one of
> general expediency; nor to limit the interference of government by any universal
> rule, save the simple and vague one that it should never be admitted but when
> the case of expediency is strong ".[7]

Mill states this after noting the following varied, legitimate (necessary
and optional) activities of government, involving as they do authoritative
and non-authoritative interference : preservation of peace and order ;
laying down laws of inheritance ; definitions of property ; laws about contracts—defining them and how to set them out and determining which are
fit to be enforced, and enforcing them ; setting up civil tribunals to settle
disputes, e.g., with laws about wills and forms of wills ; registry of births,
marriages, deaths and general statistical data ; monopoly of money ; pre-
scribing standards of weights and measures ; paving, lighting, and cleaning
streets ; making and improving harbours, lighthouses, surveys, maps, etc. ;
fostering exploration, colonization, culture, research and universities.

Mill later suggests that many of these activities can be explained in
terms of these formulae (" each is best judge ", " force and fraud ", " self-
regarding and other-regarding ", authoritative and non-authoritative interference, necessary and optional state activities) ; but his well-considered
view is that expressed above, that the function of the state consists in the
promotion of happiness and that concern for liberty and non-interference
has its justification as a dictate of expediency (which for Mill is the imposing of a moral point of view). However, he writes :—

> " The supporters of interference have been content with asserting a general
> right and duty on the part of government to intervene, wherever its intervention
> would be useful: and when those who have been called the *laisser-faire* school
> have attempted any definite limitation of the province of government, they
> have usually restricted it to the protection of person and property against force
> and fraud ; a definition to which neither they nor anyone else can deliberately
> adhere, since it excludes, as has been shown in a preceding chapter, some of the
> most indispensable, and unanimously recognized, of the duties of government.
> " Without professing entirely to supply this deficiency of a general theory, on a
> question which does not, as I conceive, admit of any universal solution, I shall
> attempt to afford some little aid towards the resolution of this class of ques-
> tions as they arise, by examining, in the most general point of view in which
> the subject can be considered, what are the advantages, and what the evils or
> inconveniences, of government interference " (Bk. v, ch. 11, sec. 1, p. 568).

This Mill does by reference to particular issues, but his " solutions ",
are often in terms of non-liberal or illiberal principles ; yet such principles
emerge from thoughtful attempts to explain the state's rights and duties.

After discussing the province of government early in the last chapter of
Principles of Political Economy, Mill states :—

> " We have observed that, as a general rule, the business of life is better per-
> formed when those who have an immediate interest in it are left to take their
> own course, uncontrolled either by the mandate of the law or by the meddling of
> any public functionary " (*Ib.*, sec. 7, p. 575).

But he then goes on to qualify this conclusion, stating : " The proposition
that the consumer is a competent judge of the commodity, can be admitted

---

[7] *Principles of Political Economy* (Longmans, Green, London : People's Edition,
1866), Bk. v, ch. 1, sec. 2, p. 482. All subsequent references in my article are to this
work.

only with numerous abatements and exceptions " (*Ib.*, sec. 8, p. 575). Mill intends his qualifications to justify state compulsion in respect of education ; state protection of children, lunatics, and animals ; state interference with joint stock companies ; compulsion in the sphere of labour and industry ; state charity ; state supervision and control of colonization ; state promotion of goods such as culture, science, research, etc. The drastic nature of some of these qualifications reveals that Mill invokes principles of a radically different kind from those usually associated with liberalism.

To look at Mill's discussion of these exceptions. First, he allows that the ordinary citizen may not be a competent judge of his own interest in certain areas, e.g. education. He argues :—

> " The uncultivated cannot be competent judges of cultivation. Those who most need to be made wiser and better, usually desire it least, and if they desired it, would be incapable of finding the way to it by their own lights " (*Ib.*, sec. 8, p. 575).
>
> " In the matter of education, the intervention of government is justifiable, because the case is not one in which the interest and judgment of the consumer are a sufficient security for the goodness of the commodity " (*Ib.*, sec. 9, p. 577).

Since this argument admits of indefinite extension if the empirical facts warrant, it may be significant that Mill uses it rather than that stated elsewhere in terms of the state's right to enforce assignable duties, or that which liberals more generally use, in terms of the rights of the child. That mature adults are not always the best judges of their own interests is also suggested in Mill's discussion of state interference where irrevocable contracts are, or may be, involved :—

> " A second exception . . . is when an individual attempts to decide irrevocably now, what will be best for his interest at some future and distant time. The presumption in favour of individual judgment is only legitimate, where the judgment is grounded on actual, and especially on present, personal experience ; not where it is formed antecedently to experience, and not suffered to be reversed even after experience has condemned it " (*Ib.*, sec. 10, p. 579).

Mill here has in mind slave and marriage contracts, but his comment suggests that the individual is the best judge of his own interest only when his judgment is grounded on personal experience. If taken seriously, this entails the illiberal conclusions that the state must insist on trial marriages, even where the parties are opposed, or alternatively, forbid the legal enactment of life-long marriage contracts, even where the parties wish to enter into unbreakable contracts. In either event, the thought behind his position represents a considerable qualification which admits of wide application.

Some of Mill's comments suggest that he invokes the same argument to justify state interference to protect children, lunatics, and animals ; but Mill also suggests the alternative account that children, lunatics, and animals are weaker parties in a " contractual " situation, in need of state protection. In either case, the argument involves the remarkable suggestion that animals have a status comparable with that of lunatics. Possibly because he is uneasy about this suggestion, Mill offers the third account :—

> " It is by the grossest misunderstanding of the principles of liberty, that the infliction of exemplary punishment on ruffianism practised towards these defenceless creatures, has been treated as a meddling by government with things beyond its province ; an interference with domestic life. . . . What it would be the

> duty of a human being, possessed of the requisite physical strength, to prevent
> by force if attempted in his presence, it cannot be less incumbent on society
> generally to repress " (*Ib.*, sec. 9. p. 578).

This illiberal suggestion is Mill's most convincing account of the state's right to punish cruelty to animals.

A further qualification condones state compulsion to ensure uniformity of action where the individual on his own cannot achieve what he judges to be his own interest. Mill sees in this a justification of labour and factory legislation—workers see their interest to lie in shorter hours under better conditions for higher wages, but only compulsory uniformity will allow them to realize their good. The argument assumes that the state has the right and competence to make this value judgment ; and in effect it is claimed to justify coercion of others against what they judge to be their own interests. Again, the judgment may apparently involve uniformity to achieve moral ends that can be achieved only by compulsory uniformity of action. Hobhouse saw in this argument a justification for restraining individuals so as to permit unpopular religious processions, whilst Joad saw it as justifying the compulsory wearing of clothing in our society, and compulsory nudism among primitives.

Mill concedes the right of the state to provide help for the needy, provided various conditions, which amount to such aid being beneficial in its total effects, are fulfilled. He argues :—

> " The argument against government interference grounded on the maxim
> that individuals are the best judges of their own interest, cannot apply to the very
> large class of cases, in which those acts of individuals with which the government
> claims to interfere, are not done by those individuals for their own interest,
> but for the interest of other people. This includes, among other things, the
> important and much agitated subject of public charity " (*Ib.*, sec. 13, p. 583).

Mill argues that the state is entitled to interfere with colonization engaged in by individuals judging rightly concerning their own interest, for the good of later generations, and that the same principle holds here as with state charity. He observes :—

> "If it is desirable, as no one will deny it to be, that the planting of colonies
> should be conducted, not with an exclusive view to the private interests of the
> first founders, but with a deliberate regard to the permanent welfare of the
> nations afterwards to arise from these small beginnings ; such regard can only
> be secured by placing the enterprise, from its commencement, under regulations
> constructed with the foresight and enlarged views of philosophical legislators ;
> and the government alone has power either to frame such regulations, or to enforce
> their observance " (*Ib.*, sec. 14, p. 585).

The principle involved here is the fundamentally distinct one of interference for the good of future generations ; and it is really an extension of the qualification about harming others, but one which amounts to a new principle, involving as it does, reference to the well-being of unborn generations. Such an extension of the principle would qualify liberty in all its contexts, and opens the way for wholesale intervention of the Russian and Chinese kinds ; yet Mill is forced to admit this principle to explain and justify what is undoubtedly a necessary and proper activity of government.

Mill further noted that there are goods which are not any one person's goods, which ought to be promoted by the state ; and he accordingly notes the desirability of state interference in the form of taxation and state subsidy to promote goods such as science, culture, research and exploration.

In brief, then, the argument "each is the best judge" holds only for rational beings ; and then only where it holds, i.e., where the goods are goods of particular individuals, and where the individual is in fact the best judge or guardian of his own interest. He is not the best *judge* of certain commodities, and where irrevocable decisions are involved, his judgment is suspect. Hence the state may properly interfere in such matters. Mill gives no clear generally applicable principle by which to judge when the individual is the best judge of his own interest, and neglects to consider here the very relevant, important areas of morality and religion. The " individual " may also not be the best *guardian* of his own interest, e.g., if he is a child, a lunatic, or an animal, or if compulsory joint action is essential for him and others to realize their interests ; and here, too, state interference is allowed. This means that much moral behaviour may properly be enforced, if it is expedient to enforce it, for compulsory observance of duties such as truth-telling, promise-keeping, marital fidelity, etc., is essential if most are to realize effectively their individual interests. Further, even where the individual is the best judge and guardian of his own interest, the state may interfere for the good of future generations, or to promote those goods which are not any one individual's goods. These essential qualifications represent a very substantial modification of the non-interference thesis. In the light of Mill's discussions here and elsewhere in *Principles of Political Economy, Liberty,* and *Representative Government,* the view of the function and proper activities of the state which results from Mill facing the concrete problems of political life is seen to be a very different theory to the non-interference theory commonly ascribed to him and which, no doubt, he sometimes believed himself to be advancing.

Mill's view is that it is the business of the state to secure and promote goods such as happiness, truth, rational belief, self-perfection, self-direction, moral character, and culture ; and that it may interfere with liberty in special cases to promote these goods, even when the behaviour of those interfered with is not harmful to others. Mill does not regard it as part of the function of the state to promote moral conduct for its own sake ; but he does argue that the state may legitimately take steps which in effect make much private immorality impossible. He suggests that it may possibly be legitimate to suppress, indirectly, those private immoralities which can usually or only be practised if organized in some way by others for their own gain. And this would make impossible or less easy to engage in, such immoralities as gambling, the private enjoyment of pornography, the practice of birth-control, and fornication. Again, all immorality which results in harm to others (where harm is construed in a very elastic way, sometimes narrowly, sometimes widely to cover offences against good manners, and harm to unborn generations) may be punished—if this results in less harm occurring. Again, any immoralities which involve failure to fulfil "assign-

H. J. McCloskey

able duties" may be suppressed ; and the state (or society) is to be judge both of what is an assignable duty, and of what is an evil practice from which gainful employment may not lawfully be made.

There are still very significant differences between Mill's view and those of the Thomists and of Devlin ; but Mill's liberal theory is not the simple theory Hart suggests that it is, nor is it the simple multiple criteria theory he suggests that it could readily be modified into becoming. It is a very complex theory and such that if it were consulted today, it would probably result in substantially more moral legislation than prevails in Great Britain and vastly more than most liberals would regard as permissible or desirable.

H. J. McCloskey

University of Melbourne.

[16]

Mill's Moral Theory and the Problem of Preference Change*

Michael S. McPherson

Like many figures of his age, John Stuart Mill placed the prospect of progressive changes in human character and motivation near the center of his thought. Mill's stress on the malleability of character under the influence of education and social institutions had a profound effect on his approach to moral, political, and economic problems. It led him away from the classical utilitarian practice of evaluating social policies and institutions solely from the standpoint of their effectiveness in satisfying existing wants, and brought him to think about them also from the standpoint of their tendency to generate improved wants and forms of character. Mill described the change in perspective this way:

> I now looked upon the choice of political institutions as a moral and educational question more than one of material interests, thinking that it ought to be decided mainly by the consideration, what great improvement in life and culture stands next in order for the people concerned, as the condition of their further progress, and what institutions are most likely to promote that.[1]

My purpose in this essay is to examine Mill's attempt to modify classical utilitarianism in order to accommodate this concern for human improvement. The problem Mill was attempting to solve, that of describing and defending an ideal of human character against which existing types of character and the institutions that sustain them could be judged, is both an ancient one, with roots going back at least to Plato, and a terribly modern one. Neoclassical welfare economics is a direct descendant of Benthamite utilitarianism and it has been roundly and perennially criticized for failing to take into account the process of preference formation and the endogeneity of preferences to the economic system.[2] But

*This paper was prepared while I was a fellow of the American Council of Learned Societies. I owe thanks to a number of people for helpful comments; especially useful were those by Albert Hirschman, Richard Krouse, Thomas Scanlon, Dennis Thompson, and Gordon Winston.

1. J. S. Mill, *Autobiography* (New York: New American Library, 1964), p. 129.

2. See, for example, John K. Galbraith, *The Affluent Society*, 2nd ed., rev. (New York: New American Library, 1969); Brian Barry, *Political Argument* (London: Routledge & Kegan Paul, 1965), pp. 75-79; and Herbert Gintis, "A Radical Analysis of Welfare Economics and Individual Development," *Quarterly Journal of Economics* 86 (November, 1972): 572-99.

Ethics 92 (January 1982): 252-273

criticism of the assumption of "given wants" has, understandably, been easier to come by than the construction of coherent and appealing alternative schemes of social evaluation.[3] Although Mill spoke of "character" where contemporary economists speak of "preferences," I believe that many of Mill's formulations remain directly relevant to contemporary concerns.[4] This provides an important motive for reexamining the logic of Mill's analysis in addition to the obvious historical interest in clarifying an aspect of Mill's thought that has sometimes been neglected or misunderstood.[5]

I by no means intend to suggest that Mill's modified utilitarianism is a completely adequate response to the moral and political problems raised by endogenous preferences. I do want to suggest that Mill's theory deserves a better hearing than it has sometimes received at the hands of critics. I also think that even in areas where Mill's own formulations are plainly inadequate, his constructions remain interesting and suggestive. By exploring both the strengths and weaknesses of Mill's analysis, I hope (1) to bring out the continuing importance of grappling with the range of issues his theory raises; (2) to show the considerable merit of the general framework within which Mill tried to address those issues; and (3) to identify some of the major areas where Mill's development of that framework is flawed or incomplete and which require further thought and research.

The structure of the paper is as follows. I begin in section 1 with a description of the central concept in Mill's ideal of human character, namely the idea of individuality, and a brief sketch of Mill's views about how social institutions could be refashioned to foster individuality. Basic to Mill's defense of individuality as a worthwhile ideal was his argument

3. For recent attempts at constructive normative analyses of the problem of endogenous preferences, see Carl C. von Weizsacker, "Notes on Endogenous Change of Tastes," *Journal of Economic Theory* 3 (December 1971), 345–72; Burton A. Weisbrod, "Comparing Utility Functions in Efficiency Terms or, What Kind of Utility Functions Do We Want?," *American Economic Review* 67 (December, 1977): 991–95; Thomas M. Scanlon, "Equality: Preference and Urgency," *Journal of Philosophy* 72 (November 7, 1975): 655–70; Menachem Yaari, "Endogenous Changes in Tastes: A Philosophical Discusssion" (unpublished, 1976); M. McManus, "Social Welfare Optimization with Tastes as Variables," *Weltwirtschaftliches Archive* 114 (1978): 101–23; and Thomas Marschak, "On the Study of Taste Changing Policies," *American Economic Review* 68 (May 1978): 386–91.

4. "Preferences" in modern economics characterize not just tastes for consumer goods, but also tastes for work vs. leisure, for alternative occupations, for one's own consumption vs. that of others, and so on. To the modern economist, a complete picture of a person's preferences is a complete picture of the person, and "character" and "preference structure" become largely synonymous.

5. For an interesting paper with related aims, see J. K. Whitaker, "Some Neglected Aspects of Alfred Marshall's Economic and Social Thought," *History of Political Economy* 9 (Summer 1977): 161–97. Herbert Gintis has preceded me in identifying Mill's theory as being importantly relevant to problems in modern welfare economics. His analysis of Mill, which in some ways parallels my own, although with some important differences in perspective and conclusions as well, appears in ch. 3 of *Alienation and Power: Toward a Radical Welfare Economics* (Ph.D. dissertation, Harvard, 1969).

that an individualized character was desirable as part of a happy life. This is a particular case of Mill's general view that some kinds of experience or ways of living could be judged objectively better or more valuable for people than others. Mill's defense of this claim—his doctrine of "higher pleasures"—is described in section 2 and criticized and in part reformulated in section 3. Section 4 takes up an important objection to Mill's theory, and to any theory which points to the implication that some wants, characters, or ways of living are better than others. The objection is that any such theory must be unacceptably paternalistic if not totalitarian, and hence cannot provide an adequate defense of individual liberty.[6] My position is that Mill's argument for the objective value of individuality actually served to strengthen and enrich his defense of liberty within a broadly utilitarian framework of social evaluation. The paper concludes by identifying two important issues raised in Mill's theory which deserve more systematic attention from economists and other social theorists. These issues are, first, exploration of the empirical links between social institutions and preference patterns and, second, analysis of the social preconditions for autonomous choice.

1. INDIVIDUALITY

One key element in Mill's departure from Bentham's utilitarianism was his attempt to make room for a conception of individual self-development or self-realization. For a Benthamite, accepting the doctrine that "push-pin is as good as poetry, quantity of pleasure being the same," the notion of self-realization is egregious nonsense. Room might easily enough be made within the basically want-regarding scheme of utilitarianism to justify modifying character on the ground that some sets of wants are more easily satisfied than others, or more productive of pleasure for other people, or the like. But the notion that a particular form of character might be regarded as more desirable or valuable intrinsically, and not just because it produces a greater quantity of pleasure, is simply meaningless for a Benthamite.

Mill early recognized this gap in Bentham's conception of human need and desire: "Man is never recognized by him as a being capable of pursuing spiritual perfection as an end, of desiring, for its own sake, the conformity of his own character to his standard of excellence, without hope of good or fear of evil from other source than his own inward consciousness."[7] The need for society to provide the basic preconditions for such self-realization is a central theme of Mill's famous essay *On Liberty*.

---

6. For such a criticism of Mill, see Maurice Cowling, *Mill and Liberalism* (Cambridge: Cambridge University Press, 1963). A convincing rebuttal is in Graeme Duncan, *Marx and Mill: Two Views of Social Conflict and Social Harmony* (Cambridge: Cambridge University Press, 1973), pp. 276–80.

7. "Bentham," in M. Cowling (ed.), *Selected Writings of John Stuart Mill* (New York: New American Library, 1968), p. 34.

On Liberty is often misread as simply a tract opposing state intervention in the private affairs of individuals. It is that in some measure, but
On Liberty is at least as much concerned with the threat of society tyran-
nizing over the individual through the enormous power of public opinion as it is with the prospect of state tyranny. In trying to articulate the
proper limits of social intervention into individual affairs, Mill is brought
to provide an account of what self-realization and individual autonomy
amount to, and to provide at least a sketch of the social prerequisites for
their achievement.

Mill's description of the man who possesses "individuality" turns on
an interpretation of what it means to choose one's way of life. The contrast with individuality is conformity to custom:

> [T]o conform to custom, merely as custom, does not educate or
> develop in a man any of the qualities which are the distinctive
> endowment of a human being. The human faculties of perception,
> judgment, discriminative feeling, mental activity, and even moral
> preference are exercised only in making a choice. He who does any-
> thing because it is the custom makes no choice.[8]

Mill's account of the meaning of "free choice" in this context is
closely bound up with the description of a form of character which is both
required for and fostered by autonomous action:

> [E]ven in what people do for pleasure, conformity is the first thing
> thought of; . . . peculiarity of taste, eccentricity of conduct, are
> shunned equally with crimes, until by dint of not following their
> own nature, they have no nature to follow; their human capacities
> are withered and starved; they become incapable of any strong
> wishes or native pleasures and are generally without either opinions
> or feelings of home growth or properly their own.[11]

In fact, as Anschutz has observed, Mill's diatribe against conformity
at times becomes so strong that he seems to be celebrating mere eccentricity for its own sake.[12]

But it is clear enough, even in *On Liberty* and especially in some of
Mill's other writings, that Mill's central concern was with cultivating
human beings who could be active and responsible, and not merely eccentric. It is also clear that Mill believed the social conditions for developing such a character went beyond the prevention of the tyranny of public
opinion. Thus, in his *Principles of Political Economy*, Mill attended
closely to the impact of economic institutions on the development of an
individualized character. Mill's preference for peasant proprietorships

8. "On Liberty," ibid., p. 174.
9. Idem.
10. Ibid., p. 176.
11. Ibid., p. 177.
12. Ralph P. Anschutz, *The Philosophy of John Stuart Mill* (Oxford: Oxford University Press, 1953), ch. 2.

over the employment of hired labor on large farms, for example, rested principally on the effects of land ownership on the peasants' industry, intelligence, and self-reliance, effects Mill valued even more for their moral than for their economic appeal.[13]

Similar but even more striking is the "moral revolution" Mill expected the cooperative movement to bring about through "the conversion of each human being's daily occupation into a school of the social sympathies and the practical intelligence."[14] In comparing peasant proprietorships with cooperative associations, Mill praised the former "as a step out of the merely animal state into the human, out of reckless abandonment to brute instinct into prudential foresight and self-government." But the latter were far superior: "if public spirit, generous sentiment, or true justice and equality are desired, association, not isolation of interests, is the school in which these excellences are nurtured."[15] Likewise, in Mill's discussions of representative government, his support for institutions that will foster citizen participation rested importantly on the tendency of participation to encourage the kind of active, intelligent, and public spirited character that Mill praised in *On Liberty*.[16]

Indeed, Mill's concern to foster human individuality was a major theme in all his mature work. But Mill always remained too much of a utilitarian simply to take the expression of individuality as itself an ultimate end, irrespective of individual desire and need for it. Mill put it this way in a letter to Carlyle in 1834: "Though I hold the good of the species (or rather of its several units) to be the *ultimate* end (which is the alpha and omega of my utilitarianism), I believe with the fullest belief that this end can in no other way be forwarded but by the means you speak of, namely by each taking for his exclusive aim the development of what is best in himself."[17] The exclusiveness of Mill's concern for individuality is undoubtedly overstated here, in deference to Carlyle's views. But the problem of how Mill brought his concern for autonomy in line with his continual allegiance to the principle of utility as the ultimate standard is one we must explore.

Mill certainly did not disdain arguments defending individuality because it tended to promote the material interests of society. There are various arguments in *On Liberty* that defend non-interference with the individual on such pragmatic grounds: the likelihood that a person

13. Mill, *Principles of Political Economy with Some of Their Applications to Social Philosophy*, 2 vols. (Toronto: University of Toronto Press, 1965), Book II, ch. 7, sec. 1–3, pp. 278–83.

14. Ibid., Book IV, ch. 7, sec. 6, p. 792.

15. Ibid., Book IV, ch. 7, sec. 4, p. 768.

16. Mill, *Considerations on Representative Government* (ed. Currin V. Shields), (Indianapolis: Bobbs–Merrill Press, 1958), ch. iii; and Dennis F. Thompson, *John Stuart Mill and Representative Government* (Princeton, N.J.: Princeton University Press, 1976), pp. 28–36.

17. Mill, *Earlier Letters, The Collected Works of John Stuart Mill*, vol. 12 (Toronto: University of Toronto Press, 1963), pp. 207–08. Quoted in John M. Robson, *The Improvement of Mankind: The Social and Political Thought of John Stuart Mill* (Toronto: University of Toronto Press, 1968), p. 128.

knows his own wants better than others do, the case for free trade on
efficiency grounds, and so on. Specifically in regard to fostering individuality of character, Mill argued the importance of allowing room for the
development of geniuses on the ground of the utilitarian benefits they
yield to society.[18] But the argument is offered grudgingly by Mill:

> Having said that Individuality is the same thing with development,
> and that it is only the cultivation of individuality which produces,
> or can produce, well-developed human beings, I might here close
> the argument. . . . Doubtless, however, these considerations will not
> suffice to convince those who most need convincing; and it is neces-
> sary further to show that these developed human beings are of some
> use to the undeveloped—to point out to those who do not desire
> liberty, and would not avail themselves of it, that they may be in
> some intelligible manner rewarded for allowing other people to
> make use of it without hindrance.[19]

Mill argues on this level because he thinks he must, but his major
thesis is not that the well-developed individual is of value to others, but
rather that autonomy is intrinsically of value for the individual himself.
This value has two sources. First, free choice is needed to permit each
person to discover for himself what best suits him. Society does not now,
and will not in the foreseeable future, know enough to be able to prescribe
for individuals those paths of development which best realize their capacities, except perhaps in very general terms.

But second, and more fundamentally, even if society could somehow
discern the good for an individual, it remains true that the cultivation and
exercise of one's own capacity for autonomous choice is in itself "one of
the principal ingredients of human happiness."[20] Conceivably, Mill allows, a person "might be guided in some good path and kept out of
harm's way" without exercising much power of choice. "But what will be
his comparative worth as a human being? It really is of importance not
only what men do, but also what manner of men they are that do it."[21]

The keystone of Mill's modified-utilitarian defense of individuality is
thus that the exercise of individuality is itself one of life's highest pleasures. Mill in fact went further than simply trying to show that the interest in self-development is one interest among others, whose importance is
to be weighed by the subjective value people place on it. Had he been
satisfied with that, his modification of Bentham's theory would have been
more limited than it really was. For the cutting edge of Mill's position was
that self-development was quite important despite the fact that most people in Mill's own time and place subjectively cared little for it:

18. *On Liberty*, pp. 179–82. See also *Considerations on Representative Government*,
pp. 48 and 51.
19. *On Liberty*, p. 179.
20. Ibid., p. 172.
21. Ibid., p. 173.

258   *Ethics   January 1982*

> If it were felt that the free development of individuality is one of the leading essentials of well being—that it is not only a coordinate element with all that is designated by the terms civilization, instruction, education, culture, but is itself a necessary part and condition of all those things—there would be no danger that liberty should be undervalued . . . but the evil is that individual spontaneity is hardly recognized by the common mode of thinking as having any intrinsic worth or deserving any regard on its own account.[22]

The doctrine of the higher pleasures in Mill's *Utilitarianism* was aimed at supporting claims of this kind that some ways of living are intrinsically more valuable than others, independently of what some (or even most) people might think. Mill was attempting with that doctrine to carve out a standard for criticizing existing preferences in terms of an ideal of human character, but without abandoning the aim of making that ideal itself rest ultimately on people's preferences. Plainly, that is not easy. How he did it, and how successfully, are our next concerns.

2. THE HIGHER PLEASURES[23]

Mill understood the "higher pleasures" to be those resulting from the exercise of what he described as man's characteristically human faculties— "the pleasures of the intellect, of the feelings and imagination, and of the moral sentiments," in contrast to the pleasures of "mere sensation."[24] Mill's theory of the higher pleasures, presented in Chapter II of *Utilitarianism*, was an attempt to establish a firmer case for the desirability of the pursuit of such elevated pleasures than his utilitarian predecessors had been able to do.

Mill observed that the earlier utilitarians had "placed the superiority of mental over bodily pleasures chiefly in the greater permanency, safety, uncostliness, etc. of the former—that is in their circumstantial advantages rather than in their intrinsic nature."[25] Although Mill paid lip service to this argument, and claimed that his own analysis was merely an attempt to move the discussion to "higher ground," it seems clear that Mill entertained grave doubts about its validity. "A being of higher pleasure," Mill observed at one point, "requires more to make him happy, is capable probably of more acute suffering, and certainly accessible to it at more points, than one of an inferior type . . . it is indisputable that the being whose capacities of enjoyment are low has the greater chance of having them fully satisfied and a highly endowed being will always feel that any happiness he can look for, as the world is constituted, is imperfect."[26] Thus, a secure defense of the higher pleasures required Mill to show that a

22. Ibid., pp. 172–73.
23. My exposition of Mill's doctrine of the higher pleasures draws heavily on Thompson, pp. 55–63.
24. *Utilitarianism*, in Cowling (ed.), *Selected Writings*, p. 250.
25. Ibid.
26. Ibid., p. 253.

life devoted to them was to be preferred even if it should in fact yield a smaller quantity of pleasure than a more swinish existence.[27] Mill was not trying to argue that the higher pleasures are morally better or more beneficial to society as a whole—he thought that was obvious—but that they are in fact more desirable for the actor—"irrespective of any feeling of moral obligation to prefer [them]"[28]—even if they provide less pleasure.

The argument Mill put forward is essentially empirical. The proof that the higher pleasures are the more desirable ones is that they are in fact preferred by those in a position to judge. There is no appeal from the verdict of these "competent judges": "On a question which is the best worth having of two pleasures, or which of two modes of existence is the most grateful to the feelings, apart from its moral attributes and from its consequences, the judgment of those who are qualified by knowledge of both . . . is final."[29] And the verdict of such judges, Mill thought, was clear: "no intelligent human being would consent to be a fool, no instructed person would be an ignoramus, no person of feeling and conscience would be selfish and base, even though they should be persuaded that the fool, the dunce, or the rascal is better satisfied with his lot than they are with theirs."[30]

Mill, of course, had to deal with the obvious counterexamples to his empirical claim—namely, all those persons who had been reasonably well-exposed to the higher pleasures in their youth, but who had turned away.[31] His answer was that they had not voluntarily chosen the lower pleasures. "Capacity for the nobler feelings is in most natures a very tender plant, easily killed not only by hostile influences, but by mere want of sustenance; and in the majority of young persons, it speedily dies away if the occupations to which their position in life has devoted them, and the society into which it has thrown them, are not favorable to keeping that higher capacity in exercise."[32]

Mill thus hoped to show that the higher pleasures were objectively more desirable—objectively, that is, not in the sense that they corresponded to some ultimate metaphysical truth about the Good (as in Plato) but only in the sense that a desire for the higher pleasures is an empirical

27. Mill cast his argument in terms of some pleasures being qualitatively better than others *as pleasures* even when equal in the quality of pleasure they produce. This is obviously confused. What Mill needs to argue is that if one experience or way of living is preferred to another which yields equal pleasure (assuming that can be measured), the preferred experience is qualitatively better (in the eyes of the chooser) on some dimension other than pleasure. See Henry J. McCloskey, *John Stuart Mill: A Critical Study* (New York: St. Martin's Press, 1971), ch. 3. This confusion does not seem to be of any substantive importance for Mill's analysis.

28. *Utilitarianism*, p. 250.

29. Ibid., pp. 252-53.

30. Ibid., p. 251.

31. A similar problem arises concerning "weak-willed" people who choose lower pleasures although they know better. This problem, which is quite parallel to that discussed in the text, I leave aside.

32. Ibid., p. 252.

260   *Ethics*   *January 1982*

fact about human nature. People prefer the higher pleasures, and choose
them whenever they can. When they do not choose them, it is because they
cannot. To the extent that this argument succeeds, it provides an under-
pinning for Mill's commitment to the intrinsic value of individuality, for
liberty and self-realization are prominent both as sources of and means to
the higher pleasures. And this commitment leads naturally on to support
for political and economic reforms which will help to foster self-
development. The quotation in the previous paragraph in fact underlines
the urgency of such reforms by stressing both the tenderness of the
"plant" and the importance of social preconditions for its growth.

But does the argument work? As described above, many of its key
elements are vaguely or ambiguously expressed. The next section puts
forward several alternative reconstructions of Mill's argument, with a
view to clarifying Mill's claims and illuminating their merits.

3. PROBLEMS IN MILL'S ANALYSIS

Mill's theory of the higher pleasures can perhaps best be seen as an attempt to analyze the question of how one would want one's character or
system of preferences to develop over time—or, more abstractly, how one
would go about choosing between two different preference systems for
oneself.[33] In claiming that a life of higher pleasures is more desirable than
other lives, Mill is arguing that this process of preference change is, under
favorable circumstances, unambiguously a process of improvement.

In much of Mill's argument, he seems to rely on the proposition that
in equipping oneself for the exercise of the higher pleasures, one is simply
adding new capacities and perspectives, without losing or changing any
of the old ones. "It is better to be Socrates dissatisfied than a fool satisfied.
And if the fool or the pig are of a different opinion, it is because they only
know their own side of the question. The other party to the comparison
knows both sides."[34] On this view, there can be genuine progress in the
course of an individual's character development in much the same sense
that there can be progress in the technology of a profit-maximizing firm:
we can be sure that an innovation employed by a firm is genuinely an
improvement (from the firm's point of view, not necessarily from society's) if we know that the technology formerly employed by the firm is still
available to it. And just as a firm will revert to the old technology only if
the new technology ceases to be available (say because of a supply bottle-
neck), so a person will revert to the lower pleasures only if he loses the
capacity for the higher ones. If this is a fair picture of the process of
character development, and if Mill is indeed right empirically that those

33. Mill did not clearly distinguish between this problem and that of choosing between
two alternative pleasures at a given time, given one's preferences. As Viner has noted, this
second problem is greatly clarified by marginal utility theory developed shortly after Mill's
death. If indeed Mill's interests were confined to this second sort of problem, as Viner seems
to think, his work would hold much less interest for us. See Jacob Viner, "Bentham and J. S.
Mill: The Utilitarian Background," *American Economic Review* 39 (March 1949): 360–82.

34. *Utilitarianism*, pp. 251–52.

with a capacity for the higher pleasures tend to pursue them, it would follow that this "revealed preference" for the higher pleasures would be proof of their superiority.

In fact, this characterization of the problem of preference change, and this argument for the higher pleasures, really need not involve any fundamental preference change at all. Socrates and the fool differ essentially in their *capacities* to obtain satisfaction from certain kinds of experiences; there need be no difference in their underlying preferences for the satisfactions these different experiences provide. This idea of reducing apparent differences in tastes between people to differences in their "consumption technologies" has been formalized in the so-called "new" theory of consumer behavior developed independently by Gary Becker and Kelvin Lancaster.[35]

In this formulation, both Socrates and the fool have a taste for the commodity, "listening to music," for example, but Socrates *knows how* to get pleasure from hearing a symphony (pardon the anachronism) and the fool does not. The superiority of Socrates' way of living is established by the (alleged) fact that the has available to him all the consumption "know-how" possessed by the fool, plus some more. Again to use modern terminology, Socrates' "opportunity set" is larger than the fool's, and *ipso facto* (assuming identical underlying tastes) Socrates' level of satisfaction is higher.

This seems a reasonable formal rendering of the main line of Mill's argument, and it seems obviously open to serious objection. For it is clear that there is much more to the process of character change or "development" than the addition of new capacities with no impairment of or even change in the old capacities. For it seems likely that such character changes are in an important sense irreversible. "Lost innocence" is an ancient theme: it is surely not the same to have been Socrates and then act the fool as it is always to have been a fool. Further, even if such decisions to return to an earlier form of life are, as it were, technically possible, it is far from clear that the educated or cultivated man is any longer a competent judge of foolish or porcine pleasures. As Dennis Thompson has argued, "Even if a more qualified individual once experienced a lower pleasure in the same way that the less qualified do, he can no longer regard the pleasure from the same perspective. . . . Only if a person's powers of imagination and memory were uncommonly acute would it be possible to say that he is 'equally capable of appreciating and enjoying' both forms of satisfaction."[36] The positions of Socrates and the fool are more nearly symmetrical than Mill would allow.

35. See Kelvin Lancaster, "A New Approach to Consumer Theory," *Journal of Political Economy* 74 (April 1966): 132-57; and Robert T. Michael and Gary S. Becker, "On the New Theory of Consumer Behavior," *Swedish Journal of Economics* 75 (1973): 378-95. See also George Stigler and Gary S. Becker, "De Gustibus Non Est Disputandum," *American Economic Review* 67 (March 1977): 76-90.

36. *Mill and Representative Government*, p. 58.

Although this core argument of Mill's cannot be judged a success, there are elements in Mill's discussion of the higher pleasures which point toward another argument for their superiority, an argument which is less conclusive in its claims but considerably more plausible than that just canvassed. Mill for the most part argues from the perspective of those who have already acquired the capacity for the higher pleasures and he claims that their choice to exercise that capacity, instead of renouncing or abandoning it, proves its superiority. But it is possible to argue instead from the perspective of those who are deciding prospectively whether to embark on acquiring such capacities. The claim then would be that those who are genuinely free to choose their plan of life, and as well informed as may practically be about the alternatives, display a strong tendency to choose a life of higher pleasures. The assertion then is that there is an innate or natural propensity for people to try to develop capacities to realize the higher pleasures. (In the language of modern preference theory, such a propensity would be characterized as a "metapreference": a preference concerning the kind of preference structure one wants to have. This notion has been interestingly developed by A. K. Sen.)[37] Mill's assertion in this form could be made more or less independently of his argument that having made such a commitment people could readily and knowledgeably abandon it if they chose. Mill seems closest to adopting this line of argument (which is very similar to John Rawls's defense of the Aristotelian principle in a *Theory of Justice*) in referring to "a sense of dignity" as a kind of natural human preference for self-development.[38]

This argument seems proof against the more obvious objections to Mill's other line of attack (although it plainly rests heavily on a nonobvious empirical generalization). In particular, in pursuing this line of argument, Mill is excused from having to claim that people choose the path of self-development because they believe it will yield them "more pleasure." Rather, it is simply a (putative) fact about people that the higher-order interest in self-development plays a central role in their lives. Whether the facts in any sense support Mill's claim is a large and complex question which cannot be entered into here,[39] but there is an important conceptual difficulty that must be looked at. For Mill intends his empirical claim to apply only to those who are genuinely free to choose. He speaks of people who begin with "youthful aspirations for everything noble" but then "lose their aspirations as they lose their intellectual tastes

37. A. K. Sen, "Choice, Orderings and Morality," in S. Koerner (ed.), *Practical Reason* (Oxford: Basil Blackwell, 1974), pp. 54–67; and Sen, "Rational Fools: A Critique of the Behavioral Foundations of Economic Theory," *Philosophy and Public Affairs* 7 (Summer 1977): 317–44.

38. Mill, *Utilitarianism*, p. 251. For John Rawls, see *A Theory of Justice* (Cambridge, Mass.: Belknap Press, 1971), ch. 7. Rawls notes the resemblance to Mill's view on p. 426.

39. Rawls's "Aristotelian principle," which (as noted in footnote 38) is similar to Mill's doctrine of higher pleasures, has been subjected to criticism on grounds of empirical plausibility. See, among others, Brian Barry, *The Liberal Theory of Justice* (Oxford: Clarendon Press, 1973), esp. ch. 3.

because they have not time or opportunity for indulging them; and they addict themselves to inferior pleasures not because they deliberately prefer them, but because they are either the only ones to which they have access or the only ones which they are any longer capable of enjoying."[40] Some such qualifier is obviously needed to make the theory empirically plausible, but the qualifier is not simply an escape clause to fend off empirical refutations. As I noted earlier, Mill wants to be able to hold out for the value of the higher pleasures even and maybe especially in a society where few care for them enough. This, indeed, is the essence of his departure from a Benthamite, want-regarding utilitarianism. Mill does want his theory to rest ultimately on people's deepest or truest preferences: he denies the possibility of getting a priori knowledge of the good people should seek.[41] But he also wants to be able to criticize existing preferences, and thus he needs a criterion for discounting some preferences as less legitimate or less genuine than others.

Mill's problem (which emerges most acutely to the extent that we construe his argument as one about the *prospective* choices made by young people among alternative "life-styles") is to state such a criterion of autonomous choice without arguing in a circle. He wants to ground the superiority of the higher pleasures on people's choices, and he wants to defend individual autonomy on the ground that it is a basic source of the higher pleasures. But it begins to appear that for the choices grounding the higher pleasures to be genuine, they have to be autonomous![42]

Mill, I think, would like to see here two different arguments for the value of autonomy, rather than a single circular one, and to some degree he is justified. To a large extent, Mill would argue, society at present is ignorant about the contents of the higher pleasures and how best to achieve them. People therefore must be allowed to discover for themselves how best to live their lives, both for the sake of their own satisfactions and because it is through such free exploration that better ways of living are discovered. But society is not *completely* ignorant about the character of the good life. And one of the things that is known is that those in a position to judge have consistently opted for a life of self-reliance, activity, and responsibility over one of passivity and conformity. Thus individuality ought to be fostered both as a precondition in the continuing search for the good life, and as a component of the good life as we know it. On this line, the two sides of the argument are seen as mutually supportive rather than circular: providing for autonomy helps establish which are the higher pleasures, while the content of the higher pleasures, to the extent it is known, confirms the importance of autonomy.

40. *Utilitarianism*, p. 252.

41. See Mill's remarks on Kant, *Utilitarianism*, p. 246, and the essay "Grote's Plato" in *Essays on Philosophy and the Classics* (*Collected Works*, vol. 11) (Toronto: University of Toronto Press, 1978), pp. 375–440.

42. This criticism is made by Robson in *The Improvement of Mankind*, p. 157.

The difficulty though is that for either side of this argument to work, Mill needs to specify some criteria for what counts as an autonomous choice which are independent of the content of the choices being made. Otherwise the circle closes. Whether it is a matter of determining who are the competent judges of the higher pleasures, or of establishing the ideal conditions of choice in the face of ignorance about the value of the alternatives, Mill must avoid simply building the "right answers" into the criteria of choice. This, it seems to me, is the key theoretical problem posed by Mill's doctrine of the higher pleasures. And it is a problem, I would argue, which any moral theory that recognizes the influence of institutions on people's tastes must come to grips with.

Mill himself never really provides a way out of this dilemma, for his descriptions of what it is to choose voluntarily or to have a character of one's own are all bound up with contentful descriptions of what such choices or such a character are like. It is, for example, never quite clear whether a person who is genuinely allowed a free choice will *in fact* always or generally decide to become active and self-reliant or whether instead a person who fails to become active and self-reliant has shown himself to be incapable of free choice *by definition*.

Although the main point of this section is to assess Mill's contribution, rather than to solve the problems he posed, it may be illuminating to indicate a direction in which resolution might be sought. One means of providing Mill's theory with the foundation it needs is a more careful and less question-begging account of the distinction between environments tending to produce "good" and "impaired" choosers. The aim would be to give a description of favorable conditions of choice which would be minimally controversial and yet have enough cutting power to actually distinguish some social environments as better than others for the process of preference formation.

"Autonomy" would then enter the theory at two levels or stages. The first, minimal, conception of autonomy would be used to pick out good choosers (or, less ambitiously, to rule out some choosers as obviously impaired). Examination of the actual choices of good choosers would then be used to support the empirical generalizations embodied in the doctrine of higher pleasures. One of the most important of these generalizations is that good choosers opt for a life of Millian individuality, which is a life of autonomy in its second, richer sense. This second conception of autonomy, as described in Section 1 above, is plainly much more contentful and controversial than a mere description of favorable conditions of choice—which of course is precisely why Mill felt the need to argue for it through the doctrine of higher pleasures.

Whether this "two-stage" strategy[43] can work depends on what a description and defense of this minimal conception of autonomy would

43. This approach is a kind of inversion of the two-stage argument about the good in Rawls's *Theory of Justice*. Rawls first develops a "thin" theory of the good which characterizes those "primary social goods" which anyone requires to fulfill a rational plan of life.

look like, and how far the good choosers it would pick out would tend in fact to choose the higher pleasures. One can think of the issue as a sort of balancing act between the two stages of the theory: the more controversial moral content is poured into the first-stage conception of autonomy, the easier it will be to get out a defense of "individuality" and the higher pleasures at the second stage. But, at the same time, the more controversial is the first stage of the theory, the more will the conception of autonomy it starts with stand in need of independent defense and the less successful will the theory be in grounding its claim on empirical choices people actually make.

This is surely not the place to try to elaborate a theory of the social preconditions of autonomous choice, but a couple of observations are in order. (It should be noted that a reasonable account of autonomy at either of these levels need not imply a commitment to "freedom of the will," in the sense in which belief in "free will" entails rejecting the thesis that human behavior and action are caused as other natural events are.) One is that a general program of the kind just outlined seems to be central to the work of a number of contemporary social theorists. The broad and essentially Kantian idea of establishing a set of minimal criteria that social institutions must satisfy in order to be compatible with rational formation of values and preferences can be found in the writings of theorists as diverse as Popper, Rawls, and Habermas.[44] A good deal of the difference among these theorists can be explained, on the one hand, in terms of differences in the character and stringency of their conceptions of rational choice and, on the other hand, in terms of the character of their reasoning from a particular conception of rationality or autonomy to criticism of social institutions. Whether anything like a consensus among these divergent views can ultimately be expected to emerge is very hard to say, but it is heartening to observe an increasing awarenesss of the centrality of these problems and of the mutual relevance of these different approaches to them.[45]

whatever it may be. This thin theory then plays a central role in Rawls's argument for the two principles of justice. These principles then enter as constraints on what sorts of rational life plans—that is, conceptions of the good for a person in the full sense—can be admitted in a just society. Rawls thus moves from a minimal conception of the good to the derivation of deontological principles which help shape the full theory of the good. My suggestion for a reformulation of Mill's view is to move from a minimal conception of individual autonomy through an analysis of what people would choose under conditions described by that conception to a fuller conception of autonomy as part of what they would choose.

44. Karl Popper, *The Open Society and Its Enemies*, 2 vols. (Princeton, N.J.: Princeton University Press, 1971); Rawls, *A Theory of Justice*; and Jürgens Habermas, *Knowledge and Human Interests* (Boston: Beacon Press, 1971), esp. the appendix, "Knowledge and Human Interests: A General Perspective," and *Theory and Practice* (Boston: Beacon Press, 1973), esp. chs. 1 and 7.

45. See, among others, Brian Fay, *Social Theory and Political Practice* (London: George Allen & Unwin, 1975); Richard J. Bernstein, *The Restructuring of Social and Political Theory* (Philadelphia: University of Pennsylvania Press, 1977); Martin Hollis, *Models of Man* (Cambridge: Cambridge University Press, 1977); and William E. Connolly, "On 'Interests' in Politics," *Politics and Society* 2 (1972): 459–77.

The second observation is that Mill's formulation of the problem of autonomy points to its close connection to the irreversibilities and uncertainties connected with the choice of life plans, and hence to the economic analysis of decision-making under uncertainty. As we have seen, it is essentially such irreversibilities and uncertainties that render Mill's Socrates/fool comparisons inconclusive—Socrates can neither recall nor return to the life of the fool—and force Mill instead to fall back on claims about the prospective choices people tend to make among alternative ways of living, when choosing under favorable conditions. In this perspective, the problem of specifying a minimal conception of autonomy becomes one of analyzing the character of a favorable environment for choice when the alternatives are only imperfectly known and the commitments involved are irreversible. Decision-theoretic analysis in economics has been concerned to date less with this range of problems than with determining the best choice to make or the best way of choosing, *given* the information available and other aspects of the environment for choosing. But this other dimension of the question, namely that of optimally structuring the environment for choice when information is costly, time for decision is limited, and rationality is "bounded" by limits on reasoning capacity, has begun to receive systematic attention in writings by Kenneth Arrow, Herbert Simon, and others.[46] These theories have indicated, for example, that the choice process can be impeded by a glut as well as by a paucity of information, and that the pre-screening of information to attend to is therefore inevitable. The nature and effectiveness of the filters that get imposed on the flow of new information will be importantly influenced by early experiences, and once in place such filters will be relatively immune to correction by later experience, precisely because such later experience is interpreted through the filters.

Considerations like these seem obviously relevant to describing optimal environments for choice under uncertainty, and they seem to bear some relation to our ideas about the kind of social background that might impair one's ability to choose well, but it is plainly a long step from such relatively abstract analyses to the criticism of particular social institutions as environments for preference formation. How far this line of thought can go in clarifying and making more rigorous our intuitive judgments about the merits of different choice environments and hence about the idea of autonomy, remains to be seen.

A summary assessment of Mill's contribution to the moral analysis of preference change might be as follows. The main line of Mill's argument, which reduces change in preferences to increases or reductions in "con-

46. Kenneth J. Arrow, *The Limits of Organization* (New York: W. W. Norton, 1974), and Herbert Simon, "Rationality as Process and as Product of Thought," *American Economic Review* 68 (May, 1978), pp. 1–16. These and other contemporary economic contributions to these problems are examined in my paper, "Want Formation, Morality, and the Interpretive Dimension of Economic Inquiry," Williams College Economics Department Research Paper No. 33 (September, 1980).

sumption capacities," does not work. A second line, which defends the life of higher pleasures as that willingly chosen by good choosers in favorable environments, is more promising, but it demands a nonquestion-begging explication of the notion of a "good environment for choice." A fully satisfactory account on these lines cannot be found in Mill, but his theory does effectively point to the need for and potential role of such a theory of "autonomous choices."

4. LIBERTY AND THE HIGHER PLEASURES

Mill's theory, if it can be made to work along the lines discussed in the preceding section, would provide a criterion of individual well-being that is to some degree independent of the preferences a person happens to have, although it is closely tied to the preferences the person would have developed under more favorable conditions. Economic institutions in particular could be evaluated not just from the standpoint of how well they satisfied existing wants, but also from the standpoint of their tendency to promote the cultivation of more valuable or desirable wants. The higher pleasures, including most notably the cultivation of an individualized, active and socially responsible character, attain in this theory a kind of objective importance as ends worth striving for, and, as I noted earlier, Mill was not hesitant to advocate social policies designed to support and further the pursuit of those ends.

It is natural to wonder whether support for such policies, apparently aimed at interfering with people's pursuit of their own aims in the name of an external judgment of their "real" interests, can be made compatible with Mill's strong commitment to individual, negative liberty. In a famous passage in the *Liberty* Mill says that "the only purpose for which power can be rightfully exercised over any member of a civilized community, against his will, is to prevent harm to others. His own good, either physical or moral, is not a sufficient warrant."[47] *Prima facie*, this rather absolute sounding stance leaves little room for promoting the higher pleasures. Part of the answer to this apparent contradiction is that Mill's commitments to individual liberty, understood as the right to freedom from interference in pursuing one's own freely chosen ends, although very strong indeed, were not so completely rigid as the language of this quotation seems to imply.[48] But more importantly for present purposes, there are several considerations suggesting that Mill's doctrine of higher pleasures, rather than undercutting his commitment to liberty, actually

47. *On Liberty*, p. 129.

48. For important recent contributions bearing on the longstanding controversy on this question, see David Lyons, "Human Rights and the General Welfare," *Philosophy and Public Affairs* 6 (Winter, 1977), pp. 113–29, Gerald Dworkin, "Paternalism," in R. A. Wasserstrom (ed.), *Morality and the Law* (Belmont, Calif.: Wadsworth Publishing Company, 1971), pp. 107–36, and Alan Ryan, *John Stuart Mill* (New York: Pantheon Books, 1970), ch. xiii. Selections from classic items in the controversy are in Peter Radcliff (ed.), *Limits of Liberty* (Belmont, Calif.: Wadsworth Publishing Company, 1966).

tended to support it and in fact to help reconcile his belief in liberty with his utilitarianism.

First is the fact that Mill did not deploy the doctrine of higher pleasures with the idea in mind mainly of interfering with the choices made by people whose preferences had already been formed under existing institutions. This sort of overriding of a person's existing preferences in the name of his own good is what is usually meant by paternalism, and it is clear from the examples in *On Liberty* that Mill's antipaternalistic commitments were extremely strong. Mill was never the sort of Old Grundy who thought people should be made to listen to "good" music or the like whether they cared to or not; rather Mill's concern was to reform the major institutions of society so that people would come to want things that were more valuable, both to themselves and to society.[49]

This is perhaps clearest in regard to education. Since children begin life with their preferences and character largely unformed, the question of how they should be taught cannot be posed as one of interference vs. noninterference by society with their existing wants, but must rather be seen as one of who in society will control the want-shaping process and of how much of society's resources will be devoted to it. Mill rejects the argument that parents have a self-evident right to this control—"it [is not] a question whether government should interfere with individuals in the direction of their own conduct and interests, but whether it should leave absolutely in their power the conduct and interests of somebody else."[50] Mill establishes a legitimate governmental role in education partly on grounds that the community at large has an interest in children acquiring a basic education (the familiar "externalities" argument in contemporary economics of education literature), and also quite directly on grounds of government's superior knowledge of the higher pleasures: "[A]ny well-intentioned and tolerably civilized government may think without presumption that it does or ought to possess a degree of civilization above the average of the community which it rules, and that it should therefore be capable of offering better education and better instruction to the people than the greater number of them would spontaneously demand."[51] Mill, however, precisely because he regarded education as so powerful an influence on people's characters, was careful to build in limitations to governmental exercise of its use: first, government ought not establish a monopoly of education and second, good instruction must pass the test of cultivating a spirit of independence in the instructed—it must be "help toward doing without help."[52]

Mill's treatment of institutional reform in fields other than education, which concerned especially alternative systems of political and eco-

49. I have expanded on this point in a comment on a recent article by Martin Bronfenbrenner, "Pushpin, Poetry, and Utility," *Economy Inquiry* 15 (January, 1977), pp. 95–110. The comment appears in *Economic Inquiry* 18 (April, 1980), pp. 314–18.

50. Mill, *Principles*, vol. 2, p. 951.

51. Ibid., pp. 947–48.

52. Ibid., pp. 949–50.

nomic organization, is analogous. The underlying point is that if institutions do indeed affect people's preferences profoundly, then it is impossible to judge the liberty of those institutions simply by the extent to which they permit people to satisfy the preferences they tend to generate. By such a definition a totalitarian regime which could restrict its subjects' wants to what it chose to make available would leave them quite free.[53] It is true as well that a change in institutions which results in people having different wants cannot automatically be presumed to curtail their freedom or to constitute a paternalistic intervention in their lives, since the preferences they had status quo have no special warrant. Instead, insofar as liberty is concerned with want-satisfaction, the liberty provided by a set of institutions has to be judged in a more complex way, including such factors as (a) the tendency of the institutions to satisfy the preferences they generate; (b) the compatibility of the institutions with the satisfaction of a wide variety of preferences; and (c) the capacity of the institutions to allow people to develop and change their own preferences without undue or arbitrary restrictions on information or the environment of choice.

It is, I think, possible to criticize Mill for never facing squarely the possibility of conflicts among these various dimensions of liberty, or the possibility that temporary infringements of certain freedoms might be needed to ensure a fuller realization of liberty in the long run.[54] Thus, for example, Mill relied on the spontaneous growth of the cooperative movement to overcome the negative effect of the wage system on individual self-development, without recognizing that the success of the cooperative movement might require serious modifications in the traditional rights of private property.[55] These are plainly serious problems for Mill's thought—and for liberal political theory in general[56]—but they cannot obscure the depth of Mill's commitment to liberty in all its dimensions, nor the advance of Mill's view of liberty over those which fail to take seriously the dependence of preferences on social institutions.

In fact, since the doctrine of the higher pleasures provided the underpinnings for Mill's defense of individuality, as we have seen above, that doctrine was not only compatible with but actually essential for Mill's deep commitment to liberty. Mill's conception of an ideal human character did not run in terms of a narrowly prescribed pattern of conduct or a

53. This point is forcefully made in Isaiah Berlin, "Two Concepts of Liberty," in *Four Essays on Liberty* (Oxford: Oxford University Press, 1969). See also the introduction to that volume, pp. xxxvii–xl.

54. This criticism is made (I think too one-sidedly) in Herbert Gintis, *Alienation and Power*, ch. 3.

55. See Richard Krouse, *From Classical Republicanism to Contemporary Democratic Theory: A study in the Revision of Political Ideas* (Ph.D. dissertation, Princeton University, 1977), ch. 3 and p. 321.

56. Related criticisms concerning a lack of sensitivity to problems of historical change have been leveled at Rawls. See Benjamin Barber, "Justifying Justice: Problems of Psychology, Politics and Measurement in Rawls," in Norman Daniels (ed.), *Reading Rawls* (Oxford: Basil Blackwell, 1975), pp. 292–318; and R. P. Wolff, *Understanding Rawls* (Princeton, 1977), part 5.

particular pattern of tastes which society was justified in forcing on the individual. Mill was rather concerned to stress certain broad features of a desirable kind of life: a concern for intellectual values, sympathy for others, and a desire for individuality. Individual liberty in this view takes on an objective importance in a desirable plan of life which goes beyond its contingent usefulness in helping men and women attain their ends, and even beyond the strength of the preference for liberty people in particular social circumstances may feel. As Alan Ryan has said,

> [F]reedom is a necessary ingredient in anything that Mill can recognize as the life which a rational man would choose. The good society is one made up of happy people, and Mill's picture of what makes a man happy is not unclear. It is the possession of a character which is self-reliant, rational in its assessment of the world, tolerant, wide-ranging in its interest, spontaneous in its sympathies. Not merely can we not make men like this by coercing them; coercion is logically at odds with the creation of such a character.[57]

This is a much stronger defense of liberty than a classical utilitarian could give. Such a theorist, aiming only at satisfying existing desires and asking no questions about their origins, could, for example, have no objections to a Brave New World in which the instrumental importance of liberty had been obviated and the empirical desire for it had been conditioned away. But Mill could still defend the value of freedom, provided anyway that the conditioning process which eliminated the desire for freedom precluded the chance for a rational, informed choice of alternative ways of living. For he could protest that such a conditioning process was incompatible with minimal conditions of human autonomy, and that the resulting preferences were not those a rational man or woman would choose under more favorable conditions.

There is a final and somewhat less direct connection between liberty and the higher pleasures. It concerns the problem of motivating and educating people to be moral. Mill thought the higher pleasures were plainly more productive of utility for society at large than the lower pleasures were. It thus followed that people were morally obligated to cultivate the higher pleasures—and society was justified within appropriate limits in encouraging their cultivation—even if the lower pleasures were more productive of utility for any one individual separately:

> [I]f it may possibly be doubted whether a noble character is always the happier for its nobleness, there can be no doubt that it makes other people happier and that the world in general is immensely a gainer by it. . . . Utilitarianism, therefore, could only attain its end by the general cultivation of nobleness of character, even if each individual were only benefited by the nobleness of others, and his own, so far as happiness is concerned, were a sheer deduction from the benefit.[58]

57. *John Stuart Mill*, pp. 254–55.
58. *Utilitarianism*, p. 253.

Now if the higher pleasures are socially productive and privately unproductive, society becomes a Prisoner's Dilemma game, with each person hoping to benefit from other people's "good" behavior, but knowing that, whatever others do, he is best off to be a swine. But if, on the other hand, the higher pleasures are both privately and socially productive, then at least within limits society becomes what Sen has termed a game of cooperation, in which the private interest of each corresponds to the social interest.

These two views of society obviously lead to very different visions of the nature of moral education and of the possible scope of individual freedom in a good society. If the "Prisoner's Dilemma" conception is correct, morality becomes a matter of constraint and the aim of moral education has to be to suppress natural human impulses and tendencies. One would also expect social institutions to have a distinctly Hobbesian flavor, being designed to hem in and subordinate destructive human inclinations. But if instead society is a game of cooperation, the pursuit of individual and social good can proceed in step. Moral education becomes education for freedom, a matter of helping each to discover and cultivate the deepest springs of his own well-being. And social institutions, properly designed, can give the widest scope to individual freedom, spontaneity, and initiative.[59]

Mill was deeply committed to this latter sort of view, which with its harmonistic implications for ultimate human possibilities is strikingly similar to Marx. Of course, for immediate purposes of social policy, Mill's reformist orientation did not require him to lean heavily on this version of ultimate perfectibility, which for him was plainly a matter for the very long run.[60] His more modest claim was concerned with directions of change: in existing social circumstances, changes in wants and character which were conducive to the well-being of each separately would also contribute to the collective good. "In proportion to the development of his individuality, each person becomes more valuable to himself and is therefore capable of being more valuable to others."[61] The doctrine of the higher pleasures was central in making out this case.

5. CONCLUSION

Even at the distance of a hundred years, Mill's moral theory provides a remarkably rich and illuminating starting point for the analysis of the

---

59. Rawls's account of moral development in a well-ordered society reflects these concerns and in some respects, as he notes, echoes Mill. See *A Theory of Justice*, ch. 8.

60. Mill's caution is well reflected in this comment in a letter to Harriet Taylor: "I cannot persuade myself that you do not greatly overrate the ease of making people unselfish. Granting that in 'ten years' the children of a community might by teaching be made 'perfect' it seems to me that to do so there must be perfect people to teach them" (Mill, *Principles*, vol. 2, appendix G ["John Stuart Mill-Harriet Taylor Correspondence"], p. 1030). See also Mill's views on revolution, *Chapters on Socialism*, in *Essays on Economics and Society, 1850–1879*, (*Collected Works*, vol. 5) (Toronto: University of Toronto Press, 1967), pp. 748–49.

61. *On Liberty*, p. 178.

moral and empirical problems raised by the social determination of wants. It is, of course, only a starting point: Mill's writings are not without ambiguities, confusions, and inadequacies only some of which have been addressed in this paper. Further, there has been much change and some progress both in moral philosophy and social science since Mill wrote, and parts of Mill's theory need to be rethought to accommodate those changes. But Mill's theory has great merits as a systematic attempt to take account of the profound influence of social institutions on human values and preferences without abandoning—and, indeed, while trying to strengthen—some of the central commitments of liberalism. Perhaps of greatest value is the way Mill shows the inevitable interconnections among the moral, political, and economic dimensions of these problems. Mill's underlying aim in revising classical utilitarianism was, I think, to retain its critical, reforming, and analytical spirit, while freeing it from an attachment to an impoverished moral psychology and a myopic view of the possibilities for social change. With neoclassical welfare economics serving as the heir apparent to Benthamite utilitarianism in both its good and bad respects, these aims have, it seems to me, retained their force.

I would like in conclusion to emphasize two particular issues raised in Mill's theory which merit renewed attention by contemporary social theorists.

The first is the empirical side of the problem of the dependence on economic and social institutions of individual preferences or character. It seems undeniable, in fact a commonplace, that such dependencies exist, but our knowledge both of what the connections are and of how they can be explained remains loose and informal. Mill himself recognized the lack of systematic knowledge of these connections in his day, and urged their study in the field he called "comparative ethology," while relying, in his own applied work, on casual empiricism and common sense to fill the gap. It matters little whether studies in this area, a large part of what Schumpeter called "economic sociology." [62] are labeled as part of economics or not—although I think it likely that the tools and conceptual standpoint of economics may have much to contribute to their study. What is important is that economists and other social theorists recognize the importance of these issues, and the need for more empirical knowledge about them, in criticizing and reforming economic institutions. If indeed institutions affect preferences in systematic ways, there is no meaningful sense in which economists can adopt a neutral stance on the problem of preference formation. [63] When economists pretend to do so, they are implicitly supporting the status quo and thus placing their assessment of

---

62. "[E]conomic analysis deals with the questions how people behave at any time and what the economic effects are they produce by so behaving; economic sociology deals with the question how they came to behave as they do" (Joseph A. Schumpeter, *History of Economic Analysis* [New York: Oxford University Press, 1954], p. 21).

63. This point is well developed in Brian Barry, *The Liberal Theory of Justice.*

alternative social arrangements "at the mercy, so to speak, of existing wants and interests."[64] To do better requires not only a richer ethical framework than neoclassical welfare economics provides, but also better knowledge of the empirical connections between preferences and institutions.

The second issue Mill's theory raises is suggested by his conception of autonomy. It seems to me clear that a commitment to autonomy, in the sense of a basic right people have to judge for themselves among alternatives and to be treated as responsible moral agents, plays a central role in our moral sentiments. Indeed, the appeal of some such notion of respect for individual autonomy goes far to provide the intuitive basis in neoclassical welfare economics for the premise that individual preferences alone should count in designing social institutions and policies. The Millian analysis I have surveyed can be viewed as an attempt to extend this commitment to autonomy to contexts where preferences cannot be treated as given.

The job of providing a clear and adequate interpretation and defense of the commitment to autonomy, and of working out the implications for the design of social institutions, was certainly not completed by Mill (or Kant, to cite the obvious alternative). While, as I noted above, this problem is being seriously addressed by a wide range of social theorists, it has been rather neglected in the recent spate of writings by economists about endogenous preferences. One reason for the neglect may be that the question of autonomy arises most naturally when uncertainty and bounded rationality are incorporated in the analysis of the choice process. These features have been assumed away in much of the recent work on preference change, and indeed in much of modern economics. Once they are incorporated, as they plainly have to be in any realistic conception of preference formation and change, it may well be that the economic framework will have as much to say about what it means to choose autonomously and about the social preconditions for such choices.

---

64. Rawls, *A Theory of Justice*, p. 261.

Part II
Libertarian Liberalism

[17]

THE COMING SLAVERY

The kinship of pity to love is shown among other ways in this, that it idealizes its object. Sympathy with one in suffering suppresses, for the time being, remembrance of his transgressions. The feeling which vents itself in "poor fellow!" On seeing one in agony, excludes the thought of "bad fellow," which might at another time arise. Naturally, then, if the wretched are unknown or but vaguely known, all the demerits they may have are ignored; and thus it happens that when the miseries of the poor are dilated upon, they are thought of as the miseries of the deserving poor, instead of being thought of as the miseries of the undeserving poor, which in large measure they should be. Those whose hardships are set forth in pamphlets and proclaimed in sermons and speeches which echo throughout society, are assumed to be all worthy souls, grievously wronged; and none of them are thought of as bearing the penalties of their misdeeds.

On hailing a cab in a London street, it is surprising how frequently the door is officiously opened by one who expects to get something for his trouble. The surprise lessens after counting the many loungers about tavern-doors, or after observing the quickness with which a street-performance, or procession, draws from neighbouring slums and stable-yards a group of idlers. Seeing how numerous they are in every small area, it becomes manifest that tens of thousands of such swarm through London. "They have no work," you say. Say rather that they either refuse work or quickly turn themselves out of it. They are simply good-for-nothings, who in one way or other live on the good-for-somethings—vagrants and sots, criminals and those on the way to crime, youths who are burdens on hard-worked parents, men who appropriate the wages of their wives, fellows who share the gains of prostitutes; and then, less visible and less numerous, there is a corresponding class of women.

Is it natural that happiness should be the lot of such? or is it natural that they should bring unhappiness on themselves and those connected with them? Is it not manifest that there must exist in our midst an immense amount of misery which is a normal result of misconduct, and ought not to be dissociated from it? There is a notion, always more or less prevalent and just now vociferously expressed, that all social suffering is removable, and that it is the duty of somebody or other to remove it. Both these beliefs are false. To separate pain from ill-doing is to fight against the constitution of things, and will be followed by far more pain. Saving men from the natural penalties of dissolute living, eventually necessitates the infliction of artificial penalties in solitary cells, on tread-wheels, and by the lash. I suppose a dictum on which the current creed and the creed of science are at one, may be considered to have as high an authority as can be found. Well, the command "if any would not work neither should he eat," is simply a Christian enunciation of that universal law of Nature under which life has reached its present height—the law that a creature not energetic enough to maintain itself must die: the sole difference being that the law which in the one case is to be artificially enforced, is, in the other case, a natural necessity. And yet this particular tenet of their religion which science so manifestly justifies, is the one which Christians seem least inclined to accept. The current assumption is that there should be no suffering, and that society is to blame for that which exists.

"But surely we are not without responsibilities, even when the suffering is that of the unworthy?"

If the meaning of the word "we" be so expanded as to include with ourselves our ancestors, and especially our ancestral legislators, I agree. I admit that those who made, and modified, and administered, the old Poor Law, were responsible for producing an appalling amount of demoralization, which it will take more than one generation to remove. I admit, too, the partial responsibility of recent and present law-makers for regulations which have brought into being a permanent body of tramps, who ramble from union to union; and also their responsibility for maintaining a constant supply of felons by sending back convicts into society under such conditions that they are almost compelled again to commit crimes. Moreover, I admit that the philanthropic are not without their share of responsibility; since, that they may aid the offspring of the unworthy, they disadvantage the offspring of the worthy through burdening their parents by increased local rates. Nay, I even admit that these swarms of good-for-nothings, fostered and multiplied by public and private agencies, have, by sundry mischievous meddlings, been made to suffer more than they would otherwise have suffered. Are these the responsibilities meant? I suspect not.

But now, leaving the question of responsibilities, however conceived, and considering only the evil itself, what shall we say of its treatment? Let me begin with a fact.

A late uncle of mine, the Rev. Thomas Spencer, for some twenty years incumbent of Hinton Charterhouse, near Bath, no sooner entered on his parish duties than he proved himself anxious for the welfare of the poor, by establishing a school, a library, a clothing club, and land-allotments, besides building some model cottages. Moreover, up to 1833 he was a pauper's friend—always for the pauper against the overseer.

There presently came, however, the debates on the Poor Law, which impressed him with the evils of the system then in force. Though an ardent philanthropist he was not a timid sentimentalist. The result was that, immediately the New Poor Law was passed, he proceeded to carry out its provisions in his parish. Almost universal opposition was encountered by him: not the poor only being his opponents, but even the farmers on

whom came the burden of heavy poor-rates. For, strange
to say, their interests had become apparently identified
with the maintenance of this system which taxed them
so largely. The explanation is that there had grown up
the practice of paying out of the rates a part of the wages
of each farm-servant—"make-wages," as the sum was
called. And though the farmers contributed most of the
fund from which "make-wages" were paid, yet, since
all other ratepayers contributed, the farmers seemed to
gain by the arrangement. My uncle, however, not easily
deterred, faced all this opposition and enforced the law.
The result was that in two years the rates were reduced
from £700 a year to £200 a year; while the condition of
the parish was greatly improved. "Those who had hitherto loitered at the corners of the streets, or at the doors
of the beer-shops, had something else to do, and one
after another they obtained employment"; so that out of
a population of 800, only 15 had to be sent as incapable
paupers to the Bath Union (when that was formed), in
place of the 100 who received out-door relief a short time
before. If it be said that the £25 telescope which, a few
years after, his parishioners presented to my uncle,
marked the gratitude of the ratepayers only; then my
reply is the fact that when, some years later still, having
killed himself by overwork in pursuit of popular welfare,
he was taken to Hinton to be buried, the procession
which followed him to the grave included not the well-
to-do only but the poor.

Several motives have prompted this brief narrative.
One is the wish to prove that sympathy with the people
and self-sacrificing efforts on their behalf, do not nec-

essarily imply approval of gratuitous aids. Another is the desire to show that benefit may result, not from multiplication of artificial appliances to mitigate distress, but, contrariwise, from diminution of them. And a further purpose I have in view is that of preparing the way for an analogy.

Under another form and in a different sphere, we are now yearly extending a system which is identical in nature with the system of "make-wages" under the old Poor Law. Little as politicians recognize the fact, it is nevertheless demonstrable that these various public appliances for working-class comfort, which they are supplying at the cost of ratepayers, are intrinsically of the same nature as those which, in past times, treated the farmer's man as half-labourer and half-pauper. In either case the worker receives in return for what he does, money wherewith to buy certain of the things he wants; while, to procure the rest of them for him, money is furnished out of a common fund raised by taxes. What matters it whether the things supplied by ratepayers for nothing, instead of by the employer in payment, are of this kind or that kind? The principle is the same. For sums received let us substitute the commodities and benefits purchased; and then see how the matter stands. In old Poor-Law times, the farmer gave for work done the equivalent, say of house-rent, bread, clothes, and fire; while the ratepayers practically supplied the man and his family with their shoes, tea, sugar, candles, a little bacon, etc. The division is, of course, arbitrary; but unquestionably the farmer and the ratepayers furnished these things between them. At the present time the artisan receives from his employer in wages, the equivalent of the consumable commodities he wants: while from the public comes satisfaction for others of his needs and desires. At the cost of ratepayers he has in some cases, and will presently have in more, a house at less than its commercial value; for of course when, as in Liverpool, a municipality spends nearly £200,000 in pulling down and reconstructing low-class dwellings, and is about to spend as much again, the implication is that in some way the ratepayers supply the poor with more accommodation than the rents they pay would otherwise have brought. The artisan further receives from them, in schooling for his children, much more than he pays for; and there is every probability that he will presently receive it from them gratis. The ratepayers also satisfy what desire he may have for books and newspapers, and comfortable places to read them in. In some cases too, as in Manchester, gymnasia for his children of both sexes, as well as recreation grounds, are provided. That is to say, he obtains from a fund raised by local taxes, certain benefits beyond those which the sum received for his labour enables him to purchase. The sole difference, then, between this system and the old system of "make-wages," is between the kinds of satisfactions obtained; and this difference does not in the least affect the nature of the arrangement.

Moreover, the two are pervaded by substantially the same illusion. In the one case, as in the other, what looks like a gratis benefit is not a gratis benefit. The amount which, under the old Poor Law, the half-pauperized labourer received from the parish to eke out his weekly income, was not really, as it appeared, a bonus; for it was accompanied by a substantially equivalent decrease of his wages, as was quickly proved when the system was abolished and the wages rose. Just so is it with these seeming boons received by working people in towns. I do not refer only to the fact that they unawares pay in part through the raised rents of their dwellings (when they are not actual ratepayers); but I refer to the fact that the wages received by them are, like the wages of the farm-labourer, diminished by these public burdens falling on employers. Read the accounts coming of late from Lancashire concerning the cotton-strikes containing proofs, given by artisans themselves, that the margin of profit is so narrow that the less skilful manufacturers, as well as those with deficient capital, fail, and that the companies of cooperators who compete with them can rarely hold their own; and then consider what is the implication respecting wages. Among the costs of production have to be reckoned taxes, general and local. If, as in our large towns, the local rates now amount to one-third of the rental or more—if the employer has to pay this, not on his private dwelling only, but on his business-premises, factories, warehouses, or the like; it results that the interest on his capital must be diminished by that amount, or the amount must be taken from the wages-fund, or partly one and partly the other. And if competition among capitalists in the same business, and in other businesses, has the effect of so keeping down interest that while some gain others lose, and not a few are ruined—if capital, not getting adequate interest, flows elsewhere and leaves labour unemployed; then it is manifest that the choice for the artisan under such conditions, lies between diminished amount of work and diminished rate of payment for it. Moreover, for kindred reasons these local burdens raise the costs of the things he consumes. The charges made by distributors are, on the average, determined by the current rates of interest on capital used in distributing businesses; and the extra costs of carrying on such businesses have to be paid for by extra prices. So that as in the past the rural worker lost in one way what he gained in another, so in the present does the urban worker: there being, too, in both cases, the loss entailed on him by the cost of administration and the waste accompanying it.

"But what has all this to do with 'the coming slavery'?" will perhaps be asked. Nothing directly, but a good deal indirectly, as we shall see after yet another preliminary section.

It is said that when railways were first opened in Spain, peasants standing on the tracks were not unfrequently run over; and that the blame fell on the engine-drivers for not stopping: rural experiences having yielded no conception of the momentum of a large mass moving at a high velocity.

The incident is recalled to me on contemplating the ideas of the so-called "practical" politician, into whose mind there enters no thought of such a thing as political momentum, still less of a political momentum which, instead of diminishing or remaining constant, increases. The theory on which he daily proceeds is that the change caused by his measure will stop where he intends it to

stop. He contemplates intently the things his act will
achieve, but thinks little of the remoter issues of the
movement his act sets up, and still less its collateral issues. When, in war-time, "food for powder" was to be
provided by encouraging population—when Mr. Pitt
said, "Let us make relief in cases where there are a number of children a matter of right and honour, instead of
a ground for opprobrium and contempt,"[1] it was not
expected that the poor-rates would be quadrupled in
fifty years, that women with many bastards would be
preferred as wives to modest women, because of their
incomes from the parish, and that hosts of ratepayers
would be pulled down into the ranks of pauperism. Legislators who in 1833 voted £30,000 a year to aid in building school-houses, never supposed that the step they
then took would lead to forced contributions, local and
general, now amounting to £6,000,000;[2] they did not intend to establish a principle that A should be made responsible for educating B's offspring; they did not dream
of a compulsion which would deprive poor widows of
the help of their elder children; and still less did they
dream that their successors, by requiring impoverished
parents to apply to Boards of Guardians to pay the fees
which School Boards would not remit, would initiate a
habit of applying to Boards of Guardians and so cause
pauperization.[3] Neither did those who in 1834 passed an
Act regulating the labour of women and children in certain factories, imagine that the system they were begin-

---

[1] Hansard's *Parliamentary History*, 32, p. 710.
[2] Since this was written the sum has risen to £10,000,000; i.e., in 1890.
[3] *Fortnightly Review*, January 1884, p. 17.

ning would end in the restriction and inspection of
labour in all kinds of producing establishments where
more than fifty people are employed; nor did they conceive that the inspection provided would grow to the
extent of requiring that before a "young person" is employed in a factory, authority must be given by a certi-
fying surgeon, who, by personal examination (to which
no limit is placed) has satisfied himself that there is no
incapacitating disease or bodily infirmity: his verdict determining whether the "young person" shall earn wages
or not.[4] Even less, as I say, does the politician who
plumes himself on the practicalness of his aims, conceive
the indirect results which will follow the direct results of
his measures. Thus, to take a case connected with one
named above, it was not intended through the system
of "payment by results," to do anything more than give
teachers an efficient stimulus: it was not supposed that
in numerous cases their health would give way under
the stimulus; it was notexpected that they would be led
to adopt a cramming system and to put undue pressure
on dull and weak children, often to their great injury; it
was not foreseen that in many cases a bodily enfeeble-
ment would be caused which no amount of grammar
and geography can compensate for.[5] The licensing of
public-houses was simply for maintaining public order:
those who devised it never imagined that there would

---

[4] Factories and Workshops Act, 41 and 42 Vic., cap. 16.
[5] Since this was written, these mischiefs have come to be recognized,
and the system is in course of abandonment; but not one word is said
about the immense injury the Government has inflicted on millions of
children during the last 20 years!

result an organized interest powerfully influencing elections in an unwholesome way. Nor did it occur to the "practical" politicians who provided a compulsory load-line for merchant vessels, that the pressure of shipowners' interests would habitually cause the putting of the load-line at the very highest limit, and that from precedent to precedent, tending ever in the same direction, the load-line would gradually rise in the better class of ships; as from good authority I learn that it has already done. Legislators who, some forty years ago, by Act of Parliament compelled railway-companies to supply cheap locomotion, would have ridiculed the belief, had it been expressed, that eventually their Act would punish the companies which improved the supply; and yet this was the result to companies which began to carry third-class passengers by fast trains; since a penalty to the amount of the passenger-duty was inflicted on them for every third-class passenger so carried. To which instance concerning railways, add a far more striking one disclosed by comparing the railway policies of England and France. The law-makers who provided for the ultimate lapsing of French railways to the State, never conceived the possibility that inferior travelling facilities would result—did not foresee that reluctance to depreciate the value of property eventually coming to the State, would negative the authorization of competing lines, and that in the absence of competing lines locomotion would be relatively costly, slow, and infrequent; for, as Sir Thomas Farrer has lately shown, the traveller in England has great advantages over the French traveller in the economy, swiftness, and frequency with which his journeys can be made.

But the "practical" politician who, in spite of such experiences repeated generation after generation, goes on thinking only of proximate results, naturally never thinks of results still more remote, still more general, and still more important than those just exemplified. To repeat the metaphor used above—he never asks whether the political momentum set up by his measure, in some cases decreasing but in other cases greatly increasing, will or will not have the same general direction with other like momenta; and whether it may not join them in presently producing an aggregate energy working changes never thought of. Dwelling only on the effects of his particular stream of legislation, and not observing how such other streams already existing, and still other streams which will follow his initiative, pursue the same average course, it never occurs to him that they may presently unite into a voluminous flood utterly changing the face of things. Or to leave figures for a more literal statement, he is unconscious of the truth that he is helping to form a certain type of social organization, and that kindred measures, effecting kindred changes of organization, tend with ever-increasing force to make that type general; until, passing a certain point, the proclivity towards it becomes irresistible. Just as each society aims when possible to produce in other societies a structure akin to its own—just as among the Greeks, the Spartans and the Athenians struggled to spread their respective political institutions, or as, at the time of the

French Revolution, the European absolute monarchies aimed to re-establish absolute monarchy in France while the Republic encouraged the formation of other republics; so within every society, each species of structure tends to propagate itself. Just as the system of voluntary cooperation by companies, associations, unions, to achieve business ends and other ends, spreads throughout a community; so does the antagonistic system of compulsory cooperation under State-agencies spread; and the larger becomes its extension the more power of spreading it gets. The question of questions for the politician should ever be—"What type of social structure am I tending to produce?" But this is a question he never entertains.

Here we will entertain it for him. Let us now observe the general course of recent changes, with the accompanying current of ideas, and see whither they are carrying us.

The blank form of an inquiry daily made is—"We have already done this; why should we not do that?" And the regard for precedent suggested by it, is ever pushing on regulative legislation. Having had brought within their sphere of operation more and more numerous businesses, the Acts restricting hours of employment and dictating the treatment of workers are now to be made applicable to shops. From inspecting lodging-houses to limit the numbers of occupants and enforce sanitary conditions, we have passed to inspecting all houses below a certain rent in which there are members of more than one family, and are now passing to a kindred inspection

of all small houses.[6] The buying and working of tele-
graphs by the State is made a reason for urging that the
State should buy and work the railways. Supplying children with food for their minds by public agency is being
followed in some cases by supplying food for their bodies; and after the practice has been made gradually more
general, we may anticipate that the supply, now proposed to be made gratis in the one case, will eventually
be proposed to be made gratis in the other: the argument
that good bodies as well as good minds are needful to
make good citizens, being logically urged as a reason for
the extension.[7] And then, avowedly proceeding on the
precedents furnished by the church, the school, and the
reading-room, all publicly provided, it is contended that
"pleasure, in the sense it is now generally admitted,
needs legislating for and organizing at least as much as
work."[8]

Not precedent only prompts this spread, but also the
necessity which arises for supplementing ineffective
measures, and for dealing with the artificial evils continually caused. Failure does not destroy faith in the agencies employed, but merely suggests more stringent use

---

[6] See letter of Local Government Board, *The Times*, 2 January 1884.
[7] Verification comes more promptly than I expected. This article has been
standing in type since 30 January, and in the interval, namely on 13
March, [the article was published on 1 April], the London School Board
resolved to apply for authority to use local charitable funds for supplying
gratis meals and clothing to indigent children. Presently the definition
of "indigent" will be widened; more children will be included, and more
funds asked for.
[8] *Fortnightly Review*, January 1884, p. 21.

of such agencies or wider ramifications of them. Laws to check intemperance, beginning in early times and coming down to our own times, not having done what was expected, there come demands for more thorough-going laws, locally preventing the sale altogether; and here, as in America, these will doubtless be followed by demands that prevention shall be made universal. All the many appliances for "stamping out" epidemic diseases not having succeeded in preventing outbreaks of smallpox, fevers, and the like, a further remedy is applied for in the shape of police-power to search houses for diseased persons, and authority for medical officers to examine any one they think fit, to see whether he or she is suffering from an infectious or contagious malady. Habits of improvidence having for generations been cultivated by the Poor-Law, and the improvident enabled to multiply, the evils produced by compulsory charity are now proposed to be met by compulsory insurance.

The extension of this policy, causing extension of corresponding ideas, fosters everywhere the tacit assumption that Government should step in whenever anything is not going right. "Surely you would not have this misery continue!" exclaims someone, if you hint a demurrer to much that is now being said and done. Observe what is implied by this exclamation. It takes for granted, first, that all suffering ought to be prevented, which is not true: much of the suffering is curative, and prevention of it is prevention of a remedy. In the second place, it takes for granted that every evil can be removed: the truth being that, with the existing defects of human nature, many evils can only be thrust out of one place or form into another place or form—often being increased by the change. The exclamation also implies the unhesitating belief, here especially concerning us, that evils of all kinds should be dealt with by the State. There does not occur the inquiry whether there are at work other agencies capable of dealing with evils, and whether the evils in question may not be among those which are best dealt with by these other agencies. And obviously, the more numerous governmental interventions become, the more confirmed does this habit of thought grow, and the more loud and perpetual the demands for intervention.

Every extension of the regulative policy involves an addition to the regulative agents—a further growth of officialism and an increasing power of the organization formed of officials. Take a pair of scales with many shot in the one and a few in the other. Lift shot after shot out of the loaded scale and put it into the unloaded scale. Presently you will produce a balance; and if you go on, the position of the scales will be reversed. Suppose the beam to be unequally divided, and let the lightly loaded scale be at the end of a very long arm; then the transfer of each shot, producing a much greater effect, will far sooner bring about a change of position. I use the figure to illustrate what results from transferring one individual after another from the regulated mass of the community to the regulating structures. The transfer weakens the one and strengthens the other in a far greater degree than is implied by the relative change of numbers. A comparatively small body of officials, coherent, having common interests, and acting under central authority, has an immense advantage over an incoherent public which has no settled policy, and can be brought to act unitedly only under strong provocation. Hence an organization of officials, once passing a certain stage of growth, becomes less and less resistible; as we see in the bureaucracies of the Continent.

Not only does the power of resistance of the regulated part decrease in a geometrical ratio as the regulating part increases, but the private interests of many in the regulated part itself, make the change of ratio still more rapid. In every circle conversations show that now, when the passing of competitive examinations renders them eligible for the public service, youths are being educated in such ways that they may pass them and get employment under Government. One consequence is that men who might otherwise reprobate further growth of officialism, are led to look on it with tolerance, if not favourably, as offering possible careers for those dependent on them and those related to them. Any one who remembers the numbers of upper-class and middle-class families anxious to place their children, will see that no small encouragement to the spread of legislative control is now coming from those who, but for the personal interests thus arising, would be hostile to it.

This pressing desire for careers is enforced by the preference for careers which are thought respectable. "Even should his salary be small, his occupation will be that of a gentleman," thinks the father, who wants to get a Government-clerkship for his son. And his relative dignity of State-servant as compared with those occupied in business increases as the administrative organization becomes a larger and more powerful element in society, and tends more and more to fix the standard of honour. The prevalent ambition with a young Frenchman is to get some small official post in his locality, to rise thence to a place in the local centre of government, and finally to reach some head-office in Paris. And in Russia, where that university of State-regulation which characterizes the militant type of society has been carried furthest, we see this ambition pushed to its extreme. Says Mr. Wallace, quoting a passage from a play: "All men, even shopkeepers and cobblers, aim at becoming officers, and the man who has passed his whole life without official rank seems to be not a human being."[9]

These various influences working from above downwards, meet with an increasing response of expectations and solicitations proceeding from below upwards. The hard-worked and over-burdened who form the great majority, and still more the incapables perpetually helped who are ever led to look for more help, are ready supporters of schemes which promise them this or the other benefit of State-agency, and ready believers of those who tell them that such benefits can be given, and ought to be given. They listen with eager faith to all builders of political air-castles, from Oxford graduates down to Irish irreconcilables; and every additional tax-supported appliance for their welfare raises hopes of further ones. Indeed the more numerous public instrumentalities become, the more is there generated in citizens the notion that everything is to be done for them, and

---

[9] *Russia*, 422.

nothing by them. Each generation is made less familiar with the attainment of desired ends by individual actions or private combinations, and more familiar with the attainment of them by governmental agencies; until, eventually, governmental agencies come to be thought of as the only available agencies. This result was well shown in the recent Trades-Unions Congress at Paris. The English delegates, reporting to their constituents, said that between themselves and their foreign colleagues "the point of difference was the extent to which the State should be asked to protect labour"; reference being thus made to the fact, conspicuous in the reports of the proceedings, that the French delegates always invoked governmental power as the only means of satisfying their wishes.

The diffusion of education has worked, and will work still more, in the same direction. "We must educate our masters," is the well-known saying of a Liberal who opposed the last extension of the franchise. Yes, if the education were worthy to be so called, and were relevant to the political enlightenment needed, much might be hoped from it. But knowing rules of syntax, being able to add up correctly, having geographical information, and a memory stocked with the dates of kings' accessions and generals' victories, no more implies fitness to form political conclusions than acquirement of skill in drawing implies expertness in telegraphing, or than ability to play cricket implies proficiency on the violin. "Surely," rejoins someone, "facility in reading opens the way to political knowledge." Doubtless; but will the way be followed? Table-talk proves that nine out of ten people read what amuses them rather than what instructs them; and proves, also, that the last thing they read is something which tells them disagreeable truths or dispels groundless hopes. That popular education results in an extensive reading of publications which foster pleasant illusions rather than of those which insist on hard realities, is beyond question. Says "A Mechanic," writing in the *Pall Mall Gazette* of 3 December 1883:

> Improved education instils the desire for culture—culture instils the desire for many things as yet quite beyond working men's reach . . . in the furious competition to which the present age is given up they are utterly impossible to the poorer classes; hence they are discontented with things as they are, and the more educated the more discontented. Hence, too, Mr. Ruskin and Mr. Morris are regarded as true prophets by many of us.

And that the connexion of cause and effect here alleged is a real one, we may see clearly enough in the present state of Germany.

Being possessed of electoral power, as are now the mass of those who are thus led to nurture sanguine anticipations of benefits to be obtained by social reorganization, it results that whoever seeks their votes must at least refrain from exposing their mistaken beliefs; even if he does not yield to the temptation to express agreement with them. Every candidate for Parliament is prompted to propose or support some new piece of *ad captandum* legislation. Nay, even the chiefs of parties—those anxious to retain office and those to wrest it from them—severally aim to get adherents by outbidding one another. Each seeks popularity by promising more than his opponent has promised, as we have lately seen. And then, as divisions in Parliament show us, the traditional loyalty to leaders overrides questions concerning the intrinsic propriety of proposed measures. Representatives are unconscientious enough to vote for Bills which they believe to be wrong in principle, because party-needs and regard for the next election demand it. And thus a vicious policy is strengthened even by those who see its viciousness.

Meanwhile there goes on out-of-doors an active propaganda to which all these influences are ancillary. Communistic theories, partially indorsed by one Act of Parliament after another, and tacitly if not avowedly favoured by numerous public men seeking supporters, are being advocated more and more vociferously by popular leaders, and urged on by organized societies. There is the movement for land-nationalization which, aiming at a system of land-tenure equitable in the abstract, is, as all the world knows, pressed by Mr. George and his friends with avowed disregard for the just claims of existing owners, and as the basis of a scheme going more than half-way to State-socialism. And then there is the thorough-going Democratic Federation of Mr. Hyndman and his adherents. We are told by them that "the handful of marauders who now hold possession [of the land] have and can have no right save brute force against the tens of millions whom they wrong." They exclaim against "the shareholders who have been allowed to lay hands upon (!) our great railway communications." They condemn "above all, the active capitalist class, the loan-mongers, the farmers, the mine exploiters, the contractors, the middlemen, the factory-lords—these, the modern slave drivers" who exact "more and yet more surplus value out of the wage-slaves whom they employ." And they think it "high time" that trade should be "removed from the control of individual greed."[10]

It remains to point out that the tendencies thus variously displayed, are being strengthened by press advocacy, daily more pronounced. Journalists, always chary of saying that which is distasteful to their readers, are some of them going with the stream and adding to its force. Legislative meddlings which they would once have condemned they now pass in silence, if they do not advocate them; and they speak of *laissez-faire* as an exploded doctrine. "People are no longer frightened at the thought of socialism," is the statement which meets us one day. On another day, a town which does not adopt the Free Libraries Act is sneered at as being alarmed by a measure so moderately communistic. And then, along with editorial assertions that this economic evolution is coming and must be accepted, there is prominence given to the contributions of its advocates. Meanwhile those who regard the recent course of legislation as disastrous, and see that its future course is likely to be still more disastrous, are being reduced to silence by the belief that it is useless to reason with people in a state of political intoxication.

See, then, the many concurrent causes which threaten continually to accelerate the transformation now going on. There is that spread of regulation caused by following precedents, which become the more authoritative

---

[10] *Socialism made Plain.* Reeves, 185 Fleet Street.

the further the policy is carried. There is that increasing need for administrative compulsions and restraints, which results from the unforeseen evils and shortcomings of preceding compulsions and restraints. Moreover, every additional State-interference strengthens the tacit assumption that it is the duty of the State to deal with all evils and secure all benefits. Increasing power of a growing administrative organization is accompanied by decreasing power of the rest of the society to resist its further growth and control. The multiplication of careers opened by a developing bureaucracy, tempts members of the classes regulated by it to favour its extension, as adding to the chances of safe and respectable places for their relatives. The people at large, led to look on benefits received through public agencies as gratis benefits, have their hopes continually excited by the prospects of more. A spreading education, furthering the diffusion of pleasing errors rather than of stern truths, renders such hopes both stronger and more general. Worse still, such hopes are ministered to by candidates for public choice, to augment their chances of success; and leading statesmen, in pursuit of party ends, bid for popular favour by countenancing them. Getting repeated justifications from new laws harmonizing with their doctrines, political enthusiasts and unwise philanthropists push their agitations with growing confidence and success. Journalism, ever responsive to popular opinion, daily strengthens it by giving it voice; while counter-opinion, more and more discouraged, finds little utterance.

Thus influences of various kinds conspire to increase corporate action and decrease individual action. And the change is being on all sides aided by schemers, each of whom thinks only of his pet plan and not at all of the general reorganization which his plan, joined with others such, are working out. It is said that the French Revolution devoured its own children. Here, an analogous catastrophe seems not unlikely. The numerous socialistic changes made by Act of Parliament, joined with the numerous others presently to be made, will by-and-by be all merged in State-socialism—swallowed in the vast wave which they have little by little raised.

"But why is this change described as 'the coming slavery'?" is a question which many will still ask. The reply is simple. All socialism involves slavery.

What is essential to the idea of a slave? We primarily think of him as one who is owned by another. To be more than nominal, however, the ownership must be shown by control of the slave's actions—a control which is habitually for the benefit of the controller. That which fundamentally distinguishes the slave is that he labours under coercion to satisfy another's desires. The relation admits of sundry gradations. Remembering that originally the slave is a prisoner whose life is at the mercy of his captor, it suffices here to note that there is a harsh form of slavery in which, treated as an animal, he has to expend his entire effort for his owner's advantage. Under a system less harsh, though occupied chiefly in working for his owner, he is allowed a short time in which to work for himself, and some ground on which to grow extra food. A further amelioration gives him power to sell the produce of his plot and keep the proceeds. Then we come to the still more moderated form which commonly arises where, having been a free man working on his own land, conquest turns him into what we distinguish as a serf; and he has to give to his owner each year a fixed amount of labour or produce, or both: retaining the rest himself. Finally, in some cases, as in Russia before serfdom was abolished, he is allowed to leave his owner's estate and work or trade for himself elsewhere, under the condition that he shall pay an annual sum. What is it which, in these cases, leads us to qualify our conception of the slavery as more or less severe? Evidently the greater or smaller extent to which effort is compulsorily expended for the benefit of another instead of for self-benefit. If all the slave's labour is for his owner the slavery is heavy, and if but little it is light. Take now a further step. Suppose an owner dies, and his estate with its slaves comes into the hands of trustees; or suppose the estate and everything on it to be bought by a company; is the condition of the slave any the better if the amount of his compulsory labour remains the same? Suppose that for a company we substitute the community; does it make any difference to the slave if the time he has to work for others is as great, and the time left for himself is as small, as before? The essential question is—How much is he compelled to labour for other benefit than his own, and how much can he labour for his own benefit? The degree of his slavery varies according to the ratio between that which he is forced to yield up and that which he is allowed to retain; and it matters not whether his master is a single person or a society. If, without option, he has to labour for the society, and receives from the general stock such portion as the society awards him, he becomes a slave to the society Socialistic arrangements necessitate an enslavement of this kind; and towards such an enslavement many recent measures, and still more the measures advocated, are carrying us. Let us observe, first, their proximate effects, and then their ultimate effects.

The policy initiated by the Industrial Dwellings Acts admits of development, and will develop. Where municipal bodies turn house-builders, they inevitably lower the values of houses otherwise built, and check the supply of more. Every dictation respecting modes of building and conveniences to be provided, diminishes the builder's profit, and prompts him to use his capital where the profit is not thus diminished. So, too, the owner, already finding that small houses entail much labour and many losses—already subject to troubles of inspection and interference, and to consequent costs, and having his property daily rendered a more undesirable investment, is prompted to sell; and as buyers are for like reasons deterred, he has to sell at a loss. And now these still-multiplying regulations, ending, it may be, as Lord Grey proposes, in one requiring the owner to maintain the salubrity of his houses by evicting dirty tenants, and thus adding to his other responsibilities that of inspector of nuisances, must further prompt sales and further deter purchasers: so necessitating greater depreciation. What must happen? The multiplication of houses, and especially small houses, being increasingly checked, there must come an increasing demand upon the local authority to make up for the deficient supply.

More and more the municipal or kindred body will have
to build houses, or to purchase houses rendered unsale-
able to private persons in the way shown—houses
which, greatly lowered in value as they must become,
it will, in many cases, pay to buy rather than to build
new ones. Nay, this process must work in a double way;
since every entailed increase of local taxation still further
depreciates property.[11] And then when in towns this
process has gone so far as to make the local authority the
chief owner of houses, there will be a good precedent
for publicly providing houses for the rural population,
as proposed in the Radical programme,[12] and as urged
by the Democratic Federation; which insists on "the
compulsory construction of healthy artisans' and agricultural labourers' dwellings in proportion to the population." Manifestly, the tendency of that which has
been done, is being done, and is presently to be done,
is to approach the socialistic ideal in which the community is sole house-proprietor.

Such, too, must be the effect of the daily-growing policy on the tenure and utilization of the land. More nu-

---

[11] If any one thinks such fears are groundless, let him contemplate the
fact that from 1867–8 to 1880–1, our annual local expenditure for the
United Kingdom has grown from £36,132,834 to £63,276,283; and that
during the same 13 years, the municipal expenditure in England and
Wales alone, has grown from 13 millions to 30 millions a year! How the
increase of public burdens will join with other causes in bringing about
public ownership, is shown by a statement made by Mr. W. Rathbone,
M.P., to which my attention has been drawn since the above paragraph
was in type. He says, "within my own experience, local taxation in New
York has risen from 12s.6d. per cent. to £2 12s. 6d. per cent. on the capital
of its citizens—a charge which would more than absorb the whole income
of an average English landlord."—*Nineteenth Century*, February 1883.
[12] *Fortnightly Review*, November 1883, pp. 619–20.

merous public benefits, to be achieved by more numerous public agencies, at the cost of augmented public burdens, must increasingly deduct from the returns on land; until, as the depreciation in value becomes greater and greater, the resistance to change of tenure becomes less and less. Already, as everyone knows, there is in many places difficulty in obtaining tenants, even at greatly reduced rents; and land of inferior fertility in some cases lies idle, or when farmed by the owner is often farmed at a loss. Clearly the profit on capital invested in land is not such that taxes, local and general, can be greatly raised to support extended public administrations, without an absorption of it which will prompt owners to sell, and make the best of what reduced price they can get by emigrating and buying land not subject to heavy burdens; as, indeed, some are now doing. This process, carried far, must have the result of throwing inferior land out of cultivation; after which there will be raised more generally the demand made by Mr. Arch, who, addressing the Radical Association of Brighton lately, and, contending that existing landlords do not make their land adequately productive for the public benefit, said "he should like the present Government to pass a Compulsory Cultivation Bill": an applauded proposal which he justified by instancing compulsory vaccination (thus illustrating the influence of precedent). And this demand will be pressed, not only by the need for making the land productive, but also by the need for employing the rural population. After the Government has extended the practice of hiring the unemployed to work on deserted lands, or lands acquired at nominal prices, there will be reached a stage whence there is but a small further step to that arrangement which, in the programme of the Democratic Federation, is to follow nationalization of the land—the "organization of agricultural and industrial armies under State control on co-operative principles."

To one who doubts whether such a revolution may be so reached, facts may be cited showing its likelihood. In Gaul, during the decline of the Roman Empire, "so numerous were the receivers in comparison with the payers, and so enormous the weight of taxation, that the labourer broke down, the plains became deserts, and woods grew where the plough had been."[13] In like manner, when the French Revolution was approaching, the public burdens had become such, that many farms remained uncultivated and many were deserted: one-quarter of the soil was absolutely lying waste; and in some provinces one-half was in heath.[14] Nor have we been without incidents of a kindred nature at home. Besides the facts that under the old Poor Law the rates had in some parishes risen to half the rental, and that in various places farms were lying idle, there is the fact that in one case the rates had absorbed the whole proceeds of the soil.

> At Cholesbury, in Buckinghamshire, in 1832, the poor rate "suddenly ceased in consequence of the impossibility to continue its collection, the landlords have given up their rents, the farmers their tenancies, and the clergyman his glebe and his tithes. The clergyman, Mr. Jeston, states that in October 1832, the parish officers threw up their books, and the poor assem-

---

[13] Lactant. *De M. Persecut.*, cc. 7, 23.
[14] Taine, *L'Ancien Régime*, pp. 337–8 (in the English Translation).

bled in a body before his door while he was in bed, asking for advice and food. Partly from his own small means, partly from the charity of neighbours, and partly by rates in aid, imposed on the neighbouring parishes, they were for some time supported."[15]

And the Commissioners add that "the benevolent rector recommends that the whole of the land should be divided among the able-bodied paupers": hoping that after help afforded for two years they might be able to maintain themselves. These facts, giving colour to the prophecy made in Parliament that continuance of the old Poor Law for another thirty years would throw the land out of cultivation, clearly show that increase of public burdens may end in forced cultivation under public control.

Then, again, comes State-ownership of railways. Already this exists to a large extent on the Continent. Already we have had here a few years ago loud advocacy of it. And now the cry, which was raised by sundry politicians and publicists, is taken up afresh by the Democratic Federation; which proposes "State-appropriation of railways, with or without compensation." Evidently pressure from above joined by pressure from below, is likely to effect this change dictated by the policy everywhere spreading; and with it must come many attendant changes. For railway-proprietors, at first owners and workers of railways only, have become masters of numerous businesses directly or indirectly connected with

---

[15] *Report of Commissioners for Inquiry into the Administration and Practical Operation of the Poor Laws*, p. 37. 20 February 1834.

railways; and these will have to be purchased. Already exclusive letter-carrier, exclusive transmitter of telegrams, and on the way to become exclusive carrier of parcels, the State will not only be exclusive carrier of passengers, goods, and minerals, but will add to its present various trades many other trades. Even now, besides erecting its naval and military establishments and building harbours, docks, break-waters, etc., it does the work of ship-builder, cannon-founder, small-arms maker, manufacturer of ammunition, army-clothier and boot-maker; and when the railways have been appropriated "with or without compensation," as the Democratic Federationists say, it will have to become locomotive-engine-builder, carriage-maker, tarpaulin and grease manufacturer, passenger-vessel owner, coal-miner, stone-quarrier, omnibus proprietor, etc. Meanwhile its local lieutenants, the municipal governments, already in many places suppliers of water, gas-makers, owners and workers of tramways, proprietors of baths, will doubtless have undertaken various other businesses. And when the State, directly or by proxy, has thus come into possession of, or has established, numerous concerns for wholesale production and for wholesale distribution, there will be good precedents for extending its function to retail distribution: following such an example, say, as is offered by the French Government, which has long been a retail tobacconist.

Evidently then, the changes made, the changes in progress, and the changes urged, will carry us not only towards State-ownership of land and dwellings and means of communication, all to be administered and worked by State-agents, but towards State-usurpation of all industries: the private forms of which, disadvantaged more and more in competition with the State, which can arrange everything for its own convenience, will more and more die away; just as many voluntary schools have, in presence of Board-schools. And so will be brought about the desired ideal of the socialists.

And now when there has been compassed this desired ideal, which "practical" politicians are helping socialists to reach, and which is so tempting on that bright side which socialists contemplate, what must be the accompanying shady side which they do not contemplate? It is a matter of common remark, often made when a marriage is impending, that those possessed by strong hopes habitually dwell on the promised pleasures and think nothing of the accompanying pains. A further exemplification of this truth is supplied by these political enthusiasts and fanatical revolutionists. Impressed with the miseries existing under our present social arrangements, and not regarding these miseries as caused by the ill-working of a human nature but partially adapted to the social state, they imagine them to be forthwith curable by this or that rearrangement. Yet, even did their plans succeed it could only be by substituting one kind of evil for another. A little deliberate thought would show that under their proposed arrangements, their liberties must be surrendered in proportion as their material welfares were cared for.

For no form of cooperation, small or great, can be carried on without regulation, and an implied submission

to the regulating agencies. Even one of their own organizations for effecting social changes yields them proof.
It is compelled to have its councils, its local and general
officers, its authoritative leaders, who must be obeyed
under penalty of confusion and failure. And the experience of those who are loudest in their advocacy of a
new social order under the paternal control of a Government, shows that even in private voluntarily-formed societies, the power of the regulative organization becomes
great, if not irresistible: often, indeed, causing grumbling and restiveness among those controlled. Trades-
unions which carry on a kind of industrial war in defence
of workers' interests *versus* employers' interests, find
that subordination almost military in its strictness is
needful to secure efficient action; for divided councils
prove fatal to success. And even in bodies of cooperators, formed for carrying on manufacturing or distributing businesses, and not needing that obedience to
leaders which is required where the aims are offensive
or defensive, it is still found that the administrative
agency gains such supremacy that there arise complaints
about "the tyranny of organization." Judge then what
must happen when, instead of relatively small combinations, to which men may belong or not as they please,
we have a national combination in which each citizen
finds himself incorporated, and from which he cannot
separate himself without leaving the country. Judge
what must under such conditions become the despotism
of a graduated and centralized officialism, holding in its
hands the resources of the community, and having behind it whatever amount of force it finds requisite to

carry out its decrees and maintain what it calls order. Well may Prince Bismarck display leanings towards State-socialism.

And then after recognizing, as they must if they think out their scheme, the power possessed by the regulative agency in the new social system so temptingly pictured, let its advocates ask themselves to what end this power must be used. Not dwelling exclusively, as they habitually do, on the material well-being and the mental gratifications to be provided for them by a beneficent administration, let them dwell a little on the price to be paid. The officials cannot create the needful supplies: they can but distribute among individuals that which the individuals have joined to produce. If the public agency is required to provide for them, it must reciprocally require them to furnish the means. There cannot be, as under our existing system, agreement between employer and employed—this the scheme excludes. There must in place of it be command by local authorities over workers, and acceptance by the workers of that which the authorities assign to them. And this, indeed, is the arrangement distinctly, but as it would seem inadvertently, pointed to by the members of the Democratic Federation. For they propose that production should be carried on by "agricultural and industrial *armies* under State-control": apparently not remembering that armies pre-suppose grades of officers, by whom obedience would have to be insisted upon; since otherwise neither order nor efficient work could be ensured. So that each would stand toward the governing agency in the relation of slave to master.

"But the governing agency would be a master which he and others made and kept constantly in check; and one which therefore would not control him or others more than was needful of the benefit of each and all."

To which reply the first rejoinder is that, even if so, each member of the community as an individual would be a slave to the community as a whole. Such a relation has habitually existed in militant communities, even under quasi-popular forms of government. In ancient Greece the accepted principle was that the citizen belonged neither to himself nor to his family, but belonged to his city—the city being with the Greek equivalent to the community. And this doctrine, proper to a state of constant warfare, is a doctrine which socialism unawares re-introduces into a state intended to be purely industrial. The services of each will belong to the aggregate of all; and for these services, such returns will be given as the authorities think proper. So that even if the administration is of the beneficent kind intended to be secured, slavery, however mild, must be the outcome of the arrangement.

A second rejoinder is that the administration will presently become not of the intended kind, and that the slavery will not be mild. The socialist speculation is vitiated by an assumption like that which vitiates the speculations of the "practical" politician. It is assumed that officialism will work as it is intended to work, which it never does. The machinery of Communism, like existing social machinery, has to be framed out of existing human nature; and the defects of existing human nature will generate in the one the same evils as in the other. The love of power, the selfishness, the injustice, the untruthfulness, which often in comparatively short times bring private organizations to disaster, will inevitably, where their effects accumulate from generation to generation, work evils far greater and less remediable; since, vast and complex and possessed of all the resources, the administrative organization once developed and consolidated, must become irresistible. And if there needs proof that the periodic exercise of electoral power would fail to prevent this, it suffices to instance the French Government, which, purely popular in origin, and subject at short intervals to popular judgement, nevertheless tramples on the freedom of citizens to an extent which the English delegates to the late Trades Unions Congress say "is a disgrace to, and an anomaly in, a Republican nation."

The final result would be a revival of despotism. A disciplined army of civil officials, like an army of military officials, gives supreme power to its head—a power which has often led to usurpation, as in medieval Europe and still more in Japan—nay, has thus so led among our neighbours, within our own times. The recent confessions of M. de Maupas have shown how readily a constitutional head, elected and trusted by the whole people, may, with the aid of a few unscrupulous confederates, paralyse the representative body and make himself autocrat. That those who rose to power in a socialistic organization would not scruple to carry out their aims at all costs, we have good reason for concluding. When we find that shareholders who, sometimes gaining but often losing, have made that railway-system

by which national prosperity has been so greatly increased, are spoken of by the council of the Democratic
Federation as having "laid hands" on the means of communication, we may infer that those who directed a socialistic administration might interpret with extreme
perversity the claims of individuals and classes under
their control. And when, further, we find members of
this same council urging that the State should take possession of the railways, "with or without compensation," we may suspect that the heads of the ideal society
desired, would be but little deterred by considerations
of equity from pursuing whatever policy they thought
needful: a policy which would always be one identified
with their own supremacy. It would need but a war with
an adjacent society, or some internal discontent demanding forcible suppression, to at once transform a
socialistic administration into a grinding tyranny like
that of ancient Peru; under which the mass of the people,
controlled by grades of officials, and leading lives that
were inspected out-of-doors and in-doors, laboured for
the support of the organization which regulated them,
and were left with but a bare subsistence for themselves.
And then would be completely revived, under a different form, that régime of status—that system of compulsory cooperation, the decaying tradition of which is
represented by the old Toryism, and towards which the
new Toryism is carrying us back.

"But we shall be on our guard against all that—we
shall take precautions to ward off such disasters," will
doubtless say the enthusiasts. Be they "practical" politicians with their new regulative measures, or commu-

nists with their schemes for re-organizing labour their reply is ever the same: "It is true that plans of kindred nature have, from unforeseen causes or adverse accidents, or the misdeeds of those concerned, been brought to failure; but this time we shall profit by past experiences and succeed." There seems no getting people to accept the truth, which nevertheless is conspicuous enough, that the welfare of a society and the justice of its arrangements are at bottom dependent on the characters of its members; and that improvement in neither can take place without that improvement in character which results from carrying on peaceful industry under the restraints imposed by an orderly social life. The belief, not only of the socialists but also of those so-called Liberals who are diligently preparing the way for them, is that by due skill an ill-working humanity may be framed into well-working institutions. It is a delusion. The defective natures of citizens will show themselves in the bad acting of whatever social structure they are arranged into. There is no political alchemy by which you can get golden conduct out of leaden instincts.

NOTE—Two replies by socialists to the foregoing article have appeared since its publication—*Socialism and Slavery* by H. M. Hyndman, and *Herbert Spencer on Socialism* by Frank Fairman. Notice of them here must be limited to saying that, as usual with antagonists, they ascribe to me opinions which I do not hold. Disapproval of socialism does not, as Mr. Hyndman assumes, necessitate approval of existing arrangements. Many things he reprobates I reprobate quite as much; but I dissent from his remedy. The gentleman who writes under the pseudonym of "Frank Fairman," reproaches me with having receded from that sympathetic defence of the labouring-classes which he finds in *Social Statics;* but I am quite unconscious of any such change as he alleges. Looking with a lenient eye upon the irregularities of those whose lives are hard, by no means involves tolerance of good-for-nothings.

[18]

THE GREAT POLITICAL SUPERSTITION

The great political superstition of the past was the divine right of kings. The great political superstition of the present is the divine right of parliaments. The oil of anointing seems unawares to have dripped from the head of the one on to the heads of the many, and given sacredness to them also and to their decrees.

However irrational we may think the earlier of these beliefs, we must admit that it was more consistent than is the latter. Whether we go back to times when the king was a god, or to times when he was a descendant of a god, or to times when he was god-appointed, we see good reason for passive obedience to his will. When, as under Louis XIV, theologians like Bossuet taught that kings "are gods, and share in a manner the Divine independence," or when it was thought, as by our own Tory party in old days, that "the monarch was the delegate of heaven"; it is clear that, given the premise, the inevitable conclusion was that no bounds could be set

123

to governmental commands. But for the modern belief such a warrant does not exist. Making no pretention to divine descent or divine appointment, a legislative body can show no supernatural justification for its claim to unlimited authority; and no natural justification has ever been attempted. Hence, belief in its unlimited authority is without that consistency which of old characterized belief in a king's unlimited authority.

It is curious how commonly men continue to hold in fact, doctrines which they have rejected in name—retaining the substance after they have abandoned the form. In Theology an illustration is supplied by Carlyle, who, in his student days, giving up, as he thought, the creed of his fathers, rejected its shell only, keeping the contents; and was proved by his conceptions of the world, and man, and conduct, to be still among the sternest of Scotch Calvinists. Similarly, Science furnishes an instance in one who united naturalism in Geology with supernaturalism in Biology—Sir Charles Lyell. While, as the leading expositor of the uniformitarian theory in Geology, he ignored only the Mosaic cosmogony, he long defended that belief in special creations of organic types, for which no other source than the Mosaic cosmogony could be assigned; and only in the latter part of his life surrendered to the arguments of Mr. Darwin. In Politics, as above implied, we have an analogous case. The tacitly-asserted doctrine, common to Tories, Whigs, and Radicals, that governmental authority is unlimited, dates back to times when the law-giver was supposed to have a warrant from God; and it survives still, though the belief that the law-giver has God's warrant has died out. "Oh, an Act of Parliament can do anything," is the reply made to a citizen who questions the legitimacy of some arbitrary State-interference; and the citizen stands paralysed. It does not occur to him to ask the how, and the when, and the whence, of this asserted omnipotence bounded only by physical impossibilities.

Here we will take leave to question it. In default of the justification, once logically valid, that the ruler on Earth being a deputy of the ruler in Heaven, submission to him in all things is a duty, let us ask what reason there is for asserting the duty of submission in all things to a ruling power, constitutional or republican, which has no Heavenly-derived supremacy. Evidently this inquiry commits us to a criticism of past and present theories concerning political authority. To revive questions supposed to be long since settled, may be thought to need some apology; but there is a sufficient apology in the implication above made clear, that the theory commonly accepted is ill-based or unbased.

The notion of sovereignty is that which first presents itself; and a critical examination of this notion, as entertained by those who do not assume the supernatural origin of sovereignty, carries us back to the arguments of Hobbes.

Let us grant Hobbes's postulate that, "during the time men live without a common power to keep them all in awe, they are in that condition which is called war . . . of every man against every man"[1]; though this is not

---

[1] T. Hobbes, *Collected Works*, vol. iii, pp. 112–13.

true, since there are some small uncivilized societies in which, without any "common power to keep them all in awe," men maintain peace and harmony better than it is maintained in societies where such a power exists. Let us suppose him to be right, too, in assuming that the rise of a ruling man over associated men, results from their desires to preserve order among themselves; though, in fact, it habitually arises from the need for subordination to a leader in war, defensive or offensive, and has originally no necessary, and often no actual, relation to the preservation of order among the combined individuals. Once more, let us admit the indefensible assumption that to escape the evils of chronic conflicts, which must otherwise continue among them, the members of a community enter into a "pact or covenant," by which they all bind themselves to surrender their primitive freedom of action, and subordinate themselves to the will of an autocrat agreed upon:[2] accepting, also, the implication that their descendants for ever are bound by the covenant which remote ancestors made for them. Let us, I say, not object to these data, but pass to the conclusions Hobbes draws. He says:

> For where no covenant hath preceded, there hath no right been transferred, and every man has a right to everything; and consequently, no action can be unjust. But when a covenant is made, then to break it is *unjust:* and the definition of INJUSTICE, is no other than *the not performance of covenant.* . . . Therefore before the names of just and unjust can have place, there must be some coercive power, to compel men equally to the performance of their covenants, by the terror of some punishment,

[2] ibid., p. 159.

greater than the benefit they expect by the breach of their covenant.[3]

Were people's characters in Hobbes's day really so bad as to warrant his assumption that none would perform their covenants in the absence of a coercive power and threatened penalties? In our day "the names of just and unjust can have place" quite apart from recognition of any coercive power. Among my friends I could name several whom I would implicitly trust to perform their covenants without any "terror of such punishment"; and over whom the requirements of justice would be as imperative in the absence of a coercive power as in its presence. Merely noting, however, that this unwarranted assumption vitiates Hobbe's argument for State-authority, and accepting both his premises and conclusion, we have to observe two significant implications. One is that State-authority as thus derived, is a means to an end, and has no validity save as subserving that end: if the end is not subserved, the authority, by the hypothesis, does not exist. The other is that the end for which the authority exists, as thus specified, is the enforcement of justice—the maintenance of equitable relations. The reasoning yields no warrant for other coercion over citizens than that which is required for preventing direct aggressions, and those indirect aggressions constituted by breaches of contract; to which, if we add protection against external enemies, the entire function implied by Hobbes's derivation of sovereign authority is comprehended.

---

[3] Hobbes, *Collected Works*, vol. iii, pp. 130–31.

Hobbes argued in the interests of absolute monarchy. His modern admirer, Austin, had for his aim to drive the authority of law from the unlimited sovereignty of one man, or a number of men, small or large compared with the whole community. Austin was originally in the army; and it has been truly remarked that "the permanent traces left" may be seen in his *Province of Jurisprudence*. When, undeterred by the exasperating pedantries—the endless distinctions and definitions and repetitions—which served but to hide his essential doctrines, we ascertain what these are, it becomes manifest that he assimilates civil authority to military authority; taking for granted that the one, as the other, is above question in respect of both origin and range. To get justification for positive law, he takes us back to the absolute sovereignty of the power imposing it—a monarch, an aristocracy, or that larger body of men who have votes in a democracy; for such a body also, he styles the sovereign, in contast with the remaining portion of the community which, from incapacity or other cause, remains subject. And having affirmed, or rather, taken for granted, the unlimited authority of the body, simple or compound, small or large, which he styles sovereign, he, of course, has no difficulty in deducing the legal validity of its edicts, which he calls positive law. But the problem is simply moved a step further back and there left unsolved. The true question is—Whence the sovereignty? What is the assignable warrant for this unqualified supremacy assumed by one, or by a small number, or by a large number, over the rest? A critic might fitly say—"We will dispense with your process of deriving positive law from unlimited sovereignty: the sequence is obvious enough. But first prove your unlimited sovereignty."

To this demand there is no response. Analyse his assumption, and the doctrine of Austin proves to have no better basis than that of Hobbes. In the absence of admitted divine descent or appointment, neither single-headed ruler nor many-headed ruler can produce such credentials as the claim to unlimited sovereignty implies.

"But surely," will come in deafening chorus the reply, "there is the unquestionable right of the majority, which gives unquestionable right to the parliament it elects."

Yes, now we are coming down to the root of the matter. The divine right of parliaments means the divine right of majorities. The fundamental assumption made by legislators and people alike, is that a majority has powers which have no bounds. This is the current theory which all accept without proof as a self-evident truth. Nevertheless, criticism will, I think, show that this current theory requires a radical modification.

In an essay on "Railway Morals and Railway Policy," published in the *Edinburgh Review* for October, 1854, I had occasion to deal with the question of a majority's powers as exemplified in the conduct of public companies; and I cannot better prepare the way for conclusions presently to be drawn, than by quoting a passage from it:

> Under whatever circumstances, or for whatever ends, a number of men cooperate, it is held that if difference of opinion arises among them, justice requires that the will of the greater number shall be executed rather than that of the smaller num-

ber; and this rule is supposed to be uniformly applicable, be
the question at issue what it may. So confirmed is this conviction, and so little have the ethics of the matter been considered,
that to most this mere suggestion of a doubt will cause some
astonishment. Yet it needs but a brief analysis to show that the
opinion is little better than a political superstition. Instances
may readily be selected which prove, by *reductio ad absurdum*,
that the right of a majority is a purely conditional right, valid
only within specific limits. Let us take a few. Suppose that at
the general meeting of some philanthropic association, it was
resolved that in addition to relieving distress the association
should employ home-missionaries to preach down popery.
Might the subscriptions of Catholics, who had joined the body
with charitable views, be rightfully used for this end? Suppose
that of the members of a book-club, the greater number, thinking that under existing circumstances rifle-practice was more
important than reading, should decide to change the purpose
of their union, and to apply the funds in hand for the purchase
of powder, ball, and targets. Would the rest be bound by this
decision? Suppose that under the excitement of news from Australia, the majority of a Freehold Land Society should determine, not simply to start in a body for the gold-diggings, but
to use their accumulated capital to provide outfits. Would this
appropriation of property be just to the minority? and must
these join the expedition? Scarcely anyone would venture an
affirmative answer even to the first of these questions; much
less to the others. And why? Because everyone must perceive
that by uniting himself with others, no man can equitably be
betrayed into acts utterly foreign to the purpose for which he
joined them. Each of these supposed minorities would properly
reply to those seeking to coerce them: "We combined with you
for a defined object; we gave money and time for the furtherance of that object; on all questions thence arising we tacitly
agreed to conform to the will of the greater number; but we did
not agree to conform on any other questions. If you induce us
to join you by professing a certain end, and then undertake
some other end of which we were not apprised, you obtain our
support under false pretences; you exceed the expressed or
understood compact to which we committed ourselves; and we
are no longer bound by your decisions." Clearly this is the only

rational interpretation of the matter. The general principle underlying the right government of every incorporated body, is, that its members contract with one another severally to submit to the will of the majority in all matters concerning the fulfilment of the objects for which they are incorporated; but in no others. To this extent only can the contract hold. For as it is implied in the very nature of a contract, that those entering into it must know what they contract to do; and as those who unite with others for a specified object, cannot contemplate all the unspecified objects which it is hypothetically possible for the union to undertake; it follows that the contract entered into cannot extend to such unspecified objects. And if there exists no expressed or understood contract between the union and its members respecting unspecified objects, then for the majority to coerce the minority into undertaking them, is nothing less than gross tyranny.

Naturally, if such a confusion of ideas exists in respect of the powers of a majority where the deed of incorporation tacitly limits those powers, still more must there exist such a confusion where there has been no deed of incorporation. Nevertheless the same principle holds. I again emphasize the proposition that the members of an incorporated body are bound "severally to submit to the will of the majority *in all matters concerning the fulfilment of the objects for which they are incorporated; but in no others.*" And I contend that this holds of an incorporated nation as much as of an incorporated company.

"Yes, but," comes the obvious rejoinder, "as there is no deed by which the members of a nation are incorporated—as there neither is, nor ever was, a specification of purposes for which the union was formed, there exist no limits; and, consequently, the power of the majority is unlimited."

Evidently it must be admitted that the hypothesis of

a social contract, either under the shape assumed by Hobbes or under the shape assumed by Rousseau, is baseless. Nay more, it must be admitted that even had such a contract once been formed, it could not be binding on the posterity of those who formed it. Moreover, if any say that in the absence of those limitations to its powers which a deed of incorporation might imply, there is nothing to prevent a' majority from imposing its will on a minority by force, assent must be given—an assent, however, joined with the comment that if the superior force of the majority is its justification, then the superior force of a despot backed by an adequate army, is also justified; the problem lapses. What we here seek is some higher warrant for the subordination of minority to majority than that arising from inability to resist physical coercion. Even Austin, anxious as he is to establish the unquestionable authority of positive law, and assuming, as he does, an absolute sovereignty of some kind, monarchic, aristocratic, constitutional, or popular, as the source of its unquestionable authority, is obliged, in the last resort, to admit a moral limit to its action over the community. While insisting, in pursuance of his rigid theory of sovereignty, that a sovereign body originating from the people "is *legally* free to abridge their political liberty, at its own pleasure or discretion," he allows that "a government may be hindered by *positive morality* from abridging the political liberty which it leaves or grants to its subjects."[4] Hence, we have to find, not a physical justification, but a moral justification, for the supposed absolute power of the majority.

---

[4] *The Province of Jurisprudence Determined.* Second Edition, p. 241.

This will at once draw forth the rejoinder—"Of course, in the absence of any agreement, with its implied limitations, the rule of the majority is unlimited; because it is more just that the majority should have its way than that the minority should have its way." A very reasonable rejoinder this seems until there comes the re-rejoinder. We may oppose to it the equally tenable proposition that, in the absence of an agreement, the supremacy of a majority over a minority does not exist at all. It is cooperation of some kind, from which there arises these powers and obligations of majority and minority; and in the absence of any agreement to cooperate, such powers and obligations are also absent.

Here the argument apparently ends in a deadlock. Under the existing condition of things, no moral origin seems assignable, either for the sovereignty of the majority or for the limitation of its sovereignty. But further consideration reveals a solution of the difficulty. For if, dismissing all thought of any hypothetical agreement to cooperate heretofore made, we ask what would be the agreement into which citizens would now enter with practical unanimity, we get a sufficiently clear answer; and with it a sufficiently clear justification for the rule of the majority inside a certain sphere but not outside that sphere. Let us first observe a few of the limitations which at once become apparent.

Were all Englishmen now asked if they would agree to cooperate for the teaching of religion, and would give the majority power to fix the creed and the forms of worship, there would come a very emphatic "No" from a large part of them. If, in pursuance of a proposal to revive sumptuary laws, the inquiry were made whether they would bind themselves to abide by the will of the majority in respect of the fashions and qualities of their clothes, nearly all of them would refuse. In like manner if (to take an actual question of the day) people were polled to acertain whether, in respect of the beverages they drank, they would accept the decision of the greater number, certainly half, and probably more than half, would be unwilling. Similarly with respect to many other actions which most men now-a-days regard as of purely private concern. Whatever desire there might be to cooperate for carrying on, or regulating, such actions, would be far from a unanimous desire. Manifestly, then, had social cooperation to be commenced by ourselves, and had its purposes to be specified before consent to cooperate could be obtained, there would be large parts of human conduct in respect of which cooperation would be declined; and in respect of which, consequently, no authority by the majority over the minority could be rightly exercised.

Turn now to the converse question—For what ends would all men agree to cooperate? None will deny that for resisting invasion the agreement would be practically unanimous. Excepting only the Quakers, who, having done highly useful work in their time, are now dying out, all would unite for defensive war (not, however, for offensive war); and they would, by so doing, tacitly bind themselves to conform to the will of the majority in respect of measure directed to that end. There would be practical unanimity, also, in the agreement to cooperate for defence against internal enemies as against external enemies. Omitting criminals, all must wish to have person and property adequately protected. Each citizen desires to preserve his life, to preserve things which conduce to maintenance and enjoyment of his life, and to preserve intact his liberties both of using these things and getting further such. It is obvious to him that he cannot do all this if he acts alone. Against foreign invaders he is powerless unless he combines with his fellows; and the business of protecting himself against domestic invaders, if he did not similarly combine, would be alike onerous, dangerous, and inefficient. In one other co-operation all are interested—use of the territory they inhabit. Did the primitive communal ownership survive, there would survive the primitive communal control of the uses to be made of land by individuals or by groups of them; and decisions of the majority would rightly prevail repecting the terms on which portions of it might be employed for raising food, making means of communication, and for other purposes. Even at present, though the matter has been complicated by the growth of private landownership, yet, since the State is still supreme owner (every landlord being in law a tenant of the Crown) able to resume possession, or authorize compulsory purchase, at a fair price; the implication is that the will of the majority is valid respecting the modes in which, and conditions under which, parts of the surface or subsurface, may be utilized: involving certain agreements made on behalf of the public with private persons and companies.

Details are not needful here; nor is it needful to discuss that border region lying between these two classes of cases, and to say how much is included in the last and

how much is excluded with the first. For present purposes, it is sufficient to recognize the undeniable truth
that there are numerous kinds of actions in respect of
which men would not, if they were asked, agree with
anything like unanimity to be bound by the will of the
majority; while there are some kinds of actions in respect
of which they would almost unanimously agree to be
thus bound. Here, then, we find a definite warrant for
enforcing the will of the majority within certain limits,
and a definite warrant for denying the authority of its
will beyond those limits.

But evidently, when analysed, the question resolves
itself into the further question—What are the relative
claims of the aggregate and of its units? Are the rights
of the community universally valid against the individual? or has the individual some rights which are valid
against the community? The judgement given on this
point underlies the entire fabric of political convictions
formed, and more especially those convictions which
concern the proper sphere of government. Here, then,
I propose to revive a dormant controversy, with the expectation of reaching a different conclusion from that
which is fashionable.

Says Professor Jevons, in his work, *The State in Relation
to Labour*,—"The first step must be to rid our minds of
the idea that there are any such things in social matters
as abstract rights." Of like character is the belief expressed by Mr. Matthew Arnold in his article on Copyright: "An author has no natural right to a property in

his production. But then neither has he a natural right to anything whatever which he may produce or acquire."[5] So, too, I recently read in a weekly journal of high repute, that "to explain once more that there is no such thing as "natural right" would be a waste of philosophy." And the view expressed in these extracts is commonly uttered by statesmen and lawyers in a way implying that only the unthinking masses hold any other.

One might have expected that utterances to this effect would have been rendered less dogmatic by the knowledge that a whole school of legists on the Continent, maintains a belief diametrically opposed to that maintained by the English school. The idea of *Natur-recht* is the root-idea of German jurisprudence. Now whatever may be the opinion held respecting German philosophy at large, it cannot be characterized as shallow. A doctrine current among a people distinguished above all others as laborious inquiries, and certainly not to be classed with superficial thinkers, should not be dismissed as though it were nothing more than a popular delusion. This, however, by the way. Along with the proposition denied in the above quotations, there goes a counter-proposition affirmed. Let us see what it is; and what results when we go behind it and seek its warrant.

On reverting to Bentham, we find this counter-proposition openly expressed. He tells us that government fulfils its office "by creating rights which it confers upon

---

[5] *Fortnightly Review*, 1880, vol. xxvii, p. 322.

individuals: rights of personal security; rights of protection for honour; rights of property" etc.[6]; Were this doctrine asserted as following from the divine right of kings,
there would be nothing in it manifestly incongruous, did
it come to us from ancient Peru, where the Ynca "was
the source from which everything flowed"[7]; or from
Shoa (Abyssinia), where "of their persons and worldly
substance he [the King] is absolute master"[8]; or from
Dahome, where "all men are slaves to the king"[9]; it
would be consistent enough. But Bentham, far from
being an absolutist like Hobbes, wrote in the interests of
popular rule. In his *Constitutional Code*[10] he fixes the sovereignty in the whole people; arguing that it is best "to
give the sovereign power to the largest possible portion
of those whose greatest happiness is the proper and chosen object," because "this proportion is more apt than
any other that can be proposed" for achievement of that
object.

Mark, now, what happens when we put these two
doctrines together. The sovereign people jointly appoint
representatives, and so create a government; the government thus created, creates rights; and then, having
created rights, it confers them on the separate members
of the sovereign people by which it was itself created.
Here is a marvellous piece of political legerdemain! Mr.
Matthew Arnold, contending, in the article above

---

[6] Bentham's Works (Bowring's edition), vol. i, p. 301.
[7] W. H. Prescott, *Conquest of Peru*, bk i, ch. i.
[8] J. Harris, *Highlands of Æthiopia*, ii, 94.
[9] R. F. Burton, *Mission to Gelele, King of Dahome*, i, p. 226.
[10] Bentham's Works, vol. ix, p. 97.

quoted, that "property is the creation of law," tells us to beware of the "metaphysical phantom of property in itself." Surely, among metaphysical phantoms the most shadowy is this which supposes a thing to be obtained by creating an agent, which creates the thing, and then confers the thing on its own creator!

From whatever point of view we consider it, Bentham's proposition proves to be unthinkable. Government, he says, fulfils its office "by creating rights." Two meanings may be given to the word "creating." It may be supposed to mean the production of something out of nothing; or it may be supposed to mean the giving form and structure to something which already exists. There are many who think that the production of something out of nothing cannot be conceived as effected even by omnipotence; and probably none will assert that the production of something out of nothing is within the competence of a human government. The alternative conception is that a human government creates only in the sense that it shapes something pre-existing. In that case, the question arises—"What is the something pre-existing which it shapes?" Clearly the word "creating" begs the whole question—passes off an illusion on the unwary reader. Bentham was a stickler for definiteness of expression, and in his *Book of Fallacies* has a chapter on "Impostor-terms." It is curious that he should have furnished so striking an illustration of the perverted belief which an impostor-term may generate.

But now let us overlook these various impossibilities of thought, and seek the most defensible interpretation of Bentham's view.

It may be said that the totality of all powers and rights, originally exists as an undivided whole in the sovereign people; and that this undivided whole is given in trust (as Austin would say) to a ruling power, appointed by the sovereign people, for the purpose of distribution. If as we have seen, the proposition that rights are created is simply a figure of speech; then the only intelligible construction of Bentham's view is that a multitude of individuals, who severally wish to satisfy their desires, and have, as an aggregate, possession of all the sources of satisfaction, as well as power over all individual actions, appoint a government, which declares the ways in which, and the conditions under which, individual actions may be carried on and the satisfactions obtained. Let us observe the implications. Each man exists in two capacities. In his private capacity he is subject to the government. In his public capacity he is one of the sovereign people who appoint the government. That is to say, in his private capacity he is one of those to whom rights are given; and in his public capacity he is one of those who, through the government they appoint, give the rights. Turn this abstract statement into a concrete statement, and see what it means. Let the community consist of a million men, who, by the hypothesis, are not only joint possessors of the inhabited region, but joint possessors of all liberties of action and appropriation: the only right recognized being that of the aggregate to everything. What follows? Each person, while not owning any product of his own labour, has, as a unit in the sovereign body, a millionth part of the ownership of the products of all others' labour. This is an unavoidable implication. As the government, in Bentham's view, is but an agent; the rights it confers are rights given to it in trust by the sovereign people. If so, such rights must be possessed *en bloc* by the sovereign people before the government, in fulfilment of its trust, confers them on individuals; and, if so, each individual has a millionth portion of these rights in his public capacity, while he has no rights in his private capacity. These he gets only when all the rest of the million join to endow him with them; while he joins to endow with them every other member of the million!

Thus, in whatever way we interpret it, Bentham's proposition leaves us in a plexus of absurdities.

Even though ignoring the opposite opinion of German and French writers on jurisprudence, and even without an analysis which proves their own opinion to be untenable, Bentham's disciples might have been led to treat less cavalierly the doctrine of natural rights. For sundry groups of social phenomena unite to prove that this doctrine is well warranted, and the doctrine they set against it unwarranted.

Tribes all over the world show us that before definite government arises, conduct is regulated by customs. The Bechuanas are controlled by "long-acknowledged customs."[11] Among the Korranna Hottentots, who only "tolerate their chiefs rather than obey them,"[12] "when ancient usages are not in the way, every man seems to

---

[11] W. J. Burchell, *Travels into the Interior of Southern Africa*, vol. i, p. 544.
[12] Arbousset and Daumas, *Voyage of Exploration*, p. 27.

act as is right in his own eyes."[13] The Araucanians are guided by "nothing more than primordial usages or tacit conventions."[14] Among the Kirghizes the judgements of the elders are based on "universally-recognized customs."[15] Similarly of the Dyaks, Rajah Brooke says that "custom seems simply to have become the law; and breaking custom leads to a fine."[16] So sacred are immemorial customs with the primitive man, that he never dreams of questioning their authority; and when government arises, its power is limited by them. In Madagascar the king's word suffices only "where there is no law, custom, or precedent."[17] Raffles tells us that in Java "the customs of the country"[18] restrain the will of the ruler. In Sumatra, too, the people do not allow their chiefs to "alter their ancient usages."[19] Nay, occasionally, as in Ashantee, "the attempt to change some customs" has caused a king's dethronement.[20] Now, among the customs which we thus find to be pre-governmental, and which subordinate governmental power when it is established, are those which recognize certain individual rights—rights to act in certain ways and possess certain things. Even where the recognition of property is least developed, there is proprietorship of weapons, tools,

---

[13] G. Thompson, *Travels and Adventures in Southern Africa*, vol. ii, p. 30.

[14] G. A. Thompson, *Alcedo's Geographical and Historical Dictionary of America*, vol. i, p. 405.

[15] Alex. Michie, *Siberian Overland Route*, p. 248.

[16] C. Brooke, *Ten Years in Sarawak*, vol. i, p. 129.

[17] W. Ellis, *History of Madagascar*, vol. i, p. 377.

[18] Sir T. S. Raffles, *History of Java*, i, 274.

[19] W. Marsden, *History of Sumatra*, p. 217.

[20] J. Beecham, *Ashantee and the Gold Coast*, p. 90.

and personal ornaments; and, generally, the recognition goes far beyond this. Among such North American Indians as the Snakes, who are without Government, there is private ownership of horses. By the Chippewayans, "who have no regular government," game taken in private traps "is considered as private property."[21] Kindred facts concerning huts, utensils, and other personal belongings, might be brought in evidence from accounts of the Ahts, the Comanches, the Esquimaux, and the Brazilian Indians. Among various uncivilized peoples, custom has established the claim to the crop grown on a cleared plot of ground, though not to the ground itself; and the Todas, who are wholly without political organization, make a like distinction between ownership of cattle and of land. Kolff's statement respecting "the peaceful Arafuras" well sums up the evidence. They "recognize the right of property in the fullest sense of the word, without there being any [other] authority among them than the decisions of their elders, according to the customs of their forefathers."[22] But even without seeking proofs among the uncivilized, sufficient proofs are furnished by early stages of the civilized. Bentham and his followers seem to have forgotten that our own common law is mainly an embodiment of "the customs of the realm." It did not give definite shape to that which it found existing. Thus, the fact and the fiction are exactly opposite to what they allege. The fact is that property was well recognized before law existed; the fiction is that "property is the creation of law." These writers and

---

[21] H. R. Schoolcraft, *Expedition to the Sources of the Mississippi River,* v, 177.
[22] G. W. Earl's *Kolff's Voyage of the Dourga,* p. 161.

statesmen who with so much scorn undertake to instruct the ignorant herd, themselves stand in need of instruction.

Considerations of another class might alone have led them to pause. Were it true, as alleged by Bentham, that Government fulfils its office "by creating rights which it confers on individuals"; then, the implication would be, that there should be nothing approaching to uniformity in the rights conferred by different governments. In the absence of a determining cause over-ruling their decisions, the probabilities would be many to one against considerable correspondence among their decisions. But there is very great correspondence. Look where we may, we find that governments interdict the same kinds of aggressions; and, by implication, recognize the same kinds of claims. They habitually forbid homicide, theft, adultery: thus asserting that citizens may not be trespassed against in certain ways. And as society advances, minor individual claims are protected by giving remedies for breach of contract, libel, false witness, etc. In a word, comparisons show that though codes of law differ in their details as they become elaborated, they agree in their fundamentals. What does this prove? It cannot be by chance that they thus agree. They agree because the alleged creating of rights was nothing else than giving formal sanction and better definition to those assertions of claims and recognitions of claims which naturally originate from the individual desires of men who have to live in presence of one another.

Comparative Sociology discloses another group of facts having the same implication. Along with social progress it becomes in an increasing degree the business of the State, not only to give formal sanction to men's rights, but also to defend them against aggressors. Before permanent goverment exists, and in many cases after it is considerably developed, the rights of each individual are asserted and maintained by himself, or by his family. Alike among savage tribes at present, among civilized peoples in the past, and even now in unsettled parts of Europe, the punishment for murder is a matter of private concern; "the sacred duty of blood revenge" devolves on some one of a cluster of relatives. Similarly, compensations for aggressions on property and for injuries of other kinds, are in early states of society independently sought by each man or family. But as social organization advances, the central ruling power undertakes more and more to secure to individuals their personal safety, the safety of their possessions, and, to some extent, the enforcement of their claims established by contract. Originally concerned almost exclusively with defence of the society as a whole against other societies, or with conducting its attacks on other societies, Government has come more and more to discharge the function of defending individuals against one another. It needs but to recall the days when men habitually carried weapons, or to bear in mind the greater safety to person and property achieved by improved police-administration during our own time, or to note the facilities now given for recovering small debts, to see that the insuring to each individual the unhindered pursuit of the objects of life, within limits set by others' like pursuits, is increasingly recognized as a duty of the State. In other words, along with social progress, there goes not only a fuller recognition of these which we call natural rights, but also a better enforcement of them by Government: Government becomes more and more the servant to these essential pre-requisites for individual welfare.

An allied and still more significant change has accompanied this. In early stages, at the same time that the State failed to protect the individual against aggression, it was itself an aggressor in multitudinous ways. Those ancient societies which advanced far enough to leave records, having all been conquering societies, show us everywhere the traits of the militant régime. As, for the effectual organization of fighting bodies, the soldiers, absolutely obedient, must act independently only when commanded to do it; so, for the effectual organization of fighting societies, citizens must have their individualities subordinated. Private claims are overridden by public claims; and the subject loses much of his freedom of action. One result is that the system of regimentation, pervading the society as well as the army, causes detailed regulation of conduct. The dictates of the ruler, sanctified by ascription of them to his divine ancestor, are unrestrained by any conception of individual liberty; and they specify men's actions to an unlimited extent—down to kinds of food eaten, modes of preparing them, shaping of beard, fringing of dresses, sowing of grain, etc. This omnipresent control, which the ancient Eastern nations in general exhibited, was exhibited also in large measure by the Greeks; and was carried to its greatest pitch in the most militant city, Sparta. Similarly during mediaeval days throughout Europe, characterized by chronic warfare with its appropriate political forms and ideas, there were scarcely any bounds to Governmental interference: agriculture, manufactures, trades, were regulated in detail; religious beliefs and observances were imposed; and rulers said by whom alone furs might be worn, silver used, books issued, pigeons kept, etc. But along with increase of industrial activities, and implied substitution of the régime of contract for the régime of status, and growth of associated sentiments, there went (until the recent reaction accompanying reversion to militant activity) a decrease of meddling with people's doings. Legislation gradually ceased to regulate the cropping of fields, or dictate the ratio of cattle to acreage, or specify modes of manufacture and materials to be used, or fix wages and prices, or interfere with dresses and games (except where there was gambling), or put bounties and penalties on imports or exports, or prescribe men's beliefs, religious or political, or prevent them from combining as they pleased, or travelling where they liked. That is to say, throughout a large range of conduct, the right of the citizen to uncontrolled action has been made good against the pretensions of the State to control him. While the ruling agency has increasingly helped him to exclude intruders from that private sphere in which he pursues the objects of life, it has itself retreated from that sphere; or, in other words—decreased its intrusions.

Not even yet have we noted all the classes of facts which tell the same story. It is told afresh in the improvements and reforms of law itself; as well as in the admissions and assertions of those who have effected them.

"So early as the fifteenth century," says Professor Pol-
lock, "we find a common-law judge declaring that, as in
a case unprovided for by known rules the civilians and
canonists devise a new rule according to 'the law of nature which is the ground of all law,' the Courts of West-
minster can and will do the like."[23] Again, our system of
Equity, introduced and developed as it was to make up
for the shortcomings of Common-law, or rectify its inequities, proceeded throughout on a recognition of men's
claims considered as existing apart from legal warrant.
And the changes of law now from time to time made
after resistance, are similarly made in pursuance of current ideas concerning the requirements of justice; ideas
which, instead of being derived from the law, are opposed to the law. For example, that recent Act which
gives to a married woman a right of property in her own
earnings, evidently originated in the consciousness that
the natural connexion between labour expended and
benefit enjoyed, is one which should be maintained in
all cases. The reformed law did not create the right, but
recognition of the right created the reformed law.

Thus, historical evidences of five different kinds unite
in teaching that, confused as are the popular notions
concerning rights, and including, as they do, a great deal
which should be excluded, yet they shadow forth a
truth.

It remains now to consider the original source of this
truth. In a previous paper I have spoken of the open
secret, that there can be no social phenomena but what,

---

[23] "The Methods of Jurisprudence: an Introductory Lecture at University
College, London," 31 October 1882.

if we analyse them to the bottom, bring us down to the laws of life; and that there can be no true understanding of them without reference to the laws of life. Let us, then, transfer this question of natural rights from the court of politics to the court of science—the science of life. The reader need feel no alarm: the simplest and most obvious facts will suffice. We will contemplate first the general conditions to individual life; and then the general conditions to social life. We shall find that both yield the same verdict.

Animal life involves waste; waste must be met by repair; repair implies nutrition. Again, nutrition presupposes obtainment of food; food cannot be got without powers of prehension, and, usually, of locomotion; and that these powers may achieve their ends, there must be freedom to move about. If you shut up a mammal in a small space, or tie its limbs together, or take from it the food it has procured, you eventually, by persistence in one or other of these courses, cause its death. Passing a certain point, hindrance to the fulfilment of these requirements is fatal. And all this, which holds of the higher animals at large, of course holds of man.

If we adopt pessimism as a creed, and with it accept the implication that life in general being an evil should be put an end to, then there is no ethical warrant for these actions by which life is maintained: the whole question drops. But if we adopt either the optimist view or the meliorist view—if we say that life on the whole yields more pleasure than pain; or that it is on the way to become such that it will yield more pleasure than pain;

then these actions by which life is maintained are justified, and there results a warrant for the freedom to perform them. Those who hold that life is valuable, hold, by implication, that men ought not to be prevented from carrying on life-sustaining activities. In other words, if it is said to be "right" that they should carry them on, then, by permutation, we get the assertion that they "have a right" to carry them on. Clearly the conception of "natural rights" originates in recognition of the truth that if life is justifiable, there must be a justification for the performance of acts essential to its preservation; and, therefore, a justification for those liberties and claims which make such acts possible.

But being true of other creatures as of man, this is a proposition lacking ethical character. Ethical character arises only with the distinction between what the individual *may* do in carrying on his life-sustaining activities, and what he *may not* do. This distinction obviously results from the presence of his fellows. Among those who are in close proximity, or even some distance apart, the doings of each are apt to interfere with the doings of others; and in the absence of proof that some may do what they will without limit, while others may not, mutual limitation is necessitated. The non-ethical form of the right to pursue ends, passes into the ethical form, when there is recognized the difference between acts which can be performed without transgressing the limits, and others which cannot be so performed.

This, which is the *a priori* conclusion, is the conclusion yielded *a posteriori*, when we study the doings of the uncivilized. In its vaguest form, mutual limitation of spheres of action, and the ideas and the sentiments associated with it, are seen in the relations of groups to one another. Habitually there come to be established, certain bounds to the territories within which each tribe obtains its livelihood; and these bounds, when not respected, are defended. Among the Wood-Veddahs, who have no political organization, the small clans have their respective portions of forest; and "these conventional allotments are always honourably recognized."[24] Of the ungoverned tribes of Tasmania, we are told that "their hunting grounds were all determined, and trespassers were liable to attack."[25] And, manifestly, the quarrels caused among tribes by intrusions on one another's territories, tend, in the long run, to fix bounds and to give a certain sanction to them. As with each inhabited area, so with each inhabiting group. A death in one, rightly or wrongly ascribed to somebody in another, prompts "the sacred duty of blood-revenge"; and though retaliations are thus made chronic, some restraint is put on new aggressions. Like causes worked like effects in those early stages of civilized societies, during which families or clans, rather than individuals, were the political units; and during which each family or clan had to maintain itself and its possessions against others such. These mutual restraints, which in the nature of things arise between small communities, similarly arise between individuals in each community; and the ideas and usages appropriate to the one are more or less appropriate to the other. Though within each group there is

---

[24] Sir J. E. Tennant, *Ceylon: an Account of the Island, etc.,* ii, p. 440.
[25] J. Bonwick, *Daily Life and Origin of the Tasmanians,* p. 83.

ever a tendency for the stronger to aggress on the weaker; yet, in most cases, consciousness of the evils resulting from aggressive conduct serves to restrain Everywhere among primitive peoples, trespasses are followed by counter-trespasses. Says Turner of the Tannese, "adultery and some other crimes are kept in check by the fear of club-law."[26] Fitzroy tells us that the Patagonian, "if he does not injure or offend his neighbour, is not interfered with by others"[27]: personal vengeance being the penalty for injury. We read of the Uapés that "they have very little law of any kind; but what they have is of strict retaliation—an eye for an eye and a tooth for a tooth."[28] And that the *lex talionis* tends to establish a distinction between what each member of the community may safely do and what he may not safely do, and consequently to give sanctions to actions within a certain range but not beyond that range, is obvious. Though, says Schoolcraft of the Chippewayans, they "have no regular government, as every man is lord in his own family, they are influenced more or less by certain principles, which conduce to their general benefit"[29]: One of the principles named being recognition of private property.

How mutual limitation of activities originates the ideas and sentiments implied by the phrase "natural rights," we are shown most distinctly by the few peaceful tribes which have either nominal governments or none at all.

---

[26] *Nineteen Years in Polynesia*, p. 86.
[27] *Voyages of the Adventure and Beagle*, ii, p. 167.
[28] A. R. Wallace, *Travels on Amazon and Rio Negro*, p. 499.
[29] H. R. Schoolcraft, *Expedition to the Sources of the Mississippi*, v, p. 177.

Beyond those facts which exemplify scrupulous regard for one another's claims among the Todas, Santals, Lepchas, Bodo, Chakmas, Jakuns, Arafuras, etc., we have the fact that the utterly uncivilized Wood-Veddahs, without any social organization at all, "think it perfectly inconceivable that any person should ever take that which does not belong to him, or strike his fellow, or say anything that is untrue."[30] Thus it becomes clear, alike from analysis of causes and observation of facts, that while the positive element in the right to carry on life-sustaining activities, originates from the laws of life, that negative element which gives ethical character to it, originates from the conditions produced by social aggregation.

So alien to the truth, indeed, is the alleged creation of rights by government, that, contrariwise, rights having been established more or less clearly before government arises, become obscured as government develops along with that militant activity which, both by the taking of slaves and the establishment of ranks, produces *status;* and the recognition of rights begins again to get definiteness only as fast as militancy ceases to be chronic and governmental power declines.

When we turn from the life of the individual to the life of the society, the same lesson is taught us.

Though mere love of companionship prompts primitive men to live in groups, yet the chief prompter is experience of the advantages to be derived from coop-

---

[30] B. F. Hartshorne in *Fortnightly Review*, March 1876. See also H. C. Sirr, *Ceylon and Ceylonese*, ii, p. 219.

eration. On what condition only can cooperation arise? Evidently on condition that those who join their efforts severally gain by doing so. If, as in the simplest cases, they unite to achieve something which each by himself cannot achieve, or can achieve less readily, it must be on the tacit understanding, either that they shall share the benefit (as when game is caught by a party of them), or that if one reaps all the benefit now (as in building a hut or clearing a plot), the others shall severally reap equivalent benefits in their turns. When, instead of efforts joined in doing the same thing, different things are effected by them—when division of labour arises, with accompanying barter of products, the arrangement implies that each, in return for something which he has in superfluous quantity, gets an approximate equivalent of something which he wants. If he hands over the one and does not get the other, future proposals to exchange will meet with no response. There will be a reversion to that rudest condition in which each makes everything for himself. Hence the possibility of cooperation depends on fulfilment of contract, tacit or overt.

Now this which we see must hold of the very first step towards that industrial organization by which the life of a society is maintained, must hold more or less fully throughout its development. Though the militant type of organization, with its system of *status* produced by chronic war, greatly obscures these relations of contracts, yet they remain partially in force. They still hold between freemen, and between the heads of those small groups which form the units of early societies; and, in a measure, they still hold within these small groups themselves; since survival of them as groups, implies such recognition of the claims of their members, even when slaves, that in return for their labours they get sufficiencies of food, clothing, and protection. And when, with diminution of warfare and growth of trade, voluntary cooperation more and more replaces compulsory cooperation, and the carrying on of social life by exchange under agreement, partially suspended for a time, gradually re-establishes itself; its re-establishment makes possible that vast elaborate industrial organization by which a great nation is sustained.

For in proportion as contracts are unhindered and the performance of them certain, the growth is great and the social life active. It is not now by one or other of two individuals who contract, that the evil effects of breach of contract are experienced. In an advanced society, they are experienced by entire classes of producers and distributors, which have arisen through division of labour; and, eventually, they are experienced by everybody. Ask on what condition it is that Birmingham devotes itself to manufacturing hardware, or part of Staffordshire to making pottery, or Lancashire to weaving cotton. Ask how the rural people who here grow wheat and there pasture cattle, find it possible to occupy themselves in their special businesses. These groups can severally thus act only if each gets from the others in exchange for its own surplus product, due shares of their surplus products. No longer directly effected by barter, this obtainment of their respective shares of one another's products is indirectly effected by money; and if we ask how each division of producers gets its due amount of the required money, the answer is—by fulfilment of contract. If Leeds makes woollens and does not, by fulfilment of contract, receive the means of obtaining from agricultural districts the needful quantity of food, it must starve, and stop producing woollens. If South Wales melts iron and there comes no equivalent agreed upon, enabling it to get fabrics for clothing, its industry must cease. And so throughout, in general and in detail. That mutual dependence of parts which we see in social organization, as in individual organization, is possible only on condition that while each other part does the particular kind of work it has become adjusted to, it receives its proportion of those materials required for repair and growth, which all the other parts have joined to produce: such proportion being settled by bargaining. Moreover, it is by fulfilment of contract that there is effected a balancing of all the various products to the various needs— the large manufacture of knives and the small manufacture of lancets; the great growth of wheat and the little growth of mustard-seed. The check on undue production of each commodity, results from finding that, after a certain quantity, no one will agree to take any further quantity on terms that yield an adequate money equivalent. And so there is prevented a useless expenditure of labour in producing that which society does not want.

Lastly, we have to note the still more significant fact that the condition under which only any specialized group of workers can grow when the community needs more of its particular kind of work, is that contracts shall be free and fulfilment of them enforced. If when, from lack of material, Lancashire failed to supply the usual quantity of cotton-goods, there had been such interference with the contracts as prevented Yorkshire from asking a greater price for its woollens, which it was enabled to do by the greater demand for them, there would have been no temptation to put more capital into the woollen manufacture, no increase in the amount of machinery and number of artisans employed, and no increase of woollens: the consequence being that the whole community would have suffered from not having deficient cottons replaced by extra woollens. What serious injury may result to a nation if its members are hindered from contracting with one another, was well shown in the contrast between England and France in respect of railways. Here, though obstacles were at first raised by classes predominant in the legislature, the obstacles were not such as prevented capitalists from investing, engineers from furnishing directive skill, or contractors from undertaking works; and the high interest originally obtained on investments, the great profits made by contractors, and the large payments received by engineers, led to that drafting of money, energy, and ability, into railway-making, which rapidly developed our railway-system, to the enormous increase of our national prosperity. But when M. Thiers, then Minister of Public Works, came over to inspect, and having been taken about by Mr. Vignoles, said to him when leaving: "I do not think railways are suited to France,"[31] there resulted, from the consequent policy of hindering free contract,

---

[31] Address of C. B. Vignoles, Esq., F.R.S., on his election as President of the Institution of Civil Engineers, Session 1869–70, p. 53.

a delay of "eight or ten years" in that material progress which France experienced when railways were made.

What do these facts mean? They mean that for the healthful activity and due proportioning of those industries, occupations and professions, which maintain and aid the life of a society, there must, in the first place, be few restrictions on men's liberties to make agreements with one another, and there must, in the second place, be an enforcement of the agreements which they do make. As we have seen, the checks naturally arising to each man's actions when men become associated, are those only which result from mutual limitation; and there consequently can be no resulting check to the contracts they voluntarily make: interference with these is interference with those rights to free action which remain to each when the rights of others are fully recognized. And then, as we have seen, enforcement of their rights implies enforcement of contracts made; since breach of contract is indirect aggression. If, when a customer on one side of the counter asks a shopkeeper on the other for a shilling's worth of his goods, and, while the shopkeeper's back is turned, walks off with the goods without leaving the shilling he tacitly contracted to give, his act differs in no essential way from robbery. In each such case the individual injured is deprived of something he possessed, without receiving the equivalent something bargained for; and is in the state of having expended his labour without getting benefit—has had an essential condition to the maintenance of life infringed.

Thus, then, it results that to recognize and enforce the

rights of individuals, is at the same time to recognize and enforce the conditions to a normal social life. There is one vital requirement for both.

Before turning to those corollaries which have practical applications, let us observe how the special conclusions drawn converge to the one general conclusion originally foreshadowed—glancing at them in reversed order.

We have just found that the pre-requisite to individual life is in a double sense the pre-requisite to social life. The life of a society, in whichever of two senses conceived, depends on maintenance of individual rights. If it is nothing more than the sum of the lives of citizens, this implication is obvious. If it consists of those many unlike activities which citizens carry on in mutual dependence, still this aggregate impersonal life rises or falls according as the rights of individuals are enforced or denied.

Study of men's politico-ethical ideas and sentiments, leads to allied conclusions. Primitive peoples of various types show us that before governments exist, immemorial customs recognize private claims and justify maintenance of them. Codes of law independently evolved by different nations, agree in forbidding certain trespasses on the persons, properties, and liberties of citizens; and their correspondences imply, not an artificial source for individual rights, but a natural source. Along with social development, the formulating in law of the rights pre-established by custom, becomes more definite and elaborate. At the same time, Government

undertakes to an increasing extent the business of enforcing them. While it has been becoming a better protector, Government has been becoming less aggressive—
has more and more diminished its intrusions on men's
spheres of private action. And, lastly, as in past times
laws were avowedly modified to fit better with current
ideas of equity; so now, law-reformers are guided by
ideas of equity which are not derived from law but to
which law has to conform.

Here, then, we have a politico-ethical theory justified
alike by analysis and by history. What have we against
it? A fashionable counter-theory, purely dogmatic,
which proves to be unjustifiable. On the one hand, while
we find that individual life and social life both imply
maintenance of the natural relation between efforts and
benefits; we also find that this natural relation, recognized before Government existed, has been all along asserting and re-asserting itself, and obtaining better
recognition in codes of law and systems of ethics. On
the other hand, those who, denying natural rights, commit themselves to the assertion that rights are artificially
created by law, are not only flatly contradicted by facts,
but their assertion is self-destructive: the endeavour to
substantiate it, when challenged, involves them in manifold absurdities.

Nor is this all. The re-institution of a vague popular
conception in a definite form on a scientific basis, leads
us to a rational view of the relation between the wills of
majorities and minorities. It turns out that those cooperations in which all can voluntarily unite, and in the
carrying on of which the will of the majority is rightly

supreme, are cooperations for maintaining the conditions requisite to individual and social life. Defence of the society as a whole against external invaders, has for its remote end to preserve each citizen in possession of such means as he has for satisfying his desires, and in possession of such liberty as he has for getting further means. And defence of each citizen against internal invaders, from murderers down to those who inflict nuisances on their neighbours, has obviously the like end—an end desired by every one save the criminal and disorderly. Hence it follows that for maintenance of this vital principle, alike of individual life and social life, subordination of minority to majority is legitimate; as implying only such a trenching on the freedom and property of each, as is requisite for the better protecting of his freedom and property. At the same time it follows that such subordination is not legitimate beyond this; since, implying as it does a greater aggression upon the individual than is requisite for protecting him, it involves a breach of the vital principle which is to be maintained.

Thus we come round again to the proposition that the assumed divine right of parliaments, and the implied divine right of majorities, are superstitions. While men have abandoned the old theory respecting the source of State-authority, they have retained a belief in that unlimited extent of State-authority which rightly accompanied the old theory, but does not rightly accompany the new one. Unrestricted power over subjects, rationally ascribed to the ruling man when he was held to be a deputy-god, is now ascribed to the ruling body, the deputy-godhood of which nobody asserts.

Opponents will, possibly, contend that discussions about the origin and limits of governmental authority are mere pedantries. "Government," they may perhaps say, is bound to use all the means it has, or can get, for furthering the general happiness. Its aim must be utility; and it is warranted in employing whatever measures are needful for achieving useful ends. The welfare of the people is the supreme law; and legislators are not to be deterred from obeying that law by questions concerning the source and range of their power." Is there really an escape here? or may this opening be effectually closed?

The essential question raised is the truth of the utilitarian theory as commonly held; and the answer here to be given is that, as commonly held, it is not true. Alike by the statements of utilitarian moralists, and by the acts of politicians knowingly or unknowingly following their lead, it is implied that utility is to be directly determined by simple inspection of the immediate facts and estimation of probable results. Whereas, utilitarianism as rightly understood, implies guidance by the general conclusions which analysis of experience yields. "Good and bad results cannot be accidental, but must be necessary consequences of the constitution of things"; and it is "the business of Moral Science to deduce, from the laws of life and the conditions of existence, what kinds of action necessarily tend to produce happiness, and what kinds to produce unhappiness."[32] Current utilitarian speculation, like current practical politics, shows inadequate consciousness of natural causation. The habitual

---

[32] *Data of Ethics*, § 21. See also § § 56–62.

thought is that, in the absence of some obvious impediment, things can be done this way or that way; and no question is put whether there is either agreement or conflict with the normal working of things.

The foregoing discussions have, I think, shown that the dictates of utility, and, consequently, the proper actions of governments, are not to be settled by inspection of facts on the surface, and acceptance of their *prima facie* meanings; but are to be settled by reference to, and deductions from, fundamental facts. The fundamental facts to which all rational judgements of utility must go back, are the facts that life consists in, and is maintained by, certain activities; and that among men in a society, these activities, necessarily becoming mutually limited, are to be carried on by each within the limits thence arising, and not carried on beyond those limits: the maintenance of the limits becoming, by consequence, the function of the agency which regulates society. If each, having freedom to use his powers up to the bounds fixed by the like freedom of others, obtains from his fellow-men as much for his services as they find them worth in comparison with the services of others—if contracts uniformly fulfilled bring to each the share thus determined, and he is left secure in person and possessions to satisfy his wants with the proceeds; then there is maintained the vital principle alike of individual life and of social life. Further, there is maintained the vital principle of social progress; inasmuch as, under such conditions, the individuals of most worth will prosper and multiply more than those of less worth. So that utility, not as empirically estimated but as rationally deter-

mined, enjoins this maintenance of individual rights;
and, by implication, negatives any course which tra-
verses them.

Here, then, we reach the ultimate interdict against
meddling legislation. Reduced to its lowest terms, every
proposal to interfere with citizens' activities further than
by enforcing their mutual limitations, is a proposal to
improve life by breaking through the fundamental conditions to life. When some are prevented from buying
beer that others may be prevented from getting drunk,
those who make the law assume that more good than
evil will result from interference with the normal relation
between conduct and consequences, alike in the few ill-
regulated and the many well-regulated. A government
which takes fractions of the incomes of multitudinous
people, for the purpose of sending to the colonies some
who have not prospered here, or for building better industrial dwellings, or for making public libraries and
public museums, etc., takes for granted that, not only
proximately but ultimately, increased general happiness
will result from transgressing the essential requirement
to general happiness—the requirement that each shall
enjoy all those means to happiness which his actions,
carried on without aggression, have brought him. In
other cases we do not thus let the immediate blind us to
the remote. When asserting the sacredness of property
against private transgressors, we do not ask whether the
benefit to a hungry man who takes bread from a baker's
shop, is or is not greater than the injury inflicted on the
baker: we consider, not the special effects, but the general effects which arise if property is insecure. But when

the State exacts further amounts from citizens, or further restrains their liberties, we consider only the direct and proximate effects, and ignore the direct and distant effects. We do not see that by accumulated small infractions of them, the vital conditions to life, individual and social, come to be so imperfectly fulfilled that the life decays.

Yet the decay thus caused becomes manifest where the policy is pushed to an extreme. Any one who studies, in the writings of MM. Taine and de Tocqueville, the state of things which preceded the French Revolution, will see that that tremendous catastrophe came about from so excessive a regulation of men's actions in all their details, and such an enormous drafting away of the products of their actions to maintain the regulating organization, that life was fast becoming impracticable. The empirical utilitarianism of that day, like the empirical utilitarianism of our day, differed from rational utilitarianism in this, that in each successive case it contemplated only the effects of particular interferences on the actions of particular classes of men, and ignored the effects produced by a multiplicity of such interferences on the lives of men at large. And if we ask what then made, and what now makes, this error possible, we find it to be the political superstition that governmental power is subject to no restraints.

When that "divinity" which "doth hedge a king," and which has left a glamour around the body inheriting his power, has quite died away—when it begins to be seen clearly that, in a popularly governed nation, the government is simply a committee of management; it will also

be seen that this committee of management has no intrinsic authority. The inevitable conclusion will be that
its authority is given by those appointing it; and has just
such bounds as they choose to impose. Along with this
will go the further conclusion that the laws it passes are
not in themselves sacred; but that whatever sacredness
they have, it is entirely due to the ethical sanction—an
ethical sanction which, as we find, is derivable from the
laws of human life as carried on under social conditions.
And there will come the corollary that when they have
not this ethical sanction they have no sacredness, and
may rightly be challenged.

The function of Liberalism in the past was that of putting a limit to the powers of kings. The function of true
Liberalism in the future will be that of putting a limit to
the powers of Parliaments.

INTRODUCTION.

———•+•———

FROM FREEDOM TO BONDAGE.

OF the many ways in which common sense inferences about social affairs are flatly contradicted by events (as when measures taken to suppress a book cause increased circulation of it, or as when attempts to prevent usurious rates of interest make the terms harder for the borrower, or as when there is greater difficulty in getting things at the places of production than elsewhere) one of the most curious is the way in which the more things improve the louder become the exclamations about their badness.

In days when the people were without any political power, their subjection was rarely complained of; but after free institutions had so far advanced in England that our political arrangements were envied by continental peoples, the denunciations of aristocratic rule grew gradually stronger, until there came a great widening of the franchise, soon followed by complaints that things were going wrong for want of still further widening. If we trace up the treatment of women from the days of savagedom, when they bore all the burdens and after the men had eaten received such food as remained, up through the middle ages when they served the men at their

B

meals, to our own day when throughout our social arrangements the claims of women are always put first, we see that
along with the worst treatment there went the least apparent
consciousness that the treatment was bad ; while now that
they are better treated than ever before, the proclaiming of
their grievances daily strengthens : the loudest outcries coming from 'the paradise of women,' America.   A century ago,
when scarcely a man could be found who was not occasionally
intoxicated, and when inability to take one or two bottles of
wine brought contempt, no agitation arose against the vice of
drunkenness ; but now that, in the course of fifty years, the
voluntary efforts of temperance societies, joined with more
general causes, have produced comparative sobriety, there are
vociferous demands for laws to prevent the ruinous effects of
the liquor traffic.   Similarly again with education.   A few
generations back, ability to read and write was practically
limited to the upper and middle classes, and the suggestion
that the rudiments of culture should be given to labourers
was never made, or, if made, ridiculed ; but when, in the days
of our grandfathers, the Sunday-school system, initiated by a
few philanthropists, began to spread and was followed by the
establishment of day-schools, with the result that among the
masses those who could read and write were no longer the
exceptions, and the demand for cheap literature rapidly
increased, there began the cry that the people were perishing
for lack of knowledge, and that the State must not simply
educate them but must force education upon them.

   And so it is, too, with the general state of the population
in respect of food, clothing, shelter, and the appliances of
life.   Leaving out of the comparison early barbaric states,
there has been a conspicuous progress from the time when most
rustics lived on barley bread, rye bread, and oatmeal, down
to our own time when the consumption of white wheaten
bread is universal—from the days when coarse jackets

Introduction. 　　　　3

reaching to the knees left the legs bare, down to the present day when labouring people, like their employers, have the whole body covered, by two or more layers of clothing—from the old era of single-roomed huts without chimneys, or from the 15th century when even an ordinary gentleman's house was commonly without wainscot or plaster on its walls, down to the present century when every cottage has more rooms than one and the houses of artisans usually have several, while all have fire-places, chimneys, and glazed windows, accompanied mostly by paper-hangings and painted doors ; there has been, I say, a conspicuous progress in the condition of the people. And this progress has been still more marked within our own time. Any one who can look back sixty years, when the amount of pauperism was far greater than now and beggars abundant, is struck by the comparative size and finish of the new houses occupied by operatives—by the better dress of workmen, who wear broad-cloth on Sundays, and that of servant girls, who vie with their mistresses—by the higher standard of living which leads to a great demand for the best qualities of food by working people : all results of the double change to higher wages and cheaper commodities, and a distribution of taxes which has relieved the lower classes at the expense of the upper classes. He is struck, too, by the contrast between the small space which popular welfare then occupied in public attention, and the large space it now occupies, with the result that outside and inside Parliament, plans to benefit the millions form the leading topics, and every one having means is expected to join in some philanthropic effort. Yet while elevation, mental and physical, of the masses is going on far more rapidly than ever before—while the lowering of the death-rate proves that the average life is less trying, there swells louder and louder the cry that the evils are so great that nothing short of a social revolution can cure them. In presence of obvious im-

provements, joined with that increase of longevity which
even alone yields conclusive proof of general amelioration, it
is proclaimed, with increasing vehemence, that things are so
bad that society must be pulled to pieces and re-organized on
another plan.   In this case, then, as in the previous cases
instanced, in proportion as the evil decreases the denun-
ciation of it increases ; and as fast as natural causes are
shown to be powerful there grows up the belief that they
are powerless.

Not that the evils to be remedied are small. Let no one
suppose that, by emphasizing the above paradox, I wish to
make light of the sufferings which most men have to bear.
The fates of the great majority have ever been, and doubtless
still are, so sad that it is painful to think of them.   Unquestionably the existing type of social organization is one which
none who care for their kind can contemplate with satisfaction;
and unquestionably men's activities accompanying this type
are far from being admirable.   The strong divisions of rank
and the immense inequalities of means, are at variance with
that ideal of human relations on which the sympathetic
imagination likes to dwell; and the average conduct, under
the pressure and excitement of social life as at present carried
on, is in sundry respects repulsive. Though the many who re-
vile competition strangely ignore the enormous benefits resulting from it—though they forget that most of all the appliances
and products distinguishing civilization from savagery, and
making possible the maintenance of a large population on a
small area, have been developed by the struggle for existence
—though they disregard the fact that while every man, as
producer, suffers from the under-bidding of competitors, yet,
as consumer, he is immensely advantaged by the cheapening
of all he has to buy—though they persist in dwelling on the
evils of competition and saying nothing of its benefits; yet it
is not to be denied that the evils are great, and form a large

Introduction.

set-off from the benefits. The system under which we at present live fosters dishonesty and lying. It prompts adulterations of countless kinds; it is answerable for the cheap imitations which eventually in many cases thrust the genuine articles out of the market; it leads to the use of short weights and false measures; it introduces bribery, which vitiates most trading relations, from those of the manufacturer and buyer down to those of the shopkeeper and servant; it encourages deception to such an extent that an assistant who cannot tell a falsehood with a good face is blamed; and often it gives the conscientious trader the choice between adopting the malpractices of his competitors, or greatly injuring his creditors by bankruptcy. Moreover, the extensive frauds, common throughout the commercial world and daily exposed in lawcourts and newspapers, are largely due to the pressure under which competition places the higher industrial classes; and are otherwise due to that lavish expenditure which, as implying success in the commercial struggle, brings honour. With these minor evils must be joined the major one, that the distribution achieved by the system, gives to those who regulate and superintend, a share of the total produce which bears too large a ratio to the share it gives to the actual workers. Let it not be thought, then, that in saying what I have said above, I under-estimate those vices of our competitive system which, thirty years ago, I described and denounced[1]. But it is not a question of absolute evils; it is a question of relative evils—whether the evils at present suffered are or are not less than the evils which would be suffered under another system—whether efforts for mitigation along the lines thus far followed are not more likely to succeed than efforts along utterly different lines.

This is the question here to be considered. I must be excused for first of all setting forth sundry truths which are,

[1] See essay on 'The Morals of Trade.'

6   *A Plea for Liberty:*

to some at any rate, tolerably familiar, before proceeding to
draw inferences which are not so familiar.

Speaking broadly, every man works that he may avoid
suffering. Here, remembrance of the pangs of hunger prompts
him ; and there, he is prompted by the sight of the slave-
driver's lash. His immediate dread may be the punishment
which physical circumstances will inflict, or may be punishment inflicted by human agency. He must have a master ;
but the master may be Nature or may be a fellow man.
When he is under the impersonal coercion of Nature, we say
that he is free ; and when he is under the personal coercion
of some one above him, we call him, according to the degree
of his dependence, a slave, a serf, or a vassal. Of course I
omit the small minority who inherit means : an incidental,
and not a necessary, social element. I speak only of the
vast majority, both cultured and uncultured, who maintain
themselves by labour, bodily or mental, and must either exert
themselves of their own unconstrained wills, prompted only
by thoughts of naturally-resulting evils or benefits, or must
exert themselves with constrained wills, prompted by thoughts
of evils and benefits artificially resulting.

Men may work together in a society under either of these
two forms of control: forms which, though in many cases
mingled, are essentially contrasted. Using the word co-
operation in its wide sense, and not in that restricted sense
now commonly given to it, we may say that social life must
be carried on by either voluntary co-operation or compulsory
co-operation; or, to use Sir Henry Maine's words, the system
must be that of *contract* or that of *status*—that in which the
individual is left to do the best he can by his spontaneous efforts
and get success or failure according to his efficiency, and that
in which he has his appointed place, works under coercive rule,
and has his apportioned share of food, clothing, and shelter.

Introduction. 7

The system of voluntary co-operation is that by which, in civilized societies, industry is now everywhere carried on. Under a simple form we have it on every farm, where the labourers, paid by the farmer himself and taking orders directly from him, are free to stay or go as they please. And of its more complex form an example is yielded by every manufacturing concern, in which, under partners, come clerks and managers, and under these, time-keepers and over-lookers, and under these, operatives of different grades. In each of these cases there is an obvious working together, or co-operation, of employer and employed, to obtain in one case a crop and in the other case a manufactured stock. And then, at the same time, there is a far more extensive, though unconscious, co-operation with other workers of all grades throughout the society. For while these particular employers and employed are severally occupied with their special kinds of work, other employers and employed are making other things needed for the carrying on of their lives as well as the lives of all others. This voluntary co-operation, from its simplest to its most complex forms, has the common trait that those concerned work together by consent. There is no one to force terms or to force acceptance. It is perfectly true that in many cases an employer may give, or an employé may accept, with reluctance : circumstances he says compel him. But what are the circumstances? In the one case there are goods ordered, or a contract entered into, which he cannot supply or execute without yielding ; and in the other case he submits to a wage less than he likes because other-wise he will have no money wherewith to procure food and warmth. The general formula is not—'Do this, or I will make you;' but it is—'Do this, or leave your place and take the consequences.'

On the other hand compulsory co-operation is exemplified by an army—not so much by our own army, the service in which is under agreement for a specified period, but in a continental army, raised by conscription. Here, in time of peace the daily duties — cleaning, parade, drill, sentry work, and the rest—and in time of war the various actions of the camp and the battle-field, are done under command, without room for any exercise of choice. Up from the private soldier through the non-commissioned officers and the half-dozen or more grades of commissioned officers, the universal law is absolute obedience from the grade below to the grade above. The sphere of individual will is such only as is allowed by the will of the superior. Breaches of subordination are, according to their gravity, dealt with by deprivation of leave, extra drill, imprisonment, flogging, and in the last resort, shooting. Instead of the understanding that there must be obedience in respect of specified duties under pain of dismissal ; the understanding now is—' Obey in everything ordered under penalty of inflicted suffering and perhaps death.'

This form of co-operation, still exemplified in an army, has in days gone by been the form of co-operation throughout the civil population. Everywhere, and at all times, chronic war generates a militant type of structure, not in the body of soldiers only but throughout the community at large. Practically, while the conflict between societies is actively going on, and fighting is regarded as the only manly occupation, the society is the quiescent army and the army the mobilized society : that part which does not take part in battle, composed of slaves, serfs, women, &c., constituting the commissariat. Naturally, therefore, throughout the mass of inferior individuals constituting the commissariat, there is maintained a system of discipline identical in nature if less elaborate. The fighting body being, under such conditions, the ruling body, and the rest of the community being incapable of resistance, those who control the fighting body will, of course, impose their control upon the non-fighting body; and the

Introduction.   9

régime of coercion will be applied to it with such modifications only as the different circumstances involve. Prisoners of war become slaves. Those who were free cultivators before the conquest of their country, become serfs attached to the soil. Petty chiefs become subject to superior chiefs; these smaller lords become vassals to over-lords; and so on up to the highest: the social ranks and powers being of like essential nature with the ranks and powers throughout the military organization. And while for the slaves compulsory co-operation is the unqualified system, a co-operation which is in part compulsory is the system that pervades all grades above. Each man's oath of fealty to his suzerain takes the form—' I am your man.'

Throughout Europe, and especially in our own country, this system of compulsory co-operation gradually relaxed in rigour, while the system of voluntary co-operation step by step replaced it. As fast as war ceased to be the business of life, the social structure produced by war and appropriate to it, slowly became qualified by the social structure produced by industrial life and appropriate to it. In proportion as a decreasing part of the community was devoted to offensive and defensive activities, an increasing part became devoted to production and distribution. Growing more numerous, more powerful, and taking refuge in towns where it was less under the power of the militant class, this industrial population carried on its life under the system of voluntary co-operation. Though municipal governments and guild-regulations, partially pervaded by ideas and usages derived from the militant type of society, were in some degree coercive; yet production and distribution were in the main carried on under agreement— alike between buyers and sellers, and between masters and workmen. As fast as these social relations and forms of activity became dominant in urban populations, they influenced the whole community: compulsory co-operation lapsed

A Plea for Liberty :

more and more, through money commutation for services,
military and civil ; while divisions of rank became less rigid
and class-power diminished. Until at length, restraints
exercised by incorporated trades having fallen into desuetude,
as well as the rule of rank over rank, voluntary co-operation
became the universal principle. Purchase and sale became
the law for all kinds of services as well as for all kinds of
commodities.

The restlessness generated by pressure against the conditions
of existence, perpetually prompts the desire to try a new
position. Every one knows how long-continued rest in one
attitude becomes wearisome—every one has found how even
the best easy chair, at first rejoiced in, becomes after many
hours intolerable ; and change to a hard seat, previously
occupied and rejected, seems for a time to be a great relief.
It is the same with incorporated humanity. Having by long
struggles emancipated itself from the hard discipline of the
ancient *régime*, and having discovered that the new *régime*
into which it has grown, though relatively easy, is not
without stresses and pains, its impatience with these prompts
the wish to try another system ; which other system is, in
principle if not in appearance, the same as that which during
past generations was escaped from with much rejoicing.

For as fast as the *régime* of contract is discarded the *régime*
of status is of necessity adopted. As fast as voluntary co-
operation is abandoned compulsory co-operation must be
substituted. Some kind of organization labour must have ;
and if it is not that which arises by agreement under free
competition, it must be that which is imposed by authority.
Unlike in appearance and names as it may be to the old order
of slaves and serfs, working under masters, who were coerced
by barons, who were themselves vassals of dukes or kings, the
new order wished for, constituted by workers under foremen

Introduction.

of small groups, overlooked by superintendents, who are subject to higher local managers, who are controlled by superiors of districts, themselves under a central government, must be essentially the same in principle. In the one case, as in the other, there must be established grades, and enforced subordination of each grade to the grades above. This is a truth which the communist or the socialist does not dwell upon. Angry with the existing system under which each of us takes care of himself, while all of us see that each has fair play, he thinks how much better it would be for all of us to take care of each of us; and he refrains from thinking of the machinery by which this is to be done. Inevitably, if each is to be cared for by all, then the embodied all must get the means—the necessaries of life. What it gives to each must be taken from the accumulated contributions; and it must therefore require from each his proportion—must tell him how much he has to give to the general stock in the shape of production, that he may have so much in the shape of sustentation. Hence, before he can be provided for, he must put himself under orders, and obey those who say what he shall do, and at what hours, and where; and who give him his share of food, clothing, and shelter. If competition is excluded, and with it buying and selling, there can be no voluntary exchange of so much labour for so much produce; but there must be apportionment of the one to the other by appointed officers. This apportionment must be enforced. Without alternative the work must be done, and without alternative the benefit, whatever it may be, must be accepted. For the worker may not leave his place at will and offer himself elsewhere. Under such a system he cannot be accepted elsewhere, save by order of the authorities. And it is manifest that a standing order would forbid employment in one place of an insubordinate member from another place: the system could not be worked if the workers were severally allowed to go or come as they pleased. With corporals and sergeants under them, the captains of industry must carry out the orders of their colonels, and these of their generals, up to the council of the commander-in-chief; and obedience must be required throughout the industrial army as throughout a fighting army. 'Do your prescribed duties, and take your apportioned rations,' must be the rule of the one as of the other.

'Well, be it so;' replies the socialist. 'The workers will appoint their own officers, and these will always be subject to criticisms of the mass they regulate. Being thus in fear of public opinion, they will be sure to act judiciously and fairly; or when they do not, will be deposed by the popular vote, local or general. Where will be the grievance of being under superiors, when the superiors themselves are under democratic control?' And in this attractive vision the socialist has full belief.

Iron and brass are simpler things than flesh and blood, and dead wood than living nerve; and a machine constructed of the one works in more definite ways than an organism constructed of the other,—especially when the machine is worked by the inorganic forces of steam or water, while the organism is worked by the forces of living nerve-centres. Manifestly, then, the ways in which the machine will work are much more readily calculable than the ways in which the organism will work. Yet in how few cases does the inventor foresee rightly the actions of his new apparatus! Read the patent-list, and it will be found that not more than one device in fifty turns out to be of any service. Plausible as his scheme seemed to the inventor, one or other hitch prevents the intended operation, and brings out a widely different result from that which he wished.

What, then, shall we say of these schemes which have to do not with dead matters and forces, but with complex living

Introduction.   13

organisms working in ways less readily foreseen, and which involve the co-operation of multitudes of such organisms? Even the units out of which this re-arranged body politic is to be formed are often incomprehensible. Every one is from time to time surprised by others' behaviour, and even by the deeds of relatives who are best known to him. Seeing, then, how uncertainly any one can foresee the actions of an individual, how can he with any certainty foresee the operation of a social structure? He proceeds on the assumption that all concerned will judge rightly and act fairly—will think as they ought to think, and act as they ought to act; and he assumes this regardless of the daily experiences which show him that men do neither the one nor the other, and forgetting that the complaints he makes against the existing system show his belief to be that men have neither the wisdom nor the rectitude which his plan requires them to have.

Paper constitutions raise smiles on the faces of those who have observed their results; and paper social systems similarly affect those who have contemplated the available evidence. How little the men who wrought the French revolution and were chiefly concerned in setting up the new governmental apparatus, dreamt that one of the early actions of this apparatus would be to behead them all! How little the men who drew up the American Declaration of Independence and framed the Republic, anticipated that after some generations the legislature would lapse into the hands of wire-pullers; that its doings would turn upon the contests of office-seekers; that political action would be everywhere vitiated by the intrusion of a foreign element holding the balance between parties; that electors, instead of judging for themselves, would habitually be led to the polls in thousands by their 'bosses'; and that respectable men would be driven out of public life by the insults and slanders of professional politicians. Nor were

A Plea for Liberty :

there better previsions in those who gave constitutions to the various other states of the New World, in which unnumbered revolutions have shown with wonderful persistence the contrasts between the expected results of political systems and the achieved results. It has been no less thus with proposed systems of social re-organization, so far as they have been tried. Save where celibacy has been insisted on, their history has been everywhere one of disaster; ending with the history of Cabet's Icarian colony lately given by one of its members, Madame Fleury Robinson, in *The Open Court*—a history of splittings, re-splittings, re-re-splittings, accompanied by numerous individual secessions and final dissolution. And for the failure of such social schemes, as for the failure of the political schemes, there has been one general cause.

Metamorphosis is the universal law, exemplified throughout the Heavens and on the Earth: especially throughout the organic world; and above all in the animal division of it. No creature, save the simplest and most minute, commences its existence in a form like that which it eventually assumes; and in most cases the unlikeness is great—so great that kinship between the first and the last forms would be incredible were it not daily demonstrated in every poultry-yard and every garden. More than this is true. The changes of form are often several: each of them being an apparently complete transformation—egg, larva, pupa, imago, for example. And this universal metamorphosis, displayed alike in the development of a planet and of every seed which germinates on its surface, holds also of societies, whether taken as wholes or in their separate institutions. No one of them ends as it begins; and the difference between its original structure and its ultimate structure is such that, at the outset, change of the one into the other would have seemed incredible. In the rudest tribe the chief, obeyed as leader in war, loses his

Introduction.   15

distinctive position when the fighting is over; and even where continued warfare has produced permanent chieftainship, the chief, building his own hut, getting his own food, making his own implements, differs from others only by his predominant influence. There is no sign that in course of time, by conquests and unions of tribes, and consolidations of clusters so formed with other such clusters, until a nation has been produced, there will originate from the primitive chief, one who, as czar or emperor, surrounded with pomp and ceremony, has despotic power over scores of millions, exercised through hundreds of thousands of soldiers and hundreds of thousands of officials. When the early Christian missionaries, having humble externals and passing self-denying lives, spread over pagan Europe, preaching forgiveness of injuries and the returning of good for evil, no one dreamt that in course of time their representatives would form a vast hierarchy, possessing everywhere a large part of the land, distinguished by the haughtiness of its members grade above grade, ruled by military bishops who led their retainers to battle, and headed by a pope exercising supreme power over kings. So, too, has it been with that very industrial system which many are now so eager to replace. In its original form there was no prophecy of the factory system or kindred organizations of workers. Differing from them only as being the head of his house, the master worked along with his apprentices and a journeyman or two, sharing with them his table and accommodation, and himself selling their joint produce. Only with industrial growth did there come employment of a larger number of assistants and a relinquishment, on the part of the master, of all other business than that of superintendence. And only in the course of recent times did there evolve the organizations under which the labours of hundreds and thousands of men receiving wages are regulated by various orders of paid officials under a single or multiple

head.   These originally small, semi-socialistic, groups of producers, like the compound families or house-communities of
early ages, slowly dissolved because they could not hold their
ground : the larger establishments, with better subdivision of
labour, succeeded because they ministered to the wants of
society more effectually.   But we need not go back through
the centuries to trace transformations sufficiently great and
unexpected.   On the day when £30,000 a year in aid of
education was voted as an experiment, the name of idiot
would have been given to an opponent who prophesied that
in fifty years the sum spent through imperial taxes and local
rates would amount to £10,000,000, or who said that the aid to
education would be followed by aids to feeding and clothing,
or who said that parents and children, alike deprived of all
option, would, even if starving, be compelled by fine or
imprisonment to conform, and receive that which, with papal
assumption, the State calls education.   No one, I say, would
have dreamt that out of so innocent-looking a germ would
have so quickly evolved this tyrannical system, tamely submitted to by people who fancy themselves free.

Thus in social arrangements, as in all other things, change
is inevitable.   It is foolish to suppose that new institutions
set up, will long retain the character given them by those
who set them up.   Rapidly or slowly they will be transformed
into institutions unlike those intended—so unlike as even to
be unrecognizable by their devisers.   And what, in the case
before us, will be the metamorphosis ?   The answer pointed to
by instances above given, and warranted by various analogies,
is manifest.

A cardinal trait in all advancing organization is the development of the regulative apparatus.   If the parts of a whole are
to act together, there must be appliances by which their
actions are directed ; and in proportion as the whole is large
and complex, and has many requirements to be met by many

Introduction.

agencies, the directive apparatus must be extensive, elaborate, and powerful. That it is thus with individual organisms needs no saying; and that it must be thus with social organisms is obvious. Beyond the regulative apparatus such as in our own society is required for carrying on national defence and maintaining public order and personal safety, there must, under the *régime* of socialism, be a regulative apparatus everywhere controlling all kinds of production and distribution, and everywhere apportioning the shares of products of each kind required for each locality, each working establishment, each individual. Under our existing voluntary co-operation, with its free contracts and its competition, production and distribution need no official oversight. Demand and supply, and the desire of each man to gain a living by supplying the needs of his fellows, spontaneously evolve that wonderful system whereby a great city has its food daily brought round to all doors or stored at adjacent shops; has clothing for its citizens everywhere at hand in multitudinous varieties; has its houses and furniture and fuel ready made or stocked in each locality; and has mental pabulum from halfpenny papers, hourly hawked round, to weekly shoals of novels, and less abundant books of instruction, furnished without stint for small payments. And throughout the kingdom, production as well as distribution is similarly carried on with the smallest amount of superintendence which proves efficient; while the quantities of the numerous commodities required daily in each locality are adjusted without any other agency than the pursuit of profit. Suppose now that this industrial *régime* of willinghood, acting spontaneously, is replaced by a *régime* of industrial obedience, enforced by public officials. Imagine the vast administration required for that distribution of all commodities to all people in every city, town and village, which is now effected by traders! Imagine, again, the still more vast administration required for doing all that farmers, manufacturers, and merchants do ; having not only its various orders of local superintendents, but its sub-centres and chief centres needed for apportioning the quantities of each thing everywhere needed, and the adjustment of them to the requisite times. Then add the staffs wanted for working mines, railways, roads, canals ; the staffs required for conducting the importing and exporting businesses and the administration of mercantile shipping ; the staffs required for supplying towns not only with water and gas but with locomotion by tramways, omnibuses, and other vehicles, and for the distribution of power, electric and other. Join with these the existing postal, telegraphic, and telephonic administrations ; and finally those of the police and army, by which the dictates of this immense consolidated regulative system are to be everywhere enforced. Imagine all this, and then ask what will be the position of the actual workers! Already on the continent, where governmental organizations are more elaborate and coercive than here, there are chronic complaints of the tyranny of bureaucracies—the *hauteur* and brutality of their members. What will these become when not only the more public actions of citizens are controlled, but there is added this far more extensive control of all their respective daily duties ? What will happen when the various divisions of this vast army of officials, united by interests common to officialism—the interests of the regulators *versus* those of the regulated—have at their command whatever force is needful to suppress insubordination and act as 'saviours of society'? Where will be the actual diggers and miners and smelters and weavers, when those who order and superintend, everywhere arranged class above class, have come, after some generations, to intermarry with those of kindred grades, under feelings such as are operative in existing classes; and when there have been so produced a series of castes rising in superiority; and when all

Introduction. 19

these, having everything in their own power, have arranged modes of living for their own advantage : eventually forming a new aristocracy far more elaborate and better organized than the old ? How will the individual worker fare if he is dissatisfied with his treatment—thinks that he has not an adequate share of the products, or has more to do than can rightly be demanded, or wishes to undertake a function for which he feels himself fitted but which is not thought proper for him by his superiors, or desires to make an independent career for himself? This dissatisfied unit in the immense machine will be told he must submit or go. The mildest penalty for disobedience will be industrial excommunication. And if an international organization of labour is formed as proposed, exclusion in one country will mean exclusion in all others—industrial excommunication will mean starvation.

That things must take this course is a conclusion reached not by deduction only, nor only by induction from those experiences of the past instanced above, nor only from consideration of the analogies furnished by organisms of all orders ; but it is reached also by observation of cases daily under our eyes. The truth that the regulative structure always tends to increase in power, is illustrated by every established body of men. The history of each learned society, or society for other purpose, shows how the staff, permanent or partially permanent, sways the proceedings and determines the actions of the society with but little resistance, even when most members of the society disapprove : the repugnance to anything like a revolutionary step being ordinarily an efficient deterrent. So is it with joint-stock companies—those owning railways for example. The plans of a board of directors are usually authorized with little or no discussion ; and if there is any considerable opposition, this is forthwith crushed by an over-whelming number of proxies sent by those who always support

the existing administration. Only when the misconduct is
extreme does the resistance of shareholders suffice to displace
the ruling body.   Nor is it otherwise with societies formed
of working men and having the interests of labour especially
at heart—the Trades Unions.   In these, too, the regulative
agency becomes all powerful.   Their members, even when
they dissent from the policy pursued, habitually yield to the
authorities they have set up.   As they cannot secede without
making enemies of their fellow workmen, and often losing
all chance of employment, they succumb.   We are shown, too,
by the late congress, that already, in the general organization
of Trades Unions so recently formed, there are complaints of
' wire-pullers' and ' bosses' and' permanent officials.' If, then,
this supremacy of the regulators is seen in bodies of quite
modern origin, formed of men who have, in many of the
cases instanced, unhindered powers of asserting their independence, what will the supremacy of the regulators
become in long-established bodies, in bodies which have
grown vast and highly organized, and in bodies which,
instead of controlling only a small part of the unit's life,
control the whole of his life ?

Again there will come the rejoinder—' We shall guard
against all that.   Everybody will be educated ; and all, with
their eyes constantly open to the abuse of power, will be
quick to prevent it.'   The worth of these expectations would
be small even could we not identify the causes which will
bring disappointment ; for in human affairs the most promising schemes go wrong in ways which no one anticipated.
But in this case the going wrong will be necessitated by
causes which are conspicuous.   The working of institutions
is determined by men's characters ; and the existing defects
in their characters will inevitably bring about the results
above indicated.   There is no adequate endowment of those

Introduction.

sentiments required to prevent the growth of a despotic bureaucracy.

Were it needful to dwell on indirect evidence, much might be made of that furnished by the behaviour of the so-called Liberal party—a party which, relinquishing the original conception of a leader as a mouthpiece for a known and accepted policy, thinks itself bound to accept a policy which its leader springs upon it without consent or warning—a party so utterly without the feeling and idea implied by liberalism, as not to resent this trampling on the right of private judgment which constitutes the root of liberalism—nay, a party which vilifies as renegade liberals, those of its members who refuse to surrender their independence! But without occupying space with indirect proofs that the mass of men have not the natures required to check the development of tyrannical officialism, it will suffice to contemplate the direct proofs furnished by those classes among whom the socialistic idea most predominates, and who think themselves most interested in propagating it—the operative classes. These would constitute the great body of the socialistic organization, and their characters would determine its nature. What, then, are their characters as displayed in such organizations as they have already formed?

Instead of the selfishness of the employing classes and the selfishness of competition, we are to have the unselfishness of a mutually-aiding system. How far is this unselfishness now shown in the behaviour of working men to one another? What shall we say to the rules limiting the numbers of new hands admitted into each trade, or to the rules which hinder ascent from inferior classes of workers to superior classes? One does not see in such regulations any of that altruism by which socialism is to be pervaded. Contrariwise, one sees a pursuit of private interests no less keen than among traders. Hence, unless we suppose that men's natures will be suddenly exalted, we must conclude that the pursuit of private interests will sway the doings of all the component classes in a socialistic society.

With passive disregard of others' claims goes active encroachment on them. 'Be one of us or we will cut off your means of living,' is the usual threat of each Trades Union to outsiders of the same trade. While their members insist on their own freedom to combine and fix the rates at which they will work (as they are perfectly justified in doing), the freedom of those who disagree with them is not only denied but the assertion of it is treated as a crime. Individuals who maintain their rights to make their own contracts are vilified as 'blacklegs' and 'traitors,' and meet with violence which would be merciless were there no legal penalties and no police. Along with this trampling on the liberties of men of their own class, there goes peremptory dictation to the employing class : not prescribed terms and working arrangements only shall be conformed to, but none save those belonging to their body shall be employed—nay, in some cases, there shall be a strike if the employer carries on transactions with trading bodies that give work to non-union men. Here, then, we are variously shown by Trades Unions, or at any rate by the newer Trades Unions, a determination to impose their regulations without regard to the rights of those who are to be coerced. So complete is the inversion of ideas and sentiments that maintenance of these rights is regarded as vicious and trespass upon them as virtuous [1].

---

[1] Marvellous are the conclusions men reach when once they desert the simple principle, that each man should be allowed to pursue the objects of life, restrained only by the limits which the similar pursuits of their objects by other men impose. A generation ago we heard loud assertions of ' the right to labour,' that is, the right to have labour provided ; and there are still not a few who think the community bound to find work for each person. Compare this with the doctrine current in France at the time when the monarchical power culminated ; namely, that 'the right of working is a royal right which the prince can sell and the

Introduction. 23

Along with this aggressiveness in one direction there goes submissiveness in another direction. The coercion of outsiders by unionists is paralleled only by their subjection to their leaders. That they may conquer in the struggle they surrender their individual liberties and individual judgments, and show no resentment however dictatorial may be the rule exercised over them. Everywhere we see such subordination that bodies of workmen unanimously leave their work or return to it as their authorities order them. Nor do they resist when taxed all round to support strikers whose acts they may or may not approve, but instead, ill-treat recalcitrant members of their body who do not subscribe.

The traits thus shown must be operative in any new social organization, and the question to be asked is—What will result from their operation when they are relieved from all restraints? At present the separate bodies of men displaying them are in the midst of a society partially passive, partially antagonistic; are subject to the criticisms and reprobations of an independent press; and are under the control of law, enforced by police. If in these circumstances these bodies habitually take courses which override individual freedom, what will happen when, instead of being only scattered parts of the community, governed by their separate sets of regulators, they constitute the whole community, governed by a consolidated system of such regulators; when functionaries of all orders, including those who officer the press, form parts of the regulative organization; and when the law is both enacted and administered by this regulative organization? The fanatical

subjects must buy.' This contrast is startling enough; but a contrast still more startling is being provided for us. We now see a resuscitation of the despotic doctrine, differing only by the substitution of Trades Unions for kings. For now that Trades Unions are becoming universal, and each artisan has to pay prescribed moneys to one or another of them, with the alternative of being a non-unionist to whom work is denied by force, it has come to this, that the right to labour is a Trade Union right, which the Trade Union can sell and the individual worker must buy!

adherents of a social theory are capable of taking any measures, no matter how extreme, for carrying out their views:
holding, like the merciless priesthoods of past times, that the
end justifies the means. And when a general socialistic organization has been established, the vast, ramified, and consolidated body of those who direct its activities, using without
check whatever coercion seems to them needful in the interests
of the system (which will practically become their own interests) will have no hesitation in imposing their rigorous rule
over the entire lives of the actual workers; until, eventually,
there is developed an official oligarchy, with its various
grades, exercising a tyranny more gigantic and more terrible
than any which the world has seen.

Let me again repudiate an erroneous inference. Any one
who supposes that the foregoing argument implies contentment with things as they are, makes a profound mistake.
The present social state is transitional, as past social states
have been transitional. There will, I hope and believe, come
a future social state differing as much from the present as the
present differs from the past with its mailed barons and
defenceless serfs. In *Social Statics*, as well as in *The Study
of Sociology* and in *Political Institutions*, is clearly shown the
desire for an organization more conducive to the happiness of
men at large than that which exists. My opposition to socialism results from the belief that it would stop the progress
to such a higher state and bring back a lower state. Nothing
but the slow modification of human nature by the discipline
of social life can produce permanently advantageous changes.

A fundamental error pervading the thinking of nearly all
parties, political and social, is that evils admit of immediate
and radical remedies. 'If you will but do this, the mischief
will be prevented.' 'Adopt my plan and the suffering will
disappear.' 'The corruption will unquestionably be cured by

Introduction.   25

enforcing this measure.' Everywhere one meets with beliefs, expressed or implied, of these kinds. They are all ill-founded. It is possible to remove causes which intensify the evils; it is possible to change the evils from one form into another; and it is possible, and very common, to exacerbate the evils by the efforts made to prevent them; but anything like immediate cure is impossible. In the course of thousands of years mankind have, by multiplication, been forced out of that original savage state in which small numbers supported themselves on wild food, into the civilized state in which the food required for supporting great numbers can be got only by continuous labour. The nature required for this last mode of life is widely different from the nature required for the first; and long-continued pains have to be passed through in remoulding the one into the other. Misery has necessarily to be borne by a constitution out of harmony with its conditions; and a constitution inherited from primitive men is out of harmony with the conditions imposed on existing men. Hence it is impossible to establish forthwith a satisfactory social state. No such nature as that which has filled Europe with millions of armed men, here eager for conquest and there for revenge—no such nature as that which prompts the nations called Christian to vie with one another in filibustering expeditions all over the world, regardless of the claims of aborigines, while their tens of thousands of priests of the religion of love look on approvingly—no such nature as that which, in dealing with weaker races, goes beyond the primitive rule of life for life, and for one life takes many lives—no such nature, I say, can, by any device, be framed into a harmonious community. The root of all well-ordered social action is a sentiment of justice, which at once insists on personal freedom and is solicitous for the like freedom of others; and there at present exists but a very inadequate amount of this sentiment.

A Plea for Liberty.

Hence the need for further long continuance of a social discipline which requires each man to carry on his activities with due regard to the like claims of others to carry on their activities; and which, while it insists that he shall have all the benefits his conduct naturally brings, insists also that he shall not saddle on others the evils his conduct naturally brings: unless they freely undertake to bear them. And hence the belief that endeavours to elude this discipline will not only fail, but will bring worse evils than those to be escaped.

It is not, then, chiefly in the interests of the employing classes that socialism is to be resisted, but much more in the interests of the employed classes. In one way or other production must be regulated; and the regulators, in the nature of things, must always be a small class as compared with the actual producers. Under voluntary co-operation as at present carried on, the regulators, pursuing their personal interests, take as large a share of the produce as they can get; but, as we are daily shown by Trades Union successes, are restrained in the selfish pursuit of their ends. Under that compulsory co-operation which socialism would necessitate, the regulators, pursuing their personal interests with no less selfishness, could not be met by the combined resistance of free workers; and their power, unchecked as now by refusals to work save on prescribed terms, would grow and ramify and consolidate till it became irresistible. The ultimate result, as I have before pointed out, must be a society like that of ancient Peru, dreadful to contemplate, in which the mass of the people, elaborately regimented in groups of 10, 50, 100, 500, and 1000, ruled by officers of corresponding grades, and tied to their districts, were superintended in their private lives as well as in their industries, and toiled hopelessly for the support of the governmental organization.

[20]

Social Philosophy & Policy 2:1 Autumn 1984 ISSN 0265-0525 $2.00

EQUALITY vs. LIBERTY: ADVANTAGE, LIBERTY

Jan Narveson

Introduction

The subject of this essay is political, and therefore social, philosophy; and therefore, ethics. We want to know whether the right thing for a society to do is to incorporate in its structure requirements that we bring about equality, or liberty, or both if they are compatible, and if incompatible then which if either, or what sort of mix if they can to some degree be mixed. But this fairly succinct statement of the issue before us requires considerable clarification, even as a statment of the issue. For it is widely, and in my view correctly, held that *some* sort of equality is utterly fundamental in these matters. We seek a principle, or principles, that apply to all, are the same for all. In that sense, certainly, equality is fundamental and inescapable. But this is a very thin sort of "equality."

It will almost equally widely be agreed that the principles in question should in some more interesting sense "treat" people equally, e.g., by allotting to all the same set of rights, and moreover, rights that are – again we have to say "in some sense" – nonarbitrary, so that whatever they are, persons of all races, sexes, and so on will have the same fundamental rights assigned to them. Taking this to be, again, essentially uncontroversial, though not without potentially worrisome points of unclarity, it needs, now, to be pointed out that this characterization does not settle the issue that this essay is concerned with. That issue is about *economic* matters in particular. The question is whether people should be required to bring about, or at least move in the direction of, economic equality, meaning by this equality of income and/or wealth, property, or possessions. There is, as I shall point out, a problem about identifying and then of measuring the variable thus to be equalized, though that problem won't be the major concern of this essay. Alternatively, should we require that people's economic *liberty* be respected? Economic liberty is generally identified with the free market, and again, I share this predilection. But again, there are questions of conceptual specification here. Some have even contended that the free market is *not* really "free," that it is itself somehow the enemy of liberty. We need a notion of liberty clear enough to enable us to discern whether there is any merit in such claims.

The procedure of this essay will be as follows. I begin by expressing some

34   JAN NARVESON

doubts about the coherence of the ideal of economic equality, and then
proceed to examine, briefly, a very few of the principal defenses of that ideal.
I then move on to the subject of liberty, and in particular economic liberty,
beginning with the project of identifying the referent of that term, and of
arguing for the coherence of the ideal. Finally, I proceed to the question of
foundations: is there a good argument for one or the other, for economic
equality or economic liberty? It will emerge that they are evidently
incompatible as sets of social requirements, and thus that we must take our
choice, or try to settle on some kind of mixture. The pure doctrine of liberty
is often defended on grounds of natural rights or of self-evidence. As these
terms are normally understood, I shall make no appeal to either of them.
The argument will be contractarian, though not in Rawls' peculiar sense of
that term, and as will be seen, the argument supports liberty, so far as I can
see. There will be little space for discussing implications, but a very few will
be noted in the course of the argument.

                              PART I: EQUALITY

Economic Equality: Some Queries

Since we are considering the claim that economic equality is a goal of
justice, it is worth pausing to ask what that goal is supposed to be. There is
certainly an obvious answer: two persons are equal if they have equal
incomes or equal wealth measured in monetary units such as dollars. Since,
one might say, the whole point of money is to enable us to compare the
diverse things of which wealth is made up, this answer would seem as natural
as the use of degrees of temperature on a thermometer for measuring heat.

The trouble with that suggestion for present purposes is that the value of a
unit of currency in an exchange or market society is determined by the
market mechanism. A unit of currency expresses a relation among batches of
goods on a market, the equivalence class any of whose members would fetch
that price on the market: for each such item, not enough people will pay
more for it to make it possible for the seller to charge more profitably,
whereas enough will pay that much for it to make that price profitable. What
makes it all go around is free exchange. But now suppose we wish to equalize
dollar-income: what now? In a market society, one expects a considerable
range of incomes to develop as time goes by, and this has concomitant effects
on the consumption patterns, hence the "demand curves," of the various
agents – and this, in turn, affects what is produced and how much those
things will bring on the market. If you begin with a market society at T_1 and
impose a totally redistributive tax at T_2, then what will it mean to say that
incomes following the redistribution, identical though they may be in point
of numbers of "dollars," are now equal? Suppose that person A purchases

with his post-redistributional income, i, bundle of goods j, whereas B purchases bundle k with hers: what *meaning* do we attach to the claim that k = j? Especially if, as is likely, the post-redistributive dollar would appear to its owner to be worth less than the pre-redistributive dollar was? Suppose that at T_1 income i would have bought j + m, or k + n, where n ≠ m? Are they now, A and B, more equal or less?

One way to solve such problems would be to pay people in kind instead of in money, giving each person as nearly as possible literally the *same* bundle of goods (as soon as there is *any* difference, the same problem quickly arises). But presumably this is not what the advocate of equality really wants. Thus, Bruce Landesman, a recent proponent of egalitarianism, writes:

> But they [anti-egalitarians] have attacked a 'straw man.' It is very implausible to think that an egalitarian has or must have uniformity as his fundamental aim. Why should he want or wish for uniformity? If he has a wish, it is that persons, all of them, do well, equally well, and it is a commonplace that equal well-being is at least logically compatible with the satisfaction of quite different preferences and the pursuit of different life-styles.[1]

But there *is* pressure toward uniformity. For in the absence of a free market, which would certainly make the desired equality impossible, it would be difficult to measure the share each was getting under the putatively egalitarian regime unless what each got was extremely similar in content.

To be sure, it is difficult to see why anyone should think that a condition of equality – in the sense in which each has pretty much the same assemblage of material (or any other, so far as possible) goods – was either required by justice or any kind of social desideratum. In fact, I shall insist that the same observation holds for any other sort of equality that might be thought to underpin the desirability of economic equality, but at the outset it must be evident that anyone driven to advocating the kind of parcel-by-parcel equality imagined above must be propelled by some other underlying vision: for example, (as in Landesman's case) equality of ultimate welfare or well-being; or, as recently advocated by Ronald Dworkin, equality of resources. And even then, surely the candidates do not have the ring of self-evidence. If someone thinks we ought all to have equal ultimate well-being as a matter of justice, it must surely be because that person thinks that we are all equally deserving, or equally entitled, or some such thing, to well-being; and similarly with resources. We can profit from having a closer look at such arguments; I shall consider each in turn, briefly.

---

[1] Bruce Landesman, "Egalitarianism," *Canadian Journal of Philosophy*, March 1983, 13 (1), p. 31.

36 JAN NARVESON

Equal Welfare?

If it is thought that all should have equal welfare, the first question is: just who is "all"? Probably all *humans*, one supposes from most advocates' writings. There is an immediate problem for one trying to be serious about this. Consider the human with the lowest welfare that is not, so far as anybody knows at present, capable of being significantly improved by any efforts of other people, no matter how strenuous, well-intended, and extensive. Does the advocate of equal welfare wish to assert, then, that it is the solemn duty of the rest of us to make ourselves as miserable as that unfortunate, in the interests of justice?

Advocates of equality usually talk as though we could all be quite happy, really: they want to fix things up by equalizing *up*, not *down*. But no one who has spent much time in a mental hospital, to say nothing of any other sort of hospital, can seriously suppose that we have it within our power to improve things for the most wretched of us to the level enjoyed by ordinary people, let alone persons of unusually blessed constitution, character, and personality. In some few of those cases, conceivably, the poor individual in question was made that way by some other human, and in such cases we could, perhaps, argue that the perpetrator of whatever deeds brought about that unhappy individual's condition should be brought down to match him, as a matter of retributive justice. And some few theorists do talk as though this were actually typical – e.g., that the miserable of the earth were all made that way by greedy capitalists. It is not easy to comprehend persons who can take such a view seriously, and I do not suppose that anything said in this essay would do much to persuade them of the utter unreality of their views (though I shall try, just a bit, in the next-but-one paragraph). But the rest of us can easily enough imagine cases in which any such assessment simply has nothing going for it. Congenital diseases and malformations that were quite beyond the ability of any current persons to predict might cause the misery I have in mind here, and what we want to know of aspiring equalitarians is: *then what?* Is it now to be inferred that we have the sacred duty, as a matter of justice, of each making himself as miserable as those worst cases?

Suppose, instead, that we *can* do something. Suppose, namely, that we can improve the lot of that worst-off individual just slightly by enormous and protracted effort of ours, with the foreseeable side effect that we would all be made about as miserable as he or she will still be after all these efforts? Does the advocate of equality want to say that this makes all the difference: that even if we are to be let off the hook concerning cases where we can do nothing, we are to be put back on it if we can do anything at all? If not, why not?

The question, Whose welfare is to be equalized?, is by no means as yet at an end. For it is hard to see why we should draw a line around humankind in particular for this purpose. What about the lower animals? And how much lower? Is it an injustice, one which we all ought to be doing whatever we can to rectify, that cuttlefish, newts, and perhaps even amoeba are incapable of the levels of welfare so unfairly enjoyed by you and I? If it isn't, why isn't it? And if it is, do we have an idea, here, that deserves to be taken seriously by any rational being?

The advocate of equality is likely, upon reflection, to declare that what he has in mind is only the welfare of normal people, people not afflicted with debilitating diseases or uncontrollably melancholy tempers, and definitely only people. We are still owed an explanation – aren't we? – for this seemingly arbitrary restriction, of course, but for the sake of argument we proceed. And we have to note immediately that the connection between equal welfare and equal economic circumstances is surely not straight-forward. If the point of equalizing Smith's and Jones' incomes and/or properties is to bring about a condition of equal well-being between them, then notoriously we can hardly be assured of success even in typical cases, and can be pretty definitely assured of failure in innumerable others. One will be of sunny temperament and robust constitution, and will take little interest in most of what she would have, given economic equality (whatever that may be), while another will not enjoy himself even tolerably with appreciably less than what a typical millionaire can now command. Or is it supposed that the new equalitarian regime will take care of such matters, supplying Smith and Jones not only with equal amenities and necessities, but also with equal dispositions and identical tastes to match? And if it is so supposed, is it not already evident that the project has gone very, very far off the rails? (Or should we say, very, very far *down* the rails, toward a condition that every serious person must surely find totally abhorrent?)

Arguing for Equal Welfare I: Desert

The big question about equality is Why? Of course, that is the question we must address to any substantive conception of justice, and we must, in the end, come up with a good idea of what justice is or should be before we could decisively answer that question in any case. For the present, I want only to ask this at the level of "intuition," though I hope reasonably sensitive and well-informed intuition, and not intuition in a sense incompatible with theory. So let us ask what sort of answers might be forthcoming at this level. The sort of terms in which we would expect them to be couched are, one supposes, such as Desert or Merit, and Fairness or perhaps Equity in the sense of equal consideration or "equal treatment." Let us begin with the former.

But equal desert or merit is what we would need in order to arrive at equal welfare – and, of course, equal desert for welfare, equal merit as pertinent to

38   JAN NARVESON

distributions of (sources of) welfare in particular. But considerations of desert have in general been pointed to as justifications of inequality, rather than equality. On any ordinary standard of desert, people will vary in their deserts. And besides, it is by no means clear that 'desert' is the only relevant variable, even if one could somehow establish equality of desert; if anything, it is quite clear that it is not the only relevant variable, at least in any ordinary understanding of desert. Both points deserve some elaboration here.

(1) To begin with, desert is in general what we might call "project-specific." One might deserve more from basketball fans for activities that would get you nowhere, or worse, in a symphony orchestra. The egalitarian who appeals to desert must evidently think that there is a general, project-indifferent notion of desert in which we are all equal and which is specifically relevant to economic distribution. But there is no such notion. Not even moral worth will do; the notion that we should pay people for being virtuous is wrong-headed from the start, and in any case people are not, by any stretch of the imagination, equal in moral worth, anyway.

Not only is desert project-specific, but it is also reward-specific. One could deserve praise without deserving an increase in pay; one could deserve the trophy without deserving a citation in Who's Who in Academia. The equalitarian requires not only a project-indifferent notion of desert, but he also requires, interestingly enough, a reward-specific response to this project-indifferent notion. For economic rewards are, at least ordinarily, considered to be specific. Moreover, what is, at least on the face of it, relevant to economic rewards – the "desert-base," the project to which economic rewards are peculiarly appropriate – is productivity, of whatever it is that the enterprise in question produces. And again, productivity, notoriously, varies enormously from one person to another.

It might, as a desperate measure, be hypothesized that although people do indeed vary greatly in any particular project-specific, desert-relevant variable, yet when we take all together, people come out equal. But this is desperate: there are persons who exceed at least some other persons in just about any respect one can think of, and at least tie them in the rest. Or at least, this is so if we take any sort of commonly recognized variables as our bases. Of course, if Jones is better-looking than Smith, it follows that Smith is worse-looking than Jones, and so if Jones deserves more of whatever good looks deserve, then Smith deserves more of whatever bad looks deserve. Let him (or her!) who will make what he (or she) can out of that one . . . ! Meanwhile, we note also that in order to make any such scheme work at all, we also need some kind of workable cardinalization over different desert bases, since again we can expect many cases where A is far better than B at x, y, and z, and B exceeds A but only just slightly in respect of u, v, and w. And to top it all off, we again need to argue that somehow the aggregated sum of these diverse variables is specifically relevant to *economic* reward. I take it that we need pursue this particular hare no further.

It has become fashionable in the recent past to proclaim a deeper theory about this matter. True, we say that Joanne is more deserving than Kenneth because, say, she can program a computer much more quickly and simply than he; *but*, it will be pointed out, this is only because she is better trained/more highly motivated/whatever than he, and this she got from her superior environment which she did *not* deserve; or ultimately, perhaps, because her native ability is greater than his and she did nothing to deserve *that*. We shall take up such maneuvers in the next section, since the argument really is now an argument from fairness rather than desert.

(2) But in any case, desert cannot reasonably be held to be the only relevant variable, as Nozick has so elegantly reminded us.[2] Most of us skew the distribution of our resources very strongly in favor of persons we merely happen to love, not because they *deserve* more of our love than others but simply because they happen to be, e.g., our own children; and the same goes for friendship and other such human relations. Again, the trophy goes to the winner of the race, and not necessarily to the one who deserved to win, by virtue of far greater effort, sacrifice, or whatnot. And finally (another Nozick-inspired observation), it may be true that Vladimir Ashkenazy, if he needed my particular liver and no one else's would do, deserves it more than I, but it does not follow that I am required, in justice, to give it to him. More will be said regarding this deep and important matter later on; and of course we must acknowledge that some will simply want to reject all such claims. The main form of this rejection will be discussed next.

Arguing for Equal Welfare II: Fairness

Notions of fairness enter our lives at many points, most especially when we undertake activities as members of groups accepting certain common rules and pursuing more or less common purposes. It is then appropriate to appeal to the rules, and/or the purposes, to establish that someone has done one down (to use Lucas' adept phrase)[3] by violating the letter or the spirit of the relevant rules or purposes. This is what we might call "ordinary fairness"; but ordinary fairness will not lead one far toward equality. The weakest player on the team might have tripped up the strongest on the opposite team; this is unfair, but rectification will only widen the gap between the teams' respective scores. There can be no general expectation that narrowing of that or any other gaps, including economic ones, must follow from us all being fairer than we currently are.

But lately there has been an appeal to fairness at a deeper level. The

---

[2] Robert Nozick, *Anarchy, State and Utopia* (New York: Basic Books, 1974), Ch. 6.
[3] J. R. Lucas, *On Justice* (Oxford: Oxford University Press, 1980), p. 5.

apostle of this appeal in its current form is, no doubt, John Rawls. The principle he invokes by way of leading up to a theory of justice which at least appears to be massively redistributivist in its implications, is to be found in his discussion of what he calls the "system of natural liberty," in which there is "equal liberty and a free market economy," but no attempt made to "preserve an equality, or similarity, of social conditions," as a result of which "the initial distribution of assets for any period of time is strongly influenced by natural and social contingencies." His comment on this is that "Intuitively, the most obvious injustice of the system of natural liberty is that it permits distributive shares to be improperly influenced by these factors so arbitrary from a moral point of view."[4] But is it intuitive that all such influences must be "improper?"

We can concede that one's native endowment, and many aspects of one's environment, both natural and social, are things which an individual cannot be said to have "deserved." In that respect, at least, they are indeed morally arbitrary. But it hardly follows that everything about this is morally arbitrary: perhaps your parents really had the right to move to North Battleford, Saskatchewan even though the foreseeable consequence is that you too would wind up there at the age of nine, forever unable to attend Phillips Andover Academy. And in particular, as has been often noted by others,[5] it does not follow from the fact that *I* did not deserve distribution D that therefore someone else *does*. What if *none* of us deserves it? And there is a further point to note. Some of these undeserved conditions are so central to one's being that the whole idea of "my" deserving *or* not deserving them can make no sense at all. Some at least of my native endowment is essential to my being me at all: those bits of genetic matter that constitute my native intelligence, for instance. If "I" had been "given" quite a different parcel of such bits, then it would not be the case that *I* had gotten a different one; rather, the individual constituted by that different lot would be a different person, not me at all. To insist that things must go only to those who deserve them, is to deny that one has the right to be whomever one is. And if we deny *that* right, what could possibly be left that is recognizable, let alone worth having?

It, of course, also needs to be observed that nobody deserves to be a human being. We could, for all that desert has to say about it, have been squirrels, or – what? Microbes, perhaps? Moral arbitrariness, obviously, does not stop at the boundaries of *homo sapiens*, once we allow talk about the

---

[4] John Rawls, *A Theory of Justice* (Cambridge, Mass.: Harvard University Press, 1971), p. 72.
[5] By Nozick, for instance (*op. cit.*, pp. 216–224 especially); and by Fred D. Miller, Jr. "The Natural Right to Private Property"' Tibor Machan, ed., *The Libertarian Reader* (Totowa, N.J.: Rowman and Littlefield, 1982), pp. 278–280 especially.

arbitrariness of native endowments. For similar reasons, it does not stop, evidently, at the boundaries of intelligibility, either.

The subject of this essay is the design of social "institutions." The point of the various moral premises being scrutinized here is to direct people's actions. A premise to the effect that it was unjust of someone to do something is a premise that supports, or may be used to support, a call for action, namely to make amends. A premise to the effect that some state of affairs is unjust, however, needs to be explained in this crucial regard: *who* is to do *what* because of this? The equalitarian calls upon all of us to redistribute, if we have more than others, or to clamor for a share in a redistribution from such people, if we have less. Now, how does a premise about the undeservedness of one's natural assets or the assets one has from one's parents and one's social environment bear upon our actions? If the premise is:

P1 – People do not deserve their initial assets,

then on the face of it, the indicated conclusion would seem to be:

C1 – We should take away all initial assets from all persons,

together, one assumes, with everything they have since got by virtue of those assets. But equalitarians don't seem to want to take that line. Their reasoning, instead, seems to be this:

P2 – No person deserves native assets *any more than any other*,

therefore,

C2 – All assets should, as nearly as possible, be distributed equally.

If the native assets themselves cannot, as they obviously often cannot, be redistributed, then at least the results in terms of differential rewards to individuals differently endowed can, and the clear intent of equilitarians is to do that. But why, we should ask, does C2 follow from P2? For P2, after all, follows from P1, and what appears to follow from P1, as we noted, is C1, not C2. In order to get C2, we need to add to P2 the premise that at least some persons *do* deserve their native assets. Assuming that this would, then, give them a claim on what they can get by utilizing those assets, then subjoining P2 will indeed yield C2. But the trouble is that the only reason for affirming P2 was precisely the impossibility of making any sense of the claim that *anyone* deserves his or her native assets *at all*. If we were to go back on this – which we hardly can, but we can fudge it a little bit – and say, instead, that at least some people *do* deserve what they get by virtue of the exercise of their native assets, then the argument would proceed as follows:

42   JAN NARVESON

P3 – Some people deserve what they acquire by the exercise of their native assets.

(P2, as before:) No person deserves native assets any more than any other.

Therefore:

(C2, as before:) All acquisitions should be distributed equally.

But this is absurd. For either P3 is understood to be compatible with P1 or it isn't. If it *is*, then it requires that we reject the inferability of any conclusion such as C2 *or* C1 from it: the desert or non-desert of native assets simply doesn't figure on behalf of normative conclusions any more, and instead the weight is shifted to what people do with them. But they do *different* things with them, and come to deserve different rewards, payments, and, in general, distributive shares as a result. And, thus, we can no longer infer anything like C2 from what we now have. And if, on the other hand, P3 is understood to be incompatible with P1, then we no longer have any argument if we retain P1, since we would then be drawing our conclusion from inconsistent premises, and obviously no conclusion has any more support than any other from such sets of premises.

The argument is, therefore, hopeless. The grand premise that we all are utterly undeserving of our native endowments and assets is quite true, but entirely useless in attempting to support equalitarian conclusions. Accordingly, it provides no support for rectification, and thus for redistribution so far as it stems from *this* source.

How much did Rawls' intuition about the arbitrariness of natural and (certain kinds of) social initial assets affect the theoretical construction in *A Theory of Justice*? As is well known, he proposed to derive the basic principles of justice from the choice of persons behind a "veil of ignorance," which operates to bar each chooser from any knowledge of his own subsequent identity: we are to choose without being influenced by that knowledge. But there are two ways to interpret this requirement. *One* way is to assume not only that these persons don't know anything about their own identity on the other side of the veil, but also that whomever they are, they will not only be quite capable of coherently choosing some principles while behind it, but also of being bound by them even after they know who they will become. In that case, the well-known arguments, give or take a few details, go through: we will, doing the best we can for ourselves but realizing that we could turn out to be just anybody at all, arguably rig things so as to favor the least favored, meaning that we choose equality except if it should turn out that somehow we can do even better. But a *different* way to interpret the veil is this: we are allowed to make what we can of the information that the people on the other side of the veil will, rationally and inevitably, act in the light of the actual, and varying, values that they will then have, and will *not* be capable of incorporating into their actual, practical bases of action any principles that make sense only if one might be somebody or anybody else. If people on the original position side of the veil know *that*, then they will choose, being constrained by these facts about people, very differently. They will choose the principles that they would choose on the other side, given full information about their fellow men and the constraints of their situation.[6]

The first of these two ways may well railroad the chooser toward strongly redistributive, equalitarian principles. But not the second! And which way is right? I shall be arguing further about this below, but to anticipate, I suggest that the second way is. If its assumptions about rational choice are right, it must be, for otherwise the output from the original position will be of purely academic interest: it will be used only by those persons whose interests happen to call for principles that coincide, at least in practice, with the original position ones. And if a case for redistribution or equalitarianism is to be made, it will have to be made on the kind of grounds that would be available to any well-informed individual placed in the sort of circumstances that call for principles of justice.

Utilitarianism

Rawls, and consequently Rawlsians and most critics of Rawls, have assumed that those in the original position à la Rawls would opt for principles other than that of the Principle of Utility. I have argued previously that this is an error, both in the sense that they should, indeed, choose that principle and, also, that one must infer from Rawls' systematic exposition that they actually have chosen it, and that given his assumptions it supports the famous Two Principles. Let us, however, view the matter independently and ask (a) what utilitarianism will imply about economic equality, and (b) what appeal utilitarianism has as a fundamental theory in this area.

Utilitarianism may be characterized sufficiently, here, as the view that utility counts and nothing else counts. All and only utility counts: acts large and small, from the nodding of one's head to a passing stranger to the establishment and operation of governments are to be appraised, ultimately, from the point of view of their promotion of aggregate utility, the sum of the utilities, positive and negative, of all affectable individuals.

What are the implications of this mighty postulate for economic justice? The equality asserted in utilitarianism, it should be noted at the outset, is

---

[6] This point was first made, to my knowledge, by David Gauthier in "Justice and Natural Endowment: A Critique of Rawls' Ideological Framework," *Social Theory and Practice*, Winter 1974, 3(1). A similar point is made in John Marshall, "The Failure of Contract as Justification," *Social Theory and Practice*, Fall 1975, 3(4).

only an equality of the like amount of utility of any two individuals. On the face of it, as commentators have been quick to point out, this means that if what we were distributing were utilities, then it would not matter how any *given* lot of it should be assigned to any given lot of individuals: 50 for A and none for B is as good as 25 for each; worse still, 150 for A and -75 for B is likewise just as good, just as recommendable a distribution. People have thought this highly unintuitive, to put the matter fairly mildly. But they speak over-hastily. We do not in fact know how unintuitive this is, or indeed whether it is so at all, until we know what relationship there is between the distribution of the various things we actually can distribute – money, for instance – and utility.[7] A standard assumption in the field is that the marginal utility of economic goods diminishes as the parcel for a given individual increases. It is an old idea – only the words used by recent writers (myself included) are new; so here is an elegant statement of it from David Hume:

> It must also be confessed, that, wherever we depart from this equality, we rob the poor of more satisfaction than we add to the rich, and that the slight gratification of a frivolous vanity, in one individual, frequently costs more than bread to many families, and even provinces.

It seems plausible, at first sight. But the standard defense of permitting inequality, adopted by Hume, Adam Smith, and for that matter Rawls, has been that if you deprive people of the incentive they have from the prospect of being able to better their own situations, then:

> . . . you reduce society to the most extreme indigence; and instead of preventing want and beggary in a few, render it unavoidable to the whole community.[8]

Such defenses – certainly also plausible, so far as they go – bring up a theoretical conundrum of rather serious proportions. For about these industrious and enterprising persons who, in the process of promoting their own well-being, also promote the public good, we must ask: should they feel guilty about not sharing the portion of their product which they keep unequally for themselves? If justice requires, after all, that incomes be equalized, then why am I not always being unjust whenever I raise the lot of myself and my family, say, above the average level of the surrounding community?[9]

Nor, of course, is this all. What about the rest of mankind, outside one's

---

[7] See J. Narveson, *Morality and Utility* (Baltimore: Johns Hopkins Press, 1967), Ch. VII, where this point is pressed.
[8] David Hume, *Inquiry Concerning the Principles of Morals* (1751), Ch. III, sec. ii.
[9] For a development of this argument in relation to Rawls, cf. J. Narveson, "A Puzzle About Economic Justice in Rawls' Theory." *Social Theory and Practice*, Fall 1976, 4(1).

community? Socialist countries, we note, seem to have no compunctions about attempting to improve the lots of their own citizens relative to those in, say, Bangladesh. And liberals generally don't seem excessively bothered by the fact that the measures they propose, often including severe restrictions on foreign trade, even if they achieved their avowed purposes, would tend to maintain or increase a gap between the average domestic welfare and that in the poorer countries these measures discriminate against. Why aren't all these things really wrong? For the point is that they can't be said to be really "necessary," *unless* we think that self-interest is not only unavoidable, but also unavoidable in such a way as to be compatible with utilitarianism. But then we can, perhaps, go farther and ask whether it might not conduce still more to the general utility if people not only *did* what they wanted to do – in particular, skewing the distributions of their products quite strongly in favor of themselves and people they like – but also did so with a clean conscience? In short, perhaps the general utility will be maximized if we reject, as our theory of justice, the equalitarian pretension outright. Perhaps the losses of those who lose whatever is lost by no longer being an automatic recipient of the involuntary charity of their fellows, would be less than what virtually the whole of humankind would gain by not having to suppose that almost everything they do in life is morally unjust.[10]

But the upshot of all this is that utilitarianism may be completely useless for settling the question before us. For if theorists on polar-opposite sides of this issue can both mount plausible arguments, armed with the very same fundamental principle, then it would appear that all of our attention might as well be turned to the "supplementary factual premises" so obviously essential for applying it to anything in particular. Moreover, it is not clear that we should regard estimates of the utility of any particular state of affairs as counting among those "factual premises!"

Besides, there remains the other question: why accept utilitarianism, anyway? The question, here, must be at an abstract level, as the above arguments, I hope, sufficiently suggest. Now at this abstract level, we are being asked to regard all and sundry persons, whatever else one might think of them, as *equally deserving*, at least *prima facie*, along with one's loved ones, friends, associates, workers toward valued causes, and oneself. And surely that is not the way we want to regard all and sundry others. It is not clear that we *can* so regard them, for that matter. But consider what sort of cases we seem to be contemplating if we do. I read in a newspaper quite some time

---

[10] Two quite different arguments within the context of utilitarianism are pressed in earlier publications of mine. See Narveson, "Aesthetics, Charity, Utility and Distributive Justice," *The Monist*, October, 1972, 56(4); and also "Rights and Utilitarianism," *Canadian Journal of Philosophy* Supplementary Volume V, Summer 1979 (Cooper, Nielsen, and Patton, eds., *New Essays on John Stuart Mill and Utilitarianism*), esp. pp. 157–160.

46   JAN NARVESON

ago of someone in a village in China who, having learned his political lessons
well, and upon finding the village being swept away by a flood, had to choose
between saving Comrade X, the local Communist Party chairman, and
saving his own wife and family – and elected to save Comrade X! Now, many
of us would have our doutbs about whether more good is brought to the
universe by Comrade X than by this man's wife, but that isn't why most
people find this case rather astonishing. What we probably think is that any
system that would require such conduct as a moral duty is outrageous on the
face of it. Similarly, we have our doubts about a system that implies – if it
does – that whenever we buy a $100 dollhouse for our children, we do grave
moral wrong, since we could, instead, have sent $99 to distant lands, thus
saving the lives of several people. Evidently, as I was at pains to argue in the
preceding pages, we don't know that utilitarianism *does* imply that. It's just
that it looks on the face of it as though it should and at least could, and the
question is whether we want to buy a system which on the face of it implies
such things. It will seem to many people that these are the wrong
implications on the face of it, even though they might agree that in some
suitably exotic circumstances which we might be able to cook up, we might
have to accept some such implications nevertheless. And the utilitarian will
insist that those on-the-face-of-it appearances are *only* that and can
comfortably be disregarded in the here and now. Not all utilitarians will take
this comfortable line, however.[11] But enough said for the moment.

Dworkin
   In some recent writings[12] Ronald Dworkin has put forward a rather
different conception of equality from any of the above, including the sort of
outright income/wealth equality whose coherence I expressed doubts about
at the outset of this essay. Instead, Dworkin proposes what he calls *equality of
resources*. This involves distinguishing what counts as the (at least logically)
external goods that the individual can be thought of as utilizing to forward
his good life as he sees it, and what is inseparable from the person in
question. And then, reminiscent of (but very different from) Rawls' original
position, one must try to envisage each person as participating in a sort of
primordial auction in which, equipped with the same purchasing power, all
the existent resources are sold to the highest bidder, who bids with a view to
supplying himself for his entire life. The idea is to divide what there is in
such a way that no one would trade his lot, post-auction, for that of any
other. This ingeniously retains the meaningful market notion of equality as

[11] Peter Singer, "Failure, Affluence, and Morality," *Philosophy and Public Affairs* Spring 1972,
    1(3).
[12] Ronald Dworkin, "What is Equality?," *Philosophy and Public Affairs*, Summer 1981 (Part I:
    Equality of Welfare), and Fall 1981 (Part II: Equality of Resources), 10(3,4)

equality-in-exchange, while properly scuttling any thought of item-by-item equality. Of course, it also means that outright income equality is not necessarily, or even probably, the indicated outcome for fundamental social policy. But Dworkin supposes – plausibly, one imagines – that the scheme would support fairly heavily redistributive taxation, and taxation *for the sake of* redistribution too, and not just to ensure, say, a minimum level of welfare for all.

Having discussed Dworkin's views at length recently,[13] I will not recapitulate here, except to cite the fundamental question that seemed to me to arise in reflection on this intriguing scheme, and that is: why would one be moved to accept its basic idea? That idea was to follow from a still more abstract one, that "From the standpoint of politics, the interests of the members of the community matter, and matter equally."[14] That, too, sounds plausible, but then we have the question why the "standpoint of politics" should *matter*, even if it could be made out – which I doubt – that the Equality of Resources idea is what is maximally supported by that abstract principle, rather than something else. Surely the standpoint of politics has to be *shown* to matter to us, for it is far from obvious that political institutions are *necessary*, strictly speaking, and even if they are, there would still be the question of how *much* they matter. Suppose we agreed that from the standpoint of politics, everyone should have equal resources, but from the standpoint of our own personal selves, they should not. Then we would seem to have to decide how much politics counts vs. how much our own lives, as we see and live them, count. And then it may seem quite rational to decide that the latter count practically 100%, the former scarcely at all. And then we would have the question, which standpoint is basic? If we can face the question just framed, how would rival answers be assessed? And the trouble is, it looks very much as though they would have to be assessed from one's personal standpoint (which might, of course, include a lot having to do with others who mattered to one) – which really means that the personal standpoint is fundamental, and thus that politics only matters as a component of one's life. In that case, however, what a Dworkinian must really show is that from the standpoint of any individual person, everyone matters and matters equally, and/or that everyone should, as a matter of justice, have equal resources. And I think it implausible, even bordering on the incredible, that such a result would be forthcoming. (So, as I noted in the aforementioned treatment, does Dworkin.)[15]

****

[13] J. Narveson, "On Dworkinian Equality"; R. Dworkin, "In Defense of Equality"; J. Narveson, "Reply to Dworkin," in this journal, Autumn 1983, 1(1), pp. 1–44.

[14] Dworkin, "In Defense of Equality," p. 24.

[15] Dworkin, "What is Equality?," Part II, pp. 31–2.

48   JAN NARVESON

Here I rest with the negative part of this essay. Certainly I have not exhausted the supply of conceptions of or arguments for equality, though I hope to have addressed several of the main ones. But even if I really had, as I don't even suppose I have, demolished all such arguments, the case for liberty, if it even makes any sense as a basic social principle, needs yet to be made. For after all, there have been regimes in plenty that gave not a fig for either liberty or equality, especially as basic principles. And perhaps they were right, for all we know as yet.[16]

II. LIBERTY

Liberty-Maximization? A Puzzle

If the equalitarian wants to enforce an equal distribution of income and wealth, what does the "libertarian" want? Presumably, to enforce an equal distribution of liberty. And there is a sense, which will be refined below, in which this is exactly right. Yet, just as the equalitarian also wishes his equal distribution to be at the highest possible equal level, so one would suppose that the libertarian would want liberty to be equally distributed at the highest possible equal level. "Maximize equal welfare/income/wealth," says one; "Maximize equal liberty," says the other.

But some reflection on this leads to a puzzle. On the one hand, we would be inclined to suppose that liberty in economic matters is compatible with (at least) considerable inequality. Start persons with equal shares, even, and ere long their free use of those resources will lead to some having much more than others. Yet some would wish to argue that the free market is not free: that a society enjoying maximum equal liberty could not be one in which people had varying levels of income. Why so? Because money is, after all, "purchasing power": the more of it you have, the more you are thereby enabled to do, hence free to do. Moreover, the goods end up being yours, which means that others may not use or enjoy them without your permission. When they are yours, you have the power to exclude others. Yet to exclude others is to restrict or limit their liberty; and the more of this power you have, the less liberty they have.[17] And so, to maximize equal liberty one must also maximize *equal* incomes! This is hardly the result that defenders of a free market would expect, and it seems odd to characterize a free market as "unfree." What is wrong?

---

[16] Roger Scruton, *The Meaning of Conservatism* (Markham, Ont.: Penguin Books, 1980) provides an example of a serious thinker who evidently thinks thus.

[17] See G. A. Cohen, "Capitalism, Freedom and the Proletariat," A. Ryan, ed., *The Idea of Freedom* (Oxford, U.K.: Oxford University Press, 1979) for one who argues thus.

Liberty: What it is

Evidently we require a closer look at the notion of liberty. But an immediate restriction may, happily, be put on the scope of the inquiry, for what is at issue, here, is *social* liberty, rather than, say, the liberty of the will in general. Liberty in general, I believe, is absence of impediment to one's actions, and it is beyond question that many such impediments are not put there – certainly not intentionally or even knowingly, at any rate – by one's fellows. Some of them, for that matter, are surely put there by oneself, and sometimes put there quite rationally. And many others are not "put" there by anyone: they're just part of the nature of things. But our specific question in this investigation concerns the class of impediments posed by the actions of one's fellow persons, and in particular those posed knowingly (intentionally or otherwise) by them, and those whose impedimentary character, even if not known or intended, is establishable and preventable by methods of social control.

When is one person's action, in the relevant sense, an "impediment" to another's? We must distinguish, at least, between two sorts:

(1) B's doing y makes it *impossible* for A to do x;
(2) B's doing y would render it (much) more costly for A to do x;

which in turn has two significantly different variants:

(2a) If B does y, then A prefers not doing x to doing x
(2b) A would prefer doing x given that B does not do y to doing x given that B does y (even though A will still do x rather than x̄)[18]

Impediments of type (1) are, as we might say, out-and-out. In the interests of liberty, we would want, and we would be able, to identify a set of acts of type (1) that are to be prohibited. But if we move to (2), and especially to (2b), things are more complicated, since B can rightly claim that he does not actually prevent A from doing x in such cases. Cases of type (2) include what we commonly term "coercions": I coerce you into doing x̄ if I threaten to do something to you if you do x that would render x, under the circumstances, a highly undesirable course of action. But what if it makes x only a little bit less desirable? Especially if, as in (2b), it still leaves A willing, as well as able, to do it? Has B interfered with A's liberty in the latter case? Can the objection to B's doing y in such a case be that it violates a right to liberty that A has? Or must we go to a theory that identifies some other rights A has, then show that this case violates one of those?

In the case where A doesn't have the right to do x in the first place, the

---

[18] (Reading "x̄" as "an act other than x")

interferences posed by B are, at least so far as A's x-ing goes, not wrong. Conversely, there might be some independent reason why B's y-ing is wrong, aside from its bearing on A's doing x. But otherwise, it seems to me that if A's doing x is something A independently has the right to do, then B should not be able to increase the cost of A's doing it either, unless there is an independent argument for his having the right to do the particular thing y whose impedimental character is in question here.

Consider, in particular, the case of coercion. If I attempt to induce A not to do x by threatening to do z if he does, where z is, for instance, killing A, then z would be independently wrong, since it would prevent A from doing anything whatever thereafter. This sort of coercion can be ruled wrong too, but not simply by virtue of being an impediment to A's x-ing. Suppose, instead, I attempt to induce A not to do x by threatening to foreclose on his mortgage, and suppose that I have, independently, the right to do that. It is not clear, then, that we can object to my doing it – indeed, it is pretty clear that we cannot, just as such. But we can still object to my doing it *qua* interference with A. If I have no other reason to foreclose, and if A has the right to do x, then my making this threat seems objectionable in that respect, and objectionable on the score of being an interference with A's liberty. The snag, however, is that we are considering the view that when actions are wrong, they are so because they violate liberty in *general*. And this raises very thorny problems. For giving A the right to do x ipso facto deprives B of the right to do y, where y interferes with x. Yet, that evidently interferes with B's liberty to do y. A right is a justifiable ground of interference. How do we establish that it is B, rather than A, who must get out of the way in the above case? If y interferes with x, doesn't x amount to an interference with y?

Answer: No, or at least we needn't give up so fast. Some interferences are simply that: the description of B's action y may be essentially that it was an interference with A's doing x and not an independent course of action that merely happened to collide with A's. That, at least, would put it squarely in the category of what we wish to rule out by proclaiming a general principle of liberty. And on the other hand, we can admit that there are many cases where the solution will be to negotiate. If the situation is that x interferes with y and y interferes with x, both can be declared in the wrong simply to proceed; negotiation could be required. The question is whether we can generate enough information from the root idea of a general right of liberty to enable us to see how such procedures are what are called for. So let us not give up yet!

And What it is Not

I interfere with your liberty when I make it impossible for you to do what you are endeavoring to do. But let us consider the case in which, though you *want* to do x, you lack some of what you would need to do it, say z. And suppose that I in fact have z. Some might wish to say that if I do not supply you with z, then I would be "interfering" with your liberty to do x. Should we go along with this? Certainly not! Or so I shall argue.

Why not? It is not a consequence of anyone else's *action* that you can't do x. It is, rather, a consequence of their inaction, in a sense. But "consequence" is misleading, here, anyway. Suppose that you are drowning 50 yards offshore, and that I could save you. Is your drowning a consequence of my not saving you? But suppose I was a thousand miles away and could do nothing about your drowning. Yet you still drown! How is it a "consequence" of something about me that you are in state S if you would be in it even if I didn't exist or was nowhere near?[19]

I could increase your ability to do various things by helping you, let us suppose. Is it the case, then, that I *increase* your *liberty*? Perhaps; though why shouldn't we just say that I increase your range of options, or your powers? However, we needn't stick at this. What we need to ask, rather, is what increasing liberty in the sense so defined has to do with a general principle that everyone has a right to liberty. And the answer is that it is not part of that right that others must increase our liberty when they have the chance to do so. We must distinguish, as has become happily customary in recent years, between "positive" and "negative" liberty, and likewise between "positive" and "negative" rights to liberty (or to anything else). The definitions go roughly thus:

> A has the "negative" liberty to do x = nothing prevents A's doing x
> A has the "positive" liberty to do x = A has whatever is needed in order for A to do x, as A wishes

And the parallel constructions for negative and positive rights go as follows:

> A has the "negative" right to do x = No one may prevent A from doing x
> A has the "positive" right to do x = Others must provide A with whatever A might need in order to do x, if A lacks it

Negative *social* liberty obtains when no other *person's* actions prevent one from doing as one wishes. Positive social liberty obtains when other persons are ready to assist one in doing as one wishes. To give persons a positive right to do as they wish is to impose a social requirement that others assist them. But to impose that requirement is to forbid them to refrain from offering that assistance, and hence to restrict their liberty. Positive rights conflict with negative ones. And so the notion of "maximizing" liberty is

---

[19] A similar argument is strongly pressed by Eric Mack in "Bad Samaritanism and the Causation of Harm," *Philosophy and Public Affairs* Spring 1980, 9(3).

ambiguous, or at least misleading. Maximization suggests promotion, not in the sense of removing obstacles but of increasing the power or ability to do things. It invites thinking in terms of positive rights. Yet positive rights cut into liberty. To be at liberty is, surely, for it to be up to you whether you do x or not, and if whenever I could help someone else do something I may be legitimately coerced into doing so, then how is this liberty? If, on the other hand, I am unable to do something because, through nobody else's fault, I have only one leg, or insufficient knowledge, then there is, nevertheless, no violation of my liberty by any other person, so far as it goes.

Maximization of positive liberty is a snare and a delusion. When do you have maximum positive liberty? When you are God, evidently: for only He lacks no powers at all. And if we were out to see to it that everyone has equal powers at a maximum level, how do we decide when two persons are equal? If Smith is proficient at ping pong, and Jones at playing the cello, are they equal? How would this be decided? More importantly for present purposes, how does this goal differ from that of maximizing equal welfare? And if it does not, then why not call a spade a spade?

To be concerned with liberty, to hold that what society should do is to respect liberty, and that it should be concerned to invoke coercion only in the interests of liberty, is to advance a distinctive project. It is to hold that people may do as they wish, even if some of the things they might have been forced to do would have done much more good for other people than the acts they chose to do. What the proponent of this idea needs to talk about under the heading of "maximization" is, actually, better construed as *minimization*: namely, minimization of interferences with liberty. People are to be constrained from doing what interferes with others' liberty; apart from that, they may do as they please – though, of course, many might greatly prefer that they do some things rather than others. Perhaps even *all* (others) might thus prefer: still, that is not sufficient reason for forcing them to do it. Here, if the idea is coherent, is a distinctive notion. The questions are: is it coherent? And even if it is, do we have good reason for embracing this idea?

Maximum Liberty as a Goal of Justice

First, let us address ourselves to the question of coherence. We want to try to fix the idea of "maximizing" liberty, which I have suggested should really be thought of as the idea of minimizing interferences with liberty. If we accept the characterization of justice as concerned with basic rights, then the social system we envisage with this as our leading idea is that in which society is concerned to give everyone the right of maximum liberty, the right to do whatever one wants to do, and thus the duty to refrain from interfering with the liberty of others.

To appreciate the looming problem of coherence in this scheme, we must ask how a society in which that was the sole basic right differed from a society in which everyone "could" do as he or she pleased with no restrictions at all. In an unguarded moment, one might entertain the idea of everyone's having the right to do *whatever* he or she wished, with literally no restrictions. But then we would have to ask what the term "right" is doing in this characterization. For to recognize a right is to accept a restriction on one's behavior. If I agree that you have the right to smoke in place X, then I agree not to attempt to stop you by any coercive means (though I may reserve the right to try to persuade you not to do so, or to request, politely, that you refrain). But on the view we are considering, I would in fact have the right to do anything I felt like in the way of stopping you, since I have the right to do anything whatever – and so do you! Obviously, this is to drain the notion of a right of all meaning, unless possibly one rather ghostly resonance. Perhaps the Hobbesian state of nature, in which we are told that "every man has a right to every thing; even to one another's body"[20] gives every man one right – the right not to be criticized:

> The Desires, and other Passions of man, are in themselves no Sin. No more are the Actions, that proceed from those Passions, till they know a Law that forbids them: which till Lawes be made they cannot know.[21]

Even this is dubious, since if we have the right to do absolutely everything, why not also the right to criticize? The most Hobbes can insist on is that any such criticism will be unreasonable in such a condition. And perhaps there he has a point.

Meanwhile, the point here is that such a condition is very different from one in which everyone has a genuine right, in the full ordinary meaning of the term, to do whatever he or she pleases, meaning by this whichever of those actions are consistent with the recognition of the same right on the part of everyone else. To envisage this is to envisage, not a state in which, in Hobbes' words, "the notions of Right and Wrong have no place," but rather one in which some actions are Wrong and all others are, at least in the weak sense of being permissible, Right.

One obvious thought is to try to quantify over the "extent" of interferences: some impediments to one's action are greater, more serious, than others. So we might be tempted to try to draw up an ordered list of interferences, ranked by their "seriousness" as impositions. But this would lead to inordinate difficulties, especially in view of the fact that one would surely expect people to rank different interferences very differently. Indeed,

---

[20] Thomas Hobbes, *Leviathan* (1651), Ch. XIV, 4th paragraph.
[21] Hobbes, *op. cit.*, Ch. XIII, 10th paragraph.

54   JAN NARVESON

perhaps there will be some people who attach greatest importance to
precisely some of the actions which we would also want to say are most
obviously and outrightly interferences with others. And, thus, they would
rank interferences with these actions as most serious. And there will arise the
question whether this isn't just going to end up as a form of negative
utilitarianism (Minimize Disutility).

Fortunately, there is a better way to handle the sort of problems to which
such measures (e.g., as rank ordering) are proposed remedies: viz., by
negotiation. Once we have a proper starting point, then when acts impinge
on each other, the indicated solution is for the parties to them to reach an
agreement concerning the area under dispute, an agreement specifying who
is to be permitted to do what. Agreements, indeed, will bear the lion's share
of the burden if liberty is our guide, since they are prototypically voluntary:
no one is (in general) required to make any agreements, but once made, the
obligations stemming from them have been self-imposed. The basis for
future complaints is agreed upon, hence accepted, in advance.

Agreements, it should be noted, will typically reflect the relative strengths
of the bargaining positions of the parties antecedently. They are not made
behind the Veil of Ignorance, and nothing about them inherently requires or
promises equality of outcome in the respects considered and rejected in Part
I. The parties may take it or leave it so far as any particular proposal is
concerned, and those taken will, provided that no fraud is involved in the
negotiation, presumably be the best offers available, so that when taken the
parties will find themselves better off, in their own views of what constitutes
being better off, than before; but there is no need to expect that the degrees
to which each will be better off will be equal, supposing that could be
objectively measured anyway. This, I suggest, is as it should be. Nor is it to
deny that, very often, the basis for agreement will be a proposal to split
something equally.

In order to make sense of minimizing interferences, we need a conception
of separate or separable areas, spheres, or "territories" – "turfs," as one
subculture has it – that define the limits within which each person may
properly operate: Mill's "appropriate region of human liberty,"[22] only with a
twist. For Mill hoped to find a region in which no human activity *could*
interfere with another, and that is in principle hopeless, at least if we allow
that human action is in the natural, causal network. But what we can try to
identify is a region in which impingements by others are necessarily
interferences, are to be reckoned interferences if anything is, and to give the
individual associated with that region the right to control such impingements, at a minimum. The initial such region is surely the person's body.

[22] J. S. Mill, *An Essay on Liberty* (1859), Introduction.

Here, surely, is a region which others may not invade without the consent of the person whose body it is.

This, of course, is equivalent to maintaining that a person's body is that person's property: if the body in question is that of A, then A may do and may permit or forbid others to do with it as A wants. A is the authority over A's body: insofar as this is controllable, others may not visit effects upon it that A does not want to have visited upon it.

Is this to be reckoned (part of) a basic right to *liberty*? Ordinarily, we would say that some damages to the body impede liberty, but not others. Broken limbs, diseases that confine one to bed, maladies that render parts of the body inoperable, are clearly enough impediments to liberty, but what of bruises, scratches, or headaches? It must be admitted that to conceive the right of liberty in such a way as to make the latter impediments to liberty is to stretch things a little. But not, I think, very much. The right to do as one likes with a thing, X, is the right to control X – to decide which states X shall be in, insofar as this is possible. If we accept this construal, then anything done to one's body without consent is a violation of one's right to liberty. And I do wish to insist that liberty rights are property rights, in general. To have the right to do x is to have the right to *use* whatever is involved in doing x in whatever *way* is involved.

The connection with property continues when we move to things that are not integral parts of one's body. When we own a certain thing, T, what we have are rights to do what we wish with T, within the limits of others' rights. That much is, I think, clear enough. But how does a right to liberty entail rights to ownership?

The general form of the answer to this question, I think, is as follows, or at any rate in the general direction indicated by what follows. To own X is to have the right to do whatever one wishes with X, within the limits imposed by others' rights. Therefore, there is an identifiable (though open-ended) set of (possible) acts the right to perform which is what ownership consists in. If none of those acts on the face of it conflicts with others' rights, then we have, by hypothesis, the right to perform any member of that set, as we wish, and, of course, if we *can*. To claim ownership is to claim the right to perform those acts. To rebut such a claim is to show that the claimant either simply isn't in a position to perform them, in which case others doing them instead cannot conflict with anything the claimant does; or to show that there are others' rights with which these *would* conflict. If somebody else already owns the thing, then the claim is invalid. But if no one does, and if there are no rival simultaneous claimants, then to be embarked upon the set of actions in question is to have a sufficient claim to be allowed to continue them. The rules of "finders, keepers" and "first come, first served" are the indicated ones, if liberty, and thus noninterference, is our maxim.

In John Locke's version, the initiating actions in question are those of producing, making – "mixing one's labour with," as he puts it. But it seems to me that this is more than we need. One must be using, and intending further use, but that the use must be productive is a problematic extra restriction. If people may do as they please, then the protected activities need not be in any special way productive. (Of course, we may take the view that all voluntary activity is intended to be "productive" at least in the thin sense of satisfying one's preferences at the moment. But Locke had more than that in mind.[23])

The strong connection between liberty and (private) property becomes clear, also, when one compares a property system to one in which decisions about who may do what and with what are always, in principle at least, in the power of a public authority or committee or deliberative body, ultimately subject to putatively democratic control. The hallmark of liberty, surely, is that one may do things "without asking the leave of any man" (Locke's phrase). Being at the beck and call of the majority of one's fellows is hardly that. And if nobody owns anything, then everything will be so subject, for we can't do anything at all unless we do it *with* something!

It will be objected, no doubt, that persons with no incomes in a society lacking social welfare systems will be at the mercy of their fellows, namely for the very rudiments of life – food, clothing, etc. Now, in a society *with* such institutions, one is also at the mercy of one's fellows, corporately rather than individually. Whether that is better or worse than being at the mercy of individuals or voluntary associations whose purpose it is to cater to such persons is surely not *a priori* decidable, even from the point of view of the indigent. But that it is worse from the point of view of all of those whose involuntary support contributes to the public institution seems beyond peradventure; that such institutions could thrive in the name of *freedom*, at any rate, seems a perversion of the notion.

The conceptual problems of initial acquisition, while appreciable, do not seem to be overwhelming, given the device of negotiation. And, of course, very little in the modern world is available for initial acquisition, and certainly only a tiny portion of the world's real wealth. Overwhelmingly, goods and services are produced by human activity. And if we aim at liberty as the guide of institutional design, then the indicated format is the free market society, in which what is produced and who gets it depends upon voluntary decisions of the persons who make and receive these goods. If I may do as I please with x, and you with y, then we may also arrange a trade of x and y if we like. And we may make such trades with anyone with whom we wish to do business.

---

[23] John Locke, *Second Treatise on Civil Government* (1690), Ch. V.

EQUALITY vs LIBERTY: ADVANTAGE, LIBERTY 57

Freedom of association is also a straightforward entailment from the general conception; and associate we do, in innumerable ways and, sometimes, at great depth. This puts in perspective the claim that liberalism presupposes "atomic individualism":

> For atomic individualists, the ultimate constituents of social reality, the atoms, are individual men and women, essentially independent of one another and of society, bearing only extrinsic relations to one another. Like atoms in an enclosed space, individuals in society do come into contact with one another. But this contact is in no way constitutive of the individual's nature. Society no more constitutes individuals than space constitutes atoms . . . Society is no more a part of social reality than physical space, in the traditional atomist view, is part of matter.[24]

It is difficult to know what to make of this, since it is difficult to be sure just what the liberal is supposed to be denying in this passage. All of us are born into and grow up in particular families and particular societies, with heritages that unquestionably shape us forever after. And we are deeply attached to, and involved in, the societies we live in — often. But if it were a universal truth that individuals are "constituted by" their societies, "intrinsically" and "essentially", then why do people sometimes reject their societies and go elsewhere, or attempt to reform, even in revolutionary ways, the ones they do live in? Should not such efforts at detachment be *impossible* on the view in question? But indeed, non-individualists don't really want to deny those possibilities. They want, instead, to insist that when people do that, they are radically wrongheaded. But how do we get *that* thesis out of the facts about people and their societies? If the claim is that there is always sufficient reason to continue all the attachments of one's society without question, that is an interesting one: but what argues for it? Once the question has been raised, the nonindividualism apparently asserted is already refuted in its most salient form. And what is left?

Since the sort of principle under consideration here permits indefinitely many associations, with whatever strength and extent of obligations people may see fit to take on (or not see fit to renounce, once an "age of reason" is reached at which the question can arise whether to do so), it is hard to see how anything further can be gained by embracing the nonindividualist thesis than the blessings of fascism, such as they are. Perhaps this makes an apt point to move to our final question: why liberty?

---

[24] Andrew Levine, *Liberal Democracy: A Critique of its Theory* (New York: Columbia University Press, 1981), p. 45.

58   JAN NARVESON

The Argument for Liberty

Defenders of liberty tend to assume that the rights they proclaim are self-evident, requiring and affording no further argument. There is some excuse for this procedure – equalitarians, after all, do no better – but still, it is hardly satisfactory. The aim of political argument, I should think, is to provide good reasons for anyone to accept the system being proposed, that is, the system which would be determined by the principle being proposed.

Now, the acceptance of a system, in the sense of a preference for it, on the part of isolated persons is hardly of any interest. One cannot get very far in public matters by acting on principles that no one else respects. And even if they respect your right to believe those principles, that is hardly going to do much for you if what you are concerned about is acting on them. Ideally, our argument should show that no rational person can do better than to accept the proposal being put forward; or that he has reason to complain about any alternative.

It is also no use insisting that rational and free beings necessarily respect the like status of other beings. Free and rational beings, I think, are simply beings with preferences that are modulated by, or capable of being modulated by, information about the world around them and by considerations of internal consistency. It hardly follows from this characterization that the beings in question will respect, in the form of granting rights to their liberty, their fellow rational animals. What follows is only that their actions might well be altered on the basis of information about their fellows; but not that it will be altered in that particular manner.

What matters about one's fellow beings is that their actions might affect one's interests and pursuits. The effects can be of all kinds. Some of these fellow beings will be people one is extremely fond of; others will at least be useful, e.g., in removing one's inflamed appendix or one's garbage. And doubtless there are various things one might *like* to have guaranteed, i.e., that one's fellows would have no right to refuse to do them for you. Indeed, everyone might conceivably like this, though I doubt it. But we can't necessarily have everything we want. These "strong" rights to "positive" services are not free. If everyone has them, so too does everyone have the obligation to contribute to them if possible. And it is not so obvious that one would want so to contribute. *Prima facie* one will be willing to do so if (1) the expected benefit is at least equal to the expected cost, and (2) there are no alternative ways of achieving a sufficient level of assurance without resorting to coercion.

Now, what are the options here? One possibility is to agree to nothing. This option, the "State of Nature", is to be understood as the situation in which, as Hobbes has it, nothing is right or wrong, i.e., there simply are no rules at all. I wish to add here the understanding that this includes the rule, say, of keeping agreements: that too goes by the board in this alternative. No objection can be made to the use of force for *any* purpose, because there are literally no rules. Hobbes' classic prediction is that such a condition would afford a life that was "nasty, brutish, miserable and short", and it is difficult to see why he would not be right, unless one sneaks in the assumption that the argument is already over and that certain rules, such as that forbidding wanton killing, are *already* in force, by virtue of being inherent in the nature of man.

If the State of Nature is rationally to be rejected, then which of the various alternatives is possibly capable of universal assent? It is likely that some persons, such as the exceedingly unlucky – paraplegics, for instance – would like to have a system in which people had no choice but to render life as tolerable for them as possible. But it is difficult to see why others should accept this. There is, of course, the possibility that one will end up a paraplegic oneself. But in a system of liberty, one has two important options here. The first is to try to ensure oneself against such options, e.g., by literally buying insurance. And the second is to appeal to the benevolence of one's fellows. And if some would find these options between them preferable to the option of being maintained by coercing all the sundry into supplying one's needs, then I propose that the argument is complete. For if any proposal fails of unanimity, we must choose either some other or we are forced back to the State of Nature. Now those who opt for coercion must ask how they are going to get unanimity on *that*, given that some reject it? For the no-agreement option is the State of Nature, and surely not only paraplegics but everyone will do worse there than in the Liberty condition; and it is hard to see how we can get agreement beyond this.

Nor is it easy to see why we need it. It is odd that so many liberals talk as though the typical human being in the very liberal society he champions is already solitary, mean, nasty, brutish, and short-sighted. Why? In fact, I hardly know any person so uncharitable that he or she would not expend some effort voluntarily aiding the desperate, given ready opportunity to do so. And on the other hand, most persons are not only able-bodied but have sufficient talent so that, given also some incentive and enterprise, they would and could do reasonably well in a society in which enterprise was not substantially impeded, or substantial incentives offered for avoiding it.

Concluding Remarks

All manner of large issues are certainly stirred up in the preceding pages. Among the largest, for example, is the question of anarchism. The strong view on individual liberty and property doubtless implies, at least on the face of it, that governments should do much less than they currently do, and no

JAN NARVESON

doubt also makes it difficult to see how they could function at all within the set of constraints proposed. But it should be appreciated that these are proposed at an extremely general level, and that one should not proceed too cavalierly from theoretical cup to practical lip: slippage, as we know, is common in such transitions. Consider the Welfare State, for example. Suppose that it is overwhelmingly popular: say, that 90% of the adult population would vote for it even if they knew (as they doubtless do not at present) what they were getting in for. A determined majority of that size acting quite without recourse to government could, in principle, readily induce the remainder to go along with programs of that sort, e.g., by boycotting their services if they didn't. Such tactics could not be forbidden within the structure of rights proposed here, and they would have the effect of reenacting the State in practical terms if used; it is hard to deny that their effective use would make life (even?) less comfortable than it now is for dissenters whose monetary support, at least, is coerced by the political system as it now operates. Whether the State can be retrieved in anything like its present form within the constraints imposed by such principles as have been argued for is not easy to say, but we should not simply assume that it must be impossible.

Nevertheless, I do suppose that the principles advocated here have teeth. The alternative to liberty, it is claimed, is always the permissibility of coercion of someone or other in order to benefit someone else or \other, and we surely need to ask whether that, as it stands, is morally acceptable. If it is not, then we must ask how practice can be made to square much more nearly with this fundamental requirement. Many others have labored on these matters;[25] it behooves us to take them seriously, if the foregoing arguments are near the truth.

Philosophy, University of Waterloo

---

[25] Most of the contributors to Machan (note 5) are cases in point. I should also mention that the original version of this paper, running to rather more than twice the present length, contains more detailed discussion of many points, and also examines several more arguments for equality than those considered here. The author can supply copies of this longer version upon request (within reason).

[21]

Libertarianism Without Foundations

Anarchy, State, and Utopia. By Robert Nozick. *New York: Basic Books,* 1974. Pp. xiii, 367. $12.95.

Reviewed by Thomas Nagel†

Liberalism is the conjunction of two ideals. The first is that of individual liberty: liberty of thought, speech, religion, and political action; freedom from government interference with privacy, personal life, and the exercise of individual inclination. The second ideal is that of a democratic society controlled by its citizens and serving their needs, in which inequalities of political and economic power and social position are not excessive. Means of promoting the second ideal include progressive taxation, public provision of a social minimum, and insulation of political affairs from the excessive influence of private wealth. To approach either of these ideals is very difficult. To pursue both of them inevitably results in serious dilemmas. In such cases liberalism tends to give priority to the respect for certain personal rights, even at substantial cost in the realization of other goods such as efficiency, equality, and social stability.

The most formidable challenge to liberalism, both intellectually and politically, is from the left. It is argued that strong safeguards of individual liberty are too great a hindrance to the achievement of economic and social equality, rapid economic progress from underdevelopment, and political stability. A majority of the people in the world are governed on this assumption. Perhaps the most difficult issue is posed by economic power and the political inequality it can create. The criticism from the left is that harmful concentrations of economic power cannot be attacked—or prevented from forming—unless individual actions are more closely restricted than is permitted by the liberal ideal of personal freedom. Radical redistribution is unlikely in a liberal democracy where private wealth controls the political process. A defense against this criticism must either challenge

† Professor of Philosophy, Princeton University.

Libertarianism Without Foundations

the factual claim or argue that the importance of freedom outweighs these disadvantages.

Liberalism is also under attack from the right. The most conspicuous attacks are not theoretical: the right in its more prominent political manifestations is not particularly attached to individual liberty when that liberty threatens the unequal distribution of wealth and power. But there is also a theoretical challenge from the right, called libertarianism, and while it does not present as serious a moral issue for liberals as does the attack from the left, the two are in some ways symmetrical. Libertarianism, like leftism, fastens on one of the two elements of the liberal ideal and asks why its realization should be inhibited by the demands of the other. Instead of embracing the ideal of equality and the general welfare, libertarianism exalts the claim of individual freedom of action, and asks why state power should be permitted even the interference represented by progressive taxation and public provision of health care, education, and a minimum standard of living.

In *Anarchy, State, and Utopia*,[1] Robert Nozick attempts to set forth the libertarian position in a way that will persuade some of those who do not already accept it. Despite its ingenuity of detail, the effort is entirely unsuccessful as an attempt to convince, and far less successful than it might be as an attempt to explain to someone who does not hold the position why anyone else does hold it. The book may come to occupy the position of an official text of libertarian political theory, but it is unlikely to add to the ranks of believers in that view unless it converts a few unwary philosophical anarchists by persuading them that the minimal state need not after all violate their austere moral requirements.

To present a serious challenge to other views, a discussion of libertarianism would have to explore the foundations of individual rights and the reasons for and against different conceptions of the relation between those rights and other values that the state may be in a position to promote. But Nozick's book is theoretically insubstantial: it does not take up the main problems, and therefore fails to make the kind of contribution to political theory that might have been hoped for from someone of his philosophical attainments.[2] In the preface

---

1. R. NOZICK, ANARCHY, STATE, AND UTOPIA (1974) [hereinafter cited to page number only].

2. Nozick is the author of three important articles: *Coercion*, in PHILOSOPHY, SCIENCE, AND METHOD 440 (S. Morgenbesser, P. Suppes & M. White eds. 1969); *Newcomb's Problem and Two Principles of Choice*, in ESSAYS IN HONOR OF CARL G. HEMPEL 114 (N. Rescher ed. 1970); *Moral Complications and Moral Structures*, 13 NAT. L. FORUM 1 (1968). The book reaches their level of trenchancy only in Chapter 4, "Prohibition, Compensation, and

The Yale Law Journal

Vol. 85: 136, 1975

he announces that he was converted to libertarianism by the decisive force of the arguments,[3] but no such arguments appear in the book. He has left the establishment of the moral foundations to another occasion, and his brief indication of how the basic views might be defended is disappointing. I shall explain below why it is unlikely to survive further development.

Nozick starts from the unargued premise that individuals have certain inviolable rights which may not be intentionally transgressed by other individuals or the state for any purpose. They are the rights not to be killed or assaulted if one is doing no harm, not to be coerced or imprisoned, not to have one's property taken or destroyed, and not to be limited in the use of one's property so long as one does not violate the rights of others. He concludes that the only morally permissible state would be the minimal nightwatchman state, a state limited to protecting people against murder, assault, theft, fraud, and breach of contract. The argument is not one which derives a surprising conclusion from plausible premises. No one (except perhaps an anarchist) who did not already accept the conclusion would accept the premise, and the implausibility of each can only serve to reinforce a conviction of the implausibility of the other.

Naturally any opposition to the power of governments will meet with a certain sympathy from observers of the contemporary scene, and Nozick emphasizes the connection between his view and the fight against legal regulation of sexual behavior, drug use, and individual life styles. It is easy to develop an aversion to state power by looking at how actual states wield it. Their activities often include murder, torture, political imprisonment, censorship, conscription for aggressive war, and overthrowing the governments of other countries—not to mention tapping the phones, reading the mail, or regulating the sexual behavior of their own citizens.

The objection to these abuses, however, is not that state power exists, but that it is used to do evil rather than good. Opposition to these evils cannot be translated into an objection to welfare, public education, or the graduated income tax. A reasonably persuasive practical argument for reducing the power of governments can perhaps be based on the unhappy results of that power. But it is doubtful that a government limited to the functions of police, courts, prisons, and

Risk," a brilliant discussion of the choice among various methods of dealing with injurious or dangerous behavior: when to prohibit, when to punish, when to require compensation, when to compensate someone who is inconvenienced by a prohibition. It is also the chapter with the greatest importance for legal theory. Pp. 54-88.
  3. P. ix.

Libertarianism Without Foundations

national defense would be conspicuously benign, or that it would be especially protective of individual rights.[4] In practice, it would probably include the worst parts of what we have now, without much of the best. That is why those concerned with individual liberty are usually not opposed to strong government with power to promote desirable ends, so long as the exercise of that power is limited by strong safeguards. Governments should promote what is good and prevent evils, as well as protecting rights. How could anyone disagree?

If there is an answer to this question, it must come from the ethical foundation of political theory. Nozick states:

> Moral philosophy sets the background for, and the boundaries of, political philosophy. What persons may and may not do to one another limits what they may do through the apparatus of a state, or do to establish such an apparatus. The moral prohibitions it is permissible to enforce are the source of whatever legitimacy the state's fundamental coercive power has.[5]

I believe that this principle is correct and important. The exercise of state power is not the action of a separate entity with moral rights greater than those of individual persons, rights to use force against persons for reasons that would not justify the use of force by individuals or groups of individuals per se. If governments have the right to coerce, it must be a right possessed by the people who establish and sustain governmental institutions, and those who act through them.

There is a problem about stating this position in a way that avoids triviality. For someone who believes that governments have much larger rights than individuals could always add that the existence of such rights implies a corresponding individual right to combine with others to institute a government and act through it to exercise those

4. This helps to account for the romantic appeal of anarchism. Nozick's attempt to refute the anarchist view that even a minimal state will violate individual rights is not, I think, successful. He argues at length that a minimal state could arise by an invisible hand process from a state of nature without the process violating anyone's rights: people could voluntarily join private protective associations, one of which would naturally achieve dominance over a territory even if not everyone had agreed to join. It could then exercise limited control without violating anyone's rights. This is supposed to show that a minimal state is morally permissible. But why should the mere conceivability of such a process persuade an anarchist of that conclusion? He would already have been prepared to admit that a minimal state established by *unanimous* agreement of the participants would be allowable. He just believes no actual state will be of this sort. Similarly, he may credit Nozick with having imagined another way in which a minimal state "could" arise which violated no one's rights, even though based on less than unanimous agreement. But the likelihood of any actual state meeting these moral conditions will be almost as low. The rejection of anarchism requires the rejection of its moral premises.

5. P. 6.

The Yale Law Journal   Vol. 85: 136, 1975

larger rights of coercion and control. But in such a view, these individual rights would be derivative from the rights of the state, and not the other way around. Nozick's position, which seems correct, is that individual rights and duties are the basis of what governments may and should do.

But he appears to infer from this ethical principle a strong epistemological consequence which it does not have: that it is possible to determine what governments may and should do by first asking what individuals, taken a few at a time in isolation from large-scale society, may do, and then applying the resultant principles to all possible circumstances, including those which involve billions of people, complicated political and economic institutions, and thousands of years of history. What is more surprising, he discovers in himself intuitions about the moral requirements on men in a state of nature which he is willing to endorse as universal principles unmodified in their cumulative effects when applied in any circumstances whatever.

Abstractly described, this procedure sounds hopelessly misguided.[6] It is hard to see how anyone could seriously arrive at firm moral opinions about the universal principles of human conduct without considering what it would be like if they were universally applied, in iterations which might create complex effects of scale. When we pass from an abstract to a more substantive description, the implausibility of the view increases. For the intuition that Nozick discovers in himself is that everyone has an absolute right to be free from coercion, and an absolute right to acquire and dispose of his property—so long as he is not violating the same rights of others and so long as his acquisition of property does not, for example, give him

---

6. Nozick defends the procedure in a section entitled "Macro and Micro." He says: [C]omplex wholes are not easily scanned; we cannot easily keep track of everything that is relevant. The justice of a whole society may depend on its satisfying a number of distinct principles. These principles, though individually compelling (witness their application to a wide range of particular microcases), may yield surprising results when combined together. . . . [O]ne should not depend upon judgments about the whole as providing the only or even the major body of data against which to check one's principles. One major path to changing one's intuitive judgments about some complex whole is through seeing the larger and often surprising implications of principles solidly founded at the micro level.
Pp. 205-06. Obviously; but another way to change one's intuitive judgments about the scope or truth of principles at the micro level is by seeing their larger implications. The fact that the rights of governments derive from the rights of individuals does not imply that we can come to know the rights of individuals without thinking about governments; just as the fact that the properties of molecules derive from the properties of atoms does not imply that we can come to know the properties of atoms without investigating molecules. The logical and the epistemological connections need not go in the same direction: even if political philosophy is logically dependent on ethics, our knowledge of some aspects of ethics may derive from an investigation of political philosophy.

Libertarianism Without Foundations

sole title to the formerly public water supply of a desert community.[7]

Nozick's intuition is that each person is entitled to his talents and abilities, and to whatever he can make, get, or buy with his own efforts, with the help of others, or with plain luck. He is entitled to keep it or do anything he wants with it, and whomever he gives it to is thereby equally entitled to it. Moreover, anyone is entitled to whatever he ends up with as a result of the indefinite repetition of this process, over however many generations. I assume that most readers of Nozick's book will find no echo of this intuition in themselves, and will feel instead that they can develop no opinion on the universal principles of entitlement, acquisition and transfer of property, or indeed whether there are any such universal principles, without considering the significance of such principles in their universal application. One might even agree in part with Nozick's views about what people should do in the limited circumstances that define interpersonal relations in the state of nature, but not agree that the proper generalization of those judgments is their unmodified application to all cases no matter how complex or extended. They might be based instead on principles which give these results for small-scale individual transactions but rather different results for the specification of general conditions of entitlement to be applied on an indefinitely large scale.[8]

The fact is, however, that Nozick's moral intuitions seem wrong even on a small scale. He denies that any of the rights he detects may be overridden merely to do good or prevent evil. But even if it is not permissible to murder or maim an innocent person to promote some highly desirable result, the protected rights do not all have the same degree of importance. The things one is supposed to be protected against are, in order of gravity: killing, injury, pain, physical force, deprivation of liberty of many different kinds (movement, association, and activity), destruction of one's property, taking of one's property; or the threat of any of the above (with all *their* variations in gravity). It is far less plausible to maintain that taking some of an innocent man's property is an impermissible means for the prevention of a serious evil, than it is to maintain that killing him is impermis-

---

7. The latter is the familiar proviso in Locke's theory of property acquisition, but according to Nozick it will not operate as a serious restriction in a free market system. P. 182.

8. The example of entitlement that he offers (p. 206) as a decisive retort to such skepticism—a natural right not to be deprived of one's vital organs for the benefit of others—is plausible partly because of the extreme character of such an assault and partly because there is no possibility that protection of this right will lead to the accumulation of vast hereditary wealth or inequalities of social and political power.

sible. These rights vary in importance and some are not absolute even in the state of nature.

The sources of morality are not simple but multiple; therefore its development in political theory will reflect that multiplicity. Rights limit the pursuit of worthwhile ends, but they can also sometimes be overridden if the ends are sufficiently important. The only way to make progress in understanding the nature of individual rights is to investigate their sources and their relations to each other and to the values on whose pursuit they set limits. Nozick says little about the basis of the inviolability of persons, but the following remark indicates where he would be inclined to look:

> [W]hy may not one violate persons for the greater social good? Individually, we each sometimes choose to undergo some pain or sacrifice for a greater benefit or to avoid a greater harm: we go to the dentist to avoid worse suffering later; we do some unpleasant work for its results; some persons diet to improve their health or looks; some save money to support themselves when they are older. In each case, some cost is borne for the sake of the greater overall good. Why not, *similarly*, hold that some persons have to bear some costs that benefit other persons more, for the sake of the overall social good? But there is no *social entity* with a good that undergoes some sacrifice for its own good. There are only individual people, different individual people, with their own individual lives. Using one of these people for the benefit of others, uses him and benefits the others. Nothing more. What happens is that something is done to him for the sake of others. Talk of an overall social good covers this up. (Intentionally?) To use a person in this way does not sufficiently respect and take account of the fact that he is a separate person, that his is the only life he has. *He* does not get some overbalancing good from his sacrifice, and no one is entitled to force this upon him—least of all a state or government that claims his allegiance (as other individuals do not) and that therefore scrupulously must be *neutral* between its citizens.[9]

It is not clear how Nozick thinks individual rights derive from the fact that each person's life is the only one he has. He appears to draw the implication that a benefit to one or more persons can never outweigh a cost borne by someone else. This, however, is far too broad a claim for Nozick's purposes. It is both obviously false and unsuitable as a basis for constraints on the treatment of individuals.

To make sense of interpersonal compensation it is not necessary to invoke the silly idea of a social entity, thus establishing an analogy

---

9. Pp. 32-33 (emphasis in original; footnote omitted).

Libertarianism Without Foundations

with intrapersonal compensation. All one needs is the belief, shared by most people, that it is better for each of 10 people to receive a benefit than for one person to receive it, worse for 10 people to be harmed than for one person to be similarly harmed, better for one person to benefit greatly than for another to benefit slightly, and so forth. The fact that each person's life is the only one he has does not render us incapable of making these judgments, and if a choice among such alternatives does *not* involve the violation of any rights or entitlements, but only the allocation of limited time or resources, then we regard those comparisons as excellent reasons for picking one alternative rather than the other. If we can help either 10 people or one person, not included in the 10, and we help the 10, then we can say that rescue of the 10 outweighs the loss of the one, despite the fact that *he* does not get some overbalancing good from his sacrifice, and his is the only life he has.

So for the purpose of comparing possible outcomes of action, where the violation of rights is not in question, it is clear that the distinctness of individuals does not prevent balancing of benefits and harms across persons. If special constraints enter in when a sacrifice is to be imposed on someone as a *means* to the achievement of a desirable outcome, their source must lie elsewhere. Such constraints should not derive from a principle which also has the consequence that practically nothing can be said about the relative desirability of situations involving numbers of different people.

Furthermore, the source of rights of the general kind Nozick advocates cannot be discovered by concentrating, as he suggests we should, on the meaning of individual human lives and the value of shaping one's own life and forming a general conception of it. Vague as his suggestions are,[10] they all suffer from an error of focus, for they concentrate solely on features of persons that make it bad for certain things to *happen* to them, and good for them to have the opportunity to do certain things. But rights of the kind that interest Nozick are not rights that certain things not *happen* to you, or rights to be provided with certain opportunities. Rather they are rights not to be deliberately treated or used in certain ways, and not to be deliberately interfered with in certain activities. They give rise to claims not against the world at large, but only against someone who contemplates deliberately violating them. The *relation* between the possessor of the right and the actor, rather than just the intrinsic nature of the possessor and of his life, must enter into the analysis of the

10. *See* pp. 49-50.

The Yale Law Journal Vol. 85: 136, 1975

right and the explication of its basis.

Any theory of rights must explain this structural feature, even if it does not follow Nozick in elevating the unimpeded exercise of the will into the supreme principle of morality. It is of the first importance that your right not to be assaulted is *not* a right that everyone do what is required to ensure that you are not assaulted. It is merely a right not to be assaulted, and it is correlated with other people's duty not to *assault* you. This cannot be explained simply by the fact that it is bad to be assaulted, which is merely an item in the catalogue of values by which the desirability or undesirability of occurrences or sets of occurrences is to be weighed. That assault is disagreeable or bad does not explain why the prohibition of it should serve as a constraint on the pursuit of other values or the avoidance of other harms, even if those other values outweigh the badness of assault in a pure calculation of the relative desirability of possible outcomes. Sometimes one is required to choose the less desirable alternative because to achieve the more desirable one would have to violate a right.

As Nozick points out,[11] the constraints on action represented by rights cannot be equivalent to an assignment of large disvalue to their violation, for that would make it permissible to violate such a right if by doing so one could prevent more numerous or more serious violations of the same right by others. This is not in general true. It is not permissible in Nozick's view (or mine) to kill an innocent person even to prevent the deliberate killing of three other innocent persons. A general feature of anything worthy of being called a right is that it is not translatable into a mere assignment of disvalue to its violation.

An explanation of the basis of rights would therefore have to concentrate on the actor and his relation to the person he is constrained not to treat in certain ways, even to achieve very desirable ends. And it would have to explore the interaction between those constraints, and the goals whose pursuit they constrain. There is no reason to think that either in personal life or in society the force of every right will be absolute or nearly absolute, *i.e.*, never capable of being overridden by consequential considerations. Rights not to be deliberately killed, injured, tormented, or imprisoned are very powerful and limit the pursuit of any goal. More limited restrictions of liberty of action, restrictions on the use of property, restrictions on contracts, are simply less serious and therefore provide less powerful

11. P. 29.

144

Libertarianism Without Foundations

constraints.[12]

Moreover, there is a big difference between suddenly expropriating half of someone's savings and attaching monetary conditions in advance to activities, expenditures, and earnings—the usual form of taxation. The latter is a much less brutal assault upon the person.[13] Whether this kind of limitation of individual liberty should be permitted, to acquire resources for the promotion of desirable ends, is a function of the gravity of the violation and the desirability of the ends. (And as I have observed, this does not mean that it is justified whenever the result is a maximal social balance of benefits and costs.)

Nozick would reply that such ends can be achieved by voluntary donations rather than by compulsion, and that people who are well-off and who deplore the existence of poverty should donate significant portions of their assets to help those who are unfortunate.[14] But this is no more plausible coming from Nozick than it was coming from Barry Goldwater. Most people are not generous when asked to give voluntarily, and it is unreasonable to ask that they should be. Admittedly there are cases in which a person should do something although it would not be right to force him to do it. But here I believe the reverse is true. Sometimes it is proper to force people to do something even though it is not true that they should do it without being forced. It is acceptable to compel people to contribute to the support of the indigent by automatic taxation, but unreasonable to insist that in the absence of such a system they ought to contribute voluntarily. The latter is an excessively demanding moral position because it requires voluntary decisions that are quite difficult to make. Most people will tolerate a universal system of compulsory taxation without feeling entitled to complain, whereas they would feel justified in refusing an appeal that they contribute the same amount volun-

12. The fact that a right can be overridden to avoid sufficiently serious consequences does not mean that its violation can be assigned a disvalue comparable to the disvalue of those consequences. For that would give the occurrence of such a violation greater weight in a calculation of outcomes (e.g., when the question is what may be done to prevent such violations by others) than it in fact has. Therefore, although rights may on occasion be overridden, the violation of some people's rights cannot automatically be justified because it leads to a reduction in the more serious violation of other people's rights. This issue arises in connection with preventive detention, wiretapping, and search and seizure, all of which might be useful in the prevention of robbery, murder, assault, and rape.

13. It may be objected that taxation must be backed up by the threat of stronger force and even violence. But this arises only if there is resistance at the first level. If the original, nonviolent demand is legitimate, escalation may occur if the subject resists it and uses stronger methods to resist each succeeding method for enforcing the previous one.

14. Pp. 265-68.

145

tarily. This is partly due to lack of assurance that others would do likewise and fear of relative disadvantage; but it is also a sensible rejection of excessive demands on the will, which can be more irksome than automatic demands on the purse.

A political theory that reflected these moral complexities would assign society the function of promoting certain goods and preventing certain evils, within limits set by the differing constraints of different individual rights. It would not judge processes and procedures solely by their tendency to produce certain outcomes, nor would it judge outcomes solely by the processes that had produced them. Social institutions and the procedures defining them would be assessed by reference both to their respect for individual rights and liberty, and to their tendency to promote desirable ends like the general welfare.

Nozick offers a classification of principles of distributive justice into which such a theory does not fit.[15] After defining a *historical* principle as one which asserts that the justice of a distribution depends on how it came about,[16] and an end-result principle as one which denies this,[17] he defines a *patterned* principle as one which specifies "that a distribution is to vary along with some natural dimension, weighted sum of natural dimensions, or lexicographic ordering of natural dimensions."[18] His own theory, the entitlement theory, is easy to describe in these terms. It is a nonpatterned historical principle, for it specifies that any distribution is just if it was arrived at by a series of individual transactions among people entitled, by natural rights of acquisition and transfer, to make them.

But suppose a theory says that a distribution is just if it results from a process governed by rules that reflect (a) the suitability of certain patterns, (b) the desirability of increasing certain good results and decreasing certain evils independently of any pattern, and (c) a respect for individual rights of differing importance. Such a theory will be at bottom neither purely historical nor purely patterned. It will be formally historical, but the "historical" or process criterion will be partially determined by considerations of pattern and considerations of total outcome. Therefore Nozick's concentrated attack on patterned principles and nonhistorical principles provides no reason to think that his alternative is correct.[19]

---

15. Of course distribution is only one of the things covered in any political theory, but we may leave others aside for the moment.
16. P. 153.
17. P. 155.
18. P. 156. "To each according to his need" would be an example.
19. More specifically, his arguments against Rawls are seriously weakened by a Procrustean attempt to portray Rawls's principle of distributive justice as a nonhistorical or

Libertarianism Without Foundations

Apart from this defect, the attack is still unsuccessful. Nozick asks us to imagine some patterned principle realized, and then argues that its preservation would require interference with individual liberty: people would have to be prevented from using their allocations under the pattern as they wish. For example, preservation of a reasonably equal distribution would require that individuals not be permitted to pay Wilt Chamberlain 25 cents for each basketball game they see him play with the understanding that he can keep it all, even if it amounts to $250,000 a year. This is perfectly obvious, and it is part of what would be *meant* by a patterned principle of distribution: the adoption of a general system of acquisition, taxation and exchange that tends to preserve a certain pattern.

It only seems a problem to Nozick, and a further violation of liberty, because he erroneously interprets the notion of a patterned principle as specifying a distribution of *absolute entitlements* (like those he believes in) to the wealth or property distributed. But absolute entitlement to property is not what would be allocated to people under a partially egalitarian distribution. Possession would confer the kind of qualified entitlement that exists in a system under which taxes and other conditions are arranged to preserve certain features of the distribution, while permitting choice, use, and exchange of property compatible with it. What someone holds under such a system will not be *his property* in the unqualified sense of Nozick's system of entitlement. To suppose otherwise is to beg the question, and that is exactly what Nozick does when he says:

> There is *no* question about whether each of the people was entitled to the control over the resources they held in D_1 [the original patterned distribution]; because that was the distribution (your favorite) that (for the purposes of argument) we assumed was acceptable. . . . If the people were entitled to dispose of the resources to which they were entitled (under D_1), didn't this include their being entitled to give it to, or exchange it with, Wilt Chamberlain?[20]

This mistake drains the argument of its force.

---

end-result principle. Rawls does not maintain that the justice of a distribution can be determined independently of how it was produced. He believes that its justice depends on the justice of the institutions, including legal institutions defining entitlement, which were involved in its production. These are assessed only partly on the basis of their tendency to promote a certain distributive end-state. Rawls, for example, gives priority to the preservation of individual liberty, and while he does not mean by this what Nozick means, it certainly restricts the procedures by which a distribution can be justly arrived at. *See generally* J. RAWLS, A THEORY OF JUSTICE (1971).

20. P. 161 (emphasis in original).

Let me turn briefly to the difficult subject of equality. While the elimination of misery, poverty, and disease are probably more important social goals than the achievement of economic equality, the latter is one of the ends some people regard as legitimate. Nozick's view is predictable. If inequality arises as a result of the free exercise of entitlements, it cannot be objected to on grounds of injustice, and liberty may not be in any way infringed to reduce it. Since people are entitled not only to the wealth they inherit but to their natural assets,[21] further inequalities resulting from the employment of these assets are just.

But there is no reason to believe in an absolute natural right to profit from one's natural assets, even if a less than absolute right to their free exercise is acknowledged as a limitation on the pursuit of equality or other social goals. Someone who regards equality as a good will assume that its achievement does not take absolute precedence over efficiency, liberty, and other values. Nevertheless, more than this is required to answer Nozick, for it it not clear what makes equality of distribution a good thing *at all*. Nozick does not acknowledge the right of the state to limit liberty to produce any merely desirable outcome. But why should someone with a more standard view about individual rights be in favor of a goal of social and economic equality? Perhaps he can argue that the average level of well-being—both in material terms and in terms of contentment and self-esteem—is likely to be higher in a relatively equal society than in an unequal one of comparable total wealth. Perhaps he will argue that the political effects of economic inequality are harmful to individual liberty and general welfare. But these considerations, though very important, are not reasons for regarding equality as a good in itself; yet that is a common moral view.

It cannot be defended by claiming that inequalities are arbitrary unless based on morally relevant differences among people. Arbitrariness is a moral defect only if it can be contrasted with an alternative that is selected on the basis of morally relevant factors. Unless there is independent justification for equality, an equal distribution is just as arbitrary from a moral point of view as any other. To defend equality as a good in itself, one would have to argue that improvements in the lot of people lower on the scale of well-being took priority over greater improvements to those higher on the scale, even if the latter improvements also affected more people. While I am sym-

21. P. 225.

Libertarianism Without Foundations

pathetic to such a view, I do not believe it has ever been successfully
defended.

I have dwelt on the book's theoretical shortcomings; there is much
in it that I have not discussed, including a final chapter which describes a pluralistic libertarian utopia,[22] and interesting analyses of
such diverse topics as Marx's labor theory of value[23] and the treatment
of animals.[24] Unlike most works of philosophy, it is funny, fast-paced
and a pleasure to read. Nozick's writing, though inelegant, has great
energy, and meets a high standard of clarity and definiteness. One
is rarely in doubt about what Nozick is claiming, or about what one
denies in rejecting his views.

22.   Pp. 297-333.
23.   Pp. 252-62.
24.   Pp. 35-41.

Part III
Social-Democratic Liberalism

A
Origins

[22]

Excerpt from L.T. Hobhouse (1964), *Liberalism*, 16–29

II

THE ELEMENTS OF LIBERALISM

I cannot here attempt so much as a sketch of the historical progress of the Liberalizing movement. I would call attention only to
the main points at which it assailed the old order, and to the
fundamental ideas directing its advance.

1. CIVIL LIBERTY.

Both logically and historically the first point of attack is arbitrary
government, and the first liberty to be secured is the right to be
dealt with in accordance with law. A man who has no legal rights
against another, but stands entirely at his disposal, to be treated
according to his caprice, is a slave to that other. He is "rightless,"
devoid of rights. Now, in some barbaric monarchies the system
of rightlessness has at times been consistently carried through in
the relations of subjects to the king. Here men and women, though
enjoying customary rights of person and property as against one
another, have no rights at all as against the king's pleasure. No
European monarch or seignior has ever admittedly enjoyed power
of this kind, but European governments have at various times and
in various directions exercised or claimed powers no less arbitrary
in principle. Thus, by the side of the regular courts of law which
prescribe specific penalties for defined offences proved against a
man by a regular form of trial, arbitrary governments resort to
various extrajudicial forms of arrest, detention, and punishment,
depending on their own will and pleasure. Of such a character is
punishment by "administrative" process in Russia at the present

16

day; imprisonment by *lettre de cachet* in France under the *ancien régime;* all executions by so-called martial law in times of rebellion, and the suspension of various ordinary guarantees of immediate and fair trial in Ireland. Arbitrary government in this form was one of the first objects of attack by the English Parliament in the seventeenth century, and this first liberty of the subject was vindicated by the Petition of Right, and again by the Habeas Corpus Act. It is significant of much that this first step in liberty should be in reality nothing more nor less than a demand for law. "Freedom of men under government," says Locke, summing up one whole chapter of seventeenth-century controversy, "is to have a standing rule to live by, common to every one of that society and made by the legislative power erected in it."

The first condition of universal freedom, that is to say, is a measure of universal restraint. Without such restraint some men may be free but others will be unfree. One man may be able to do all his will, but the rest will have no will except that which he sees fit to allow them. To put the same point from another side, the first condition of free government is government not by the arbitrary determination of the ruler, but by fixed rules of law, to which the ruler himself is subject. We draw the important inference that there is no essential antithesis between liberty and law. On the contrary, law is essential to liberty. Law, of course, restrains the individual; it is therefore opposed to his liberty at a given moment and in a given direction. But, equally, law restrains others from doing with him as they will. It liberates him from the fear of arbitrary aggression or coercion, and this is the only way, indeed, the only sense, in which liberty *for an entire community* is attainable.

There is one point tacitly postulated in this argument which should not be overlooked. In assuming that the reign of law guarantees liberty to the whole community, we are assuming that it is impartial. If there is one law for the Government and another for its subjects, one for noble and another for commoner, one for rich and another for poor, the law does not guarantee liberty for all. Liberty in this respect implies equality. Hence the demand of Liberalism for such a procedure as will ensure the impartial application of law. Hence the demand for the independence of the judiciary to secure equality as between the Government and its subjects. Hence the demand for cheap procedure and accessible

18   LIBERALISM

courts. Hence the abolition of privileges of class.[1] Hence will come in time the demand for the abolition of the power of money to purchase skilled advocacy.

2. FISCAL LIBERTY.

Closely connected with juristic liberty, and more widely felt in everyday life, is the question of fiscal liberty. The Stuarts brought things to a head in this country by arbitrary taxation. George III brought things to a head in America by the same infallible method. The immediate cause of the French Revolution was the refusal of the nobles and the clergy to bear their share of the financial burden. But fiscal liberty raises more searching questions than juristic liberty. It is not enough that taxes should be fixed by a law applying universally and impartially, for taxes vary from year to year in accordance with public needs, and while other laws may remain stable and unchanged for an indefinite period, taxation must, in the nature of the case, be adjustable. It is a matter, properly considered, for the Executive rather than the Legislature. Hence the liberty of the subject in fiscal matters means the restraint of the Executive, not merely by established and written laws, but by a more direct and constant supervision. It means, in a word, responsible government, and that is why we have more often heard the cry, "No taxation without representation," than the cry, "No legislation without representation." Hence, from the seventeenth century onwards, fiscal liberty was seen to involve what is called political liberty.

3. PERSONAL LIBERTY.

Of political liberty it will be more convenient to speak later. But let us here observe that there is another avenue by which it can be, and, in fact, was, approached. We have seen that the reign of

---

[1] In England "benefit of clergy" was still a good plea for remission of sentence for a number of crimes in the seventeenth century. At that time all who could read could claim benefit, which was therefore of the nature of a privilege for the educated class. The requirement of reading, which had become a form, was abolished in 1705, but peers and clerks in holy orders could still plead their clergy in the eighteenth century, and the last relics of the privilege were not finally abolished till the nineteenth century.

law is the first step to liberty. A man is not free when he is controlled by other men, but only when he is controlled by principles and rules which all society must obey, for the community is the true master of the free man. But here we are only at the beginning of the matter. There may be law, and there may be no attempt, such as the Stuarts made, to set law aside, yet (1) the making and maintenance of law may depend on the will of the sovereign or of an oligarchy, and (2) the content of the law may be unjust and oppressive to some, to many, or to all except those who make it. The first point brings us back to the problem of political liberty, which we defer. The second opens questions which have occupied a great part of the history of Liberalism, and to deal with them we have to ask what types of law have been felt as peculiarly oppressive, and in what respects it has been necessary to claim liberty not merely through law, but by the abolition of bad law and tyrannical administration.

In the first place, there is the sphere of what is called personal liberty—a sphere most difficult to define, but the arena of the fiercest strife of passion and the deepest feelings of mankind. At the basis lies liberty of thought—freedom from inquisition into opinions that a man forms in his own mind[1]—the inner citadel where, if anywhere, the individual must rule. But liberty of thought is of very little avail without liberty to exchange thoughts —since thought is mainly a social product; and so with liberty of thought goes liberty of speech and liberty of writing, printing, and peaceable discussion. These rights are not free from difficulty and dubiety. There is a point at which speech becomes indistinguishable from action, and free speech may mean the right to create disorder. The limits of just liberty here are easy to draw neither in theory nor in practice. They lead us immediately to one of the points at which liberty and order may be in conflict, and it is with conflicts of this kind that we shall have to deal. The possibilities of conflict are not less in relation to the connected right of liberty in religion. That this liberty is absolute cannot be contended. No modern state would tolerate a form of religious worship which should include cannibalism, human sacrifice, or the burning of

---

[1] See an interesting chapter in Faguet's *Liberalisme*, which points out that the common saying that thought is free is negated by any inquisition which compels a man to disclose opinions, and penalizes him if they are not such as to suit the inquisitor.

witches. In point of fact, practices of this kind—which follow quite naturally from various forms of primitive belief that are most sincerely held—are habitually put down by civilized peoples that are responsible for the government of less developed races. The British law recognizes polygamy in India, but I imagine it would not be open either to a Mahommedan or a Hindu to contract two marriages in England. Nor is it for liberty of this kind that the battle has been fought.

What, then, is the primary meaning of religious liberty? Externally, I take it to include the liberties of thought and expression, and to add to these the right of worship in any form which does not inflict injury on others or involve a breach of public order. This limitation appears to carry with it a certain decency and restraint in expression which avoids unnecessary insult to the feelings of others; and I think this implication must be allowed, though it makes some room for strained and unfair applications. Externally, again, we must note that the demand for religious liberty soon goes beyond mere toleration. Religious liberty is incomplete as long as any belief is penalized, as, for example, by carrying with it exclusion from office or from educational advantages. On this side, again, full liberty implies full equality. Turning to the internal side, the spirit of religious liberty rests on the conception that a man's religion ranks with his own innermost thought and feelings. It is the most concrete expression of his personal attitude to life, to his kind, to the world, to his own origin and destiny. There is no real religion that is not thus drenched in personality; and the more religion is recognized for spiritual the starker the contradiction is felt to be that any one should seek to impose a religion on another. Properly regarded, the attempt is not wicked, but impossible. Yet those sin most against true religion who try to convert men from the outside by mechanical means. They have the lie in the soul, being most ignorant of the nature of that for which they feel most deeply.

Yet here again we stumble on difficulties. Religion is personal. Yet is not religion also eminently social? What is more vital to the social order than its beliefs? If we send a man to gaol for stealing trash, what shall we do to him whom, in our conscience and on our honour, we believe to be corrupting the hearts of mankind, and perhaps leading them to eternal perdition? Again, what in the name of liberty are we to do to men whose preaching, if followed out in act, would bring back the rack and the stake? Once more there is a difficulty of delimitation which will have to be fully sifted. I will only remark here that our practice has arrived at a solution which, upon the whole, appears to have worked well hitherto, and which has its roots in principle. It is open to a man to preach the principles of Torquemada or the religion of Mahomet. It is not open to men to practise such of their precepts as would violate the rights of others or cause a breach of the peace. Expression is free, and worship is free as far as it is the expression of personal devotion. So far as they infringe the freedom, or, more generally, the rights of others, the practices inculcated by a religion cannot enjoy unqualified freedom.

4. SOCIAL LIBERTY.

From the spiritual we turn to the practical side of life. On this side we may observe, first, that Liberalism has had to deal with those restraints on the individual which flow from the hierarchic organization of society, and reserve certain offices, certain forms of occupation, and perhaps the right or at least the opportunity of education generally, to people of a certain rank or class. In its more extreme form this is a caste system, and its restrictions are religious or legal as well as social. In Europe it has taken more than one form. There is the monopoly of certain occupations by corporations, prominent in the minds of eighteenth-century French reformers. There is the reservation of public appointments and ecclesiastical patronage for those who are "born," and there is a more subtly pervading spirit of class which produces a hostile attitude to those who could and would rise; and this spirit finds a more material ally in the educational difficulties that beset brains unendowed with wealth. I need not labour points which will be apparent to all, but have again to remark two things. (1) Once more the struggle for liberty is also, when pushed through, a struggle for equality. Freedom to choose and follow an occupation, if it is to become fully effective, means equality with others in the opportunities for following such occupation. This is, in fact, one among the various considerations which lead Liberalism to support a national system of free education, and will lead it further yet on the same lines. (2) Once again, though we may insist on the rights of the individual, the social value of the corporation or quasi-corporation, like the Trade Union, cannot be ignored. Experience shows the necessity of some measure of collective regulation in industrial matters, and in the adjustment of such regulation to individual liberty serious difficulties of principle emerge. We shall have to refer to these in the next section. But one point is relevant at this stage. It is clearly a matter of Liberal principle that membership of a corporation should not depend on any hereditary qualification, nor be set about with any artificial difficulty of entry, where by the term artificial is meant any difficulty not involved in the nature of the occupation concerned, but designed for purposes of exclusiveness. As against all such methods of restriction, the Liberal case is clear.

It has only to be added here that restrictions of sex are in every respect parallel to restrictions of class. There are, doubtless, occupations for which women are unfit. But, if so, the test of fitness is sufficient to exclude them. The "open road for women" is one application, and a very big one, of the "open road for talent," and to secure them both is of the essence of Liberalism.

5. ECONOMIC LIBERTY.

Apart from monopolies, industry was shackled in the earlier part of the modern period by restrictive legislation in various forms, by navigation laws, and by tariffs. In particular, the tariff was not merely an obstruction to free enterprise, but a source of inequality as between trade and trade. Its fundamental effect is to transfer capital and labour from the objects on which they can be most profitably employed in a given locality, to objects on which they are less profitably employed, by endowing certain industries to the disadvantage of the general consumer. Here, again, the Liberal movement is at once an attack on an obstruction and on an inequality. In most countries the attack has succeeded in breaking down local tariffs and establishing relatively large Free Trade units. It is only in England, and only owing to our early manufacturing supremacy, that it has fully succeeded in overcoming the Protective principle, and even in England the Protectionist reaction would undoubtedly have gained at least a temporary victory but for our dependence on foreign countries for food and the materials of industry. The most striking victory of Liberal ideas is one of the most precarious. At the same time, the battle

is one which Liberalism is always prepared to fight over again.
It has led to no back stroke, no counter-movement within the
Liberal ranks themselves.

It is otherwise with organized restrictions upon industry. The
old regulations, which were quite unsuited to the conditions of
the time, either fell into desuetude during the eighteenth century,
or were formally abolished during the earlier years of the industrial revolution. For a while it seemed as though wholly unrestricted industrial enterprise was to be the progressive watchword,
and the echoes of that time still linger. But the old restrictions had
not been formally withdrawn before a new process of regulation began. The conditions produced by the new factory system
shocked the public conscience; and as early as 1802 we find the
first of a long series of laws, out of which has grown an industrial
code that year by year follows the life of the operative, in his
relations with his employer, into more minute detail. The first
stages of this movement were contemplated with doubt and distrust by many men of Liberal sympathies. The intention was,
doubtless, to protect the weaker party, but the method was that of
interference with freedom of contract. Now the freedom of the
sane adult individual—even such strong individualists as Cobden
recognized that the case of children stood apart—carried with it
the right of concluding such agreements as seemed best to suit his
own interests, and involved both the right and the duty of determining the lines of his life for himself. Free contract and personal
responsibility lay close to the heart of the whole Liberal movement. Hence the doubts felt by so many Liberals as to the regulation of industry by law. None the less, as time has gone on, men
of the keenest Liberal sympathies have come not merely to accept
but eagerly to advance the extension of public control in the
industrial sphere, and of collective responsibility in the matter of
the education and even the feeding of children, the housing of the
industrial population, the care of the sick and aged, the provision
of the means of regular employment. On this side Liberalism
seems definitely to have retraced its steps, and we shall have to
inquire closely into the question whether the reversal is a change
of principle or of application.

Closely connected with freedom of contract is freedom of association. If men may make any agreement with one another in
their mutual interest so long as they do not injure a third party,

they may apparently agree to act together permanently for any purposes of common interest on the same conditions. That is, they may form associations. Yet at bottom the powers of an association are something very different from the powers of the individuals composing it; and it is only by legal pedantry that the attempt can be made to regulate the behavior of an association on principles derived from and suitable to the relations of individuals. An association might become so powerful as to form a state within the state, and to contend with government on no unequal terms. The history of some revolutionary societies, of some ecclesiastical organizations, even of some American trusts might be quoted to show that the danger is not imaginary. Short of this, an association may act oppressively towards others and even towards its own members, and the function of Liberalism may be rather to protect the individual against the power of the association than to protect the right of association against the restriction of the law. In fact, in this regard, the principle of liberty cuts both ways, and this double application is reflected in history. The emancipation of trade unions, however, extending over the period from 1824 to 1906, and perhaps not yet complete, was in the main a liberating movement, because combination was necessary to place the workman on something approaching terms of equality with the employer, and because tacit combinations of employers could never, in fact, be prevented by law. It was, again, a movement to liberty through equality. On the other hand, the oppressive capacities of a trade union could never be left out of account, while combinations of capital, which might be infinitely more powerful, have justly been regarded with distrust. In this there is no inconsistency of principle, but a just appreciation of a real difference of circumstance. Upon the whole it may be said that the function of Liberalism is not so much to maintain a general right of free association as to define the right in each case in such terms as make for the maximum of real liberty and equality.

6. DOMESTIC LIBERTY.

Of all associations within the State, the miniature community of the Family is the most universal and of the strongest independent vitality. The authoritarian state was reflected in the authoritarian family, in which the husband was within wide limits absolute lord of the person and property of wife and children. The movement of liberation consists (1) in rendering the wife a fully responsible individual, capable of holding property, suing and being sued, conducting business on her own account, and enjoying full personal protection against her husband; (2) in establishing marriage as far as the law is concerned on a purely contractual basis, and leaving the sacramental aspect of marriage to the ordinances of the religion professed by the parties; (3) in securing the physical, mental, and moral care of the children, partly by imposing definite responsibilities on the parents and punishing them for neglect, partly by elaborating a public system of education and of hygiene. The first two movements are sufficiently typical cases of the interdependence of liberty and equality. The third is more often conceived as a Socialistic than a Liberal tendency, and, in point of fact, the State control of education gives rise to some searching questions of principle, which have not yet been fully solved. If, in general, education is a duty which the State has a right to enforce, there is a countervailing right of choice as to the lines of education which it would be ill to ignore, and the mode of adjustment has not yet been adequately determined either in theory or in practice. I would, however, strongly maintain that the general conception of the State as Over-parent is quite as truly Liberal as Socialistic. It is the basis of the rights of the child, of his protection against parental neglect, of the equality of opportunity which he may claim as a future citizen, of his training to fill his place as a grown-up person in the social system. Liberty once more involves control and restraint.

7. LOCAL, RACIAL, AND NATIONAL LIBERTY.

From the smallest social unit we pass to the largest. A great part of the liberating movement is occupied with the struggle of entire nations against alien rule, with the revolt of Europe against Napoleon, with the struggle of Italy for freedom, with the fate of the Christian subjects of Turkey, with the emancipation of the Negro, with the national movement in Ireland and in India. Many of these struggles present the problem of liberty in its simplest form. It has been and is too often a question of securing the most elementary rights for the weaker party; and those who are not touched by the appeal are deficient rather in imagination than in logic or ethics. But at the back of national movements very diffi-cult questions do arise. What is a nation as distinct from a state? What sort of unity does it constitute, and what are its rights? If Ireland is a nation, is Ulster one? and if Ulster is a British and Protestant nation, what of the Catholic half of Ulster? History has in some cases given us a practical answer. Thus, it has shown that, enjoying the gift of responsible government, French and British, despite all historical quarrels and all differences of reli-gious belief, language, and social structure, have fused into the nation of Canada. History has justified the conviction that Ger-many was a nation, and thrown ridicule on the contemptuous say-ing of Metternich that Italy was a geographical expression. But how to anticipate history, what rights to concede to a people that claims to be a self-determining unit, is less easy to decide. There is no doubt that the general tendency of Liberalism is to favour autonomy, but, faced as it is with the problems of subdivision and the complexity of group with group, it has to rely on the concrete teaching of history and the practical insight of statesmanship to determine how the lines of autonomy are to be drawn. There is, however, one empirical test which seems generally applicable. Where a weaker nation incorporated with a larger or stronger one can be governed by ordinary law applicable to both parties to the union, and fulfilling all the ordinary principles of liberty, the ar-rangement may be the best for both parties. But where this sys-tem fails, where the government is constantly forced to resort to exceptional legislation or perhaps to de-liberalize its own institu-tions, the case becomes urgent. Under such conditions the most liberally-minded democracy is maintaining a system which must undermine its own principles. The Assyrian conqueror, Mr. Her-bert Spencer remarks, who is depicted in the bas-reliefs leading his captive by a cord, is bound with that cord himself. He forfeits his liberty as long as he retains his power.

Somewhat similar questions arise about race, which many peo-ple wrongly confuse with nationality. So far as elementary rights are concerned there can be no question as to the attitude of Liberalism. When the political power which should guarantee such rights is brought into view, questions of fact arise. Is the Negro or the Kaffir mentally and morally capable of self-govern-ment or of taking part in a self-governing State? The experience of Cape Colony tends to the affirmative view. American experience of the Negro gives, I take it, a more doubtful answer. A specious extension of the white man's rights to the black may be the best way of ruining the black. To destroy tribal custom by introducing conceptions of individual property, the free disposal of land, and the free purchase of gin may be the handiest method for the expropriator. In all relations with weaker peoples we move in an atmosphere vitiated by the insincere use of high-sounding words. If men say equality, they mean oppression by forms of justice. If they say tutelage, they appear to mean the kind of tutelage extended to the fattened goose. In such an atmosphere, perhaps, our safest course, so far as principles and deductions avail at all, is to fix our eyes on the elements of the matter, and in any part of the world to support whatever method succeeds in securing the "coloured" man from personal violence, from the lash, from expropriation, and from gin; above all, so far as it may yet be, from the white man himself. Until the white man has fully learnt to rule his own life, the best of all things that he can do with the dark man is to do nothing with him. In this relation, the day of a more constructive Liberalism is yet to come.

8. INTERNATIONAL LIBERTY.

If non-interference is the best thing for the barbarian many Liberals have thought it to be the supreme wisdom in international affairs generally. I shall examine this view later. Here I merely remark: (1) It is of the essence of Liberalism to oppose the use of force, the basis of all tyranny. (2) It is one of its practical necessities to withstand the tyranny of armaments. Not only may the military force be directly turned against liberty, as in Russia, but there are more subtle ways, as in Western Europe, in which the military spirit eats into free institutions and absorbs the public resources which might go to the advancement of civilization. (3) In proportion as the world becomes free, the use of force becomes meaningless. There is no purpose in aggression if it is not to issue in one form or another of national subjection.

9. POLITICAL LIBERTY AND POPULAR SOVEREIGNTY.

Underlying all these questions of right is the question how they are to be secured and maintained. By enforcing the responsibility of the executive and legislature to the community as a whole? Such is the general answer, and it indicates one of the lines of connection between the general theory of liberty and the doctrine of universal suffrage and the sovereignty of the people. The answer, however, does not meet all the possibilities of the case. The people as a whole might be careless of their rights and incapable of managing them. They might be set on the conquest of others, the expropriation of the rich, or on any form of collective tyranny or folly. It is perfectly possible that from the point of view of general liberty and social progress a limited franchise might give better results than one that is more extended. Even in this country it is a tenable view that the extension of the suffrage in 1884 tended for some years to arrest the development of liberty in various directions. On what theory does the principle of popular sovereignty rest, and within what limits does it hold good? Is it a part of the general principles of liberty and equality, or are other ideas involved? These are among the questions which we shall have to examine.

We have now passed the main phases of the Liberal movement in very summary review, and we have noted, first, that it is co-extensive with life. It is concerned with the individual, the family, the State. It touches industry, law, religion, ethics. It would not be difficult, if space allowed, to illustrate its influence in literature and art, to describe the war with convention, insincerity, and patronage, and the struggle for free self-expression, for reality, for the artist's soul. Liberalism is an all-penetrating element of the life-structure of the modern world. Secondly, it is an effective historical force. If its work is nowhere complete, it is almost everywhere in progress. The modern State as we see it in Europe outside Russia, in the British colonies, in North and South America, as we begin to see it in the Russian empire and throughout the vast continent of Asia, is the old authoritarian society modified in greater or less degree by the absorption of Liberal principles. Turning, thirdly, to those principles themselves, we have recognized Liberalism in every department as a movement fairly denoted by the name—a movement of liberation, a clearance of obstructions, an opening of channels for the flow of free spontaneous vital activity. Fourthly, we have seen that in a large number of cases what is under one aspect a movement for liberty is on another side a movement towards equality, and the habitual association of these principles is so far confirmed. On the other hand, lastly, we have seen numerous cases in which the exacter definition of liberty and the precise meaning of equality remain obscure, and to discuss these will be our task. We have, moreover, admittedly regarded Liberalism mainly in its earlier and more negative aspect. We have seen it as a force working within an old society and modifying it by the loosening of the bonds which its structure imposed on human activity. We have yet to ask what constructive social scheme, if any, could be formed on Liberal principles; and it is here, if at all, that the fuller meaning of the principles of Liberty and Equality should appear, and the methods of applying them be made out. The problem of popular sovereignty pointed to the same need. Thus the lines of the remainder of our task are clearly laid down. We have to get at the fundamentals of Liberalism, and to consider what kind of structure can be raised upon the basis which they offer. We will approach the question by tracing the historic movement of Liberal thought through certain well-marked phases. We shall see how the problems which have been indicated were attacked by successive thinkers, and how partial solutions gave occasion for deeper probings. Following the guidance of the actual movement of ideas, we shall reach the centre and heart of Liberalism, and we shall try to form a conception of the essentials of the Liberal creed as a constructive theory of society. This conception we shall then apply to the greater questions, political and economic, of our own day; and this will enable us finally to estimate the present position of Liberalism as a living force in the modern world and the prospect of transforming its ideals into actualities.

[23]

Excerpt from L.T. Hobhouse (1964), *Liberalism*, 63–73

VI

THE HEART OF LIBERALISM

The teaching of Mill brings us close to the heart of Liberalism. We learn from him, in the first place, that liberty is no mere formula of law, or of the restriction of law. There may be a tyranny of custom, a tyranny of opinion, even a tyranny of circumstance, as real as any tyranny of government and more pervasive. Nor does liberty rest on the self-assertion of the individual. There is scope abundant for Liberalism and illiberalism in personal conduct. Nor is liberty opposed to discipline, to organization, to strenuous conviction as to what is true and just. Nor is it to be identified with tolerance of opposed opinions. The Liberal does not meet opinions which he conceives to be false with toleration, as though they did not matter. He meets them with justice, and exacts for them a fair hearing as though they mattered just as much as his own. He is always ready to put his own convictions to the proof, not because he doubts them, but because he believes in them. For, both as to that which he holds for true and as to that which he holds for false, he believes that one final test applies. Let error have free play, and one of two things will happen. Either as it develops, as its implications and consequences become clear, some elements of truth will appear within it. They will separate themselves out; they will go to enrich the stock of human ideas; they will add something to the truth which he himself mistakenly took as final; they will serve to explain the root of the error; for error itself is generally a truth misconceived, and it is only when it is explained that it is finally and satisfactorily confuted. Or, in the alternative, no element of truth will appear. In that case the

63

more fully the error is understood, the more patiently it is followed up in all the windings of its implications and consequences, the more thoroughly will it refute itself. The cancerous growth cannot be extirpated by the knife. The root is always left, and it is only the evolution of the self-protecting anti-toxin that works the final cure. Exactly parallel is the logic of truth. The more the truth is developed in all its implications, the greater is the opportunity of detecting any element of error that it may contain; and, conversely, if no error appears, the more completely does it establish itself as the whole truth and nothing but the truth. Liberalism applies the wisdom of Gamaliel in no spirit of indifference, but in the full conviction of the potency of truth. If this thing be of man, *i.e.* if it is not rooted in actual verity, it will come to nought. If it be of God, let us take care that we be not found fighting against God.

Divergences of opinion, of character, of conduct are not unimportant matters. They may be most serious matters, and no one is called on in the name of Liberalism to overlook their seriousness. There are, for example, certain disqualifications inherent in the profession of certain opinions. It is not illiberal to recognize such disqualifications. It is not illiberal for a Protestant in choosing a tutor for his son to reject a conscientious Roman Catholic who avows that all his teaching is centred on the doctrine of his Church. It would be illiberal to reject the same man for the specific purpose of teaching arithmetic, if he avowed that he had no intention of using his position for the purpose of religious propagandism. For the former purpose the divergence of religious opinion is an inherent disqualification. It negates the object propounded, which is the general education of the boy on lines in which the father believes. For the latter purpose the opinion is no disqualification. The devout Catholic accepts the multiplication table, and can impart his knowledge without reference to the infallibility of the Pope. To refuse to employ him is to impose an extraneous penalty on his convictions. It is not illiberal for an editor to decline the services of a member of the opposite party as a leader writer, or even as a political reviewer or in any capacity in which his opinions would affect his work. It is illiberal to reject him as a compositor or as a clerk, or in any capacity in which his opinions would not affect his work for the paper. It is not illiberal to refuse a position of trust to the man whose record shows that

THE HEART OF LIBERALISM   65

he is likely to abuse such a trust. It is illiberal—and this the "moralist" has yet to learn—to punish a man who has done a wrong in one relation by excluding him from the performance of useful social functions for which he is perfectly fitted, by which he could at once serve society and re-establish his own self-respect. There may, however, yet come a time when Liberalism, already recognized as a duty in religion and in politics, will take its true place at the centre of our ethical conceptions, and will be seen to have its application not only to him whom we conceive to be the teacher of false opinions, but to the man whom we hold a sinner.

The ground of Liberalism so understood is certainly not the view that a man's personal opinions are socially indifferent, nor that his personal morality matters nothing to others. So far as Mill rested his case on the distinction between self-regarding actions and actions that affect others, he was still dominated by the older individualism. We should frankly recognize that there is no side of a man's life which is unimportant to society, for whatever he is, does, or thinks may affect his own well-being, which is and ought to be matter of common concern, and may also directly or indirectly affect the thought, action, and character of those with whom he comes in contact. The underlying principle may be put in two ways. In the first place, the man is much more than his opinions and his actions. Carlyle and Sterling did not differ "except in opinion." To most of us that is just what difference means. Carlyle was aware that there was something much deeper, something that opinion just crassly formulates, and for the most part formulates inadequately, that is the real man. The real man is something more than is ever adequately expressed in terms which his fellows can understand; and just as his essential humanity lies deeper than all distinctions of rank, and class, and colour, and even, though in a different sense, of sex, so also it goes far below those comparatively external events which make one man figure as a saint and another as a criminal. This sense of ultimate oneness is the real meaning of equality, as it is the foundation of social solidarity and the bond which, if genuinely experienced, resists the disruptive force of all conflict, intellectual, religious, and ethical.

But, further, while personal opinions and social institutions are like crystallized results, achievements that have been won by certain definite processes of individual or collective effort, human

66   LIBERALISM

personality is that within which lives and grows, which can be
destroyed but cannot be made, which cannot be taken to pieces
and repaired, but can be placed under conditions in which it will
flourish and expand, or, if it is diseased, under conditions in which
it will heal itself by its own recuperative powers. The foundation
of liberty is the idea of growth. Life is learning, but whether in
theory or practice what a man genuinely learns is what he absorbs, and what he absorbs depends on the energy which he himself puts forth in response to his surroundings. Thus, to come at
once to the real crux, the question of moral discipline, it is of
course possible to reduce a man to order and prevent him from
being a nuisance to his neighbours by arbitrary control and harsh
punishment. This may be to the comfort of the neighbours, as is
admitted, but regarded as a moral discipline it is a contradiction
in terms. It is doing less than nothing for the character of the man
himself. It is merely crushing him, and unless his will is killed the
effect will be seen if ever the superincumbent pressure is by
chance removed. It is also possible, though it takes a much higher
skill, to teach the same man to discipline himself, and this is to
foster the development of will, of personality, of self control, or
whatever we please to call that central harmonizing power which
makes us capable of directing our own lives. Liberalism is the belief that society can safely be founded on this self-directing power
of personality, that it is only on this foundation that a true community can be built, and that so established its foundations are so
deep and so wide that there is no limit that we can place to the extent of the building. Liberty then becomes not so much a right of
the individual as a necessity of society. It rests not on the claim of
A to be let alone by B, but on the duty of B to treat A as a rational
being. It is not right to let crime alone or to let error alone, but it
is imperative to treat the criminal or the mistaken or the ignorant
as beings capable of right and truth, and to lead them on instead
of merely beating them down. The rule of liberty is just the application of rational method. It is the opening of the door to the
appeal of reason, of imagination, of social feeling; and except
through the response to this appeal there is no assured progress of
society.

Now, I am not contending that these principles are free from
difficulty in application. At many points they suggest difficulties
both in theory and in practice, with some of which I shall try to

deal later on. Nor, again, am I contending that freedom is the universal solvent, or the idea of liberty the sole foundation on which a true social philosophy can be based. On the contrary, freedom is only one side of social life. Mutual aid is not less important than mutual forbearance, the theory of collective action no less fundamental than the theory of personal freedom. But, in an inquiry where all the elements are so closely interwoven as they are in the field of social life, the point of departure becomes almost indifferent. Wherever we start we shall, if we are quite frank and consistent, be led on to look at the whole from some central point, and this, I think, has happened to us in working with the conception of 'liberty.' For, beginning with the right of the individual, and the antithesis between personal freedom and social control, we have been led on to a point at which we regard liberty as primarily a matter of social interest, as something flowing from the necessities of continuous advance in those regions of truth and of ethics which constitute the matters of highest social concern. At the same time, we have come to look for the effect of liberty in the firmer establishment of social solidarity, as the only foundation on which such solidarity can securely rest. We have, in fact, arrived by a path of our own at that which is ordinarily described as the organic conception of the relation between the individual and society—a conception towards which Mill worked through his career, and which forms the starting-point of T. H. Green's philosophy alike in ethics and in politics.

The term organic is so much used and abused that it is best to state simply what it means. A thing is called organic when it is made up of parts which are quite distinct from one another, but which are destroyed or vitally altered when they are removed from the whole. Thus, the human body is organic because its life depends on the functions performed by many organs, while each of these organs depends in turn on the life of the body, perishing and decomposing if removed therefrom. Now, the organic view of society is equally simple. It means that, while the life of society is nothing but the life of individuals as they act one upon another, the life of the individual in turn would be something utterly different if he could be separated from society. A great deal of him would not exist at all. Even if he himself could maintain physical existence by the luck and skill of a Robinson Crusoe, his mental and moral being would, if it existed at all, be something quite dif-

ferent from anything that we know. By language, by training, by
simply living with others, each of us absorbs into his system the
social atmosphere that surrounds us. In particular, in the matter of
rights and duties which is cardinal for Liberal theory, the relation
of the individual to the community is everything. His rights and
his duties are alike defined by the common good. What, for example, is my right? On the face of it, it is something that I claim.
But a mere claim is nothing. I might claim anything and everything. If my claim is of right it is because it is sound, well
grounded, in the judgment of an impartial observer. But an impartial observer will not consider me alone. He will equally weigh
the opposed claims of others. He will take us in relation to one another, that is to say, as individuals involved in a social relationship. Further, if his decision is in any sense a rational one, it must
rest on a principle of some kind; and again, as a rational man, any
principle which he asserts he must found on some good result
which it serves or embodies, and as an impartial man he must take
the good of every one affected into account. That is to say, he
must found his judgment on the common good. An individual
right, then, cannot conflict with the common good, nor could any
right exist apart from the common good.

The argument might seem to make the individual too subservient to society. But this is to forget the other side of the original
supposition. Society consists wholly of persons. It has no distinct
personality separate from and superior to those of its members. It
has, indeed, a certain collective life and character. The British nation is a unity with a life of its own. But the unity is constituted by
certain ties that bind together all British subjects, which ties are in
the last resort feelings and ideas, sentiments of patriotism, of kinship, a common pride, and a thousand more subtle sentiments that
bind together men who speak a common language, have behind
them a common history, and understand one another as they can
understand no one else. The British nation is not a mysterious entity over and above the forty odd millions of living souls who
dwell together under a common law. Its life is their life, its well-
being or ill-fortune their well-being or ill-fortune. Thus, the common good to which each man's rights are subordinate is a good in
which each man has a share. This share consists in realizing his
capacities of feeling, of loving, of mental and physical energy, and

in realizing these he plays his part in the social life, or, in Green's phrase, he finds his own good in the common good.

Now, this phrase, it must be admitted, involves a certain assumption, which may be regarded as the fundamental postulate of the organic view of society. It implies that such a fulfilment or full development of personality is practically possible not for one man only but for all members of a community. There must be a line of development open along which each can move in harmony with others. Harmony in the full sense would involve not merely absence of conflict but actual support. There must be for each, then, possibilities of development such as not merely to permit but actively to further the development of others. Now, the older economists conceived a natural harmony, such that the interests of each would, if properly understood and unchecked by outside interference, inevitably lead him in courses profitable to others and to society at large. We saw that this assumption was too optimistic. The conception which we have now reached does not assume so much. It postulates, not that there is an actually existing harmony requiring nothing but prudence and coolness of judgment for its effective operation, but only that there is a possible ethical harmony, to which, partly by discipline, partly by the improvement of the conditions of life, men might attain, and that in such attainment lies the social ideal. To attempt the systematic proof of this postulate would take us into the field of philosophical first principles. It is the point at which the philosophy of politics comes into contact with that of ethics. It must suffice to say here that, just as the endeavour to establish coherent system in the world of thought is the characteristic of the rational impulse which lies at the root of science and philosophy, so the impulse to establish harmony in the world of feeling and action—a harmony which must include all those who think and feel—is of the essence of the rational impulse in the world of practice. To move towards harmony is the persistent impulse of the rational being, even if the goal lies always beyond the reach of accomplished effort.

These principles may appear very abstract, remote from practical life, and valueless for concrete teaching. But this remoteness is of the nature of first principles when taken without the connecting links that bind them to the details of experience. To find some of these links let us take up again our old Liberal principles, and see how they look in the light of the organic, or, as we may now call it, the harmonic conception. We shall readily see, to begin with, that the old idea of equality has its place. For the common good includes every individual. It is founded on personality, and postulates free scope for the development of personality in each member of the community. This is the foundation not only of equal rights before the law, but also of what is called equality of opportunity. It does not necessarily imply actual equality of treatment for all persons any more than it implies original equality of powers.[1] It does, I think, imply that whatever inequality of actual treatment, of income, rank, office, consideration, there be in a good social system, it would rest, not on the interest of the favoured individual as such, but on the common good. If the existence of millionaires on the one hand and of paupers on the other is just, it must be because such contrasts are the result of an economic system which upon the whole works out for the common good, the good of the pauper being included therein as well as the good of the millionaire; that is to say, that when we have well weighed the good and the evil of all parties concerned we can find no alternative open to us which could do better for the good of all. I am not for the moment either attacking or defending any economic system. I point out only that this is the position which according to the organic or harmonic view of society must be made good by any rational defence of grave inequality in the distribution of wealth. In relation to equality, indeed, it appears, oddly enough, that the harmonic principle can adopt wholesale, and even expand, one of the "Rights of Man" as formulated in 1789— "Social distinctions can only be founded upon common utility." If it is really just that A should be superior to B in wealth or power or position, it is only because when the good of all concerned is considered, among whom B is one, it turns out that there is a net gain in the arrangement as compared with any alternative that we can devise.

If we turn from equality to liberty, the general lines of argument have already been indicated, and the discussion of difficulties in detail must be left for the next chapter. It need only be repeated here that on the harmonic principle the fundamental importance of liberty rests on the nature of the "good" itself, and that

[1] An absurd misconception fostered principally by opponents of equality for controversial purposes.

whether we are thinking of the good of society or the good of the individual. The good is something attained by the development of the basal factors of personality, a development proceeding by the widening of ideas, the awakening of the imagination, the play of affection and passion, the strengthening and extension of rational control. As it is the development of these factors in each human being that makes his life worth having, so it is their harmonious interaction, the response of each to each, that makes of society a living whole. Liberty so interpreted cannot, as we have seen, dispense with restraint; restraint, however, is not an end but a means to an end, and one of the principal elements in that end is the enlargement of liberty.

But the collective activity of the community does not necessarily proceed by coercion or restraint. The more securely it is founded on freedom and general willing assent, the more it is free to work out all the achievements in which the individual is feeble or powerless while combined action is strong. Human progress, on whatever side we consider it, is found to be in the main social progress, the work of conscious or unconscious co-operation. In this work voluntary association plays a large and increasing part. But the State is one form of association among others, distinguished by its use of coercive power, by its supremacy, and by its claim to control all who dwell within its geographical limits. What the functions of such a form of association are to be we shall have to consider a little further in connection with the other questions which we have already raised. But that, in general, we are justified in regarding the State as one among many forms of human association for the maintenance and improvement of life is the general principle that we have to point out here, and this is the point at which we stand furthest from the older Liberalism. We have, however, already seen some reason for thinking that the older doctrines led, when carefully examined, to a more enlarged conception of State action than appeared on the surface; and we shall see more fully before we have done that the "positive" conception of the State which we have now reached not only involves no conflict with the true principle of personal liberty, but is necessary to its effective realization.

There is, in addition, one principle of historic Liberalism with which our present conception of the State is in full sympathy. The conception of the common good as it has been explained can be realized in its fullness only through the common will. There are, of course, elements of value in the good government of a benevolent despot or of a fatherly aristocracy. Within any peaceful order there is room for many good things to flourish. But the full fruit of social progress is only to be reaped by a society in which the generality of men and women are not only passive recipients but practical contributors. To make the rights and responsibilities of citizens real and living, and to extend them as widely as the conditions of society allow, is thus an integral part of the organic conception of society, and the justification of the democratic principle. It is, at the same time, the justification of nationalism so far as nationalism is founded on a true interpretation of history. For, inasmuch as the true social harmony rests on feeling and makes use of all the natural ties of kinship, of neighbourliness, of congruity of character and belief, and of language and mode of life, the best, healthiest, and most vigorous political unit is that to which men are by their own feelings strongly drawn. Any breach of such unity, whether by forcible disruption or by compulsory inclusion in a larger society of alien sentiments and laws, tends to mutilate—or, at lowest, to cramp—the spontaneous development of social life. National and personal freedom are growths of the same root, and their historic connection rests on no accident, but on ultimate identity of idea.

Thus in the organic conception of society each of the leading ideas of historic Liberalism has its part to play. The ideal society is conceived as a whole which lives and flourishes by the harmonious growth of its parts, each of which in developing on its own lines and in accordance with its own nature tends on the whole to further the development of others. There is some elementary trace of such harmony in every form of social life that can maintain itself, for if the conflicting impulses predominated society would break up, and when they do predominate society does break up. At the other extreme, true harmony is an ideal which it is perhaps beyond the power of man to realize, but which serves to indicate the line of advance. But to admit this is to admit that the lines of possible development for each individual or, to use a more general phrase, for each constituent of the social order are not limited and fixed. There are many possibilities, and the course that will in the end make for social harmony is only one among them, while the possibilities of disharmony and conflict are many. The progress of society like that of the individual depends, then, ultimately on choice. It is not "natural," in the sense in which a physical law is natural, that is, in the sense of going forward automatically from stage to stage without backward turnings, deflections to the left, or fallings away on the right. It is natural only in this sense, that it is the expression of deep-seated forces of human nature which come to their own only by an infinitely slow and cumbersome process of mutual adjustment. Every constructive social doctrine rests on the conception of human progress. The heart of Liberalism is the understanding that progress is not a matter of mechanical contrivance, but of the liberation of living spiritual energy. Good mechanism is that which provides the channels wherein such energy can flow unimpeded, unobstructed by its own exuberance of output, vivifying the social structure, expanding and ennobling the life of mind.

[24]

Excerpt from L.T. Hobhouse (1964), *Liberalism*, 74–87

VII

THE STATE AND THE INDIVIDUAL

We have seen something of the principle underlying the Liberal idea and of its various applications. We have now to put the test question. Are these different applications compatible? Will they work together to make that harmonious whole of which it is easy enough to talk in abstract terms? Are they themselves really harmonious in theory and in practice? Does scope for individual development, for example, consort with the idea of equality? Is popular sovereignty a practicable basis of personal freedom, or does it open an avenue to the tyranny of the mob? Will the sentiment of nationality dwell in unison with the ideal of peace? Is the love of liberty compatible with the full realization of the common will? If reconcilable in theory, may not these ideals collide in practice? Are there not clearly occasions demonstrable in history when development in one direction involves retrogression in another? If so, how are we to strike the balance of gain and loss? Does political progress offer us nothing but a choice of evils, or may we have some confidence that, in solving the most pressing problem of the moment, we shall in the end be in a better position for grappling with the obstacles that come next in turn?

I shall deal with these questions as far as limits of space allow, and I will take first the question of liberty and the common will upon which everything turns. Enough has already been said on this topic to enable us to shorten the discussion. We have seen that social liberty rests on restraint. A man can be free to direct his own life only in so far as others are prevented from molesting and interfering with him. So far there is no real departure from the

74

strictest tenets of individualism. We have, indeed, had occasion to examine the application of the doctrine to freedom of contract on the one hand, and to the action of combinations on the other, and have seen reason to think that in either case nominal freedom, that is to say, the absence of legal restraint, might have the effect of impairing real freedom, that is to say, would allow the stronger party to coerce the weaker. We have also seen that the effect of combination may be double edged, that it may restrict freedom on one side and enlarge it on the other. In all these cases our contention has been simply that we should be guided by real and not by verbal considerations,—that we should ask in every case what policy will yield effective freedom—and we have found a close connection in each instance between freedom and equality. In these cases, however, we were dealing with the relations of one man with another, or of one body of men with another, and we could regard the community as an arbiter between them whose business it was to see justice done and prevent the abuse of coercive power. Hence we could treat a very large part of the modern development of social control as motived by the desire for a more effective liberty. The case is not so clear when we find the will of the individual in conflict with the will of the community as a whole. When such conflict occurs, it would seem that we must be prepared for one of two things. Either we must admit the legitimacy of coercion, avowedly not in the interests of freedom but in furtherance, without regard to freedom, of other ends which the community deems good. Or we must admit limitations which may cramp the development of the general will, and perchance prove a serious obstacle to collective progress. Is there any means of avoiding this conflict? Must we leave the question to be fought out in each case by a balance of advantages and disadvantages, or are there any general considerations which help us to determine the true sphere of collective and of private action?

Let us first observe that, as Mill pointed out long ago, there are many forms of collective action which do not involve coercion. The State may provide for certain objects which it deems good without compelling any one to make use of them. Thus it may maintain hospitals, though any one who can pay for them remains free to employ his own doctors and nurses. It may and does maintain a great educational system, while leaving every one free to maintain or to attend a private school. It maintains parks and picture galleries without driving any one into them. There is a municipal tramway service, which does not prevent private people from running motor 'buses along the same streets, and so on. It is true that for the support of these objects rates and taxes are compulsorily levied, but this form of compulsion raises a set of questions of which we shall have to speak in another connection, and does not concern us here. For the moment we have to deal only with those actions of State which compel all citizens, or all whom they concern, to fall in with them and allow of no divergence. This kind of coercion tends to increase. Is its extension necessarily an encroachment upon liberty, or are the elements of value secured by collective control distinct from the elements of value secured by individual choice, so that within due limits each may develop side by side?

We have already declined to solve the problem by applying Mill's distinction between self-regarding and other-regarding actions, first because there are no actions which may not directly or indirectly affect others, secondly because even if there were they would not cease to be matter of concern to others. The common good includes the good of every member of the community, and the injury which a man inflicts upon himself is matter of common concern, even apart from any ulterior effect upon others. If we refrain from coercing a man for his own good, it is not because his good is indifferent to us, but because it cannot be furthered by coercion. The difficulty is founded on the nature of the good itself, which on its personal side depends on the spontaneous flow of feeling checked and guided not by external restraint but by rational self-control. To try to form character by coercion is to destroy it in the making. Personality is not built up from without but grows from within, and the function of the outer order is not to create it, but to provide for it the most suitable conditions of growth. Thus, to the common question whether it is possible to make men good by Act of Parliament, the reply is that it is not possible to compel morality because morality is the act or character of a free agent, but that it is possible to create the conditions under which morality can develop, and among these not the least important is freedom from compulsion by others.

The argument suggests that compulsion is limited not by indifference—how could the character of its members be matter of indifference to the community?—but by its own incapacity to

THE STATE AND THE INDIVIDUAL

achieve its ends. The spirit cannot be forced. Nor, conversely, can it prevail by force. It may require social expression. It may build up an association, a church for example, to carry out the common objects and maintain the common life of all who are like-minded. But the association must be free, because spiritually everything depends not on what is done but on the will with which it is done. The limit to the value of coercion thus lies not in the restriction of social purpose, but in the conditions of personal life. No force can compel growth. Whatever elements of social value depend on the accord of feeling, on comprehension of meaning, on the assent of will, must come through liberty. Here is the sphere and function of liberty in the social harmony.

Where, then, is the sphere of compulsion, and what is its value? The reply is that compulsion is of value where outward conformity is of value, and this may be in any case where the nonconformity of one wrecks the purpose of others. We have already remarked that liberty itself only rests upon restraint. Thus a religious body is not, properly speaking, free to march in procession through the streets unless people of a different religion are restrained from pelting the procession with stones and pursuing it with insolence. We restrain them from disorder not to teach them the genuine spirit of religion, which they will not learn in the police court, but to secure to the other party the right of worship unmolested. The enforced restraint has its value in the action that it sets free. But we may not only restrain one man from obstructing another—and the extent to which we do this is the measure of the freedom that we maintain—but we may also restrain him from obstructing the general will; and this we have to do whenever uniformity is necessary to the end which the general will has in view. The majority of employers in a trade we may suppose would be willing to adopt certain precautions for the health or safety of their workers, to lower hours or to raise the rate of wages. They are unable to do so, however, as long as a minority, perhaps as long as a single employer, stands out. He would beat them in competition if they were voluntarily to undertake expenses from which he is free. In this case, the will of a minority, possibly the will of one man, thwarts that of the remainder. It coerces them, indirectly, but quite as effectively as if he were their master. If they, by combination, can coerce him no principle of liberty is violated. It is coercion against coercion, differing possibly in form and method, but not in principle or in spirit. Further, if the community as a whole sympathizes with the one side rather than the other, it can reasonably bring the law into play. Its object is not the moral education of the recusant individuals. Its object is to secure certain conditions which it believes necessary for the welfare of its members, and which can only be secured by an enforced uniformity.

It appears, then, that the true distinction is not between self-regarding and other-regarding actions, but between coercive and non-coercive actions. The function of State coercion is to override individual coercion, and, of course, coercion exercised by any association of individuals within the State. It is by this means that it maintains liberty of expression, security of person and property, genuine freedom of contract, the rights of public meeting and association, and finally its own power to carry out common objects undefeated by the recalcitrance of individual members. Undoubtedly it endows both individuals and associations with powers as well as with rights. But over these powers it must exercise supervision in the interests of equal justice. Just as compulsion failed in the sphere of liberty, the sphere of spiritual growth, so liberty fails in the external order wherever, by the mere absence of supervisory restriction, men are able directly or indirectly to put constraint on one another. This is why there is no intrinsic and inevitable conflict between liberty and compulsion, but at bottom a mutual need. The object of compulsion is to secure the most favourable external conditions of inward growth and happiness so far as these conditions depend on combined action and uniform observance. The sphere of liberty is the sphere of growth itself. There is no true opposition between liberty as such and control as such, for every liberty rests on a corresponding act of control. The true opposition is between the control that cramps the personal life and the spiritual order, and the control that is aimed at securing the external and material conditions of their free and unimpeded development.

I do not pretend that this delimitation solves all problems. The "inward" life will seek to express itself in outward acts. A religious ordinance may bid the devout refuse military service, or withhold the payment of a tax, or decline to submit a building to inspection. Here are external matters where conscience and the State come into direct conflict, and where is the court of appeal that is to decide between them? In any given case the right, as judged by the ultimate effect on human welfare, may, of course, be on the one side, or on the other, or between the two. But is there anything to guide the two parties as long as each believes itself to be in the right and sees no ground for waiving its opinion? To begin with, clearly the State does well to avoid such conflicts by substituting alternatives. Other duties than that of military service may be found for a follower of Tolstoy, and as long as he is willing to take his full share of burdens the difficulty is fairly met. Again, the mere convenience of the majority cannot be fairly weighed against the religious convictions of the few. It might be convenient that certain public work should be done on Saturday, but mere convenience would be an insufficient ground for compelling Jews to participate in it. Religious and ethical conviction must be weighed against religious and ethical conviction. It is not number that counts morally, but the belief that is reasoned out according to the best of one's lights as to the necessities of the common good. But the conscience of the community has its rights just as much as the conscience of the individual. If we are convinced that the inspection of a convent laundry is required in the interest, not of mere official routine, but of justice and humanity, we can do nothing but insist upon it, and when all has been done that can be done to save the individual conscience the common conviction of the common good must have its way. In the end the external order belongs to the community, and the right of protest to the individual.

On the other side, the individual owes more to the community than is always recognized. Under modern conditions he is too much inclined to take for granted what the State does for him and to use the personal security and liberty of speech which it affords him as a vantage ground from which he can in safety denounce its works and repudiate its authority. He assumes the right to be in or out of the social system as he chooses. He relies on the general law which protects him, and emancipates himself from some particular law which he finds oppressive to his conscience. He forgets or does not take the trouble to reflect that, if every one were to act as he does, the social machine would come to a stop. He certainly fails to make it clear how a society would subsist in which every man should claim the right of unrestricted disobedience to a law which he happens to think wrong. In fact, it is pos-

sible for an over-tender conscience to consort with an insufficient
sense of social responsibility. The combination is unfortunate; and
we may fairly say that, if the State owes the utmost consideration
to the conscience, its owner owes a corresponding debt to the
State. With such mutual consideration, and with the development
of the civic sense, conflicts between law and conscience are capable of being brought within very narrow limits, though their complete reconciliation will always remain a problem until men are
generally agreed as to the fundamental conditions of the social
harmony.

It may be asked, on the other hand, whether in insisting on the
free development of personality we have not understated the duty
of society to its members. We all admit a collective responsibility
for children. Are there not grown-up people who stand just as
much in need of care? What of the idiot, the imbecile, the feeble-
minded or the drunkard? What does rational self-determination
mean for these classes? They may injure no one but themselves
except by the contagion of bad example. But have we no duty
towards them, having in view their own good alone and leaving
every other consideration aside? Have we not the right to take
the feeble-minded under our care and to keep the drunkard from
drink, purely for their own good and apart from every ulterior
consideration? And, if so, must we not extend the whole sphere
of permissible coercion, and admit that a man may for his own
sake and with no ulterior object, be compelled to do what we think
right and avoid what we think wrong?

The reply is that the argument is weak just where it seeks to
generalize. We are compelled to put the insane under restraint for
social reasons apart from their own benefit. But their own benefit
would be a fully sufficient reason if no other existed. To them, by
their misfortune, liberty, as we understand the term, has no application, because they are incapable of rational choice and therefore of the kind of growth for the sake of which freedom is valuable. The same thing is true of the feebleminded, and if they are
not yet treated on the same principle it is merely because the
recognition of their type as a type is relatively modern. But the
same thing is also in its degree true of the drunkard, so far as he
is the victim of an impulse which he has allowed to grow beyond
his own control; and the question whether he should be regarded
as a fit object for tutelage or not is to be decided in each case by

THE STATE AND THE INDIVIDUAL 81

asking whether such capacity of self-control as he retains would be impaired or repaired by a period of tutelar restraint. There is nothing in all this to touch the essential of liberty which is the value of the power of self-governance where it exists. All that is proved is that where it does not exist it is right to save men from suffering, and if the case admits to put them under conditions in which the normal balance of impulse is most likely to be restored. It may be added that, in the case of the drunkard—and I think the argument applies to all cases where overwhelming impulse is apt to master the will—it is a still more obvious and elementary duty to remove the sources of temptation, and to treat as anti-social in the highest degree every attempt to make profit out of human weakness, misery, and wrong-doing. The case is not unlike that of a very unequal contract. The tempter is coolly seeking his profit, and the sufferer is beset with a fiend within. There is a form of coercion here which the genuine spirit of liberty will not fail to recognize as its enemy, and a form of injury to another which is not the less real because its weapon is an impulse which forces that other to the consent which he yields.

I conclude that there is nothing in the doctrine of liberty to hinder the movement of general will in the sphere in which it is really efficient, and nothing in a just conception of the objects and methods of the general will to curtail liberty in the performance of the functions, social and personal, in which its value lies. Liberty and compulsion have complementary functions, and the self-governing State is at once the product and the condition of the self-governing individual.

Thus there is no difficulty in understanding why the extension of State control on one side goes along with determined resistance to encroachments on another. It is a question not of increasing or diminishing, but of reorganizing, restraints. The period which has witnessed a rapid extension of industrial legislation has seen as determined a resistance to anything like the establishment of doctrinal religious teaching by a State authority,[1] and the distinction is perfectly just. At bottom it is the same conception of liberty and the same conception of the common will that prompts the regulation of industry and the severence of religious worship and doctrinal teaching from the mechanism of State control.

[1] The objection most often taken to "undenominationalism" itself is that it is in reality a form of doctrinal teaching seeking State endowment.

So far we have been considering what the State compels the individual to do. If we pass to the question what the State is to do for the individual, a different but parallel question arises, and we have to note a corresponding movement of opinion. If the State does for the individual what he ought to do for himself what will be the effect on character, initiative, enterprise? It is a question now not of freedom, but of responsibility, and it is one that has caused many searchings of heart, and in respect of which opinion has undergone a remarkable change. Thus, in relation to poverty the older view was that the first thing needful was self-help. It was the business of every man to provide for himself and his family. If, indeed, he utterly failed, neither he nor they could be left to starve, and there was the Poor Law machinery to deal with his case. But the aim of every sincere friend of the poor must be to keep them away from the Poor Law machine. Experience of the forty years before 1834 had taught us what came of free resort to public funds by way of subvention to inadequate wages. It meant simply that the standard of remuneration was lowered in proportion as men could rely on public aid to make good the deficiency, while at the same time the incentives to independent labour were weakened when the pauper stood on an equal footing with the hard-working man. In general, if the attempt was made to substitute for personal effort the help of others, the result would only sap individual initiative and in the end bring down the rate of industrial remuneration. It was thought, for example—and this very point was urged against proposals for Old Age Pensions— that if any of the objects for which a man will, if possible, provide were removed from the scope of his own activity, he would in consequence be content with proportionally lower wages; if the employer was to compensate him for accident, he would fail to make provision for accidents on his own account; if his children were fed by the ratepayers, he would not earn the money wherewith to feed them. Hence, on the one hand, it was urged that the rate of wages would tend to adapt itself to the necessities of the wage earner, that in proportion as his necessities were met from other sources his wages would fall, that accordingly the apparent relief would be in large measure illusory, while finally, in view of the diminished stimulus to individual exertion, the productivity of labour would fall off, the incentives to industry would be diminished, and the community as a whole would be poorer. Upon the other hand, it was conceived that, however deplorable the condition of the working classes might be, the right way of raising them was to trust to individual enterprise and possibly, according to some thinkers, to voluntary combination. By these means the efficiency of labour might be enhanced and its regular remuneration raised. By sternly withholding all external supports we should teach the working classes to stand alone, and if there were pain in the disciplinary process there was yet hope in the future. They would come by degrees to a position of economic independence in which they would be able to face the risks of life, not in reliance upon the State, but by the force of their own brains and the strength of their own right arms.

These views no longer command the same measure of assent. On all sides we find the State making active provision for the poorer classes and not by any means for the destitute alone. We find it educating the children, providing medical inspection, authorizing the feeding of the necessitous at the expense of the ratepayers, helping them to obtain employment through free Labour Exchanges, seeking to organize the labour market with a view to the mitigation of unemployment, and providing old age pensions for all whose incomes fall below thirteen shillings a week, without exacting any contribution. Now, in all this, we may well ask, is the State going forward blindly on the paths of broad and generous but unconsidered charity? Is it and can it remain indifferent to the effect on individual initiative and personal or parental responsibility? Or may we suppose that the wiser heads are well aware of what they are about, have looked at the matter on all sides, and are guided by a reasonable conception of the duty of the State and the responsibilities of the individual? Are we, in fact—for this is really the question—seeking charity or justice?

We said above that it was the function of the State to secure the conditions upon which mind and character may develop themselves. Similarly we may say now that the function of the State is to secure conditions upon which its citizens are able to win by their own efforts all that is necessary to a full civic efficiency. It is not for the State to feed, house, or clothe them. It is for the State to take care that the economic conditions are such that the normal man who is not defective in mind or body or will can by useful labour feed, house, and clothe himself and his family. The "right to work" and the right to a "living wage" are just as valid

as the rights of person or property. That is to say, they are integral
conditions of a good social order. A society in which a single honest man of normal capacity is definitely unable to find the means
of maintaining himself by useful work is to that extent suffering
from malorganization. There is somewhere a defect in the social
system, a hitch in the economic machine. Now, the individual
workman cannot put the machine straight. He is the last person
to have any say in the control of the market. It is not his fault if
there is over-production in his industry, or if a new and cheaper
process has been introduced which makes his particular skill, perhaps the product of years of application, a drug in the market.
He does not direct or regulate industry. He is not responsible for
its ups and downs, but he has to pay for them. That is why it is
not charity but justice for which he is asking. Now, it may be
infinitely difficult to meet his demand. To do so may involve a
far-reaching economic reconstruction. The industrial questions involved may be so little understood that we may easily make matters worse in the attempt to make them better. All this shows the
difficulty in finding means of meeting this particular claim of justice, but it does not shake its position as a claim of justice. A right
is a right none the less though the means of securing it be imperfectly known; and the workman who is unemployed or underpaid
through economic malorganization will remain a reproach not
to the charity but to the justice of society as long as he is to be
seen in the land.

If this view of the duty of the State and the right of the workman is coming to prevail, it is owing partly to an enhanced sense
of common responsibility, and partly to the teaching of experience. In the earlier days of the Free Trade era, it was permissible
to hope that self-help would be an adequate solvent, and that with
cheap food and expanding commerce the average workman would
be able by the exercise of prudence and thrift not only to maintain himself in good times, but to lay by for sickness, unemployment, and old age. The actual course of events has in large measure disappointed these hopes. It is true that the standard of living
in England has progressively advanced throughout the nineteenth
century. It is true, in particular, that, since the disastrous period
that preceded the Repeal of the Corn Laws and the passing of
the Ten Hours' Act, social improvement has been real and marked.
Trade Unionism and co-operation have grown, wages upon the

whole have increased, the cost of living has diminished, housing and sanitation have improved, the death rate has fallen from about twenty-two to less than fifteen per thousand. But with all this improvement the prospect of a complete and lifelong economic independence for the average workman upon the lines of individual competition, even when supplemented and guarded by the collective bargaining of the Trade Union, appears exceedingly remote. The increase of wages does not appear to be by any means proportionate to the general growth of wealth. The whole standard of living has risen; the very provision of education has brought with it new needs and has almost compelled a higher standard of life in order to satisfy them. As a whole, the working classes of England, though less thrifty than those of some Continental countries, cannot be accused of undue negligence with regard to the future. The accumulation of savings in Friendly Societies, Trade Unions, Co-operative Societies, and Savings Banks shows an increase which has more than kept pace with the rise in the level of wages; yet there appears no likelihood that the average manual worker will attain the goal of that full independence, covering all the risks of life for self and family, which can alone render the competitive system really adequate to the demands of a civilized conscience. The careful researches of Mr. Booth in London and Mr. Rowntree in York, and of others in country districts, have revealed that a considerable percentage of the working classes are actually unable to earn a sum of money representing the full cost of the barest physical necessities for an average family; and, though the bulk of the working classes are undoubtedly in a better position than this, these researches go to show that even the relatively well-to-do gravitate towards this line of primary poverty in seasons of stress, at the time when the children are still at school, for example, or from the moment when the principal wage-earner begins to fail, in the decline of middle life. If only some ten per cent. of the population are actually living upon the poverty line at any given time,[1] twice or three times that number, it is reasonable to suppose, must approach the line in one period or other of their lives. But when we ascend from the

---

[1] I do not include those living in "secondary poverty," as defined by Mr. Rowntree, as the responsibility in this case is partly personal. It must, however, be remembered that great poverty increases the difficulty of efficient management.

86   LIBERALISM

conception of a bare physical maintenance for an average family
to such a wage as would provide the real minimum requirements
of a civilized life and meet all its contingencies without having to
lean on any external prop, we should have to make additions to
Mr. Rowntree's figure which have not yet been computed, but as
to which it is probably well within the mark to say that none but
the most highly skilled artisans are able to earn a remuneration
meeting the requirements of the case. But, if that is so, it is clear
that the system of industrial competition fails to meet the ethical
demand embodied in the conception of the "living wage." That
system holds out no hope of an improvement which shall bring the
means of such a healthy and independent existence as should be
the birthright of every citizen of a free state within the grasp of
the mass of the people of the United Kingdom. It is this belief
slowly penetrating the public mind which has turned it to new
thoughts of social regeneration. The sum and substance of the
changes that I have mentioned may be expressed in the principle
that the individual cannot stand alone, but that between him and
the State there is a reciprocal obligation. He owes the State the
duty of industriously working for himself and his family. He is
not to exploit the labour of his young children, but to submit to
the public requirements for their education, health, cleanliness
and general well-being. On the other side society owes to him the
means of maintaining a civilized standard of life, and this debt
is not adequately discharged by leaving him to secure such wages
as he can in the higgling of the market.

This view of social obligation lays increased stress on public
but by no means ignores private responsibility. It is a simple principle of applied ethics that responsibility should be commensurate
with power. Now, given the opportunity of adequately remuner-
ated work, a man has the power to earn his living. It is his right
and his duty to make the best use of his opportunity, and if he
fails he may fairly suffer the penalty of being treated as a pauper
or even, in an extreme case, as a criminal. But the opportunity itself he cannot command with the same freedom. It is only within
narrow limits that it comes within the sphere of his control. The
opportunities of work and the remuneration for work are determined by a complex mass of social forces which no individual,
certainly no individual workman, can shape. They can be controlled, if at all, by the organized action of the community, and

THE STATE AND THE INDIVIDUAL 87

therefore, by a just apportionment of responsibility, it is for the community to deal with them.

But this, it will be said, is not Liberalism but Socialism. Pursuing the economic rights of the individual we have been led to contemplate a Socialistic organization of industry. But a word like Socialism has many meanings, and it is possible that there should be a Liberal Socialism, as well as a Socialism that is illiberal. Let us, then, without sticking at a word, seek to follow out the Liberal view of the State in the sphere of economics. Let us try to determine in very general terms what is involved in realizing those primary conditions of industrial well-being which have been laid down, and how they consort with the rights of property and the claims of free industrial enterprise.

[25]

Excerpt from L.T. Hobhouse (1964), *Liberalism*, 88–109

VIII

ECONOMIC LIBERALISM

There are two forms of Socialism with which Liberalism has nothing to do. These I will call the mechanical and the official. Mechanical Socialism is founded on a false interpretation of history. It attributes the phenomena of social life and development to the sole operation of the economic factor, whereas the beginning of sound sociology is to conceive society as a whole in which all the parts interact. The economic factor, to take a single point, is at least as much the effect as it is the cause of scientific invention. There would be no world-wide system of telegraphy if there was no need of world-wide intercommunication. But there would be no electric telegraph at all but for the scientific interest which determined the experiments of Gauss and Weber. Mechanical Socialism, further, is founded on a false economic analysis which attributes all value to labour, denying, confounding or distorting the distinct functions of the direction of enterprise, the unavoidable payment for the use of capital, the productivity of nature, and the very complex social forces which, by determining the movements of demand and supply actually fix the rates at which goods exchange with one another. Politically, mechanical Socialism supposes a class war, resting on a clear-cut distinction of classes which does not exist. Far from tending to clear and simple lines of cleavage, modern society exhibits a more and more complex interweaving of interests, and it is impossible for a modern revolutionist to assail "property" in the interest of "labour" without finding that half the "labour" to which he appeals has a direct or indirect interest in "property." As to the future, mechanical

88

Socialism conceives a logically developed system of the control of industry by government. Of this all that need be said is that the construction of Utopias is not a sound method of social science; that this particular Utopia makes insufficient provision for liberty, movement, and growth; and that in order to bring his ideals into the region of practical discussion, what the Socialist needs is to formulate not a system to be substituted as a whole for our present arrangements but a principle to guide statesmanship in the practical work of reforming what is amiss and developing what is good in the actual fabric of industry. A principle so applied grows if it has seeds of good in it, and so in particular the collective control of industry will be extended in proportion as it is found in practice to yield good results. The fancied clearness of Utopian vision is illusory, because its objects are artificial ideas and not living facts. The "system" of the world of books must be reconstructed as a principle that can be applied to the railway, the mine, the workshop, and the office that we know, before it can even be sensibly discussed. The evolution of Socialism as a practical force in politics has, in point of fact, proceeded by such a reconstruction, and this change carries with it the end of the materialistic Utopia.

Official Socialism is a creed of different brand. Beginning with a contempt for ideals of liberty based on a confusion between liberty and competition, it proceeds to a measure of contempt for average humanity in general. It conceives mankind as in the mass a helpless and feeble race, which it is its duty to treat kindly. True kindness, of course, must be combined with firmness, and the life of the average man must be organized for his own good. He need not know that he is being organized. The socialistic organization will work in the background, and there will be wheels within wheels, or rather wires pulling wires. Ostensibly there will be a class of the elect, an aristocracy of character and intellect which will fill the civil services and do the practical work of administration. Behind these will be committees of union and progress who will direct operations, and behind the committees again one or more master minds from whom will emanate the ideas that are to direct the world. The play of democratic government will go on for a time, but the idea of a common will that should actually undertake the organization of social life is held the most childish of illusions. The master minds can for the moment work

more easily through democratic forms, because they are here, and
to destroy them would cause an upheaval. But the essence of
government lies in the method of capture. The ostensible leaders
of democracy are ignorant creatures who can with a little management be set to walk in the way in which they should go, and
whom the crowd will follow like sheep. The art of governing consists in making men do what you wish without knowing what they
are doing, to lead them on without showing them whither until
it is too late for them to retrace their steps. Socialism so conceived
has in essentials nothing to do with democracy or with liberty.
It is a scheme of the organization of life by the superior person,
who will decide for each man how he should work, how he should
live, and indeed, with the aid of the Eugenist, whether he should
live at all or whether he has any business to be born. At any rate,
if he ought not to have been born—if, that is, he comes of a stock
whose qualities are not approved—the Samurai will take care that
he does not perpetuate his race.

Now the average Liberal might have more sympathy with this
view of life if he did not feel that for his part he is just a very
ordinary man. He is quite sure that he cannot manage the lives
of other people for them. He finds it enough to manage his own.
But with the leave of the Superior he would rather do this in his
own way than in the way of another, whose way may be much
wiser but is not his. He would rather marry the woman of his own
choice, than the one who would be sure to bring forth children
of the standard type. He does not want to be standardized. He
does not conceive himself as essentially an item in a census return.
He does not want the standard clothes or the standard food, he
wants the clothes which he finds comfortable and the food which
he likes. With this unregenerate Adam in him, I fear that the
Liberalism that is also within him is quite ready to make terms.
Indeed, it incites him to go still further. It bids him consider that
other men are, on the whole, very like himself and look on life
in much the same way, and when it speaks within him of social
duty it encourages him to aim not at a position of superiority
which will enable him to govern his fellow creatures for their own
good, but at a spirit of comradeship in which he will stand shoulder to shoulder with them on behalf of common aims.

If, then, there be such a thing as a Liberal Socialism—and
whether there be is still a subject for inquiry—it must clearly fulfil

ECONOMIC LIBERALISM

two conditions. In the first place, it must be democratic. It must come from below, not from above. Or rather, it must emerge from the efforts of society as a whole to secure a fuller measure of justice, and a better organization of mutual aid. It must engage the efforts and respond to the genuine desires not of a handful of superior beings, but of great masses of men. And, secondly, and for that very reason, it must make its account with the human individual. It must give the average man free play in the personal life for which he really cares. It must be founded on liberty, and must make not for the suppression but for the development of personality. How far, it may be asked, are these objects compatible? How far is it possible to organize industry in the interest of the common welfare without either overriding the freedom of individual choice or drying up the springs of initiative and energy? How far is it possible to abolish poverty, or to institute economic equality without arresting industrial progress? We cannot put the question without raising more fundamental issues. What is the real meaning of "equality" in economics? Would it mean, for example, that all should enjoy equal rewards, or that equal efforts should enjoy equal rewards, or that equal attainments should enjoy equal rewards? What is the province of justice in economics? Where does justice end and charity begin? And what, behind all this, is the basis of property? What is its social function and value? What is the measure of consideration due to vested interest and prescriptive right? It is impossible, within the limits of a volume, to deal exhaustively with such fundamental questions. The best course will be to follow out the lines of development which appear to proceed from those principles of Liberalism which have been already indicated and to see how far they lead to a solution.

We saw that it was the duty of the State to secure the conditions of self-maintenance for the normal healthy citizen. There are two lines along which the fulfilment of this duty may be sought. One would consist in providing access to the means of production, the other in guaranteeing to the individual a certain share in the common stock. In point of fact, both lines have been followed by Liberal legislation. On the one side this legislation has set itself, however timidly and ineffectively as yet, to reversing the process which divorced the English peasantry from the soil. Contemporary research is making it clear that this divorce was not the inevitable result of slowly operating economic forces. It was brought about by the deliberate policy of the enclosure of the common fields begun in the fifteenth century, partially arrested from the middle of the sixteenth to the eighteenth, and completed between the reigns of George II and Queen Victoria. As this process was furthered by an aristocracy, so there is every reason to hope that it can be successfully reversed by a democracy, and that it will be possible to reconstitute a class of independent peasantry as the backbone of the working population. The experiment, however, involves one form or another of communal ownership. The labourer can only obtain the land with the financial help of the State, and it is certainly not the view of Liberals that the State, having once regained the fee simple, should part with it again. On the contrary, in an equitable division of the fruits of agriculture all advantages that are derived from the qualities or position of the soil itself, or from the enhancement of prices by tariffs would, since they are the product of no man's labour, fall to no man's share, or, what is the same thing, they should fall to every man, that is, to the community. This is why Liberal legislation seeks to create a class not of small landlords but of small tenants. It would give to this class access to the land and would reward them with the fruits of their own work—and no more. The surplus it would take to itself in the form of rent, and while it is desirable to give the State tenant full security against disturbance, rents must at stated periods be adjustable to prices and to cost. So, while Conservative policy is to establish a peasant proprietary which would reinforce the voting strength of property, the Liberal policy is to establish a State tenantry from whose prosperity the whole community would profit. The one solution is individualist. The other, as far as it goes, is nearer to the Socialist ideal.

But, though British agriculture may have a great future before it, it will never regain its dominant position in our economic life, nor are small holdings ever likely to be the prevalent form of agriculture. The bulk of industry is, and probably will be, more and more in the hands of large undertakings with which the individual workman could not compete whatever instruments of production were placed in his hands. For the mass of the people, therefore, to be assured of the means of a decent livelihood must mean to be assured of continuous employment at a living wage, or, as an alternative, of public assistance. Now, as has been remarked, experience goes to show that the wage of the average worker, as fixed by competition, is not and is not likely to become sufficient to cover all the fortunes and misfortunes of life, to provide for sickness, accident, unemployment and old age, in addition to the regular needs of an average family. In the case of accident the State has put the burden of making provision on the employer. In the case of old age it has, acting, as I think, upon a sounder principle, taken the burden upon itself. It is very important to realize precisely what the new departure involved in the Old Age Pensions Act amounted to in point of principle. The Poor Law already guaranteed the aged person and the poor in general against actual starvation. But the Poor Law came into operation only at the point of sheer destitution. It failed to help those who had helped themselves. Indeed, to many it held out little inducement to help themselves if they could not hope to lay by so much as would enable them to live more comfortably on their means than they would live in the workhouse. The pension system throws over the test of destitution. It provides a certain minimum, a basis to go upon, a foundation upon which independent thrift may hope to build up a sufficiency. It is not a narcotic but a stimulus to self help and to friendly aid or filial support, and it is, up to a limit, available for all alike. It is precisely one of the conditions of independence of which voluntary effort can make use, but requiring voluntary effort to make it fully available.

The suggestion underlying the movement for the break up of the Poor Law is just the general application of this principle. It is that, instead of redeeming the destitute, we should seek to render generally available the means of avoiding destitution, though in doing so we should uniformly call on the individual for a corresponding effort on his part. One method of meeting these conditions is to supply a basis for private effort to work upon, as is done in the case of the aged. Another method is that of State-aided insurance, and on these lines Liberal legislators have been experimenting in the hope of dealing with sickness, invalidity, and one portion of the problem of unemployment. A third may be illustrated by the method by which the Minority of the Poor Law Commissioners would deal with the case, at present so often full of tragic import, of the widowed or deserted mother of young children. Hitherto she has been regarded as an object of charity. It has been a matter for the benevolent to help her to retain her home, while it has been regarded as her duty to keep "off the rates" at the cost of no matter what expenditure of labour away from home. The newer conception of rights and duties comes out clearly in the argument of the commissioners, that if we take in earnest all that we say of the duties and responsibilities of motherhood, we shall recognize that the mother of young children is doing better service to the community and one more worthy of pecuniary remuneration when she stays at home and minds her children than when she goes out charing and leaves them to the chances of the street or to the perfunctory care of a neighbour. In proportion as we realize the force of this argument, we reverse our view as to the nature of public assistance in such a case. We no longer consider it desirable to drive the mother out to her charing work if we possibly can, nor do we consider her degraded by receiving public money. We cease, in fact, to regard the public money as a dole, we treat it as a payment for a civic service, and the condition that we are inclined to exact is precisely that she should not endeavour to add to it by earning wages, but rather that she should keep her home respectable and bring up her children in health and happiness.

In defence of the competitive system two arguments have been familiar from old days. One is based on the habits of the working classes. It is said that they spend their surplus incomes on drink, and that if they have no margin for saving, it is because they have sunk it in the public-house. That argument is rapidly being met by the actual change of habits. The wave of temperance which two generations ago reformed the habits of the well-to-do in England is rapidly spreading through all classes in our own time. The drink bill is still excessive, the proportion of his weekly wages spent on drink by the average workman is still too great, but it is a diminishing quantity, and the fear which might have been legitimately expressed in old days that to add to wages was to add to the drink bill could no longer be felt as a valid objection to any improvement in the material condition of the working population in our own time. We no longer find the drink bill heavily increasing in years of commercial prosperity as of old. The second argument has experienced an even more decisive fate. Down to my own time it was forcibly contended that any improvement in the material condition of the mass of the people would result in an increase of the birth rate which, by extending the supply of labour, would bring down wages by an automatic process to the old level. There would be more people and they would all be as miserable as before. The actual decline of the birth rate, whatever its other consequences may be, has driven this argument from the field. The birth rate does not increase with prosperity, but diminishes. There is no fear of over-population; if there is any present danger, it is upon the other side. The fate of these two arguments must be reckoned as a very important factor in the changes of opinion which we have noted.

Nevertheless, it may be thought that the system that I have outlined is no better than a vast organization of State charity, and that as such it must carry the consequences associated with charity on a large scale. It must dry up the sources of energy and undermine the independence of the individual. On the first point, I have already referred to certain cogent arguments for a contrary view. What the State is doing, what it would be doing if the whole series of contemplated changes were carried through to the end, would by no means suffice to meet the needs of the normal man. He would still have to labour to earn his own living. But he would have a basis to go upon, a substructure on which it would be possible for him to rear the fabric of a real sufficiency. He would have greater security, a brighter outlook, a more confident hope of being able to keep his head above water. The experience of life suggests that hope is a better stimulus than fear, confidence a better mental environment than insecurity. If desperation will sometimes spur men to exceptional exertion the effect is fleeting, and, for a permanence, a more stable condition is better suited to foster that blend of restraint and energy which makes up the tissue of a life of normal health. There would be those who would abuse their advantages as there are those who abuse every form of social institution. But upon the whole it is thought that individual responsibility can be more clearly fixed and more rigorously insisted on when its legitimate sphere is properly defined, that is to say, when the burden on the shoulders of the individual is not too great for average human nature to bear.

But, it may be urged, any reliance on external assistance is destructive of independence. It is true that to look for support to private philanthropy has this effect, because it makes one man dependent on the good graces of another. But it is submitted that

96   **LIBERALISM**

a form of support on which a man can count as a matter of legal
right has not necessarily the same effect. Charity, again, tends to
diminish the value of independent effort because it flows in the
direction of the failures. It is a compensation for misfortune which
easily slides into an encouragement to carelessness. What is matter of right, on the other hand, is enjoyed equally by the successful and the unsuccessful. It is not a handicap in favour of the one,
but an equal distance deducted from the race to be run against
fate by both. This brings us to the real question. Are measures of
the kind under discussion to be regarded as measures of philanthropy or measures of justice, as the expression of collective benevolence or as the recognition of a general right? The full discussion of the question involves complex and in some respects
novel conceptions of economics and of social ethics to which I
can hardly do justice within the limits of this chapter. But I will
endeavour to indicate in outline the conception of social and economic justice which underlies the movement of modern Liberal
opinion.

We may approach the subject by observing that, whatever the
legal theory, in practice the existing English Poor Law recognizes
the right of every person to the bare necessaries of life. The destitute man or woman can come to a public authority, and the public
authority is bound to give him food and shelter. He has to that
extent a lien on the public resources in virtue of his needs as a
human being and on no other ground. This lien, however, only
operates when he is destitute; and he can only exercise it by
submitting to such conditions as the authorities impose, which
when the workhouse test is enforced means loss of liberty. It was
the leading "principle of 1834" that the lot of the pauper should
be made "less eligible" than that of the independent labourer.
Perhaps we may express the change of opinion which has come
about in our day by saying that according to the newer principle
the duty of society is rather to ensure that the lot of the independent labourer be more eligible than that of the pauper. With this
object the lien on the common wealth is enlarged and reconsti-
tuted. Its exercise does not entail the penal consequence of the
loss of freedom unless there is proved misfeasance or neglect on
the part of the individual. The underlying contention is that, in
a State so wealthy as the United Kingdom, every citizen should
have full means of earning by socially useful labour so much

material support as experience proves to be the necessary basis of a healthy, civilized existence. And if in the actual working of the industrial system the means are not in actual fact sufficiently available he is held to have a claim not as of charity but as of right on the national resources to make good the deficiency.

That there are rights of property we all admit. Is there not perhaps a general right *to* property? Is there not something radically wrong with an economic system under which through the laws of inheritance and bequest vast inequalities are perpetuated? Ought we to acquiesce in a condition in which the great majority are born to nothing except what they can earn, while some are born to more than the social value of any individual of whatever merit? May it not be that in a reasoned scheme of economic ethics we should have to allow a true right of property in the member of the community as such which would take the form of a certain minimum claim on the public resources? A pretty idea, it may be said, but ethics apart, what are the resources on which the less fortunate is to draw? The British State has little or no collective property available for any such purpose. Its revenues are based on taxation, and in the end what all this means is that the rich are to be taxed for the benefit of the poor, which we may be told is neither justice nor charity but sheer spoliation. To this I would reply that the depletion of public resources is a symptom of profound economic disorganization. Wealth, I would contend, has a social as well as a personal basis. Some forms of wealth, such as ground rents in and about cities, are substantially the creation of society, and it is only through the misfeasance of government in times past that such wealth has been allowed to fall into private hands. Other great sources of wealth are found in financial and speculative operations, often of distinctly anti-social tendency and possible only through the defective organization of our economy. Other causes rest in the partial monopolies which our liquor laws, on the one side, and the old practice of allowing the supply of municipal services to fall into private hands have built up. Through the principle of inheritance, property so accumulated is handed on; and the result is that while there is a small class born to the inheritance of a share in the material benefits of civilization, there is a far larger class which can say "naked we enter, naked we leave." This system, as a whole, it is maintained, requires revision. Property in this condition of things ceases, it is urged, to be essentially an institution by which each man can secure to himself the fruits of his own labour, and becomes an instrument whereby the owner can command the labour of others on terms which he is in general able to dictate. This tendency is held to be undesirable, and to be capable of a remedy through a concerted series of fiscal, industrial, and social measures which would have the effect of augmenting the common stock at the disposal of society, and so applying it as to secure the economic independence of all who do not forfeit their advantages by idleness, incapacity, or crime. There are early forms of communal society in which each person is born to his appropriate status, carrying its appropriate share of the common land. In destroying the last relics of this system economic individualism has laid the basis of great material advances, but at great cost to the happiness of the masses. The ground problem in economics is not to destroy property, but to restore the social conception of property to its right place under conditions suitable to modern needs. This is not to be done by crude measures of redistribution, such as those of which we hear in ancient history. It is to be done by distinguishing the social from the individual factors in wealth, by bringing the elements of social wealth into the public coffers, and by holding it at the disposal of society to administer to the prime needs of its members.

The basis of property is social, and that in two senses. On the one hand, it is the organized force of society that maintains the rights of owners by protecting them against thieves and depredators. In spite of all criticism many people still seem to speak of the rights of property as though they were conferred by Nature or by Providence upon certain fortunate individuals, and as though these individuals had an unlimited right to command the State, as their servant, to secure them by the free use of the machinery of law in the undisturbed enjoyment of their possessions. They forget that without the organized force of society their rights are not worth a week's purchase. They do not ask themselves where they would be without the judge and the policeman and the settled order which society maintains. The prosperous business man who thinks that he has made his fortune entirely by self help does not pause to consider what single step he could have taken on the road to his success but for the ordered tranquillity which has made commercial development possible, the security by road, and rail, and sea, the masses of skilled labour, and the sum of intelligence which civilization has placed at his disposal, the very demand for the goods which he produces which the general progress of the world has created, the inventions which he uses as a matter of course and which have been built up by the collective effort of generations of men of science and organizers of industry. If he dug to the foundations of his fortune he would recognize that, as it is society that maintains and guarantees his possessions, so also it is society which is an indispensable partner in its original creation.

This brings us to the second sense in which property is social. There is a social element in value and a social element in production. In modern industry there is very little that the individual can do by his unaided efforts. Labour is minutely divided; and in proportion as it is divided it is forced to be co-operative. Men produce goods to sell, and the rate of exchange, that is, price, is fixed by relations of demand and supply the rates of which are determined by complex social forces. In the methods of production every man makes use, to the best of his ability, of the whole available means of civilization, of the machinery which the brains of other men have devised, of the human apparatus which is the gift of acquired civilization. Society thus provides conditions or opportunities of which one man will make much better use than another, and the use to which they are put is the individual or personal element in production which is the basis of the personal claim to reward. To maintain and stimulate this personal effort is a necessity of good economic organization, and without asking here whether any particular conception of Socialism would or would not meet this need we may lay down with confidence that no form of Socialism which should ignore it could possibly enjoy enduring success. On the other hand, an individualism which ignores the social factor in wealth will deplete the national resources, deprive the community of its just share in the fruits of industry and so result in a one-sided and inequitable distribution of wealth. Economic justice is to render what is due not only to each individual but to each function, social or personal, that is engaged in the performance of useful service, and this due is measured by the amount necessary to stimulate and maintain the efficient exercise of that useful function. This equation between function and sustenance is the true meaning of economic equality.

Now to apply this principle to the adjustment of the claims of the community on the one hand and the producers or inheritors of wealth on the other would involve a discrimination of the factors of production which is not easy to make in all instances. If we take the case of urban land, referred to above, the distinction is tolerably clear. The value of a site in London is something due essentially to London, not to the landlord. More accurately a part of it is due to London, a part to the British empire, a part, perhaps we should say, to Western civilization. But while it would be impossible to disentangle these subsidiary factors, the main point that the entire increment of value is due to one social factor or another is sufficiently clear, and this explains why Liberal opinion has fastened on the conception of site value as being by right communal and not personal property. The monopoly value of licensed premises, which is the direct creation of laws passed for the control of the liquor traffic, is another case in point. The difficulty which society finds in dealing with these cases is that it has allowed these sources of wealth to pass out of its hands, and that property of these kinds has freely passed from one man to another in the market, in the belief that it stood and would stand on the same basis in law as any other. Hence, it is not possible for society to insist on the whole of its claim. It could only resume its full rights at the cost of great hardship to individuals and a shock to the industrial system. What it can do is to shift taxation step by step from the wealth due to individual enterprise to the wealth that depends on its own collective progress, thus by degrees regaining the ownership of the fruits of its own collective work.

Much more difficult in principle is the question of the more general elements of social value which run through production as a whole. We are dealing here with factors so intricately interwoven in their operation that they can only be separated by an indirect process. What this process would be we may best understand by imagining for a moment a thoroughgoing centralized organization of the industrial system endeavouring to carry out the principles of remuneration outlined above. The central authority which we imagine as endowed with such wisdom and justice as to find for every man his right place and to assign to every man his due reward would, if our argument is sound, find it necessary to assign to each producer, whether working with hand or brain, whether directing a department of industry or serving under direction, such remuneration as would stimulate him to put forth his best efforts and would maintain him in the condition necessary for the life-long exercise of his function. If we are right in considering that a great part of the wealth produced from year to year is of social origin, it would follow that, after the assignment of this remuneration, there would remain a surplus, and this would fall to the coffers of the community and be available for public purposes, for national defence, public works, education, charity, and the furtherance of civilized life.

Now, this is merely an imaginary picture, and I need not ask whether such a measure of wisdom on the part of a Government is practically attainable, or whether such a measure of centralization might not carry consequences which would hamper progress in other directions. The picture serves merely to illustrate the principles of equitable distribution by which the State should be guided in dealing with property. It serves to define our conception of economic justice, and therewith the lines on which we should be guided in the adjustment of taxation and the reorganization of industry. I may illustrate its bearing by taking a couple of cases.

One important source of private wealth under modern conditions is speculation. Is this also a source of social wealth? Does it produce anything for society? Does it perform a function for which our ideal administration would think it necessary to pay? I buy some railway stock at 110. A year or two later I seize a favourable opportunity and sell it at 125. Is the increment earned or unearned? The answer in the single case is clear, but it may be said that my good fortune in this case may be balanced by ill luck in another. No doubt. But, to go no further, if on balance I make a fortune or an income by this method it would seem to be a fortune or an income not earned by productive service. To this it may be replied that the buyers and sellers of stocks are indirectly performing the function of adjusting demand and supply, and so regulating industry. So far as they are expert business men trained in the knowledge of a particular market this may be so. So far as they dabble in the market in the hope of profiting from a favourable turn, they appear rather as gamblers. I will not pretend to determine which of the two is the larger class. I would point out only that, on the face of the facts, the profits derived from this particular source appear to be rather of the nature of a tax which

astute or fortunate individuals are able to levy on the producer
than as the reward which they obtain for a definite contribution
on their own part to production. There are two possible empirical
tests of this view. One is that a form of collective organization
should be devised which should diminish the importance of the
speculative market. Our principle would suggest the propriety of
an attempt in that direction whenever opportunity offers. Another
would be the imposition of a special tax on incomes derived from
this source, and experience would rapidly show whether any such
tax would actually hamper the process of production and distribution at any stage. If not, it would justify itself. It would prove that
the total profit now absorbed by individuals exceeds, at least by
the amount of the tax, the remuneration necessary to maintain
that particular economic function.

The other case I will take is that of inherited wealth. This is the
main determining factor in the social and economic structure of
our time. It is clear on our principle that it stands in quite a different position from that of wealth which is being created from
day to day. It can be defended only on two grounds. One is prescriptive right, and the difficulty of disturbing the basis of the
economic order. This provides an unanswerable argument against
violent and hasty methods, but no argument at all against a gentle
and slow-moving policy of economic reorganization. The other
argument is that inherited wealth serves several indirect functions. The desire to provide for children and to found a family
is a stimulus to effort. The existence of a leisured class affords
possibilities for the free development of originality, and a supply
of disinterested men and women for the service of the State. I
would suggest once again that the only real test to which the
value of these arguments can be submitted is the empirical test.
On the face of the facts inherited wealth stands on a different footing from acquired wealth, and Liberal policy is on the right lines
in beginning the discrimination of earned from unearned income.
The distinction is misconceived only so far as income derived from
capital or land may represent the savings of the individual and
not his inheritance. The true distinction is between the inherited
and the acquired, and while the taxation of acquired wealth may
operate, so far as it goes, to diminish the profits, and so far to
weaken the motive springs, of industry, it is by no means self-
evident that any increase of taxation on inherited wealth would

necessarily have that effect, or that it would vitally derange any other social function. It is, again, a matter on which only experience can decide, but if experience goes to show that we can impose a given tax on inherited wealth without diminishing the available supply of capital and without losing any service of value, the result would be net gain. The State could never be the sole producer, for in production the personal factor is vital, but there is no limit set by the necessities of things to the extension of its control of natural resources, on the one hand, and the accumulated heritage of the past, on the other.

If Liberal policy has committed itself not only to the discrimination of earned and unearned incomes but also to a super-tax on large incomes from whatever source, the ground principle, again, I take to be a respectful doubt whether any single individual is worth to society by any means as much as some individuals obtain. We might, indeed, have to qualify this doubt if the great fortunes of the world fell to the great geniuses. It would be impossible to determine what we ought to pay for a Shakespere, a Browning, a Newton, or a Cobden. Impossible, but fortunately unnecessary. For the man of genius is forced by his own cravings to give, and the only reward that he asks from society is to be let alone and have some quiet and fresh air. Nor is he in reality entitled, notwithstanding his services, to ask more than the modest sufficiency which enables him to obtain those primary needs of the life of thought and creation, since his creative energy is the response to an inward stimulus which goads him on without regard to the wishes of any one else. The case of the great organizers of industry is rather different, but they, again, so far as their work is socially sound, are driven on more by internal necessity than by the genuine love of gain. They make great profits because their works reach a scale at which, if the balance is on the right side at all, it is certain to be a big balance, and they no doubt tend to be interested in money as the sign of their success, and also as the basis of increased social power. But I believe the direct influence of the lust of gain on this type of mind to have been immensely exaggerated; and as proof I would refer, first, to the readiness of many men of this class to accept and in individual cases actively to promote measures tending to diminish their material gain, and, secondly, to the mass of high business capacity which is at the command of the public administration for salaries which, as their recipient must be perfectly conscious, bear no relation to the income which it would be open to him to earn in commercial competition.

On the whole, then, we may take it that the principle of the super-tax is based on the conception that when we come to an income of some £5,000 a year we approach the limit of the industrial value of the individual.[1] We are not likely to discourage any service of genuine social value by a rapidly increasing surtax on incomes above that amount. It is more likely that we shall quench the anti-social ardour for unmeasured wealth, for social power, and the vanity of display.

These illustrations may suffice to give some concreteness to the conception of economic justice as the maintenance of social function. They serve also to show that the true resources of the State are larger and more varied than is generally supposed. The true function of taxation is to secure to society the element in wealth that is of social origin, or, more broadly, all that does not owe its origin to the efforts of living individuals. When taxation, based on these principles, is utilized to secure healthy conditions of existence to the mass of the people it is clear that this is no case of robbing Peter to pay Paul. Peter is not robbed. Apart from the tax it is he who would be robbing the State. A tax which enables the State to secure a certain share of social value is not something deducted from that which the taxpayer has an unlimited right to call his own, but rather a repayment of something which was all along due to society.

But why should the proceeds of the tax go to the poor in particular? Granting that Peter is not robbed, why should Paul be paid? Why should not the proceeds be expended on something of common concern to Peter and Paul alike, for Peter is equally a member of the community? Undoubtedly the only just method of dealing with the common funds is to expend them in objects which

[1] It is true that so long as it remains possible for a certain order of ability to earn £50,000 a year, the community will not obtain its services for £5,000. But if things should be so altered by taxation and economic reorganization that £5,000 became in practice the highest limit attainable, and remained attainable even for the ablest only by effort, there is no reason to doubt that that effort would be forthcoming. It is not the absolute amount of remuneration, but the increment of remuneration in proportion to the output of industrial or commercial capacity, which serves as the needed stimulus to energy.

subserve the common good, and there are many directions in which public expenditure does in fact benefit all classes alike. This, it is worth noting, is true even of some important branches of expenditure which in their direct aim concern the poorer classes. Consider, for example, the value of public sanitation, not merely to the poorer regions which would suffer first if it were withheld, but to the richer as well who, seclude themselves as they may, cannot escape infection. In the old days judge and jury, as well as prisoners, would die of gaol fever. Consider, again, the economic value of education, not only to the worker, but to the employer whom he will serve. But when all this is allowed for it must be admitted that we have throughout contemplated a considerable measure of public expenditure in the elimination of poverty. The prime justification of this expenditure is that the prevention of suffering from the actual lack of adequate physical comforts is an essential element in the common good, an object in which all are bound to concern themselves, which all have the right to demand and the duty to fulfil. Any common life based on the avoidable suffering even of one of those who partake in it is a life not of harmony, but of discord.

But we can go further. We said at the outset that the function of society was to secure to all normal adult members the means of earning by useful work the material necessaries of a healthy and efficient life. We can see now that this is one case and, properly understood, the largest and most far reaching case falling under the general principle of economic justice. This principle lays down that every social function must receive the reward that is sufficient to stimulate and maintain it through the life of the individual. Now, how much this reward may be in any case it is probably impossible to determine otherwise than by specific experiment. But if we grant, in accordance with the idea with which we have been working all along, that it is demanded of all sane adult men and women that they should live as civilized beings, as industrious workers, as good parents, as orderly and efficient citizens, it is, on the other side, the function of the economic organization of society to secure them the material means of living such a life, and the immediate duty of society is to mark the points at which such means fail and to make good the deficiency. Thus the conditions of social efficiency mark the minimum of industrial remuneration, and if they are not secured without the deliberate action of the

State they must be secured by means of the deliberate action of
the State. If it is the business of good economic organization to
secure the equation between function and maintenance, the first
and greatest application of this principle is to the primary needs.
These fix the minimum standard of remuneration beyond which
we require detailed experiment to tell us at what rate increased
value of service rendered necessitates corresponding increase of
reward.

It may be objected that such a standard is unattainable. There
are those, it may be contended, who are not, and never will be,
worth a full efficiency wage. Whatever is done to secure them such
a remuneration will only involve net loss. Hence it violates our
standard of economic justice. It involves payment for a function
of more than it is actually worth, and the discrepancy might be
so great as to cripple society. It must, of course, be admitted that
the population contains a certain percentage of the physically
incapable, the mentally defective, and the morally uncontrolled.
The treatment of these classes, all must agree, is and must be
based on other principles than those of economics. One class requires punitive discipline, another needs life-long care, a third—
the mentally and morally sound but physically defective—must
depend, to its misfortune, on private and public charity. There is
no question here of payment for a function, but of ministering to
human suffering. It is, of course, desirable on economic as well as
on broader grounds that the ministration should be so conceived
as to render its object as nearly as possible independent and self-
supporting. But in the main all that is done for these classes of the
population is, and must be, a charge on the surplus. The real
question that may be raised by a critic is whether the considerable
proportion of the working class whose earnings actually fall short,
as we should contend, of the minimum, could in point of fact earn
that minimum. Their actual value, he may urge, is measured by
the wage which they do in fact command in the competitive market, and if their wage falls short of the standard society may make
good the deficiency if it will and can, but must not shut its eyes
to the fact that in doing so it is performing, not an act of economic
justice, but of charity. To this the reply is that the price which
naked labour without property can command in bargaining with
employers who possess property is no measure at all of the addition which such labour can actually make to wealth. The bargain

is unequal, and low remuneration is itself a cause of low efficiency which in turn tends to react unfavourably on remuneration. Conversely, a general improvement in the conditions of life reacts favourably on the productivity of labour. Real wages have risen considerably in the last half century, but the income-tax returns indicate that the wealth of the business and professional man has increased even more rapidly. Up to the efficiency minimum there is, then, every reason to think that a general increase of wages would positively increase the available surplus whether that surplus goes to individuals as profits or to the State as national revenue. The material improvement of working-class conditions will more than pay its way regarded purely as an economic investment on behalf of society.

This conclusion is strengthened if we consider narrowly what elements of cost the "living wage" ought in principle to cover. We are apt to assume uncritically that the wages earned by the labour of an adult man ought to suffice for the maintenance of an average family, providing for all risks. It ought, we think, to cover not only the food and clothing of wife and children, but the risks of sickness, accident, and unemployment. It ought to provide for education and lay by for old age. If it fails we are apt to think that the wage earner is not self supporting. Now, it is certainly open to doubt whether the actual addition to wealth made by an unskilled labourer denuded of all inherited property would equal the cost represented by the sum of these items. But here our further principle comes into play. He ought not to be denuded of all inherited property. As a citizen he should have a certain share in the social inheritance. This share should be his support in the times of misfortune, of sickness, and of worklessness, whether due to economic disorganization or to invalidity and old age. His children's share, again, is the State-provided education. These shares are charges on the social surplus. It does not, if fiscal arrangements are what they should be, infringe upon the income of other individuals, and the man who without further aid than the universally available share in the social inheritance which is to fall to him as a citizen pays his way through life is to be justly regarded as self-supporting.

The central point of Liberal economics, then, is the equation of social service and reward. This is the principle that every function of social value requires such remuneration as serves to stimulate and maintain its effective performance; that every one who performs such a function has the right, in the strict ethical sense of that term, to such remuneration and to no more; that the residue of existing wealth should be at the disposal of the community for social purposes. Further, it is the right, in the same sense, of every person capable of performing some useful social function that he should have the opportunity of so doing, and it is his right that the remuneration that he receives for it should be his property, *i.e.* that it should stand at his free disposal enabling him to direct his personal concerns according to his own preferences. These are rights in the sense that they are conditions of the welfare of its members which a well-ordered State will seek by every means to fulfil. But it is not suggested that the way of such fulfilment is plain, or that it could be achieved at a stroke by a revolutionary change in the tenure of property or the system of industry. It is, indeed, implied that the State is vested with a certain overlordship over property in general and a supervisory power over industry in general, and this principle of economic sovereignty may be set side by side with that of economic justice as a no less fundamental conception of economic Liberalism. For here, as elsewhere, liberty implies control. But the manner in which the State is to exercise its controlling power is to be learnt by experience and even in large measure by cautious experiment. We have sought to determine the principle which should guide its action, the ends at which it is to aim. The systematic study of the means lies rather within the province of economics; and the teaching of history seems to be that progress is more continuous and secure when men are content to deal with problems piecemeal than when they seek to destroy root and branch in order to erect a complete system which has captured the imagination.

It is evident that these conceptions embody many of the ideas that go to make up the framework of Socialist teaching, though they also emphasize elements of individual right and personal independence, of which Socialism at times appears oblivious. The distinction that I would claim for economic Liberalism is that it seeks to do justice to the social and individual factors in industry alike, as opposed to an abstract Socialism which emphasizes the one side and an abstract Individualism which leans its whole weight on the other. By keeping to the conception of harmony as our clue we constantly define the rights of the individual in terms of the common good, and think of the common good in terms of the welfare of all the individuals who constitute a society. Thus in economics we avoid the confusion of liberty with competition, and see no virtue in the right of a man to get the better of others. At the same time we are not led to minimize the share of personal initiative, talent, or energy in production, but are free to contend for their claim to adequate recognition. A Socialist who is convinced of the logical coherence and practical applicability of his system may dismiss such endeavours to harmonize divergent claims as a half-hearted and illogical series of compromises. It is equally possible that a Socialist who conceives Socialism as consisting in essence in the co-operative organization of industry by consumers, and is convinced that the full solution of industrial problems lies in that direction, should in proportion as he considers the psychological factors in production and investigates the means of realizing his ideal, find himself working back along the path to a point where he will meet the men who are grappling with the problems of the day on the principles here suggested, and will find himself able to move forward in practice in the front ranks of economic Liberalism. If this is so, the growing co-operation of political Liberalism and Labour, which in the last few years has replaced the antagonism of the 'nineties, is no mere accident of temporary political convenience, but has its roots deep in the necessities of Democracy.

[26]

Excerpt from *The Sickness of an Acquisitive Society*, 7–48

II.

RIGHTS AND FUNCTIONS.

A function may be defined as an activity which embodies and expresses the idea of social purpose. The essence of it is that the agent does not perform it merely for personal gain or to gratify himself, but recognizes that he is responsible for its discharge to some higher authority. The purpose of industry is obvious. It is to supply man with things which are necessary, useful or beautiful, and thus to bring life to body or spirit. In so far as it is governed by this end, it is among the most important of human activities. In so far as it is diverted from it, it may be harmless, amusing, or even exhilarating to those who carry it on, but it possesses no more social significance than the orderly business of ants and bees, the strutting of peacocks, or the struggles of carnivorous animals over carrion. Men have normally appreciated this fact, however unwilling or unable they may have been to act upon it ; and therefore from time to time, in so far as they have been able to control the forces of violence and greed, they have adopted various expedients for emphasizing the social quality of economic activity. It is not easy, however, to emphasize it effectively, because to do so requires a constant effort of will, against which egotistical instincts are in rebellion, and because, if that will is to prevail, it must be embodied in some social and political organization, which may itself become so arbitrary, tyrannical and corrupt as to thwart the performance of function instead of promoting it. When this process of degeneration has gone far, as in most European countries it had by the middle of the eighteenth century, the indispensable thing is to break the dead organization up and to clear the ground. In the course of doing so, the individual is emancipated and his rights are enlarged ; but the idea of social purpose is discredited by the discredit justly attaching to the obsolete order in which it is embodied.

It is not surprising, therefore, that in the new industrial societies which arose on the ruins of the old régime the dominant note should have been the insistence upon individual rights, irrespective of any social purpose to which their exercise contributed. The change of social quality was profound. But in England, at least, it was gradual, and the " industrial revolution," though catastrophic in its effects, was only the visible climax of generations of subtle moral change. The rise of modern economic relations, which may be dated in England from the latter half of the seventeenth century, was coincident with the growth of a political theory which replaced the conception of purpose by that of mechanism. During a great part of history men had found the significance of their social order in its relation'to the universal purposes of religion. It stood as one rung in a ladder which stretched from hell to Paradise, and the classes who composed it were the hands, the feet, the head of a corporate body which was itself a microcosm imperfectly reflecting a larger universe. When the Reformation made the Church a department of the secular government, it undermined the already enfeebled spiritual forces which had erected that sublime, but too much elaborated, synthesis. But its influence remained for nearly a century after the roots which fed it had been severed. It was the atmosphere into which men were born, and from which, however practical, or even Machiavellian, they could not easily disengage their spirits. Nor was it inconvenient for the new statecraft to see the weight of a traditional religious sanction added to its own concern in the subordination of all classes and interests to the common end, of which it conceived itself, and during the greater part of the sixteenth century was commonly conceived, to be the guardian. The lines of the social structure were no longer supposed to reproduce in miniature the plan of a universal order. But common habits, common traditions and beliefs, common pressure from above gave them a unity of direction, which restrained the forces of individual variation and lateral expansion ; and the centre towards which they converged, formerly a Church possessing some of the characteristics of a State, was now a State that had clothed itself with many of the attributes of a Church.

The difference between the England of Shakespeare, still visited by the ghosts of the Middle Ages, and the England which emerged in 1700 from the fierce polemics of the last two generations, was a difference of social and political theory even more than of constitutional and political arrangements. Not only the facts, but the minds which appraised them, were profoundly modified. The essence of the change was the disappearance of the idea that social institutions and economic activities were related to common ends, which gave them their significance and which served as their criterion. In the eighteenth century both the State and the Church had abdicated that part of their sphere which had consisted in the maintenance of a common body of social ethics ; what was left of it was the repression of a class, not the discipline of a nation. Opinion ceased to regard social institutions and economic activity as amenable, like personal conduct, to moral criteria, because it was no longer influenced by the spectacle of institutions which, arbitrary, capricious, and often corrupt in their practical operation, had been the outward symbol and expression of the subordination of life to purposes transcending private interests. That part of government which had been concerned with social administration, if it did not end, became at least obsolescent. For such democracy as had existed in the Middle Ages was dead, and the democracy of the Revolution was not yet born, so that government passed into the lethargic hand of classes who wielded the power of the State in the interests of an irresponsible aristocracy.   And the Church was even more remote from the daily life of mankind than the State.   Philanthropy abounded ;   but religion, once the greatest social force, had become a thing as private and individual as the estate of the squire or the working clothes of the labourer.   There were special dispensations and occasional interventions, like the acts of a monarch who reprieved a criminal or signed an order for his execution.   But what was familiar, and human and loveable—what was Christian in Christianity had largely disappeared. God had been thrust into the frigid altitudes of infinite space.   There was a limited monarchy in Heaven, as well as upon earth.   Providence was the spectator of the curious machine which it had constructed and set in motion, but the operation of which it was neither able nor willing to control.   Like the occasional intervention of the Crown in the proceedings of Parliament, its wisdom was revealed in the infrequency of its interference.

The natural consequence of the abdication of authorities which had stood, however imperfectly, for a common purpose in social organization, was the gradual disappearance from social thought of the idea of purpose itself.   Its place in the eighteenth century was taken by the idea of mechanism.   The conception of men as united to each other, and of all mankind as united to God, by mutual obligations arising from their relation to a common end, which vaguely conceived and imperfectly realized, had been the keystone holding together the social fabric, ceased to be impressed upon men's minds, when Church and State withdrew from the centre of social life to its circumference.   What remained when the keystone of the arch was removed, was private rights and private interests, the materials of a society rather than a society itself.   These rights and interests were the natural order which had been distorted by the ambitions of kings and priests, and which emerged when the artificial superstructure disappeared, because they were the creation, not of man, but of Nature herself.   They had been regarded in the past as relative to some public end, whether religion or national welfare.   Henceforward they were thought to be absolute and indefeasible, and to stand by their own virtue.   They were the ultimate political and social reality ;   and since they were the ultimate reality, they were not subordinate to other aspects of society, but other aspects of society were subordinate to them.   The State could not encroach upon them, for the State existed for their maintenance.   They determined the relation of classes, for the most obvious and fundamental of all rights was property—property absolute and unconditioned—and those who possessed it were regarded as the natural governors of those who did not.   Society arose from their exercise, through the contracts of individual with individual.   It fulfilled its object in so far as, by maintaining contractual freedom, it secured full scope for their unfettered exercise.   It failed in so far as, like the French monarchy, it overrode them by the use of an arbitrary authority.   Thus conceived, society assumed something of the appearance of a great joint-stock company, in which political power and the receipt of dividends were justly assigned to those who held the most numerous shares. The currents of social activity did not converge upon common ends, but were dispersed through a multitude of channels, created by the private interests of the individuals who composed society. But in their very variety and spontaneity, in the very absence of any attempt to relate them to a larger purpose than that of the individual, lay the best security of its attainment. There is a mysticism of reason as well as of emotion, and the eighteenth century found, in the beneficence of natural instincts, a substitute for the God whom it had expelled from contact with society, and did not hesitate to identify them.

> " Thus God and nature planned the general frame
> And bade self-love and social be the same."

The result of such ideas in the world of practice was a society which was ruled by law, not by the caprice of Governments, but which recognized no moral limitation on the pursuit by individuals of their economic self-interest. In the world of thought, it was a political philosophy which made rights the foundation of the social order, and which considered the discharge of obligations, when it considered it at all, as emerging by an inevitable process from their free exercise. The first famous exponent of this philosophy was Locke, in whom the dominant conception is the indefeasibility of private rights, not the pre-ordained harmony between private rights and public welfare. In the great French writers who prepared the way for the Revolution, while believing that they were the servants of an enlightened absolutism, there is an almost equal emphasis upon the sanctity of rights and upon the infallibility of the alchemy by which the pursuit of private ends is transmuted into the attainment of public good. Though their writings reveal the influence of the conception of society as a self-adjusting mechanism, which afterwards became the most characteristic note of the English individualism, what the French Revolution burned into the mind of Europe was the former not the latter. In England the idea of right had been negative and defensive, a barrier to the encroachment of Governments. The French leapt to the attack from trenches which the English had been content to defend, and in France the idea came affirmative and militant, not a weapon of defence, but a principle of social organization. The attempt to refound society upon rights, and rights springing not from musty charters, but from the very nature of man himself, was at once the triumph and the limitation of the Revolution. It gave it the enthusiasm and infectious power of religion.

What happened in England might seem at first sight to have been precisely the reverse. English practical men, whose thoughts were pitched in a lower key, were a little shocked by the pomp and brilliance of that tremendous creed. They had scanty sympathy with the absolute affirmations of France. What captured their imagination was not the right to liberty, which made no appeal to their commercial instincts, but the expediency of liberty, which did ; and when the Revolution had revealed the explosive power of the idea of natural

[10]

right, they sought some less menacing formula. It had been offered them first by Adam Smith and his precursors, who showed how the mechanism of economic life converted " as with an invisible hand," the exercise of individual rights into the instrument of public good. Bentham, who despised metaphysical subtleties, and thought the Declaration of the Rights of Man as absurd as any other dogmatic religion, completed the new orientation by supplying the final criterion of political institutions in the principle of utility. Henceforward emphasis was transferred from the right of the individual to exercise his freedom as he pleased to the expediency of an undisturbed exercise of freedom to society.

The change is significant. It is the difference between the universal and equal citizenship of France, with its five million peasant proprietors, and the organized inequality of England established solidly upon class traditions and class institutions ; the descent from hope to resignation, from the fire and passion of an age of illimitable vistas to the monotonous beat of the factory engine, from Turgot and Condorcet to the melancholy mathematical creed of Bentham and Ricardo and James Mill. Mankind has, at least, this superiority over its philosophers that great movements spring from the heart and embody a faith, not the nice adjustments of the hedonistic calculus. So in the name of the rights of property France abolished in three years a great mass of property rights which, under the old régime had robbed the peasant of part of the produce of his labour, and the social transformation survived a whole world of political changes. In England the glad tidings of democracy were broken too discreetly to reach the ears of the hind in the furrow or the shepherd on the hill ; there were political changes without a social transformation. The doctrine of Utility, though trenchant in the sphere of politics, involved no considerable interference with the fundamentals of the social fabric. Its exponents were principally concerned with the removal of political abuses and legal anomalies. They attacked sinecures and pensions and the criminal code and the procedure of the law courts. But they touched only the surface of social institutions. They thought it a monstrous injustice that the citizen should pay one-tenth of his income in taxation to an idle Government, but quite reasonable that he should pay one-fifth of it in rent to an idle landlord.

The difference, nevertheless, was one of emphasis and expression, not of principle. It mattered very little in practice whether private property and unfettered economic freedom were described as natural rights, or whether they were merely assumed once for all to be expedient. In either case they were taken for granted as the fundamentals upon which social organization was to be based, and about which no further argument was admissible. Though Bentham argued that rights were derived from utility, not from nature, he did not push his analysis so far as to argue that any particular right was relative to any particular function, and thus endorsed indiscriminately rights which were not accompanied by service as well as rights which were. While eschewing, in

[11]

short, the phraseology of natural rights, the English Utilitarians retained something not unlike the substance of them. For they assumed that private property in land, and the private ownership of capital, were natural institutions, and gave them, indeed, a new lease of life, by proving to their own satisfaction that social well-being must result from their continued exercise. Their negative was as important as their positive teaching. It was a conductor which diverted the lightning. Behind their political theory, behind the practical conduct, which as always, continues to express theory long after it has been discredited in the world of thought, lay the acceptance of absolute rights to property and to economic freedom as the unquestioned centre of social organization.

III.

THE ACQUISITIVE SOCIETY.

This doctrine has been qualified in practice by particular limitations to avert particular evils and to meet exceptional emergencies. But it is limited in special cases precisely because its general validity is regarded as beyond controversy, and, up to the eve of the present war, it was the working faith of modern economic civilization. What it implies is, that the foundation of society is found, not in functions, but in rights ; that rights are not deducible from the discharge of functions, so that the acquisition of wealth and the enjoyment of property are contingent upon the performances of services, but that the individual enters the world equipped with rights to the free disposal of his property and the pursuit of his economic self-interest, and that these rights are anterior to, and independent of, any service which he may render. True, the service of society will, in fact, it is assumed, result from their exercise. But it is not the primary motive and criterion of industry, but a secondary consequence, which emerges incidentally through the exercise of rights, a consequence which is attained, indeed, in practice, but which is attained without being sought. It is not the end at which economic activity aims, or the standard by which it is judged, but a bye-product, as coal-tar is a bye-product of the manufacture of gas ; whether that bye-product appears or not, it is not proposed that the rights themselves should be abdicated. For they are regarded, not as a conditional trust, but as a property, which may, indeed give way to the special exigencies of extraordinary emergencies, but which resumes its sway when the emergency is over, and in normal times is above discussion.

That conception is written large over the history of the nineteenth century. The doctrine which it inherited was that property was held by an absolute right on an individual basis, and to this fundamental it added another, which can be traced in principle far back into history, but which grew to its full stature only after the rise of capitalist industry, that societies act both unfairly and unwisely when they limit opportunities of economic enterprize. Hence every attempt to impose obligations as a condition of the tenure of property or of the exercise of economic activity has been met by uncompromising resistance. The story of the struggle between humanitarian sentiment and the theory of property transmitted from the eighteenth century is familiar. No one has forgotten the opposition offered in the name of the rights of property to factory legislation, to housing reform, to interference with the adulteration of goods, even to the compulsory sanitation of private houses. " May I not do what I like with my own ? " was the answer to the proposal to require a minimum standard of safety and sanitation from the owners of mills and houses. Even to this day, while an English urban landlord can

[13]

cramp or distort the development of a whole city by withholding land except at fancy prices, English municipalities are without adequate powers of compulsory purchase, and must either pay through the nose or see thousands of their members overcrowded. The whole body of procedure by which they may acquire land, or indeed new powers of any kind, has been carefully designed by lawyers to protect owners of property against the possibility that their private rights may be subordinated to the public interest, because their rights are thought to be primary and absolute and public interests secondary and contingent. No one needs to be reminded, again, of the influence of the same doctrine in the sphere of taxation. Thus the income tax was excused as a temporary measure, because the normal society was conceived to be one in which the individual spent his whole income for himself and owed no obligations to society on account of it. The death duties were denounced as robbery, because they implied that the right to benefit by inheritance was conditional upon a social sanction. The Budget of 1909 created a storm, not because the taxation of land was heavy—in amount the land-taxes were trifling—but because it was felt to involve the doctrine that property is not an absolute right, but that it may properly be accompanied by special obligations, a doctrine which, if carried to its logical conclusion, would destroy its sanctity by making ownership no longer absolute but conditional.

Such an implication seems intolerable to an influential body of public opinion, because it has been accustomed to regard the free disposal of property and the unlimited exploitation of economic opportunities, as rights which are absolute and unconditioned. On the whole, until recently, this opinion had few antagonists who could not be ignored. As a consequence the maintenance of property rights has not been seriously threatened even in those cases in which it is evident that no service is discharged, directly or indirectly, by their exercise. No one supposes, that the owner of urban land, performs *qua* owner, any function. He has a right of private taxation ; that is all. But the private ownership of urban land is as secure to-day as it was a century ago ; and Lord Hugh Cecil, in his interesting little book on Conservatism, declares that whether private property is mischievous or not, society cannot interfere with it, because to interfere with it is theft, and theft is wicked. No one supposes that it is for the public good that large areas of land should be used for parks and game. But our country gentlemen are still settled heavily upon their villages and still slay their thousands. No one can argue that a monopolist is impelled by " an invisible hand " to serve the public interest. But over a considerable field of industry competition, as the recent Report on Trusts shows, has been replaced by combination, and combinations are allowed the same unfettered freedom as individuals in the exploitation of economic opportunities. No one really believes that the production of coal depends upon the payment of mining royalties or that ships will not go to and fro unless ship-owners can earn fifty per cent. upon their capital. But coal-mines, or rather the coal miner, still pays royalties, and shipowners still make fortunes and are made Peers.   At the very moment when everybody is talking about the importance of increasing the output of wealth, the last question, apparently, which it occurs to any statesman to ask is why wealth should be squandered on futile activities, and in expenditure which is either disproportionate to service or made for no service at all.   So inveterate, indeed, has become the practice of payment in virtue of property rights, without even the pretence of any service being rendered, that when, in a national emergency, it is proposed to extract oil from the ground, the government actually proposes that every gallon shall pay a tax to landowners who never even suspected its existence, and the ingenuous proprietors are full of pained astonishment at any one questioning whether the nation is under a moral obligation to endow them further.   Such rights are, strictly speaking, privileges.   For the definition of a privilege is a right to which no corresponding function is attached.

The enjoyment of property and the direction of industry are considered, in short, to require no social justification, because they are regarded as rights which stand by their own virtue, not functions to be judged by the success with which they contribute to a social purpose.   To-day that doctrine, if intellectually discredited, is still the practical foundation of social organization.   How slowly it yields even to the most insistent demonstration of its inadequacy is shown by the attitude which the heads of the business world have adopted to the restrictions imposed on economic activity during the war.   The control of railways, mines and shipping, the distribution of raw materials through a public department instead of through competing merchants, the regulation of prices, the attempts to check " profiteering "—the detailed application of these measures may have been effective or ineffective, wise or injudicious.   It is evident, indeed, that some of them have been foolish, like the restriction of imports when the world has five years destruction to repair, and that others, if sound in conception, have been questionable in their execution.   If they were attacked on the ground that they obstruct the efficient performance of function—if the leaders of industry came forward and said generally, as some, to their honour, have :—"We accept your policy, but we will improve its execution ; we desire payment for service and service only and will help the state to see that it pays for nothing else "—there might be controversy as to the facts, but there could be none as to the principle.   In reality, however, the gravamen of the charges brought against these restrictions appears generally to be precisely the opposite.   They are denounced by most of their critics not because they limit the opportunity of service but because they diminish the opportunity for gain, not because they prevent the trader enriching the community but because they make it more difficult for him to enrich himself, not, in short, because they have failed to convert economic activity into a social function, but because they have come too near succeeding.   If the financial adviser to the Coal Controller may be trusted, the shareholders in coal-mines would appear to have done fairly well during the war.   But the proposal to limit their profits to 1/2 per ton is described by Lord Gainford as " sheer

[15]

robbery and confiscation." With some honourable exceptions, what is demanded is that in the future as in the past the directors of industry should be free to handle it as an enterprise conducted for their own convenience or advancement, instead of being compelled, as they have been partially compelled during the war, to subordinate it to a social purpose. For to admit that the criterion of commerce and industry is its success in discharging a social purpose is at once to turn property and economic activity from rights which are absolute into rights which are contingent and derivative, because it is to affirm that they are relative to functions and that they may justly be revoked when the functions are not performed. It is, in short, to imply that property and economic activity exist to promote the ends of society, whereas hitherto society has been regarded in the world of business as existing to promote them. To those who hold their position, not as functionaries, but by virtue of their success in making industry contribute to their own wealth and social influence, such a reversal of means and ends appears little less than a revolution. For it means that they must justify before a social tribunal rights which they have hitherto taken for granted as part of an order which is above criticism.

During the greater part of the nineteenth century the significance of the opposition between the two principles of individual rights and social functions was masked by the doctrine of the inevitable harmony between private interests and public good. Competition, it was argued, was an effective substitute for honesty. To-day that subsidiary doctrine has fallen to pieces under criticism ; few now would profess adherence to the compound of economic optimism and moral bankruptcy which led a nineteenth century economist to say : " Greed is held in check by greed, and the desire for gain sets limits to itself." The disposition to regard individual rights as the centre and pivot of society is still, however, the most powerful element in political thought and the practical foundation of industrial organization. The laborious refutation of the doctrine that private and public interests are coincident, and that man's self-love is God's Providence, which was the excuse of the last century for its worship of economic egotism, has achieved, in fact, surprisingly small results. Economic egotism is still worshipped ; and it is worshipped because that doctrine was not really the centre of the position. It was an outwork, not the citadel, and now that the outwork has been captured, the citadel is still to win. What gives its special quality and character, its toughness and cohesion, to the industrial system built up in the last century and a half, is not its exploded theory of economic harmonies. It is the doctrine that economic rights are anterior to, and independent of economic functions, that they stand by their own virtue, and need adduce no higher credentials. The practical result of it is that economic rights remain, whether economic functions are performed or not. They remain to-day in a more menacing form than in the age of early industrialism. For those who control industry no longer compete but combine, and the rivalry between property in capital and property in land has long since ended. The basis of the New

[16]

Conservatism appears to be a determination so to organize society, both by political and economic action, as to make it secure against every attempt to extinguish payments which are made, not for service, but because the owners possess a right to extract income without it. Hence the fusion of the two traditional parties, the proposed " strengthening " of the second chamber, the return to protection, the swift conversion of rival industrialists to the advantages of monopoly, and the attemps to buy off with concessions the more influential section of the working classes. Revolutions, as a long and bitter experience reveals, are apt to take their colour from the régime which they overthrow. Is it any wonder that the creed which affirms the absolute rights of property should sometimes be met with a counter-affirmation of the absolute rights of labour, less anti-social, indeed, and inhuman, but almost as dogmatic, almost as intolerant and thoughtless as itself ?

A society which aimed at making the acquisition of wealth contingent upon the discharge of social obligations, which sought to proportion remuneration to service and denied it to those by whom no service was performed, which inquired first not what men possess but what they can make or create or achieve, might be called a Functional Society, because in such a society the main subject of social emphasis would be the performance of functions. But such a society does not exist, even as a remote ideal, in the modern world, though something like it has hung, an unrealized theory, before men's minds in the past. Modern societies aim at protecting economic rights, while leaving economic functions, except in moments of abnormal emergency, to fulfil themselves. The motive which gives colour and quality to their public institutions, to their policy and political thought, is not the attempt to secure the fulfilment of tasks undertaken for the public service, but to increase the opportunities open to individuals of attaining the objects which they conceive to be advantageous to themselves. If asked the end or criterion of social organization, they would give an answer reminiscent of the formula the greatest happiness of the greatest number. But to say that the end of social institutions is happiness, is to say that they have no common end at all. For happiness is individual, and to make happiness the object of society is to resolve society itself into the ambitions of numberless individuals, each directed towards the attainment of some personal purpose.

Such societies my be called Acquisitive Societies, because their whole tendency and interest and preoccupation is to promote the acquisition of wealth. The appeal of this conception must be powerful, for it has laid the whole modern world under its spell. Since England first revealed the possibilities of industrialism, it has gone from strength to strength, and as industrial civilization invades countries hitherto remote from it, as Russia and Japan and India and China are drawn into its orbit, each decade sees a fresh extension of its influence. The secret of its triumph is obvious. It is an invitation to men to use the powers with which they have been endowed by nature or society, by skill or energy or relentless egotism or mere good fortune, without enquiring whether there is any principle by which their exercise should be limited. It assumes the social organization which determines the opportunities which different classes shall in fact possess, and concentrates attention upon the right of those who possess or can acquire power to make the fullest use of it for their own self-advancement. By fixing men's minds, not upon the discharge of social obligations, which restricts their energy, because it defines the goal to which it should be directed, but upon the exercise of the right to pursue their own self-interest, it offers unlimited scope for the acquisition of riches, and therefore gives free play to one of the most powerful of human instincts. To the strong it promises unfettered freedom for the exercise of their strength; to the weak the hope that they too one day may be strong. Before the eyes of both it suspends a golden prize, which not all can attain, but for which each may strive, the enchanting vision of infinite expansion It assures men that there are no ends other than their ends, no law other than their desires, no limit other than that which they think advisable. Thus it makes the individual the centre of his own universe, and dissolves moral principles into a choice of expediences. And it immensely simplifies the problems of social life in complex communities. For it relieves them of the necessity of discriminating between different types of economic activity and different sources of wealth, between enterprise and avarice, energy and unscrupulous greed, property which is legitimate and property which is theft, the just enjoyment of the fruits of labour and the idle parasitism of birth or fortune, because it treats all economic activities as standing upon the same level, and suggests that excess or defect, waste or superfluity, require no conscious effort of the social will to avert them, but are corrected almost automatically by the mechanical play of economic forces.

Under the impulse of such ideas men do not become religious or wise or artistic; for religion and wisdom and art imply the acceptance of limitations. But they become powerful and rich. They inherit the earth and change the face of nature, if they do not possess their own souls; and they have that appearance of freedom which consists in the absence of obstacles between opportunities for self-advancement and those whom birth or wealth or talent or good fortune has placed in a position to seize them. It is not difficult either for individuals or for societies to achieve their object, if that object be sufficiently limited and immediate, and if they are not distracted from its pursuit by other considerations. The temper which dedicates itself to the cultivation of opportunities, and leaves obligations to take care of themselves, is set upon an object which is at once simple and practicable. The eighteenth century defined it. The twentieth century has very largely attained it. Or, if it has not attained it, it has at least grasped the possibilities of its attainment. The national output of wealth per head of population is estimated to have been approximately £40 in 1914. Unless mankind chooses to continue the sacrifice of prosperity to the ambitions and terrors of nationalism, there is no reason why by the year 2000 it should not be doubled.

IV.

THE NEMESIS OF INDUSTRIALISM.

Such happiness is not remote from achievement. In the course of achieving it, however, the world has been confronted by a group of unexpected consequences, which are the cause of its *malaise*, as the obstruction of economic opportunity was the cause of social *malaise* in the eighteenth century. And these consequences are not, as is often suggested, accidental mal-adjustments, but flow naturally from its dominant principle : so that there is a sense in which the cause of its perplexity is not its failure, but the quality of its success, and its light itself a kind of darkness. The will to economic power, if it is sufficiently single-minded, brings riches. But if it is single-minded it destroys the moral restraints which ought to condition the pursuit of riches, and therefore also makes the pursuit of riches meaningless. For what gives meaning to economic activity, as to any other activity is, as we have said, the purpose to which it is directed. But the faith upon which our economic civilization reposes, the faith that riches are not a means but an end, implies that all economic activity is equally estimable, whether it is subordinated to a social purpose or not. Hence it divorces gain from service, and justifies rewards for which no function is performed, or which are out of all proportion to it. Wealth in modern societies is distributed according to opportunity ; and while opportunity depends partly upon talent and energy, it depends still more upon birth, social position, access to education and inherited wealth ; in a word, upon property. For talent and energy can create opportunity. But property need only wait for it. It is the sleeping partner who draws the dividends which the firm produces, the residuary legatee who always claims his share in the estate.

Because rewards are divorced from services, so that what is prized most is not riches obtained in return for labour but riches the economic origin of which, being regarded as sordid, is concealed, two results follow. The first is the creation of a class of pensioners upon industry, who levy toll upon its product, but contribute nothing to its increase, and who are not merely tolerated, but applauded and admired and protected with assiduous care, as though the secret of prosperity resided in them. They are admired because in the absence of any principle of discrimination between incomes which are payment for functions and incomes which are not, all incomes, merely because they represent wealth, stand on the same level of appreciation, and are estimated solely by their magnitude, so that in all societies which have accepted industrialism there is an upper layer which claims the enjoyment of social life, while it repudiates its responsibilities. The *rentier* and his ways, how familiar they were in England before the war ! A public school and then club life in Oxford and Cambridge, and then another club in town ; London in June, when London is pleasant, the moors in August, and pheasants in October, Cannes in December and hunting in February and March ; and a whole world of rising bourgeoisie eager to imitate them, sedulous to make their expensive watches keep time with this preposterous calendar !

The second consequence is the degradation of those who labour, but who do not by their labour command large rewards ; that is of the great majority of mankind. And this degradation follows inevitably from the refusal of men to give the purpose of industry the first place in their thought about it. When they do that, when their minds are set upon the fact that the meaning of industry is the service of man, all who labour appear to them honourable, because all who labour serve, and the distinction which separates those who serve from those who merely spend is so crucial and fundamental as to obliterate all minor distinctions based on differences of income. But when the criterion of function is forgotten, the only criterion which remains is that of wealth, and an Acquisitive Society reverences the possession of wealth, as a Functional Society would honour, even in the person of the humblest and most laborious craftsman, the arts of creation. So wealth becomes the foundation of public esteem, and the mass of men who labour, but who do not acquire wealth, are thought to be vulgar and meaningless and insignificant compared with the few who acquire wealth by good fortune, or by the skilful use of economic opportunities. They come to be regarded, not as the ends for which alone it is worth while to produce wealth at all, but as the instruments of its acquisition by a world that declines to be soiled by contact with what is thought to be the dull and sordid business of labour. They are not happy, for the reward of all but the very mean is not merely money, but the esteem of their fellow-men, and they know they are not esteemed, as soldiers, for example, are esteemed, though it is because they give their lives to making civilization that there is a civilization which it is worth while for soldiers to defend. They are not esteemed, because their work is not esteemed, because the admiration of society is directed towards those who get, not towards those who give ; and though workmen give much they get little. And the *rentiers* whom they support are not happy ; for in discarding the idea of function, which sets a limit to the acquisition of riches, they have also discarded the principle which alone give riches their meaning. Hence unless they can persuade themselves that to be rich is in itself meritorious, they may bask in social admiration, but they are unable to esteem themselves. For they have abolished the principle which makes activity significant, and therefore estimable. They are, indeed, more truly pitiable than some of those who envy them. For like the spirits in the Inferno, they are punished by the attainment of their desires.

A society ruled by these notions is necessarily the victim of inequality. To escape inequality it is necessary to recognise that there is some principle which ought to limit the gains of particular classes and particular individuals, because gains drawn from certain sources or exceeding certain amounts are illegitimate.   But such a limitation implies a standard of discrimination, which is inconsistent with the assumption that each man has a right to what he can get, irrespective of any service rendered for it.   Thus privilege, which was to have been exorcised by the gospel of 1789, returns in a new guise, the creature no longer of unequal legal rights thwarting the natural exercise of equal powers of hand and brain, but of unequal powers springing from the exercise of equal rights in a world where property and inherited wealth and the apparatus of class institutions have made opportunities unequal.   Inequality, again, leads to the mis-direction of production.   For, since the demand of one income of £50,000 is as powerful a magnet as the demand of 500 incomes of £100, it diverts energy from the creation of wealth to the multiplication of luxuries, so that, for example, while one-tenth of the people of England are overcrowded, a considerable part of them are engaged, not in supplying that deficiency, but in making rich men's hotels, luxurious yachts, and motor-cars like that used by the Secretary of State for War, " with an interior inlaid with silver in quartered mahogany, and upholstered in fawn suede and morocco," which was recently bought by a suburban capitalist, by way of encouraging useful industries and rebuking public extravagance with an example of private economy, for the trifling sum of 3,550 guineas.

Thus part of the goods which are annually produced, and which are called wealth, is, strictly speaking, waste, because it consists of articles, which, though reckoned as part of the income of the nation, either should not have been produced until other articles had already been produced in sufficient abundance, or should not have been produced at all.   And some part of the population is employed in making goods which no man can make with happiness, or indeed without loss of self-respect, because he knows that they had much better not be made, and that his life is wasted in making them.   Everybody recognizes that the army contractor who, in time of war, set several hundred navvies to dig an artificial lake in his grounds, was not adding to, but subtracting from, the wealth of the nation.   But in time of peace many hundred thousand workmen, if they are not digging ponds, are doing work which is equally foolish and wasteful; though, in peace as in war, there is important work, which is waiting to be done, and which is neglected.   It is neglected because, while the effective demand of the mass of men is only too small, there is a small class which wears several men's clothes, eats several men's dinners, occupy several families' houses, and lives several men's lives.   As long as a minority has so large an income that part of it, if spent at all, must be spent on trivialities, so long will part of the human energy and mechanical equipment of the nation be diverted from serious work, which enriches it, to making trivialities, which impoverishes it, since they can only be made at the cost of not making other things.   And if the peers and millionaires who are now preaching the duty of production to miners and dock labourers desire that more wealth, not more waste, should be produced, the simplest way in which they can achieve their aim is to transfer to the public their whole incomes over (say) £1,000 a year, in order that it may be spent in setting to work, not gardeners, chauffeurs, domestic servants and shopkeepers in the West end of London, but builders, mechanics and teachers.

So to those who clamour, as many now do, " Produce ! Produce ! " one simple question may be addressed :—" Produce what ? " Food, clothing, house-room, art, knowledge ? By all means ! But if the nation is scantily furnished with these things had it not better stop producing a good many others which fill shop windows in Regent Street ? If it desires to re-equip its industries with machinery and its railways with wagons, had it not better refrain from holding exhibitions designed to encourage rich men to re-equip themselves with motor-cars ? What can be more childish than to urge the necessity that pro-ductive power should be increased, if part of the productive power which exists already is misapplied ? Is not *less* production of futilities as important as, indeed a condition of *more* production of things of moment ? Would not " Spend less on private luxuries " be as wise a cry as " produce more " ? Yet this result of inequality, again, is a phenomenon which cannot be prevented, or checked, or even recog-nized by a society which excludes the idea of purpose from its social arrangements and industrial activity. For to recognize it is to admit that there is a principle superior to the mechanical play of economic forces, which ought to determine the relative importance of different occupations, and thus to abandon the view that all riches, however composed, are an end, and that all economic activity is equally justifiable.

The rejection of the idea of purpose involves another consequence which every one laments, but which no one can prevent, except by abandoning the belief that the free exercise of rights is the main interest of society and the discharge of obligations a secondary and incidental consequence which may be left to take care of itself. It is that social life is turned into a scene of fierce antagonisms, and that a considerable part of industry is carried on in the intervals of a dis-guised social war. The idea that industrial peace can be secured merely by the exercise of tact and forbearance is based on the idea that there is a fundamental identity of interest between the different groups engaged in it, which is occasionally interrupted by regrettable misunderstandings. Both the one idea and the other are an illusion. The disputes which matter are not caused by a misunderstanding of identity of interests, but by a better understanding of diversity of interests. Though a formal declaration of war is an episode, the conditions which issue in a declaration of war are permanent ; and what makes them permanent is the conception of industry which also makes inequality and functionless incomes permanent. It is the denial that industry has any end or purpose other than the satisfaction of those engaged in it. That motive produces industrial warfare, not as a regrettable incident, but as an inevitable result. It produces industrial war, because its teaching is that each individual or group has a right to what they can get, and denies that there is any prin-ciple, other than the mechanism of the market, which determines what they ought to get. For, since the income available for distribution is limited, and since, therefore, when certain limits have been passed, what one group gains another group must lose, it is evident that if the relative incomes of different groups are not to be determined by their functions, there is no method other than mutual self-assertion which is left to determine them. Self-interest indeed, may cause them to refrain from using their full strength to enforce their claims, and, in so far as this happens, peace is secured in industry, as men have attemped to secure it in international affairs, by a balance of power. But the maintenance of such a peace is contingent upon the estimate of the parties to it that they have more to lose than to gain by an overt struggle, and is not the result of their aceptance of any standard of remuneration as an equitable settlement of their claims. Hence it is precarious, insincere and short. It is without finality, because there can be no finality in the mere addition of increments of income, any more than in the gratification of any other desire for material goods. When demands are conceded the old struggle recommences upon a new level, and will always recommence as long as men seek to end it merely by increasing remuneration, not by finding a principle upon which all remuneration, whether large or small, should be based.

Such a principle is offered by the idea of function, because its application would eliminate the surpluses which are the subject of contention, and would make it evident that remuneration is based upon service, not upon chance or privilege or the power to use opportunities to drive a hard bargain. But the idea of function is incompatible with the doctrine that every person and organization have an unlimited right to exploit their economic opportunities as fully as they please, which is the working faith of modern industry ; and, since it is not accepted, men resign themselves to the settlement of the issue by force, or propose that the state should supersede the force of private associations by the use of its force, as though the absence of a principle could be compensated by a new kind of machinery. Yet all the time the true cause of industrial warfare is as simple as the true cause of international warfare. It is that if men recognize no law superior to their desires, then they must fight when their desires collide. For though groups or nations which are at issue with each other may be willing to submit to a principle which is superior to them both, there is no reason why they should submit to each other. Hence the idea, which is popular with rich men, that industrial disputes would disappear if only the output of wealth were doubled, and every one were twice as well off, not only is refuted by all practical experience, but is in its very nature founded upon an illusion. For the question is one not of amounts but of proportions ; and men will fight to be paid £30 a week, instead of £20, as readily as they will fight to be paid £5 instead of £4, as long as there is no reason why they should be paid £20 instead of £30, and as long as other men who do not work are paid anything at all. If miners demanded higher wages when every superfluous charge upon coal getting had been eliminated, there would be a principle with which to meet their claim, the principle that one group of workers ought not to encroach upon the livelihood of others.

But as long as mineral owners extract royalties, and exceptionally productive mines pay 30 per cent to absentee shareholders, there is no valid answer to a demand for higher wages. For if the community pays anything at all to those who do not work, it can afford to pay more to those who do. The naive complaint, that workmen are never satisfied, is, therefore, strictly true. It is true, not only of workmen, but of all classes in a society which conducts its affairs on the principle that wealth, instead of being proportioned to function, belongs to those who can get it. They are never satisfied, nor can they be satisfied. For as long as they make that principle the guide of their individual lives and of their social order, nothing short of infinity could bring them satisfaction.

So here, again, the prevalent insistence upon rights, and prevalent neglect of functions, brings men into a vicious circle which they cannot escape, without escaping from the false philosophy which dominates them. But it does something more. It makes that philosophy itself seem plausible and exhilarating, and a rule not only for industry, in which it had its birth, but for politics and culture and religion and the whole compass of social life. The possibility that one aspect of human life may be so exaggerated as to overshadow, and in time to atrophy, every other, has been made familiar to Englishmen by the example of " Prussian militarism." Militarism is the characteristic, not of an army, but of a society. Its essence is not any particular quality or scale of military preparation, but a state of mind, which, in its concentration on one particular element in social life, ends finally by exalting it until it becomes the arbiter of all the rest. The purpose for which military forces exist is forgotten. They are thought to stand by their own right and to need no justification. Instead of being regarded as an instrument which is necessary in an imperfect world, they are elevated into an object of superstitious veneration, as though the world would be a poor insipid place without them, so that political institutions and social arrangements and intellect and morality and religion are crushed into a mould made to fit one activity, which in a sane society is a subordinate activity, like the police, or the maintenance of prisons, or the cleansing of sewers, but which in a militarist state is a kind of mystical epitome of society itself.

Militarism, as Englishmen see plainly enough, is fetich worship. It is the prostration of men's souls before, and the laceration of their bodies to appease, an idol. What they do not see is that their reverence for economic activity and industry and what is called business is also fetich worship, and that in their devotion to that idol they torture themselves as needlessly and indulge in the same mean- ingless antics as the Prussians did in their worship of militarism. For what the military tradition and spirit have done for Prussia, with the result of creating militarism, the commercial tradition and spirit have done for England, with the result of creating industrialism. Industrialism is no more a necessary characteristic of an economically developed society, than militarism is a necessary characteristic of a nation which maintains military forces. It is no more the result of applying science to industry, than militarism is the result of the application of science to war, and the idea that it is something inevitable in a community which uses coal and iron and machinery, so far from being the truth, is itself a product of the perversion of mind which industrialism produces. Men may use what mechanical instruments they please and be none the worse for their use. What kills their souls is when they allow their instruments to use them. The essence of industrialism, in short, is not any particular method of industry, but a particular estimate of the importance of industry, which results in it being thought the only thing that is important at all, so that it is elevated from the subordinate place which it should occupy among human interests and activities into being the standard by which all other interests and activities are judged.

When a Cabinet Minister declares that the greatness of this country depends upon the volume of its exports, so that France, which exports comparatively little, and Elizabethan England, which exported next to nothing, are presumably to be pitied as altogether inferior civilizations, that is Industrialism. It is the confusion of one minor department of life with the whole of life. When manufacturers cry and cut themselves with knives, because it is proposed that boys and girls of fourteen shall attend school for eight hours a week, and the President of the Board of Education is so gravely impressed by their apprehensions, that he at once allows the hours to be reduced to seven, that is Industrialism. It is fetich worship. When the Government obtains money for a war, which costs £7,000,000 a day, by closing the Museums, which cost £20,000 a year, that is Industrialism. It is a contempt for all interests which do not contribute obviously to economic activity. When the Press clamours that the one thing needed to make this island an Arcadia is productivity, and more productivity, and yet more productivity, that is Industrialism. It is the confusion of means with ends. Men will always confuse means with ends if they are without any clear conception that it is the ends, not the means, which matter—if they allow their minds to slip from the fact that it is the social purpose of industry which gives it meaning and makes it worth while to carry it on at all. And when they do that, they will turn their whole world upside down, because they do not see the poles upon which it ought to move. So when, like England, they are thoroughly industrialized, they behave like Germany, which was thoroughly militarized. They talk as though man existed for industry, instead of industry existing for man, as the Prussians talked of man existing for war. They resent any activity which is not coloured by the predominant interest, because it seems a rival to it. So they destroy religion and art and morality, which cannot exist unless they are disinterested; and having destroyed these, which are the end, for the sake of industry, which is a means, they make their industry itself what they make their cities, a desert of unnatural dreariness, which only forgetfulness can make endurable, and which only excitement can enable them to forget.

Torn by suspicions and recriminations, avid of power, and oblivious of duties, desiring peace, but unable to " seek peace and ensue it," because unwilling to surrender the creed which is the cause of war, to what can one compare such a society but to the international world, which also has been called a society and which also is social in nothing but name? And the comparison is more than a play upon words. It is an analogy which has its roots in the facts of history. It is not a chance that the last two centuries, which saw the new growth of a new system of industry, saw also the growth of the system of international politics which came to a climax in the period from 1870 to 1914. Both the one and the other are the expression of the same spirit and move in obedience to similar laws. The essence of the former was the repudiation of any authority superior to the individual reason. It left men free to follow their own interests or ambitions or appetites, untrammelled by subordination to any common centre of allegiance. The essence of the latter was the repudiation of any authority superior to the sovereign state, which again was conceived as a compact self-contained unit—a unit which would lose its very essence if it lost its independence of other states. Just as the one emancipated economic activity from a mesh of anti-quated traditions, so the other emancipated nations from arbitrary subordination to alien races or Governments, and turned them into nationalities with a right to work out their own destiny. Nationalism is, in fact, the counterpart among nations of what individualism is within them. It has similar origins and tendencies, similar triumphs and defects. For nationalism, like individualism, lays its emphasis on the rights of separate units, not on their subordination to common obligations, though its units are races or nations, not individual men. Like individualism it appeals to the self-assertive instincts, to which it promises opportunities of unlimited expansion. Like individualism it is a force of immense explosive power, the just claims of which must be conceded before it is possible to invoke any alternative principle to control its operations. For one cannot impose a super-national authority upon irritated or discontented or oppressed nationalities, any more than one can subordinate economic motives to the control of society, until society has recognized that there is a sphere which they may legitimately occupy. And, like individualism, if pushed to its logical conclusion, it is self-destructive. For as nationalism, in its brilliant youth, begins as a claim that nations, because they are spiritual beings, shall determine themselves, and passes too often into a claim that they shall dominate others, so individualism begins by asserting the right of men to make of their own lives what they can, and ends by condoning the subjection of the majority of men to the few whom good fortune or special opportunity or privilege have enabled most successfully to use their rights. They rose together. It is probable that, if ever they decline, they will decline together. For life cannot be cut in compartments. In the long run the world reaps in war what it sows in peace. . And to expect that international rivalry can be exorcised as long as the industrial order within each nation is such as to give success to those whose whole existence is a struggle for self-aggrandisement is a dream which has not even the merit of being beautiful.

[26]

So the perversion of nationalism is imperialism, as the perversion of individualism is industrialism. And the perversion comes, not through any flaw or vice in human nature, but by the force of the idea, because the principle is defective and reveals its defects as it reveals its power. For it asserts that the rights of nations and individuals are absolute, which is false, instead of asserting that they are absolute in their own sphere, but that their sphere itself is contingent upon the part which they play in the community of nations and individuals, which is true. Thus it constrains them to a career of indefinite expansion, in which they devour continents and oceans, law, morality, and religion, and last of all their own souls, in an attempt to attain infinity by the addition to themselves of all that is finite. In the meantime their rivals, and their subjects, and they themselves are conscious of the danger of opposing forces, and seek to purchase security and to avoid a collision by organizing a balance of power. But the balance, whether in international politics or in industry, is unstable, because it reposes not on the common recognition of a principle by which the claims of nations and individuals are limited, but on an attempt to find an equipoise which may avoid a conflict without abjuring the assertion of unlimited claims. No such equipoise can be found, because, in a world where the possibilities of increasing military or industrial power are illimitable, no such equipoise can exist.

Thus, as long as men move on this plane, there is no solution. They can obtain peace only by surrendering the claim to the unfettered exercise of their rights, which is the cause of war. What we have been witnessing, in short, during the past five years, both in international affairs and in industry, is the breakdown of the organization of society on the basis of rights divorced from obligations. Sooner or later the collapse was inevitable, because the basis were too narrow. For a right is simply a power which is secured by legal sanctions, "a capacity," as the lawyers define it, "residing in one man, of controlling, with the assistance of the State, the action of others," and a right should not be absolute for the same reason that a power should not be absolute. No doubt it is better that individuals should have absolute rights than that the State or the Government should have them ; and it was the reaction against the abuses of absolute power by the State which led in the eighteenth century to the declaration of the absolute rights of individuals. The most obvious defence against the assertion of one extreme was the assertion of the other. Because Governments and the relics of feudalism had encroached upon the property of individuals it was affirmed that the right of property was absolute; because they had strangled enterprize, it was affirmed that every man had a natural right to conduct his business as he pleased. But, in reality, both the one assertion and the other are false, and, if applied to practice, must lead to disaster. The State has no absolute rights; they are limited by its commission. The individual has no absolute rights; they are relative to the function which he performs in the community of which he is a member, because, unless they are so limited, the consequences must be something in the

[27]

nature of private war.   All rights, in short are conditional and derivative, because all power should be conditional and derivative.   They are derived from the end or purpose of the society in which they exist. They are conditional on being used to contribute to the attainment of that end, not to thwart it.   And this means in practice that, if society is to be healthy, men must regard themselves not as the owners of rights, but as trustees for the discharge of functions and the instruments of a social purpose.

V.

PROPERTY AND CREATIVE WORK.

THE application of the principle that society should be organised upon the basis of functions, is not recondite, but simple and direct. It offers in the first place, a standard for discriminating between those types of private property which are legitimate and those which are not. During the last century and a half, political thought has oscillated between two conceptions of property, both of which, in their different ways, are extravagant. On the one hand, the practical foundation of social organization has been the doctrine that the particular forms of private property which exist at any moment are a thing sacred and inviolable, that anything may properly become the object of property rights, and that, when it does, the title to it is absolute and unconditioned. The modern industrial system took shape in an age· when this theory of property was triumphant. The American Constitution and the French Declaration of the Rights of Man both treated property as one of the fundamental rights which governments exist to protect. The English Revolution of 1688, undogmatic and reticent though it was, had in effect done the same. The great individualists from Locke to Turgot, Adam Smith and Bentham all repeated, in different language, a similar conception. Though what gave the Revolution its diabolical character in the eyes of the English upper classes was its treatment of property, the dogma of the sanctity of private property was maintained as tenaciously by French Jacobins as by English Tories ; and the theory that property is an absolute, which is held by many modern Conservatives, is identical, if only they knew it, with that not only of the men of 1789, but of the Convention itself. On the other hand, the attack has been almost as undiscriminating as the defence. Private property has been the central position against which the social movement of the last hundred years has directed its forces. The criticism of it has ranged from an imaginative communism in the most elementary and personal of necessaries, to prosaic and partially realized proposals to transfer certain kinds of property from private to public ownership, or to limit their exploitation by restrictions imposed by the State. But, however varying in emphasis and in method, the general note of what may conveniently be called the Socialist criticism of property is what the word Socialism itself implies. Its essence is the statement that the economic evils of society are primarily due to the unregulated operation, under modern conditions of industrial organization, of the institution of private property.

The divergence of opinion is natural, since in most discussions of property the opposing theorists have usually been discussing different things. Property is the most ambiguous of categories. It covers a multitude of rights which have nothing in common except that they are exercised by persons and enforced by the State. Apart from these formal characteristics, they vary indefinitely in economic character, in social effect, and in moral justification. They may be conditional like the grant of patent rights, or absolute like the ownership of ground rents, terminable like copyright, or permanent like a freehold, as comprehensive as sovereignty or as restricted as an easement, as intimate and personal as the ownership of clothes and books, or as remote and intangible as shares in a goldmine or rubber plantation. It is idle, therefore, to present a case for or against private property without specifying the particular forms of property to which reference is made, and the journalist who says that " private property is the foundation of civilization " agrees with Proudhon, who said it was theft, in this respect at least that, without further definition, the words of both are meaningless. Arguments which support or demolish certain kinds of property may have no application to others ; considerations which are conclusive in one stage of economic organization may be almost irrelevant in the next. The course of wisdom is neither to attack private property in general nor to defend it in general ; for things are not similar in quality, merely because they are identical in name. It is to discriminate between the various concrete embodiments of what, in itself, is, after all, little more than an abstraction.

The origin and development of different kinds of proprietary rights is not material to this discussion. Whatever may have been the historical process by which they have been established and recognized, the *rationale* of private property traditional in England is that which sees in it the security that each man will reap where he has sown. " If I despair of enjoying the fruits of my labour," said Bentham, " I shall only live from day to day ; I shall not undertake labours which will only benefit my enemies." Property, it is argued, is a moral right, and not merely a legal right, because it ensures that the producer will not be deprived by violence of the result of his efforts. The period from which that doctrine was inherited differed from our own in three obvious, but significant, respects. Property in land and in the simple capital used in most industries was widely distributed. Before the rise of capitalist agriculture and capitalist industry, the ownership, or at any rate the secure and effective occupation, of land and tools by those who used them, was a condition precedent to effective work in the field or in the workshop. The forces which threatened property were the fiscal policy of governments and in some countries, for example France, the decaying relics of feudalism. The interference both of the one and of the other involved the sacrifice of those who carried on useful labour to those who did not. To resist them was to protect not only property but industry, which was indissolubly connected with it. Too often, indeed, resistance was ineffective. Accustomed to the misery of the rural proprietor in France, Voltaire remarked with astonishment that in England the peasant may be rich, and " does not fear to increase the number of his beasts to or cover his roof with tiles." And the English Parliamentarians and the French philosophers who made the inviolability of property rights the centre of their political theory, when they defended those who owned, were incidentally, if sometimes unintentionally, defending those who laboured. They were protecting the yeoman or the master craftsman or the merchant from seeing the fruits of his toil squandered by the hangers-on at St. James or the courtly parasites of Versailles.

In such circumstances the doctrine which found the justification of private property in the fact that it enabled the industrious man to reap where he had sown, was not a paradox, but, as far as the mass of the population was concerned, almost a truism. Property was defended as the most sacred of rights. But it was defended as a right which was not only widely exercised, but which was indispensable to the performance of the active function of providing food and clothing. For it consisted predominantly of one of two types, land or tools which were used by the owner for the purpose of production, and personal possessions which were the necessities or amenities of civilized existence. The former had its *rationale* in the fact that the land of the peasant or the tools of the craftsman were the condition of his rendering the economic services which society required ; the latter because furniture and clothes are indispensable to a life of decency and comfort. The proprietary rights—and, of course, they were numerous—which had their source, not in work, but in predatory force, were protected from criticism by the wide distribution of some kind of property among the mass of the population, and in England, at least, the cruder of them were gradually whittled down. When property in land and what simple capital existed were generally diffused among all classes of society, when, in most parts of England, the typical workman was not a labourer but a peasant farmer or small master, who could point to the strips which he had ploughed or the cloth which he had woven, when the greater part of the wealth passing at death consisted of land, household furniture and a stock in trade which was hardly distinguishable from it, the moral justification of the title to property was self-evident. It was obviously, what theorists said that it was, and plain men knew it to be, the labour spent in producing, acquiring and administering it.

Such property was not a burden upon society, but a condition of its health and efficiency, and indeed, of its continued existence. To protect it was to maintain the organization through which public necessities were supplied. If, as in Tudor England, the peasant was evicted from his holding to make room for sheep, or crushed, as in eighteenth century France, by arbitrary taxation and seignurial dues, land went out of cultivation and the whole community was short of food. If the tools of the carpenter or smith were seized, ploughs were not repaired or horses shod. Hence, before the rise of a commercial civilization, it was the mark of statesmanship, alike in the England of the Tudors and in the France of Henry IV, to cherish the small property-owner even to the point of offending the great. Popular sentiment idealized the yeoman—" the Joseph of the country

[31]

who keeps the poor from starving"—not merely because he owned property, but because he worked on it, denounced that " bringing of the livings of many into the hands of one " which capitalist societies regard with equanimity as an inevitable, and, apparently, a laudable result of economic development, cursed the usurer who took advantage of his neighbour's necessities to live without labour, was shocked by the callous indifference to public welfare shown by those who " not having before their eyes either God or the profit and advantage of the realm, have enclosed with hedges and dykes towns and hamlets," and was sufficiently powerful to compel governments to intervene to prevent the laying of field to field, and the engrossing of looms—to set limits, in short, to the scale to which property might grow.   When Bacon, who commended Henry VII. for protecting the tenant right of the small farmer, and pleaded in the House of Commons for more drastic land legislation, wrote " Wealth is like muck.   It is not good but if it be spread," he was expressing in an epigram what was the commonplace of every writer on politics from Fortescue at the end of the fifteenth century to Harrington in the middle of the seventeenth. The modern conservative, who is inclined to take *au pied de la lettre* the vigorous argument in which Lord Hugh Cecil denounces the doctrine that the maintenance of proprietary rights ought to be contingent upon the use to which they are put, may be reminded that Lord Hugh's own theory is of a kind to make his ancestors turn in their graves.   Of the two members of the family who achieved distinction before the nineteenth century, the elder advised the Crown to prevent landlords evicting tenants, and actually proposed to fix a pecuniary maximum to the property which different classes might possess, while the younger attacked enclosing in Parliament, and carried legislation compelling landlords to build cottages, to let them with small holdings, and to plough up pasture.

William and Robert Cecil were sagacious and responsible men, and their view that the protection of property should be accompanied by the enforcement of obligations upon its owners was shared by most of their contemporaries.   The idea that the institution of private property involves the right of the owner to use it, or refrain from using it, in such a way as he may please, and that its principle significance is to supply him with an income, irrespective of any duties which he may discharge, would not have been understood by most public men of that age, and, if understood, would have been repudiated with indignation by the more reputable among them.   They found the meaning of property in the public purposes to which it contributed, whether they were the production of food, as among the peasantry, or the management of public affairs, as among the gentry, and hesitated neither to maintain those kinds of property which met these obligations nor to repress those uses of it which appeared likely to conflict with them.   Property was to be an aid to creative work, not an alternative to it.   The patentee was secured protection for a new invention, in order to secure him the fruits of his own brain, but the monopolist who grew fat on the industry of others was to be put down.   The law of the village bound the peasant to use his land, not as he himself might find most profitable, but to grow the corn the village needed. Long after political changes had made direct interference impracticable, even the higher ranks of English land-owners continued to discharge, however capriciously and tyrannically, duties which were vaguely felt to be the contribution which they made to the public service in virtue of their estates. When as in France, the obligations of ownership were repudiated almost as completely as they have been by the owner of to-day, nemesis came in an onslaught upon the position of a *noblesse* which had retained its rights and abdicated its functions. Property reposed, in short, not merely upon convenience, or the appetite for gain, but on a moral principle. It was protected not only for the sake of those who owned, but for the sake of those who worked and of those for whom their work provided. It was protected, because, without security for property, wealth could not be produced or the business of society carried on.

Whatever the future may contain, the past has shown no more excellent social order than that in which the mass of the people were the masters of the holdings which they ploughed and of the tools with which they worked, and could boast, with the English freeholder, that " it is a quietness to a man's mind to live upon his own and to know his heir certain." With this conception of property and its practical expression in social institutions those who urge that society should be organized on the basis of function have no quarrel. It is in agreement with their own doctrine, since it justifies property by reference to the services which it enables its owner to perform. All that they need ask is that it should be carried to its logical conclusion.

The argument has evidently more than one edge. If it justifies cer-tain types of property, it condemns others; and in the conditions of modern industrial civilization, what it justifies is less than what it condemns. For this theory of property and the institutions in which it is embodied have survived into an age in which the whole structure of society is radically different from that in which it was formulated, and which made it a valid argument, if not for all, at least for the most common and characteristic kinds of property. It is not merely that the ownership of any substantial share in the national wealth is concentrated to-day in the hands of a few hundred thousand families, and that at the end of an age which began with an affirmation of the rights of property, proprietary rights are, in fact, far from being widely distributed. Nor is it merely that what makes property insecure to-day is not the arbitrary taxation of unconstitutional monarchies or the privileges of an idle *noblesse*, but the insatiable expansion and aggregation of property itself, which menaces with absorption all property less than the greatest, the small master, the little shop-keeper, the country bank, and has turned the mass of mankind into a proletariat working under the agents and for the profit of those who own. The characteristic fact, which differentiates most modern property from that of the pre-industrial age, and which turns against it the very reasoning by which formerly it was supported, is that in modern economic conditions ownership is not active, but passive, that to most of those who own property to-day it is not a means of work but an instrument for the acquisition of gain or the exercise of power, and that there is no guarantee that gain bears any relation to service, or power to responsibility. For property which can be regarded as a condition of the performance of function, like the tools of the craftsman, or the holding of the peasant, or the personal possessions which contribute to a life of health and efficiency, forms an insignificant proportion, as far as its value is concerned, of the property rights existing at present. In modern industrial societies the great mass of property consists, as the annual review of wealth passing at death reveals, neither of personal acquisitions such as household furniture, nor of the owner's stock-in-trade, but of rights of various kinds, such as royalties, ground-rents, and, above all, of course, shares in industrial undertakings, which yield an income irrespective of any personal service rendered by their owners. Owner-ship and use are normally divorced. The greater part of modern property has been attenuated to a pecuniary lien or bond on the product of industry, which carries with it a right to payment, but which is normally valued precisely because it relieves the owner from any obligation to perform a positive or constructive function.

Such property may be called passive property, or property for acquisition, for exploitation, or for power, to distinguish it from the property which is actively used by its owner for the conduct of his profession or the upkeep of his household. To the lawyer the first is, of course, as fully property as the second. It is questionable, however, whether economists should call it " Property " at all, and not rather, as Mr. Hobson has suggested, "Improperty," since it is not identical with the rights which secure the owner the produce of his toil, but is the opposite of them. A classification of proprietary rights based upon this difference would be instructive. If they were arranged according to the closeness with which they approximate to one or other of these two extremes, it would be found that they were spread along a line stretching from property which is obviously the payment for, and condition of, personal services, to property which is merely a right to payment from the services ren-dered by others, in fact a private tax. The rough order which would emerge, if all details and qualification were omitted, might be something as follows :—

1. Property in payments made for personal services.
2. Property in personal possessions necessary to health and comfort.
3. Property in land and tools used by their owners.
4. Property in copyright and patent rights owned by authors and inventors.
5. Property in pure interest, including much agricultural rent.
6. Property in profits of luck and good fortune : " quasi-rents."
7. Property in monopoly profits.
8. Property in urban ground rents.
9. Property in royalties.

The first four kinds of property obviously accompany, and in some sense condition, the performance of work. The last four obviously do not. Pure interest has some affinities with both. It represents a necessary economic cost, the equivalent of which must be born, whatever the legal arrangements under which property is held, and is thus unlike the property represented by profits (other than the equivalent of salaries and payment for necessary risk), urban ground-rents and royalties. It relieves the recipient from personal services, and thus resembles them.

The crucial question for any society is, under which each of these two broad groups of categories the greater part (measured in value) of the proprietary rights which it maintains are at any given moment to be found. If they fall in the first group creative work will be encouraged and idleness will be depressed ; if they fall in the second, the result will be the reverse. The facts vary widely from age to age and from country to country. Nor have they ever been fully revealed ; for the lords of the jungle do not hunt by daylight. It is probable, at least, that in the England of 1550 to 1750, a larger proportion of the existing property consisted of land and tools used by their owners than either in contemporary France, where feudal dues absorbed a considerable proportion of the peasants' income, or than in the England of 1800 to 1850, where the new capitalist manufacturers made hundreds per cent while manual workers were goaded by starvation into ineffectual revolt. It is probable that in the nineteenth century, thanks to the Revolution, France and England changed places, and that in this respect not only Ireland but the British Dominions resemble the former rather than the latter. The transformation can be studied best of all in the United States, in parts of which the population of peasant proprietors and small masters of the early nineteenth century were converted in three generations into a capitalist plutocracy. The abolition of the economic privileges of agrarian feudalism, which, under the name of equality, was the driving force of the French Revolution, and which has taken place, in one form or another, in all countries touched by its influence, has been largely counterbalanced since 1800 by the growth of the inequalities springing from Industrialism.

In England the general effect of recent economic development has been to swell proprietary rights which entitle the owners to payment without work, and to diminish those which can properly be described as functional. The expansion of the former, and the process by which the simpler forms of property have been merged in them, are movements the significance of which it is hardly possible to over-estimate. There is, of course, a considerable body of property which is still of the older type. But though working landlords, and capitalists who manage their own businesses, are still in the aggregate a numerous body, the organization for which they stand is not that which is most representative of the modern economic world. The general tendency for the ownership and administration of property to be separated, the general refinement of property into a claim on goods produced by an unknown worker, is as unmistakeable as the growth of capitalist industry and urban civilization themselves. Villages are turned into towns and property in land changes

[85]

from the holding worked by a farmer or the estate administered by a landlord into " rents," which are advertized and bought and sold like any other investment. Mines are opened and the rights of the land-owner are converted into a tribute for every ton of coal which is brought to the surface. As joint-Stock Companies take the place of the individual enterprise which was typical of the earlier years of the factory system, organization passes from the employer who both owns and manages his business, into the hands of salaried officials, and again the mass of property-owners is swollen by the multiplication of *rentiers* who put their wealth at the disposal of industry, but who have no other connection with it. The change is taking place in our day most conspicuously, perhaps, through the displacement in retail trade of the small shopkeeper by the multiple store, and the substitution in manufacturing industry of combines and amalgamations for separate businesses conducted by competing employers. And, of course, it is not only by economic development that such claims are created. " Out of the eater came forth meat, and out of the strong came forth sweet-ness." It is probable that war, which in barbarous ages used to be blamed as destructive of property, has recently created more titles to property than almost all other causes put together.

Infinitely diverse as are these proprietary rights, they have the common characteristic of being so entirely separated from the actual objects over which they are exercised, so rarified and generalized, as to be analogous almost to a form of currency rather than to the property which is so closely united to its owner as to seem a part of him. Their isolation from the rough environment of economic life, where the material objects of which they are the symbol are shaped and handled, is their charm. It is also their danger. The hold which a class has upon the future depends on the function which it performs. What nature demands is work : few working aristocracies, however tyrannical, have fallen ; few functionless aristocracies have survived. In society, as in the world of organic life, atrophy is but one stage removed from death. In proportion as the landowner becomes a mere *rentier* and industry is conducted, not by the rude energy of the competing employers who dominated its infancy, but by the salaried servants of shareholders, the argument for private property which reposes on the impossibility of finding any organization to supersede them loses its application, for they are already superseded.

Whatever may be the justification of these types of property, it cannot be that which was given for the property of the peasant or the craftsman. It cannot be that they are necessary in order to secure to each man the fruits of his own labour. For if a legal right which gives £50,000 a year to a mineral owner in the North of England and to a ground landlord in London " secures the fruits of labour " at all, the fruits are the proprietor's and the labour that of someone else. Property has no more insidious enemies than those well-meaning anarchists who, by defending all forms of it as equally valid, involve the institution in the discredit attaching to its extravagances. In reality, whatever conclusion may be drawn from the fact, the greater part of modern property, whether, like mineral rights and urban ground-rents, it is merely a form of private taxation which the law allows certain persons to levy on the industry of others, or whether, like property in capital, it consists of rights to payment for instruments which the capitalist cannot himself use but puts at the disposal of those who can, has as its essential feature that it confers upon its owners income unaccompanied by personal service. In this respect the ownership of land and the ownership of capital are normally similar, though from other points of view their differences are important. To the economist rent and interest are distinguished by the fact that the latter, though it is often accompanied by surplus elements which are merged with it in dividends, is the price of an instrument of production which would not be forthcoming for industry if the price were not paid, while the former is a differential surplus which does not affect the supply. To the business community and the solicitor land and capital are equally investments, between which, since they possess the common characteristic of yielding income without labour it is inequitable to discriminate ; and though their significance as economic categories may be different, their effect as social institutions is the same. It is to separate property from creative activity, and to divide society into two classes, of which one has its primary interest in passive ownership, while the other is mainly dependent upon active work.

Hence the real analogy to many kinds of modern property is not the simple property of the small landowner or the craftsman, still less the household gods and dear domestic amenities, which is what the word suggests to the guileless minds of clerks and shopkeepers, and which stampede them into displaying the ferocity of terrified sheep when the cry is raised that " Property " is threatened. It is the feudal dues which robbed the French peasant of part of his produce till the Revolution abolished them. How do royalties differ from *quintaines* and *lods et ventes ?* They are similar in their origin and similar in being a tax levied on each increment of wealth which labour produces. How do urban ground-rents differ from the payments which were made to English sinecurists before the Reform Bill of 1832 ? They are equally tribute paid by those who work to those who do not. If the monopoly profits of the owner of *banalités*, whose tenant must grind corn at his mill and make wine at his press, were an intolerable oppression, what is the sanctity attaching to the monopoly profits of the capitalists, who, as the Report of the Government Committee on trusts tells us, " in soap, tobacco, wall-paper, salt, cement and in the textile trades . . . . . are in a position to control output and prices," or, in other words, can compel the consumer to buy from them, at the figure they fix, on pain of not buying at all ?

All these rights—royalties, ground rents, monopoly profits—are " Property." The criticism most fatal to them is not that of Socialists. It is contained in the arguments by which property is usually defended. For if the meaning of the institution is to encourage industry by securing that the worker shall receive the produce of his toil, then precisely in proportion as it is important to preserve the property which a man has in the results of his own efforts, is it important to abolish that which he has in the results of the efforts of someone else. The considerations which justify ownership as a function are those which condemn it as a tax. Property is not theft, but a good deal of theft becomes property. The owner of royalties who, when asked why he should be paid £50,000 a year from minerals which he has neither discovered nor developed nor worked but only owned, replies " But it's Property ! " may feel all the awe which his language suggests. But in reality he is behaving like the snake which sinks into its background by pretending that it is the dead branch of a tree, or the lunatic who tried to catch rabbits by sitting behind a hedge and making a noise like a turnip. He is practising protective—and sometimes aggressive—mimicry. His sentiments about property are those of the simple toiler who fears that what he has sown another may reap. His claim is to be allowed to continue to reap what another has sown.

It is sometimes suggested that the less attractive characteristics of our industrial civilization, its combination of luxury and squalor, its class divisions and class warfare, are accidental maladjustments which are not rooted in the centre of its being, but are excrescences which economic progress itself may in time be expected to correct. That agreeable optimism will not survive an examination of the operation of the institution of private property in land and capital in industrialized communities. In countries where land is widely distributed, in France or in Ireland, its effect may be to produce a general diffusion of wealth among a rural middle class who at once work and own. In countries where the development of industrial organization has separated the ownership of property and the performance of work, the normal effect of private property is to transfer to functionless owners the surplus arising from the more fertile sites, the better machinery, the more elaborate organization. No clearer exemplifications of this "law of rent" has been given than the figures supplied to the Coal Industry Commission by Sir Arthur Lowes Dickenson, which showed that in a given quarter the costs per ton of producing coal varied from 12/6 to 48/- per ton, and the profits from *nil* to 16/6. The distribution in dividends to shareholders of the surplus accruing from the working of richer and more accessible seams, from special opportunities and access to markets, from superior machinery, management and organization, involves the establishment of Privilege as a national institution, as much as the most arbitrary exactions of a feudal *seigneur*. It is the foundation of an inequality which is not accidental or temporary, but necessary and permanent. And on this inequality is erected the whole apparatus of class institutions, which make not only the income, but the housing, education, health and manners, indeed the very physical appearance of different classes of Englishmen almost as different from each other as though the minority were alien settlers established amid the rude civilization of a race of impoverished aborigines.

[38]

So the justification of private property traditional in England, which saw in it the security that each man would enjoy the fruits of his own labour, though largely applicable to the age in which it was formulated, has undergone the fate of most political theories. It has been refuted not by the doctrines of rival philosophers, but by the prosaic course of economic development. As far as the mass of mankind are concerned, the need which private property other than personal possessions does still often satisfy, though imperfectly and precariously, is the need for security. To the small investors, who are the majority of property-owners, though owning only an insignificant fraction of the property in existence, its meaning is simple. It is not wealth or power, or even leisure from work. It is safety. They work hard. They save a little money for old age, or sickness, or for their children. They invest it, and the interest stands between them and all that they dread most. Their savings are of convenience to industry, the income from them is convenient to themselves. " Why " they ask, " should we not reap in old age the advantage of energy and thrift in youth ? " And this hunger for security is so imperious that those who suffer most from the abuses of property, as well as those who, if they could profit by them, would be least inclined to do so, will tolerate and even defend them, for fear lest the knife which trims dead matter should cut into the quick. They have seen too many men drown to be critical of dry land, though it be an inhospitable rock. They are haunted by the nightmare of the future, and, if a burglar broke it, would welcome a burglar.

This need for security is fundamental, and almost the gravest indictment of our civilization is that the mass of mankind are without it. Property is one way of securing it. It is quite comprehensible therefore, that the instrument should be confused with the end, and that any proposal to modify it should create dismay. In the past, human beings, roads, bridges and ferries, civil, judicial and clerical offices, and commissions in the army have all been private property. Whenever it was proposed to abolish the rights exercised over them, it was protested that their removal would involve the destruction of an institution in which thrifty men had invested their savings, and on which they depended for protection amid the chances of life and for comfort in old age. In fact, however, property is not the only method of assuring the future, nor, when it is the way selected, is security dependent upon the maintenance of all the rights which are at present normally involved in ownership. In so far as its psychological foundation is the necessity for securing an income which is stable and certain, which is forthcoming when its recipient cannot work, and which can be used to provide for those who cannot provide for themselves, what is really demanded is not the command over the fluctuating proceeds of some particular undertaking, which accompanies the ownership of capital, but the security which is offered by an annuity. Property is the instrument, security is the object, and when some alternative way is forthcoming of providing the latter, it does not appear in practice that any loss of confidence, or freedom or independence is caused by the absence of the former. Hence not only the manual workers, who since the rise of capitalism, have rarely in England been able to accumulate property sufficient to act as a guarantee of income when their period of active earning is past, but also the middle and professional classes, increasingly seek security to-day, not in investment, but in insurance against sickness and death, in the purchase of annuities, or in what is in effect the same thing, the accumulation of part of their salary towards a pension which is paid when their salary ceases. The professional man may buy shares in the hope of making a profit on the transaction. But when what he desires to buy is security, the form which his investment takes is usually one kind or another of insurance. The teacher, or nurse, or government servant looks forward to a pension. Women, who fifty years ago would have been regarded as dependent almost as completely as if femininity were an incurable disease with which they had been born, and whose fathers, unless rich men, would have been tormented with anxiety for fear lest they should not save sufficient to provide for them, now receive an education, support themselves in professions, and save in the same way. It is still only in comparatively few cases that this type of provision is made ; almost all wage earners outside government employment, and many in it, as well as large numbers of professional men, have nothing to fall back upon in sickness or old age. But that does not alter the fact that, when it is made, it meets the need for security, which, apart, of course, from personal possessions and household furniture, is the principle meaning of property to by far the largest element in the population, and that it meets it more completely and certainly than property itself.

Nor, indeed, even when property is the instrument used to provide for the future, is such provision dependent upon the maintenance in its entirety of the whole body of rights which accompany ownership to-day. Property is not simple but complex. That of a man who has invested his savings as an ordinary shareholder comprises at least three rights, the right to interest, the right to profits, the right to control. In so far as what is desired is the guarantee for the maintenance of a stable income, not the acquisition of additional wealth without labour—in so far as his motive is not gain but security—the need is met by interest on capital. It has no necessary connection either with the right to residuary profits or the right to control the management of the undertaking from which the profits are derived, both of which are vested to-day in the shareholder. If all that were desired were to use property as an instrument for purchasing security, the obvious course—from the point of view of the investor desiring to insure his future the safest course—would be to assimilate his position as far as possible to that of a debenture holder or mortgagee, who obtains the stable income which is his motive for investment, but who neither incurs the risks nor receives the profits of the speculator. To insist that the elaborate apparatus of proprietary rights which distributes dividends of thirty per cent to the shareholders in Coats, and several thousands a year to the owner of mineral royalties and ground-rents, and then

[40]

allows them to transmit the bulk of gains which they have not earned to descendants who in their turn will thus be relieved from the necessity of earning, must be maintained for the sake of the widow and the orphan, the vast majority of whom have neither and would gladly part with them all for a safe annuity if they had, is, to say the least of it, extravagantly *mal-à-propos*. It is like pitching a man into the water because he expresses a wish for a bath, or presenting a tiger cub to a householder who is plagued with mice, on the ground that tigers and cats both belong to the genus *felis*. The tiger. hunts for itself not for its masters, and when game is scarce will hunt them. The classes who own little or no property may reverence it because it is security. But the classes who own much prize it for quite different reasons, and laugh in their sleeve at the innocence which supposes that anything as vulgar as the saving of the *petite bourgeosie* have, except at elections, any interest for them. They prize it because it is the order which quarters them on the community and which provides for the maintenance of a leisure class at the public expense.

"Possession," said the Egoist, "without obligation to the object possessed, approaches felicity." Functionless property appears natural to those who believe that society should be organized for the acquisition of private wealth, and attacks upon it perverse or malicious, because the question which they ask of any institution is, "What does it yield?" And such property yields much to those who own it. Those, however, who hold that social unity and effective work are possible only if society is organized and wealth distributed on the basis of function, will ask of an institution, not, "What dividends does it pay?" but "What service does it perform?" To them the fact that much property yields income irrespective of any service which is performed or obligation which is recognized by its owners will appear not a quality but a vice. They will see in the social confusion which it produces, payments disproportionate to service here, and payments without any service at all there, and dissatisfaction everywhere, a convincing confirmation of their argument that to build on a foundation of rights and of rights alone is to build on a quicksand. From the portentous exaggeration into an absolute of what once was, and still might be, a sane and social institution most other social evils follow, the power of those who do not work over those who do, the alternate subservience and rebelliousness of those who work towards those who do not, the starving of science and thought and creative effort for fear that expenditure upon them should impinge on the comfort of the sluggard and the *fainéant*, and the arrangement of society in most of its subsidiary activities to suit the convenience not of those who work usefully but of those who spend gaily, so that the most hideous, desolate and parsimonious places in the country are those in which the greatest wealth is produced, the Clyde valley, or the cotton towns of Lancashire, or the mining villages of Scotland and Wales, and the gayest and most luxurious those in which it is consumed. From the point of view of social health and economic efficiency, society should obtain its material equipment at the cheapest price possible, and after providing for depreciation and expansion should distribute the whole product to its working members and their dependents. What happens at present, however, is that its workers are hired at the cheapest price which the market (as modified by organization) allows, and that the surplus, somewhat diminished by taxation, is distributed to the owners of property. Profits may vary in a given year from a loss to 100 per cent. But wages are fixed at a level which will enable the marginal firm to continue producing one year with another; and the surplus, even when due partly to efficient management, goes neither to managers nor manual workers, but to shareholders. The meaning of the process becomes startlingly apparent when, as in Lancashire to-day, large blocks of capital change hands at a period of abnormal activity. The existing shareholders receive the equivalent of the capitalized expectation of future profits. The workers, as workers, do not participate in the immense increment in value; and when, in the future, they demand an advance in wages, they will be met by the answer that profits, which before the transaction would have been reckoned large, yield shareholders after it only a low rate of interest on their investment.

The truth is that whereas in earlier ages the protection of property was normally the protection of work, the relationship between them has come in the course of the economic development of the last two centuries to be very nearly reversed. The two elements which compose civilization are active effort and passive property, the labour of human things are the tools which human beings use. Of these two elements those who supply the first maintain and improve it, those who own the second normally dictate its character, its development and its administration. Hence, though politically free, the mass of mankind live in effect under rules imposed to protect the interests of the small section among them whose primary concern is ownership. From this subordination of creative activity to passive property, the worker who depends upon his brains, the organizer, inventor, teacher or doctor suffers almost as much embarrassment as the craftsman. The real economic cleavage is not, as is often said, between employers and employed, but between all who do constructive work, from scientist to labourer, on the one hand, and all whose main interest is the preservation of existing proprietary rights upon the other, irrespective of whether they contribute to constructive work or not. If the world is to be governed for the advantages of those who own, it is only incidentally and by accident that the results will be agreeable to those who work. In practice there is a constant collision between them. Turned into another channel, half the wealth distributed in dividends to functionless shareholders could secure every child a good education up to 18, could re-endow English Universities, and (since more efficient production is important) could equip English industries for more efficient production. Half the ingenuity now applied to the protection of property could have made most industrial diseases as rare as smallpox, and most English cities into places of health and even of beauty. What stands in the way is the doctrine that the rights of property are absolute, irrespec-

[42]

tive of any social function which its owners may perform. So the laws which are most stringently enforced are still the laws which protect property, though the protection of property is no longer likely to be equivalent to the protection of work, and the interests which govern industry and predominate in public affairs are proprietary interests. A mill-owner may poison or mangle a generation of operatives; but his brother magistrates will let him off with a caution or a nominal fine to poison and mangle the next. For he is an owner of property. A landowner may draw rents from slums in which young children die at the rate of 200 per 1000; but he will be none the less welcome in polite society. For property has no obligations and therefore can do no wrong. Urban land may be held from the market on the outskirts of cities in which human beings are living three to a room, and rural land may be used for sport when villagers are leaving it to overcrowd them still more. No public authority intervenes, for both are property. To those who believe that institutions which repudiate all moral significance must sooner or later collapse, a society which confuses the protection of property with the preservation of its functionless perversions will appear as precarious as that which has left the memorials of its tasteless frivolity and more tasteless ostentation in the gardens of Versailles.

Do men love peace ?   They will see the greatest enemy of   social   unity   in   rights   which   involve   no   obligation to co-operate for the service of society.   Do they value equality ?   Property rights which dispense their owners from the   common   human   necessity   of   labour   make   inequality an institution permeating every corner of society, from the distribution of material wealth to the training of intellect itself.   Do they desire greater industrial efficiency ?   There is no more fatal obstacle to efficiency than the revelation that idleness has the same privileges. as industry, and that for every additional blow with the pick or hammer an additional profit will be distributed among shareholders who wield neither.   Indeed, functionless property is the greatest enemy of legitimate property itself.   It is the parasite which kills the organism that produced it.   Bad money drives out good, and, as the history of the last two hundred years shows, when property for acquisition or power and property for service or for use jostle each other freely in the market, without restrictions such as some legal systems have imposed on alienation and inheritance, the latter tends normally to be absorbed by the former, because it has less resisting power.   Thus functionless property grows, and as it grows it undermines the creative energy which produced property and which in earlier ages it protected.   It cannot unite men, for what unites them is the bond of service to a common purpose, and that bond it repudiates, since its very essence is the maintenance of rights irrespective of service. It cannot create ; it can only spend, so that the number of scientists, inventors, artists or men of letters who have sprung in the course of the last century from hereditary riches can be numbered on one hand.   It values neither culture nor beauty, but only the power which belongs to wealth and the ostentation which is the symbol of it.

[43]

So those who dread these qualities, energy and thought and the creative spirit—and they are many—will not discriminate, as we have tried to discriminate, between different types and kinds of property, in order that they may preserve those which are legitimate and abolish those which are not. They will endeavour to preserve all private property, even in its most degenerate forms. And those who value those things will try to promote them by relieving property of its perversions, and thus enabling it to return to its true nature. They will not desire to establish any visionary communism, for they will realize that the free disposal of a sufficiency of personal possessions is the condition of a healthy and self-respecting life, and will seek to distribute more widely the property rights which make them to-day the privilege of a minority. But they will refuse to submit to the naïve philosophy which would treat all proprietary rights as equal in sanctity merely because they are identical in name. They will distinguish sharply between property which is used by its owner for the conduct of his profession or the upkeep of his household, and property which is merely a claim on wealth produced by another's labour. They will insist that property is moral and healthy only when it is used as a condition not of idleness but of activity, and when it involves the discharge of definite personal obligations. They will endeavour, in short, to base it upon the principle of function.

VI.

THE FUNCTIONAL SOCIETY.

THE application to property and industry of the principle of function is compatible with several different types of social organization, and is as unlikely as more important revelations to be the secret of those who cry " Lo here ! " and " Lo there ! " The essential thing is that men should fix their minds upon the idea of purpose, and give that idea pre-eminence over all subsidiary issues. If, as is patent, the purpose of industry is to provide the material foundation of a good social life, then any measure which makes that provision more effective, so long as it does not conflict with some still more important purpose, is wise, and any institution which thwarts or encumbers it is foolish. It is foolish, for example, to cripple education, as it is crippled in England for the sake of industry ; for one of the uses of industry is to provide the wealth which may make possible better education. It is foolish to maintain property rights for which no service is performed, for payment without service is waste ; and if it is true, as statisticians affirm, that, even were income equally divided, income per head would be small, then it is all the more foolish, for sailors in a boat have no room for first-class passengers, and it is all the more important that none of the small national income should be misapplied. It is foolish to leave the direction of industry in the hands of servants of private property-owners who themselves know nothing about it but its balance sheets, because this is to divert it from the performance of service to the acquisition of gain, and to subordinate those who do creative work to those who do not. The course of wisdom in the affairs of industry is, after all, what it is in any other department of organized life. It is to consider the end for which economic activity is carried on and then to adapt economic organization to it. It is to pay for service and for service only, and when capital is hired to make sure that it is hired at the cheapest possible price. It is to place the responsibility for organizing industry on the shoulders of those who work and use, not of those who own, because production is the business of the producer and the proper person to see that he discharges his business is the consumer for whom, and not for the owner of property, it ought to be carried on. Above all it is to insist that all industries shall be conducted in complete publicity as to costs and profits, because publicity ought to be the antiseptic both of economic and political abuses, and no man can have confidence in his neighbour unless both work in the light.

As far as property is concerned, such a policy would possess two edges. On the one hand, it would aim at abolishing those forms of property in which ownership is divorced from obligations. On the other hand, it would seek to encourage those forms of economic organization under which the worker, whether owner or not, is free to carry on his work without sharing its control or its profits with the mere *rentier*. Thus, if in certain spheres it involved an extension of public ownership, it would in others foster an extension of private property. For it is not private ownership, but private ownership divorced from work, which is corrupting to the principle of industry ; and the idea of some socialists that private property in land or capital is necessarily mischievous is a piece of scholastic pedantry as absurd as that of those conservatives who would invest all property with some kind of mysterious sanctity. It all depends what sort of property it is and for what purpose it is used. Provided that the State retains its eminent domain, and controls alienation, as it does under the Homestead laws of the Dominions, with sufficient stringency to prevent the creation of a class of functionless property-owners, there is no inconsistency between encouraging simultaneously a multiplication of peasant farmers and small masters who own their own farms or shops, and the abolition of private ownership in those industries, unfortunately to-day the most conspicuous, in which the private owner is an absentee share-holder. Indeed, the second would help the first. In so far as the community tolerates functionless property it makes difficult, if not impossible, the restoration of the small master in agriculture or in industry, who cannot easily hold his own in a world dominated by great estates or capitalist finance. In so far as it abolishes those kinds of property which are merely parasitic, it facilitates the restoration of the small property owner in those kinds of industry for which small ownership is adapted. A socialistic policy towards the former is not antagonistic to the " distributive state," but, in modern economic conditions, a necessary preliminary to it, and if by " Property " is meant the personal possessions which the word suggests to nine-tenths of the population, the object of socialists is not to undermine property but to protect and increase it. The boundary between large scale and small scale production will always be uncertain and fluctuating, depending, as it does, on technical conditions which cannot be foreseen : a cheapening of electrical power, for example, might result in the decentralization of manufactures, as steam resulted in their concentration. The fundamental issue, however, is not between different scales of ownership, but between ownership of different kinds, not between the large farmer or master and the small, but between property which is used for work and property which yields income without it. The Irish landlord was abolished, not because he owned upon a large scale, but because he was an owner and nothing more ; if, and when English landownership has been equally attenuated, as in towns it already has been, it will deserve to meet the same fate. Once the issue of the character of ownership has been settled, the question of the size of the economic unit can be left to settle itself.

The first step, then, towards the organization of economic life for the performance of function is to abolish those types of private property in return for which no function is performed. The man who lives by owning without working is necessarily supported by the industry of someone else, and is, therefore, too expensive a luxury to be encouraged. Though he deserves to be treated with the leniency which ought to be, and usually is not, shown to those who have been brought up from infancy to any other disreputable trade, indulgence to individuals must not condone the institution of which both they and their neighbours are the victims. Judged by this standard, certain kinds of property are obviously anti-social. The rights in virtue of which the owner of the surface is entitled to levy a tax, called a royalty, on every ton of coal which the miner brings to the surface, to levy another tax, called a way-leave, on every ton of coal transported under the surface of his land though its amenity and value may be quite unaffected, to distort, if he pleases, the development of a whole district by refusing access to the minerals except upon his own terms, and to cause some 3500 to 4000 million tons to be wasted in barriers between different properties, while he in the meantime contributes to a chorus of lamentation over the wickedness of the miners in not producing more tons of coal for the public and incidentally more private taxes for himself— all this adds an agreeable 'touch of humour to the drab quality of our industrial civilization for which mineral owners deserve perhaps some recognition, though not the £100,000 odd a year which is paid to each of the four leading players, or the £6,000,000 a year which is distributed among the crowd.

The alchemy by which a gentleman who has never seen a coalmine distils the contents of that place of gloom into elegant chambers in London and a place in the country is not the monopoly of royalty owners. A similar feat of presdigitation is performed by the owner of urban ground rents. In rural districts some landlords, perhaps many landlords, are partners in the hazardous and difficult business of agriculture, and, though they may often exercize a power which is socially excessive, the position which they hold and the income which they receive are, in part at least, a return for the functions which they perform. The ownership of urban land has been refined till of that crude ore only the pure gold is left. It is the perfect sinecure, for the only function it involves is that of collecting its profits, and in an age when the struggle of Liberalism against sinecures was still sufficiently recent to stir some chords of memory, the last and greatest of liberal thinkers drew the obvious deduction. " The reasons which form the justification . . . of property in land," wrote Mill in 1848, " are valid only in so far as the proprietor of land is its improver . . . In no sound theory of private property was it ever contemplated that the proprietor of land should be merely a sinecurist quartered on it." Urban ground-rents and royalties are, in fact, as the Prime Minister in his unregenerate days suggested, a tax which some persons are permitted by the law to levy upon the industry of others. They differ from public taxation only in that their amount increases in proportion not to the nation's need of revenue but to its need of the coal and space on which they are levied, that their growth enures to private gain not to public benefit, and that if the proceeds are wasted on frivolous expenditure no one has any right to complain, because the arrangement by which Lord Smith spends wealth produced by Mr. Brown on objects which do no good to either is part of the system which, under the name of private property, Mr. Brown as well as Lord Smith have learned to regard as essential to the higher welfare of mankind.

But if we accept the principle of function we shall ask what is the *purpose* of this arrangement, and for what *end* the inhabitants of, for example, London pay £16,000,000 a year to their ground landlords. And if we find that it is for no purpose and no end, but that these things are like the horse shoes and nails which the City of London presents to the Crown on account of land in the Parish of St. Clement Danes, then we shall not deal harshly with a quaint historical survival, but neither shall we allow it to distract us from the business of the present, as though there had been history but there were not history any longer. We shall close these channels through which wealth leaks away by resuming the ownership of minerals and of urban land, as some communities in the British Dominions and on the Continent of Europe have resumed it already. We shall secure that such large accumulations as remain change hands at least once in every generation, by increasing our taxes on inheritance till what passes to the heir is little more than personal possessions, not the right to a tribute from industry which, though qualified by death-duties, is what the son of a rich man inherits to-day. We shall treat mineral owners and land owners, in short, as Plato would have treated the poets, whom in their ability to make something out of nothing and to bewitch mankind with words they a little resemble, and crown them with flowers and usher them politely out of the State.

B
Recent Formulations

A Kantian Conception of Equality*

John Rawls

My aim in these remarks is to give a brief account of the conception of equality that underlies the view expressed in *A Theory of Justice* and the principles considered there. I hope to state the fundamental intuitive idea simply and informally; and so I make no attempt to sketch the argument from the original position.[1] In fact, this construction is not mentioned until the end and then only to indicate its role in giving a Kantian interpretation to the conception of equality already presented.

I

When fully articulated, any conception of justice expresses a conception of the person, of the relations between persons, and of the general structure and ends of social cooperation. To accept the principles that represent a conception of justice is at the same time to accept an ideal of the person; and in acting from these principles we realise such an ideal. Let us begin, then, by trying to describe the kind of person we might want to be and the form of society we might wish to live in and to shape our interests and character. In this way we arrive at the notion of a well-ordered society. I shall first describe this notion and then use it to explain a Kantian conception of equality.

First of all, a well-ordered society is effectively regulated by a public conception of justice. That is, it is a society all of whose members accept, and know that the others accept, the same principles (the same conception) of justice. It is also the case that basic social institutions and their arrangement into one scheme (the basic structure) actually satisfy, and are on good grounds believed by everyone to satisfy, these principles. Finally, publicity also implies that the public conception is founded on reasonable beliefs that have been established by generally accepted methods of inquiry; and the same is true of the application of its principles to basic social arrangements. This last aspect of publicity does not mean that everyone holds the same religious, moral, and theoretical beliefs; on the contrary, there are assumed to be sharp and indeed irreconcilable differences on such questions. But at the same time there is a shared understanding that the principles of justice, and their application to the basic structure of society, should be determined by considerations and evidence that are supported by rational procedures commonly recognised.

Secondly, I suppose that the members of a well-ordered society are, and view themselves as, free and equal moral persons. They are moral persons in that, once they have reached the age of reason, each has, and

views the others as having, a realised sense of justice; and this sentiment informs their conduct for the most part. That they are equal is expressed by the supposition that they each have, and view themselves as having, a right to equal respect and consideration in determining the principles by which the basic arrangements of their society are to be regulated. Finally, we express their being free by stipulating that they each have, and view themselves as having, fundamental aims and higher-order interests (a conception of their good) in the name of which it is legitimate to make claims on one another in the design of their institutions. At the same time, as free persons they do not think of themselves as inevitably bound to, or as identical with, the pursuit of any particular array of fundamental interests that they may have at any given time; instead, they conceive of themselves as capable of revising and altering these final ends and they give priority to preserving their liberty in this regard.

In addition, I assume that a well-ordered society is stable relative to its conception of justice. This means that social institutions generate an effective supporting sense of justice. Regarding society as a going concern, its members acquire as they grow up an allegiance to the public conception and this allegiance usually overcomes the temptations and strains of social life.

Now we are here concerned with a conception of justice and the idea of equality that belongs to it. Thus, let us suppose that a well-ordered society exists under circumstances of justice. These necessitate some conception of justice and give point to its special role. First, moderate scarcity obtains. This means that although social cooperation is productive and mutually advantageous (one person's or group's gain need not be

---

* Sections I, III and IV of this discussion draw upon sections I and III of 'Reply to Alexander and Musgrave', *Quarterly Journal of Economics*, November, 1974. Sections II, V and VI of that paper take up some questions about the argument from the original position.

[1] The argument in *A Theory of Justice* was likewise informal in that I argued for the principles of justice by considering the balance of reasons in their favor given a short list of traditional philosophical conceptions. It appears, however, that formal arguments may be possible. Steven Strasnick has found a proof that certain familiar conditions on social choice functions (which it seems natural to associate with the original position), when conjoined with a principle of preference priority, entail the difference principle. He has also shown that a form of the difference principle follows once Arrow's independence condition (used in the proof of the impossibility theorem) is modified to accommodate the notion of preference priority.

CAMBRIDGE REVIEW FEBRUARY 1975

another's loss), natural resources and the state of technology are such that the fruits of joint efforts fall short of the claims that people make. And second, persons and associations have contrary conceptions of the good that lead them to make conflicting claims on one another; and they also hold opposing religious, philosophical, and moral convictions (on matters the public conception leaves open) as well as different ways of evaluating arguments and evidence in many important cases. Given these circumstances, the members of a well-ordered society are not indifferent as to how the benefits produced by their cooperation are distributed. A set of principles is required to judge between social arrangements that shape this division of advantages. Thus the role of the principles of justice is to assign rights and duties in the basic structure of society and to specify the manner in which institutions are to influence the overall distribution of the returns from social cooperation. The basic structure is the primary subject of justice and that to which the principles of justice in the first instance apply.

It is perhaps useful to observe that the notion of a well-ordered society is an extension of the idea of religious toleration. Consider a pluralistic society, divided along religious, ethnic, or cultural, lines in which the various groups have reached a firm understanding on the scheme of principles to regulate their fundamental institutions. While they have deep differences about other things, there is public agreement on this framework of principles and citizens are attached to it. A well-ordered society has not attained social harmony in all things, if indeed that would be desirable; but it has achieved a large measure of justice and established a basis for civic friendship, which makes people's secure association together possible.

II

The notion of a well-ordered society assumes that the basic structure, the fundamental social institutions and their arrangement into one scheme, is the primary subject of justice. What is the reason for this assumption? First of all, any discussion of social justice must take the nature of the basic structure into account. Suppose we begin with the initially attractive idea that the social process should be allowed to develop over time as free agreements fairly arrived at and fully honored require. Straightaway we need an account of when agreements are free and the conditions under which they are reached are fair. In addition, while these conditions may be satisfied at an earlier time, the accumulated results of agreements in conjunction with social and historical contingencies are likely to change institutions and opportunities so that the conditions for free and fair agreements no longer hold. The basic structure specifies the background conditions against which the actions of individuals, groups, and associations take place. Unless this structure is regulated and corrected so as to be just over time, the social process with its procedures and outcomes is no longer just, however free and fair parti-

cular transactions may look to us when viewed by themselves. We recognise this principle when we say that the distribution resulting from voluntary market transactions will not in general be fair unless the antecedent distribution of income and wealth and the structure of the market is fair. Thus we seem forced to start with an account of a just basic structure. It's as if the most important agreement is that which establishes the principles to govern this structure. Moreover, these principles must be acknowledged ahead of time, as it were. To agree to them now, when everyone knows their present situation, would enable some to take unfair advantage of social and natural contingencies, and of the results of historical accidents and accumulations.

Other considerations also support taking the basic structure as the primary subject of justice. It has always been recognised that the social system shapes the desires and aspirations of its members; it determines in large part the kind of persons they want to be as well as the kind of persons they are. Thus an economic system is not only an institutional device for satisfying existing wants and desires but a way of fashioning wants and desires in the future. By what principles are we to regulate a scheme of institutions that has such fundamental consequences for our view of ourselves and for our interests and aims? This question becomes all the more crucial when we consider that the basic structure contains social and economic inequalities. I assume that these are necessary, or highly advantageous, for various reasons: they are required to maintain and to run social arrangements, or to serve as incentives; or perhaps they are a way to put resources in the hands of those who can make the best social use of them; and so on. In any case, given these inequalities, individuals' life-prospects are bound to be importantly affected by their family and class origins, by their natural endowments and the chance contingencies of their (particular early) development, and by other accidents over the course of their lives. The social structure, therefore, limits people's ambitions and hopes in different ways, for they will with reason view themselves in part according to their place in it and take into account the means and opportunities they can realistically expect.

The justice of the basic structure is, then, of predominant importance. The first problem of justice is to determine the principles to regulate inequalities and to adjust the profound and long-lasting effects of social, natural, and historical contingencies, particularly since these contingencies combined with inequalities generate tendencies that, when left to themselves, are sharply at odds with the freedom and equality appropriate for a well-ordered society. In view of the special role of the basic structure, we cannot assume that the principles suitable to it are natural applications, or even extensions, of the familiar principles governing the actions of individuals and associations in everyday life which take place within its framework. Most likely we shall have to loosen ourselves from our ordinary perspective and take a more comprehensive viewpoint.

III

I shall now state and explain two principles of justice, and then discuss the appropriateness of these principles for a well-ordered society. They read as follows:

1. Each person has an equal right to the most extensive scheme of equal basic liberties compatible with a similar scheme of liberties for all.
2. Social and economic inequalities are to meet two conditions: they must be (a) to the greatest expected benefit of the least advantaged; and (b) attached to offices and positions open to all under conditions of fair opportunity.

The first of these principles is to take priority over the second; and the measure of benefit to the least advantaged is specified in terms of an index of social primary goods. These goods I define roughly as rights, liberties, and opportunities, income and wealth, and the social bases of self-respect. Individuals are assumed to want these goods whatever else they want, or whatever their final ends. The least advantaged are defined very roughly, as the overlap between those who are least favored by each of the three main kinds of contingencies. Thus this group includes persons whose family and class origins are more disadvantaged than others, whose natural endowments have permitted them to fare less well, and whose fortune and luck have been relatively less favourable, all within the normal range (as noted below) and with the relevant measures based on social primary goods. Various refinements are no doubt necessary, but this definition of the least advantaged suitably expresses the link with the problem of contingency and should suffice for our purposes here.

I also suppose that everyone has physical needs and psychological capacities within the normal range, so that the problems of special health care and of how to treat the mentally defective do not arise. Besides prematurely introducing difficult questions that may take us beyond the theory of justice, the consideration of these hard cases can distract our moral perception by leading us to think of people distant from us whose fate arouses pity and anxiety. Whereas the first problem of justice concerns the relations among those who in the normal course of things are full and active participants in society and directly or indirectly associated together over the whole course of their life.

Now the members of a well-ordered society are free and equal; so let us first consider the fittingness of the two principles to their freedom, and then to their equality. These principles reflect two aspects of their freedom, namely, liberty and responsibility, which I take up in turn. In regard to liberty, recall that people in a well-ordered society view themselves as having fundamental aims and interests which they must protect, if this is possible. It is partly in the name of these interests that they have a right to equal consideration and respect in the design of their society. A familiar historical example is the religious interest; the interest in the integrity of the person, freedom from psychological oppression and from physical assault and dismemberment is another. The notion of a well-ordered society leaves open what particular expression these interests take; only their general form is specified. But individuals do have interests of the requisite kind and the basic liberties necessary for their protection are guaranteed by the first principle.

It is essential to observe that these liberties are given by a list of liberties; important among these are freedom of thought and liberty of conscience, freedom of the person and political liberty. These liberties have a central range of application within which they can be limited and compromised only when they conflict with other basic liberties. Since they may be limited when they clash with one another, none of these liberties is absolute; but however they are adjusted to form one system, this system is to be the same for all. It is difficult, perhaps impossible, to give a complete definition of these liberties independently from the particular circumstances, social, economic, and technological, of a given well-ordered society. Yet the hypothesis is that the general form of such a list could be devised with sufficient exactness to sustain this conception of justice. Of course, liberties not on the list, for example, the right to own certain kinds of property (e.g., means of production), and freedom of contract as understood by the doctrine of laissez-faire, are not basic; and so they are not protected by the priority of the first principle.[2]

One reason, then, for holding the two principles suitable for a well-ordered society is that they assure the protection of the fundamental interests that members of such a society are presumed to have. Further reasons for this conclusion can be given by describing in more detail the notion of a free person. Thus we may suppose that such persons regard themselves as having a highest-order interest in how all their other interests, including even their fundamental ones, are shaped and regulated by social institutions. As I noted earlier, they do not think of themselves as unavoidably tied to any particular array of fundamental interests; instead they view themselves as capable of revising and changing these final ends. They wish, therefore, to give priority to their liberty to do this, and so their original allegiance and continued devotion to their ends are to be formed and affirmed under conditions that are free. Or, expressed another way, members of a well-ordered society are viewed as responsible for their fundamental interests and ends. While as members of particular associations some may decide in practice to yield much of this responsibility to others, the basic structure cannot be arranged so as prevent people from developing their capacity to be responsible, or to obstruct their exercise of it once they attain it. Social arrangements must respect their autonomy and this points to the appropriateness of the two principles.

IV

These last remarks about responsibility may be elaborated further in connection with the role of social

[2] This paragraph confirms H. L. A. Hart's interpretation. See his discussion of liberty and its priority, *Chicago Law Review*, April, 1973, pp. 536–540.

primary goods. As already stated, these are things that people in a well-ordered society may be presumed to want, whatever their final ends. And the two principles assess the basic structure in terms of certain of these goods: rights, liberties, and opportunities, income and wealth, and the social bases of self-respect. The latter are features of the basic structure that may reasonably be expected to affect people's self-respect and self-esteem (these are not the same) in important ways.[3] Part (a) of the second principle (the difference principle, or as economists prefer to say, the maximin criterion) uses an index of these goods to determine the least advantaged. Now certainly there are difficulties in working out a satisfactory index, but I shall leave these aside. Two points are particularly relevant here: first, social primary goods are certain objective characteristics of social institutions and of people's situation with respect to them; and second, the same index of these goods is used to compare everyone's social circumstances. It is clear, then, that although the index provides a basis for interpersonal comparisons for the purposes of justice, it is not a measure of individuals' overall satisfaction or dissatisfaction. Of course, the precise weights adopted in such an index cannot be laid down ahead of time, for these should be adjusted, to some degree at least, in view of social conditions. What can be settled initially is certain constraints on these weights, as illustrated by the priority of the first principle.

Now, that the responsibility of free persons is implicit in the use of primary goods can be seen in the following way. We are assuming that people are able to control and to revise their wants and desires in the light of circumstances and that they are to have responsibility for doing so, provided that the principles of justice are fulfilled, as they are in a well-ordered society. Persons do not take their wants and desires as determined by happenings beyond their control. We are not, so to speak, assailed by them, as we are perhaps by disease and illness so that wants and desires fail to support claims to the means of satisfaction in the way that disease and illness support claims to medicine and treatment.

Of course, it is not suggested that people must modify their desires and ends whatever their circumstances. The doctrine of primary goods does not demand the stoic virtues. Society for its part bears the responsibility for upholding the principles of justice and secures for everyone a fair share of primary goods (as determined by the difference principle) within a framework of equal liberty and fair equality of opportunity. It is within the limits of this division of responsibility that individuals and associations are expected to form and moderate their aims and wants. Thus among the members of a well-ordered society there is an understanding that as citizens they will press claims for only certain kinds of things, as allowed for by the principles of justice. Passion-

ate convictions and zealous aspirations do not, as such, give anyone a claim upon social resources or the design of social institutions. For the purposes of justice, the appropriate basis of interpersonal comparisons is the index of primary goods and not strength of feeling or intensity of desire. The theory of primary goods is an extension of the notion of needs, which are distinct from aspirations and desires. One might say, then, that as citizens the members of a well-ordered society collectively take responsibility for dealing justly with one another founded on a public and objective measure of (extended) needs, while as individuals and members of associations they take responsibility for their preferences and devotions.

V

I now take up the appropriateness of the two principles in view of the equality of the members of a well-ordered society. The principles of equal liberty and fair opportunity (part (b) of the second principle) are a natural expression of this equality; and I assume, therefore, that such a society is one in which some form of democracy exists. Thus our question is: by what principle can members of a democractic society permit the tendencies of the basic structure to be deeply affected by social chance, and natural and historical contingencies?

Now since we are regarding citizens as free and equal moral persons (the priority of the first principle of equal liberty gives institutional expression to this), the obvious starting point is to suppose that all other social primary goods, and in particular income and wealth, should be equal: everyone should have an equal share. But society must take organizational requirements and economic efficiency into account. So it is unreasonable to stop at equal division. The basic structure should allow inequalities so long as these improve everyone's situation, including that of the least advantaged, provided these inequalities are consistent with equal liberty and fair opportunity. Because we start from equal shares, those who benefit least have, so to speak, a veto; and thus we arrive at the difference principle. Taking equality as the basis of comparison those who have gained more must do so on terms that are justifiable to those who have gained the least.

In explaining this principle, several matters should be kept in mind. First of all, it applies in the first instance to the main public principles and policies that regulate social and economic inequalities. It is used to adjust the system of entitlements and rewards, and the standards and precepts that this system employs. Thus the difference principle holds, for example, for income and property taxation, for fiscal and economic policy; it does not apply to particular transactions or distributions, nor, in general, to small scale and local decisions, but rather to the background against which these take place. No observable pattern is required of actual distributions, nor even any measure of the degree of equality (such as

---

[3] I discuss certain problems in interpreting the account of primary goods in 'Fairness to Goodness', to appear in the *Philosophical Review*.

the Gini coefficient) that might be computed from these.[4] What is enjoined is that the inequalities make a functional contribution to those least favoured. Finally, the aim is not to eliminate the various contingencies, for some such contingencies seem inevitable. Thus even if an equal distribution of natural assets seemed more in keeping with the equality of free persons, the question of redistributing these assets (were this conceivable) does not arise, since it is incompatible with the integrity of the person. Nor need we make any specific assumptions about how great these variations are; we only suppose that, as realized in later life, they are influenced by all three kinds of contingencies. The question, then, is by what criterion a democratic society is to organize cooperation and arrange the system of entitlements that encourages and rewards productive efforts? We have a right to our natural abilities and a right to whatever we become entitled to by taking part in a fair social process. The problem is to characterise this process.[5]

At first sight, it may appear that the difference principle is arbitrarily biased towards the least favoured. But suppose, for simplicity, that there are only two groups, one significantly more fortunate than the other. Society could maximise the expectations of either group but not both, since we can maximise with respect to only one aim at a time. It seems plain that society should not do the best it can for those initially more advantaged; so if we reject the difference principle, we must prefer maximising some weighted mean of the two expectations. But how should this weighted mean be specified? Should society proceed as if we had an equal chance of being in either group (in proportion to their size) and determine the mean that maximises this purely hypothetical expectation? Now it is true that we sometimes agree to draw lots but normally only to things that cannot be appropriately divided or else cannot be enjoyed or suffered in common.[6] And we are willing to use the lottery principle even in matters of lasting importance if there is no other way out. (Consider the example of conscription). But to appeal to it in regulating the basic structure itself would be extraordinary. There is no necessity for society as an enduring system to invoke the lottery principle in this case; nor is there any reason for free and equal persons to allow their relations over the whole course of their life to be significantly affected by contingencies to the greater advantage of those already favored by these accidents. No one had an antecedent claim to be benefited in this way; and so to maximise a weighted mean is, so to speak, to favour the more fortunate twice over. Society can, however, adopt the difference principle to arrange inequalities so that social and natural contingencies are efficiently used

to the benefit of all, taking equal division as a benchmark. So while natural assets cannot be divided evenly, or directly enjoyed or suffered in common, the results of their productive efforts can be allocated in ways consistent with an initial equality. Those favoured by social and natural contingencies regard themselves as already compensated, as it were, by advantages to which no one (including themselves) had a prior claim. Thus they think the difference principle appropriate for regulating the system of entitlements and inequalities.

VI

The conception of equality contained in the principles of justice I have described as Kantian. I shall conclude by mentioning very briefly the reasons for this description. Of course, I do not mean that this conception is literally Kant's conception, but rather that it is one of no doubt several conceptions sufficiently similar to essential parts of his doctrine to make the adjective appropriate. Much depends on what one counts as essential. Kant's view is marked by a number of dualisms, in particular, the dualisms between the necessary and the contingent, form and content, reason and desire, and noumena and phenomena. To abandon these dualisms as he meant them is, for many, to abandon what is distinctive in his theory. I believe otherwise. His moral conception has a characteristic structure that is more clearly discernible when these dualisms are not taken in the sense he gave them but reinterpreted and their moral force reformulated within the scope of an empirical theory. One of the aims of *A Theory of Justice* was to indicate how this might be done.

To suggest the main idea, think of the notion of a well-ordered society as an interpretation of the idea of a kingdom of ends thought of as a human society under circumstances of justice. Now the members of such a society are free and equal and so our problem is to find a rendering of freedom and equality that it is natural to describe as Kantian; and since Kant distinguished between positive and negative freedom, we must make room for this contrast. At this point I resorted to the idea of the original position: I supposed that the conception of justice suitable for a well-ordered society is the one that would be agreed to in a hypothetical situation that is fair between individuals conceived as free and equal moral persons, that is, as members of such a society. Fairness of the circumstances under which agreement is reached transfers to the fairness of the principles agreed to. The original position was designed so that the conception of justice that resulted would be appropriate.

Particularly important among the features of the original position for the interpretation of negative freedom are the limits on information, which I called the veil of ignorance. Now there is a stronger and a weaker form of these limits. The weaker supposes that we begin with full information, or else that which we possess in everyday life, and then proceed to eliminate only the

---

[4] For a discussion of such measures, see A. K. Sen, *On Economic Inequality* (Oxford, 1973), chap. 2.

[5] The last part of this paragraph alludes to some objections raised by Robert Nozick in his *Anarchy, State, and Utopia* (New York, 1974), esp. pp. 213–229.

[6] At this point I adapt some remarks of Hobbes. See The *Leviathan*, Ch. 15, under the thirteenth and fourteenth laws of nature.

CAMBRIDGE REVIEW FEBRUARY 1975

information that would lead to partiality and bias. The stronger form has a Kantian explanation: we start from no information at all; for by negative freedom Kant means being able to act independently from the determination of alien causes; to act from natural necessity is to subject oneself to the heteronomy of nature. We interpret this as requiring that the conception of justice that regulates the basic structure, with its deep and long-lasting effects on our common life, should not be adopted on grounds that rest on a knowledge of the various contingencies. Thus when this conception is agreed to, knowledge of our social position, our peculiar desires and interests, or of the various outcomes and configurations of natural and historical accident is excluded. One allows only that information required for a rational agreement. This means that, so far as possible, only the general laws of nature are known together with such particular facts as are implied by the circumstances of justice.

Of course, we must endow the parties with some motivation, otherwise no acknowledgement would be forthcoming. Kant's discussion in the *Groundwork* of the second pair of examples indicates, I believe, that in applying the procedure of the categorical imperative he tacitly relied upon some account of primary goods. In any case, if the two principles would be adopted in the original position with its limits on information, the conception of equality they contain would be Kantian in the sense that by acting from this conception the members of a well-ordered society would express their negative freedom. They would have succeeded in regulating the basic structure and its profound consequences on their persons and mutual relationships by principles the grounds for which are suitably independent from chance and contingency.

In order to provide an interpretation of positive freedom, two things are necessary: first, that the parties are conceived as free and equal moral persons must play a decisive part in their adoption of the conception of justice; and second, the principles of this conception must have a content appropriate to express this determining view of persons and must apply to the controlling institutional subject. Now if correct, the argument from the original position seems to meet these conditions. The assumption that the parties are free and equal moral persons does have an essential role in this argument; and as regards content and application, these principles express, on their public face as it were, the conception of the person that is realised in a well-ordered society. They give priority to the basic liberties, regard individuals as free and responsible masters of their aims and desires, and all are to share equally in the means for the attainment of ends unless the situation of everyone can be improved, taking equal division as the starting point. A society that realised these principles would attain positive freedom, for these principles reflect the features of persons that determined their selection and so express a conception they give to themselves.

[28]

Political Studies (1987), XXXV, 537–551

Towards a Social Democratic Theory of the State

PHILIP PETTIT*

Australian National University

The paper attempts two tasks. The first is to provide a characterization of the social democratic approach which sets it in contrast to liberal democratic theories. This is pursued by contrasting the different interpretations of the ideal of equal respect which are associated with the two approaches. The second task is to establish that the social democratic approach is, if not clearly superior, at least worth considering further. This task is pursued by the attempt to vindicate three assumptions which the social democratic approach must make about the state.

What kind of institution is the state to be; what sort of requirements ought it to satisfy? I wish to sketch one answer to this question, setting it up in contrast to a more established type of response. The answer I sketch constitutes what I shall describe as a social democratic theory of the state; equally well perhaps, it might be cast as a democratic socialist one. The sort of response from which I distinguish it is the liberal democratic approach to the state, an approach which has been rather better articulated in the recent literature.

My definitions of the social democratic and liberal democratic theories, and the further distinctions with which I embroider those definitions, are stipulative rather than historical. I say this to guard against the charge of under-documenting them. But I hope that the definitions are not rootless either. They are designed to regiment and idealize commonly accepted ideas; their rationale is to further a familiar debate, not initiate a foreign one.

The paper is in four sections. First I introduce a distinction between two ways of taking the ideal of equal respect for all; one associated with the liberal democratic approach, the other with the social democratic. In the second section I examine the significance of adopting the liberal construal and in the third the significance of espousing the alternative. Finally, in the fourth section, I try to establish the tenability, if not the actual preferability, of the social democratic viewpoint. Specifically, I provide a sketch defence of three assumptions which it involves: first, that the state can be a reliable agent; secondly, that

* I am grateful for comments, written and oral, from Ruth Abbey, Paul Bourke, Geoff Brennan, Jerry Gaus, Alan Hamlin, Peter Self, Kim Sterelny, Mark Thomas and Peter Wilensky. I benefited greatly from comments received when the paper was presented at the Research School of Social Sciences, Australian National University, in December 1985. A successor piece, 'The freedom of the city', appears in Alan Hamlin and Philip Pettit (eds), *The Good Polity* (Oxford, Basil Blackwell, forthcoming).

0032-3217/87/04/0537-15/$03.00 © 1987 *Political Studies*

it can be a respectful one; and thirdly, that it is an agent that ought to be given responsibility for the goals espoused by social democrats.

The paper may go some way towards a social democratic theory of the state but it certainly does not constitute one. It does not outline in any detail the agenda for the social democratic state, and it does not try to defend that agenda against standard liberal objections. Those tasks are ones which I hope to take up elsewhere.[1]

1. Two Democratic Viewpoints

I shall take it as axiomatic that democratic theories of the state agree on one crucial matter. This is that the social ideal of equal respect for all persons ought to be central to the organization of society. What makes such theories democratic—better perhaps, democentric—is precisely the notion that every citizen enjoys or ought to enjoy equal respect. However far short of being by the people, government is certainly to be for the peopole. Each to count for one, and none for more than one.[2]

The division between liberal democratic and social democratic theory comes of a difference in how they understand the ideal of equal respect for all. The difference does not bear in the first place on the content of that ideal but rather on the agent perspective from which it is seen. Equal respect for all is a goal designed to guide the organization of social life. How it is understood depends on who is taken to conduct that organization.

There are two salient possibilities. Equal respect may be taken as a goal for the guidance of individuals, because it is individuals who are in principle responsible for social life: after all, nothing is done in society except by the human hand. On this approach, we will take the point of view of all the individuals in the community, given that all play some part in the reproduction of social pattern, and we will ask what such individuals should seek of the institutions they live by, in particular of the state, if they are concerned with the realization of equal respect.

Alternatively, equal respect may be taken as a goal for the guidance of the state, since it is the state which is responsible in practice for the shape of the society. If we adopt this line, then we will view the social world from the vantage point of a potentially beneficient government and we will ask what the state can and ought to do—what changes in the social and political institutions it can and ought to initiate—in order to maximize equal respect for all.

Liberal democratic theory is distinguished, I believe, by the assumption that equal respect for all is an ideal addressed to individuals; social democratic theory by the assumption that it is an ideal addressed to the state. In the one case we ask what individuals ought to require of the social and political institutions they generate, given a concern that they be equally respected. In the other

---

[1] I have done so to some extent in 'Democratic socialism as a political ideology', in Don Rawson (ed.), *Blast, Budge or Bypass: Towards a Social Democratic Australia* (Canberra, Australian Academy of the Social Sciences, 1986); in Italian translation, *State e Mercato*, Vol. 16 (1986).

[2] See for example C. B. Macpherson, *The Real World of Democracy* (Oxford, Clarendon Press, 1966), p. 29; Steven Lukes, *Individualism* (Oxford, Basil Blackwell, 1973), Chs 7 and 18; and Ronald Dworkin, 'Liberalism', in Stuart Hampshire (ed.), *Public and Private Morality* (Cambridge, Cambridge University Press, 1978), pp. 121, 126, 145.

we ask what the state ought to choose in their name, given a similar concern.

If we ask the liberal democratic question, then we intrude the assumption that as things stand people are equally respect-able individuals. After all, they are taken to be autonomous individuals equally responsible for the moulding of society. If we ask the social democratic question, we leave open the possibility that in view of asymmetries of capacity and power people are not equally respect-able. The difference of assumption has a crucial effect on how the two sorts of theory approach the task of detailing the requirements of their shared ideal.

There are two ways in which an agent or agency can take an ideal like that of equal respect. The ideal may be seen as something to be exemplified whatever the consequences, even consequences of there being less respect overall. Alternatively it may be seen as something to be promoted or maximized, even when the promotion requires behaviour that is not itself particularly respectful: this will happen if a local act of disrespect provides a greater amount of respect globally.

The difference in assumption between them means that the liberal democrat requires social institutions to exemplify equal respect, the social democrat requires them to promote it.

The liberal democrat asks what equally respect-able individuals, concerned with the value of equal respect, ought to require of their institutions; in particular what they ought to require of their state, assuming that the institutions amount to a state. If the individuals are equally respect-able, then the answer is clear. All that the ideal can lead them to require is that these institutions should exemplify equal respect all round.

The social democrat does not assume equal respect-ability, since he takes the state as the given agent and asks what the ideal of equal respect requires of it. Since equal respect-ability is often clearly lacking among people, he is naturally led to see the ideal as something that calls for promotion rather than exemplification. He will want the state to exemplify equal respect where that is the way also to maximize it, but not otherwise. The state will be allowed to show the inequality of respect involved in redistribution for example, so long as that promises to increase equal respect-ability and equal respect overall.

These comments serve to introduce the difference between the liberal democratic and social democratic viewpoints. It is now time to examine each in greater detail.

2. The Liberal Democratic Point of View

A person or institution X respects a person Y so far as X takes appropriate account of some aspect of Y's attitudes or actions: say, Y's beliefs or desires or commitments. What it is to take appropriate account of that aspect—that *respiciendum*, we may say—varies, depending on the sort of factor in question.

The liberal democrat might look for institutions which equally exemplify respect with regard to a mix—perhaps the largest possible mix—of aspects. But in practice each liberal democratic theory tends to select one *respiciendum* as primary and to elaborate an account of the sort of institutions, in particular the sort of state, required, if people are to be institutionally respected under that aspect.

The range of liberal democratic theories includes approaches such as the utilitarian, the libertarian, the unanimitarian and the contractarian. Such theories can be, and indeed frequently are, defended on a number of grounds. It is striking, however, and surely not accidental, that they can be readily seen as different interpretations, under the liberal democratic approach, of the ideal of exemplifying equal respect. They can each be represented as identifying a distinctive *respiciendum*.[3]

The utilitarian theory of social organization, including the theory of the state, takes that *respiciendum* to be people's preferences or, in a now less fashionable version, their hedonistic sensibilities.[4] Each is to count equally, as Bentham insists, but the way in which they are to count is by having their preferences—or at least their relevant preferences—considered equally in the identification of the optimific social pattern: that is, the pattern which maximizes preference-satisfaction overall.[5]

Utilitarianism prescribes different sorts of organization, and different types of state, under different empirical assumptions. Thus, under certain assumptions, it leads to the economic theory of the state. According to this theory, preference-satisfaction is guaranteed of maximization in the free market and the only task for the state is to compensate, where it can, for market failure.[6]

The libertarian theory takes the primary *respiciendum* to be, not people's preferences, but rather the choices they make within certain bounds, whether or not those choices promise to maximize preference-satisfaction.[7] This libertarian view is implicit in any approach that stresses natural rights, for such rights serve to define the bounds within which choices are to be respected. It is perhaps the purest form of liberal democratic theory, for even if it acknowledges the need

---

[3] The egalitarian approach which Ronald Dworkin has been exploring can be seen as the liberal democratic response that is motivated by taking people's life-projects as the primary *respiciendum*. See his 'In defence of equality', *Social Philosophy and Policy*, 1 (1983). Similarly, the 'consensualist' approaches associated with Jürgen Habermas and David Gauthier can be cast as interpretations of the demands of equal respect. On Habermas see my 'Habermas on truth and justice', in G. H. R. Parkinson (ed.), *Marx and Marxisms* (Cambridge, Cambridge University Press, 1982); for Gauthier's rather different approach see his *Morals by Agreement* (Oxford, Oxford University Press, 1984). My reading of utilitarianism and contractarianism as each serving to interpret the ideal of equal respect is motivated by Dworkin's *Taking Rights Seriously* (London, Duckworth, 1977).

[4] On the variety of utilitarian doctrines see James Griffin, 'Modern utilitarianism', *Revue Internationale de Philosophie*, 36 (1982).

[5] The identification of relevant preferences is matter for debate. See Griffin, 'Modern utilitarianism' and my *Judging Justice* (London, Routledge and Kegan Paul, 1980), Ch. 13.

[6] The economic theory of the state is usually tied to the assumption that preference-satisfaction is interpersonally incommensurable, and perhaps non-cardinal. It recommends different types of state, depending on different estimates of the relative capacities of market and polity. For a minimalist extreme see Milton and Rose Friedman, *Free to Choose* (Harmondsworth, Penguin, 1980).

[7] John Hospers, *Libertarianism* (Los Angeles, Nash Publishing, 1971) offers a good example of a libertarian attitude, though his arguments often betray utilitarian presuppositions. The outstanding contemporary statement is Robert Nozick, *Anarchy, State, and Utopia* (New York, Basic Books, 1974). F. A. Hayek puts such a premium on liberties that he ought also to be counted among libertarians but it is worth noticing that he prizes liberty, as utilitarian theorists often do, for what it makes possible, rather than for its own sake. See Anthony de Crespigny, 'F. A. Hayek: freedom for progress', in A. de Crespigny and Kenneth Minogue (eds), *Contemporary Political Philosophers* (London, Methuen, 1976).

for a state it leaves the state little to do for its citizens.[8]

Unanimitarian theory is one of a family of electoral theories, of which majoritarianism is also a member. It goes beyond preferences and choices to present people's votes as the primary *respiciendum*; people are equally respected so far as each has a veto over any institutional arrangement.[9] A vote in this context is the expression of a preference—not yet a choice, since it is not effective—for one sort of social and political arrangement rather than another.[10] The domain of preferences and choices elevated under the other approaches is largely personal and private; the domain of votes includes public and institutional matters.

Unanimitarian theory is in principle open to the adoption of any sort of state, so long as that state secures unanimous support. In practice it will endorse only that type of state of which it can reasonably be held that it would secure unanimous support. Such a state will be as minimal as any favoured by libertarians.[11]

Finally, contractarian theory argues that what ought primarily to be respected in the design of social and political institutions is not preferences or choices or votes, but evaluations. There ought to be such institutions, and only such institutions, as warrant the evaluative assent of the people living under them. The approach is contractarian, because it is assumed that the institutions that warrant assent are those which individuals would contract into, were they free of bias; in particular, were they required to choose a set of institutions in ignorance of their own life-chances.[12]

Contractarianism is like the utilitarian theory, and unlike the libertarian and unanimitarian, in so far as it is liable to select a much more extensive state than the night-watchman variety. Thus the state selected under John Rawls's application of the approach is one which seeks to implement his two principles of justice: the first requires maximum equal liberty; the second allows only such inequality in other regards as improves the position of the worst-off in the society.[13]

This is sufficient to illustrate the range and variety of liberal democratic theories, as I understand the genre. All endorse the ideal of equal respect and all insist on seeing that ideal as something to be exemplified by the state. Each claims to give the appropriate interpretation of the notion of what is owed to individuals, as equal partners in the making of society, by the institutions under which they live.

---

[8] The problem of whether there should be a state at all is discussed in Hospers, *Libertarianism*, Ch. 11, and is at the centre of Nozick's concerns.

[9] See J. M. Buchanan and Gordon Tullock, *The Calculus of Consensus* (Michigan, Ann Arbor, 1962). For a discussion see Brian Barry, *Political Argument* (London, Routledge and Kegan Paul, 1965), Chs 14 and 15.

[10] On the complications surrounding the idea of a vote see Geoffrey Brennan and James Buchanan, 'Voter choice', *American Behavioural Scientist*, 28 (1984).

[11] But there are difficulties in store. See Geoffrey Brennan and Loren Lomasky, 'Inefficient unanimity', *Journal of Applied Philosophy*, 1 (1984).

[12] Evaluations correspond to the notion of ethical preferences in J. C. Harsanyi, 'Cardinal welfare, individualistic ethics, and interpersonal comparisons of utility', *Journal of Political Economy*, 63 (1955).

[13] John Rawls, *A Theory of Justice* (Oxford, Oxford University Press, 1971).

3. The Social Democratic Point of View

The social democratic approach is impatient of the theoretical conceits favoured by liberal democratic philosophies. It is an abstraction to think of all individuals as equal partners in the organization of social and political life and to consider what institutions they might approve, for example, in a hypothetical state of nature. The social democrat rejects this sort of idealization. His starting point is the actual historical condition within which the state is already a potent reality.[14]

Given the difference of starting point, the social democrat adopts quite a different perspective on the shared ideal of a society in which individuals enjoy maximum equal respect. He does not ask what equally respect-able individuals should require of the institutions under which they live, and in particular of the state, if they are to enjoy equal respect. He asks rather what the state should do in the world as it is now in order to promote this ideal.

It is a matter of uncontestable fact that individuals do not equally command respect in the actual world. Inequalities of information, influence and the like ensure this. People may be equally respect-able in the higher-order sense that they each have the capacity to perform in a manner, and with an effect, which is as worthy of respect as anyone else's performance. But they are not equally respect-able in the sense of actually performing to that standard or with such an effect.

Once this fact is brought into focus, then the ideal of equal respect takes on a rather different aspect. It calls for a response to the inequalities that spring from the fact of unequal respect-ability. It counsels the exemplification of equal respect only so far as that is compatible with its maximum promotion.

People command respect from one another in varying degrees because of variations in at least two sorts of factor: (1) the capacity to form preferences and other attitudes in an informed and justifiable manner; and (2) the power to make such attitudes felt. These inequalities are neglected by the liberal democrat for whom respect is already available equally to all.[15]

When it is granted that mutual respect is based on such capacities and powers, and that these vary between individuals, the social democratic response is to require the state, so far as possible, to reduce differences in those capacities and powers. The state will have to concern itself with equalizing personal respect-ability, with promoting equal dignity for all. This is not the place to spell out the demands of that goal but we can identify the broad sorts of requirements it is likely to impose.

In order to redress people's inequality in capacity and power, the social democratic state will have to try to emancipate and empower those who are relatively deprived. The twin goals of emancipation and empowering can be identified in the range of policies which social democrats have been distinctively

---

[14] It is no accident that the tradition of social democratic thinkers is more political than academic: its protagonists are people like Bernstein, Tawney, the Webbs, G. D. H. Cole, Anthony Crossland, and Barbara Wootton. There are some contemporary statements of course that are of a more academic kind. A good example is Albert Weale, *Political Theory and Social Policy* (London, Macmillan, 1983).

[15] See Lukes, *Individualism*, p. 126, where respect is said to be based on the existence of certain characteristics, rather than on the degree to which they are developed.

prepared to propose and contemplate. A quick check-list will serve to make the point; nothing more detailed is possible here.

In order to equalize capacities, the state must emancipate people from such conditions as penury, ignorance and vulnerability; in particular, vulnerability to sickness and disability. It is no surprise therefore to find that social democrats emphasize the importance of social security, public housing, compulsory education, public health care, and the like. And equally it is not surprising that they have proposed or contemplated, where appropriate, that the state provision of these goods be in kind, be universal, and be monopolistic.

In-kind provision of housing, education, or medical care serves the ideal of equal dignity in a manner that cash support, where the cash was used for other purposes, would not. Universal provision will promote such dignity if it is necessary to guard against social stigma. And monopolistic provision will be necessary for equal dignity if, as is sometimes alleged, the positional aspect of a good like education means that a private sector can give its clients an advantage that damages others.

So much for the emancipatory imperatives of equal dignity, under the social democratic approach. What now of the empowering requirements? Here the major problems are: coercion, exploitation, manipulation, discrimination, marginalization, and the like.[16] The other distinctive aspect of social democratic policies derives from the attempt to combat such melancholy phenomena.

In view of their shared ideal, social democrats join liberals in arguing for such staples as trial by jury, separation of powers and the universal franchise. But with their different reading of the ideal, they naturally go further. They argue too for a level of social security that prevents employer exploitation; for a freedom of information that guards against manipulation; for a system of review to monitor and eliminate discrimination; and for forms of participatory democracy, industrial and communal, designed to stop people being marginalized and alienated.

This check-list may serve to elucidate what the requirements of equal dignity are and to justify the claim that equal dignity is indeed the goal that social democrats distinctively pursue. But it should not be taken as more than an indication of the drift of social democratic thinking. As I see it, social democratic theory is a philosophy for policy-making, not a closed list of political programmes.

The open-endedness of the social democratic perspective means that what is ultimately supported may even be non-statist in character. The fact that we start with the potent state does not mean that we are prohibited from arguing, for example, that the way for the state to maximize equal dignity is for it to restrict or devolve its own power: to efface itself, if not to wither away. The social democratic perspective is distinguished by the broad domain which it assigns to democratic concern, not by any detailed presuppositions about where the concern will lead.

---

[16] The terms are probably self-explanatory but for the distinction between coercion and exploitation. As I use the terms, coercion occurs when one is forced to do or accept something because one is threatened with worse, exploitation when one is forced to do or accept something because one's initial situation is unacceptably bad and means that the alternative is worse anyhow.

One further remark may be made in conclusion. If my argument is sound, then liberal and social democratic theories, albeit they start out from the common ideal of equal respect, press that ideal in rather different directions. But that claim should not obscure the fact that the sort of state for which social democrats argue may coincide in many important respects with the state supported by, for example, certain utilitarians and contractarians. The difference between liberal democratic and social democratic theory is precisely a difference of theory; it does not always show up as a difference in practical recommendations.

4. The Tenability of the Social Democratic Point of View

The social democratic point of view is attractive, so far as it does not depend on the historical abstraction which characterizes liberal democratic perspectives. But the final judgement on whether it is tenable must rest on where it is found to lead and whether the commitments that it generates can be assembled in a reflective equilibrium: an internally consistent set that includes all the relevant considered judgements of the theorist.[17] Such an assessment is beyond the scope of this paper.

In lieu of a final vindication, however, we can see whether the social democratic viewpoint possesses the prior virtue of offering at least a plausible perspective on questions of institutional design. There are three assumptions involved in the social democratic approach which can be, and have been, challenged. What I propose to do by way of fulfilling this interim task is to see if these can be justified. I shall not be able to argue in detail for the defensibility of these assumptions but I can at least indicate how I think that the defence should go.

The first assumption is that the state envisaged by social democrats is a potentially reliable agent: an agent capable of systematically furthering an institutional goal like equal dignity. The second assumption is that the state can coherently seek to promote that particular goal, being capable of dealing respectfully with the persons for whom it wishes to procure respect. And the third is that the state is an agent—indeed the agent—which ought to be assigned responsibility for the maximization of equal dignity.

The Reliability Assumption

Two counsels of despair challenge the assumption of reliability. One, from the left, holds that classes are the dominant social forces and that in a class-divided society the state will be just a pawn of the ruling class. The other, from the right, holds that individuals are the motor agents of social life and that the state is merely an arena within which such individuals will pursue their own goals, not an agent with a life of its own.

The leftist challenge is familiar from a more or less vulgar tradition of Marxist theory. Within this tradition it is axiomatic that the capitalist class in contemporary western society acts in its class interest so that, given its power, it

---

[17] The notion of reflective equilibrium comes from Rawls, *A Theory of Justice*. It is discussed in my *Judging Justice*, Ch. 4.

will pre-empt any genuine state reform. Given such an assumption, there is room only for despair about the prospects for a state committed, ostensibly, to social democratic ideals; even indeed about the prospects for a state dedicated to liberal democratic ends.[18]

The axiom on which this challenge rests, however, is decidedly shaky. The individuals and corporations who constitute the capitalist class are admitted on all sides to be agents concerned only with their private gains. We can expect them to act as a collective agent, therefore, only where contingent circumstances or some sort of organization ensure that it is in their private interest to do so. But in the actual world both of these conditions are often lacking.

The constituent members of the capitalist class find themselves in a collective action predicament in which each stands to benefit most by defecting on any potential class action, leaving it to others to carry the burden, and where the organization necessary to ensure compliance is often lacking. They might all benefit by a price-fixing or wage-fixing or state-pressurizing campaign, but none is automatically motivated to do his bit for the cause.[19]

Once this is recognized, the leftist counsel of despair loses its paralysing force. There emerges some ground for hope that even in a society where capitalist forces are dominant, the state can achieve goals, like the promotion of equal dignity, which are not in the capitalist interest. I say some ground for hope, because the fact remains that the state will certainly be subject to a variety of capitalist pressures, applied through a variety of political means. Recognition of such problems however need not induce paralysis; on the contrary, it ought rather to motivate reflection on how the problems may be circumvented in a social democratic régime.[20]

The rightist counsel of despair derives from a dogma with roots as deep as the dogma of class agency. This is the belief that individuals are the only agents on the social scene; and this not just in the sense that even corporate agents act via individuals. The thesis is, rather more strongly, that individuals are the only centres for the systematic formation and production of goals.[21]

This thesis springs from two more basic assumptions, each associated with economics: first, that every individual is a rational utility-maximizing animal; and secondly, that utilities are bound up with more or less egocentric and competitive goals like wealth and status and power.[22] 'You can't make a silk purse out of a sow's ear.' And, similarly, the idea is that you can't make an

[18] See Bob Jessop, *The Capitalist State* (Oxford, Martin Robertson, 1982), for a survey.

[19] On the free rider problem see my 'The Prisoner's Dilemma and social theory', *Politics*, 20 (1985) and 'Free riding and foul dealing', *Journal of Philosophy*, 83 (1986). See also Jon Elster, *Making Sense of Marx* (Cambridge, Cambridge University Press, 1985), Ch. 6.2. Elster (Ch. 7) offers a further reason for resisting the leftist counsel of despair: that, as Elster thinks that Marx claims, it may be in the ultimate capitalist interest to leave the state alone.

[20] See Martin Carnoy, *The State and Political Theory* (Princeton, N.J., Princeton University Press, 1984) for a survey of less state-despairing Marxist views. See also Jessop, *The Capitalist State*.

[21] See James Buchanan, *What Should Economists Do?* (Indianapolis, Liberty Press, 1979), p. 144.

[22] The first comes of standard axioms governing preferences; the second, less obviously, from the assumption that preferences are either exogenous or are explained by exogenous preferences: see Geoffrey Brennan and James Buchanan, 'The normative purpose of economic "science"', *International Review of Law and Economics*, 1 (1981), pp. 159–60.

agent which can be relied upon to further corporate goals, independently of how those goals relate to personal priorities, out of beings whose only motivation is the promotion of self-interest.

The problem is to find reliable corporate policy-makers for those corporations where policy is meant to be guided by criteria which are unconnected with, or even cut across, the self-interest of those individuals. There is no problem with an agent like a firm, since the self-interest of the directors is tied up with the criterion of profit-maximization. There is a problem, however, with the social democratic state, or so it is alleged, since the self-interest of top ministers and civil servants is often going to suggest a different line from that dictated by the goal of equal dignity for all.[23]

As a counsel of principled despair, the rightist thesis is no more compelling than its leftist counterpart. The literature with which it is associated may be a useful source of warnings on how politicians may be bought off, but those warnings can be heeded in the design of political institutions. They do not constitute grounds for total despair.

The rightist thesis falls foul, in my view, of considerations like the following.

1. The point about egocentric concerns is unpersuasive, except in this weak form: that agents may not generally be relied upon to promote any goals whose fulfilment is, at some level, inimical to their income or status or power; self-interest serves as a constraint, not a maximand.

2. In this weaker form, the point is consistent with the possibility, substantiated in everyday experience, that individuals internalize the goals of corporate agents like the social democratic state, promoting them as if the ends were their own; individuals have a tendency to identify loyally with the agencies they serve.[24]

3. Even in its stronger form, the point is consistent with a slightly less dramatic possibility: that individuals, under pressure of appropriate sanctions—and it is important that these be constantly reviewed—find it optimal to pursue the ends corporately assigned to them, without constant reference to their self-interest. Such a line may save them time, provide them with a simple decision procedure, ensure the public legitimacy of what they decide, and promise better career prospects than unrelentingly self-interested calculation.[25]

4. These possibilities are supported by the observation that the politicians and public servants who run a state are in a different position from the agents

---

[23] This is the so-called public choice critique of the state. For an overview see Dennis Mueller, *Public Choice* (Cambridge, Cambridge University Press, 1979). The public choice point of view often passes unremarked into contemporary textbooks. See for example Norman P. Barry, *An Introduction to Modern Political Theory* (London, Macmillan, 1981), p. 53: 'The acts of the state, however, are always the acts of officials authorised by the rules of the state and the ends of the state are always the ends of the individuals and groups that use its machinery'.

[24] This is to say that people's operative preferences are not always generated instrumentally by what they exogenously prefer. See note 22 above.

[25] Their egoism, to pick up a phrase I have used elsewhere, would have to be restrictive; it might serve as an evaluation criterion but not as a basis for selecting actions. See Philip Pettit and Geoffrey Brennan, 'Restrictive consequentialism', *Australasian Journal of Philosophy*, 64 (1986). This point explains why I am not persuaded by the claim that the worst scenario of rational economic agents ought to drive us towards a liberal democratic approach. See Brennan and Buchanan, 'The normative purpose of economic "science"' for a defence of that claim.

who constitute, for example, the capitalist class; they are not typically involved in a collective action problem, for there is not an inverse relationship between the pursuit of the corporate goal and the satisfaction of their personal interests.[26]

Before leaving the issue of the reliability of a corporate agent like the social democratic state, it may be useful to add a philosophical gloss. I distinguish two doctrines that I describe, respectively, as atomism and collectivism. Atomism goes quite naturally with the rightist counsel of despair, collectivism with the leftist. Contrary to common opinion, the doctrines are not mutually contradictory, and I reject both.[27]

Atomism is the doctrine that the states in virtue of which people act do not consist in, or necessarily presuppose, relations to outside objects: in particular, relations to aspects of social context. The beliefs, desires and other intentional states that drive people to action are essentially individualistic; without a causal effect, no change of context on its own would mean any change in them. Such an atomistic image would go naturally with the rightist despair, for if people act under pre-social pressures, than it is easy to imagine that they may not be capable of constituting certain sorts of stable corporations.

Collectivism is the theory that the intentional states which seem to prompt behaviour are not really its effective sources: they come and go, by whatever institutional magic, so that what the agent does in their name will always serve to promote the ends of some larger group. Given this view, the individual drops away as the relevant explanatory unit; his place is taken by the collectivity, with its causally potent ends. Such a collectivistic picture would serve nicely to support the leftist despair, since if classes can be treated as effective collectivities, then class agency will not be any matter for surprise.

I hold to a middle position between these two extremes, maintaining that intentional states are the sources of action but denying that they are essentially unrelational. This position allows that among the beliefs and desires which motivate individuals are some states that intrinsically involve reference to social and other objects: judgements built around particular people and groups and practices, affections involving this or that specific particular, and the like. If we adopt this context-bound image of individual agents, then we will find it natural that people are capable of the loyalty and commitment necessary for the formation of a stable corporation like the social democratic state.

[26] This perspective is often lost in the pluralist view of the state. For some background see the references in Brian Galligan, 'The state in Australian political thought', *Politics*, 18 (1983).

[27] On collectivism see the characterization and critique in Graham Macdonald and Philip Pettit, *Semantics and Social Science* (London, Routledge and Kegan Paul, 1981), Ch. 3; also my 'In defence of "A New Methodological Individualism"', *Ratio*, 26 (1984) and 'The varieties of collectivism', in O. Neumaier (ed.), *Mind, Language and Society* (Vienna, 1984). On atomism see my 'Social holism and moral theory', *Proceedings of the Aristotelian Society*, 86 (1985–86) and, by way of background: 'A priori principles and action-explanation', *Analysis*, 45 (1986) and 'Broad-minded explanation and psychology', in John McDowell and Philip Pettit (eds), *Subject, Thought and Context* (Oxford, Oxford University Press, 1986). I work out my own position most fully in 'Social holism without collectivism', in Edna Margalit (ed.), *1986 Israel Colloquium in Philosophy of Science* (Dordrecht, Reidel, forthcoming).

The Respectfulness Assumption

So much for the assumption about reliability that is involved in the social democratic viewpoint. The next task is to vindicate the further assumption that the social democratic state is not only generally reliable, it is also capable, in particular, of promoting a goal like equal dignity. Here the challenge is to show that there is nothing self-defeating about the enterprise. The claim is that there are certain things which no agent, corporate or personal, can do for another and that the promotion of an individual's dignity is one of them.

There are indeed certain benefits which no one can set out, with the full knowledge of the beneficiary, to confer on another. These are benefits which the person enjoys so far as the agent, far from setting out to confer them, finds himself more or less compelled to treat the person in a certain way. Let the compulsion be that associated with admiration and the beneficiary enjoys esteem; let it be that associated with love and he enjoys affection; and so on. Such benefits cannot be bestowed out of good will; they are essentially by-products of a more or less involuntary response.[28]

Dignity, like esteem and affection, is an essential by-product in this sense. You enjoy dignity, because others find themselves compelled to take you into account, according respect to your wishes, opinions, actions, or whatever. You do not enjoy dignity, however, if others behave in this way merely because they want you to have the benefit. In that case you are at their mercy and in their debt: you are a pawn in their beneficent enterprises. Far from having the dignity that goes with knowing that they have no choice but to honour you, what you enjoy is the good fortune of having kindly masters and fellows. This is the stuff of servility, not respect.

The challenge is clear. The social democratic state sets out to promote equal respect overall by trying at once to ensure equal personal respect-ability and to accord equal institutional respect. The question is whether the state can confer benefits on those whose respect-ability it wishes to raise without turning them into debtors and depriving them of the very dignity it wishes to promote. The considerations brought forward suggest that it cannot do so, because dignity comes of treatment that is in some way compelled, not of ex gratia beneficence.

I have spent some time getting the challenge clear, for once it is clear, then so is the response. Suppose that you are in a position in which you want to confer dignity on someone: say your teenage daughter. You will not do that if you retain discretion in how you treat her, even though your treatment is designed, as you think, to promote dignity. Yet you need not despair for, as common lore has it, there is an alternative strategy. You can commit yourself, even bind yourself by means of sanction, to exercising no control over certain aspects of your daughter's behaviour. Do that and there is no doubt but that she will gain immediately in dignity.

The lesson for the social democratic state is immediatly obvious. If the state is to confer certain material benefits on people, and is yet to preserve their dignity, then it must commit itself to making those benefits available under

---

[28] The notion of essential by-products is introduced in Jon Elster, *Sour Grapes* (Cambridge, Cambridge University Press, 1983), Ch. 3. I elaborate it in 'Satisficing consequentialism', *Proceedings of the Aristotelian Society*, Supp. Vol. 56 (1984), and in Pettit and Brennan, 'Restrictive consequentialism'.

appropriate conditions, and not just at state discretion. The individuals who benefit must be given suitable claims; they must not be left to linger in the rôle of passive beneficiaries.

The claims which are accorded will have to exhibit two features. They will have to be personalized, in the sense that each can make a claim that is not contingent on how the balance of overall claims is best satisfied; otherwise no one enjoys the dignity of being able personally to activate a response. And secondly the claims will have to be privileged, in the sense that they cannot readily be overriden by competing social goals; otherwise no one can be sure of being able to exercise the control associated with the claim.

Personalized and privileged claims constitute rights; or so a number of standard accounts go.[29] The upshot then is that the social democratic state is capable of promoting a goal like equal dignity, so long as the beneficence which it exercises is made available under a strict dispensation of rights. The welfare which it dispenses must not be distributed at any functionary's discretion; it must be removed from the realm of will.[30]

The Responsibility Assumption

The third assumption associated with the social democratic viewpoint is that the state is not just a reliable and respectful agent but the agent which ought to be assigned responsibility for the promotion of equal dignity. I shall try to indicate what needs to be done to vindicate this assumption though, as in the other cases, the argument will be sketched rather than elaborated.

The assumption will be challenged on two fronts: first, by those who think that moral duty does not encompass the promotion of a goal like equal dignity; and secondly, by those who agree that it does but who are unwilling to allow that the state ought to be given special responsibility for the task.

To defend the assumption on the first front, it is necessary to establish the case for a distinctively consequentialist thesis. This is that if there is a certain sort of good that can be promoted, such that the world is the better for its promotion, then someone or other has the duty of furthering that good. Duty is a function of the good and if equal dignity is a good that can be furthered then someone ought to pursue that enterprise.

Short of a wholesale defence of consequentialism, there is little that can be said in support of the thesis.[31] It will have to be sufficient to record that, on the face of it, the thesis is more plausible than the rival deontological claim that the basis of duty is distinct from reference to the good. What can be so compelling about duty, one wants to ask, if the discharge of duty does not produce the goods?

---

[29] For example, the accounts of rights offered by Robert Nozick, *Anarchy, State, and Utopia* and Ronald Dworkin, *Taking Rights Seriously*. See my 'Rights, constraints, and trumps', *Analysis*, 46 (1987).

[30] See my 'Can the welfare state take rights seriously?', in Denis Galligan and Charles Sampford (eds), *Law, Rights and the Welfare State* (London, Croom Helm, 1986), and 'The consequentialist can recognise rights', *Philosophical Quarterly* (forthcoming).

[31] A full defence would seek to establish that consequentialist theories do not resist reflective equilibrium. One strand in the defence is offered by Pettit and Brennan, 'Restrictive consequentialism'.

But our assumption also needs to be defended on a second front. It will be challenged, not just by deontologists, but also by consequentialists who argue that the state should not be given special responsibility for the promotion of equal dignity. Their case is that equal dignity will be better promoted if responsibility for it is not pre-empted by the state but is left in the hands of the community at large.

The defence on this front will have to be mounted on considerations like the following.[32]

1. The promotion of equal dignity is a good such that if different agents try to further it, they are liable to cut across, or undercut, one another's efforts.
2. With such goods, it must be for the best (overall) to have a scheme of coordination assigning special responsibility for their promotion.
3. Responsibility should be assigned in each case to the agent which occupies such a position, or enjoys such power, that he can best promote the good in question.
4. In the case of promoting equal dignity, the state is the obvious agent to assume responsibility: *pouvoir oblige*.

This completes our sketch vindication of the three assumptions that go with the social democratic point of view. I hope that the argument is sufficient to establish that the social democratic point of view deserves a fuller consideration than it has often received in the past. Democratic theories of the state are not the preserve of liberals and it is time that the academic literature began to reflect the fact.

Conclusion

It may be useful in conclusion to try to draw together the main points that we have argued:

1. Liberal democratic theories ask the abstract question of what equally respect-able individuals ought to require of the institutions by which they live, including the state, if their ideal is equal respect. Social democratic theory asks the historically more concrete question of what the state ought to do in the actual world where people are not equally respect-able, if it is given charge of this ideal.
2. The liberal democratic question leads to the view that the state ought to exemplify equal respect, the social democratic question to the view that the state ought to promote it.
3. Liberal democratic theories diverge from one another, so far as they provide different interpretations of what it is for the state to exemplify equal respect. Utilitarian, libertarian, unanimitarian and contractarian theories can be cast as different interpretations of this exemplifying ideal.
4. Social democratic theory is distinguished by a concern for working out the requirements of equal respect-abilty. It is not a body of doctrine so much as

---

[32] The approach mentioned here is more fully elaborated in Philip Pettit and Robert Goodin, 'The possibility of special duties', *Canadian Journal of Philosophy*, 16 (1986). See also Goodin's, *Protecting the Vulnerable* (Chicago, Chicago University Press, 1985).

a policy-making programme and it has been associated with political rather than academic figures.

5. The social democratic approach—like some of the less minimal liberal democratic approaches—makes certain assumptions about the state and these need to be vindicated if it is to have any plausibility.

6. A first assumption is that the sort of powerful state sought by social democrats can be an agent reliable for the pursuit of its assigned ends. This can be vindicated only under psychological assumptions that challenge vulgar Marxists on one side, public-choice enthusiasts on the other.

7. A second assumption is that the state can simultaneously enhance the respect-ability of citizens and be respectful of them. It can, if it institutes a régime under which the services it provides can be claimed as rights.

8. A third and last assumption is that the state is the proper agent to be made responsible for the promotion of equal respect-ability. It is, under the principle for allocating responsibility which we sum up in the phrase: *pouvoir oblige.*

[29]

B.J.Pol.S. 18, 415–443
Printed in Great Britain

Citizenship, Social Citizenship and the Defence of Welfare Provision

DESMOND S. KING and JEREMY WALDRON

This article analyses the normative status of claims to the social rights of citizenship in the light of New Right criticisms of the welfare state. The article assesses whether there is any normative justification for treating welfare provision and citizenship as intrinsically linked. After outlining T. H. Marshall's conception of citizenship the article reviews its status in relation to: traditional arguments about citizenship of the polity; relativist arguments about the embedded place of citizenship within current societies; and, drawing upon Rawlsian analysis, absolutist arguments about what being a member of a modern society implies. Each argument has some strengths and together they indicate the importance of retaining the idea of citizenship at the centre of modern political debates about social and economic arrangements.

From the Second World War until very recently, most Western societies have treated an expanding public sector as the norm. Citizens in these countries have grown used to a consistent expansion in the state's provision of goods and services, in particular goods and services associated with the welfare state like education, health, social security and employment.[1] The 1945 election of the Labour party in Britain is often seen as a watershed in this regard – an emphatic popular endorsement of state planning as a promoter of the collective good through the pursuit of welfare policies and creation of welfare institutions like the National Health Service.[2] It is striking how universal this process has been amongst advanced industrial democracies: in most OECD countries, including the United States, the proportion of national income allocated to social welfare services has

Department of Politics, University of Edinburgh; Jurisprudence and Social Policy Program, School of Law, University of California, Berkeley, respectively. This is a joint work, authorship is listed alphabetically. The authors wish to thank the following for comments upon an earlier draft: Mike Adler, Ruth Adler, Nigel Bowles, Vinit Haksar, Neil MacCormick, Peter Morriss, Kim Scheppele, Janet Siltanen, Albert Weale and participants in the University of Edinburgh's Department of Politics seminar. They are also grateful for the advice and suggestions of Robert Goodin, co-editor of this Journal.

[1] See, for example, Peter Taylor-Gooby, *Public Opinion, Ideology and State Welfare* (London: Routledge & Kegan Paul, 1985). The 1986 British social attitudes survey revealed growing support for the institutions of the welfare state: see Nick Bosanquet, 'Interim Report: Public Spending and the Welfare State', in Roger Jowell, Sharon Witherspoon and Lindsay Brook, eds, *British Social Attitudes: The 1986 Report* (Aldershot: Gower Publishers, 1986). For an alternative view, and criticisms of these opinion polls, see Ralph Harris and Arthur Seldon, *Welfare Without the State: A Quarter-Century of Suppressed Choice* (London: Hobart Paperback No. 26, Institute of Economic Affairs, 1987).

[2] See: John Dryzek and Robert E. Goodin, 'Risk-Sharing and Social Justice: The Motivational Foundations of the Post-War Welfare State', *British Journal of Political Science*, 16 (1986), 1–34; Desmond S. King, *The New Right: Politics, Markets and Citizenship* (London: Macmillan, 1987); and Kenneth O. Morgan, *Labour in Power 1945–1951* (Oxford: Oxford University Press, 1984).

increased steadily (in some instances dramatically) since the late 1940s, frequently absorbing as much as 50 per cent of GDP, and there has been a dramatic expansion in public employment and in the number of citizens receiving their primary income from the state in one form or another.[3]

However, since the mid-1970s this orthodoxy has suffered a serious material and ideological challenge. Materially, the post-1973 economic crisis rapidly undermined any expectation that economic growth would continue to supply the wealth necessary to sustain extensive public provision of welfare services. As a result, most developed countries have had to initiate some control of welfare spending (however modest or unsuccessful), and in many of them 'bringing welfare spending under control' has become a major political imperative. In the United States and Britain particularly, such policies have received ideological support from the major political development of the late 1970s and 1980s, the so-called 'New Right'. The New Right has many forms (both intellectual and political) but the core features of the movement include: a critique of the economics of state interventionism, particularly Keynesianism; an economic and moral critique of the welfare state; and an advocacy of free market mechanisms in all areas of public policy including the meeting of welfare needs in society. New Right theorists and politicians have sought to bring about a reversal in the post-1945 expansion of the public sector, as manifested primarily in the growth of the welfare state.[4]

New Right theorists are troubled by the welfare state for both economic and moral reasons. Economically, the provision of public welfare is thought to erode market incentives, for it provides people with a guaranteed source of income during difficult circumstances, making their search for work (especially for low-paying jobs) less diligent than it would be if such income protection were not available. Further, the welfare state is said to be economically damaging by virtue of its size (for example, crowding out private investment) and by virtue of its negative impact on individual savings as a basis for investment.[5]

In addition, the welfare state has regularly been cited as a source of moral corruption through its effect on the family: it provides support when families break down and therefore encourages their disintegration or encourages some people not to enter into them at all. Some New Right theorists complain that it saps the authority of the male breadwinner and encourages feminism.[6] As well as the

[3] See chapters in Richard Rose, ed., *Public Employment in Western Nations* (Cambridge: Cambridge University Press, 1985).

[4] See, for example: Milton Friedman, *Capitalism and Freedom* (Chicago: University of Chicago Press, 1962); F. A. Hayek, *The Road to Serfdom* (London: Routledge & Kegan Paul, 1944); and Hayek, *The Constitution of Liberty* (London: Routledge & Kegan Paul, 1960).

[5] See David G. Davies, *United States' Taxes and Tax Policy* (Cambridge: Cambridge University Press, 1986) regarding the United States.

[6] See George Gilder, *Poverty and Wealth* (New York: Basic Books, 1981). For a similar, but more effectively developed, thesis see Charles A. Murray, 'The Two Wars Against Poverty: Economic Growth and the Great Society', *The Public Interest*, 69 (1982), 3–16. Murray attributes the drop in husband–wife family units in the United States during the 1960s to the federal anti-poverty programmes associated with the Great Society: during the 1960s, he argues, 'fundamental changes

effect on morals, there is also the effect on values such as liberty. New Right theorists claim that the bureaucracy of welfare institutions reduces individual freedom and enhances state power. Collective provision limits the role of market processes, which are the most powerful guarantors of political liberty and economic prosperity, according to writers like Friedman and Hayek.[7] And, being financed out of taxation, it involves interference with private property and direct coercion of those individual taxpayers who would rather not contribute to 'compulsory charity' in this way.[8]

Despite the influence enjoyed by the New Right challenge (for example, in the public policies of the Thatcher and Reagan administrations), it is striking how little the welfare state has actually been eroded. There have certainly been cuts, and there are disputes about how welfare spending should be measured. In part, the maintenance of high levels of welfare spending reflects the impact of the economic recession: high unemployment has obviously raised the volume of direct income support from the state. But on the whole the main institutions – in Britain, the National Health Service, the education system and the benefit system – remain largely intact, and it is noticeable that politicians (even those on the Right) still feel constrained to assure the electorate that these institutions are 'safe in our hands'; for example, the stance of the Conservative party in the 1983 and 1987 elections. Some commentators argue that this is not just a superficial whim of the electorate; it is an indication of the extent to which welfare provision is now conceived of as a core element of citizenship in Western society.[9]

One way of putting the point is to say that the publicly guaranteed provision of welfare goods and services associated with the post-1945 expansion of the welfare state is no longer seen as a contingency of public policy, as something which might be changed whenever the administration changes its political hue. Instead, collective provision for welfare is associated now with an idea of social citizenship, and is taken to be comparable in status and importance to other aspects of citizenship such as the right to own property and the right to vote. Such a perception implies that if governments try to cut the welfare state, they will confront resistance based upon a belief that people have rights embedded in welfare services which no one ought to tamper with: such welfare 'rights' are integral to the contemporary sense of citizenship – so the argument goes – and therefore cannot simply be abrogated or whittled away at the whim of a particular government.

occurred in the philosophy, administration, and magnitude of social welfare programs for low-income families, and these changes altered – both directly and indirectly – the social risks and rewards, and the financial costs and benefits, of maintaining a husband-wife family' (p. 15).

[7] Friedman, *Capitalism and Freedom*; Hayek, *Road to Serfdom* and *Constitution of Liberty*.

[8] See, for example, Robert Nozick, *Anarchy, State and Utopia* (New York: Basic Books, 1974), Chaps 7-8.

[9] See figures in: King, *New Right*; Desmond S. King, 'The State and the Social Structures of Welfare in Advanced Industrial Democracies', *Theory and Society*, 16 (1987), 841-68; and Ray Robinson, 'Restructuring the Welfare State: An Analysis of Public Expenditure, 1979/80-1984/85', *Journal of Social Policy*, 15 (1986), 1-21.

That this is a widely held opinion cannot be doubted. But in this article we are going to attempt to *evaluate* it. We want to consider whether there is any normative justification for treating welfare provision and citizenship as linked in this way. Such provision should constitute more than a simple safety-net; it refers to the universal provision of education, health, social security and welfare benefits (financed through a system of redistributive taxation), available as attributes of citizenship and not granted as a residual fund to help the least well-off cope with excessive hardship as Hayek and Friedman would accept.

We should perhaps emphasize that there are other defences of the welfare state apart from those that can be developed through the citizenship idea.[10] The focus of the present article does not, of course, imply any disparagement of these other approaches. But it is the citizenship argument with which we are concerned. It is one which has enjoyed considerable prominence recently, in Britain and elsewhere.[11] Moreover, the claim that social provision is an attribute of citizenship is an important and interesting one, and it warrants a more thorough and searching examination, particularly in normative theory, than it has received up till now.

1. T. H. MARSHALL AND SOCIAL CITIZENSHIP

The principal theorist of the 'social citizenship' idea is the British sociologist, T. H. Marshall. In an essay entitled 'Citizenship and Social Class', published originally in 1949, Marshall contended that social provision constituted one of three sets of rights associated with citizenship in modern Britain, the others being civil and political rights.[12] He began by defining citizenship in the following general terms:

Citizenship is a status bestowed on those who are full members of a community. All who possess the status are equal with respect to the rights and duties with which the status is endowed. There is no universal principle that determines what those rights and duties shall be, but societies in which citizenship is a developing institution create an image of an ideal citizenship against which achievement can be measured and towards which aspiration can be directed. The urge forward along the path thus plotted is an urge towards a fuller measure of equality, an enrichment of the stuff of which the status is made and an increase in the number of those on whom the status is bestowed ... Citizenship requires a ... direct sense of community membership based on loyalty to a civilization which is a

[10] Robert E. Goodin, *Reasons for Welfare* (Princeton, NJ: Princeton University Press, forthcoming 1988); Raymond Plant, *Equality, Markets and the State* (London: Fabian Tract no. 494, 1984); and Plant, 'Needs, Agency and Rights' in C. J. G. Sampford and D. J. Galligan, eds, *Law, Rights, and the Welfare State* (London: Croom Helm, 1986).

[11] See, for the general argument, Gosta Esping-Andersen, *Politics Against Markets* (Princeton, NJ: Princeton University Press, 1985) and 'Power and Distributional Regimes', *Politics and Society*, 14 (1985), 223–56; and, for Britain, King, *New Right*, and recent publications of the Fabian Society, for example, Michael Mann, *Socialism Can Survive* (London: Fabian Tract no. 502, 1985).

[12] T. H. Marshall, 'Citizenship and Social Class', *Class, Citizenship and Social Development* (New York: Doubleday, 1964). This essay was first published in 1949.

common possession. It is a loyalty of free men endowed with rights and protected by a common law. Its growth is stimulated both by the struggle to win those rights and by their enjoyment when won.[13]

What are these rights and how have they evolved? In his 1949 essay Marshall differentiated between three layers of citizenship rights and the institutions which supported them. The first layer comprised *civil rights*: that is, those rights concerning individual freedom which were associated with the sphere of 'civil society': 'liberty of the person, freedom of speech, thought and faith, the right to own property and to conclude valid contracts, and the right to justice.'[14] Civil rights are associated principally with the institutions of legal justice, such as the courts; they are rights held by discrete individuals which they may come to law to vindicate. The second layer comprised *political rights*, that is, democratic rights of participation: 'the right to participate in the exercise of political power, as a member of a body invested with political authority or as an elector of the members of such a body.'[15] The institutions of representative democracy (Parliament and the electoral system) are central to the realization and maintenance of these political rights. Thirdly, there are *social rights*. By these, Marshall meant economic and welfare rights, rights to a minimum standard of welfare and income: 'the whole range from the right to a modicum of economic welfare and security to the right to share to the full in the social heritage and to live the life of a civilised being according to the standards prevailing in the society.'[16] Welfare state policies and institutions – the educational system and the social services – are the main expression of this third layer. The idea is that by providing civil rights, society mitigates the impact of force and violence in relations between people. By providing political rights, it ensures that power is not confined to an elite. And by providing minimum standards in these areas the state offsets the vagaries of market processes and corrects the gross inequalities of distribution arising from the market.

Now the first thing to note about these three types of citizenship rights is that they are not rigid or mutually exclusive as categories. Free speech, for example, can be regarded both as a civil right and as a political right. This point has particular importance for some of the items on the social agenda. Take, for instance, the case of education. Education is a facility important both for individual life-chances and for participation in other citizenship activities, such as voting or seeking redress through the courts.[17] This view is consonant with many

---

[13] Marshall, 'Citizenship and Social Class', pp. 84, 92.

[14] Marshall, 'Citizenship and Social Class', p. 71.

[15] Marshall, 'Citizenship and Social Class', p. 72.

[16] Marshall, 'Citizenship and Social Class', p. 72.

[17] As Marshall himself notes, 'education ... is a service of a unique kind' since 'the education of children has a direct bearing on citizenship, and, when the State guarantees that all children shall be educated, it has the requirements and the nature of citizenship definitely in mind. It is trying to stimulate the growth of citizens in the making. The right to education is a genuine social right of citizenship, because the aim of education during childhood is to shape the future adult ... Education is a necessary prerequisite of civil freedom'. Marshall, 'Citizenship and Social Class', pp. 81, 82.

traditional opinions in political theory about citizenship, as we shall show below. Like many citizenship arguments, it establishes a tight reciprocity between the duties individuals owe to the community and the duties the community owes to them. As Marshall notes, 'we have here a personal right combined with a public duty to exercise the right'.[18]

In other words, one and the same good can have several different aspects. In its contribution to a person's own well-being, free education is a social good; in its contribution to her or his political status and capabilities, it is a political right and, indeed, a political duty. And much the same can be said about the other aspects of social provision like health, social security and employment. The fact that Marshall's categories are not rigid should not worry us. Indeed, sometimes it is the very fluidity of the boundaries that provides the best case for the idea of social citizenship. One of the strongest arguments in favour of welfare provision is the empirical one that securing basic social standards does in fact promote the existence and exercise of other citizenship rights. We will explore this argument in section 3.

Consideration of the way in which these various aspects of citizenship have evolved plays an important part in Marshall's argument. In each case the evolution can be considered in two ways: in relation to its content; and in relation to its status as something which is universally enjoyed in a society. For example, when the concept of political citizenship emerged, it was first confined to a minority of the members of the polity: only recently has it been extended to all. Of these two aspects of evolution, it is the second which is of interest to us in this article – the gradual universalization of social provision, to the point where it is available equally to all.

Marshall suggests that the three kinds of citizenship right were originally part and parcel of a single core: 'in early times these three strands were wound into a single thread', in which there was a

fusion of political and civil institutions and rights. But a man's social rights, too, were part of the same amalgam, and derived from the status which also determined the kind of justice he could get and where he could get it, and the way in which he could take part in the administration of the affairs of the community of which he was a member.[19]

However, this earlier notion of citizenship is by no means a direct equivalent of citizenship according to contemporary conceptions. Modern citizenship began in the twelfth century, according to Marshall, but it is the eighteenth, nineteenth and twentieth centuries which are crucial for the transformation of civil, political and social rights successively into universal rights.

Civil rights were established, in Britain, between the Revolution and the first Reform Act. During the eighteenth century the rule of law was established, mainly through the 'work of the courts, both in their daily practice and also in a series of famous cases in some of which they were fighting against parliament in

[18] Marshall, 'Citizenship and Social Class', p. 82.
[19] Marshall, 'Citizenship and Social Class', p. 72.

defence of individual liberty.'[20] There also developed a civil right in the economic sphere, the right to work, that is, the right to economic freedom as a complement to the rule of law, resultant, in no small degree, upon the development of markets. Thus individual freedom, as embodied in civil rights, became a universal feature of citizenship with the emergence and growth of the bourgeoisie. *Political rights* emerged in the nineteenth century, according to Marshall, as the franchise was steadily extended (to some extent as a consequence of working-class pressure for equal citizen rights) and the status of citizenship expanded to include rights of democratic participation. It was not until the present century, however, that political rights were universalized through universal franchise based on the equality of individuals as an attribute of citizenship. Thus by the 1920s in Britain civil and political rights reflected the position each person enjoyed as implicit in the status of citizen. All citizens enjoyed equal rights in civil and political spheres, and these rights were understood to be part and parcel of what it was to be a member of a society like our own.

Social citizenship is largely a twentieth-century phenomenon. Twentieth-century rights to education, health and an assured income are in many ways diametrically opposed to earlier practice in this area. For example, the 1834 Poor Law implemented an exclusionary principle of citizenship, since it

> treated the claims of the poor, not as an integral part of the rights of the citizen, but as an alternative to them — as claims which could be met only if the claimants ceased to be citizens in any true sense of the word. For paupers forfeited in practice the civil right of personal liberty, by internment in the workhouse, and they forfeited by law any political rights they might possess.[21]

Likewise, the Factory Acts initially narrowed the meaning of citizenship by applying to children and women exclusively, though 'by the end of the nineteenth century, such arguments had become obsolete, and the factory code had become one of the pillars of the edifice of social rights.'[22] In the twentieth century these social rights have undergone enormous expansion as state responsibility for education, health, welfare and employment has been increasingly expanded and taken for granted. For Marshall this expanded responsibility constitutes social or welfare rights and thus transforms them into legitimate attributes of citizenship. These developments were stimulated, in part, by growth in money incomes (unequally distributed), the introduction of direct taxation, and mass production or consumerism which fuelled demands for reductions in inequality.[23] Welfare state institutions directly counter market processes by

---

[20] Marshall, 'Citizenship and Social Class', p. 75.

[21] Marshall, 'Citizenship and Social Class', p. 80.

[22] Marshall, 'Citizenship and Social Class', p. 81.

[23] As another scholar argues, 'welfare statism is the twentieth century's response to the demands of citizens — however articulated — for material protection from contingencies that are beyond their privately organized capacity to resist', Kathi V. Friedman, *Legitimation of Social Rights and the Western Welfare State: A Weberian Perspective* (Chapel Hill, NC: University of North Carolina Press, 1981), p. 15.

providing citizens with a minimum income, a basic standard of social services (health and education) and respite against economic uncertainty.[24]

Marshall's account of the development of the rights of citizenship has been the subject of controversy in two ways: there have been disputes about its descriptive plausibility and disputes about its normative claims. The second set of issues are our central concern, and we will deal with them in the sections that follow.[25]

2. IS THERE AN ARGUMENT FOR SOCIAL RIGHTS?

In saying that welfare provision was part and parcel of citizenship in the modern state, Marshall was describing how it had evolved and how it was viewed by the people who enjoyed it. But we think he was also doing more than this: we think he was talking about the way in which welfare provision *ought* to be viewed, and intimating an argument about how it might be defended.

At the minimum, to associate welfare provision with citizenship is to make a proposal about how welfare should be handled in society. For example, as we have seen, it is to endorse the replacement of the Poor Law approach to welfare with provision for need that is given universally, that is provided without supplication or stigma, and that avoids as far as possible the invidious operation of official discretion.[26] But associating it with citizenship is not just a way of making this proposal; it is also a way of defending it. The suggestion may be that

---

[24] See also King, *New Right*, and Julia Parker, *Social Policy and Citizenship* (London: Macmillan, 1975).

[25] With regard to the first set of issues, much of the debate has occurred within stratification studies, where Marshall's essay was 'one of the seminal works which resulted in the reorientation of the whole discussion of the class structure in capitalist societies' according to David Lockwood, 'For T. H. Marshall', *Sociology*, 8 (1974), 363–7. Arguments about citizenship informed Ralf Dahrendorf's *Class and Class Conflict in Industrial Society* (Stanford, Calif.: Stanford University Press, 1957) in which he considers the accuracy of Marshall's claims about the equalizing impact of social rights. The argument here is about empirical accuracy not normative validity. Dahrendorf contends that Marshall's thesis neglects the social distribution of power: though greater equalization through citizenship rights has certainly occurred, it has not resolved the conflicts centred on class. More recently, Giddens considers also the utility of Marshall's claims as a possible refutation of the centrality of class conflict. He argues that citizenship rights cannot be separated from the contradictory forms of modern capitalism, and more specifically, since the rights of citizenship do not extend to the workplace – where class conflict is most persistent according to Giddens – Marshall's thesis is an inadequate account of contemporary Western democracies: see Anthony Giddens, *A Contemporary Critique of Historical Materialism* (London: Macmillan, 1981), pp. 226–9. A more sympathetic treatment of Marshall's arguments is contributed by Turner who argues that the pursuit and establishment of citizenship rights has altered the nature of capitalist society in a fundamental and positive way: Bryan S. Turner, *Citizenship and Capitalism* (London: George Allen & Unwin, 1986).

[26] Such a proposal is advanced by Parker when she observes that, 'the idea of citizenship implies that there should be no stigma attached to the use of public services, either because of popular attitudes condemning dependency or as a result of deterrent administrative procedures or poor standards of provision'. Parker, *Social Policy and Citizenship*, pp. 145–6. In this regard, the provision of education and health services in Britain conforms more closely to the model of citizenship rights than, say, the provision of supplementary benefit. We will examine such distinctions in a little more detail in section 4.

we *ought* to associate welfare with citizenship because our concept of citizenship will be radically impoverished if we do not. Citizenship, on this account, *demands* welfare provision; we cannot have an adequate or attractive notion of citizenship without it.

Is there any justification for this claim? In normative terms, does our concept of citizenship provide us with a reason for continuing to assure health, education, social services and income support to everyone in our society? To put it another way, is there anything in the idea of social citizenship to trouble the theorists of the New Right in the normative arguments that they are making against the welfare state?

One way into these questions is through Marshall's focus upon equality. We have already mentioned that, for Marshall, citizenship seems to be about expanding and enriching society's notion of equality by extending its scope through civil, political and social rights. The development of universal rights of citizenship has pushed forward the meaning of equality by broadening the scope of its application. Marshall stresses that it is not 'absolute equality' he is aiming at nor is it any rigid equality of wealth:

The extension of the social services is not primarily a means of equalizing incomes. In some cases it may, in others it may not. The question is relatively unimportant ... What matters is that there is *a general enrichment of the concrete substance of civilized life, a general reduction of risk and insecurity, an equalization between the more and the less fortunate at all levels* ... Equalization is not so much between classes as between individuals within a population which is now treated for this purpose as though it were one class. Equality of status is more important than equality of income.[27]

To talk about equality in the context of citizenship is to talk about a progressive enlargement and enrichment of people's life chances. Citizenship does this principally by altering existing patterns of social inequality, and making it less likely that extremes can be sustained: 'the preservation of inequalities has been made more difficult by the enrichment of the status of citizenship. There is less room for them and there is more and more likelihood of their being challenged'.[28] But, again, what if someone simply denies that this is an *enrichment* of the notion of equality, or that the value of equality, so enriched, is attractive? Does the notion of citizenship give us any basis for rebuttal?

There are two ways in which it might help. First, we might be able to show that citizenship as it has been traditionally understood is a concept which requires social provision and enriched equality for its effective realization. Or secondly, even if this is not the case, we might be able to show that a new concept of citizenship which *does* include a guarantee of social provision is nevertheless more attractive as an ideal than one which does not. The first line of argument takes us from a familiar value to one that is in dispute, asserting an empirical connection between welfare provision and the possibility of effective participation by everyone as a citizen. The second line of argument challenges us directly

[27] Marshall, 'Citizenship and Social Class', pp. 102–3, our emphasis.
[28] Marshall, 'Citizenship and Social Class', p. 117.

to adopt the disputed conception of citizenship as our modern social ideal. Instead of asserting an empirical connection between welfare and citizenship, it challenges us to adopt a new account of citizenship of which the guarantee of welfare rights is partly constitutive.[29]

We will explore the first line of argument in section 3. But most often it seems to be the second line of argument that Marshall is hinting at. His thesis seems to be that social rights derive from a widely shared notion of ideal citizenship within a given society – that is, there is a historically based public conviction in the appropriateness of social welfare as a characteristic of the status of equal citizenship. Certainly his evolutionary argument seems to advance such a position. He contends that 'societies in which citizenship is a developing institution create an image of an ideal citizenship against which the achievement can be measured and towards which aspiration can be directed'.[30] The image of ideal citizenship emerges in the struggle for rights. Given that this process has involved the extension of citizenship rights to more and more members of society – their universal application – through processes of conflict and demand (for example, working-class pressure for universal suffrage), then it would seem that at least those to whom those rights have historically been denied share a sense of the sort of citizenship they aspire to enjoy. It would not be remarkable if such a conception of the rights of citizenship expanded historically from civil through political to social rights as Marshall depicts.[31] Indeed, citizenship remains a dynamic process likely to expand into other areas in the future.

The limitation of such a view is that it requires us to impose some sort of teleology or purpose on what may be in fact a purely accidental and contingent process of evolution. It also makes social provision vulnerable to the course that social evolution happens to take. What if society lurches away from the welfare state, under the impact of New Right policies and ideologies? Does that show that the ideal of citizenship now no longer involves social rights? Or does it show that, as a society, we have abandoned this idea of citizenship? And how might we decide between these interpretations?

In sections 4 and 5, we explore two different ways in which social citizenship might be vindicated as an ideal. One of the arguments is relative to the actual course of development in our society, while the other purports to be more absolute. In section 4, we argue that – whether we like it or not – Marshall's idea of social citizenship captures something that has as a matter of fact become embedded in the expectations of ordinary people, and that it is not now something which can easily be done away with without grave disruption to people's lives. In section 5, we develop a Rawlsian argument about what it is to be a *member* of a modern society. Whatever course social development has taken so far, it cannot claim to treat its citizens equally as members unless it provides socio-

---

[29] We are grateful to Robert Goodin for drawing this distinction to our attention. See Goodin's *Reasons for Welfare*, Chap. 4 on 'Community'.

[30] Marshall, 'Citizenship and Social Class', p. 84.

[31] This is the view which Giddens appears to ascribe to Marshall's analysis. See Anthony Giddens's *Profiles and Critiques in Social Theory* (London: Macmillan, 1982).

economic structures that they could all have agreed to live under. We argue that a society without welfare provision would not be a structure that satisfied this condition.

But before we explore these arguments for the ideal of social citizenship, let us see how far we can get with the notion of citizenship as it has been traditionally understood.

3. CITIZENSHIP AND POLITICAL PARTICIPATION

Marshall, it will be remembered, distinguished between the political rights and the social rights associated with citizenship. But we know that these are not rigid categories, and an obvious starting point for our inquiry is to ask whether there is any deep or important connection between the two.

The most familiar notion of political citizenship that we have is of the citizen as a participator particularly a participator in republican or democratic politics. In classical political thought, a citizen was a full member of a city, a *polis*, or a republic. He was not merely subject to its laws and under its protection – these were often characteristics of non-citizens as well (resident aliens, for example). His citizenship consisted in the fact that he could hold public office, that he could join in the determination of the laws and (as a juror) in their application, and that he could be called upon to discharge patriotic duties such as the defence of his polity against external attack. The classic definition was that of Aristotle. 'A citizen is one who has a share in both ruling and being ruled. Deliberative or judicial, we deem him to be a citizen of that state.'[32] The idea of citizenship is connected, then, with the view that political power should be exercised, not by a specialist elite who have made politics their vocation, but by ordinary members of the polity, acting either together or in rotation. Citizenship does not necessarily imply democracy: roughly, a democracy is a republic in which all adult men and women are citizens. In ancient Athens slaves and women were excluded from citizenship, and in the ideal polity that Aristotle proposed, workers and artisans would be excluded as well. In Britain (to the extent that we have ever had a genuine notion of the citizen, as opposed to the subject) citizenship was restricted until the late nineteenth century to men, and to men who held more than a specified amount of property. But citizenship in Britain is now universal: every adult participates in ruling to the extent that each can vote for representative legislators in elections, and any adult may be called to serve on a jury.

It may be thought that this idea of citizenship is *simply* a matter of political rights and that no conclusions can be drawn about the social or economic position that the citizen, as such, ought to be in. But, in fact, the tradition of Western political thought about political citizenship completely contradicts this. Almost all the great theorists of citizenship Aristotle, Cicero, Machiavelli, Burke, de

---

[32] Aristotle, *Politics*, trans. T. A. Sinclair (Harmondsworth, Middx: Penguin Books, 1962), Bk III, Chaps 1, 13.

Tocqueville, Mill and, in the twentieth century, Hannah Arendt – have believed that in order to be a citizen of a *polis*, in order to be able to participate fully in public life, one needed to be in a certain socio-economic position. Or they certainly believed that a *well-ordered* city or republic would be one in which political participants were in a certain socio-economic position. People, it was said, could not act as citizens at all, or could not be expected to act well in the political sphere and to make adequate decisions, unless some attention was paid to matters of their wealth, their well-being and their social and economic status.

Two things have always been thought particularly important in this connection: the absence of great inequality, and the possession by all of some modicum of wealth (for example, a property qualification). We want to discuss them both.

Among theorists of citizenship, there has always been a consensus that some sort of rough equality among citizens is desirable. We find this in the Greek thinkers. While Plato did not develop a theory of citizenship in *The Republic*, he did stress there the danger of the struggle between rich and poor as a source of political instability, and in his later and less Utopian work, *The Laws*, he suggested that no citizen should be permitted to own an amount of wealth above a norm set at a level five times greater than the property of the poorest citizen.[33] Aristotle agreed that extremes of riches and poverty were likely to be a destabilizing factor, though he shied away from the imposition of any egalitarian norm.[34]

In later political thought, Machiavelli argued in the *Discourses*, that political solidarity was greatest among those who shared a reasonably austere style of life (the image was Sparta), and he suggested that republican institutions could survive in a territory only if the richer members of the gentry were eliminated.[35] Rousseau, too, insisted that extreme inequality was dangerous: it was the cause 'of mutual hatred among the citizens, of indifference to the common cause, of the corruption of the people, and of the weakening of all the springs of government'.[36]

We are not citing these writers because we think they are sages to whose authority we should submit on matters of citizenship; their works are not, as it were, sacred texts. But there is a long tradition of thinking about citizenship, and in our thought about modern institutions and practices we should take advantage of whatever insights and arguments they offer. The theme linking inequality and instability is an important one: if those who are radically unequal share in the exercise of political authority and the determination of the laws, there will be a constant and understandable tendency for one group of citizens to challenge the existing distribution of property, for another group of citizens to defend that distribution, and for both the challenge and the defence to be fired up by con-

[33] Plato, *The Republic*, trans. Desmond Lee (Harmondsworth, Middx: Penguin Books, 1974) and *The Laws*, trans. T. J. Sound (Harmondsworth, Middx: Penguin Books, 1980).

[34] Aristotle, *Politics*, Bk II, Chap. 7.

[35] N. Machiavelli, *The Discourses* (Harmondsworth, Middx: Penguin Books, 1970).

[36] J. J. Rousseau, *Discourse on Political Economy*, trans. and ed. G. D. H. Cole (London: Dent, 1966), p. 134.

siderations of intense personal advantage as well as, and perhaps at the expense of, whatever sense of justice there is on either side. In modern terms, reductions in inequality may enhance social integration and therefore promote stability.

Put more positively, the suggestion may be that there is a need for a certain spirit of fraternity to exist among citizens; they must regard one another as friends and work on a basis of goodwill and mutual understanding. That goodwill and understanding are required if civic politics is to be undertaken in good faith, and if debate and disagreement are to be possible without suspicion and paranoia creeping in. But that sort of solidarity and mutual trust may depend upon rough equality as well as on a sense of community and belonging, for the more inequality there is, the more cleavages there are likely to be in things like consumption patterns and life-style, and in a sense the less comprehensible citizens are likely to be to one another. (It is partly these ideas that are being appealed to, when concern is voiced about 'two nations' in British society.)

Besides stability and solidarity, other arguments for equality in the civic tradition have focused on the need for citizens to be economically independent of one another; as Rousseau put it, no one must be rich enough to be able to purchase the dependence of another, and none poor enough to be bought in that way. The argument rests on the premise that a citizen should be one who is in a position to bring his or her *own* judgement to public issues, rather than one who responds as a member of a faction or retinue or as a mere mouthpiece for another. As independent individuals, citizens can have some hope of reaching agreement on the common good; and no citizen would ever be interested in purchasing the vote or opinion of another unless he or she wanted to promote some sectional or peculiar interest of his or her own. There are, therefore, good civic reasons for ensuring, on the one hand, that no one is in a position to do this, and, on the other, that no one is so economically vulnerable that he or she would be tempted to sell his or her civic obligations for the food and shelter he or she needs to live. These concerns have been amplified in modern political theory, with an awareness of how easily the opinions, preferences and perceived interests of the poorer groups can be manipulated by those who have economic power over them – those with whom they must come to terms if they are to secure a living.[37]

So far we have presented this in terms of an attack on inequality. It does not follow that citizens should be rigidly equal in their wealth and income; these are arguments against extremes of inequality, arguments for narrowing the range between rich and poor, not arguments for making everyone the same or levelling all differences. Moreover, though extreme inequality undermines civic life *qua* inequality, because of the lack of fraternity between rich and poor, it also corrupts the citizens at either end of the social scale. Luxury and wealth corrupt the rich – that was Machiavelli's concern about the gentry. And poverty and vulnerability corrupt the poor. Now, a defence of welfare provision in terms of citizenship will naturally focus mainly on this last concern; the predicament of poverty,

[37] See Steven Lukes, *Power: A Radical View* (London: Macmillan, 1974) and Herbert Marcuse, *One-Dimensional Man* (London: Sphere, 1964).

and the insistence, by almost every writer in this tradition, that those who are poor cannot be citizens, that, in Aristotle's words, 'you could no more make a city out of paupers than out of slaves'.[38]

The view that the poor cannot be citizens is based in part on the way in which desperate need is conceived to interfere with the processes of reflection and deliberation that civic politics requires. It is trite to say that hunger is something of a distraction so far as politics is concerned. Perhaps it is more telling to reflect that people who are completely unsure about food and shelter in the coming days for themselves and their families will be worried sick and, as it were, understandably obsessed with this issue all the time, in a way which leaves little room, very little mental space, for any general and long-term reflection on issues that go very far beyond their present predicament. Similar concerns were voiced by the English Idealists (T. H. Green and others) when they argued that political participants could not develop into moral citizens, capable of contributing to the common good, if they were absorbed all the time by the pressure of material need.

Now, of course, we should take care not to exaggerate the point. We do not need to agree with Hegel that such a situation is one of 'savagery and unfreedom', nor do we need to go as far as Hobbes who suggests that the drive for elementary survival is psychologically irresistible and simply short-circuits all the apparatus of rational deliberation and consent on which political structures depend. We do not need to agree even with Hannah Arendt that the domination of politics by questions of need signals the entrance of violence and terror into the political realm. But there is something to Arendt's conviction that civic politics in a republic cannot be expected to survive for very long if there is constant clamouring for bread and constant demands for 'action now, not words' to meet the predicaments of those who may perish while the politicians talk. To clamour for 'action now, not words' to meet the social problem is, in effect, to dismiss as instantly irrelevant any articulate consideration of the means whereby the social problem may be addressed and any reflective discussion of the way in which those means might fit with the other goals and priorities of the republic. It is, in other words, to dismiss as irrelevant politics as the civic tradition understands it. Need, then, and the urgency of the demands that it generates, can radically undermine the possibility of civic politics and distort the contribution that an individual participator can make.

Another way of putting this is to note that Plato and Aristotle more or less took it for granted that the poverty of the masses, if given a political voice, would drive them to rapacious greed rather than to a genuine concern for justice. The hidden assumption of that view is, not that the masses are inherently depraved, but that poverty itself blocks and interferes with the articulate and deliberative reflection that a genuine concern for justice necessarily involves. Those who are in desperate need cannot be expected to take time to reflect on the issue of what resources they are justly entitled to; they are too taken up with the business of literally getting a living to concern themselves with that. But if articulate reflec-

[38] Aristotle, *Politics*, Bk III, Chap. 13.

tion about justice is, as Aristotle believed, the essence of political activity, need must somehow be banished from the forum before political activity can take place.

The point is one that can be taken conservatively or liberally. At the very least, it seems to imply that hungry people must not be let loose in the political forum, for their needs will impel them to make demands that subvert and short-circuit the leisurely course of citizens' deliberations. This implies that citizenship should be the privilege of those who are economically secure. But that may not be enough to meet the concern, for, as Arendt quite rightly points out, the compassion which desperate need kindles in others can often be as violent and anti-political in character as the original needs themselves. This sometimes leads her to the odd suggestion that citizens must steel themselves to resist the siren charms of compassion, and that they must blind themselves to any concern with the economic predicament of those languishing in poverty outside the doors of the assembly. Politics, she sometimes claims, must not concern itself with the life process. But that is fatuous, first, because people cannot always succeed in distancing themselves in that way, and secondly, because it implies that citizens should be unconcerned with the conditions that make their civic life possible. A more sensible and liberal solution is to say that the removal of need *from society* is one of the great and urgent issues of civic life, for as long as it remains, whether the poor are admitted to citizenship or not, there is always the danger that – directly or relayed through compassion – the clamour for bread *now* will subvert the processes of political debate.

Apart from the threat posed by need itself, there is also concern amongst civic theorists about the sort of life the poorest members of society are likely to lead. Aristotle wrote that 'the best state will not make the labourer a citizen',[39] and Plato spoke in *The Republic* of the 'stunted natures' of the working classes – 'their minds being as cramped and crushed by their mechanical lives as their bodies are deformed by manual trades'.[40] In ancient thought the concern was that the long hours of work necessary to secure a living for those who had no independent means would not leave them time or leisure to acquaint themselves with and deliberate upon the issues that citizens ought to be addressing. In modern political thought, this has combined with concern about the effects of the division of labour and the way that it contracts a person's mind and strength to the performance of just one task.[41]

---

[39] Aristotle, *Politics*, Bk III, Chap. 5.

[40] Plato, *The Republic*, Bk VI, 495e.

[41] As de Tocqueville puts it, once the workman becomes habituated to the concerns of, say, his particular place on the assembly line, 'he no longer belongs to himself, but to the calling which he has chosen ... In proportion as the principle of the division of labour is more extensively applied, the workman becomes more weak, more narrow-minded, and more dependent'; Alexis de Tocqueville *Democracy in America*, ed. J. P. Mayer and Max Lerner (New York, Harper & Row, 1970), Bk II, Chap. 20. This seems to mean then that the workman lacks the necessary qualities for citizenship: an open and broad mind, an independent point of view, and sufficient experience of the world beyond his own hovel or workshop to allow him to address himself intelligently to the great and general issues of politics.

Inevitably, these lines of thought direct the civic tradition towards the idea of a property franchise. The property-owner is independent of others, and he or she can hold independent views. Unlike the propertyless members of the proletariat, he or she does not have to come to terms with and submit himself or herself to the members of another class in order to secure a living. He or she can live off his or her own resources or the income which they generate.[42] To get a living he or she does not have to work long hours and preoccupy himself or herself exclusively with one task; his or her independent income gives the time and leisure to reflect on broader political issues.

As well as these considerations, there are several other arguments for restricting the class of citizens to property-holders. One is the narrow, pragmatic view favoured by Locke, that the tasks of the citizen in the modern state may not necessarily involve much more than periodic consent to taxation; and consent to taxation is morally required only from those on whom the burden of taxation falls. But Locke had an impoverished notion of citizenship. More interesting are the arguments of Edmund Burke, that only property-holders have something solid and permanently at stake in the commonwealth, or (if one is unconvinced by that argument, thinking perhaps that *everyone* has something solid at stake in the commonwealth, namely their lives and well-being), only property-holders can be expected to have a proper sense of caution, prudence, responsibility and permanence in their thought and action in public affairs.[43]

The theme of the ethical importance of property-owning is also taken up by Hegel in the *Philosophy of Right*. Owning property, he said, allows the individual's will to transcend and supersede 'the pure subjectivity of personality'.[44] People have all sorts of schemes and good ideas whizzing about in their heads, constantly changing and replacing one another. But once they have property to work on, the objects themselves start to register and embody the effects of their schemes and purposes in a more or less inerasable form, and so they have to start taking the business of settling upon some particular purpose or project seriously; you cannot always be changing your mind once you are working on external objects, for you will soon learn that the whimsicality of subjective thinking can wreck and undermine everything when it is applied in the real

[42] As John Stuart Mill puts it: 'those whose bread is already secured, and who desire no favours from men in power, or from bodies of men, or from the public, have nothing to fear from the open avowal of opinions'. *On Liberty* (London: Dent, 1972), Chap. 2, para. 19.

[43] 'We receive, we hold, we transmit our government and our privileges, in the same manner as we enjoy and transmit our property', Burke claimed, as an inheritance from the past and a responsibility for the future (Edmund Burke, *Reflections on the French Revolution* (Harmondsworth, Middx: Penguin Books, 1969), p. 120). He insisted therefore that 'by the spirit of philosophic analogy', we should conclude that the skills which are developed in those who are used to handling landed property are the very skills which we should want the citizen to exercise. These are skills which are unavailable to the common masses, who 'immersed in hopeless poverty, could regard all property ... with no other eye than that of envy. Nothing lasting, and therefore in human life nothing useful, could be expected from such men' (Burke, *Reflections*, p. 134).

[44] G. W. Hegel, *The Philosophy of Right*, ed. T. M. Knox (Oxford: Oxford University Press, 1967), para. 4.

world. Along Burkean lines, then, there is an emphasis on a sense of permanence, a sense of responsibility, and a stable sense of purpose which property-owners can be expected to have, and which those who are propertyless are likely to lack.

Enough has been said, we hope, to indicate that the traditional notion of citizenship is not independent of considerations of social and economic concerns. Everyone in the civic republican tradition of Western political thought – that is, everyone who has ever thought seriously about citizenship in a political sense – has reached certain conclusions about what the economic situation of the citizen ought to be. But one may still think that we are miles away from social citizenship in Marshall's sense. Indeed, if anything we seem to be going in the opposite direction; instead of just taking welfare rights away from the poor, the tendency of the civic tradition seems to be that we should take political rights away from them too!

The interesting thing, though, is that each of the arguments we have been considering can be pushed in either of two directions. On the one hand, as we have seen they can be used as arguments for restricting citizenship to those who happen to be in a certain socio-economic position – those who own property, those of independent means, or those who are economically secure in some other sense. But on the other hand, they can be used as a basis for exactly the opposite conclusion: if we are going to have universal citizenship, in a political sense, for our society, then we should do it properly and see to it that *everyone* is put in the socio-economic position that we have reason to believe citizens ought to be in. In other words, if we take the idea of universal suffrage seriously, then we should not be content simply to give everybody a vote; we should set about the task of giving them the economic security, which, on the arguments we have been considering, is the necessary precondition for good citizenship.

It is true that the arguments we have been considering are not in themselves arguments for universal suffrage. In the modern democratic age, we think we have independent arguments for that: ethical ideas about equal respect; utilitarian ideas about the necessity to get governments to promote the general interest; Aristotlean ideas about participation being part of human nature, not just the nature of a few; arguments about what political obligation presupposes; and so on. Our thesis is a conditional one. *If* we accept any of these independent arguments for universal suffrage, *then*, taking seriously the arguments we have been outlining about fraternity, economic independence and security, we will have powerful reasons for associating political citizenship with at least some of the welfare rights that Marshall spoke about when he referred to citizenship in a social sense.

4. BELONGING TO OUR SOCIETY

So far we have explored the connections that there might be between what Marshall calls political citizenship and what he calls social citizenship. The other arguments we want to discuss appeal, however, to a broader notion of citizenship than this. Often when we say 'X is a citizen of the United Kingdom', what we mean is that he or she is a fully-fledged *member* of this community, entitled to live here and make a life here. We may not be implying any theory about political participation; we may be saying, rather, that this is where he or she belongs. What is the normative force of this idea? Is there anything in the concept of membership or belonging that lends support to Marshall's idea of social citizenship?

Let us start modestly with a discussion of what it is to belong to a society *like our own*. Then in section 5, we will consider whether any normative argument can be drawn out of the concept of belonging itself, quite apart from the history of the particular community with which it is associated. The argument we want to consider in this section goes roughly like this.

Over the last fifty years in Britain, we have taken it upon ourselves collectively to provide for much of the basic welfare of the members of society. Over that period, people who live here have become familiar with that provision: they are familiar with the way welfare is provided and they are familiar with the way it is paid for, out of taxation. Both taxpayers and potential recipients have taken all this on board, and organized their expectations, and the way they run their lives, accordingly. Of course, there is disagreement at the margins: the precise array of goods and services that are on offer, and about the precise extent and incidence of taxation. But the broad idea that this is what our society does for its members and this is how, has caught on, and is used as a primary point of reference for the way people organize their lives. To launch an attack, then, on *the very idea* of welfare provision, in the way that some New Right thinkers suggest, would be to challenge the way people have grown accustomed to think about themselves and the planning of their lives. For that reason, it is to attack their basic sense of what it is to live here, to make a life here, to belong here. It is, in that way, to attack their sense of citizenship.

Notice a few things about this argument. It does not proceed, as the previous argument did, from an antecedent notion of citizenship to the demand that there should be welfare provision. Instead it proceeds from the contingent fact that welfare guarantees have been established in this society (for whatever reason) to the claim that they are now part of what we understand by citizenship. The suggestion is that what it is to be a member is not something fixed in stone for all time, but is expandable, as new ways develop in which the state can offer various benefits that accrue from collective organization, and in which members can participate in those arrangements to make benefits available to each other.

Secondly, the concept of citizenship here is somewhat broader than that used in the previous discussion. Now it means not only political participation, but all aspects of what it is to be a *member* of a society. Many political scientists argue that political participation is not what people think is most important about their lives (though some regret that this is so). The present argument is realistic, then, in focusing on a sense of citizenship which connects more comprehensively with people's sense of their social selves, and of the organization of their lives.

The third thing to note is that, in so far as it has any normative force, this argument is primarily a conservative one, with a small 'c' (and we shall have to consider shortly whether it is not *too* conservative). According to this conservative approach, the reasons for keeping welfare guarantees in existence once they have become established are not confined to the reasons there were for establishing them in the first place. Once a certain form of provision is established, people build their expectations around it, in a way that they would not build their expectations around a mere demand that welfare provision *ought* to be established. But when people do start building their expectations, the fact of establishment takes on a moral significance of its own.

The point can be put as one about security. When Jeremy Bentham wrote about security as one of the ends of law, he said that 'security consists in receiving no check, no shock, no derangement to the expectation founded on the laws, of enjoying such and such a portion of good: the legislator owes the greatest respect to this expectation which he has himself produced'.[45] Security of expectation, he argued, is the basis of people's ability to plan their lives: 'It is hence that we have the power of forming a general plan of conduct; it is hence that the successive instants which compose the duration of life are not like isolated and independent points, but become continuous parts of a whole'.[46] Similar points have been made in the New Right context itself by F. A. Hayek and others, stressing the need for stable and predictable laws.[47]

As Bentham stated it, the point was mainly about property law. Though there are good utilitarian reasons for redistributing property (utilitarianism favours equality on the basis of the law of diminishing marginal utility of resources), there are also powerful utilitarian reasons for resisting redistribution on the ground of security of expectations. Bentham believed it was possible to calculate in advance that the property-owner who suffers a shock to his or her expectations and those who are frightened or made anxious by the example of what is happening to him or her, will suffer more, directly and indirectly, than the beneficiaries of redistribution could possibly gain, even taking into account diminishing marginal utility. But everything that Bentham says about property expectations can be applied to welfare expectations, once they too have become established. Indeed, once they are established there is as much of a case for regarding them as part of the overall property scheme as there is for regarding, say, home-ownership in this way. In each case, someone has a recognized legal claim over certain of the resources available in society, and that claim forms the basis of his or her expectations and his or her ability to plan his or her life. (This is why a number of American writers have argued, for example, that welfare entitlements should be given protection under the Fifth Amendment to the US Constitution, which prohibits the taking of private property for public use without just compensation.)

Of course, many welfare benefits are awarded on a discretionary basis and this

[45] Jeremy Bentham, *The Theory of Legislation*, ed. C. K. Ogden (London: Routledge & Kegan Paul, 1931), p. 113.

[46] Bentham, *Theory of Legislation*, p. 111.

[47] See F. A. Hayek, *Law, Legislation and Liberty* (London: Routledge & Kegan Paul, 1973, 1976 and 1979), 3 vols.

raises issues about whether it is possible to describe them strictly speaking as
rights. Though Marshall uses the terminology of rights, there is not space to
consider here in any detail the issue of whether welfare provision is a matter of
rights or even whether the idea of welfare rights makes sense. That is a subject
for another paper.[48] Our point is about the morality of discontinuing or dis-
mantling welfare provision (however this is described in the terminology of
meta-ethics). Some welfare benefits are in fact distributed as a matter of legal
right (for example, education and child benefits) but even those that are discretionary are still capable of giving rise to strong expectations amongst the
members of a community. In other words, the fact that some aspects of social
welfare are discretionary does not prevent people from forming expectations
about it, and organizing their lives in often quite important ways on the basis of
those expectations. Though people know that there is discretion in the award of
these payments, still they expect that discretion to be exercised in their favour, at
least if they become a clearly needy case, and they will be shocked, taken aback
and outraged if it is not. That is the key to our argument.

To violate these expectations is not merely to disappoint people; it is also to
radically disrupt their personal planning. In particular, there is one very important aspect of the way people run their lives which is bound up with the integrity
of their social security expectations. Social security expectations radically affect
the risks people think they can take in making their decisions. We have in mind
here things like forming and breaking marital or quasi-marital relationships,
conceiving children, moving away from close-knit communities, employment
decisions, taking certain attitudes to one's employment on the shop floor, starting a small business, opting for higher education and so on, across a wide array
of areas. In all these areas, people are taking chances, entering into gambles if
you like, on certain assumptions and against the background of certain conditions. Now attitudes to social risk are crucial in establishing social identity,
and beliefs about welfare provision are crucial to that. My sense of what it is to
be a member of this community is going to be centrally linked to my awareness
of the conditions under which I am to think about making a life for myself in this
community and taking the various risks that that involves.

It is clear that people are willing to take much greater risks when they know
that there is a safety net – a limit to the catastrophic losses that they may incur.
They can say to themselves, 'I will go into this new relationship, or I will take the
risk of university education rather than a secure school-leaver's job, or I will
start this new business, knowing that if things work out badly at least I will not
starve.' We shou|I stress too that many of these risks are long-term, and the will-
ingness to undert|ke them is based therefore on long-run expectations. We can
see then immediately the force of the argument that would say it is wrong or
unfair to, as it were, change the terms of the gamble – by abolishing the welfare
safety net – half-way through.

[48] Some of these points are discussed in T. H. Marshall, *The Right to Welfare* (London: Heine-
mann, 1981), pp. 83–4. For the notion of a *right* to welfare, see Jeremy Waldron, *Nonsense Upon
Stilts: Bentham, Burke and Marx on the Rights of Man* (London: Methuen, 1987), pp. 156–60.

Some New Right theorists have seized on this aspect of welfare provision as the very thing they are objecting to: welfare provision, they say, encourages people to run irresponsible risks, so that people become less prudent in their decisions about families, industrial action, education and so on. As we mentioned at the beginning of this article, they claim that the mitigation of risk undermines market discipline and other forms of discipline in the society. We do not want to get into that argument except to say attitudes towards risk in *any* society are going to be relative to institutional expectations; and so the New Right view presupposes already that there is some other good argument for choosing markets-without-safety nets as the baseline in terms of which personal responsibility is to be assessed. We should say, too, that there are arguments on the other side – particularly feminist and modernist (as well as economic) arguments – for increasing mobility and choice in modern society for everyone in it. Mitigating the risks of choice and mobility is one way of doing this.

But eventually we have to come back to the point about conservatism. Suppose the New Right theorists are even half right, and we do suffer harm as a society in terms of unemployment and erosion of incentives – because this social security is on offer. Is it our argument that no expectations can *ever* be overturned no matter how socially harmful they are?

The question is a good one, and the argument we have put forward should not be regarded as absolute. There are all sorts of traditional privileges in society, which are the centre of people's established expectations, but which nevertheless are socially harmful and ought to be abolished. For example, one of the issues at stake in the American Civil War was not whether slavery was wrong but whether it was right to violate all the expectations and life-plans that had become bound up with this (admittedly undesirable) institution. The danger is that people can organize their lives around harmful systems as well as good ones; and then the force of a conservative argument would be to perpetuate the evil. Indeed, if this had been accepted as a general argument in 1945 social provision in its modern form might never have been established.

The force of this objection, however, should not be exaggerated in the present context. It is important in the case of social citizenship that we are talking, not about an institution like slavery, but about benefits and privileges that are universal that is part of the significance of drawing attention to their status as aspects of 'citizenship'. Since this is so, we need to be quite clear about what is being said when it is alleged they are socially harmful. Is it the case that *everybody* would be better off if welfare benefits were withdrawn, if the risks people run were not socially underwritten, and if unmitigated market discipline were allowed to operate? Or is it merely that *some* would be better off and their gains would outweigh others' losses? We may be dealing here with a clash between the common good and the greatest good, familiar to all involved in the modern discussion of utilitarianism. The fact that a conservative argument protects a universal entitlement in the face of aggregate social utility is hardly a devastating objection, unless more is said.

Secondly, a conservative argument does not imply absolute and slavish adherence to the expectations of the past. It implies rather that if one wants to make changes in the basis of people's expectations, one must do so slowly, over decades or even generations, rather than (say) in the space of one parliament. Otherwise one is not sufficiently respecting the people one is dealing with — the people who have to live their lives in the environment one is manipulating — and the need that they have to get a settled sense of the basis on which they can make their plans and choices.

Thirdly, it should be noted that, though the objection is an important one, it does nothing to diminish the *concern* which is at the basis of our argument: it does not deny that people do form expectations, and that their lives may be disrupted and disoriented if these are shattered, by even well-intentioned reform. The present argument is not a cast-iron defence of welfare provision. But it uses the notions of citizenship, membership and belonging — as they relate to our society – to sound a serious note of caution about any attempt to roll back the welfare state. The virtue of the social citizenship argument, or this interpretation, is to draw attention to certain costs, which might otherwise be underestimated, attendant upon any such anti-welfare initiative. That cost is not merely the material loss to the people concerned: it is also the disruption of a whole array of plans and decisions about how to organize their lives, and therefore a loss of people's social sense of themselves as members of this community, living and choosing within its social structures. We must bear in mind that the argument to be made here is not necessarily an argument for a massive welfare state or a welfare state expanding inexorably toward socialism. The argument we are making is for public provision of a minimum level of welfare as a universal entitlement, defining a threshold below which people will not be allowed to fall without diminishing their sense and their capacities of citizenship. That is something one ought to be very wary about disrupting, for it is most unlikely that the alienation, disappointment and disorientation that results would have no effects on other aspects of social action and social integration. If the idea of citizenship can be associated with that of membership, then we can say what is disrupted is people's whole sense of what it is to be a citizen in Britain.

5. MEMBERSHIP IN GENERAL

The argument we have just made is a relative one: the set of welfare provision that has been established in Britain helps to constitute citizens' sense of what it is to be a member of this society. Some writers however have taken the citizenship–membership–welfare link even further, and argued that provision for welfare is not just an incident of particular conceptions of community and membership in particular countries, but partly constitutive of *the very concept* of community and membership. If there is any force to this argument, then it provides a universal rather than a merely relative case for welfare based on citizenship. Though some of Marshall's arguments seem oriented towards the relative approach – this is where *we* have got to in the evolution of citizenship – some of his arguments, as we have seen, seem to imply that a more absolute case can be made: that there is, in some sense, an ideal of social citizenship towards which the evolution of modern citizenship is taking us.

To make this case, it is not sufficient to establish merely that welfare provision is, in fact, a characteristic of all modern societies. In Humean terms, the 'constant conjunction' of citizenship and welfare in the modern world does not establish that one is *implied* by the other. It may be mere coincidence; or it may be that all societies have accepted other arguments for welfare provision that have nothing to do with citizenship. (We did not want to say that the arguments we are considering are the only arguments for welfare.) Moreover, we should remember that the New Right proposal, that universal practice should be altered in this regard, is one which is also made in all modern societies. One does not have to be a firm believer in the fact/value gap to see that a normative argument for resisting that proposal cannot simply be inferred from the very state of affairs that New Right critics are proposing to challenge.

Nor are we likely to get very far with purely conceptual or linguistic analysis of ideas like 'citizenship', 'membership' and 'community'. We can stare at the words for as long as we like, but the dictionary will not do our moral thinking for us. Anyone who thinks that these terms can be linked *definitionally* to the pursuit of certain ends, such as the provision of welfare, needs to bear in mind Max Weber's dictum that 'the state cannot be defined in terms of its end. There is scarcely any task that some political association has not taken in hand'.[49] Equally one might say with Weber that there is no task that has not sometime been neglected by some political association or community. Political societies have neglected welfare provision in the past, and there are proposals from people on the Right that they should neglect welfare provision in the future. One can make the move of insisting that such societies are not really entitled to be called '*communities*' in some defined sense; but that is simply rhetoric and happy talk, and begs the morally much more important question of why people should be interested in the application of *that* definition, rather than some other.

In a recent book, *Spheres of Justice*, Michael Walzer has suggested that 'every political community is in principle a "welfare state"',[50] and insisted that the very idea of a community connotes some distribution according to need: 'Every political community must attend to the needs of its members as they collectively understand those needs; ... the goods that are distributed must be distributed in proportion to need; and that distribution must recognize and uphold the underlying equality of membership.'[51] If Walzer is right about this, then citizenship in the sense of membership has a direct implication of welfare provision. Unfortunately, his argument for these assertions falls into both the traps we have mentioned. First, he takes the fact that welfare provision is a universal feature of all

[49] Max Weber, 'Politics as a Vocation' in *From Max Weber*, ed. Hans Gerth and C. Wright Mills (London: Routledge & Kegan Paul, 1948), p. 77.

[50] Michael Walzer, *Spheres of Justice* (Oxford: Martin Robertson, 1983), p. 62.

[51] Walzer, *Spheres of Justice*, p. 84.

societies as a basis for his normative claim that proposals to end welfare provision are misguided:

There has never been a political community that did not provide, or try to provide, or claim to provide, for the needs of its members as its members understood those needs. And there has never been a political community that did not engage its collective strength – its capacity to direct, regulate, pressure and coerce – in this project.[52]

Now, that fact, if it is true, is no doubt interesting; but it does not in itself imply any reason not to try something new in this regard. As it happens, Walzer's factual claim is false. He himself cites the example of Athens as a society which recognized and understood a much wider range of poverty-related needs than it attempted to cater for; it was well understood, for example, that all widows were potentially in need of economic assistance, but there was state provision only for the widows of fallen soldiers. Athens certainly recognized the importance of economic support for political citizenship; public money was paid out to make it possible for poorer citizens to miss a day's work to come to the Assembly or serve on juries, and this charge often amounted to more than half the public revenue of the city. This was in recognition of some of the arguments we mentioned in section 3. But beyond that, it is simply untrue to say that Athens catered for all the needs, or even all the pressing needs, that it recognized its members to have.

There are two moves Walzer uses to deal with such counterexamples. On the one hand, he argues that certain societies do not count as communities in the appropriate sense. Thus, for example, 'the indifference of Britain's rulers during the Irish potato famine is a sure sign that Ireland was a colony', not part of the British community; and he says also that his principles, such as the principle that if distribution *is* undertaken it is distribution according to need, 'probably don't apply to a society organized hierarchically, as in traditional India, where the fruits of the harvest are distributed not according to need but according to caste'.[53] But the question then arises: what moral reason is there for having a Walzerian community rather than a colony or caste society in this sense? Walzer gives no answer.

Secondly, and connected with that, Walzer stresses the vagueness of welfare provision as a concept which applies to all communities: 'the idea of need and the commitment to communal provision do not by themselves yield any clear determination of priorities and degrees'.[54] That is something, Walzer believed, every society works out for itself, in terms of its own history, its politics and its social understandings. (It is not for the philosopher to second-guess from his or her armchair the process of the evolution Marshall has described.) But then, Walzer is moving back towards the relativist position we have already considered in section 4:

---

[52] Walzer, *Spheres of Justice*, p. 68.
[53] Walzer, *Spheres of Justice*, p. 84.
[54] Walzer, *Spheres of Justice*, p. 66.

The ancient Athenians, for example, provided public baths and gymnasiums for the citizens but never provided anything remotely resembling unemployment insurance or social security. They made a choice about how to spend public funds, a choice shaped presumably by their understanding of what the common life required. It would be hard to argue that they made a mistake. I suppose there are notions of need that would yield such a conclusion, but these would not be notions acceptable to – they might not even be comprehensible to – the Athenians themselves.[55]

In fact the main interest of Walzer's book has been in his relativist suggestion that different standards of distribution are morally appropriate to the social understandings established in different societies. For our purposes the important point is that there is no longer any sense of an argument that membership and community, as such, imply a commitment to welfare provision, in anything other than a notional sense.

Are there then no substantive conclusions we can reach about membership as such, only the relativist conclusions with which we ended the previous section? We think that there is one other approach that may be promising.

The work of John Rawls has been very influential in political philosophy, for its revival of contractarianism as a method of argument, and for the liberal egalitarianism of its conclusions.[56] Rawls's argument is usually considered in terms of justice and injustice. A just society, he argues, will be one in which people enjoy equal basic liberties and in which inequalities of wealth and power are tolerated only if they contribute positively to the well-being of the least advantaged group of society. Though Rawls is agnostic about whether these principles are capable of legitimating a market economy and the institutions of capitalism, there is no doubt at all that they require social redistribution and the establishment of a welfare state.[57] Rawls's theory has been subject, of course, to many criticisms by New Right philosophers. Some, like Anthony Flew, accuse him of distorting the very notion of justice;[58] others, like Nozick, take him to task for ignoring the primacy of property and for assuming that society simply has at its disposal goods it may distribute in accordance with Rawlsian principles;[59] and still others, like Hayek, extend a cautious welcome to Rawls's work mainly because they misunderstood its tendency.[60]

For our purposes, the interest lies not only in the welfarist and redistributivist *conclusions* of Rawls's discussion, but also in the way they are presented. We believe Rawls's work can be understood as a discussion of what it is to be a citizen or member of a given society. A person is a mere *subject* of a regime and not

---

[55] Walzer, *Spheres of Justice*, p. 67. See Goodin, *Reasons for Welfare*, Chap. 4, for a general critique of 'community' in arguments of this sort.

[56] John Rawls, *A Theory of Justice* (Cambridge, Mass.: Harvard University Press, 1971).

[57] Rawls, *Theory of Justice*, pp. 275–84. Minimum provision in this context is discussed in Jeremy Waldron, 'John Rawls and the Social Minimum', *Journal of Applied Philosophy*, 3 (1986), 21–34.

[58] Anthony Flew, *The Politics of Procrustes: Contradictions of Enforced Equality* (London: Temple-Smith, 1981).

[59] Nozick, *Anarchy, State and Utopia*.

[60] F. A. Hayek, *Law, Legislation and Liberty* (London: Routledge, Kegan & Paul, 1976), p. 100.

a citizen, if its rules and policies will be applied to him or her whether he or she likes it or not and whether they serve his or her interests or not. They are applied without reference to his or her consent. But, since Locke, the liberal tradition has always been that we should try and think of subjects as though they were founding members of the society in which they live. Even though they cannot actually choose the regime they live under, nevertheless in our attempts to evaluate and to legitimize such a regime, we should at least ask what sort of order they would have chosen if they had had the choice. This is the tradition Rawls pursues. For Rawls, being a member of a society is not just a matter of living in and being subject to a social framework, it is also a matter of how that framework is justified. A person is a *member* of a society if and only if the design of its basic institutions fairly reflects a concern for his or her interests along with those of everyone else.

As everyone knows, the way Rawls chooses to express this idea is through the myth of the social contract. A society is just, and the people living in it are members rather than subjects, if we can show that its institutions satisfy certain principles that people would have agreed to as basic terms of co-operation, had they been given the opportunity to decide. If its institutions do not satisfy such principles, or if they are based on principles that would not or could not have been agreed to in advance by those who have to live with them, then they cannot be regarded as just, for they do not embody sufficient respect for the persons they apply to. Thus understood, the social contract myth attractively expresses the idea of a veto. You cannot be voted into a contract; everyone has to agree, everyone has to be convinced, and everyone has to gain. Now, of course, Rawls is the first to concede that in fact nothing like the 'original position' ever takes place: it is a moral perspective or a thought-experiment, not a historical speculation:[61]

No society can, of course, be a scheme of co-operation which men enter voluntarily in a literal sense; each person finds himself placed at birth in some particular position in some particular society, and the nature of his position materially affects his life prospects. Yet a society satisfying the principles of justice comes as close as a society can to being a voluntary scheme, for it meets the principles which free and equal people *would assent to* under circumstances that are fair. In this sense, its members are autonomous and the obligations they recognize self-imposed.[62]

If people learn to think about their society in this way, then they can say to one another 'that they are co-operating on terms to which they would agree if they were free and equal'[63] or, if they are critical, they can say that what is wrong with their society is that it would *not* pass this test of agreement by everyone under conditions of fairness. The terms that would be agreed to can be used then as a basis for evaluating both present arrangements and proposals for change in the future.

Rawls argues that people in his 'original position' would choose a mix of principles. They would choose a principle of equal political liberty and they would

[61] Rawls, *Theory of Justice*, pp. 138-9.
[62] Rawls, *Theory of Justice*, p. 13, our emphasis.
[63] Rawls, *Theory of Justice*, p. 13.

choose a principle of fair equality of opportunity and what he calls 'the Difference Principle' to govern the distribution of social and economic goods. The Difference Principle is our concern here. Rawls argues that it would be impossible in the 'original position' to secure general agreement for a set of social institutions that did not make collective provision for the plight of the members of the worst-off group. Social institutions that did not include the securing of a social minimum, the familiar apparatus of welfare provision, and perhaps more substantial methods of redistribution as well, would not command unanimous agreement in the original position. People would not be willing to accept an economic system or a system of property unless it had all this built into it. Those who feared they might fall into the worst-off group in the community would be reluctant to accept anything less than this, because they would be unsure of their ability to *live with* anything less. Agreeing to terms of co-operation that did not include such gurantees would impose what Rawls refers to as 'strains of commitment' on the parties:

> they cannot enter into agreements that may have consequences they cannot accept. They will avoid those that they can adhere to only with great difficulty. Since the original agreement is final and made in perpetuity, there is no second chance. In view of the serious nature of the possible consequences, the question of burden of commitment is especially acute ... Looking at the question from the standpoint of the original position, the parties recognise that it would be highly unwise if not irrational to choose principles which may have consequences so extreme that they could not accept them in practice.[64]

In other words, the Rawlsian argument takes us from what he refers to as 'a general knowledge of human psychology' to conclusions about the sort of social arrangements people could live with. Faced with great deprivation and inequality, people cannot be expected to live quiet and satisfied lives. They therefore cannot in good faith undertake or agree to live with such deprivation and inequality. So a political theory which gives any weight to the question of what people would agree to has an argument against the acceptability of such arrangements.

His argument connects with our concerns then in two ways. First, a political theory treats people as citizens and members (as opposed to subjects) only if it concerns itself with what social arrangements those people would agree to. Secondly, Rawls argues that people would agree only to principles which focused concern on the plight of the poorest members of society. His principles certainly require a welfare state; indeed they may require much more. They therefore provide the backbone of a powerful argument connecting citizenship or membership as such with at least basic welfare provision.

As Rawls presents it, *no one* would sign up for an economic system without welfare provision. That is because one of the features of his 'original position' is that the people taking this perspective must pretend to be ignorant of their wealth, class and talents, and Rawls argues that no one would want to take the risk of turning out to be poor and untalented in a society that lacked a safety net.

[64] Rawls, *Theory of Justice*, pp. 176–8.

But it is worth noting that the argument can be made out even without Rawls's controversial 'veil of ignorance'. All one needs is a veto and the requirement of unanimous agreement. Those who happen to be poor or untalented may be expected to veto the adoption of any social system that does not attempt to ameliorate their plight. If they have to live under such a system, they will be unable to give it their support and they will be driven by their need to subvert it where they can. Knowing this, they will be unable in good faith to agree to such a system from the standpoint of the original position. If nevertheless they find themselves in a society which lacks a safety net, or which lacks a basic welfare system, they are perfectly entitled to say to themselves, 'This society does not treat us as members, as citizens, or as people who belong here, for it is operating a system which could not possibly have commanded our consent'. So once again, the warning of the social citizenship argument, on this interpretation, is that the cost of rolling back welfare provision may be the acceptance of this sort of alienation.

If an argument like this can be made, then there is a reason for having welfare rights in a society whether it has a tradition of such institutions or not. Social rights of citizenship are a necessary condition for genuine and meaningful consent to social and political arrangements. It is true that in his more recent work Rawls has drawn back a little from the apparent universalism of *A Theory of Justice*: he now maintains that the principles of justice and the reasoning that leads to them do not represent moral conclusions valid for all times and places but rather moral conclusions whose validity is in some sense relative to the 'social and historical conditions' which have produced what he calls 'an overlapping consensus' about the basic values of a democratic society.[65] Rawls appears to be adopting a very deep and general relativism about social and political thought here. But the relativism which distinguished our argument in section 4 was more concerned with existing institutional arrangements like the welfare state and their effect on people's expectations. It is therefore a more 'surface-level' relativism than that to which Rawls has recently committed himself. The argument we have made in this section may be relative in Rawls's terms – that is, it only makes sense to people who have been brought up in a certain sort of culture with a certain sense of history. All the same, some of the societies with this history have had welfare arrangements, others have not. The Rawlsian argument reaches very deeply into the underlying values of our culture to show that welfare arguments are necessary if we are to keep faith with those values.

6. CONCLUSION

In this article we have sought to explore different arguments which might underlie, and give normative substance to, the notion of citizenship. Our analysis has

---

[65] J. Rawls, 'The Idea of an Overlapping Consensus', *Oxford Journal of Legal Studies*, 7 (1987), 4; see also Rawls, 'Kantian Constructivism in Moral Theory', *Journal of Philosophy*, 77 (1980), 515–72. For a critique of this relativism, see Waldron, *Nonsense Upon Stilts*, pp. 166–72.

been framed with reference to two possible views of the relationship between welfare provision and citizenship: an idealistic argument whereby social welfare is presented as an attribute of citizenship in a statement about the most desirable form of social organization,and an empirical argument about the necessity of welfare for effective citizenship in a traditional sense. The first branch of the argument in turn divides in two: one branch arguing from the impact of expectations of existing welfare provision, the other not being so directly relative to actual social institutions. The arguments are separate but they are not meant to be mutually exclusive: we have presented them here as partially overlapping, partially complementary ways of teasing out the normative implications of social citizenship.

The importance of this discussion lies in its relevance to contemporary political and social discourse. In an effort to rebut New Right arguments and policies, some scholars and politicians have drawn upon social right and citizenship arguments to defend the policies and institutions of the welfare state. We have tried to evaluate the strength of such claims through examination of their analytical basis and to suggest various ways in which those claims might be understood. Above all, we think it important that the idea of citizenship should remain at the centre of modern political debates about social and economic arrangements. The concept of a citizen is that of a person who can hold her or his head high and participate fully and with dignity in the life of her or his society. Although, as we have seen, there are many competing conceptions of what it is to be a citizen in the modern state, and although, as our argument has shown, none of these conceptions is particularly straightforward, nevertheless the underlying idea is one that must not ever be lost sight of when we are considering in our political discussions what life in this society is to be like.

C
Beyond the Welfare State?

[30]

A capitalist road to communism

ROBERT J. VAN DER VEEN AND PHILIPPE VAN PARIJS
University of Amsterdam; University of Louvain-la-Neuve and the Belgian National Science Foundation

Prospects for the Left look bleak indeed. Electoral disasters (on the British pattern) and policy U-turns (on the French pattern) have reinforced the suspicion that socialism may forever remain out of reach. Even worse, actually existing socialist societies have repeatedly failed to provide an attractive picture of socialism. Compounded by mounting disillusionment with the achievements of State intervention in the West, this failure has shaken many people's faith in the very desirability of socialism.

In this article, we argue that this predicament provides no legitimate ground for dismay, cynicism, or despondency – not because true socialism is different, or because it is possible after all, but because the Left need not be committed to socialism. We believe there is another way forward, a radical alternative to socialism, that combines feasibility and desirability to a surprising extent and that is, therefore, well worth considering.

This belief is unorthodox enough. It implies, among other things, that the "working class," even rather broadly defined, is not the social force that the Left should systematically identify and side with.[1] Nonetheless, the arguments we shall put forward in support of this belief are fairly orthodox. Indeed, we believe they are fully consistent with Marx's ultimate views on the sort of future we should struggle to realize, as well as with his claim that material conditions determine which struggles make historical sense. Our putting forward these arguments does not mean we are fully convinced by the conclusion to which they lead. But we *are* fully convinced that a serious discussion of this sort of conclusion and argument is urgently needed.

Theory and Society 15: 635–655 (1987)
© *Martinus Nijhoff Publishers, Dordrecht – Printed in the Netherlands*

636

There is one question about our scenario that many readers are likely to ask and to which no reply can be found in this article: granted, if only for the sake of the argument, that the path we sketch is economically feasible as well as ethically desirable, where are the social movements and political forces that are both willing and able to help our societies along it? We believe that this question is of the utmost importance and that some lineaments of an answer exist.[2] But we also think that the questions we tackle in this article are logically prior, and hence that it is with them, and not with political feasibility, that we should be concerned in the first place. We have sympathy for those − mainly economists − who say one should not waste time investigating the ethical desirability of a scheme that is not economically workable. And we understand those − mainly philosophers − who say there is no point in investigating the economic feasibility of a proposal that is ethically unacceptable. But denying the usefulness of investigating either economic feasibility or ethical desirability before having established, or at least discussed, a scheme's political chances, is unwarranted and irresponsible. For what is politically feasible depends largely on what has been shown to make economic and ethical sense. In any case, our ambition, in writing and publishing this article, is not to provide a full-fledged plea − at several junctures, we will point out important gaps that would need to be filled − but merely to set the stage for a meaningful discussion about whether the transition path described is, if feasible, desirable and, if desirable, feasible.

Does communism require socialism?

From a Marxian standpoint, "socialism" is not an end in itself. It is a means, indeed the best means or even the only means, to reach true communism. The term "socialism" here covers what Marx calls the lower stage of communism in the *Critique of the Gotha Programme*. It refers to a society in which workers collectively own the means of production − and in which therefore they collectively decide what these should be used for and how the resulting product should be distributed, namely according to the principle "To each according to his labor." "Communism," on the other hand, refers to the higher stage of communism, as characterized in the *Critique of the Gotha Programme*. It is defined by the distribution principle "From each according to his abilities, to each according to his needs" − which implies at least that the social product is distributed in such a way (1) that everyone's basic needs are adequately met, and (2) that each individual's share is entirely indepen-

dent of his or her (freely provided) labor contribution.[3] Socialism, as
defined, implies that "exploitation" is abolished — workers appropriate
the whole of the social product — while communism, as defined, implies
that "alienation" is abolished — productive activities need no longer be
prompted by external rewards.

Why then do we need socialism? Why can't we move straight into communism? There are two standard answers to these questions. One is that
communism is utopian as long as man is what capitalism has made him:
we need socialism to reshape man, to get rid of his selfishness, his *Selbst-
sucht*, and to turn him into the altruistic person communism requires.
The second answer is that communism is bound to fail under conditions
of scarcity: we need socialism to develop the productive powers of humankind and thus create the state of abundance in which alone communism can flourish. Both these answers consist in a conjunction of two
propositions: (1) the possibility of communism depends on the development of altruism/productivity, and (2) such development is better served
by socialism than by capitalism, by the collective ownership of the means
of production rather than by their private ownership. Both answers fail,
we believe, because at least one of the propositions of which they consist
is indefensible.

Is altruism really necessary?

One may well doubt that (democratic) socialism is better than capitalism
at promoting altruism, i.e., that involvement in collective decision-
making about production would make people less selfish than they are
in a system in which production decisions are mediated by the market.
For the sake of argument, however, let us suppose that this is the case.
This does not give socialism a decisive advantage over capitalism as a
way of approaching communism, because the latter does *not* require
altruism. (Indeed, if it did, those who reject communism as irredeemably
utopian would be right.) To see this, let us look more closely at how the
transition to communism is supposed to proceed.

Even at the lower stage of communism, as Marx describes it in the *Critique of the Gotha Programme*, part of the social product is distributed
according to needs — whether to meet the individual needs of those unable to work or to fulfil collective needs. The transition to full communism can then be viewed as a gradual increase of the part of the social
product distributed according to needs vis-à-vis the part distributed ac-

638

cording to labor contributions.[4] Progress along this dimension does require that material rewards should gradually lose their significance, but does not entail that workers should be increasingly driven by altruistic motives. To start with, nonmaterial rewards (respect, esteem, prestige, fame, glory, and the like) could be substituted for material ones as a way of motivating people to perform the required amount of work.[5] Moreover, the content of work, its organization, and the human relations associated with it could and should be so altered that extrinsic rewards, whether material or not, would be less and less necessary to prompt a sufficient supply of labor. Work, to use Marx's phrase, could and should become "life's prime want."[6]

By proceeding along this dimension — the improvement of work up to the point where it is no longer work — the transition to communism need not rely in any way on the development of altruism, nor indeed on any other transformation of human nature. It takes persons and their preferences as they are, but alters the nature of (paid) work up to a point where it is no longer distinguishable from free time. Even if we grant that only socialism can turn people into altruistic beings, therefore, it does not follow that socialism is indispensable to reaching communism.

Is socialism better suited to the pursuit of abundance?

Though socialism is not needed to get rid of selfishness, it may still be needed to get rid of scarcity. For as Marx repeatedly stressed, the growth of the productive forces (in a sense to be specified below) plays an irreplaceable role in the transition scenario sketched above. More precisely, productivity growth defined as an increase of output per unit of effort — taking both the length *and* the unattractiveness of labor into account — is essential to make room for a substantial improvement in the quality of work, and hence for an increase in the proportion of the social product that can be distributed regardless of labor contributions.[7]

The question, then, is not whether productivity growth, in the relevant sense, is indispensable to the advent of communism — it certainly is — but rather whether socialism is superior to capitalism as a means of achieving productivity growth. Marx did believe that there is a decisive argument to this effect. In both the 1859 *Critique* and in various passages of *Capital*, he argues that the development of the productive forces is *fettered* under advanced capitalism: the productivity of labor grows at a rate that is lower than it would be if relations of production were changed, i.e., if socialism were substituted for capitalism. This is because profit maximization, which competition forces capitalists to seek, does not necessarily coincide with the maximization of labor productivity or – what comes down to the same thing – with the minimization of the amount of labor that is required directly (as "living labor") or indirectly (as "means of production") to produce one unit of output. Suppose a technique that uses comparatively much capital (or indirect labor) and little living (or direct) labor performs better, according to the latter criterion, than another technique, which requires more direct labor but less capital. It may nonetheless be against the capitalist's interest to introduce it, essentially because, when using direct labor, he need pay only the workers' wages, but when using indirect labor, the price he must pay includes not only the wages of the workers who performed it, but also the profits derived from it by the capitalists employing these workers. Hence there are techniques that would enhance the productivity of labor but will never be introduced under capitalist relations of production. This argument plays an absolutely crucial role in Marx's overall vision of history, because this "fettering" of the productive forces is the fundamental reason why, in his view, capitalism is but a transient mode of production. Marx gives no other argument in support of his claim that capitalism fetters the development (as distinct from the use) of the productive forces. And nothing but such fettering can, according to historical materialism, necessitate the replacement of capitalism by socialism.[8]

This argument is flawed, however, not because capitalism really does select techniques so as to maximize the productivity of labor, but because a rational socialist planner would not do so either. This is the case, first of all, because labor is not the only primary factor. Natural resources are scarce, and how much of them various possible techniques use up is clearly relevant to making a rational choice among them. Moreover, even if labor were the sole primary factor, selecting techniques in such a way as to maximize labor productivity would be justified only under very special conditions, if one is to maximize utility from consumption per capita for a given working time. (And what is the point of producing if not to consume, and the point of consuming if not to derive utility from it?) That there may be situations in which choosing the technique that minimizes labor time makes no sense becomes obvious if you consider the following example.

Suppose you have ten more years to live. You now produce your bread with a highly labor-intensive technique. If you build a mill, the labor

640

time required, whether directly or indirectly, to produce one loaf of bread will be cut by half. Nonetheless, if it takes you ten years to build the mill, you will wisely stick to your less "productive" old ways. Moreover, even if you lift the assumption of a finite time horizon (which makes some sense for a rational planner) and disregard the transition period from one technique to another (to consider so-called "steady states"), it can still be shown that the maximization of labor productivity is only defensible as a criterion of technical choice if both the rate of accumulation and the rate of time preference are zero, i.e., if there is no growth and future consumption is valued as much as present consumption. When these strong conditions do not hold, rational socialist planning will deviate from such a criterion by attributing a greater weight to labor that needs to be performed one or several periods in advance of the production of consumption goods. (How great the weights need to be depends on the rates of accumulation and of time preference). In so doing, socialist planning uses a criterion that need not coincide with, but is bound to approximate pretty closely, capitalist profit maximization. Consequently, if rational socialist planning is the appropriate baseline for comparison, no significant "fettering" can be expected from technical choice under profit-maximizing capitalism.[9]

Thus, the central theoretical argument in favor of socialism's superiority for productive development is flawed. Moreover, the empirical evidence is hardly encouraging. On the opposite side, apologists of capitalism are keen to stress that the rules of the capitalist game provide producers with strong incentives to introduce productivity-enhancing innovations. Indeed, they often force them, if they are to survive at all, to fight off the routine and inertia into which they would sink under a mellower system, and to further develop the productive powers of humankind. If "abundance" in some sense is a key condition for the realization of communism and if the development of the productive forces, as understood above, constitutes the way of reaching it, should not a rational pursuer of communism frankly opt for capitalism? Of course, capitalism as such offers no guarantee that the quality of work will be improved, that more and more will be distributed according to needs, or that increased productivity will be reflected in reduced effort rather than in growing output. But as we shall see shortly, one key institutional change *within* capitalism could turn such tendencies into endogenous features of the system.

Is socialism morally superior?

Before describing this institutional change and examining its consequences, let us briefly pause to consider an alternative tack that defenders of socialism might want to take. The whole discussion so far assumes that the superiority claimed for socialism over capitalism is of an instrumental nature: socialism is (normatively) superior to capitalism because it is a better instrument for helping society along on the road to communism, whether by promoting the development of altruistic dispositions or by fostering more effectively the growth of labor productivity.

But there is another, *directly* ethical way of justifying socialism against capitalism: not as a more effective way of getting somewhere else, but as *intrinsically* more just, and therefore better, than capitalism. After all, as pointed out earlier, it follows from the very definition of (ideal) socialism that it abolishes exploitation. One may therefore expect exploitation to be much less present, if at all, in actual socialism than in any version of capitalism we may dream of. And this in itself may suffice to justify our preference for socialism over capitalism, especially when one realizes that communism only constitutes the notional and unreachable end of a transition that is bound to drag on forever, even under the most favorable circumstances. Even if capitalism could take us more safely or faster in the direction of communism, therefore, it may still be wise to choose socialism, because choosing capitalism would have the intolerable implication that exploitation would be with us forever.

This objection presupposes that exploitation can be precisely defined so that it is possible both (1) to say that exploitation is intrinsic to capitalism, and (2) to construct a cogent case in support of the claim that exploitation is ethically unacceptable. And showing that this is possible is far trickier than is commonly assumed. Nonetheless, we believe the objection is a serious one and one that deserves careful consideration.[10] In this article, however, we want to stick to a fairly orthodox Marxian framework. And for Marx, questions of justice and other ethical considerations were, if relevant at all, secondary. What really matters, when assessing a mode of production, is not how fairly the social product is shared out, but how effectively it spurs productive development in the direction of full communism. We therefore keep to the instrumental perspective adopted in the previous sections, and now turn to the question of how capitalist development could be geared to the advent of communism.

642

"Social income" and the pursuit of communism

Capitalism as such does not imply that any part of the social product should be granted to anyone who contributes neither labor, nor capital, nor natural resources. But it does not exclude it either. It does not exclude the possibility of a "social income" whose recipients need not contribute anything to production at the time they receive it. It is of crucial importance, however, to distinguish between different formulas of "social income" in this sense.

Some of them are just indirect wages. They involve an indirect connection with labor contribution. For example, the right to a "social income" may be restricted to those who are unable to work or unable to find work, as is roughly the case with unemployment benefits in advanced capitalist countries. Or it may be extended to people who freely choose not to work, but subject to the proviso that they have in the past performed some specified amount of labor, as in Edward Bellamy's utopia recently revived, in a less rigid version, by Gunnar Adler-Karlsson, André Gorz, and Marie-Louise Duboin.[11] In all such cases, labor — or at least the willingness to work — remains the basis of the entitlement to a "social income," and increasing the size of the latter cannot be construed as a move toward distribution according to needs.

Other formulas, however, grant a genuine guaranteed income: the connection with labor contribution is completely severed. This is the case, for example, when any household whose income from other sources falls below some specified minimum is entitled to a transfer payment *making up for the difference* — which is roughly the way in which basic social security actually works in several advanced capitalist societies. And it is also the case when every individual, whatever his or her income from other sources, is entitled to an *unconditional grant*, the level of which depends only on such variables as age and degree of handicap (as rough proxies for basic needs) — an old idea advocated by Bertrand Russell[12] that has recently become the focus of growing interest throughout Western Europe.[13]

In the case of these last two formulas, it makes sense to say that an increase in the level of the "social income" moves us closer (ceteris paribus) to communism, as defined by distribution according to needs. In both cases, it is possible to say that in any economy (defined by its technological level, its stock of labor power and capital, and the preference schedules of its members) some positive levels of a "guaranteed income" are sustainable, while others are not. And in both cases, it is therefore in principle possible to determine a maximum sustainable level of the "guaranteed income" (with given technology, stocks, and preferences), which the pursuit of communism within capitalism should constantly aim for.[14] Nonetheless, it is of paramount importance to see that the consequences associated with these two versions are by no means the same: whereas the former version would lock the transition to communism in a dead end, the latter provides a promising way of effecting it.

The case for a universal grant

The key point is that a *make-up guaranteed income* — whereby transfer payments are added to income from other sources up to the level of the guaranteed income — not only stigmatizes all those who "live off benefits." It also unavoidably imposes a minimum wage: no one will accept a job (even a job one would much like to do, though not for nothing) for less than the guaranteed income, because accepting it would mean becoming financially worse off than one would be without working (due to the cost of child care, of transport to and from work, etc.). At first sight, this seems to be a consequence we should welcome. But as soon as the make-up guaranteed income reaches a level that is not negligible, it catches all those whose skills are such that they could not market them for a higher wage, in the so-called unemployment trap. Moreover, it constitutes a strong disincentive against sharing out the jobs of those whose part-time work would only earn them less or little more than the guaranteed income. Of course, the higher the relative level of the guaranteed income, the more people get caught in the unemployment trap, and the more one's choice is restricted to working a lot (to make it "worth it") and not working at all (and "living off" the others' work). Capitalism with a substantial make-up guaranteed income, therefore, will be attractive neither to those who will feel excluded from work nor to those who will feel they bear all the burden. Moreover, it will be very expensive financially speaking, because the taxes required to support it will need to be raised from a shrinking tax base.

If, on the other hand, guaranteed income takes the form of a *universal grant*, unconditionally awarded to every citizen, things are different indeed. Because citizens have an absolute right to this grant whatever their income from other sources, they start earning additional net income as soon as they do any work, however little and however poorly paid it may be. Combined with some deregulation of the labor market (no adminis-

644

trative obstacles to part-time work, no compulsory minimum wage, no compulsory retirement age, etc.), the universal grant would make it possible to spread paid employment much more widely than it is now. Consequently, if the guaranteed income takes this form, its growth need no longer generate acute tensions between the overworked who feel exploited and the jobless who feel excluded. Moreover, it also follows – however paradoxical it may seem – that awarding a decent basic income to all may be, under appropriate conditions, much "cheaper" (in terms of marginal tax rates), and therefore more realistic, than awarding it only to those who "need" it.[15]

The economic consequences of a universal grant

Consequently, if communism is to be approached within a capitalist society, it must be by way of raising as much as possible the guaranteed income in the form of a universal grant. Note that this maximization could be conceived in either absolute or relative terms. Maximizing the guaranteed income in absolute terms could be justified on the basis of John Rawls's well-known "difference principle": it would amount to eliminating all income inequalities that are not required if the least advantaged – here identified as those who have no income, in cash or kind, apart from the guaranteed minimum – are to be as well off as possible.[16] Such an elegant way of combining the imperatives of equality and efficiency may seem attractive to many.[17] But it does not coincide with the Marxian objective of abolishing alienation, which implies instead, at least as a first approximation, that the guaranteed income should be maximized in relative terms. Communism is achieved when the whole social product is distributed irrespective of each person's contribution, *not* when the share each gets irrespective of his contribution reaches some absolute threshold.

Of course, whatever the level of technology, the amounts of labor and capital available, and individual preferences, it is always "possible" to set the universal grant (and hence the tax rate) at 100 percent of per capita disposable income, i.e., to tax all gross incomes so that everyone has the same net income after taxes. But this would, in all likelihood, generate such a drastic fall in the supply of both capital and labor, and hence in the size of the social product, that per capita income (now equal to the universal grant) would no longer cover fundamental needs. Consequently, the Marxian criterion should be construed as implicitly imposing a constraint on the maximization of the relative share of society's total product distributed according to needs: this share should be and remain large enough, in absolute terms, to secure the satisfaction of each individual's fundamental needs. Due to insufficient technical progress, insufficient capital or skill accumulation, or excessive aversion to working or saving, some economies are unable to meet this constraint. But others may have reached a state of "abundance" in the weak sense that an unconditional guaranteed income could viably cover everyone's fundamental needs. As productivity (in the comprehensive sense, which takes the unattractiveness of labor into account) increases, the maximum relative share of the guaranteed income compatible with this constraint increases steadily, up to the point where "abundance" is reached in the stronger sense that all fundamental needs could sustainably be met without labor being differentially rewarded.[18]

We do not believe that advanced capitalist countries have achieved anything like abundance in this strong sense required for the implementation of full communism. But we do believe that they have achieved abundance in the weaker sense specified above: they could grant each of their members a sustainable universal grant — though not necessarily a sustainable make-up guaranteed income — that would be sufficient to cover his or her fundamental needs. Of course, such a claim, once made precise (what are "fundamental needs"?), can only be established by informed simulation and actual experiments. It is not the purpose of this article to undertake the important task of assessing this empirical claim. In the remaining pages, we want to focus instead on the following question. Let us suppose that the empirical claim just made is correct. Let us suppose, in other words, that technology, stocks, and preferences are such, in advanced capitalist countries, that it is possible to provide everyone with a universal grant sufficient to cover his or her "fundamental needs" without this involving the economy in a downward spiral. How does the economy evolve once such a universal grant is introduced?

A precise answer to this question would obviously require that one specify the way the universal grant would be financed (indirect or direct taxation, progressive or proportional), the way it would be modulated according to age, the extent to which it would replace or supplement other public expenditures, and so on. In very general terms, however, it can be said that introducing such a universal grant need not cancel capitalism's endogenous tendencies toward productivity increases. But it would twist these tendencies so that productivity in the comprehensive sense (amount of effort, rather than simply of labor time, per unit of product) will be promoted more effectively than before. For workers' uncondition-

646

al entitlement to a substantial universal grant will simultaneously push
up the wage rate for unattractive, unrewarding work (which no one is
now forced to accept in order to survive) and bring down the *average*
wage rate for attractive, intrinsically rewarding work (because fundamental needs are covered anyway, people can now accept a high-
quality job paid far below the guaranteed income level). Consequently,
the capitalist logic of profit will, much more than previously, foster technical innovation and organizational change that improve the quality of
work and thereby reduce the drudgery required per unit of product.

The growth of productivity in this comprehensive sense does not guarantee that the economy will move toward communism as defined above. It
only provides a necessary condition for it. When less drudgery, less disutility, is required to produce a given social product, more of the latter
could be distributed according to needs rather than according to contributions, without this reducing the absolute level of the universal grant.
Whether and to what extent the relative share of the universal grant will
actually rise, however, depends on whether and how far this possibility
is seized through political decisions to raise the average rate at which
gross income is (directly or indirectly) taxed. It is obvious that nothing
of the sort will be done if growth is the overriding objective. *If* instead
there is a political will to use increased productivity for changing the distribution pattern (and thereby reducing the effort prompted by differential rewards) rather than for increasing output, capitalist societies will
smoothly move toward full communism.

From supply-side economics to political ecology

The "Laffer curve" of supply-side economics provides us with an effective (though oversimplified) device for depicting the range of choices
open to a society.[19] For a given technology, a given pattern of individual
preferences between income and leisure, and a given (potential) labor
force, one can picture both the amount of effort elicited from the population and (consequently) the total product as decreasing functions of
the tax rate (supposed to be uniform). On the other hand, total receipts,
which are given by the total product multiplied by the tax rate, and coincide (to keep things simple) with the part of the total product distributed
in the form of a universal grant, first increase and then decrease as the
rate of tax rises. Note, however, that the total product (or income) we are
talking about here only corresponds to the *taxable* product (or income).
As the tax rate increases, the actual total product may well fall at a much

slower rate, as people replace market production by household production, monetary by non-monetary transactions, and consumption outside the firm (wages) by consumption within the firm (say, comfortable offices and business trips).

A policy that gives a guaranteed income for all a high priority could be guided by at least four distinct principles: it could attempt

> (1) to maximize the total product (both actual and taxable) under the constraint that the universal grant should reach a given minimum level (*"growth-oriented" criterion*);
>
> (2) to maximize the absolute level of the universal grant (*"Rawlsian" criterion*);
>
> (3) to maximize the relative level of the universal grant (as a proportion of total taxable income) – which amounts, under our assumptions, to maximizing the tax rate – under the constraint that its absolute level should not fall below some given minimum level (*"Marxian" criterion*); and
>
> (4) to maximize equality, as approximated by the ratio of the universal grant to the actual total product, subject again to the (not necessarily binding) constraint that the universal grant does not fall below some minimum level (*"equality-oriented" criterion*).

The tax rate set in accord with criterion (4) must necessarily lie somewhere between the tax rates set in accord with criteria (2) and (3). For suppose that actual income and taxable income behave in nearly the same way, i.e., that, as the tax rate goes up, people tend to replace activities yielding taxable income by pure leisure. Then the ratio of the universal grant to taxable income will hardly be different from the ratio of the universal grant to actual income, and maximizing equality (criterion (4)) will then practically be equivalent to maximizing the rate at which market incomes are taxed (criterion (3)). At the other extreme, suppose that taxable income is strongly affected by changes in the tax rate, while actual income is hardly affected at all – i.e., that taxable production is nearly fully replaced by (just as unequally distributed) nontaxable production. Then the ratio of the universal grant to the actual total product mirrors closely the absolute level of the universal grant, and maximizing equality (criterion (4)) is then practically equivalent to maximizing the tax yield (criterion (2)). One possible configuration of the four choices is given in Fig. 1.

The Laffer curve and the universal grant

The Y curve represents the level of a country's taxable social product.

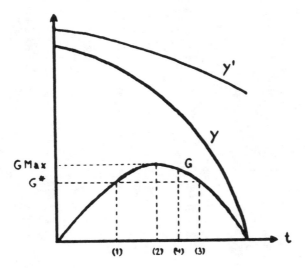

Fig. 1. Static criteria of choice

t: uniform tax rate
Y: taxable social product
Y':   total social product
G: aggregate universal grant
G*:   level of G covering everyone's basic needs
GMax: maximum sustainable level of G

(1):   growth-oriented criterion
(2):   "Rawlsian" criterion
(3):   "Marxian" criterion
(4):   equality-oriented criterion

The G curve represents the part of that product absorbed by taxes (the total tax yield). The shape of these curves indicates how a labor force will respond to changes in the tax rate t when the entire tax yield tY is redistributed among the general population by means of the universal grant (i.e., when tY equals G). As the tax rate rises from 0 to 100 percent, the workers' incentive to supply productive effort will decline steadily to 0, and (assuming a given technique of production) the taxable social product Y will fall correspondingly.

To explain the shape of the Laffer curve (the tax yield curve G), consider the net effect of a small rise in the tax rate. Raising the tax rate increases the proportion of the taxable social product going to grant recipients (the redistributive effect) but also reduces the amount of labor supplied, and therefore the size of the taxable social product itself (the incentive effect). The relative impact of these two effects, and hence the net effect of the small rise of t on G, varies with the absolute level of the tax rate. If t is relatively low, the redistributive effect will dominate the incentive effect: the rise of t will be greater than the fall of Y it induces, and therefore the level of the universal grant G will rise as the tax rate rises above 0. If t is relatively high, however, the incentive effect will dominate the redistributive effect, and G will fall as t rises to 100 percent. At a tax rate somewhere between 0 and 100 percent, the incentive effect will exactly offset the redistributive effect. This is GMax, the peak of the Laffer curve.

Figure 1 describes a state of abundance in the weak sense that the maximum sustainable level of the universal grant exceeds the minimum level required to cover everyone's fundamental needs. In such a state, as argued earlier, the most obviously Marxian criterion is criterion (3): pursuing communism means that the tax rate is raised as high as possible, but not high enough to jeopardize the satisfaction of everyone's fundamental needs. Yet the diagram makes it clear that this choice can be justified neither in terms of making those who are worst off as well off as possible, nor in terms of equality. What criterion (3) does guarantee, however, is that the "realm of freedom" will be expanded as much as possible without letting the universal grant fall below what is required to satisfy fundamental needs. By requiring the minimization of taxable income under this constraint, criterion (3) ensures that work, and in particular unpleasant work, is discouraged as much as possible. In other words, it promotes the expansion of freedom both in the sense of shortening the average working day and in the sense of improving the average quality of work. As productivity (in the comprehensive sense) grows (see Fig. 2), the total product generated by a given amount of effort increases, and so, therefore, does the tax yield corresponding to a given tax rate. This makes it possible for the tax rate to rise without violating the constraint that the universal grant should keep exceeding the chosen minimum. As the process goes on, the share of total (taxable) income that is not distributed in the form of a universal grant gradually shrinks. At the same time — and this is what justifies the choice of criterion (3) — the working day keeps growing shorter and the quality of work keeps rising. At the limit, both processes converge in the abolition of work: free time fills the day and work is so attractive that it is no longer work.[20]

Consequently, for the Marxian criterion (3) to be acceptable, material growth must have, to say the least, a low priority.[21] Such a transition has the best chance when for some independent reasons (say, the physical

650

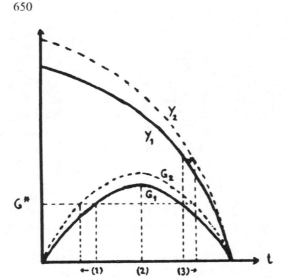

Fig. 2. Possible transitions to communism, as
productivity rises over time

t: uniform tax rate
Y_1, Y_2:   taxable social product at times 1,2
G_1, G_2:   aggregate universal grant at times 1,2
G^*:   level of G covering everyone's basic needs

(1):   growth-oriented criterion
(2):   "Rawlsian" criterion
(3):   "Marxian" criterion

and social "limits to growth") the society concerned finds the expansion
of GNP sufficiently unattractive. And an increase of free time combined
with a stagnation (or even a fall, as Fig. 2 shows to be possible) of incomes can be perceived as tolerable only if the quality of the living environment is sufficiently high. (What is the point of having more free
time if you live stuck between a motorway and a rubbish dump, and get
no additional money to escape?) Restrained (or even negative) growth
and environmental protection, it turns out, are key conditions for the full
success of our Marxian scenario. And ecologism, not socialism, is required if we are ever to be able to write on our banners: "From each according to his abilities, to each according to his needs!"

Freedom, equality, and growth

Still, one may doubt whether the "Marxian" criterion (3) is really the most appropriate criterion. First, as already mentioned, the choice of criterion (3) may not be the most *egalitarian* one. Expanding the "realm of freedom" may mean that an increasing part of society's wealth is produced outside the formal sector, in the form of self-production, mutual help, volunteer work, etc. And nothing guarantees that the benefits of this production will be evenly spread: a childless old-age pensioner stuck in a third-floor flat in an anonymous city is not likely to get as large a share of this "autonomous" production as vigorous young people living in a rural area and firmly integrated in a closely knit network of neighbors, relatives, and friends. Precisely because of the growth of the "autonomous" sphere, therefore, even full communism would go hand in hand with quite a high level of avoidable inequality. This may incline us to favor criterion (4). But it need not. If what really matters to us − as it arguably did to Marx − is the expansion of freedom, the abolition of alienation, we need not be bothered by the persistence of substantial inequalities, because everyone's fundamental needs are covered anyway.

A second and stronger argument against criterion (3) is that the expansion of freedom should not mean only an increase in the quantity of free time vis-à-vis working time and an improvement in the quality of work, but also an improvement in the *quality of free time*. And the latter is nothing but the degree to which people are able to fulfill their desires in their free time − which is itself closely related to the level of production (stripped of externalities). Two possibilities must be distinguished here. Suppose, first, that what matters (as regards the quality of free time) is only the extent to which those who are *worst off* can fulfill their needs. One could then choose any criterion in the range between criteria (3) and (2). At one extreme, the "Marxian" criterion (3) requires only that the quality of free time enjoyed by those who are worst off should not decrease, while the "Rawlsian" criterion (2) requires that the quality of their free time should be as high as possible, at the cost of a lower share of free time in total time or of a poorer quality of working time. But suppose, next, that what one cares about is the quality of the *average person's* free time. One could then, at one extreme, maximize production under the constraint that the universal grant remains sufficient to cover fundamental needs, i.e., select our "growth-oriented" criterion (1), with the further proviso that, as productivity grows, the amount of effort required for production should not increase (i.e., the other dimensions of the realm of freedom should not shrink). At the other extreme, one could initially choose our "Marxian" criterion (3) but with the proviso that, as productivity rises, total income should not go down. There is, clearly,

652

a trade-off between the freedom to satisfy one's needs and freedom from drudgery. The more importance one attaches to the former, the more inclined one will be to retreat from the austere criterion (3) toward the more expansive criterion (2) or even (1).

Such a retreat receives further support if one brings in, thirdly, the causal link between growth and productivity. Restrained or negative growth, as implied by the "Marxian" criterion (3), may conceivably hinder labor-saving and labor-quality-improving innovations to such an extent that the potential for any further transition may be undermined. Using criterion (1) and maximizing growth forever, on the other hand, means that this potential builds up without ever being used. Here again there is a trade-off: between using all the existing potential to maximize freedom from drudgery for the current generation and refraining from doing so in order to improve the prospects for the next generation — assuming higher production does not deplete other resources that generation would need.

If one aims to expand the realm of freedom, the choice of the appropriate tax rate may thus be, even at this abstract level, a rather complex matter. The optimal transition towards communism may not be the one that proceeds by simply maximizing the tax rate — and thus minimizing drudgery. It may be argued that the choice of the tax rate should not only be constrained by the provision of a universal grant covering everyone's fundamental needs, but that it should be further constrained by the need to keep (actual) inequality within bounds and by the need to keep growth at a sufficiently high level for productive development to continue.

But suppose something like a universal grant is introduced — because of the intolerable consequences of having no guaranteed income system at all and because of the perverse effects associated with alternative formulas. The choice of the tax rate (and hence of the level of the universal grant) will of course not be determined by any abstract optimality calculus, whether conducted in a Marxian framework or not. It will be determined by power relationships in the context of current material conditions. It is these material conditions — basically, rapid labor-saving technical change combined with compelling constraints on economic growth — that will turn the capitalist transition to communism from a utopian dream into a *historical necessity*, not in the sense that it will happen automatically, no matter what people think or do, but in the sense that, given the material conditions, human rationality can be relied upon

653

to generate, sooner or later, political forces that will bring it about. A crucial part is played in this process by the exploration of alternative futures, by the investigation of their possibility and desirability — the central component of human rationality. Consequently, however sketchy and tentative, this article's argument is of a piece with the historical necessity it ends up asserting.

Acknowledgments

Earlier versions of this article were presented at the Universities of Manchester (May 1983), London (September 1983), Berlin (May 1984), and Amsterdam (May 1985). We are particularly grateful to Rod Aya, Heiner Ganssmann, Norman Geras, Andrew Glyn, André Gorz, Staf Hellemans, Cornelia von Kleist, Michael Kraetke, David Purdy, Ian Steedman, and "Titanic," as well as to our colleagues in the "September Group" (especially G. A. Cohen, Jon Elster, Adam Przeworski, and Erik Wright), to three anonymous referees, and to each other, for stimulating discussions or comments from which the final version of this article has benefited greatly. Because most of these people, to put it mildly, remain rather critical of our central idea, they can hardly be held responsible for whatever the reader may find objectionable, indeed scandalous, in the preceding pages.

Notes

1. This claim does not contradict the view — to which we adhere — that, by definition, the Left systematically sides with those who own nothing but their labor power (if that).

2. See Robert J. van der Veen and Philippe Van Parijs, "Capitalism, Communism and the Realm of Freedom: A Formal Presentation" (Louvain-la-Neuve: Institut des Sciences Economiques, Working Paper no. 8501, 1985), section 5, and Philippe Van Parijs, "A Revolution in Class Theory," *Politics and Society* (forthcoming) section 6, for an inchoate answer.

3. Note that "communism," as defined, does not entail collective ownership of the means of production by the workers, i.e., "socialism" as defined above. But it does entail collective ownership of the social product by society as a whole: while the owners of means of production, labor power, and skills decide whether and how to put them to productive use, society appropriates all income flows in order to distribute them "according to needs" to all its members. This constitutes the etymological justification for our "thin" definition of "communism."

4. For a formal model of this transition from socialism to communism, see Robert J. van der Veen, "From Contribution to Needs. A Normative-Economic Essay on the Transition towards Full Communism," *Acta Politica* 18 (1984): 463–492.

5. See Joseph H. Carens, *Equality, Moral Incentives and the Market* (Chicago: Universi-

654

ty of Chicago Press, 1981). If the motivation to work is provided by fear of nonmaterial penalties (social disapproval, contempt, resentment, etc.), it is questionable whether alienation has really been abolished.

6. Using Sen's terminology, it must be conceded that any society, whether capitalist or socialist, that effectively guarantees a minimum consumption level (if only to those who are unable to work) needs to rely to some extent on "sympathy" (giving weight to other people's preferences) or "commitment" (letting moral considerations override one's preferences). See Amartya Sen, "Rational Fools," in *Philosophy and Economic Theory*, ed. F. Hahn and M. Hollis (Oxford: Oxford University Press, 1979), 87–109, section iv. However, the possibility of increasing the part that is being distributed independently of labor contributions by no means requires *increasing* reliance on sympathy or commitment.

7. Elsewhere, we present a very simple model in which the exact nature of relations between the rise in productivity, increase in the proportion of the social product distributed according to needs, and expansion of the realm of freedom, can be rigorously explored (van der Veen and Van Parijs, "Capitalism, Communism and the Realm of Freedom").

8. For a lucid discussion of the concept of "fettering," in particular of the distinction between use-fettering and development-fettering, see G. A. Cohen, "Forces and Relations of Production," in *Marxism: A Hundred Years On*, ed. B. Matthews (London: Lawrence and Wishart, 1983). Some Marxists might think that Marx's work contains (implicitly) a distinct argument (based on the theory of the falling rate of profit) that could do the job much better than the explicit argument here considered. But the difficulties raised by this theory are fatal to it. See Philippe Van Parijs, "The Falling-Rate-of-Profit Theory of Crisis: A Rational Reconstruction by Way of Obituary," *Review of Radical Political Economics* 12 (1980): 1–16, and "Why Marxist Economics Needs Microfoundations: Postscripts to an Obituary," *Review of Radical Political Economics* 15 (1983): 111–124, for a systematic discussion. Moreover, the argument derived from it would equally apply to socialist economies – indeed, even more so if Marx's explicit argument discussed in the main text were correct: if socialism did not filter out some of the capital-intensive techniques that are not viable under capitalism, the organic composition of capital would rise faster and the rate of accumulation would fall more rapidly under socialism than under capitalism. Less common but more cogent arguments, may, however, be found. See Philippe Van Parijs, *What (if Anything) is Wrong with Capitalism?* (work in progress, tentative title), part 2.

9. The formal points are made by Christian C. von Weiszäcker and Paul A. Samuelson, "A New Labor Theory of Value for Rational Planning through Use of the Bourgeois Profit Rate," *Proceedings of the National Academy of Sciences* 68 (1971): 1192–1194; Paul A. Samuelson, "Optimality of Profit-Including Prices under Ideal Planning," *Proceedings of the American Academy of Sciences* 70 (1973): 2109–2122; and Paul A. Samuelson, "The Normative and Positivistic Inferiority of Marx's Value Paradigm," *Southern Economic Journal* 49 (1982): 11–18. For illuminating discussions of their relevance to the Marxist view of the difference between capitalism and socialism, see John E. Roemer, "Choice of Technique under Capitalism, Socialism and Nirvana: Reply to Samuelson" (University of California, Davis, Department of Economics, Working Paper no. 213, 1983); and Jon Elster, *Making Sense of Marx* (Cambridge: Cambridge University Press, 1985), sections 3.2.2 and 5.1.3.

10. See Philippe Van Parijs, "What (if Anything) Is Intrinsically Wrong with Capitalism?" *Philosophica* 34 (1984): 85–102; idem, *What (if Anything) Is Wrong with Capitalism?* part 1; and Robert J. van der Veen, "Can Socialism Be Non-Exploitative?" in *Modern Theories of Exploitation*, ed. A. Reeve, (London: Sage, 1987, forthcoming).

11. See Gunnar Adler-Karlsson, "Probleme des Wirtschaftswachstums und der Wirtschaftsgesinnung: Utopie eines besseren Lebens," *Mitteilungen zur Arbeits- und Berufsforschung* 4 (1979): 481 – 505; André Gorz, *Les chemins du paradis: L'agonie du capital* (Paris: Galilée, 1983), and "L'allocation universelle: Version de droite et version de gauche," *La revue nouvelle* 81 (1985) 419 – 428; and Marie-Louise Duboin, *Les affranchis de l'an 2000* (Paris: Syros, 1984).

12. Bertrand Russell, *Roads to Freedom: Socialism, Anarchism and Syndicalism* (London: Allen and Unwin, 1918), 81.

13. In English, see for example Bill Jordan, *Paupers: The Making of the New Claiming Class* (London: Routledge and Kegan Paul, 1973), and *The State. Authority and Autonomy* (Oxford: Blackwell, 1985), part 3; Stephen Cook, "Can a Social Wage Solve Unemployment?" (Birmingham: University of Aston Management Center, Working Paper no. 165, 1979); Keith Roberts, *Automation, Unemployment and the Distribution of Income* (Maastricht: European Center for Work and Society, 1982); Anne Miller, "In Praise of Social Dividends" (Edinburgh: Heriot Watt University, Department of Economics, Working Paper no. 1, 1983), and Peter Ashby, *Social Security after Beveridge: What Next?* (London: National Council for Voluntary Organizations, 1984). For a survey of the discussion in various European countries, see *L'allocation universelle: Une idée pour vivre autrement*, ed. Paul-Marie Boulanger, Philippe Defeyt, and Philippe Van Parijs, special issue of *La revue nouvelle* 81 (April 1985), part 2.

14. Or so it seems. Several qualifications are introduced below.

15. This point is developed in Philippe De Villé and Philippe Van Parijs, "Quelle stratégie contre la pauvreté? Du salaire minimum garanti à l'allocation universelle," *La revue nouvelle* 81 (1985): 361 – 372.

16. See John Rawls, *A Theory of Justice* (Oxford: Oxford University Press, 1972), section 13.

17. See for example Elster, *Making Sense of Marx*, 230, who argues that Rawls's difference principle is better than the labor contribution principle as a second best to distribution according to needs.

18. This stronger sense is akin to the one Ian Steedman, "Some Socialist Questions" (University of Manchester: Department of Economics, unpublished, 1982), gives the term. The distinction could also be made in terms of a contrast between individual and collective freedom, which G. A. Cohen, "The Structure of Proletarian Unfreedom," *Philosophy and Public Affairs* 12 (1983): 3 – 33, uses in a different context. Under weak abundance, every single individual is (not just formally) free not to do any paid work, but only because a sufficient number of individuals do not make use of this freedom (individual freedom). Under strong abundance, this condition no longer applies: everyone retains the freedom not to do any paid work, even if no one else engages in it (collective freedom).

19. The simplifications include the abstraction from any public expenditure other than the universal grant, and the absence of a capital stock constraint.

20. For further discussion of the growth of the "autonomous" sphere see André Gorz, *Adieux au prolétariat* (Paris: Seuil, 1980) 142 – 155; and Philippe Van Parijs, "Marx, l'écologisme et la transition directe du capitalisme au communisme," in *Marx en perspective*, ed. Bernard Chavance (Paris: Editions de l'École des Hautes Études en Sciences Sociales, 1985), 135 – 155, section 2.

21. As one advocate of some form of universal grant puts it: "If we want to enter the realm of freedom, then it is absolutely certain that we must impose limits on ourselves as regards the amount of material goods" (Adler-Karlsson, "Probleme des Wirtschaftswachstums," 63).

Name Index